The Ultimate Problem Solver

When the makefile won't go to completion, when a schedule-buster bug can't be found, when the proof-of-concept demo of your strategic application *must* be running reliably before tomorrow, *time* is the enemy. We created the Coriolis *Black Book* series to give you a weapon in this War Against Time. Our goal is to gather essential technical facts and techniques on the title topic into single, focused volumes, and make those facts easy to find when you most need them. (And if you want to focus on the syntax and semantics of the programming language you're using, we also publish the Coriolis Little Black Book series—the most concise and readily searchable reference on the major languages in use by professionals today.)

When the network goes down, when a schedule-buster bug can't be found, when your program keeps crashing, when you absolutely have to have your program finished tomorrow, *time* is the enemy. We created the Coriolis *Black Book* series to give you a weapon in this War Against Time. Our goal is to gather essential technical facts and techniques on the title topic into single, focused volumes, and make those facts easy to find when you most need them. (And if you need additional focus, we also publish the Coriolis *Little Black Book* series, in which more compact volumes zoom in on significant technical niche topics.)

Every Coriolis Black Book is highly structured and focused on its topic, so you won't be furiously flipping past pages and pages of irrelevant material. Every fact and solution we publish is designed to be located quickly, with minimal searching.

Each chapter begins with an in-depth technical discussion of the topic at hand. After the technical discussion are the solutions, which tell you step-by-step how to handle even the ugliest programming problems.

We've put a lot of thought into making this format work. Please write to us at **blackbookinfo@coriolis.com** and let us know what you think.

If you're reading this, you're probably on the firing line and need to return to the battle. Good luck—with this book in your hand, time is now on your side!

Keith Weiskamp
Publisher
Coriolis Group Books

Jeff Duntemann
Editorial Director
Coriolis Group Books

Also Look For These Other Black Book Titles:

AFC Black Book

Oracle8 & Windows NT Black Book

Dynamic HTML Black Book

Michael Abrash's Graphics Programming Black Book

Microsoft SQL Server Black Book

Oracle8 Black Book

Oracle8 PL/SQL Black Book

Web Design & Development Black Book

Windows NT 4 Administrator's Black Book

Windows 98 Black Book

Active Server Pages Black Book

CORIOLIS
Technology Press

VISUAL
BASIC 6

Black Book

Indispensable Problem Solver

even Holzner

Visual Basic 6 Black Book

The Coriolis Group, LLC
14455 N. Hayden Road, Suite 220
Scottsdale, Arizona 85260

480/483-0192
FAX 480/483-0193
http://www.coriolis.com

Library of Congress Cataloging-in-Publication Data
Holzner, Steven.
    Visual Basic 6 black book / by Steven Holzner.
        p.   cm.
    Includes index.
    ISBN 1-57610-283-1
    1. Microsoft Visual BASIC.   2. BASIC (Computer program language)
I. Title.
QA73.73.B3H75   1998
005.2'768–dc21

98-27200
CIP

Printed in the United States of America
10 9 8 7 6 5 4

President, CEO
Keith
Weiskamp

Publisher
Steve Sayre

Acquisitions
Stephanie
Wall

Marketing Specialist
Jody Kent

Project Editor
Jeff
Kellum

Production Coordinator
Wendy
Littley

Layout Design
April
Nielsen

Cover Design
Anthony
Stock

CD-ROM Development
Robert
Clarfield

CORIOLIS

*To my Sweetie, Nancy, the best editor in the world,
with more kisses than there are pages in this book
(and every one of those kisses is well deserved).*

About The Author

Steven Holzner wrote the book on Visual Basic…a number of times. He co-authored with Peter Norton the bestseller *Peter Norton's Visual Basic for Windows* and *Peter Norton's Guide to Visual Basic 4 for Windows 95*. He also wrote *Advanced Visual Basic 4.0 Programming*, a 650-pager that came out in three editions, and *Internet Programming With Visual Basic 5*, as well as several other Visual Basic books. All in all, this former contributing editor for *PC Magazine* has authored 43 books ranging in subjects from assembly language to Visual C++, but Visual Basic is his favorite topic. Steven's books have sold over a million copies and have been translated into 15 languages around the world.

Steven was on the faculty of Cornell University for 10 years, where he earned his Ph.D. He's also been on the faculty at his undergraduate school, Massachusetts Institute of Technology. Steven loves to travel, and has been to over 30 countries, from Afghanistan to India, from Borneo to Iran, from Sweden to Thailand, with more to come. He and Nancy live in a small, picturesque town on the New England coast and spend summers in their house in the Austrian Alps.

Acknowledgments

The book you are holding is the result of many people's dedication. I would especially like to thank Stephanie Wall, Acquisitions Editor, for her hard work; Jeff Kellum, the Project Editor who did such a great job of bringing this project together and shepherding it along, as well as Wendy Littley, the Production Coordinator who kept things on track; Joanne Slike, the copyeditor who waded through everything and got it into such good shape; and April Nielsen, who did the interior design. Special thanks to Harry Henderson for the terrific tech edit. Thanks to all: great job!

Table Of Contents

Introduction xxxiii

Chapter 1
Visual Basic Overview 1
    Creating A Project In Visual Basic   2
    The Parts Of A Visual Basic Project   9
    Project Scope   11
    Projects On Disk   13
    Using The Visual Basic Application Wizard   22
    Visual Basic Programming Conventions   28
    Code Commenting Conventions   33
    Best Coding Practices In Visual Basic   34
    Getting Down To The Details   39

Chapter 2
The Visual Basic Development Environment 41
    In Depth
    Overview Of The Integrated Development Environment   42
    Immediate Solutions
    Selecting IDE Colors, Fonts, And Font Sizes   50
    Aligning, Sizing, And Spacing Multiple Controls   51
    Setting A Startup Form Or Procedure   54
    Using Visual Basic Predefined Forms, Menus, And Projects   56
    Setting A Project's Version Information   59
    Setting An EXE File's Name And Icon   60
    Displaying The Debug, Edit, And Form Editor Toolbars   61
    Turning Bounds Checking On Or Off   63
    Checking For Pentium Errors   65
    Managing Add-Ins   65
    Adding ActiveX Controls And Insertable Objects To Projects   66
    Customizing Menus And Toolbars   67
    Setting Forms' Initial Positions   69
    Enabling Or Disabling Quick Info, Auto List Members, Data Tips,
        And Syntax Checking   70

Displaying Or Hiding IDE Windows   73
Searching An Entire Project For Specific Text Or A Variable's Definition   74
Optimizing For Fast Code, Small Code, Or A Particular Processor   75
Adding And Removing Forms, Modules, And Class Modules   76
Using Bookmarks   78
Using The Object Browser   79

Chapter 3
The Visual Basic Language 81

In Depth

How Does Visual Basic Code Look?   82

Immediate Solutions

Declaring Constants   85
Declaring Variables   86
Selecting Variable Types   88
Converting Between Data Types   90
Setting Variable Scope   90
Verifying Data Types   91
Declaring Arrays And Dynamic Arrays   93
Declaring Subroutines   96
Declaring Functions   97
Preserving Variables' Values Between Calls To Their Procedures   99
Handling Strings   100
Converting Strings To Numbers And Back Again   102
Handling Operators And Operator Precedence   102
Using **If...Else** Statements   104
Using **Select Case**   105
Making Selections With **Switch()** And **Choose()**   106
Looping   107
Using Collections   110
Sending Keystrokes To Other Programs   110
Handling Higher Math   113
Handling Dates And Times   114
Handling Financial Data   116
Ending A Program At Any Time   116

Chapter 4
Managing Forms In Visual Basic 117

In Depth

The Parts Of A Form   118
The Parts Of An MDI Form   119

Immediate Solutions

Setting Title Bar Text   121
Adding/Removing Min/Max Buttons And Setting A Window's Border   122
Adding Toolbars To Forms   123
Adding Status Bars To Forms   126
Referring To The Current Form   128
Redrawing Form Contents   129
Setting Control Tab Order   129
Moving And Sizing Controls From Code   131
Showing And Hiding Controls In A Form   132
Measurements In Forms   133
Working With Multiple Forms   134
Loading, Showing, And Hiding Forms   136
Setting The Startup Form   137
Creating Forms In Code   138
Using The Multiple Document Interface   139
Arranging MDI Child Windows   140
Opening New MDI Child Windows   141
Arrays Of Forms   142
Coordinating Data Between MDI Child Forms (Document Views)   144
Creating Dialog Boxes   145
All About Message Boxes And Input Boxes   148
Passing Forms To Procedures   150
Minimizing/Maximizing And Enabling/Disabling Forms From Code   151

Chapter 5
Visual Basic Menus 153

In Depth

Menu Design Considerations   155

Immediate Solutions

Using The Visual Basic Application Wizard To Set Up Your Menus   157
What Item Goes In What Menu?   163
Adding A Menu To A Form   165
Modifying And Deleting Menu Items   168
Adding A Menu Separator   169
Adding Access Characters   170
Adding Shortcut Keys   171
Creating Submenus   173
Creating Immediate ("Bang") Menus   175
Using The Visual Basic Predefined Menus   176
Adding A Checkmark To A Menu Item   178
Disabling (Graying Out) Menu Items   180

Handling MDI Form And MDI Child Menus   181
Adding A List Of Open Windows To An MDI Form's Window Menu   182
Making Menus And Menu Items Visible Or Invisible   184
Creating And Displaying Pop-Up Menus   184
Adding And Deleting Menu Items At Runtime   187
Adding Bitmaps To Menus   190
Using The Registry To Store A Most Recently Used (MRU) Files List   192

Chapter 6
Text Boxes And Rich Text Boxes 197

In Depth
Use Of Text Boxes And RTF Boxes In Windows Programs   198

Immediate Solutions
Creating Multiline, Word-Wrap Text Boxes   200
Aligning Text In Text Boxes   200
Adding Scroll Bars To Text Boxes   201
Making A Text Box Read-Only   202
Accessing Text In A Text Box   203
Selecting And Replacing Text In A Text Box   204
Copying Or Getting Selected Text To Or From The Clipboard   204
Creating A Password Control   205
Controlling Input In A Text Box   206
Adding An RTF Box To A Form   207
Accessing Text In A Rich Text Box   208
Selecting Text In Rich Text Boxes   208
Using Bold, Italic, Underline, And Strikethru   209
Indenting Text In Rich Text Boxes   211
Setting Fonts And Font Sizes In Rich Text Boxes   212
Using Bullets In Rich Text Boxes   214
Aligning Text In A Rich Text Box   216
Setting Text Color In RTF Boxes   216
Moving The Insertion Point In RTF Boxes   217
Adding Superscripts And Subscripts In Rich Text Boxes   219
Setting The Mouse Pointer In Text Boxes And Rich Text Boxes   220
Searching For (And Replacing) Text In RTF Boxes   221
Saving RTF Files From Rich Text Boxes   222
Reading RTF Files Into A Rich Text Box   223
Printing From A Rich Text Box   223

Chapter 7
Command Buttons, Checkboxes, And Option Buttons 225

In Depth
How This Chapter Works   227

Immediate Solutions
Setting A Button's Caption   229
Setting A Button's Background Color   229
Setting Button Text Color   230
Setting Button Fonts   231
Reacting To Button Clicks   232
Creating Button Control Arrays   233
Resetting The Focus After A Button Click   234
Giving Buttons Access Characters   235
Setting Button Tab Order   236
Disabling Buttons   236
Showing And Hiding Buttons   237
Adding Tool Tips To Buttons   238
Resizing And Moving Buttons From Code   239
Adding A Picture To A Button   239
Adding A Down Picture To A Button   241
Adding Buttons At Runtime   242
Passing Buttons To Procedures   243
Handling Button Releases   244
Making A Command Button Into A Cancel Button   244
Getting A Checkbox's State   245
Setting A Checkbox's State   245
Grouping Option Buttons Together   246
Getting An Option Button's State   247
Setting An Option Button's State   247
Using Graphical Checkboxes And Radio Buttons   248
Using Checkboxes And Option Buttons Together   249

Chapter 8
List Boxes And Combo Boxes 251

In Depth
Immediate Solutions
Adding Items To A List Box   254
Referring To Items In A List Box By Index   255
Responding To List Box Events   256
Removing Items From A List Box   257

Sorting A List Box 258
Determining How Many Items Are In A List Box 259
Determining If A List Box Item Is Selected 259
Using Multiselect List Boxes 261
Making List Boxes Scroll Horizontally 263
Using Checkmarks In A List Box 264
Clearing A List Box 264
Creating Simple Combo Boxes, Drop-Down Combo Boxes, And Drop-Down List
   Combo Boxes 265
Adding Items To A Combo Box 266
Responding To Combo Box Selections 267
Removing Items From A Combo Box 269
Getting The Current Selection In A Combo Box 270
Sorting A Combo Box 271
Clearing A Combo Box 272
Locking A Combo Box 272
Getting The Number Of Items In A Combo Box 273
Setting The Topmost Item In A List Box Or Combo Box 274
Adding Numeric Data To Items In A List Box Or Combo Box 275
Determining Where An Item Was Added In A Sorted List Box Or Combo Box 276
Using Images In Combo Boxes 277

Chapter 9
Scroll Bars And Sliders 281

In Depth
Adding Scroll Bars And Sliders To A Program 284

Immediate Solutions
Adding Horizontal Or Vertical Scroll Bars To A Form 286
Setting Scroll Bars' Minimum And Maximum Values 286
Setting Up Scroll Bar Clicks (Large Changes) 287
Setting Up Scroll Bar Arrow Clicks (Small Changes) 288
Getting A Scroll Bar's Current Value 289
Handling Scroll Bar Events 289
Handling Continuous Scroll Bar Events 291
Showing And Hiding Scroll Bars 292
Coordinating Scroll Bar Pairs 293
Adding Scroll Bars To Text Boxes 293
Creating And Using Flat Scroll Bars 294
Customizing Flat Scroll Bar Arrows 295
Creating Slider Controls 296
Setting A Slider's Orientation 297
Setting A Slider's Range 298

Setting Up Slider Groove Clicks   298
Adding Ticks To A Slider   299
Setting A Slider's Tick Style   300
Getting A Slider's Current Value   301
Handling Slider Events   301
Handling Continuous Slider Events   302
Handling Slider Selections   303
Clearing A Selection In A Slider   306
Creating An Updown Control   307
Setting An Updown Control's Minimum And Maximum   308
Handling Updown Events   308

Chapter 10
Picture Boxes And Image Controls 311

In Depth

Image Controls   312
Picture Boxes   313

Immediate Solutions

Adding A Picture Box To A Form   315
Setting Or Getting The Picture In A Picture Box   316
Adjusting Picture Box Size To Contents   317
Aligning A Picture Box In A Form   317
Handling Picture Box Events (And Creating Image Maps)   318
Picture Box Animation   320
Grouping Other Controls In A Picture Box   322
Using A Picture Box In An MDI Form   322
Drawing Lines And Circles In A Picture Box   323
Using Image Lists With Picture Boxes   326
Adding Text To A Picture Box   327
Formatting Text In A Picture Box   329
Clearing A Picture Box   330
Accessing Individual Pixels In A Picture Box   331
Copying Pictures To And Pasting Pictures From The Clipboard   332
Stretching And Flipping Images In A Picture Box   333
Printing A Picture   335
Using Picture Box Handles   336
Setting Measurement Scales In A Picture Box   337
Saving Pictures To Disk   338
Adding An Image Control To A Form   338
Stretching An Image In An Image Control   339

Chapter 11
Windows Common Dialogs 341

In Depth
The Common Dialog Control   342

Immediate Solutions
Creating And Displaying A Windows Common Dialog   345
Setting A Common Dialog's Title   346
Did The User Click OK Or Cancel?   347
Using A Color Dialog Box   348
Setting Color Dialog Flags   350
Using The Open And Save As Dialogs   350
Setting Open And Save As Flags   352
Getting The File Name In Open, Save As Dialogs   354
Setting Maximum File Name Size In Open And Save As Dialog Boxes   354
Setting Default File Extensions   355
Set Or Get The Initial Directory   355
Setting File Types (Filters) In Open, Save As Dialogs   356
Using A Font Dialog Box   358
Setting Font Dialog Flags   360
Setting **Max** And **Min** Font Sizes   361
Using The Print Dialog Box   363
Setting Print Dialog Flags   365
Setting The Minimum And Maximum Pages To Print   366
Setting Page Orientation   367
Showing Windows Help From A Visual Basic Program   368

Chapter 12
The Chart And Grid Controls 371

In Depth
The Chart Control   372
Grid Controls   373

Immediate Solutions
Adding A Chart Control To A Program   375
Adding Data To A Chart Control   376
Working With A Multiple Data Series   379
Setting Chart And Axis Titles And Chart Colors   382
Creating Pie Charts   382
Creating 2D And 3D Line Charts   384
Creating 2D And 3D Area Charts   385
Creating 2D And 3D Bar Charts   387

Creating 2D And 3D Step Charts   388
Creating 2D And 3D Combination Charts   390
Adding A Flex Grid Control To A Program   392
Working With Data In A Flex Grid Control   393
Typing Data Into A Flex Grid   397
Setting Flex Grid Grid Lines And Border Styles   400
Labeling Rows And Columns In A Flex Grid   400
Formatting Flex Grid Cells   401
Sorting A Flex Grid Control   401
Dragging Columns In A Flex Grid Control   402
Connecting A Flex Grid To A Database   403

Chapter 13
The Timer And Serial Communications Controls 405

In Depth

The Timer Control   406
The Communications Control   407
The MonthView And DateTimePicker Controls   410

Immediate Solutions

Adding A Timer Control To A Program   412
Initializing A Timer Control   412
Handling **Timer** Events   413
Formatting Times And Dates   413
Creating A Clock Program   415
Creating A Stopwatch   416
Creating An Alarm Clock   417
Creating Animation Using The Timer Control   419
Adding A Communications Control To A Program   421
Setting Up The Receive And Transmit Buffers   422
Opening The Serial Port   423
Working With A Modem   423
Reading Data With The Communications Control   424
Sending Data With The Communications Control   425
Setting Up Communications Handshaking   425
Handling Communications Events   426
Closing The Serial Port   427
Adding A MonthView Control To Your Program   428
Getting Dates From A MonthView Control   428
Adding A DateTimePicker Control To Your Program   429
Using A DateTimePicker Control   430

Chapter 14
The Frame, Label, Shape, And Line Controls 433

In Depth
The Frame Control   435
The Label Control   435
The Shape Control   436
The Line Control   437
Form Drawing Methods   438

Immediate Solutions
Adding A Frame To A Program   439
Setting Frame Size And Location   440
Dragging And Dropping Controls   440
Grouping Controls In A Frame   442
Adding A Label To A Program   443
Using Labels Instead Of Text Boxes   444
Formatting Text In Labels   445
Aligning Text In Labels   446
Handling Label Control Events   446
Using Labels To Give Access Keys To Controls Without Captions   447
Adding A Shape Control To A Program   448
Drawing Rectangles   449
Drawing Squares   449
Drawing Ovals   450
Drawing Circles   450
Drawing Rounded Rectangles   451
Drawing Rounded Squares   451
Setting Shape Borders: Drawing Width, Dashes, And Dots   451
Filling Shapes   452
Drawing A Shape Without The IDE Grid   453
Moving Shapes At Runtime   454
Adding A Line Control To A Program   455
Drawing Thicker, Dotted, And Dashed Lines   456
Drawing A Line Without The IDE Grid   456
Changing A Line Control At Runtime   457
Using Form Methods To Draw Lines   458
Using Form Methods To Draw Circles   459

Chapter 15
Toolbars, Status Bars, Progress Bars, And Coolbars 463

In Depth
Toolbars   465

Status Bars   465
Progress Bars   466
Coolbars   467

Immediate Solutions

Adding A Toolbar To A Form   469
Aligning Toolbars In A Form   470
Adding Buttons To A Toolbar   471
Handling Toolbar Buttons Clicks   471
Connecting Toolbar Buttons To Menu Items   473
Adding Separators To A Toolbar   474
Adding Images To Toolbar Buttons   475
Adding Check (Toggle) Buttons To A Toolbar   477
Creating Button Groups In A Toolbar   478
Adding Combo Boxes And Other Controls To A Toolbar   479
Setting Toolbar Button Tool Tips   481
Letting The User Customize The Toolbar   482
Adding Toolbar Buttons At Runtime   482
Adding A Status Bar To A Program   484
Aligning Status Bars In A Form   485
Adding Panels To A Status Bar   485
Displaying Text In A Status Bar   486
Displaying Time, Dates, And Key States In A Status Bar   487
Customizing A Status Bar Panel's Appearance   488
Displaying Images In A Status Bar   489
Handling Panel Clicks   490
Adding New Panels To A Status Bar At Runtime   490
Creating Simple Status Bars   491
Adding A Progress Bar To A Form   491
Using A Progress Bar   492
Adding A Coolbar To A Form   493
Aligning Coolbars In A Form   494
Adding Bands To A Coolbar   494
Adding Controls To Coolbar Bands   495
Handling Coolbar Control Events   496

Chapter 16
Image Lists, Tree Views, List Views, And Tab Strips 499

In Depth

Image Lists   501
Tree Views   502
List Views   504
Tab Strips   504

Immediate Solutions

Adding An Image List To A Form   507
Adding Images To Image Lists   507
Using The Images In Image Lists   508
Setting Image Keys In An Image List   509
Adding A Tree View To A Form   510
Selecting Tree View Styles   511
Adding Nodes To A Tree View   511
Adding Subnodes To A Tree View   513
Adding Images To A Tree View   515
Expanding And Collapsing Nodes (And Setting Node Images To Match)   517
Handling Tree View Node Clicks   518
Adding A List View To A Form   518
Adding Items To A List View   520
Adding Icons To List View Items   522
Adding Small Icons To List View Items   523
Selecting The View Type In List Views   524
Adding Column Headers To A List View   525
Adding Column Fields To A List View   527
Handling List View Item Clicks   529
Handling List View Column Header Clicks   530
Adding A Tab Strip To A Form   531
Inserting Tabs Into A Tab Strip Control   532
Setting Tab Captions   533
Setting Tab Images   534
Using A Tab Strip To Display Other Controls   535
Handling Tab Clicks   536

Chapter 17
File Handling And File Controls 539

In Depth

Sequential Access Files   541
Binary Files   543
The FileSystemObject   543

Immediate Solutions

Using The Common Dialogs File Open And File Save As   544
Creating A File   546
Getting A File's Length   548
Opening A File   549
Writing To A Sequential File   550
Writing To A Random Access File   552

Writing To A Binary File 554
Reading From Sequential Files 554
Reading From Random Access Files 558
Reading From Binary Files 561
Accessing Any Record In A Random Access File 563
Closing A File 564
Saving Files From Rich Text Boxes 564
Opening Files In Rich Text Boxes 565
Saving Files From Picture Boxes 566
Opening Files In Picture Boxes 566
Using The Drive List Box Control 567
Using The Directory List Box Control 568
Using The File List Box Control 569
Creating And Deleting Directories 572
Changing Directories 572
Copying A File 572
Moving A File 573
Deleting A File 574
When Was A File Created? Last Modified? Last Accessed? 574
Creating A TextStream 575
Opening A TextStream 576
Writing To A TextStream 577
Reading From A TextStream 578
Closing A TextStream 578

Chapter 18
Working With Graphics 581

In Depth

Graphics Methods Vs. Graphics Controls 582
About Visual Basic Coordinates 583

Immediate Solutions

Redrawing Graphics In Windows: **AutoRedraw** And **Paint** 584
Clearing The Drawing Area 585
Setting Colors 585
Drawing Text 588
Working With Fonts 589
Drawing Lines 591
Drawing Boxes 593
Drawing Circles 594
Drawing Ellipses 596
Drawing Arcs 597

Drawing Freehand With The Mouse   599
Filling Figures With Color   601
Filling Figures With Patterns   602
Setting Figure Drawing Style And Drawing Width   602
Drawing Points   604
Setting The Drawing Mode   604
Setting Drawing Scales   606
Using The Screen Object   608
Resizing Graphics When The Window Is Resized   608
Copying Pictures To And Pasting Pictures From The Clipboard   609
Printing Graphics   610
Layering Graphics With The **AutoRedraw** And **ClipControls** Properties   611

Chapter 19
Working With Images 613

In Depth
Picture Boxes Vs. Image Controls   614
Image Effects: Working With Images Bit By Bit   615

Immediate Solutions
Adding Images To Controls   616
Adding Images To Forms   617
Using Image Controls   617
Using Picture Boxes   618
AutoSizing Picture Boxes   619
Loading Images In At Runtime   619
Clearing (Erasing) Images   621
Storing Images In Memory Using The Picture Object   621
Using Arrays Of Picture Objects   623
Adding Picture Clip Controls To A Program   623
Selecting Images In A Picture Clip Control Using Coordinates   625
Selecting Images In A Picture Clip Control Using Rows And Columns   629
Flipping Images   630
Stretching Images   632
Creating Image Animation   634
Handling Images Bit By Bit   635
Creating Grayscale Images   637
Lightening Images   640
Creating "Embossed" Images   642
Creating "Engraved" Images   644
Sweeping Images   645
Blurring Images   646
Freeing Memory Used By Graphics   647

Chapter 20
Creating ActiveX Controls And Documents 649

In Depth

All About ActiveX Components   650
In-Process Vs. Out-Of-Process Components   652
Which ActiveX Component Do I Want To Build?   652

Immediate Solutions

Creating An ActiveX Control   653
Designing An ActiveX Control From Scratch   654
Giving ActiveX Controls Persistent Graphics   657
Basing An ActiveX Control On An Existing Visual Basic Control   657
Handling Constituent Control Events In An ActiveX Control   659
Adding Controls To An ActiveX Control (A Calculator ActiveX Control)   660
Testing An ActiveX Control   661
Creating A Visual Basic Project Group To Test An ActiveX Control   662
Registering An ActiveX Control   664
Using A Custom ActiveX Control In A Visual Basic Program   664
Adding A Property To An ActiveX Control   666
Making ActiveX Control Properties Persistent (PropertyBag Object)   671
Adding A Method To An ActiveX Control   674
Adding An Event To An ActiveX Control   678
Adding Design Time Property Pages   680
Creating An ActiveX Document   682
ActiveX Document DLLs Vs. EXEs   684
Adding Controls To An ActiveX Document (A Tic-Tac-Toe Example)   684
Handling Constituent Control Events In An ActiveX Document   689
Testing An ActiveX Document   690
Creating ActiveX Documents That Run Outside Visual Basic   690
Distributed Computing: ActiveX Documents And Integrated Browsers   691
Making ActiveX Document Properties Persistent (PropertyBag Object)   693

Chapter 21
Visual Basic And The Internet: Web Browsing, Email, HTTP,
FTP, And DHTML 695

In Depth

Creating A Web Browser   696
Creating A Dynamic HTML Page   696
Working With Email   697
Using FTP   697
Using HTTP   697

Immediate Solutions

Creating A Web Browser   699
Specifying URLs In A Web Browser   700
Adding Back And Forward Buttons To A Web Browser   704
Adding Refresh, Home, And Stop Buttons To A Web Browser   705
Creating DHTML Pages   706
Adding Text To DHTML Pages   709
Adding Images To DHTML Pages   710
Adding HTML Controls To DHTML Pages   712
Adding ActiveX Controls To DHTML Pages   713
Adding Tables To DHTML Pages   715
Adding Hyperlinks To DHTML Pages   716
Using MAPI Controls To Support Email   717
Sending Email From Visual Basic   721
Reading Email In Visual Basic   725
Using The Internet Transfer Control For FTP And HTTP Operations   727
Handling FTP Operations In Visual Basic   728
Handling HTTP Operations In Visual Basic   734

Chapter 22
Multimedia 739

In Depth

The Multimedia MCI Control   740
Using The Multimedia Control From Code   741

Immediate Solutions

Using The Animation Control   742
Adding A Multimedia Control To A Program   743
Setting The Device Type And Opening The Device   744
Setting File Information And Opening Files   745
Setting A Multimedia Control's Time Format   746
Controlling The Multimedia Control From Code   747
Stopping And Pausing The Multimedia Control   749
Displaying The Multimedia Control's Status   750
Closing The Multimedia Control   753
Playing CDs From Your CD-ROM Drive   753
Playing WAV Files   755
Playing MID Files   757
Playing AVI Files   759
Playing MPG Files   761
Keeping Track Of Multimedia Command Execution Using Notification   763
Handling Multimedia Errors   764
Stepping A Multimedia Control Forward Or Backward Frame By Frame   769

Starting From And To In A Multimedia Control 770
Making The Multimedia Control Wait 770
Multimedia Without Multimedia Controls 771

Chapter 23
Connecting To The Windows API And Visual C++ 773

In Depth
Declaring And Using DLL Procedures In Visual Basic 775
Handling C/C++ And Windows Data Types 776
What's Available In The Windows API? 779

Immediate Solutions
Getting Or Creating A Device Context (Including The Whole Screen) 780
Drawing Lines In A Device Context 782
Drawing Ellipses In A Device Context 784
Drawing Rectangles In A Device Context 785
Setting Drawing Colors And Styles (Using Pens) 786
Setting Drawing Modes (ROP2) 788
Handling The Mouse Outside Your Program's Window 789
Copying Bitmaps Between Device Contexts Quickly 793
Capturing Images From The Screen 794
Getting A Window Handle For Any Window On The Screen 800
Getting A Window's Text 802
Playing Sounds With API Functions 804
Allocating Memory And Storing Data 805
Reading Data From Memory And Deallocating Memory 808
Making A Window Topmost 810
Determining Free And Total Disk Space 813
Determining The Windows Directory 814
Connecting To Visual C++ 816

Chapter 24
Databases: Using DAO, RDO, And ADO 821

In Depth
What Are Databases? 823
DAO 824
RDO 826
ADO 827
The Data-Bound Controls 828

Immediate Solutions
Creating And Managing Databases With The Visual Data Manager 830
Creating A Table With The Visual Data Manager 831

Creating A Field With The Visual Data Manager   831
Entering Data In A Database With The Visual Data Manager   833
Adding A Data Control To A Program   834
Opening A Database With The Data Control   835
Connecting A Data Control To A Bound Control   835
Registering An ODBC Source   836
Opening A Database With A Remote Data Control   838
Connecting A Remote Data Control To A Bound Control   838
Opening A Database With An ADO Data Control   839
Connecting An ADO Data Control To A Bound Control   840
The Data Form Wizard: Creating A Data Form   841
Using Database Control Methods: Adding, Deleting, And Modifying Records   843
Adding Records To Databases   844
Deleting Records In Databases   844
Refreshing A Data Control   845
Updating A Database With Changes   845
Moving To The Next Record   845
Moving To The Previous Record   846
Moving To The First Record   846
Moving To The Last Record   846
The Data-Bound Controls: From Text Boxes To Flex Grids   847
The ADO Data-Bound Controls   848

Chapter 25
Working With Database Objects In Code 851
In Depth
DAO   853
RDO   854
ADO   854
Immediate Solutions
A Full-Scale DAO Example   856
Using The Daocode Example To Create And Edit A Database   856
DAO: Creating A Database   857
DAO: Creating A Table With A TableDef Object   859
DAO: Adding Fields To A TableDef Object   860
DAO: Adding An Index To A TableDef Object   861
DAO: Creating A Record Set   863
DAO: Opening A Database   865
DAO: Adding A Record To A Record Set   867
DAO: Editing A Record In A Record Set   868
DAO: Updating A Record In A Record Set   868
DAO: Moving To The First Record In A Record Set   869

DAO: Moving To The Last Record In A Record Set   870
DAO: Moving To The Next Record In A Record Set   870
DAO: Moving To The Previous Record In A Record Set   871
DAO: Deleting A Record In A Record Set   872
DAO: Sorting A Record Set   872
DAO: Searching A Record Set   873
DAO: Executing SQL   874
A Full-Scale RDO Example   875
RDO: Opening A Connection   876
RDO: Creating A Result Set   877
RDO: Moving To The First Record In A Result Set   879
RDO: Moving To The Last Record In A Result Set   880
RDO: Moving To The Next Record In A Result Set   881
RDO: Moving To The Previous Record In A Result Set   882
RDO: Executing SQL   883
A Full-Scale ADO Example   883
ADO: Opening A Connection   884
ADO: Creating A Record Set From A Connection   885
ADO: Binding Controls To Record Sets   887
ADO: Adding A Record To A Record Set   888
ADO: Refreshing The Record Set   888
ADO: Updating A Record In A Record Set   889
ADO: Moving To The First Record In A Record Set   890
ADO: Moving To The Last Record In A Record Set   890
ADO: Moving To The Next Record In A Record Set   891
ADO: Moving To The Previous Record In A Record Set   891
ADO: Deleting A Record In A Record Set   892
ADO: Executing SQL In A Record Set   893

Chapter 26
OLE 895

In Depth

Linking Vo. Embodding   807

Immediate Solutions

Adding An OLE Control To A Form   900
Creating And Embedding An OLE Object At Design Time   900
Linking Or Embedding An Existing Document At Design Time   902
Autosizing An OLE Control   903
Determining How An Object Is Displayed In An OLE Container Control   903
Using The OLE Control's Pop-Up Menus At Design Time   904
Inserting An OLE Object Into An OLE Control At Runtime   905
Deactivating OLE Objects   907

Using Paste Special To Insert A Selected Part Of A Document Into An OLE Control   908
How To Activate The OLE Objects In Your Program   912
Activating OLE Objects With A Pop-Up Menu That Lists All OLE Verbs   912
Activating OLE Objects From Code   913
Is An Object Linked Or Embedded?   914
Handling Multiple OLE Objects   914
Using OLE Control Arrays To Handle Multiple OLE Objects   916
Loading New OLE Controls At Runtime   920
Dragging OLE Objects In A Form   924
Deleting OLE Objects   926
Copying And Pasting OLE Objects With The Clipboard   927
Zooming OLE Objects   928
Saving And Retrieving Embedded Object's Data   929
Handling OLE Object Updated Events   930
Disabling In-Place Editing   931

Chapter 27
Creating Code Components (OLE Automation) 933

In Depth
Code Components: Classes And Objects   934
Code Components And Threads   935

Immediate Solutions
Using A Code Component From A Client Application   938
Creating An Object From A Class   940
Using A Code Component's Properties And Methods   942
Creating A Code Component   942
Setting A Code Component's Project Type: In-Process Or Out-Of-Process   945
Adding A Property To A Code Component   946
Adding A **Get/Let** Property To A Code Component   947
Adding A Method To A Code Component   950
Passing Arguments To A Code Component Method   951
Passing Optional Arguments To A Code Component Method   953
Testing A Code Component With A Second Instance Of Visual Basic   954
Creating And Registering An In-Process Code Component   957
Creating And Registering An Out-Of-Process Code Component   958
Using The Class **Initialize** Event   958
Using The Class **Terminate** Event   958
Global Objects: Using Code Components Without Creating An Object   959
Destroying A Code Component Object   960
Using Forms From Code Components   961
Creating Dialog Box Libraries In Code Components   962
Designing Multithreaded In-Process Components   963

Designing Multithreaded Out-Of-Process Components   963

Chapter 28
Advanced Form, Control, And Windows Registry Handling 965

In Depth
Drag And Drop And OLE Drag And Drop   969
The Windows Registry   969

Immediate Solutions
Passing Controls To Procedures   970
Passing Control Arrays To Procedures   970
Determining The Active Control   971
Determining Control Type At Runtime   972
Creating/Loading New Controls At Runtime   973
Changing Control Tab Order   975
Changing Control Stacking Position With Z-Order   976
Drag/Drop: Dragging Controls   976
Drag/Drop: Dropping Controls   978
Handling "Self-Drops" When Dragging And Dropping   981
Drag/Drop: Handling **DragOver** Events   982
OLE Drag/Drop: Dragging Data   983
OLE Drag/Drop: Dropping Data   986
OLE Drag/Drop: Reporting The Drag/Drop Outcome   989
Using The Lightweight Controls   990
Passing Forms To Procedures   992
Determining The Active Form   992
Using The Form Object's **Controls** Collection   993
Using the **Forms** Collection   994
Setting A Form's Startup Position   995
Keeping A Form's Icon Out Of The Windows 95 Taskbar   995
Handling Keystrokes In A Form Before Controls Read Them   995
Making A Form Immovable   996
Showing Modal Forms   996
Saving Values In The Windows Registry   997
Getting Values From The Windows Registry   997
Getting All Registry Settings   999
Deleting A Registry Setting   999

Chapter 29
Error Handling And Debugging 1001

In Depth
Testing Your Programs   1007

Immediate Solutions

Writing Error Handlers   1009
Using **On Error GoTo** *Label*   1012
Using **On Error GoTo** *line#*   1014
Using **On Error Resume Next**   1015
Using **On Error GoTo 0**   1015
Using **Resume** In Error Handlers   1016
Using **Resume** *Label* In Error Handlers   1017
Using **Resume** *line#* In Error Handlers   1018
Using **Resume Next** In Error Handlers   1019
Getting An Error's Error Code   1020
Getting An Error's Description   1021
Determining An Error's Source Object   1022
Handling Errors In DLLs: The **LastDLLError** Property   1023
Creating An Intentional (User-Defined) Error   1023
Nested Error Handling   1024
Creating An Error Object Directly In Visual Basic   1026
Trappable Cancel Errors In Common Dialogs   1028
Debugging In Visual Basic   1029
Setting Debugging Breakpoints   1031
Single-Stepping While Debugging   1032
Examining Variables And Expressions   1033
Adding Debug Watch Windows   1034
Using The Immediate Window While Debugging   1035
Clearing All Debugging Breakpoints   1036
Executing Code Up To The Cursor While Debugging   1036
Skipping Over Statements While Debugging   1036

Chapter 30
Deploying Your Program: Creating Setup Programs, Help Files, And Online Registration 1037

In Depth

Setup Programs   1039
Help Files   1040
Online Registration   1040
The "Designed For Microsoft Windows" Logo   1041

Immediate Solutions

Creating Your Application's EXE File   1043
Using The Package And Deployment Wizard   1043
Step 1: Package Type   1044
Step 2: Build Folder   1044
Step 3: Files   1045

Step 4: Distribution Type   1045

Step 5: Installation Title   1046

Step 6: Icons   1046

Step 7: Install Locations   1047

Step 8: Shared Files   1048

Step 9: Finished!   1048

Creating Help Files With The Microsoft Help Workshop   1049

Creating A Help Project's RTF File   1051

Entering Text In A Help File   1052

Creating A Help Hotspot   1053

Creating A Help Hotspot Target   1055

Titling A Help Page   1057

Adding Help Topics To The Help Index   1058

Creating Help Pop-Up Links   1058

Creating Help "Tool Tips" Targets   1060

Compiling Help Files With The Help Workshop   1060

Displaying A Help File From Visual Basic   1061

Building Online Help Into Your Application   1063

Creating Online User Registration   1065

Uploading Online Registration Information To An FTP Server   1066

Concluding The FTP Transfer Of The Online Registration Information   1068

Index 1069

Introduction

Welcome to your Visual Basic support package. That's what this book has been designed to be: your complete VB support package. Have we reached that goal yet? It's up to you to decide. If what you're looking for is not in this edition, we'll work hard to make sure it's in the next—I encourage your suggestions. Please feel free to write. We'll put in the time to make sure this book is the most complete one available on Visual Basic, edition after edition. This is the book we want you to come back to again and again.

I've used Visual Basic back before version 1 even came out publicly and have written many books on the program. I put Visual Basic to work for a very wide range of uses day after day; in fact, it's is my favorite programming package of all, and it comes close to being my favorite program period. But I've never written a book on Visual Basic as complete as this one and never included as many features, documented or undocumented, examples, and tips in one volume.

This book has been designed to give you the coverage you just won't find in any other book. Other books often omit not only the larger topics, like deploying your program after you've created it and creating Help files, but also the smaller ones, like covering in depth just about every control that comes with Visual Basic, including the ActiveX controls—from the MS chart control to flat scroll bars, from the serial port comm control to the Internet transfer control.

Reluctantly, I must admit that it's impossible for one volume to be utterly comprehensive on the subject of Visual Basic (impossible because it's not physically possible to bind a book that big yet), but we're trying our best. It's true that some specialty books might have more coverage on a few topics, but if you want to see more on a particular topic, write in and we'll work seriously on adding more of that topic to the next edition.

How This Book Works

The task-based format we use in this book is the one most programmers appreciate because programming is a task-based business. Rather than reading about subjects in the order the author thinks best, you can go directly to your topic of interest and find the bite-sized nugget of information you need, such as opening an FTP connection, adding a Web browser to your program, supporting online user registration from Visual Basic, adding a method to an ActiveX control, creating an error handler, flipping or stretching an image, opening an RDO database connection, playing CDs from the computer's CD-ROM drive, and literally hundreds of other topics.

And best of all, there's a working example in code for almost every programming topic in the book. The actual process of programming is not abstract; it's very applied. So instead of vague generalities, we get down to the specifics—all the specifics—that give you everything you need to understand and use Visual Basic.

In the old days, programming books used to be very top-down, with chapters on subjects like conditional branching, loop structures, variable declarations, and so forth. But who sits down to program by saying, "I'm about to create a conditional program flow branch"? Instead, programmers are more interested in performing useful tasks, like adding buttons, menus, list boxes, or toolbars to a window; creating graphics animation; creating dialog boxes; creating setup programs; working with files; supporting online Help; and so on. And this book is written for programmers.

Because this book is written for programmers, each chapter is broken up into dozens of practical programming tasks. After selecting the chapter you want, you can turn to the table of contents, or to the first page in that chapter, to find the task you're interested in. Hundreds of tasks are covered in this book, chosen as those that programmers most want to see. In addition, this book is filled with nearly 800 examples, covering just about every Visual Basic programming area there is. These examples are bite-sized and to the point, so you don't have to wade through a dozen files trying to understand one simple topic. And they're as comprehensive as we could make them, covering every programming area in the book.

Besides programming tasks and examples, the book also has overviews designed to bring all the pieces together into a coherent whole, giving you the entire picture. The first chapter is designed specifically to give you an overview of Visual Basic itself, along with some of the best programming practices to use, including those recommended by Microsoft. Every subsequent chapter starts with an overview of the subject it covers before digging into the specifics, making sure we never get lost in details. We'll also see discussions on best programming practices, program design, program testing, what makes a professional Windows application professional, and much more, as befits a book that wants to be your complete Visual Basic support package. In addition, the CD that accompanies this book holds the code for all the major projects we develop. To open and use a project, look for the Visual Basic project file (for example, browser.vbp for the browser project) and open that project file with Visual Basic.

Besides the code from the book, note that the CD has *hundreds* of megabytes of tools and software, ready for you to use.

What's In This Book

Just about everything we could write about Visual Basic is in this book, and that's a lot of ground to cover. From language reference to ADO database handling, from creating Web browsers to dragging and dropping data across applications, from email applications to multimedia players, from creating ActiveX controls and ActiveX documents to setup programs, it's all here.

Here's some of what we'll see how to create in this book:

- ActiveX controls
- ActiveX documents
- ADO, DAO, and RDO database applications
- Multimedia AVI, MPG, WAV, and MID players
- CD players that play CDs from the computer's CD-ROM drive
- Bitmapped menu items
- Full Web browsers
- Pie charts, line charts, bar charts, and others
- Code clients that call methods in programs like Microsoft Excel
- Code components (OLE automation servers)
- Graphics animation
- Applications that use the Windows Common Dialogs
- Customized toolbars with embedded controls like combo boxes
- Data entry forms
- Database editing applications
- Direct connections to the Windows API
- Direct connections to code written in Visual C++
- Drag/drop operations
- Graphics applications that draw arcs, circles, rectangles, lines, and more
- Email applications
- Error handlers
- Applications that use the printer
- Word processor applications
- File handlers for text and binary data
- FTP applications

- Dialog boxes
- Windows Help files
- MDI applications
- Pop-up menus activated with right mouse clicks
- Application deployment
- HTTP applications
- Image handling: blur, emboss, engrave, flip, sweep, stretch images, and more
- OLE applications
- Applications that use the Windows Registry
- List views and tree views
- Applications that create controls at runtime
- Mouse capture
- OLE drags (dragging data between applications)
- Online user registration
- Picture clip applications
- Setup programs
- Screen capture
- Spreadsheets
- Status bars and toolbars
- Tab strips, progress bars, and others

That's just some of what's coming up. Visual Basic is a very large topic, and the topics we'll cover number in the hundreds. And if you have suggestions for more, please send them in.

What You'll Need

To use this book profitably, you should have some experience with Visual Basic—not necessarily a lot, but enough to get through Chapter 1 without trouble. We assume you have some familiarity with the essentials of Visual Basic in this book, although those essentials are not very hard to pick up. If you do have trouble with Chapter 1, you might take a look at an introductory book before proceeding.

As far as software goes, just about all you need to use this book is already in Microsoft Visual Basic (we'll use version 6 in this book). Visual Basic comes with an enormous set of tools and resources, and we'll have our hands full putting them to work.

We try to be as self-contained in this book as possible—even creating the database files we'll use in examples with Visual Basic itself, not with a database application. The graphics files we use in various examples are on the CD, and the multimedia files we'll play in our multimedia examples come with Windows. Some of our OLE and OLE automation examples use Microsoft Excel, but Excel is not essential to those examples—any OLE server and OLE automation server program will do. Note that to use email from Visual Basic, you must have the Windows MAPI system installed (as represented by the Inbox icon on the Windows desktop).

Where can you go for additional Visual Basic support? You can find Visual Basic user groups all over, and more are appearing every day. You can also find Visual Basic information (and advertising) at the Microsoft Visual Basic home page at www.microsoft.com/vbasic/, free Visual Basic downloads at http://www.microsoft.com/vbasic/download/, and technical documents (white papers) at http://www.microsoft.com/vbasic/techmat/.

Although the content varies in accuracy, there are many Usenet groups dedicated to Visual Basic as well, but be careful what you read there—there's no guarantee it's accurate. About two dozen of those groups are hosted by Microsoft, including:

- microsoft.public.vb.bugs
- microsoft.public.vb.addins
- microsoft.public.vb.controls
- microsoft.public.vb.database
- microsoft.public.vb.installation
- microsoft.public.vb.ole
- microsoft.public.vb.ole.automation
- microsoft.public.vb.syntax

Other, non-Microsoft groups include some of these popular Usenet forums:

- comp.lang.basic.visual
- comp.lang.basic.visual.3rdparty
- comp.lang.basic.visual.announce
- comp.lang.basic.visual.database
- comp.lang.basic.visual.misc

And that all the introduction we need—it's time to start digging into Visual Basic. As we've said, we intend this book to be your complete support package for Visual Basic, so, again, if you see something that should be covered and isn't, let us know. In the meantime, happy reading!

Chapter 1

Visual Basic Overview

Welcome to our big book on Visual Basic. It's no secret that Visual Basic is the favorite programming environment of many programmers. (In fact, you're reading a book written by one of those programmers right now.) When Visual Basic first appeared, it created a revolution in Windows programming, and that revolution continues to this day. Never before had Windows programming been so easy—just build the program you want, right before your eyes, and then run it. Visual Basic introduced unheard-of ease to Windows programming and changed programming from a chore to something very fun.

In time, Visual Basic has gotten more complex, as well as more powerful. In this book, we're going to see how to use Visual Basic in a task-oriented way, which is the best way to write about programming. Instead of superimposing some abstract structure on the material in this book, we'll organize it the way programmers want it—task by task.

This book assumes you have some familiarity with Visual Basic; when you use this book, you'll usually have some task in mind—setting a program's startup form, for example, or optimizing for a specific processor—and this book will provide the answer. We'll try to be as complete as possible (*unlike* the frustrating recordings of frequently asked questions—which never seem to address your particular problem—you can access while on hold for tech support). This book is designed to be the one you come back to time and time again. It's not just to learn new techniques, but it is also to reacquaint yourself with the forgotten details of familiar methods.

We'll start with an overview of Visual Basic, taking a look at topics common to the material in the rest of the text. In this chapter, we'll create the foundation we'll rely on later as we take a look at the basics of Visual Basic, including how to create Visual Basic projects and seeing what's in such projects. We'll also get an overview of essential Visual Basic concepts like forms, controls, events, properties, methods, and so on. And we'll examine the structure of a Visual Basic program, taking a look at variables, variable scope, and modules. In other words, we're going to lay bare the anatomy of a Visual Basic program here.

We'll also take a look at programming practices common to all Visual Basic programs. This overview chapter is the place to take a look at those practices because they involve the rest of the book.

Most Visual Basic programmers do not have formal programming training and have to learn a lot of this material the hard way. As programming has matured, programmers have learned more and more about what are called "best practices"— the programming techniques that make robust, easily debugged programs. We'll take a look at those practices in this chapter, because they are becoming more and more essential for programmers in commercial environments these days, especially those programmers that work in teams. And we'll look at those practices from the viewpoint of programmers who program for a living; frequently there's a gap between the way best practices are taught by academics and how they are actually needed by programmers facing the prospect of writing a 20,000-line program as part of a team of programmers.

We'll start our overview chapter by creating and dissecting a Visual Basic project, jumping right into the code.

Creating A Project In Visual Basic

There are three different editions of Visual Basic:

- *The Learning Edition*, which is the most basic edition. This edition allows you to write many different types of programs, but lacks a number of tools that the other editions have.

- *The Professional Edition*, designed for professionals. This edition contains all that the Learning Edition contains and more, such as the capability to write ActiveX controls and documents.

- *The Enterprise Edition*, which is the most complete Visual Basic edition. This edition is targeted towards professional programmers who may work in a team and includes additional tools such as Visual SourceSafe, a version-control system that coordinates team programming.

We'll use the Enterprise Edition in this book, so if you have either of the other two editions, we might occasionally use something not supported in your Visual Basic edition. We'll try to keep such occurrences to a minimum.

Start Visual Basic now, bringing up the New Project dialog box, as shown in Figure 1.1.

In Figure 1.1 you see some of the project types that Visual Basic supports:

- Standard Windows EXE programs
- ActiveX EXE files

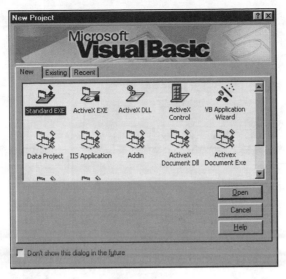

Figure 1.1   Creating a new Visual Basic project.

- ActiveX DLLs
- ActiveX controls
- Programs written by the Visual Basic Application Wizard
- Data projects
- IIS (the Microsoft Internet Information Server) applications
- Visual Basic add-ins
- ActiveX document DLLs
- ActiveX document EXE files
- DHTML applications
- VB Enterprise Edition controls

This list of project types indicates some of the ways Visual Basic has grown over the years. As you can see, there's a whole galaxy of power here (and we'll cover that galaxy in this book). In this case, we just want to take a look at the basics of a standard Visual Basic project, so double-click the Standard EXE item in the New Project dialog box, opening Visual Basic itself. Figure 1.2 shows the Visual Basic Integrated Development Environment (IDE). (We're going to cover all parts of the Visual Basic Integrated Development Environment in the next chapter—here, we'll just use it to create our first project.)

For our first example, we might create a small tic-tac-toe program using nine buttons in a form, as shown in Figure 1.3.

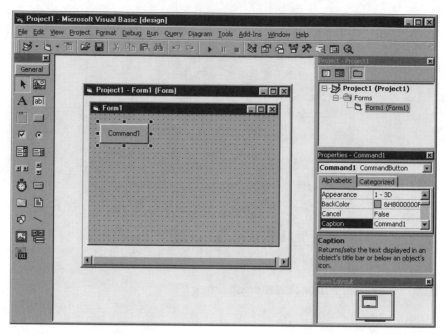

Figure 1.2   A new Visual Basic project.

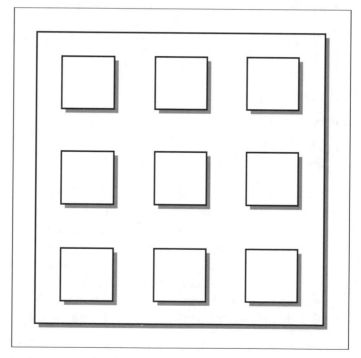

Figure 1.3   Designing our first project.

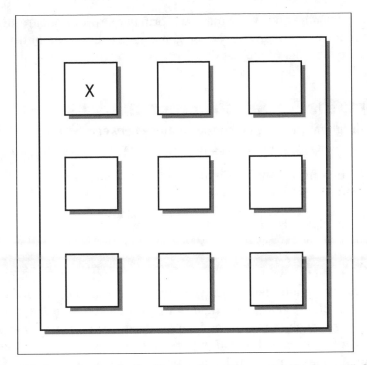

Figure 1.4   *Clicking a button in the tic-tac-toe program to display an "x".*

When the user clicks a button, we can display an "x" in the button's caption, as shown in Figure 1.4.

If the user clicks another button, we can display an "o", and so forth.

This example will create a program that lets us take a look at Visual Basic projects, controls, control arrays, events, properties, coding, variables, and variable scope.

Designing The Tic-Tac-Toe Program

Using the Command Button tool in the Visual Basic toolbox, add a new command button to the main form in our program now, as shown earlier in Figure 1.2. Next, in the Properties window, change the **Name** property of this button from **Command1** to **Command** in preparation for setting up a control array, and clear its **Caption** property so the button appears blank.

Next, add a second button to the form, and set its **Name** property to **Command** as well. When you do, Visual Basic opens a dialog box that states: "You already have a control named 'Command'. Do you want to set up a control array?" Click Yes to create a control array, which means we will be able to refer to our controls using an index instead of simply by name.

Add a total of nine buttons to the main form in our program, arranged in a 3×3 grid similar to a standard tic-tac-toe game, give each of the buttons the name **Command**, and clear their captions. That completes the preliminary design—now we're ready to write some code.

Coding The Tic-Tac-Toe Program

In this program, we'll toggle button captions between "x" and "o". To start coding, double-click any button, opening the code window, as shown in Figure 1.5.

Double-clicking a button creates an event handler subroutine named **Command_Click( )** and opens that subroutine in the code window:

```
Private Sub Command_Click(Index As Integer)

End Sub
```

Visual Basic programs like this one are centered around *events*, and most events occur when the user triggers them. In this case, a **Click** event is triggered when the user clicks a button, and we're passed the button's index in the control array of buttons as the **Index** parameter in **Command_Click( )**, as with this line of code from the earlier snippet:

```
Private Sub Command_Click(Index As Integer)
```

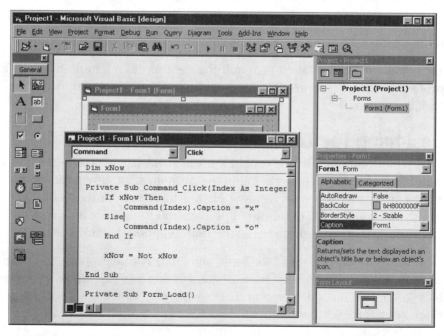

Figure 1.5   Using the Visual Basic code window.

When the user clicks a button, we need to know which character to display, and we'll keep track of that in a form-wide variable named **xNow**; if **xNow** is True, we should display an x, if False, an o.

To add that form-wide variable, click the (General) entry in the left drop-down list box in the code window, and add this code to the general section of our form:

```
Dim xNow
```

You can indicate the type of a variable when declaring it with **Dim**—to indicate that **xNow** is a Boolean variable, we could declare it this way:

```
Dim xNow As Boolean
```

(Declaring it without a type makes it a variant, which means it can operate as any type of variable.) The possible variable types and their ranges appear in Table 1.1.

Table 1.1 Variable types.

Variable Type	Bytes Of Storage	Range
Boolean	2	True or False
Byte	1	0 to 255
Currency	8	-922,337,203,685,477.5808 to 922,337,203,685,477.5807
Date	8	1 January 100 to 31 December 9999 and times from 0:00:00 to 23:59:59
Decimal	12	-79,228,162,514,264,337,593,543,950,335 to 79,228,162,514,264,337,593,543,950,335
Double	8	-1.79769313486232E308 to 4.94065645841247E-324 for negative values and from 4.94065645841247E-324 to 1.79769313486232E308 for positive values
Integer	2	-32,768 to 32,767
Long	4	-2,147,483,648 to 2,147,483,647
Object	4	N/A
Single	4	-3.402823E38 to -1.401298E-45 for negative values and from 1.401298E-45 to 3.402823E38 for positive values
String	N/A	A variable-length string can contain up to approximately 2 billion characters; a fixed-length string can contain 1 to approximately 64K characters

(continued)

Table 1.1   Variable types (continued).

Variable Type	Bytes Of Storage	Range
User-defined data type	N/A	N/A
Variant	N/A	N/A

We need to initialize that form-wide variable, **xNow**, and we do that when the form first loads in the **Form_Load( )** procedure, which is run when the form is first loaded. Open that procedure now by selecting the Form item in the code window's left drop-down list box, or by double-clicking the form itself; here, we just initialize **xNow** to True:

```
Private Sub Form_Load()
    xNow = True
End Sub
```

Now we will toggle the clicked button's caption depending on the current setting of **xNow**. To reach the clicked button in **Command_Click( )**, we use the control array index passed to us this way:

```
Private Sub Command_Click(Index As Integer)
    If xNow Then
        Command(Index).Caption = "x"
    Else
        Command(Index).Caption = "o"
    End If
...
End Sub
```

Finally, we toggle **xNow** (from True to False or False to True) this way:

```
Private Sub Command_Click(Index As Integer)
    If xNow Then
        Command(Index).Caption = "x"
    Else
        Command(Index).Caption = "o"
    End If

    xNow = Not xNow

End Sub
```

Figure 1.6   Running the tic-tac-toe program.

And that's all we need—the tic-tac-toe program is complete. Run it now, as shown in Figure 1.6, and click a few buttons. The captions toggle between x and o as they should.

It's not a very exciting program as it stands, of course, because it was just designed to give us a look into how Visual Basic projects work. Now we'll take a closer look at the parts of a project, starting with the one we've just created.

The Parts Of A Visual Basic Project

Projects can become quite advanced in Visual Basic, even containing sub-projects of different types. From a programming point of view, however, standard Visual Basic projects usually contain just three types of items: global items, forms, and modules, as outlined in Figure 1.7.

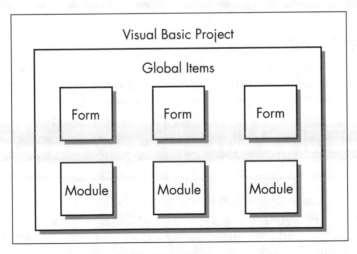

Figure 1.7   The parts of a Visual Basic project.

Forms

Forms are familiar to all Visual Basic programmers, of course—they're the templates you base windows on. Besides standard forms, Visual Basic also supports Multiple Document Interface (MDI) forms, as well as a whole number of predefined forms that we'll see in the next chapter.

Modules

Modules are collections of code and data that function something like objects in object-oriented programming (OOP), but without defining OOP characteristics like inheritance, polymorphism, and so on. The point behind modules is to enclose procedures and data in a way that hides them from the rest of the program. We'll discuss the importance of doing this later in this chapter when we cover Visual Basic programming techniques and style; breaking a large program into smaller, self-contained modules can be invaluable for creating and maintaining code.

You can think of well-designed modules conceptually as programming objects; for example, you might have a module that handles screen display that includes a dozen internal (unseen by the rest of the program) procedures and one or two procedures accessible to the rest of the program. In this way, the rest of the program only has to deal with one or two procedures, not a dozen.

Besides modules, Visual Basic also supports *class modules*, which we'll see later in this book when we discuss how to create ActiveX components in Chapter 20. Programming with class modules will bring us much closer to true OOP programming.

Global Items

Global items are accessible to all modules and forms in a project, and you declare them with the **Public** keyword. However, Microsoft recommends that you keep the number of global items to an absolute minimum and, in fact, suggests their use only when you need to communicate between forms. One reason to avoid global variables is their accessibility from anywhere in the program; while you're working with a global variable in one part of a program, another part of the program might be busy changing that variable, giving you unpredictable results.

Now that we've gotten an overview of the major parts of a project, we'll take a look at how the parts of a project interact, which brings up the idea of *scope*, or visibility in a project.

Project Scope

An object's scope indicates how much visibility it has throughout the project—in the procedure where it's declared, throughout a form or module, or global scope (which means it's accessible everywhere). There are two types of scope in Visual Basic projects: variable scope (including object variables) and procedure scope. We'll take a look at both of them here as we continue our overview of Visual Basic projects and how the parts of those projects interact.

Variable Scope

You declare variables in a number of ways. Most often, you use the **Dim** statement to declare a variable. If you do not specify the variable type when you use **Dim**, it creates a variant, which can operate as any variable type. You can specify the variable type using the **As** keyword like this:

```
Dim IntegerValue As Integer
```

Besides **Dim**, you can also use **ReDim** to redimension space for dynamic arrays, **Private** to restrict it to a module or form, **Public** to make it global—that is, accessible to all modules or forms—or **Static** to make sure its value doesn't change between procedure calls. These ways of declaring variables are summarized in Table 1.2.

There are three levels of variable scope in Visual Basic: at the procedure level, at the form or module level, and at the global level. Schematically, Figure 1.8 shows how project scope works.

When you're designing your program, Microsoft suggests you limit your variables to the minimum possible scope in order to make things simpler and to avoid conflicts. Next, we'll take a look at the other type of scope: procedure scope.

Table 1.2   Visual Basic declaring statements.

Keyword	Does This
Dim	Using **Dim** alone creates variants. Use the **As** keyword to specify variable type.
Private	Makes variable available only in the current form/module.
Public	Makes variable global—variable is available to the rest of program.
ReDim	Reallocates storage space for dynamic array variables.
Static	Variable preserves its value between procedure calls.
Type	Declares a user type.

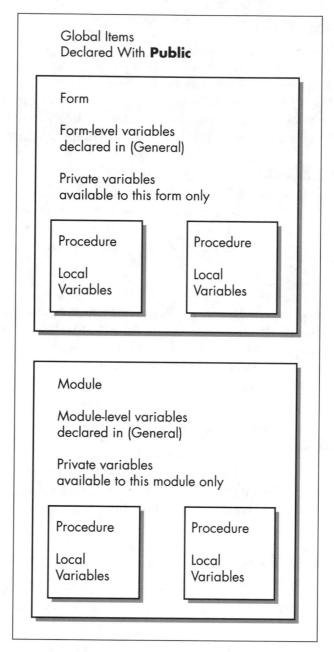

Figure 1.8   Schematic of Visual Basic project scope.

Procedure Scope

As with variables, you can restrict the scope of procedures, and you do that with the **Private**, **Public**, **Friend**, and **Static** keywords. The **Private** and **Public** keywords are the main keywords here; using them, you can specify if a subroutine or function is private to the module or form in which it is declared or public (that is, global) to all forms and modules. You use these keywords before the **Sub** or **Function** keywords like this:

```
Private Function Returns7()
    Dim Retval
    Retval = 7
    Returns7 = Retval
End Function
```

You can also declare procedures as *friend* procedures with the **Friend** keyword. Friend procedures are usually used in class modules (they are not available in standard modules, although you can declare them in forms) to declare that the procedure is available outside the class, but not outside the current project. This restricts those functions from being called if the current project serves as an OLE automation server, for example.

Besides the earlier declarations, you can also declare procedures as **Static**, which means that the variables in the procedure do not change between procedure calls, and that can be very useful in cases like this, where we support a counter variable that is incremented each time a function is called:

```
Static Function Counter()
    Dim CounterValue as Integer
    CounterValue = CounterValue + 1
    Counter = CounterValue
End Sub
```

That completes our overview of projects in memory now—we've seen how such projects are organized, what parts they have, and what scope their parts have. We'll take a look at storing projects on disk next.

Projects On Disk

Now that we've created our first project—the tic-tac-toe project—we'll save it to disk. Turn to Visual Basic now and select the Save Project As item in the Visual Basic File menu to save our new project to disk.

Visual Basic first saves the files associated with the project, and places a Save File As dialog box on the screen to save the program's form, which Visual

Basic gives the default name of Form1.frm. Change that name to tictactoe.frm now, and save it to disk (in this book, we'll save projects in the C:\vbbb directory, so this project will go into the C:\vbbb\tictactoe directory).

Next, Visual Basic displays the Save Project As dialog box. Each project has at least one project file, and it gives the default name Project1.vbp to ours. Change that to tictactoe.vbp now, and save that project file to disk.

In the Enterprise Edition of Visual Basic, another dialog box, labeled Source Code Control, will pop up with the prompt: Add This Project To SourceSafe? SourceSafe is a special utility to coordinate teams of programmers. For now, click No.

This saves our project to disk, which really means the new files tictactoe.vbp, tictactoe.vbw, and tictactoe.frm are created (and, if you have the Enterprise Edition, Mssccprj.scc, which is used by SourceSafe). The VBP file is the project file itself and stores overall information about the project. The VBW file is the workspace file and stores information used by the Visual Basic development environment (such as which windows are open, and where they are placed; if your project doesn't include this file, one will be created when you start editing the project in the Visual Basic IDE). The FRM files are for forms, and if you have any modules in your project, they are stored as BAS files. An overview of a project's files appears in Figure 1.9.

We'll take a look at these kinds of files in turn, starting with the project file, tictactoe.vbp.

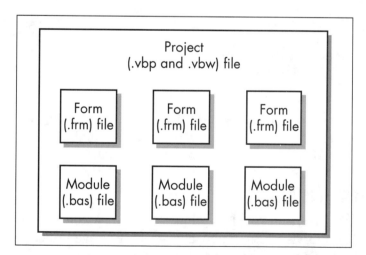

Figure 1.9   *The types of files in a Visual Basic project.*

Project Files

The project file, tictactoe.vbp, coordinates the overall project. This is the file that specifies what type your project is; what forms are in your project; what the startup form (if any) is; what the name, version, and compiler options are for your project; and much more. For example, here's how our project is recorded in tictactoe.vbp—as an EXE.exe project with the startup form **Form1**, and as version 1.0 of this program:

```
Type=Exe
Form=tictactoe.frm
...
MajorVer=1
MinorVer=0
```

Besides this information, the project file includes compiler options of the type we'll see in the next chapter (the **FDIVCheck** item is to check for bad Pentiums processors):

```
CompilationType=0
OptimizationType=0
FavorPentiumPro(tm)=0
CodeViewDebugInfo=0
NoAliasing=0
BoundsCheck=0
OverflowCheck=0
FlPointCheck=0
FDIVCheck=0
UnroundedFP=0
StartMode=0
Unattended=0
ThreadPerObject=0
MaxNumberOfThreads=1
```

Overall, then, the project file coordinates the project as far as Visual Basic is concerned. The listing for tictactoe.vbp appears in Listing 1.1.

Listing 1.1 *tictactoe.vbp*

```
Type=Exe
Form=tictactoe.frm
Reference=*\G{00020430-0000-0000-C000-_
    000000000046}#2.0#0#..\..\WINDOWS\SYSTEM\STDOLE2.TLB#OLE Automation
Startup="Form1"
Command32=""
```

```
Name="Project1"
HelpContextID="0"
CompatibleMode="0"
MajorVer=1
MinorVer=0
RevisionVer=0
AutoIncrementVer=0
ServerSupportFiles=0
VersionCompanyName="SteveCo"
CompilationType=0
OptimizationType=0
FavorPentiumPro(tm)=0
CodeViewDebugInfo=0
NoAliasing=0
BoundsCheck=0
OverflowCheck=0
FlPointCheck=0
FDIVCheck=0
UnroundedFP=0
StartMode=0
Unattended=0
ThreadPerObject=0
MaxNumberOfThreads=1
```

The other type of project file, the tictactoe.vbw file, which holds workspace information, is really used by the Integrated Development Environment (IDE).

Workspace Files

The tictactoe.vbw file holds information about what windows are open where in the IDE, and other information. In our very simple example, our VBW file only contains information about the form we've been working on, **Form1**, and its location in the IDE:

```
Form1 = 16, 123, 410, 430, , 44, 44, 395, 351,
```

For our purposes, VBW files aren't very interesting.

Form Files

Form files are more interesting, however. In tictactoe.frm, for example, we start with the general properties of the form: its caption, height, width, and so on:

```
Begin VB.Form Form1
    Caption        =   "Form1"
    ClientHeight   =   3195
```

```
ClientLeft      =   60
ClientTop       =   345
ClientWidth     =   4680
LinkTopic       =   "Form1"
ScaleHeight     =   3195
ScaleWidth      =   4680
StartUpPosition =   3   'Windows Default
```

TIP: *Distances are measured in what was supposed to be a device-independent way in Visual Basic using twips (a twip is 1/1440 of an inch). You don't have to use twips, though—you can change the measurement scale in a form by setting its **ScaleMode** property to 0 for user-defined units, 1 for twips, 2 for points (1/72 of an inch), 3 for pixels, 4 for characters (120 twips horizontally, 240 twips vertically), 5 for inches, 6 for millimeters, and 7 for centimeters. This can be very useful if your user interface depends on measurements of distance.*

Next comes the command buttons in our form, specified by name, location, and tab index:

```
Begin VB.Form Form1
...
   Begin VB.CommandButton Command
      Height      =   495
      Index       =   8
      Left        =   3120
      TabIndex    =   8
      Top         =   2160
      Width       =   1215
   End
   Begin VB.CommandButton Command
      Height      =   495
      Index       =   7
      Left        =   1680
      TabIndex    =   7
      Top         =   2160
      Width       =   1215
   End
   Begin VB.CommandButton Command
      Height      =   495
      Index       =   6
      Left        =   240
      TabIndex    =   6
      Top         =   2160
      Width       =   1215
   End
```

```
Begin VB.CommandButton Command
   Height          =   495
   Index           =   5
   Left            =   3120
   TabIndex        =   5
   Top             =   1200
   Width           =   1215
End
Begin VB.CommandButton Command
   Height          =   495
   Index           =   4
   Left            =   1680
   TabIndex        =   4
   Top             =   1200
   Width           =   1215
End
Begin VB.CommandButton Command
   Height          =   495
   Index           =   3
   Left            =   240
   TabIndex        =   3
   Top             =   1200
   Width           =   1215
End
Begin VB.CommandButton Command
   Height          =   495
   Index           =   2
   Left            =   3120
   TabIndex        =   2
   Top             =   240
   Width           =   1215
End
Begin VB.CommandButton Command
   Height          =   495
   Index           =   1
   Left            =   1680
   TabIndex        =   1
   Top             =   240
   Width           =   1215
End
Begin VB.CommandButton Command
   Height          =   495
   Index           =   0
   Left            =   240
   TabIndex        =   0
   Top             =   240
```

```
        Width            =    1215
    End
End
```

TIP: *A control's tab index indicates its position as the user moves from control to control using the Tab key. You can change the tab order of controls using this index property. If you set a control's **TabStop** property to False, the user cannot tab to that control.*

Some distance after the controls in the tictactoe.frm file comes the code we've put into this form:

```
Dim xNow

Private Sub Command_Click(Index As Integer)
    If xNow Then
        Command(Index).Caption = "x"
    Else
        Command(Index).Caption = "o"
    End If

    xNow = Not xNow

End Sub

Private Sub Form_Load()
    xNow = True
End Sub
```

As you can see, the complete specification for our form appears in the FRM file, and it's in readable format. It's worthwhile understanding the basic structures of FRM files, because if something's going wrong (for example, a FRM file got corrupted), you can sometimes find the answer here yourself. The listing for this file, tictactoe.frm, appears in Listing 1.2; note that if you re-create this project by hand, some measurements, like heights and widths, will differ in your FRM file.

Listing 1.2   tictactoe.frm

```
VERSION 6.00
Begin VB.Form Form1
    Caption          =    "Form1"
    ClientHeight     =    3195
    ClientLeft       =    60
    ClientTop        =    345
    ClientWidth      =    4680
```

```
LinkTopic        =    "Form1"
ScaleHeight      =    3195
ScaleWidth       =    4680
StartUpPosition =    3    'Windows Default
Begin VB.CommandButton Command
   Height        =    495
   Index         =    8
   Left          =    3120
   TabIndex      =    8
   Top           =    2160
   Width         =    1215
End
Begin VB.CommandButton Command
   Height        =    495
   Index         =    7
   Left          =    1680
   TabIndex      =    7
   Top           =    2160
   Width         =    1215
End
Begin VB.CommandButton Command
   Height        =    495
   Index         =    6
   Left          =    240
   TabIndex      =    6
   Top           =    2160
   Width         =    1215
End
Begin VB.CommandButton Command
   Height        =    495
   Index         =    5
   Left          =    3120
   TabIndex      =    5
   Top           =    1200
   Width         =    1215
End
Begin VB.CommandButton Command
   Height        =    495
   Index         =    4
   Left          =    1680
   TabIndex      =    4
   Top           =    1200
   Width         =    1215
End
Begin VB.CommandButton Command
   Height        =    495
```

```
                Index          =    3
                Left           =    240
                TabIndex       =    3
                Top            =    1200
                Width          =    1215
            End
            Begin VB.CommandButton Command
                Height         =    495
                Index          =    2
                Left           =    3120
                TabIndex       =    2
                Top            =    240
                Width          =    1215
            End
            Begin VB.CommandButton Command
                Height         =    495
                Index          =    1
                Left           =    1680
                TabIndex       =    1
                Top            =    240
                Width          =    1215
            End
            Begin VB.CommandButton Command
                Height         =    495
                Index          =    0
                Left           =    240
                TabIndex       =    0
                Top            =    240
                Width          =    1215
            End
        End
End
Attribute VB_Name = "Form1"
Attribute VB_GlobalNameSpace = False
Attribute VB_Creatable = False
Attribute VB_PredeclaredId = True
Attribute VB_Exposed = False
Dim xNow

Private Sub Command_Click(Index As Integer)
    If xNow Then
        Command(Index).Caption = "x"
    Else
        Command(Index).Caption = "o"
    End If

    xNow = Not xNow
```

```
End Sub

Private Sub Form_Load()
    xNow = True
End Sub
```

We'll take a look at module files next.

Module Files

We don't have any module files in the tic-tac-toe project, but if we did, it would be stored in a BAS file. BAS files hold code and data and might look something like this (note the name of the module, which is stored in the first line, followed by the code in this module):

```
Attribute VB_Name = "Module1"
Sub CheckData(value1 As Integer)
    If value1 = 1 Then
        MsgBox ("Value OK")
    Else
        MsgBox ("Uh oh")
    End If
End Sub

Function Returns7()
    Dim Retval
    Retval = 7
    Returns7 = Retval
End Function
```

This completes our overview of the standard parts of a standard Visual Basic project. We've seen how simple projects work in Visual Basic now. Besides this simple kind of project, you can design quite advanced projects using a tool like the Visual Basic Application Wizard, and we'll take a look at that now.

Using The Visual Basic Application Wizard

The Visual Basic Application Wizard is a Visual Basic add-in that lets you use some advanced project features when you first create a project. The Application Wizard is usually used by beginning programmers, but we'll take a look at it here to get an idea of what more involved projects can look like.

You start the Application Wizard from the New Project box, opened either from the New item in the File menu or when Visual Basic first starts. The Application Wizard appears in Figure 1.10.

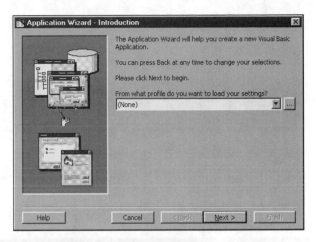

Figure 1.10   The Visual Basic Application Wizard.

TIP: *In Figure 1.10, the Application Wizard is asking for a profile. You can save Application Wizard profiles (something like project templates) in the last step of the Application Wizard, which lets you save all the options you've specified. Loading them in later can save you some time if you just want to alter a few settings.*

Click the Next button in the Application Wizard now, opening the next screen, shown in Figure 1.11. The Multiple Document Interface (MDI) option is already selected, and we'll leave it selected. Click the Next button to move to the next screen.

The next screen lets you select menu options, the next screen toolbar options, and the one after that resource options. Keep clicking Next to accept all the defaults. The Internet Connectivity screen, which opens next, lets you add a

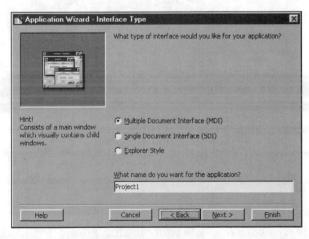

Figure 1.11   Selecting MDI support in the Visual Basic Application Wizard.

Figure 1.12   Adding a Web browser with the Visual Basic Application Wizard.

Web browser window to your project if you like. This can be very useful, so click Yes as shown in Figure 1.12, then click Next again to move on.

The next step in the Application Wizard, as shown in Figure 1.13, lets you add a *splash screen*. A splash screen comes up while the program is loading and can give the impression that something is really happening while the program is loaded. We add a splash screen to our program by selecting the Splash Screen At Application Start Up option.

TIP: Originally, splash screens were very popular—in fact, virtually every piece of Microsoft software has one these days—but users are catching on that they are just razzle-dazzle.

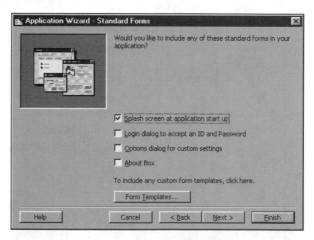

Figure 1.13   Adding a splash screen with the Visual Basic Application Wizard.

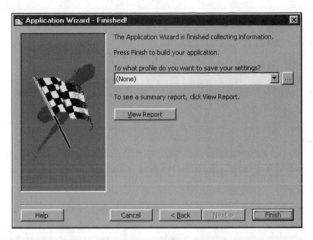

Figure 1.14   Finishing a Visual Basic Application Wizard project.

The next screen asks about database connectivity; click Next to open the last Application Wizard screen, shown in Figure 1.14.

Click Finish in the last Application Wizard screen now to create the project, and run that project, as shown in Figure 1.15.

This new program has a great deal of programming power. As you can see in Figure 1.15, this program is an MDI program, capable of opening multiple documents and even displaying a Web browser in a window. In fact, you can even use the File menu's Open, Save, and Save As items to open and display files.

There's a lot of power here, and we'll see how to do all these things ourselves in this book. It's instructive to take a look at the project file for this project, where we see that this project makes use of these ActiveX controls:

• Common dialogs (COMDLG32.OCX)

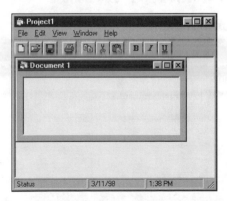

Figure 1.15   Running our Visual Basic Application Wizard program.

- Common windows controls (MSCOMCTL.OCX)
- Rich text control (RICHTX32.OCX)
- Web browser DLL (SHDOCVW.DLL)

Here is the code snippet:

```
Type=Exe
Reference=*\G{00020430-0000-0000-C000-_
    000000000046}#2.0#0#..\..\WINDOWS\SYSTEM\STDOLE2.TLB#OLE Automation
Module=Module1; Module1.bas
Form=frmMain.frm
Object={F9043C88-F6F2-101A-A3C9-08002B2F49FB}#1.2#0; COMDLG32.OCX
Object={6B7E6392-850A-101B-AFC0-4210102A8DA7}#1.3#0; MSCOMCTL.OCX
Form=frmSplash.frm
Object={3B7C8863-D78F-101B-B9B5-04021C009402}#1.1#0; RICHTX32.OCX
Form=frmDocument.frm
Object={EAB22AC0-30C1-11CF-A7EB-0000C05BAE0B}#1.1#0; SHDOCVW.DLL
Form=frmBrowser.frm
Startup="Sub Main"
...
```

Note the last of the statements, **Startup="Sub Main"**. This indicates that this program starts with a **Main( )** procedure, not a startup form (we'll see more about this in the next chapter). In the **Main( )** procedure, the program first loads the splash screen, then the MDI frame window. The MDI frame window in turn loads its first child window, based on the **frmDocument** form. Taking a look at frmDocument.frm, which appears in Listing 1.3, indicates that this child window displays a rich text control (as you can see by the inclusion of the rich text control), which in fact handles all the text. As you can see, taking apart projects file by file this way removes all the mystery, and it's a good skill for the Visual Basic programmer to have.

Listing 1.3 frmDocument.frm

```
VERSION 6.00
Object = "{3B7C8863-D78F-101B-B9B5-04021C009402}#1.1#0"; "RICHTX32.OCX"
Begin VB.Form frmDocument
    Caption         =   "frmDocument"
    ClientHeight    =   3195
    ClientLeft      =   60
    ClientTop       =   345
    ClientWidth     =   4680
    LinkTopic       =   "Form1"
    MDIChild        =   -1  'True
    ScaleHeight     =   3195
```

```
        ScaleWidth      =   4680
        Begin RichTextLib.RichTextBox rtfText
            Height        =   2000
            Left          =   100
            TabIndex      =   0
            Top           =   100
            Width         =   3000
            _ExtentX      =   5292
            _ExtentY      =   3519
            _Version      =   393216
            Enabled       =   -1  'True
            ScrollBars    =   3
            RightMargin   =   8e6
            TextRTF       =   $"frmDocument.frx":0000
        End
    End
End
Attribute VB_Name = "frmDocument"
Attribute VB_GlobalNameSpace = False
Attribute VB_Creatable = False
Attribute VB_PredeclaredId = True
Attribute VB_Exposed = False
Private Sub rtfText_SelChange()
    fMainForm.tbToolBar.Buttons("Bold").Value = IIf(rtfText.SelBold, _
        tbrPressed, tbrUnpressed)
    fMainForm.tbToolBar.Buttons("Italic").Value = IIf(rtfText.SelItalic, _
        tbrPressed, tbrUnpressed)
    fMainForm.tbToolBar.Buttons("Underline").Value = _
        IIf(rtfText.SelUnderline, tbrPressed, tbrUnpressed)
    fMainForm.tbToolBar.Buttons("Align Left").Value = _
        IIf(rtfText.SelAlignment = rtfLeft, tbrPressed, tbrUnpressed)
    fMainForm.tbToolBar.Buttons("Align Right").Value = _
        IIf(rtfText.SelAlignment = rtfRight, tbrPressed, tbrUnpressed)
    fMainForm.tbToolBar.Buttons("Center").Value = _
        IIf(rtfText.SelAlignment = rtfCenter, tbrPressed, tbrUnpressed)
End Sub


Private Sub Form_Load()
    Form_Resize
End Sub



Private Sub Form_Resize()
    On Error Resume Next
    rtfText.Move 100, 100, Me.ScaleWidth - 200, Me.ScaleHeight - 200
    rtfText.RightMargin = rtfText.Width - 400
End Sub
```

That completes our overview of Visual Basic projects for now, although there will be more about projects throughout the book. We'll turn to an overview of another kind now: discussing topics that impact every chapter in the book. In this overview, we're going to cover general Visual Basic programming issues, including Visual Basic conventions, best coding practices, and code optimization. This discussion touches practically every aspect of our book, so it's best to consider it first.

Visual Basic Programming Conventions

Microsoft has set up a number of conventions for programming Visual Basic, including naming conventions. These conventions are not necessary if you program alone, but they can still be helpful. If you program as part of a team, these conventions can be very valuable, because they provide clues to a variable's scope and type to someone reading your code. Because many Visual Basic programmers work in teams these days, we'll cover the Microsoft programming conventions here, beginning with variable scope prefixes.

Variable Scope Prefixes

You use a variable prefix in front of its name to indicate something about that variable. For example, if you have a global variable named **ErrorCount**, you can use the **g** prefix to indicate that that variable is global this way: **gErrorCount**. Microsoft has established scope prefixes for variables as shown in Table 1.3.

The scope prefixes come before all other prefixes—and there are many other types, such as variable prefixes, control prefixes, and so on. We'll continue with variable prefixes.

Variable Prefixes

Ideally, variable names should be prefixed to indicate their data type. Table 1.4 lists the prefixes that Microsoft recommends for all the Visual Basic data types.

Table 1.3   Variable scope prefix conventions.

Scope	Prefix
Global	g
Module-level or form-level	m
Local to procedure	None

Table 1.4   Variable prefixes.

Data Type	Prefix
Boolean	bln
Byte	byt
Collection object	col
Currency	cur
Date (Time)	dtm
Double	dbl
Error	err
Integer	int
Long	lng
Object	obj
Single	sng
String	str
User-defined type	udt
Variant	vnt

Here are some prefixed variable names using the recommended variable prefixes:

```
blnTrueFalse          'Boolean
intCounter            'Integer
sngDividend           'Single
```

Using variable prefixes this way provides some clue as to the variable's type, and that can be extraordinarily helpful if someone else will be reading your code. Note that it's also a good idea to prefix function names using the above prefixes to indicate the return type of the function.

Besides variable prefixes, Microsoft also has a set of prefixes for the standard control types.

Control Prefixes

The suggested Microsoft control prefixes appear in Table 1.5. As you can see, there's a suggested prefix for every standard type of control.

Table 1.5   Control prefixes.

Control Type	Prefix
3D panel	pnl
ADO data	ado
Animated button	ani
Checkbox	chk
Combo box, drop-down list box	cbo
Command button	cmd
Common dialog	dlg
Communications	com
Control (used within procedures when the specific type is unknown)	ctr
Data	dat
Data-bound combo box	dbcbo
Data-bound grid	dbgrd
Data-bound list box	dblst
Data combo	dbc
Data grid	dgd
Data list	dbl
Data repeater	drp
Date picker	dtp
Directory list box	dir
Drive list box	drv
File list box	fil
Flat scroll bar	fsb
Form	frm
Frame	fra
Gauge	gau
Graph	gra
Grid	grd
Header	hdr
Hierarchical flex grid	flex
Horizontal scroll bar	hsb
Image	img

(continued)

Table 1.5   Control prefixes (continued).

Control Type	Prefix
Image combo	imgcbo
Image list	ils
Label	lbl
Lightweight checkbox	lwchk
Lightweight combo box	lwcbo
Lightweight command button	lwcmd
Lightweight frame	lwfra
Lightweight horizontal scroll bar	lwhsb
Lightweight list box	lwlst
Lightwoight option button	lwopt
Lightweight text box	lwtxt
Lightweight vertical scroll bar	lwvsb
Line	lin
List box	lst
List view	lvw
MAPI message	mpm
MAPI session	mps
MCI	mci
Menu	mnu
Month view	mvw
MS chart	ch
MS flex grid	msg
MS tab	mst
OLE container	ole
Option button	opt
Picture box	pic
Picture clip	clp
Progress bar	prg
Remote data	rd
Rich text box	rtf
Shape	shp

(continued)

Table 1.5   Control prefixes (continued).

Control Type	Prefix
Slider	sld
Spin	spn
Status bar	sta
System info	sys
Tab strip	tab
Text box	txt
Timer	tmr
Toolbar	tlb
Tree view	tre
Up-down	upd
Vertical scroll bar	vsb

If you work with databases, take a look at Table 1.6, which holds the prefixes for Data Access Objects (DAO).

Besides the prefixes in Table 1.6, Microsoft recommends prefixes for menus and constants as well, and we'll take a look at these now to round off our discussion on this topic.

Table 1.6   Data Access Object prefixes.

Database Object	Prefix
Container	con
Database	db
DBEngine	dbe
Document	doc
Field	fld
Group	grp
Index	ix
Parameter	prm
QueryDef	qry
Recordset	rec
Relation	rel
TableDef	tbd
User	usr
Workspace	wsp

Menu And Constant Prefixes

Microsoft recommends that you prefix menu controls with **mnu** and then the menu name followed by the menu item name. For example, the File menu's Open item would be named **mnuFileOpen**, and the Edit menu's Cut item would be named **mnuEditCut**. Microsoft also recommends that constant names (you declare constants with the **Const** statement) should be mixed case with capitals starting each word, for example:

```
Const DiskDriveNumber = 1        'Constant
Const MaximumFileCount = 1024    'Constant
```

TIP: *Although standard Visual Basic constants do not include data type and scope information, prefixes like* ***i***, ***s***, ***g***, *and* ***m*** *can be useful in understanding the value or scope of a constant.*

That completes the prefix and naming conventions. As you can see, there are prefixes for just about every type of programming construct available. You're not constrained to use them, but if you work in a team, they can be extremely helpful.

Microsoft also has a set of suggestions on commenting your code, and we'll take a look at those suggestions now.

Code Commenting Conventions

In general, you should add a new comment when you declare a new and important variable, or wish to make clear some implementation method. Ideally, procedures should only have one purpose and be named clearly enough so that excessive comments are not required. In addition, procedures should begin with a comment describing what the procedure does, and that comment should be broken up into various sections. The Microsoft recommendations for those sections appear in Table 1.7; note that not all sections may be applicable for all procedures.

Table 1.7   *Procedures for starting comment block sections.*

Section Heading	Comment Description
Purpose	What the procedure does
Assumptions	List of each external variable, control, open file, or other element that is not obvious
Effects	List of each affected external variable, control, or file and the effect it has (only if this is not obvious)

(continued)

Table 1.7 Procedures for starting comment block sections (continued).

Section Heading	Comment Description
Inputs	Each argument that may not be obvious; arguments are on a separate line with inline comments
Returns	Explanation of the values returned by functions

Here's an example showing how to set up a comment preceding a function named **dblSquare( )**:

```
'*****************************************************
' dblSquare()
' Purpose: Squares a number
' Inputs: sngSquareMe, the value to be squared
' Returns: The input value squared
'*****************************************************
Function dblSquare() (sngSquareMe As Integer) As Double
    dblSquare = sngSquareMe * sngSquareMe    'Use *, not ^2, for speed
End Function
```

TIP: You might notice that **dblSquare()** takes a Single parameter and returns a Double value; that's because squaring a Single can create a larger number, which might not fit into a Single value, or it can add more decimal places. Note also that we multiply the parameter **sngSquareMe** by itself to square it instead of using the exponentiation operator, because doing so saves a lot of processor time.

Note that it's particularly important to list all the global variables a procedure uses or affects in this initial comment block, because they are not listed in the parameter list.

That completes our overview of the Visual Basic programming conventions. We'll finish the chapter with a look at what we might call *best coding practices*, as targeted at Visual Basic. Through the years, some definite programming practices have proven themselves better than others, and we'll take a look at some of them now before digging into the rest of the book.

Best Coding Practices In Visual Basic

The full construction of a commercial program is usually a project that involves many clear and definite steps. There have been whole volumes written on this topic, which are usually only interesting if you are a software project manager (or write computer books and have to know the details so you can write about them!). Such books get pretty involved, encompassing ideas like module coupling and cohesion, bottom-up composition, incremental integration, and much more.

On the whole, however, one can break the software design process into steps like these (note that the explanation of each step is very flexible; there is no one-size-fits-all here):

- *Requirements analysis*—Identify the problem for the software to tackle.
- *Creating specifications*—Determine what *exactly* the software should do.
- *Overall design*—Break the overall project into parts, modules, and so on.
- *Detailed design*—Design the actual data structures, procedures, and so on.
- *Coding*—Go from PDL to code.
- *Debugging*—Solve design-time, compilation, and obvious errors.
- *Testing*—Try to break the software.
- *Maintenance*—React to user feedback and *keep testing*.

Each of these steps may have many subparts, of course. (For example, the maintenance part may take up as much time as the rest of the project taken together.)

As the design process continues, a *model* of what the program does evolves. You use this model to get a conceptual handle on the software (while keeping in mind that models are usually flawed at some level). Keeping the model in mind, then, many programmers use a program design language to start the actual coding process.

Program Design Language

Everyone seems to think that programmers use flowcharts, but the reality is usually different (flowcharts are nice to show to nonprogrammers, though). One tool that commercial programmers do find useful is *program design language (PDL)*. Although there are formal specifications for PDL, many programmers simply regard this step as writing out what a program does in English as a sort of pseudo-code.

For example, if we want to create a new function named **dblSqrt( )** that returns a number's square root, we might write its PDL this way in English, where we break what the function does into steps:

```
Function dblSqrt()
    Check if the input parameter is negative
        If the input parameter is negative, return -1
        If the input parameter is positive, return its square root
End Function
```

When you actually write the code, the PDL can often become the comments in that code; for example, here's the completed function:

```
'*******************************************************
' dblSqrt()
' Purpose: Returns the passed parameter's square root
' Inputs: dblParameter, the parameter whose square root we need
' Returns: The input value's square root
'*******************************************************
Function dblSqrt(dblParameter As Double) As Double

    'Check if the input parameter is negative
    If dblParameter < 0 Then
        'If the input parameter is negative, return -1
        dblSqrt = -1

    Else
        'If the input parameter is positive, return its square root
        dblSqrt = Sqr(dblParameter)

    End If
End Function
```

In this way, developing your program using PDL, where every line of PDL has one (and only one) specific task, can be very useful. So much for overview—let's turn to particulars that affect us as Visual Basic programmers.

Coding To Get The Most From Visual Basic

In this section, we'll discuss some best practices coding for Visual Basic. All of these practices come from professional programmers, but of course whether you implement them or not is up to you. Here we go:

- *Avoid "magic numbers" when you can.* A magic number is a number (excluding 0 or 1) that's hardwired right into your code like this:

```
Function blnCheckSize(dblParameter As Double) As Boolean

    If dblParameter > 1024 Then
        blnCheckSize = True

    Else
        blnCheckSize = False

    End If
End Function
```

Here, 1024 is a magic number. It's better to declare such numbers as constants, especially if you have a number of them. When it's time to change your code, you just have to change the constant declaration in one place, not try to find all the magic numbers scattered around your code.

- *Be modular.* Putting code and data together into modules hides it from the rest of the program, makes it easier to debug, makes it easier to work with conceptually, and even makes load-time of procedures in the same module quicker. Being modular—also called *information-hiding* (and *encapsulation* in true OOP)—is the backbone of working with larger programs. Divide and conquer is the idea here.

- *Program defensively.* An example of programming defensively would be to check data passed to you in a procedure before using it. This can save a bug from propagating throughout your program and help pinpoint its source. Make no assumptions.

- *Visual Basic procedures should have only one purpose, ideally.* This is also an aid in larger programs when things start to get complex. Certainly if a procedure has two distinct tasks, consider breaking it up.

- *Avoid deep nesting of conditionals or loops.* Debugging deeply nested conditionals visually is very, very inefficient. If you need to, place some of the inner loops or conditionals in new procedures and call them. Three levels of nesting should be about the maximum.

- *Use access procedures to protect sensitive data.* (This is part of programming defensively.) Access procedures are also called Get/Set procedures, and they are called by the rest of the program when you want to work with sensitive data. If the rest of the program must call a **Set( )** procedure to set that data, you can test to make sure that the new value is acceptable, providing a screen between that data and the rest of the program.

- *Ideally, variables should always be defined with the smallest scope possible.* Global variables can create enormously complex conditions. (In fact, Microsoft recommends that global variables should be used only when there is no other convenient way to share data between forms.)

- *Do not pass global variables to procedures.* If you pass global variables to procedures, the procedure you pass that variable to might give it one name (as a passed parameter) and also reference it as a global variable. This can lead to some serious bugs, because now the procedure has two different names for the variable.

- *Use the & operator when linking strings and the + operator when working with numerical values.* This is per Microsoft's recommendations.

- *When you create a long string, use the underscore line-continuation character to create multiple lines of code.* This is so you can read or debug the string easily. For example:

```
Dim Msg As String
Msg = "Well, there is a problem " _
    & "with your program. I am not sure " _
    & "what the problem is, but there is " _
    & "definitely something wrong."
```

- *Avoid using variants if you can.* Although convenient, they waste not only memory but time. You may be surprised by this. Remember, however, that Visual Basic has to convert the data in a variant to the proper type when it learns what is required, and that conversion actually takes a great deal of time.

- *Indent your code with four spaces per Microsoft's recommendations.* Believe it or not, there have been serious studies undertaken here, and 2 to 4 spaces were found to be best. Be consistent.

- *Finally, watch out for one big Visual Basic pitfall: misspelled variables.* Because you don't have to declare a variable in Visual Basic to use it, you might end up surprised when Visual Basic creates a new variable after you've misspelled a variable's name. For example, here's some perfectly legal code modified from our tic-tac-toe project that compiles and runs, but because of a misspelling—**xNoww** for **xNow**—it doesn't work at all:

```
Private Sub Command_Click(Index As Integer)
    If xNow Then
        Command(Index).Caption = "x"
    Else
        Command(Index).Caption = "o"
    End If

    xNoww = Not xNow

End Sub
```

Because Visual Basic treats **xNoww** as a legal variable, this kind of bug is very hard to find when debugging.

TIP: *Because Visual Basic auto-declares variables, it's usually better to use variable names that say something (like **intCurrentIndex**) instead of ones that don't (like **intDD35A**) to avoid declaring a variable through misspelling its name. A better idea is to use **Option Explicit** to make sure all variables must be explicitly declared.*

If you work in teams, use version control. There are several well-known utilities that help programmers work in teams, such as Microsoft's Visual SourceSafe. This utility, which is designed to work with programming environments like Visual Basic, restricts access to code so that two programmers don't end up modifying independent copies of the same file.

That's it for our best practices tips for now. We'll see more throughout the book.

Getting Down To The Details

That completes our overview of topics common to the rest of the book. In this chapter, we've seen an overview of a Visual Basic project, including what goes into a project, how it's stored on disk, and how the idea of scope works in a project. We've also seen a number of Visual Basic programming considerations, from naming conventions to best programming practices, including a list of Visual Basic-specific topics.

We're ready for the rest of the book, and we'll turn to the first natural topic now—the Visual Basic IDE.

Chapter 2

The Visual Basic Development Environment

If you need an immediate solution to:	See page:
Selecting IDE Colors, Fonts, And Font Sizes	50
Aligning, Sizing, And Spacing Multiple Controls	51
Setting A Startup Form Or Procedure	54
Using Visual Basic Predefined Forms, Menus, And Projects	56
Setting A Project's Version Information	59
Setting An EXE File's Name And Icon	60
Displaying The Debug, Edit, And Form Editor Toolbars	61
Turning Bounds Checking On Or Off	63
Checking For Pentium Errors	65
Managing Add-Ins	65
Adding ActiveX Controls And Insertable Objects To Projects	66
Customizing Menus And Toolbars	67
Setting Forms' Initial Positions	69
Enabling Or Disabling Quick Info, Auto List Members, Data Tips, And Syntax Checking	70
Displaying Or Hiding IDE Windows	73
Searching An Entire Project For Specific Text Or A Variable's Definition	74
Optimizing For Fast Code, Small Code, Or A Particular Processor	75
Adding And Removing Forms, Modules, And Class Modules	76
Using Bookmarks	78
Using The Object Browser	79

In Depth

In this chapter, we're going to get started with Visual Basic at the logical place to start: the Visual Basic Integrated Development Environment (IDE). The IDE is where you do your programming work in Visual Basic—just as the name says, you develop your projects in the Integrated Development Environment.

Over the years, the IDE has become more powerful, and with that power has come complexity. The IDE used to be more or less invisible to the programmer, but now that there are all kinds of project options, ActiveX controls to add, version resource data to set, and so much more, the IDE has become a worthy object of study. In this chapter, we'll cover IDE tasks so you don't have to dig out that information when you have more important things to do. We'll start with an overview of the IDE, and then go directly to the Practical Guide for the IDE, showing how to get things done.

Overview Of The Integrated Development Environment

The Visual Basic IDE appears in Figure 2.1, and as a Visual Basic programmer, this is where you'll spend most of your programming time. If you're not already familiar with the parts of the IDE, you will be in time.

The Visual Basic IDE has three distinct *states*: Design, Run, and Debug. The current state appears in Visual Basic's title bar. This chapter concentrates on the Design state. We'll cover the Debug state later in the book. (In the Run state, Visual Basic is in the background while your program runs.) It's the Design state that's become complex over the years, and we'll lay it bare in this chapter.

The IDE is composed of these parts:

- The menu bar
- The toolbar
- The Project Explorer
- The Properties window
- The Form Layout window
- The toolbox

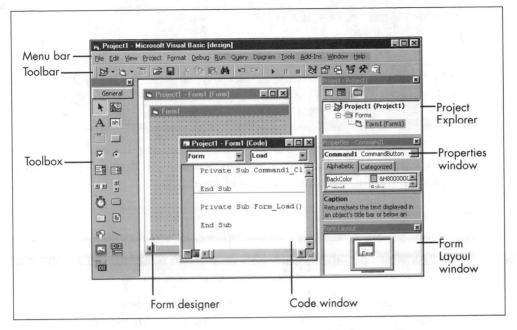

Figure 2.1   *The Visual Basic Integrated Development Environment.*

- Form designers
- Code windows

We'll take a look at all of these parts in this overview.

The Menu Bar

The menu bar presents the Visual Basic menus. Here's a list of those menus and what they do:

- *File*—File handling and printing; also used to make EXE files

- *Edit*—Standard editing functions, undo, searches

- *View*—Displays or hides windows and toolbars

- *Project*—Sets project properties, adds/removes forms and modules, and adds/removes references and components

- *Format*—Aligns or sizes controls

- *Debug*—Starts/stops debugging and stepping through programs

- *Run*—Starts a program, or compiles and starts it

- *Tools*—Adds procedures, starts the Menu Editor, sets IDE options

- *Add-Ins*—Add-in manager, lists add-ins like Application Wizard and API Viewer

- *Window*—Arranges or selects open windows
- *Help*—Handles Help and the About box

TIP: *Note that one important job of the File menu is to create EXE files for your program. When you run a program from the Run menu, no EXE file is created; if you want to run the program outside of Visual Basic, you must create that EXE file, and you do that with the File menu's Make ProjectName.exe item (where ProjectName is the name you've set for the project).*

We'll see a great deal more about these menus and the items they contain in the Immediate Solutions section of this chapter.

The Toolbar

The main Visual Basic toolbar appears in Figure 2.2. This toolbar contains buttons matching popular menu items, as you can see in Figure 2.2; clicking the button is the same as selecting a menu item and can save you some time.

Besides the main toolbar, you can also display other dockable toolbars in Visual Basic: the Debug, Edit, and Form Editor toolbars. To display one of these toolbars, just select it using the Toolbars item in the View menu; the toolbar appears free-floating at first, but you can dock it as you like in the IDE.

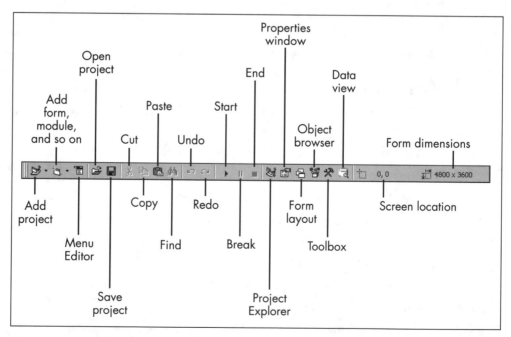

Figure 2.2   The main Visual Basic toolbar.

The Project Explorer

The Project Explorer appears in Figure 2.3. This is the window that allows you to coordinate the parts of your program into folders for easy manipulation, because all parts of that project appear in the Project Explorer arranged in a tree view.

The Project Explorer can be very useful when you're working in a larger project and the IDE is filled with design and code windows. To pick out the part of the project you want to work on, you only have to find it in the Project Explorer and double-click it. Doing so brings the appropriate window to the foreground and, if you've clicked a form, opens that form in the Properties window.

You can also add and remove items by right-clicking them with the mouse in the Project Explorer. For example, you can add new forms, MDI forms, modules, class modules, and so on just by right-clicking the project's icon in the Project Explorer. You can remove forms by right-clicking them and selecting the Remove item in the pop-up menu that appears, or you can save them to disk or switch between the form's code window and the form itself.

The buttons at the top of the Project Explorer in Figure 2.3 allow you to switch between views. The left button displays an object's code window, the middle button displays the object itself, and the right button toggles the folders open and closed in the Project Explorer as in a standard tree view (of course, you can click the folders themselves to do that as well).

To sum up, then, the Project Explorer gives us a valuable overview of our entire project, which is really very useful when a project gets large and contains many components.

Figure 2.3   The Visual Basic Project Explorer.

TIP: *Like the other windows in the IDE, the Project Explorer is dockable, which means that you can move it around with the mouse and size it as you like. In fact, you can rearrange all the windows as you like in the IDE. This can sometimes be disconcerting when you move the mouse and inadvertently drag a window to a new size and location (and you find yourself asking "What's the Project Explorer doing at the bottom of the IDE?").*

The Properties Window

The Properties window appears in Figure 2.4. This is where you set an object's properties; for example, you can set the caption of command buttons, the text in text boxes, and literally hundreds of other properties here.

When you select an object like a control in Visual Basic using the mouse, that object's properties appear in the Properties window. To change or examine a property setting in the Properties window, you just find that property's item in that window (the properties appear on the left in the Properties window and their settings on the right). If you want to change that property, nothing could be easier—just click the current setting. For properties that you set yourself, the current property value is highlighted, and you just type in the new setting (such as placing new text in a text box). If the property can only be set to one of a specific range of properties, a downwards arrow will appear in the property setting box; click this button to see the possible values this property can have.

We should note that there are really two kinds of properties in Visual Basic: *design-time* and *runtime* properties (for example, a Web browser control might have a runtime property to hold its current URL, because it doesn't make sense to set that property at design time). The properties that appear in the Properties window are design-time properties. (Microsoft does have other utilities,

Figure 2.4   The Properties window.

such as the ActiveX Control Test Container to allow you to work with runtime properties interactively.)

In the absence of adequate documentation, it can sometimes be difficult to determine what properties a specific ActiveX control has. To find out, it's easy to create a control of that type and open it in the Properties window, where the properties will be listed. (This applies only to properties available at design time, of course.) That's a quick and dirty way to get an object's properties; a better way is to use the Visual Basic Object Browser (which you can open from the toolbar or the View menu). The Object Browser provides you with an overview of all the objects in a project, including their properties and methods and what parameters to pass. For example, we take a look at rich text boxes in the Object Browser in Figure 2.5.

The Form Layout Window

The Form Layout window appears in Figure 2.6. Using this window, you can position forms as you want them to appear on the screen when they are first displayed.

To give a form a new initial location, just drag that form in the Form Layout window to that new location. You'll see the new screen position of the form's

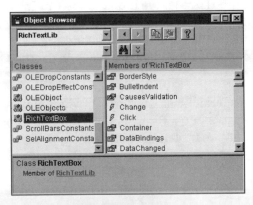

Figure 2.5   The Object Browser at work.

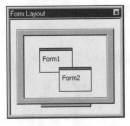

Figure 2.6   The Form Layout window.

upper-left corner (in twips) displayed in the toolbar (that position is the first set of numbers in the toolbar; see Figure 2.2). To *resize* the form, on the other hand, you have to use a form designer, which we'll see in a minute.

The Toolbox

The Visual Basic toolbox appears in Figure 2.7. This window is a mainstay of Visual Basic and indicates what was so revolutionary about Visual Basic in the first place. You use the toolbox to add controls to your projects, and you do so in a very easy way—just click a tool, such as the Command Button tool, and draw the new button in a form. That's all it takes.

The toolbox is loaded with controls you can add to your forms—text boxes, labels, list boxes, image controls, checkboxes, timers, and much more. When you add a new ActiveX control to your project (using the Project menu's Components item), that control appears in the toolbox, and you're ready to add it to your form.

All in all, the toolbox is a prime example of what's right about Visual Basic. We'll see how to add our own controls to the toolbox in Chapter 20.

Form Designers And Code Windows

The last parts of the IDE that we'll take a look at in our overview are form designers and code windows, which appear in the center of Figure 2.8. (The form designer displays the current form under design, complete with command button, and the code window displays the code for the **Command1_Click()** procedure.)

Form designers are really just windows in which a particular form appears. You can place controls into a form simply by drawing them after clicking the corresponding control's tool in the toolbox.

Figure 2.7   The Visual Basic toolbox.

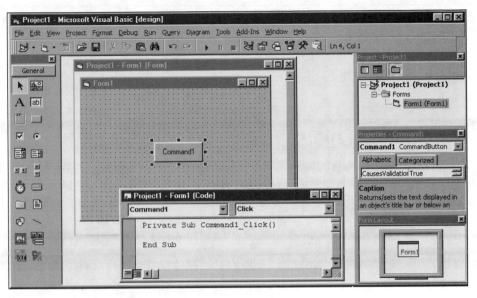

Figure 2.8   A form designer and code window.

Code windows are similarly easy to understand: you just place the code you want to attach to an object in the code window (to open an object's code in the code window, just double-click that object). There are two drop-down list boxes at the top of the code window: the left list lets you select the object to add code to, and the right list lets you select the procedure to add (all the methods the object supports appear in this list).

That completes our overview of the IDE. Let's get into the actual meat of the chapter now, task by task.

Immediate Solutions

Selecting IDE Colors, Fonts, And Font Sizes

The Visual Basic IDE comes with all kinds of preset colors—blue for keywords, green for comments, black for other code, and so on. But as when you move into a new house, you might want to do your own decorating. Visual Basic allows you to do that. Just open the Options box by clicking the Options item in the Visual Basic Tools menu, and click the Editor Format tab, as shown in Figure 2.9.

Here are the text items whose colors you can select:

- Normal Text
- Selection Text
- Syntax Error Text
- Execution Point Text
- Breakpoint Text
- Comment Text
- Keyword Text
- Identifier Text
- Bookmark Text
- Call Return Text

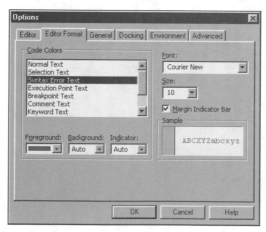

Figure 2.9   Selecting IDE colors.

To set a particular type of text's color and background color, just select the appropriate color from the drop-down list boxes labeled Foreground and Background, and click on OK. You can also set text font and font sizes in the same way—just specify the new setting and click on the OK button to customize the text the way you want it.

Aligning, Sizing, And Spacing Multiple Controls

Visual Basic is very...well...*visual*, and that includes the layout of controls in your programs. If you've got a number of controls that should be aligned in a straight line, it can be murder to have to squint at the screen, aligning those controls in a line down to the very last pixel. Fortunately, there's an easier way to do it:

1. Hold down the Ctrl key and click all the controls you want to align.

2. Make sure you have one control in the correct position, and click that one last.

Sizing handles, the eight small boxes that you can grasp with the mouse to resize a control, appear around all the clicked controls. The sizing handles appear hollow around all but the last control you clicked, as shown in Figure 2.10; the last control you clicked has solid sizing handles, and it will act as the key control. The other controls will be aligned using this key control's position.

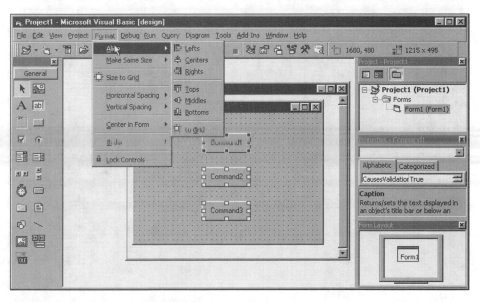

Figure 2.10   Aligning new controls.

To *align* all the selected controls to the same left, right, or center position of the key control, you continue with these steps:

3. Select the Align item in the Format menu, opening the Align submenu, as shown in Figure 2.10.

4. Select the type of alignment you want in the Align submenu: align the left, the center, the right, the top, the middle, or the bottom edges of the controls with the key control.

5. While the controls are still collectively selected, you can move them, if you like, as a group to any new location now that they are aligned as you want them.

To *size* all selected controls the same as the key control, follow Steps 1 and 2, and then continue this way:

3. Select the Make Same Size item in the Format menu, opening that submenu, as shown in Figure 2.11.

4. Choose the appropriate item in the Make Same Size submenu to size the controls as you want them: matching the key control's width, height, or both.

To *space* multiple controls vertically or horizontally, follow Steps 1 and 2 and then continue:

3. Select the Horizontal Spacing or Vertical Spacing item in the Format menu, opening that submenu, as shown in Figure 2.12.

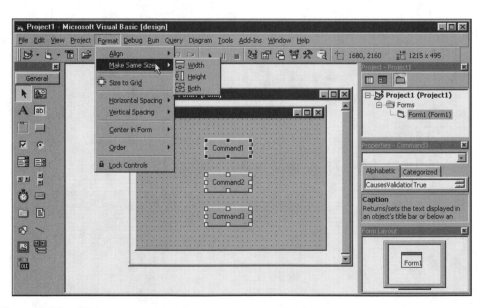

Figure 2.11   Sizing new controls.

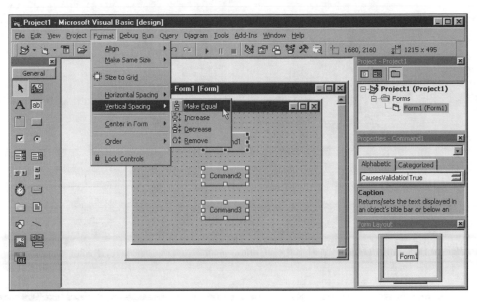

Figure 2.12   Spacing controls.

4. To space the controls horizontally or vertically, select one of the items in the corresponding submenu:

- *Make Equal*—Sets the spacing to the average of the current spacing
- *Increase*—Increases by one grid line
- *Decrease*—Decreases by one grid line
- *Remove*—Removes spacing

The Design Time Grid

Spacing depends on grid lines. The grid is made up of the array of dots you see on a form at design time. This grid is to help you place controls on a form, and by default, controls are aligned to the grid (which means they are sized to fit along vertical and horizontal lines of dots). You can change the grid units (in twips) in the Options box when you click the General tab, as shown in Figure 2.13. (To open the Options box, select the Options item in the Tools menu.)

Besides setting the units of the grid, you can also specify whether or not controls must be aligned to the grid by checking the Align Controls To Grid checkbox.

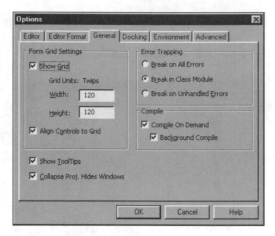

Figure 2.13   Modifying the grid settings.

Setting A Startup Form Or Procedure

Visual Basic programs mean windows, right? Not necessarily. Visual Basic programs do not need to have any windows at all, in fact. That case is a little extreme, but there are times when you don't want to start your program with code in a form. For example, you might want to display a flash screen when your program first starts, without waiting for the first (possibly complex) form to load, and then switch to the form when it does load.

Creating A Form-Free Startup Procedure

To start a program from code not in any form, you add a subroutine named **Main( )** to your program. Follow these steps:

1. Select the Properties item in the Project menu to open the Project Properties box, as shown in Figure 2.14.

2. Click the General tab in the Project Properties box (if it's not already selected), select Sub Main in the Startup Object drop-down list, and click on OK.

3. Select Add Module in the Project menu, and double-click the Module icon in the Add Module box that opens.

4. Add this code to the new module's (General) section in the code window:

```
Sub Main()

End Sub
```

5. Place the code you want in the **Main( )** subroutine.

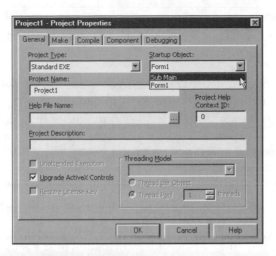

Figure 2.14   The Project Properties box.

Selecting The Startup Form

On the other hand, you might have a number of forms in a project—how do you specify which one is displayed first? You do that with the General tab of the Project Properties box, just as we've added a **Main()** subroutine to our program.

To specify the startup form for a project, just open the Project Properties box as we've done in the previous section and select the appropriate form in the Startup Object box, as shown in Figure 2.15. Now when your program starts, that form will act as the startup form.

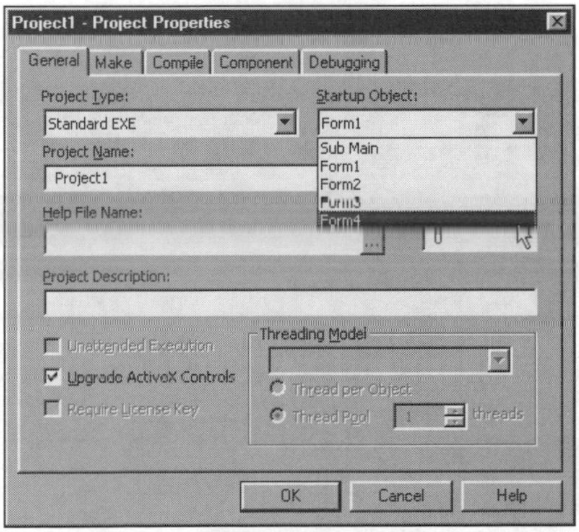

Figure 2.15   Setting a project's startup form.

Using Visual Basic Predefined Forms, Menus, And Projects

You're designing a new program, and you want a form with a complete File menu on it. You don't want to use the Application Wizard, because that add-in would redesign your whole project for you. Rather than designing a complete standard File menu from scratch, there's an easier way: you can use one of the predefined menus that come with Visual Basic.

To add one of the predefined Visual Basic menus, follow these steps:

1. Select the form you want to add the menu to by clicking it with the mouse.

2. Open the Visual Component Manager from the Tools menu. If the Visual Component Manager is not already loaded into Visual Basic, open the Add-In Manager in the Add-Ins menu, click the box labeled Visual Component Manager, and close the Add-In Manager. If your version of Visual Basic does not come with the Visual Component Manager, refer to the discussion after these steps.

3. Open the Visual Basic folder in the Visual Component Manager.

4. Open the Templates folder in the Visual Basic folder.

5. Open the Menus folder in the Templates folder, as shown in Figure 2.16.

6. Select the type of menu you want and double-click it. These are the available menus:

- Edit menu

- File menu

- Help menu

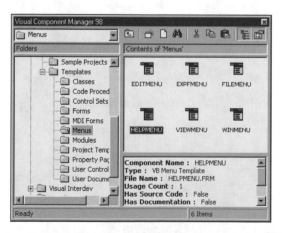

Figure 2.16   Opening the Menus folder in the Visual Component Manager.

- View menu
- Window menu

7. The new menu will be added to the form you selected, as shown in Figure 2.17.

Besides menus, you can add a whole selection of predefined forms to your projects by finding the Forms folder in the Templates folder in the Visual Component Manager. Here are the available forms, ready to be added to your project with a click of the mouse:

- Blank forms
- About dialog boxes (two types)
- Addin forms
- Browser forms
- Data grid forms
- Dialog forms
- Tip forms
- Log-in forms
- ODBC log-in forms
- Options forms
- Query forms

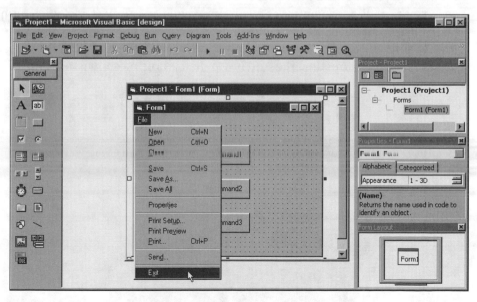

Figure 2.17   Adding a predefined Visual Basic menu to a form.

As you'll see in the Visual Component Manager's Templates folder, you can add the following pre-defined elements to a Visual Basis Project:

- Classes
- Code procedures
- Control sets
- Forms
- MDI forms
- Menus
- Modules
- Project templates
- Property pages
- User controls
- User documents

After you've created components like these in Visual Basic, you can add them to other projects using the Visual Component Manager—in fact, reusing components like this is one of the things professional programmers and programming teams do best.

If You Don't Have The Visual Component Manager

If your version of Visual Basic does not come with the Visual Component Manager, you can still add many predefined components to a project, including forms, MDI forms, modules, class modules, user controls, and property pages. For example, to add a predefined form to your project, just select Add Form from the Project menu, opening the Add Form dialog box, as shown in Figure 2.18.

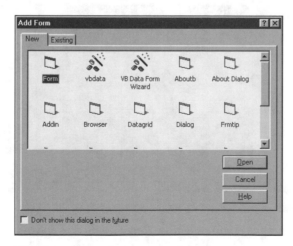

Figure 2.18   The Add Form dialog box.

As you can see, the predefined forms are here, so you can add them to your project with a simple click of the mouse.

Adding menus is a little different here, because you actually add a whole new form with that menu, instead of adding that menu to an already-existing form. For example, to add a new form with a File menu already in place, click the Existing tab in the Add Form dialog box, click the Menus folder, and double-click the Filemenu.frm entry. This adds a new form to your project, complete with File menu.

Setting A Project's Version Information

Five years from now, a user stumbles across your EXE file, which you've conveniently named CDU2000.exe. This makes perfect sense to you—what else would you name the EXE file for a utility named Crop Dusting Utility 2000? However, the user is a little puzzled. How can he get more information directly from the EXE file to know just what CDU2000.exe does? He can do that by interrogating the file's *version information.*

A program's version information includes more than just the version number of the program; it also can include the name of the company that makes the software, general comments to the user, legal copyrights, legal trademarks, the product name, and the product description. All these items are available to the user, and if you're releasing your software commercially, you should fill these items in. Here's how you do it:

1. Open the Project Properties box in Visual Basic now by selecting the Properties item in the Project menu.

2. Select the Make tab, as shown in Figure 2.19.

3. Fill in the information you want, including the program's version number, product name, and so on.

4. Create the EXE file, which in our case is CDU2000.exe, using the Make CDU2000.exe item in the File menu.

5. To look at the version information in CDU2000.exe, find that file in the Windows Explorer and right-click the file, selecting Properties from the pop-up menu that opens. As you can see in Figure 2.20, our version information—including the name of the product—appears in the Properties box.

Sometimes, version information is all that users have to go on when they encounter your program, so be sure to include it before releasing that product.

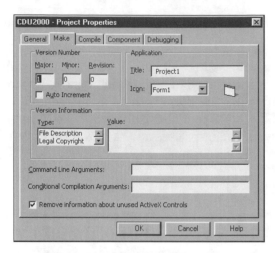

Figure 2.19   *Setting a project's version information.*

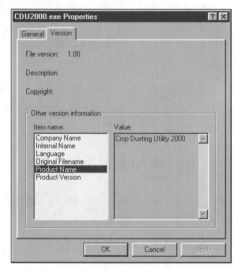

Figure 2.20   *Reading a program's version information.*

Setting An EXE File's Name And Icon

You're about to release your software commercially, but you suddenly realize that Project1.exe might not be the best name for your product's executable file. The stockholders' meeting is in five minutes—how can you change your EXE file's name?

To set the EXE file's name, you just set the project's name. Here's how you do it:

1. Select the Properties item in the Project menu to open the Project Properties box, as shown in Figure 2.21.

2. Select the General tab in the Project Properties box (if it's not already selected).

3. Enter the name of the project you want to use, such as CDU2000 in Figure 2.21.

4. The project's name will become the name of the EXE file when you create it with the Make CDU2000.exe item in the File menu.

Now you've named your EXE file, but how do you set the program's icon that will appear in Windows? The program's icon is just the icon of the startup form, and you can set that by setting that form's Icon property in the Properties window. If you have a new icon in ICO file format, you can load that icon right into that form by setting the form's **Icon** property to the ICO file name.

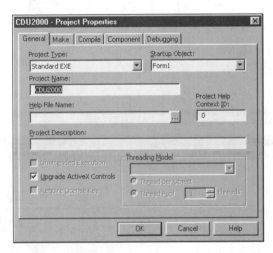

Figure 2.21   Setting a project's name.

Displaying The Debug, Edit, And Form Editor Toolbars

By default, Visual Basic displays one toolbar, the standard toolbar. However, there are other toolbars available—the Debug, Edit, and Form Editor toolbars. If you want them, you add those toolbars with the Toolbars submenu of the Visual Basic View menu—just click the new toolbar you want to add. You can also remove one or all toolbars the same way.

The Debug toolbar has the following buttons:

- Start
- Break
- End
- Toggle Breakpoint
- Step Into
- Step Over
- Step Out
- Locals Window
- Immediate Window
- Watch Window
- Quick Watch
- Call Stack

The Edit toolbar includes these buttons:

- List Properties/Methods
- List Constants
- Quick Info
- Parameter Info
- Complete Word
- Indent
- Outdent
- Toggle Breakpoint
- Comment Block
- Uncomment Block
- Toggle Bookmark
- Next Bookmark
- Previous Bookmark
- Clear All Bookmarks

The Form Editor toolbar includes these buttons:

- Bring To Front
- Send To Back
- Align

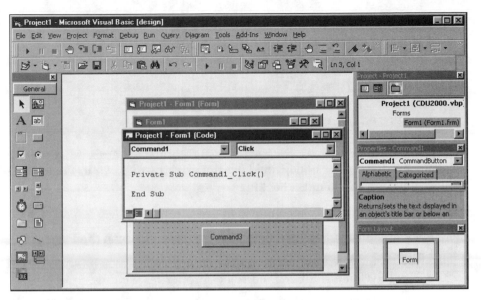

Figure 2.22   Visual Basic with the Debug, Edit, and Form toolbars.

- Center
- Width
- Lock Controls

The Debug, Edit, and Form Editor toolbars appear from left to right in the top toolbar in Figure 2.22.

Turning Bounds Checking On Or Off

When you use arrays, Visual Basic checks to make sure that you don't inadvertently try to access memory past the end or before the beginning of the array when the program runs, which is an error that could corrupt memory. In the early days of programming, however, you could use array index values that were past the end of an array without causing a compiler error, and some programmers used to rely on that to create some programming tricks involving accessing memory far beyond what they were supposed to stick with (especially in C, where the name of an array is really a pointer). That practice is heavily discouraged today, but some programmers must still have a soft spot for it, because Visual Basic allows you to turn off array bounds checking. (In fairness, there are one or two other reasons you might want to turn off bounds checking, such as not having the program halt for bounds violations while you're trying to track down a bug or, conceivably, for performance reasons.)

What does a bounds violation look like? Here's an example in code where we set up an array and then try to access a location past the end of it:

```
Private Sub Command1_Click()
    Dim Addresses(1 To 10) As Integer
    Addresses(1) = 1                        'Fine
    Addresses(11) = 11                      'Problem!
End Sub
```

If you were to run this code, you'd get the error box shown in Figure 2.23—unless you turn off bounds checking.

You can turn off bounds checking by following these steps:

1. Select the Properties item in the Project menu to open the Project Properties box.

2. Select the Compile tab in the Project Properties window.

3. Click the Advanced Optimizations button in the Project Properties window to open the Advanced Optimizations box, as shown in Figure 2.24.

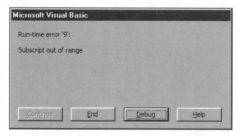

Figure 2.23   An out-of-bounds error.

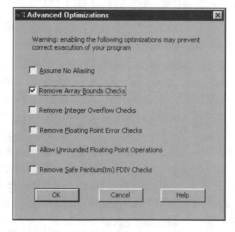

Figure 2.24   Turning off bounds checking.

4. Select the Remove Array Bounds Checks checkbox to turn off array bounds checking.

That's it—now you've turned off array bounds checking.

WARNING! *Before turning off array bounds checking, however, make sure you have a really good reason for doing so; you may find your program crashing Windows as it makes illegal use of memory.*

Checking For Pentium Errors

Some time ago, one version of the Intel Pentium suffered from a well-publicized hardware bug in the floating point instruction named FDIV. Intel responded quickly and offered to replace the defective chips, but it's reasonable to expect some are still out there.

For that reason, Visual Basic has a check to make sure the Pentium your program runs on is safe. That check is enabled by default, but if for some reason you want to turn it off (although it is hard to see why you would), you can turn off the Pentium FDIV check with these steps:

1. Select the Properties item in the Project menu to open the Project Properties box.

2. Select the Compile tab in the Project Properties window.

3. Click the Advanced Optimizations button in the Project Properties window to open the Advanced Optimizations box (as shown earlier in Figure 2.24).

4. Select the Remove Safe Pentium FDIV Checks checkbox.

That's it—you've disabled the FDIV Pentium check. Although you might want to do this yourself if you know what you're doing, it's not recommended that you do this in any software you release commercially.

Managing Add-Ins

The deadline for your project is fast approaching, and the pressure is on. Suddenly it occurs to you that you've already written a lot of the components you need to use—the day is saved! But how can you access those components? One easy way is to use the Visual Component Manager. But when you check

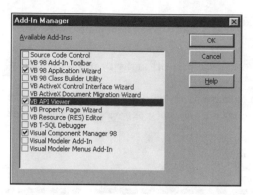

Figure 2.25   The Visual Basic Add-In Manager.

the Visual Basic Add-Ins menu, you don't see the Visual Component Manager there. How do you add it?

You use the Visual Basic Add-In Manager to add this—and any other—add-in. Here's how to use the Add-In Manager:

1. Select the Add-In Manager item in the Visual Basic Add-In menu.

2. The Add-In Manager opens, as shown in Figure 2.25.

3. Select the add-ins you want, as also shown in Figure 2.25, and close the Add-In Manager.

That's it—now you've added the add-in you want. To remove it, simply de-select the add-in's box in the Add-In Manager. (Some add-ins have an annoy-ing habit of starting when Visual Basic starts, grinding on for a long time while it loads and taking up a lot of memory, which can be annoying if you don't need the add-in any more.)

Adding ActiveX Controls And Insertable Objects To Projects

Been away from Visual Basic for a while and need to get back into the swing of things? You've been designing your project but suddenly realize you need a Microsoft Grid control. That's an ActiveX control—how do you add those again? Use the Add File To Project menu item? Double-click the toolbox and hope an Insert dialog box comes up? Add a reference to the actual Grid control's OCX file, asctrls.ocx, to the project?

None of those—here's how you do it:

1. Select the Project menu's Components item.

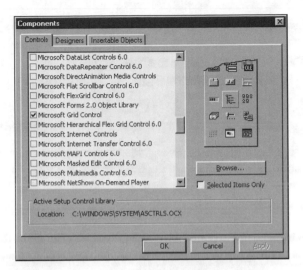

Figure 2.26   The Visual Basic Components dialog box.

2. The Visual Basic Components box opens, as shown in Figure 2.26; click the Controls tab in the Components dialog box.

3. Select the ActiveX control you want to add in the Components box, then close the Components box. The new control will appear in the toolbox.

TIP: *If the ActiveX control you want to add to a Visual Basic project doesn't appear in the Components dialog box, it may not have been registered with Windows properly. Try using the regsvr32.exe tool in the Windows\system directory to register it again.*

You can also add insertable objects like Microsoft Word or Microsoft Excel objects to a Visual Basic project by using the Components dialog box. Instead of the Controls tab in the Components box, however, you use the Insertable Objects tab and select the object you want; that object will appear in the toolbox, and you can use it in your project from then on. For example, we've inserted an Excel worksheet into the Visual Basic project in Figure 2.27.

Customizing Menus And Toolbars

*Customizing
Menus And
Toolbars*

Visual Basic might be nice, but it's just not set up as you'd like it. You might think, for example, that the Start menu item—to run programs—surely should be in the Edit menu. Well, if you'd like to place it there, it's possible (just don't expect anyone else to be able to use Visual Basic after you've customized it that way...).

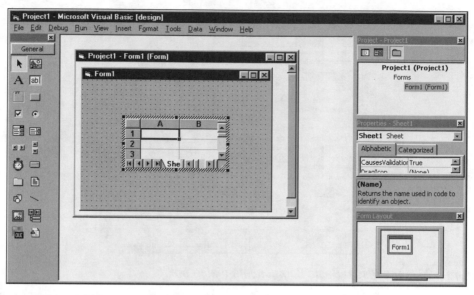

Figure 2.27 A Microsoft Excel worksheet in a Visual Basic project.

Here's how you move items between menus or toolbars:

1. Right-click the menu bar to open the Customize box.

2. Next, find the menu item you want to add to another menu or to a toolbar; here, we'll move the Start menu item to the Edit menu.

3. Using the mouse, drag the menu item from the Customize dialog's Command box to the new location in a menu or a toolbar, as shown in Figure 2.28, where we drag the Start item to the Edit menu.

4. Releasing the mouse adds the menu item to its new location. Finally, click Close in the Customize box to close that dialog.

Besides moving menu items to new locations in menus and toolbars, you can also move whole menus. For example, to move the Edit menu in the menu bar, just open the Customize box and find the Built-in Menus item in the Categories box of the Commands tab. Next, drag the menu you want to move—such as the Edit menu—from the Commands box to its new location in the menu bar. You can move menus to either the menu bar or other toolbars this way.

TIP: If you use one particular menu item a lot, you might consider moving it directly into the menu bar (where it will appear among all the menu names). You can do that the same way you'd drag that item to a new menu—just drag it into the menu bar instead.

The toolbars in Visual Basic are dockable, of course, so that means you can move them around as you'd like—even above the menu bar. Just grasp the

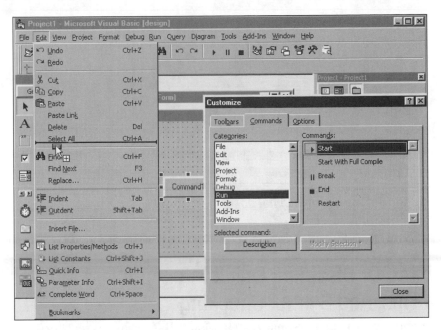

Figure 2.28   Add the Start menu item to the Visual Basic Edit menu.

double upright bars at left in the toolbar (Visual Basic uses Explorer-style toolbars) and move the toolbar to its new location.

Setting Forms' Initial Positions

You've completed the project—on schedule and under budget even. But you're not crazy about where Visual Basic displays the startup form on the screen when the program starts. You can set the form's Left and Top properties if you like, but there's an easier and more interactive way using the Form Layout window.

The Form Layout window is part of the IDE, and its default position is at the lower right in the IDE. This window appears in Figure 2.29.

Setting a form's initial position couldn't be easier—just drag the form into the new location using the mouse. If you want to know the form's exact new position, watch the first set of numbers in the toolbar—those numbers record the location of the upper left of the form (in twips).

TIP: Using the Form Layout window, you can even place forms off screen, beyond the edges of the display. That means, of course, that if you want to see the form when the program runs, you'll have to move it, either by setting its Left and Top properties or with the Move method.

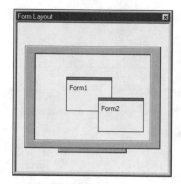

Figure 2.29   Setting a form's initial position.

Enabling Or
Disabling Quick
Info, Auto List
Members, Data
Tips, And Syntax
Checking

Enabling Or Disabling Quick Info, Auto List Members, Data Tips, And Syntax Checking

Depending on your personal tastes, Visual Basic has a great/terrible set of features/bugs that assist/hobble you while working on your code. These features are as follows:

- Quick Info
- Auto List Members
- Data Tips
- Syntax Checking

The Quick Info feature lets you know what parameters a procedure takes as you're actually typing the procedure's name, as in Figure 2.30. This is a useful feature that can save you time looking up parameter order or type.

The Auto List Members feature lists the members of an object as you're typing the object's name (actually when you type the dot [.] after the object's name, as in Figure 2.31). This is useful if you can't remember exactly what property you want to work with (for example, do I want the **Text** property, or was it the **Caption** property?).

Visual Basic Data Tips are tip tools that appear while you're debugging a program, and they're a truly useful innovation. When Visual Basic is in the Debug state, you can let the mouse rest over a variable name in your code, and Visual Basic will display that variable's current value in a Data Tip, as shown in Figure 2.32.

TIP: Note that Data Tips can only display the values of simple variables, not complex ones like objects or arrays. For those objects, you must use either the Immediate window or the Watch window.

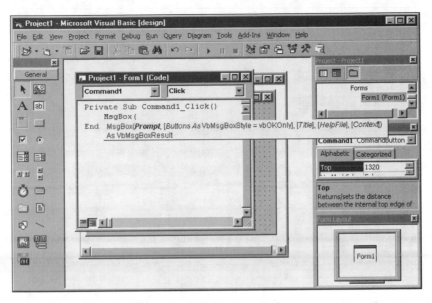

Figure 2.30 *The Visual Basic Quick Info feature.*

Syntax Checking speaks for itself—when you move the text insertion point away from a line of Visual Basic code while writing that code, Visual Basic will check the line's syntax and display an error box if there is an error. That can get annoying if you're the type of programmer who likes to move around in a file while writing code ("What was the name of that variable again?").

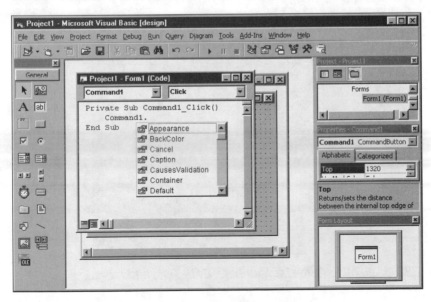

Figure 2.31 *The Visual Basic Auto List Members feature.*

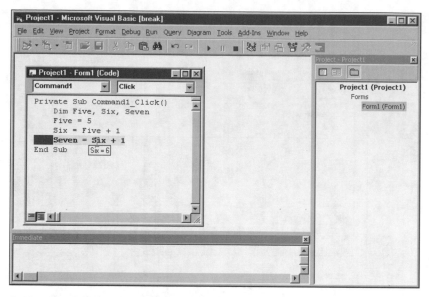

Figure 2.32   The Visual Basic Data Tips feature.

You can turn all of these features on and off following these steps:

1. Select the Options item in the Tools menu.

2. Select the Editor tab in the Options box, as shown in Figure 2.33.

3. Select the options you want from the checkboxes: Auto Syntax Check, Auto List Members, Auto Quick Info, and Auto Data Tips. That's all it takes.

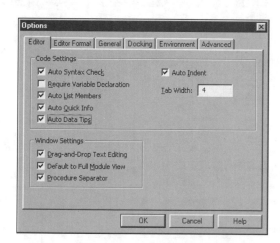

Figure 2.33   Selecting Auto List Members, Data Tips, and more.

Displaying Or Hiding IDE Windows

You're feeling cramped—is it your chair? Your office? No, this time, it's your screen. With the proliferation of windows in the Visual Basic IDE, there seems to always be more and more of them clamoring for your attention. Want to clear some IDE windows out to make room for the important ones? Just close the windows by clicking their close buttons (the button marked "x" in the top right of the window).

Whoops—now you need the Form Layout window back. But how do you get it back? Or how would you get the toolbox back if it disappeared? Or the Properties window? The solution is easy: All you have to do is to select the window you want to show again in the View menu, and it'll reappear. Open the View menu as shown in Figure 2.34, and click the name of the window you want to make visible again—it's that simple.

This is a simple task indeed, but it's worth including here; more than one programmer has panicked after closing the toolbox by mistake and wondering if Visual Basic must be reinstalled to get it back!

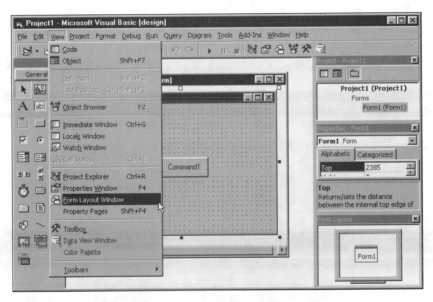

Figure 2.34   Specifying visible IDE windows in the View menu.

Searching An Entire Project For Specific Text Or A Variable's Definition

Forms, modules, class modules, MDI forms—how are you supposed to keep them all straight? These days, there are more files than ever in a Visual Basic project, and anything that can give you an overview can help. The Project Explorer is one such tool. This window gives you an overview of your entire project, organized into folders.

However, there are times when that's not good enough—times when you need more details. One such occasion is when you want to find all the occurrences of specific text throughout an entire project—for example, you might want to find all the places a particularly troublesome variable is used. To do that, you can now just use the Edit menu's Find item. Selecting that item opens the Find box, as shown in Figure 2.35. Now you can search all the code in an entire project if the code window is open—just click the Current Project option button before searching, as shown in Figure 2.35.

Even if you're familiar with searching for text throughout an entire project, there's one more capability that you might not know about—jumping to a variable's or procedure's definition just by clicking it. To jump to a variable's or procedure's definition, just right-click that variable or procedure any place it's used in the code. Doing so opens a pop-up menu, as shown in Figure 2.36.

To jump to the variable's or procedure's definition, just select the Definition item in the pop-up menu. This is very useful when, for example, you've set up a new procedure somewhere but can't quite remember what parameters you pass to that procedure, and in what order.

TIP: *Besides jumping to a variable or procedure's definition in code, you can also jump to its previous use in code—just select the pop-up menu's Last Position item.*

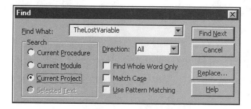

Figure 2.35   *Searching for text throughout a whole project.*

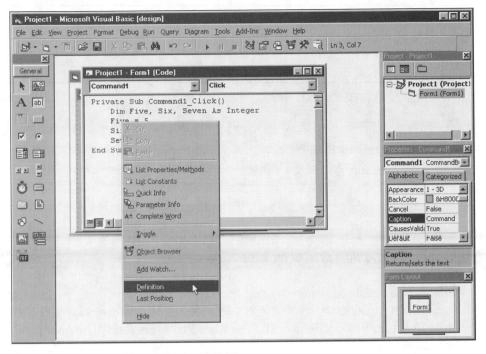

Figure 2.36   Finding a variable's definition.

Optimizing For Fast Code, Small Code, Or A Particular Processor

Your project works the way you want it, but now the users are complaining about the size of the EXE file. Isn't there any way to make it less than 500MB? Well, that might be a bit of an exaggeration, but Visual Basic does let you optimize your project in several different ways, and one of them is to optimize the code for size.

To optimize your program for code size or speed, follow these steps.

1. Select the Properties item in the Visual Basic Project menu.

2. The Project Properties box opens, as shown in Figure 2.37. Select the Compile tab in that box.

3. Select the kind of code optimization you want in the Properties box:

   • Optimize For Fast Code

   • Optimize For Small Code

   • No Optimization

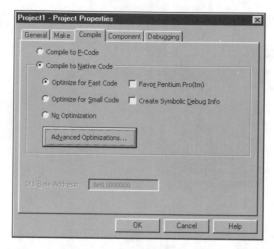

Figure 2.37   Optimizing a project for speed or code size.

Besides optimizing for code size and speed, you can optimize the code for the Pentium Pro processor in the Project Properties box as well—just click the Favor Pentium Pro checkbox. The Pentium Pro is currently the only processor Visual Basic lets you optimize for, but it does have one automatic check: the FDIV check to check for bad Pentiums (see "Checking For Pentium Errors" earlier in this chapter).

Adding And Removing Forms, Modules, And Class Modules

Your project is nearly finished. Now it's time to add an About dialog box. So how do you add new forms to a project? You do that in one of a couple of ways: First, you can use the View menu, as shown in Figure 2.38.

The Visual Basic Project menu allows you to add these items to a project:

- Form
- MDI form
- Module
- Class module
- User control
- Property page

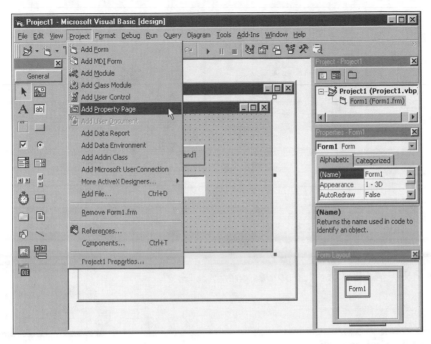

Figure 2.38   Adding forms and modules with the Visual Basic Project menu.

You can also add these items to a project by right-clicking any item in the Project Explorer window and selecting the Add item in the resulting pop-up menu. The Add submenu opens, and it holds the same items.

Adding ActiveX Designers

Besides ready-made objects like forms and modules, you can add ActiveX designers to the Visual Basic Project menu. These designers let you design new objects that are part of your project. For example, to add the Visual Basic Add-In Designer, you follow these steps:

1. Select the Components item in the Project menu, opening the Components box as shown in Figure 2.39.

2. Select the Designers tab in the Components box.

3. Select the designer you want to add, such as the Add-In Designer, and close the Components box.

4. You can reach the new object designer to design the addition to your project with the Add ActiveX Designer item in the Project menu. That item opens a submenu showing the available designers, including the one we've just added, the Visual Basic Add-In Designer.

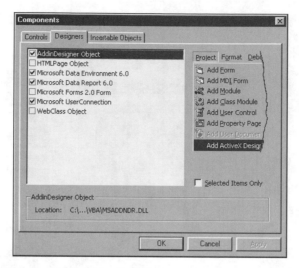

Figure 2.39   Adding the Add-In Designer.

Using Bookmarks

It's been a long night and it's nearly dawn, but you're still programming because the deadline's in a few hours. Now you've lost your place in the dozen separate code files that make up the project. There are 10 separate windows open in the IDE and you're switching back and forth between them. Isn't there a better way to mark a location and jump back to it when you need to?

There certainly is—you can use a bookmark. You mark a line of code by toggling a bookmark on or off at that location, and when you're ready you can jump back to that bookmark.

Setting Bookmarks

You set a bookmark at a particular line of code by clicking that line of code and selecting the Toggle Bookmark item in the Bookmarks submenu of the Edit menu, as shown in Figure 2.40. Selecting this same item again would remove the bookmark.

Jumping To A Bookmark

Now that you've set a bookmark and moved away from it while editing your code, how do you get back to it? You jump back to a bookmark with the two items in the Bookmarks submenu marked Next Bookmark and Previous Bookmark. (It would be convenient if Visual Basic allowed you to name bookmarks and select from a list of them where to jump to; perhaps that will appear in some future version of Visual Basic.)

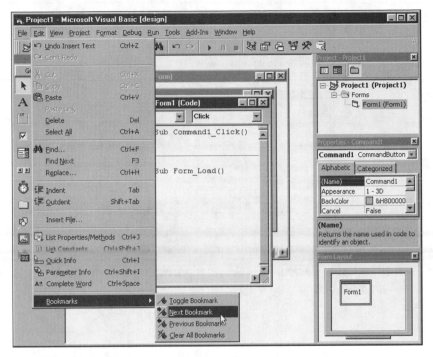

Figure 2.40   Using bookmarks in the Visual Basic IDE.

Using The Object Browser

One of the best ways of getting an overview of your project is to use the Object Browser. The Object Browser is very useful to get overviews, especially in larger projects. If your version of Visual Basic includes the Visual Basic Object Browser, you open it by selecting the Object Browser item in the View menu or by clicking its icon in the toolbar. The Object Browser opens, as shown in Figure 2.41.

You can scan through all the objects in the project by moving up and down in the Classes list. When you find the type of object you want to examine, select it; its properties and methods appear in the Members pane, as also shown in Figure 2.41.

If you want to learn more about a property or method, just select it with the mouse; you'll see an explanation of the property or method and the list of parameters for methods.

Figure 2.41   The Visual Basic Object Browser provides an overview of the objects in a project.

Chapter 3

The Visual Basic Language

If you need an immediate solution to:	See page:
Declaring Constants	85
Declaring Variables	86
Selecting Variable Types	88
Converting Between Data Types	90
Setting Variable Scope	90
Verifying Data Types	91
Declaring Arrays And Dynamic Arrays	93
Declaring Subroutines	96
Declaring Functions	97
Preserving Variables' Values Between Calls To Their Procedures	99
Handling Strings	100
Converting Strings To Numbers And Back Again	102
Handling Operators And Operator Precedence	102
Using **If...Else** Statements	104
Using **Select Case**	105
Making Selections With **Switch()** And **Choose()**	106
Looping	107
Using Collections	110
Sending Keystrokes To Other Programs	110
Handling Higher Math	113
Handling Dates And Times	114
Handling Financial Data	116
Ending A Program At Any Time	116

In Depth

This chapter is all about what makes the various parts of a Visual Basic program work: the Visual Basic language itself. In this chapter, we'll see the components of the Visual Basic language and how to use them. After designing and creating the interface for your application using the Visual Basic IDE, and filling your program with forms and controls, you'll need to write the code that makes those controls and forms *do* something.

The Visual Basic language supports a large number of programming constructs and elements, and that language is the foundation on which we'll build in this book. A good start here is essential for the work we'll do throughout the book.

If you've programmed in other languages, much of the material in this chapter will probably be familiar to you—and once you understand the basics, you will be able to create powerful applications using Visual Basic.

How Does Visual Basic Code Look?

We're going to take a look at the elements of the Visual Basic language that will let us make Visual Basic code work. What will that code look like? Some of our code will be short, such as when we check for multimedia device errors like this in Chapter 22:

```
Private Sub MMControl1_Done(NotifyCode As Integer)
    If MMControl1.Error <> 0 Then
        MsgBox MMControl1.ErrorMessage
    End If
End Sub
```

Some of our code will be a little longer, such as this code, where we display the status of a CD-ROM drive that's playing a music CD:

```
Private Sub MMControl1_StatusUpdate()
    Dim strMode As String
    strMode = ""

    Select Case MMControl1.Mode
```

```
        Case mciModeReady
            strMode = "Ready."

        Case mciModeStop
            strMode = "Stopped."

        Case mciModeSeek
            strMode = "Seeking."

        Case mciModePlay
            strMode = "Playing."

        Case mciModeRecord
            strMode = "Recording."

        Case mciModePause
            strMode = "Paused."

    End Select

    Label1.Caption = strMode

End Sub
```

That's what the Visual Basic language looks like at work. As you can imagine, knowing how to write the code is necessary to get anywhere in Visual Basic.

In the topics coming up, then, we'll see how to declare variables, functions, and subroutines—and what those elements mean. We'll see how to use text strings, conditionals, operators, loops, and math techniques. We'll even see how to handle special Visual Basic formats like dates and financial data. And we'll see some items that programmers like but don't often encounter in programming books, such as how to use **Switch( )** and **Choose( )**.

We'll cover tasks that involve some complexity and whose syntax is hard to remember. In this way, this chapter also acts as a reference for easy lookup of those hard-to-remember items—and can save you from reinventing the wheel.

We'll see a lot of syntax in this chapter, and there's one convention you should be aware of before starting: we'll use brackets for optional elements and keywords like this for the **Dim** statement:

```
Dim [WithEvents] varname[([subscripts])] [As [New] type] [, [WithEvents]
varname[([subscripts])] [As [New] type]]
```

Here, all the elements in square brackets are optional, and the variable names in italics are placeholders—you fill them in with the names of your variables as appropriate for your program

It's time to turn to the Immediate Solutions now—no further introduction is needed.

Immediate Solutions

Declaring Constants

You've filled your code with numeric values—and now it's time to change them all as you start work on the new version of the software. What a pain to have to track down and change all the numeric values (called *magic numbers*) throughout all the code. Isn't there a better way?

There is: Use constants and declare them all in one place, then refer to the constants by name throughout the code instead of hardwiring numeric values in the code. When it's time to change those values, you just change the constants, all in one well-defined part of the code.

How do you use constants? You declare constants in Visual Basic with the **Const** statement:

```
[Public | Private] Const constname [As type] = expression
```

The **Public** keyword is used at the module level to make a constant global. This keyword is not allowed in procedures. The **Private** keyword is used at the module or form level to declare constants that are private, which means only available within the module or form where the declaration is made. Like the **Public** keyword, **Private** is not allowed in procedures (constants in procedures are always private anyway). The *constname* identifier is the actual name of the constant. The *type* identifier is the data type of the constant, which may be **Byte**, **Boolean**, **Integer**, **Long**, **Currency**, **Single**, **Double**, **Date**, **String**, or **Variant**. The *expression* identifier holds the value you want for this constant. It may be a literal, other constant, or any combination that in cludes all arithmetic or logical operators (except the **Is** operator).

You can use a constant anywhere you can use any Visual Basic expression, and you usually use them for numeric or string values that you want to use many places in a program. That way, when you want to modify the value of the constant, you only have to change it in its declaration, not in many places around the program. Also, constants don't change their values, which can make them more useful than variables in certain circumstances.

TIP: *You can't use variables, user-defined functions, or intrinsic Visual Basic functions in expressions assigned to constants.*

Here's an example showing how to declare and use a constant:

```
Private Sub Command1_Click()
    Const Pi = 3.14159
    Dim Radius, Area
    Radius = 1#
    Area = Pi * Radius * Radius
    MsgBox ("Area = " & Str(Area))
End Sub
```

Declaring Variables

Before using variables, you have to set aside memory space for them—after all, that's what they are, locations in memory. Usually, you use the **Dim** statement to declare variables, although you can also use the **Private** (declare a private variable), **Public** (declare a global variable), **Static** (declare a variable that holds its value between procedure calls), **ReDim** (redimension a dynamic array), or **Type** (declare a user-defined type) keywords to declare variables, as we'll see in the tasks covered in this chapter.

The **Dim** Statement

Here's how you use the **Dim** statement:

```
Dim [WithEvents] varname[([subscripts])] [As [New] type] [, [WithEvents]
varname [([subscripts])] [As [New] type]] . . .
```

The **WithEvents** keyword is valid only in class modules. This keyword specifies that *varname* is an object variable used to respond to events triggered by an ActiveX object. The *varname* identifier is the name of the variable you are declaring. You use *subscripts* if you're declaring an array.

You set up the *subscripts* argument this way:

```
[lower To] upper [, [lower To] upper]
```

TIP: *In Visual Basic, you may declare up to 60 dimensions for an array.*

The **New** keyword enables creation of an object. If you use **New** when declaring the object variable, a new instance of the object is created on first reference to it. This means you don't have to use the **Set** statement to assign the object reference. Here's an example:

```
Dim DataSheet As New Worksheet
```

The *type* argument specifies the data type of the variable, which may be **Byte**, **Boolean**, **Integer**, **Long**, **Currency**, **Single**, **Double**, **Date**, **String** (for variable-length strings), **String * length** (for fixed-length strings), **Object**, **Variant**, a user-defined type, or an object type. If you don't specify a type, the default is **Variant**, which means the variable can act as any type.

TIP: By default in Visual Basic, numeric variables are initialized to 0, variable-length strings are initialized to a zero-length string (""), and fixed-length strings are filled with zeros. Variant variables are initialized to **Empty**.

Here's an example of declaring variables using **Dim**:

```
Dim EmployeeID As Integer
Dim EmployeeName As String
Dim EmployeeAddress As String
```

Implicit Declarations And Option Explicit

Following the traditions of earlier versions of Basic, you don't actually need to declare a variable at all to use it—just *using* it in code declares it as a variant if it's not been declared. It's better to require all variables to be explicitly declared, however, because misspelling a variable name can declare a new variable and cause problems, as we saw in this code from Chapter 1, where we think we're toggling a Boolean variable named **xNow** but are placing the result in a new and misspelled variable named **xNoww**:

```
Private Sub Command_Click(Index As Integer)
    If xNow Then
        Command(Index).Caption = "x"
    Else
        Command(Index).Caption = "o"
    End If

    xNoww = Not xNow

End Sub
```

To force variable declarations to be explicit (that is, to insist that each variable be declared), add the **Option Explicit** statement at the module or form level to the (General) declarations object.

Selecting Variable Types

It's time to create a new variable—but what type should you use? For that matter, exactly what type of variable types are there and what do they do? Even if you remember what types there are, you probably won't remember the range of possible values that variable type allows.

There's a wide range of data types, so we'll use a table here. The Visual Basic variable types appear in Table 3.1 for reference, making selecting the right type a little easier (note that although Visual Basic lists a **Decimal** variable type, that type is not yet actually supported). We also include the literal suffix symbols for numeric values in Table 3.1—those are the suffixes you can add to the end of values or variables to tell Visual Basic their type, like **strUserFormatString$**.

As you can see in Table 3.1, Visual Basic has a large number of data formats. The **Variant** type deserves special mention, because it's the default variable type. If you don't declare a type for a variable, it is made a variant:

```
Private Sub Command1_Click()
    Dim NumberTrains
...
End Sub
```

In this case, the variable **NumberTrains** is a variant, which means it can take any type of data. For example, here we place an integer value into **NumberTrains** (note that we specify that 5 is an integer by using the percent sign [%] suffix as specified in Table 3.1):

```
Private Sub Command1_Click()
    Dim NumberTrains
    NumberTrains = 5%
End Sub
```

We could have used other data types as well; here, for example, we place a string into **NumberTrains**:

```
Private Sub Command1_Click()
    Dim NumberTrains
    NumberTrains = "Five"
End Sub
```

Table 3.1   Variable types.

Variable Type	Bytes Of Storage	Literal Suffix	Range
Boolean	2	N/A	True, False
Byte	1	N/A	0 to 255
Currency	8	@	-922,337,203,685,477.5808 to 922,337,203,685,477.5807
Date	8	#...#	1 January 100 to 31 December 9999 and times from 0:00:00 to 23:59:59
Decimal	12	N/A	-79,228,162,514,264,337,593,543,950,335 to 79,228,162,514,264,337,593,543,950,335
Double	8	#	-1.79769313486232E308 to -4.94065645841247E-324 for negative values and from 4.94065645841247E-324 to 1.79769313486232E308 for positive values
Integer	2	%	-32,768 to 32,767
Long	4	&	-2,147,483,648 to 2,147,483,647
Object	4	N/A	N/A
Single	4	!	-3.402823E38 to -1.401298E-45 for negative values and from 1.401298E-45 to 3.402823E38 for positive values
String	N/A	$	A variable-length string can contain up to approximately 2 billion characters; a fixed-length string can contain 1 to approximately 64K characters
User-defined data type	N/A	N/A	N/A
Variant	N/A	N/A	N/A

And here we use a floating point value (! is the suffix for single values):

```
Private Sub Command1_Click()
    Dim NumberTrains
    NumberTrains = 5.00!
End Sub
```

Be careful of variants, however—they waste time because Visual Basic has to translate them into other data types before using them, and they also take up more space than other data types.

Converting Between Data Types

Visual Basic supports a number of ways of converting from one type of variable to another—in fact, that's one of the strengths of the language. The possible conversion statements and procedures appear in Table 3.2.

TIP: Note that you can cast variables from one type to another in Visual Basic using the functions **CBool()**, **CByte()**, and so on.

Table 3.2   *Visual Basic data conversion functions.*

To Do This	Use This
ANSI value to string	Chr
String to lowercase or uppercase	Format, LCase, UCase
Date to serial number	DateSerial, DateValue
Decimal number to other bases	Hex, Oct
Number to string	Format, Str
One data type to another	CBool, CByte, CCur, CDate, CDbl, CDec, CInt, CLng, CSng, CStr, CVar, CVErr, Fix, Int
Date to day, month, weekday, or year	Day, Month, Weekday, Year
Time to hour, minute, or second	Hour, Minute, Second
String to ASCII value	Asc
String to number	Val
Time to serial number	TimeSerial, TimeValue

Setting Variable Scope

You've just finished creating a new dialog box in your greeting card program, and it's a beauty. However, you realize there's a problem: the user enters the new number of balloons to display the greeting card in **TextBox1** of the dialog box, but how do you read that value in the rest of the program when the user closes the dialog box?

It's tempting to set up a global variable, **intNumberBalloons**, which you fill in the dialog box when the user clicks on the OK button. That way, you'll be able to use that variable in the rest of the program when the dialog box is closed. But in this case, you should resist the temptation to create a global variable—it's much better to refer to the text in the text box this way (assuming the name of the dialog form you've created is **Dialog**):

```
intNumberBalloons = Dialog.TextBox1.Text
```

This avoids setting up a global variable needlessly. In fact, one of the most important aspects of Visual Basic programming is *variable scope*. In general, you should restrict variables to the smallest scope possible.

There are three levels of variable scope in Visual Basic, as follows:

- Variables declared in procedures are private to the procedure.

- Variables declared at the form or module level in the form or module's (General) section using **Dim**, **ReDim**, **Private**, **Static**, or **Type** are form- or module-level variables. These variables are available throughout the module.

- Variables declared at the module level in the module's (General) section using **Public** are global and are available throughout the project, in all forms and modules. Note that you cannot use **Public** in procedures.

You can get an overview of the scope of variables in a Visual Basic project in Figure 3.1.

For more information, see the discussion of variable scope in Chapter 1.

TIP: *If you use the **Option Private Module** statement in a module or form, all variables in the module or form become private to the module, no matter how they are declared.*

Verifying Data Types

You can change a variable's type with **ReDim** in Visual Basic, assign objects to variables using **Set**, and even convert standard variables into arrays. For these and other reasons, Visual Basic has a number of data verification functions, which appear in Table 3.3, and you can use these functions to interrogate objects and determine their types.

Note in particular the **IsMissing()** function, which many programmers don't know about; this function tells you if the call to the current procedure included a value for a particular variant. For example, here's how we check if the call to a subroutine **CountFiles()** included a value in the optional parameter **intMaxFiles**:

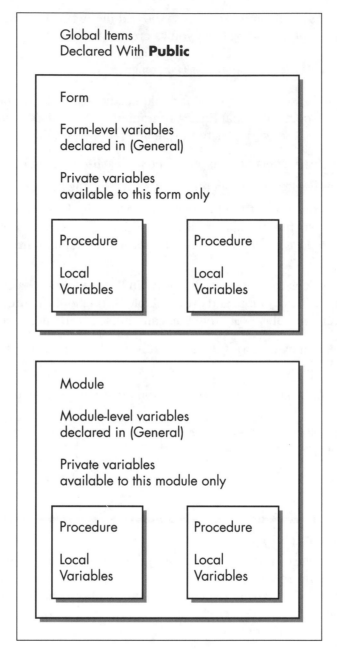

Figure 3.1   Visual Basic's variable scope schematic.

```
Sub CountFiles(Optional intMaxFile As Variant)
    If IsMissing(intMaxFile) Then
        'intMaxFiles was not passed
...
    Else
...
    End If
End Sub
```

Table 3.3   Data verification functions.

Function	Does This
IsArray()	Returns True if passed an array
IsDate()	Returns True if passed a date
IsEmpty()	Returns True if passed variable is uninitialized
IsError()	Returns True if passed an error value
IsMissing()	Returns True if value was not passed for specified parameter in procedure call
IsNull()	Returns True if passed **NULL**
IsNumeric()	Returns True if passed a numeric value
IsObject()	Returns True if passed an object

Declaring Arrays And Dynamic Arrays

Declaring Arrays And Dynamic Arrays

It's time to start coding that database program. But wait a moment—how are you going to handle the data? It's just a simple program, so you don't want to start tangling with the full Visual Basic database techniques. An array would be perfect; how do you set them up again?

You can use **Dim** (standard arrays), **ReDim** (dynamic arrays), **Static** (arrays that don't change when between calls to the procedure they're in), **Private** (arrays private to the form or module they're declared in), **Public** (arrays global to the whole program), or **Type** (for arrays of user-defined types) to dimension arrays.

We'll start with standard arrays now.

Standard Arrays

You usually use the **Dim** statement to declare a standard array (note that in Visual Basic, arrays can have up to 60 dimensions):

```
Dim [WithEvents] varname[([subscripts])] [As [New] type] [, [WithEvents]
varname [([subscripts])] [As [New] type]] ...
```

The **WithEvents** keyword is valid only in class modules. This keyword specifies that *varname* is an object variable used to respond to events triggered by an ActiveX object. The *varname* identifier is the name of the variable you are declaring.

You use *subscripts* to declare the array. You set up the *subscripts* argument this way:

```
[lower To] upper [, [lower To] upper]
```

The **New** keyword enables creation of an object. If you use **New** when declaring the object variable, a new instance of the object is created on first reference to it.

The *type* argument specifies the data type of the variable, which may be **Byte**, **Boolean**, **Integer**, **Long**, **Currency**, **Single**, **Double**, **Date**, **String** (for variable-length strings), **String * length** (for fixed-length strings), **Object**, **Variant**, a user-defined type, or an object type. If you don't specify a type, the default is **Variant**, which means the variable can act as any type.

Here are a few examples of standard array declarations:

```
Private Sub Command1_Click()
    Dim Data(30)
    Dim Strings(10) As String
    Dim TwoDArray(20, 40) As Integer
    Dim Bounds(5 To 10, 20 To 100)
    Strings(3) = "Here's a string!"
End Sub
```

TIP: *You use the **Option Base** statement at the form- or module-level to set the lower bound for all arrays. The default value is 0, but you can use either of these two statements: **Option Base 0** or **Option Base 1**.*

Dynamic Arrays

You can use the **Dim** statement to declare an array with empty parentheses to declare a *dynamic array*. Dynamic arrays can be dimensioned or redimensioned as you need them with the **ReDim** statement (which you must also do the first time you want use a dynamic array). Here's how you use **ReDim**:

```
ReDim [Preserve] varname(subscripts) [As type] [, varname(subscripts)
[As type]] ...
```

You use the **Preserve** keyword to preserve the data in an existing array when you change the size of the last dimension. The *varname* argument holds the name of the array to (re)dimension.

The *subscripts* term specifies the dimensions of the array using this syntax:

```
[lower To] upper [,[lower To] upper]
```

The *type* argument specifies the type of the array. The type may be **Byte**, **Boolean**, **Integer**, **Long**, **Currency**, **Single**, **Double**, **Date**, **String** (for variable-length strings), **String * length** (for fixed-length strings), **Object**, **Variant**, a user-defined type, or an object type.

This is one of those topics that is made easier with an example, so here's an example using dynamic arrays, where we declare an array, dimension it, and then redimension it, like this:

```
Private Sub Command1_Click()
    Dim DynaStrings() As String
    ReDim DynaStrings(10)
    DynaStrings(1) = "The first string"
    'Need more data space!
    ReDim DynaStrings(100)
    DynaStrings(50) = "The fiftieth string"
End Sub
```

The **Array()** Function

You can also use the **Array()** function to create a new variant holding an array. Here's how you use **Array()**:

```
Array(arglist)
```

The *arglist* argument is a list of values that are assigned to the elements of the array contained within the variant. Here's an example that creates an array with the values 0, 1, and 2:

```
Dim A As Variant
A = Array(0,1,2)
```

TIP: *If you don't specify any arguments, the **Array()** function returns an array of zero length.*

We'll finish this topic with a summary of array-handling techniques.

Array-Handling Techniques Summary

Visual Basic has a number of statements and functions for working with arrays, and they appear in overview in Table 3.4 for easy reference.

Table 3.4   Array-handling techniques.

To Do This	Use This
Verify an array	IsArray
Create an array	Array
Change default lower limit	Option Base
Declare and initialize an array	Dim, Private, Public, ReDim, Static
Find the limits of an array	LBound, UBound
Reinitialize an array	Erase, ReDim

Declaring Subroutines

Everyone knows about subroutines: they're the handy blocks of code that can organize your code into single-purposed sections to make programming easier. Unlike functions, subroutines do not return values; but like functions, you can pass values to subroutines in an argument list.

For reference's sake, here's how you declare a subroutine:

```
[Private | Public | Friend] [Static] Sub name [(arglist)]
...
[statements]
...
[Exit Sub]
...
[statements]
...
End Sub
```

The **Public** keyword makes a procedure accessible to all other procedures in all modules and forms. The **Private** keyword makes a procedure accessible only to other procedures in the module or form in which it is declared. The **Friend** keyword is used only in class modules and specifies that the procedure is visible throughout the project, but not visible to a controller of an instance of an object. The **Static** keyword specifies that the procedure's local variables should be preserved between calls. The *name* identifier is the name of the procedure. The *arglist* identifier is a list of variables representing arguments that are passed to the procedure when it is called. You separate multiple variables with commas. The *statements* identifier is the group of statements to be executed within the procedure.

The *arglist* identifier has the following syntax:

```
[Optional] [ByVal | ByRef] [ParamArray] varname[( )] [As type]
[= defaultvalue]
```

In *arglist*, **Optional** means that an argument is not required; **ByVal** means that the argument is passed by value; **ByRef** means that the argument is passed by reference (**ByRef** is the default in Visual Basic); **ParamArray** is used as the last argument in *arglist* to indicate that the final argument is an array of Variant elements; *varname* is the name of the variable passed as an argument; *type* is the data type of the argument; and *defaultvalue* is any constant or constant expression, which is used as the argument's default value if you've used the **Optional** keyword.

TIP: *When you use* **ByVal***, you pass a copy of a variable to a procedure; when you use* **ByRef***, you pass a reference to the variable, and if you make changes to that reference, the original variable is changed.*

The **Exit Sub** keywords cause an immediate exit from a **Sub** procedure. Finally, **End Sub** ends the procedure definition.

You call a **Sub** procedure using the procedure name followed by the argument list. Here's an example of a subroutine:

```
Sub CountFiles(Optional intMaxFile As Variant)
    If IsMissing(intMaxFile) Then
        'intMaxFiles was not passed
        MsgBox ("Did you forget something?")
    Else
...
    End If
End Sub
```

TIP: *For an overview of how to comment procedures, see the discussion in Chapter 1.*

Declaring Functions

Declaring Functions

There are two types of procedures in Visual Basic: subroutines and functions. Subroutines can take arguments passed in parentheses but do not return a value; functions do the same but do return values (which can be discarded). A function is a block of code that you call and pass arguments to, and using functions helps break your code up into manageable parts.

For reference's sake, here's how you declare a function:

```
[Private | Public | Friend] [Static] Function name [(arglist)] [As type]
...
[statements]
...
[name = expression]
...
[Exit Function]
...
[statements]
...
End Function
```

The **Public** keyword makes a procedure accessible to all other procedures in all modules and forms. The **Private** keyword makes a procedure accessible only to other procedures in the module or form in which it is declared. The **Friend** keyword is used only in class modules and specifies that the procedure is visible throughout the project, but not visible to a controller of an instance of an object. The **Static** keyword specifies that the procedure's local variables should be preserved between calls. The *name* identifier is the name of the procedure. The *arglist* identifier is a list of variables representing arguments that are passed to the procedure when it is called. You separate multiple variables with commas. The *statements* identifier is the group of statements to be executed within the procedure.

The *arglist* identifier has this following syntax:

```
[Optional] [ByVal | ByRef] [ParamArray] varname[( )] [As type]
[= defaultvalue]
```

In *arglist*, **Optional** means that an argument is not required; *ByVal* means that the argument is passed by value; **ByRef** means that the argument is passed by reference (**ByRef** is the default in Visual Basic); **ParamArray** is used as the last argument in *arglist* to indicate that the final argument is an array of Variant elements; *varname* is the name of the variable passed as an argument; *type* is the data type of the argument; and *defaultvalue* is any constant or constant expression, which is used as the argument's default value if you've used the **Optional** keyword. The *type* identifier is the data type returned by the function. The **Exit Function** keywords cause an immediate exit from a **Function** procedure.

You call a **Function** procedure using the function name, followed by the argument list in parentheses. You return a value from a function by assigning the value you want to return to the function's name like this: ***name = expression***. Finally, **End Function** ends the procedure definition.

Here's an example showing how to use a function:

```
Private Sub Command1_Click()
    Dim intResult As Integer
    intResult = Add1(5)
    MsgBox ("Result = " & Str$(intResult))
End Sub

Function Add1(intAdd1ToMe As Integer) As Integer
    Add1 = intAdd1ToMe + 1
End Function
```

Preserving Variables' Values Between Calls To Their Procedures

Preserving Variables' Values Between Calls To Their Procedures

You've written a function named **Counter()** to keep track of the number of times the user clicks a particular button. Each time the user clicks the button, you call the **Counter()** function to increment the count of button clicks, and then display the result in a message box. But the counter never seems to be incremented; instead it always returns 1. Why?

Let's look at the code:

```
Private Sub Command1_Click()
    Dim intResult As Integer
    intResult = Counter()
    MsgBox ("Result = " & Str$(intResult))
End Sub

Function Counter() As Integer
    Dim intCountValue As Integer
    intCountValue = intCountValue + 1
    Counter = intCountValue
End Function
```

The problem here is that the counter variable, **intCountValue**, in the **Counter()** function is reinitialized each time the **Counter()** function is called (because a new copy of all the variables local to procedures is allocated each time you call that procedure).

The solution is to declare **intCountValue** as *static*. This means it will retain its value between calls to the **Counter()** function. Here's the working code:

```
Private Sub Command1_Click()
    Dim intResult As Integer
    intResult = Counter()
    MsgBox ("Result = " & Str$(intResult))
End Sub

Function Counter() As Integer
    Static intCountValue As Integer
    intCountValue = intCountValue + 1
    Counter = intCountValue
End Function
```

In fact, you could declare the whole function static, which means that all the variables in it will be static. That looks like this:

```
Private Sub Command1_Click()
    Dim intResult As Integer
    intResult = Counter()
    MsgBox ("Result = " & Str$(intResult))
End Sub

Static Function Counter() As Integer
    Dim intCountValue As Integer
    intCountValue = intCountValue + 1
    Counter = intCountValue
End Function
```

Besides declaring variables with **Static**, you can also use it as a keyword when declaring functions or subroutines.

Handling Strings

You've decided to lead the way into the future by letting your users type in English sentences as commands to your program. Unfortunately, this means that you have to *parse* (that is, break down to individual words) what they type. So what was that string function that lets you break a string into smaller strings again? We'll get an overview of string handling in this topic.

Two Kinds Of Strings

There are two kinds of strings: variable-length and fixed-length strings. You declare a variable-length string this way:

```
Dim strVariableString As String
```

A variable-length string can contain up to approximately 2 billion characters, and it can grow or shrink to match the data you place in it.

You declare a fixed-length string this way, with an asterisk character (*) followed by the string's length:

```
Dim strFixedString As String * 20
```

Here, we give our fixed-length string 20 characters. A fixed-length string can contain 1 to approximately 64K characters.

The String-Handling Functions

There are quite a number of string-handling functions in Visual Basic. For example, you use **Left( )**, **Mid( )**, and **Right( )** to divide a string into substrings, you find the length of a string with **Len( )**, and so on.

For reference, the Visual Basic string-handling functions appear in Table 3.5.

Table 3.5   String-handling functions.

To Do This	Use This
Compare two strings	StrComp
Convert strings	StrConv
Convert to lowercase or uppercase	Format, LCase, UCase
Create string of repeating character	Space, String
Find length of a string	Len
Format a string	Format
Justify a string	LSet, RSet
Manipulate strings	InStr, Left, LTrim, Mid, Right, RTrim, Trim
Set string comparison rules	Option Compare
Work with ASCII and ANSI values	Asc, Chr

Converting Strings To Numbers And Back Again

You're all set to write your *SuperDeluxe* calculator program in Visual Basic—but suddenly you realize that the user will be entering numbers in text form, not in numeric form. How can you translate text into numbers, and then numbers into text to display your results?

It's common in Visual Basic to have to convert values from numbers to strings or from strings to numbers, and it's easy to do. You can use the **Str( )** to return a string representation of a number, and you use **Val( )** to convert a string to a number. That's all there is to it, but it's easy to forget those two functions, so we include them here for reference.

Besides **Str( )** and **Val( )**, you can also use **Format( )**, which lets you format an expression into a string this way:

```
Format (expression[, format[, firstdayofweek[, firstweekofyear]]])
```

Here, *expression* is the expression to format into the string, *format* is a valid named or user-defined format expression, *firstdayofweek* is a constant that specifies the first day of the week, and *firstweekofyear* is a constant that specifies the first week of the year.

For more information about how to use this function and format strings, see "Handling Dates And Time Using Dates" later in this chapter.

Handling Operators And Operator Precedence

You've done well in your computer class—so well that the instructor has asked you to calculate the average grade on the final. Nothing could be easier, you think, so you put together the following program:

```
Private Sub Command1_Click()
    Dim intGrade1, intGrade2, intGrade3, NumberStudents As Integer
    intGrade1 = 60
    intGrade2 = 70
    intGrade3 = 80
    NumberStudents = 3
    MsgBox ("Average grade = " &_
        Str(intGrade1 + intGrade2 + intGrade3 / NumberStudents))
End Sub
```

When you run the program, however, it calmly informs you that the average score is 156.66666667. That doesn't look so good—what's wrong?

The problem lies in this line:

```
Str(intGrade1 + intGrade2 + intGrade3 / NumberStudents))
```

Visual Basic evaluates the expression in parentheses from left to right, using pairs of operands and their associated operator, so it adds the first two grades together first. Instead of adding the final grade, however, it first divides that grade by **NumberStudents**, because the division operation has higher precedence than addition. So the result is $60 + 70 + (80/3) = 156.66666667$.

The solution here is to group the values to add together this way using parentheses:

```
Private Sub Command1_Click()
    Dim intGrade1, intGrade2, intGrade3, NumberStudents As Integer
    intGrade1 = 60
    intGrade2 = 70
    intGrade3 = 80
    NumberStudents = 3
    MsgBox ("Average grade = " &_
        Str((intGrade1 + intGrade2 + intGrade3)/ NumberStudents))
End Sub
```

Running this new code gives us an average of 70, as it should be.

This example points out the need to understand how Visual Basic evaluates expressions involving operators. In general, such expressions are evaluated left to right, and when it comes to a contest between two operators (such as + and / in the last term of our original program), the operator with the higher precedence is used first.

Visual Basic's operator precedence, arranged by category, appears in Table 3.6.

Table 3.6   Operators and operator precedence.

Arithmetic	Comparison	Logical
Exponentiation (^)	Equality (=)	Not
Negation (−)	Inequality (<>)	And
Multiplication and division (*, /)	Less than (<)	Or
Integer division (\)	Greater than (>)	Xor
Modulus arithmetic (Mod)	Less than or equal to (<=)	Eqv
Addition and subtraction (+, −)	Greater than or equal to (>=)	Imp
String concatenation (&)	Like	Is

When expressions contain operators from more than one category in Table 3.6, arithmetic operators are evaluated first, comparison operators are evaluated next, and logical operators are evaluated last. Also, comparison operators actually all have equal precedence, which means they are evaluated in the left-to-right order in which they appear.

If in doubt, use parentheses—operations within parentheses are always performed before those outside. Within parentheses, however, operator precedence is maintained.

Using **If...Else** Statements

The **If** statement is the bread and butter of Visual Basic conditionals, but you can forget the syntax every now and then (that is, is it **ElseIf** or **Else If**?), so here's the **If** statement:

```
If condition Then
[statements]
[ElseIf condition-n Then
[elseifstatements]]...
[Else
[elsestatements]]
End If
```

And here's an example showing how to use the various parts of this popular statement:

```
Dim intInput
intInput = -1

While intInput < 0
    intInput = InputBox("Enter a positive number")
Wend

If intInput = 1 Then
    MsgBox ("Thank you.")
ElseIf intInput = 2 Then
    MsgBox ("That's fine.")
ElseIf intInput >= 3 Then
    MsgBox ("Too big.")
End If
```

Using **Select Case**

You have to get a value from the user and respond in several different ways, but you don't look forward to a long and tangled series of **If...Then...Else** statements. What can you do?

If your program can handle multiple values of a particular variable and you don't want to stack up a lot of **If...Else** statements to handle them, you should consider **Select Case**. You usc **Select Case** to test an expression, seeing which of several *cases* it matches, and execute the corresponding code. Here's the syntax:

```
Select Case testexpression
[Case expressionlist-n
[statements-n]]
[Case Else
[elsestatements]]
End Select
```

Here's an example using **Select Case**. In this example, we read a positive value from the user and test it, responding according to its value. Note that we also use the **Select Case Is** keyword (not the same as the **Is** operator) to check if the value we read in is greater than a certain value, and **Case Else** to handle values we don't explicitly provide code for. Here's the example:

```
Dim intInput
intInput = -1

While intInput < 0
    intInput = InputBox("Enter a positive number")
Wend

Const intMax = 100

Select Case intInput
    Case 1:
        MsgBox ("Thank you.")
    Case 2:
        MsgBox ("That's fine.")
    Case 3:
        MsgBox ("Your input is getting pretty big now...")
    Case 4 To 10:
        MsgBox ("You are approaching the maximum!")
    Case Is > intMax:
        MsgBox ("Too big, sorry.")
```

```
    Case Else:
        MsgBox ("Please try again.")
End Select
```

Making Selections With **Switch()** And **Choose()**

For some reason, few books on Visual Basic cover the **Switch()** and **Choose()** functions. They certainly have their uses, however, and we'll take a look at them here.

The **Switch()** Function

The **Switch()** function evaluates a list of expressions and returns a **Variant** value or an expression associated with the first expression in the list that is true. Here's the syntax:

```
Switch (expr-1, value-1[, expr-2, value-2 ... [, expr-n, value-n]])
```

In this case, *expr-1* is the first expression to evaluate; if true, **Switch()** returns *value-1*. If *expr-1* is not True but *expr-2* is, **Switch()** returns *value-2* and so on.

Here's an example showing how to use **Switch()**. In this case, we ask the user to enter a number and use **Switch()** to calculate the absolute value of that value (having temporarily forgotten how to use the built-in Visual Basic absolute value function, **Abs()**):

```
Dim intValue

intValue = InputBox("Enter a number")

intAbsValue = Switch(intValue < 0, -1 * intValue, intValue >= 0, intValue)

MsgBox "Absolute value = " & Str(intAbsValue)
```

The **Choose()** Function

You use the **Choose()** function to return one of a number of choices based on an index. Here's the syntax:

```
Choose (index, choice-1[, choice-2, ... [, choice-n]])
```

If the index value is 1, the first choice is returned, if index equals 2, the second choice is returned, and so on.

Here's an example using **Choose()**. In this case, we have three employees—Bob, Denise, and Ted—with employee IDs 1, 2, and 3. This code snippet accepts an ID value from the user and uses **Choose()** to display the corresponding employee name:

```
Dim intID
intID = -1

While intID < 1 Or intID > 3
    intID = InputBox("Enter employee's ID")
Wend

MsgBox "Employee name = " & Choose(intID, "Bob", "Denise", "Ted")
```

Looping

Many programmers have a love/hate relationship with looping, based primarily on syntax. Programmers often have to switch back and forth these days between languages, and can find themselves writing, for example, a C++ loop in the middle of a Visual Basic program and being taken by surprise when the compiler objects.

To make it easier, we'll include examples here of all the Visual Basic loops, starting with the **Do** loop.

The **Do** Loop

The **Do** loop has two versions; you can either evaluate a condition at the beginning

```
Do [{While | Until} condition]
[statements]
[Exit Do]
[statements]
Loop
```

or at the end:

```
Do
[statements]
[Exit Do]
[statements]
Loop [{While | Until} condition]
```

Here's an example where we read from a file, looping until we reach the end of the file, which we check with the end-of-file function, **EOF()**:

```
Do Until EOF(1)
    Line Input #1, Data$
    Form1.TextBox1.Text = Form1.TextBox1.Text + Data$
Loop
```

TIP: *Note that the second form of the* **Do** *loop ensures that the body of the loop is executed at least once. On the other hand, you sometimes want to make sure the loop doesn't run even once if the condition is not met. For example, when reading from a file, you shouldn't read from a file before checking for the end of file in case the file is empty.*

The **For** Loop

The **Do** loop doesn't need a loop index, but the **For** loop does. Here's the syntax for the **For** loop:

```
For index = start To end [Step step]
[statements]
[Exit For]
[statements]
Next [index]
```

Here's how to put it to work:

```
Dim intLoopIndex, Total
Total = 0
For intLoopIndex = 1 To 10
    Total = Total + 1
Next intLoopIndex
```

TIP: *Although it's been common practice to use a loop index after a loop completes (to see how many loop iterations were executed), that practice is now discouraged by people who make it their business to write about good and bad programming practices.*

The **For Each** Loop

You use the **For Each** loop to loop over elements in an array or collection. Here's its syntax:

```
For Each element In group
[statements]
[Exit For][statements]
Next [element]
```

You can get a look at this loop in action with an example like this one, where we display all the elements of an array in message boxes:

```
Dim IDArray(1 To 3)
IDArray(1) = 1
IDArray(2) = 2
IDArray(3) = 3

For Each ArrayItem In IDArray
    MsgBox (Str(ArrayItem))
Next ArrayItem
```

The **While** Loop

You use a **While** loop if you if you want to stop looping when a condition is no longer true. Here's the **While** loop's syntax:

```
While condition
[statements]
Wend
```

And here's an example putting **While** to work:

```
Dim intInput
intInput = -1

While intInput < 0
    intInput = InputBox("Enter a positive number")
Wend
```

TIP: *Many Visual Basic functions, like **EOF()**, are explicitly constructed to return values of True or False so that you can use them to control loops such as **Do** and **While** loops.*

The **With** Statement

Properly speaking, the **With** statement is not a loop, but it can be as useful as a loop—and in fact, many programmers actually think of it as a loop. You use the **With** statement to execute statements using a particular object. Here's the syntax:

```
With object
[statements]
End With
```

Here's an example showing how to put **With** to work. Here, we use a text box, **Text1**, and set several of its properties in the **With** statement:

```
With Text1
    .Height = 1000
    .Width = 3000
    .Text = "Welcome to Visual Basic"
End With
```

Using Collections

Using collections, you can group related items together. Collections can be heterogeneous—that is, members of a collection don't have to share the same data type, and that can be very useful, because life doesn't always present you with collections made up of items of the same type.

You create a collection as you would any other object:

```
Dim GarageSaleItems As New Collection
```

You can add members to the collection with the **Add** method and remove them with the **Remove** method.

You can also reach specific members in the collection using the **Item** method. Most importantly, from a programming point of view, you can loop over the entire collection using the **For Each...Next** statement (see the previous section, "Looping").

Collections are very useful and are one of the high points of Visual Basic. However, because of the heterogeneous nature of their contents, they don't necessarily lend themselves to tight and uniform coding practices (which makes some C and C++ programmers look down their noses at Visual Basic).

Sending Keystrokes To Other Programs

It's time to print out the 349 screen spreadsheets you've created in your new spreadsheet program to show the boss. Regrettably, there just doesn't seem to be any way to print them out except one at a time, using the File menu's Print item. Can Visual Basic help here?

Yes. You can use the **SendKeys()** function to send keys to the program that currently has the Windows focus, just as if you typed in those keys yourself. Using the Alt key, you can reach the menu items in your spreadsheet's File menu. The day is saved, because now you can automate your printing job, even waiting until the spreadsheet program processes the current keystroke before continuing. Here's how you use **SendKeys()**:

```
SendKeys string[, wait]
```

The *string* expression is the string you want to send to the other program. The *wait* argument is a Boolean value indicating the wait mode. If False (which is the default), control returns right after the keys are sent. If True, the keystrokes must be processed by the other program before control returns.

If the keys you want to send are not simple text, just embed the codes you see in Table 3.7 in the text you send to **SendKeys()**.

Table 3.7   SendKeys() key codes.

Key	Code
Backspace	{BACKSPACE}, {BS}, or {BKSP}
Break	{BREAK}
Caps Lock	{CAPSLOCK}
Del or Delete	{DELETE} or {DEL}
Down arrow	{DOWN}
End	{END}
Enter or Return	{ENTER} or ~
Esc	{ESC}
Help	{HELP}
Home	{HOME}
Ins or Insert	{INSERT} or {INS}
Left arrow	{LEFT}
Num Lock	{NUMLOCK}
Page Down	{PGDN}
Page Up	{PGUP}
Print Screen	{PRTSC}
Right arrow	{RIGHT}
Scroll Lock	{SCROLLLOCK}

(continued)

Table 3.7   SendKeys() key codes (continued).

Key	Code
Tab	{TAB}
Up arrow	{UP}
F1	{F1}
F2	{F2}
F3	{F3}
F4	{F4}
F5	{F5}
F6	{F6}
F7	{F7}
F8	{F8}
F9	{F9}
F10	{F10}
F11	{F11}
F12	{F12}
F13	{F13}
F14	{F14}
F15	{F15}
F16	{F16}
Shift	+
Ctrl	^
Alt	%

Here's an example showing how to use **SendKeys()**. Here, we give the Windows WordPad program the focus with the Visual Basic **AppActivate()** function, passing it the title of that program (which appears in its title bar), and send the string "Hello from Visual Basic!" to that program as follows:

```
AppActivate ("Document - WordPad")
SendKeys ("Hello from Visual Basic!")
```

The result appears in Figure 3.2—now we're able to send keystrokes to another program.

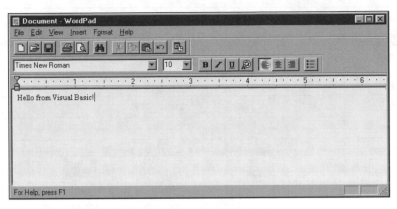

Figure 3.2   Sending keystrokes to Windows WordPad.

Handling Higher Math

Well, it may have been a mistake taking on that programming job from the astrophysics department. How do you calculate a hyperbolic cosecant anyway? Can Visual Basic do it?

Yes, although not directly. The built-in Visual Basic math functions appear in Table 3.8.

Table 3.8   Visual Basic math functions.

Function	Calculates This
Abs	Absolute value
Atn	Arc tangent
Cos	Cosine
Exp	Exponentiation
Fix	Fix places
Int	Integer value
Log	Log
Rnd	Random number
Sgn	Sign
Sin	Sine
Sqr	Square root
Tan	Tangent

Table 3.9   Calculated math functions.

Function	Calculate This Way
Secant	Sec(X) = 1 / Cos(X)
Cosecant	Cosec(X) = 1 / Sin(X)
Cotangent	Cotan(X) = 1 / Tan(X)
Inverse sine	Arcsin(X) = Atn(X / Sqr(-X * X + 1))
Inverse cosine	Arccos(X) = Atn(-X / Sqr(-X * X + 1)) + 2 * Atn(1)
Inverse secant	Arcsec(X) = Atn(X / Sqr(X * X − 1)) + Sgn((X) − 1) * (2 * Atn(1))
Inverse cosecant	Arccosec(X) = Atn(X / Sqr(X * X - 1)) + (Sgn(X) − 1) * (2 * Atn(1))
Inverse cotangent	Arccotan(X) = Atn(X) + 2 * Atn(1)
Hyperbolic sine	HSin(X) = (Exp(X) − Exp(-X)) / 2
Hyperbolic cosine	HCos(X) = (Exp(X) + Exp(-X)) / 2
Hyperbolic tangent	HTan(X) = (Exp(X) − Exp(-X)) / (Exp(X) + Exp(-X))
Hyperbolic secant	HSec(X) = 2 / (Exp(X) + Exp(-X))
Hyperbolic cosecant	HCosec(X) = 2 / (Exp(X) − Exp(-X))
Hyperbolic cotangent	HCotan(X) = (Exp(X) + Exp(-X)) / (Exp(X) − Exp(-X))
Inverse hyperbolic sine	HArcsin(X) = Log(X + Sqr(X * X + 1))
Inverse hyperbolic cosine	HArccos(X) = Log(X + Sqr(X * X − 1))
Inverse hyperbolic tangent	HArctan(X) = Log((1 + X) / (1 − X)) / 2
Inverse hyperbolic secant	HArcsec(X) = Log((Sqr(-X * X + 1) + 1) / X)
Inverse hyperbolic cosecant	HArccosec(X) = Log((Sgn(X) * Sqr(X * X + 1) + 1) / X)
Inverse hyperbolic cotangent	HArccotan(X) = Log((X + 1) / (X − 1)) / 2
Logarithm to base N	LogN(X) = Log(X) / Log(N)

If what you want, like hyperbolic cosecant, is not in Table 3.8, use Table 3.9, which shows you how to calculate other results using the built-in Visual Basic functions. There's enough math power in Table 3.9 to keep most astrophysicists happy.

Handling Dates And Times

One of the biggest headaches a programmer can have is working with dates. Handling hours, minutes, and seconds can be as bad as working with pounds, shillings, and pence. Fortunately, Visual Basic has a number of date- and time-handling functions, which appear in Table 3.10—you can even add or subtract dates using those functions.

Table 3.10   Visual Basic date keywords.

To Do This	Use This
Get the current date or time	Date, Now, Time
Perform date calculations	DateAdd, DateDiff, DatePart
Return a date	DateSerial, DateValue
Return a time	TimeSerial, TimeValue
Set the date or time	Date, Time
Time a process	Timer

There's something else you should know—the **Format$( )** function makes it easy to format dates into strings, including times. For easy reference, see Table 3.11, which shows how to display the date and time in a string—note how many ways there are to do this.

You can also compare dates and times directly. For example, here's how you loop until the current time (returned as a string by **Time$**) exceeds the time the user has entered in a text box (for example, "15:00:00"); when the time is up, the program beeps and displays a message box:

```
While Time$ < Text1.Text
Wend
Beep
MsgBox ("Time's up!")
```

Warning! *Don't use this code snippet for more than an example of how to compare times! The eternal looping while waiting for something to happen is a bad idea in Windows, because your program monopolizes a lot of resources that way. Instead, set up a Visual Basic Timer object and have a procedure called, say, every second.*

Table 3.11   Using Format$() to display dates and times.

Format Expression	Yields This on January 1, 2000 at 1:00 A M
Format$(Now, "m - d - yy")	"1-1-00"
Format$(Now, "m / d / yy")	"1 / 1 / 00"
Format$(Now, "mm - dd - yy")	"01-01-00"
Format$(Now, "ddd, mmmm d, yyy")	"Friday, January 1, 2000"
Format$(Now, "d mmm, yyy")	"1 Jan, 2000"
Format$(Now, "hh:mm:ss mm/dd/yy")	"01:00:00 01/01/00"
Format$(Now, "hh:mm:ss AM/PM mm - dd- yy")	"01:00:00 AM 01-01-00"

Handling Financial Data

You finally landed that big programming job at MegaMegaBank—congratulations! But now there's some trouble—just what is an "internal rate of return" anyway? Visual Basic to the rescue—there are 13 Visual Basic functions devoted entirely to financial work, and they appear in Table 3.12.

TIP: If you're going to be working with financial data, checkout the Visual Basic currency data in "Declaring Variables" earlier in this chapter. The currency data type can hold values from -922,337,203,685,477.5808 to 922,337,203,685,477.5807.

Table 3.12   The Visual Basic financial functions.

To Do This	Use This
Calculate depreciation	DDB, SLN, SYD
Calculate future value	FV
Calculate interest rate	Rate
Calculate internal rate of return	IRR, MIRR
Calculate number of periods	NPer
Calculate payments	IPmt, Pmt, PPmt
Calculate present value	NPV, PV

Ending A Program At Any Time

Our last topic in this chapter will be about ending programs. There are times when you want to end a program without any further ado—for example, to make an Exit menu item active. How do you do that?

You use the **End** statement. This statement stops execution of your program—but note that it does so immediately, which means that no **Unload( )** or similar event handling functions are called. **End** just brings the program to an end, which is what it should do.

---

*TIP: The **Stop** statement is similar to **End**, except that it puts the program in a break state. Executing a **Stop** statement, therefore, is just like running into a breakpoint—the debugger will come up.*

Chapter 4

Managing Forms In Visual Basic

If you need an immediate solution to:	See page:
Setting Title Bar Text	121
Adding/Removing Min/Max Buttons And Setting A Window's Border	122
Adding Toolbars To Forms	123
Adding Status Bars To Forms	126
Referring To The Current Form	128
Redrawing Form Contents	129
Setting Control Tab Order	129
Moving And Sizing Controls From Code	131
Showing And Hiding Controls In A Form	132
Measurements In Forms	133
Working With Multiple Forms	134
Loading, Showing, And Hiding Forms	136
Setting The Startup Form	137
Creating Forms In Code	138
Using The Multiple Document Interface	139
Arranging MDI Child Windows	140
Opening New MDI Child Windows	141
Arrays Of Forms	142
Coordinating Data Between MDI Child Forms (Document Views)	144
Creating Dialog Boxes	145
All About Message Boxes And Input Boxes	148
Passing Forms To Procedures	150
Minimizing/Maximizing And Enabling/Disabling Forms From Code	151

In Depth

In this chapter, we'll take a look at handling forms in Visual Basic. There's a great deal to see about form handling, and we'll look at it all. We'll see how to customize forms, how to work with multiple forms, how to support the multiple document interface (MDI), how to coordinate MDI child forms, how to use the **MsgBox( )** and **InputBox( )** functions, how to load, hide, show, and unload forms, and much more. We'll begin the chapter by getting an overview of Visual Basic forms.

The Parts Of A Form

Forms are the names for windows in Visual Basic (originally, you called windows under design *forms*, and the actual result when running a *window*, but common usage has named both forms now), and you add controls to forms in the Integrated Development Environment (IDE).

We're designing a form in the Visual Basic IDE in Figure 4.1, and you can see several aspects of forms there. At the top of the form is the *title bar*, which

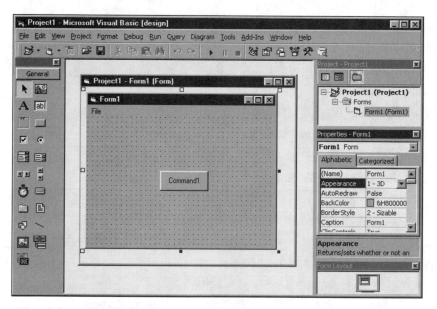

Figure 4.1   A form under design.

displays the form's title; here that's just Form1. At right in the title bar is the control box, including the minimizing/maximizing buttons and the close button. These are controls the user takes for granted in most windows, although we'll see they are inappropriate in others (such as dialog boxes).

Under the title bar comes the *menu bar*, if there is one. In Figure 4.1, the form has one menu: the File menu (we'll see how to work with menus in the next chapter). Under the menu bar, forms can have *toolbars*, as you see in the IDE itself.

The main area of a form—the area where everything takes place—is called the *client area*. In general, Visual Basic code works with controls in the client area and leaves the rest of the form to Visual Basic (in fact, the client area is itself a window). In Figure 4.1, we've added a control—a command button—to the form.

Finally, the whole form is surrounded by a *border*, and there are several types of borders that you can use.

The Parts Of An MDI Form

Besides standard forms, Visual Basic also supports MDI forms. An MDI form appears in Figure 4.2.

You can see that an MDI form looks much like a standard form, with one major difference, of course—the client area of an MDI form acts like a kind of corral for other forms. That is, an MDI form can display MDI child forms in it, which is how the multiple document interface works. In Figure 4.2, we have two documents open in the MDI form.

Figure 4.2   An MDI form.

That's the third type of form you can have in Visual Basic—MDI child forms. These forms appear in MDI child windows, but otherwise are very similar to standard forms.

Those, then, are the three types of forms available to us in Visual Basic: standard forms, MDI forms, and MDI child forms. We'll work with all of them in this chapter. In fact, we're ready to start getting into the details now as we turn to the Immediate Solutions section of this chapter.

Immediate Solutions

Setting Title Bar Text

You've submitted your project to the user-testing stage and feel smug. What could go wrong? Suddenly the phone rings—seems they don't like the title in the program's title bar: "Project1". How can you change it?

This stymies a lot of Visual Basic programmers, because the text in the title bar seems like something that Windows itself manages, not the program. In fact, it's up to the program, and setting the text in the title bar couldn't be easier. At design time, you just change the form's **Caption** property, as shown in Figure 4.3.

You can also set the **Caption** property at runtime in code like this (note that we use the **Me** keyword here to refer to the current form—see "Referring to the Current Form" later in this chapter):

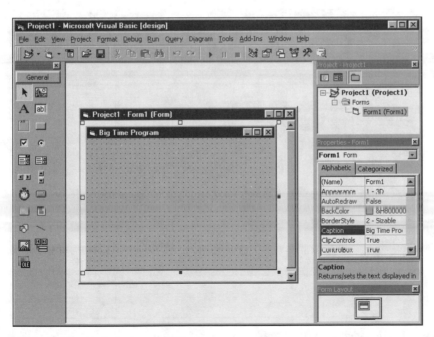

Figure 4.3   Setting a form's caption.

```
Private Sub Command1_Click()
    Me.Caption = "Hello from Visual Basic!"
End Sub
```

Adding/
Removing
Min/Max
Buttons
And Setting A
Window's
Border

Adding/Removing Min/Max Buttons And Setting A Window's Border

Forms usually come with minimizing and maximizing buttons, as well as a close box at the upper right. However, that's not appropriate in all cases, as we'll see when we design dialog boxes later in this chapter.

To remove these buttons, you can set the form's **ControlBox** property to False, as shown in Figure 4.4. Note that the usual buttons are missing from the form at the upper right.

TIP: *If you are thinking of designing a dialog box, take a look at "Creating Dialog Boxes" later in this chapter—besides removing the control box, you should also set the dialog's border correctly, add OK and Cancel buttons, and take care of a few more considerations.*

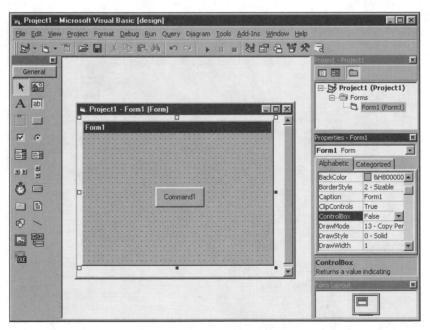

Figure 4.4   Removing the control box from a form.

You can also set what buttons are in a form by setting its border type. For example, if you set the border style to a fixed type, the minimizing and maximizing buttons will disappear.

Setting A Form's Border

You set a form's border style with its **BorderStyle** property; here are the possible values for that property:

- *0*—None
- *1*—Fixed Single
- *2*—Sizable
- *3*—Fixed Dialog
- *4*—Fixed Tool window
- *5*—Sizable Tool window

We'll see more about using the **BorderStyle** property when we work with dialog boxes in this chapter.

Adding Toolbars To Forms

For some reason, adding toolbars to forms isn't covered in a lot of Visual Basic books. However, users have come to expect toolbars in more complex programs, and we'll see how to add them here. Toolbars provide buttons that correspond to menu items and give the user an easy way to select the commands those items correspond to.

Adding A Toolbar With The Application Wizard

The easiest way to design a toolbar and add it to a program is with the Application Wizard. When you create a new application using the Application Wizard, it lets you design the toolbar, as shown in Figure 4.5.

This is a great way to put a toolbar in a program, because the support is already there for all these buttons by default. When you create the program, here's how it handles the buttons in the toolbar, with a **Select Case** statement that looks at the button's **Key** value:

```
Private Sub tbToolBar_ButtonClick(ByVal Button As MSComCtlLib.Button)
    On Error Resume Next
    Select Case Button.Key
```

```
        Case "New"
            LoadNewDoc
        Case "Open"
            mnuFileOpen_Click
        Case "Save"
            mnuFileSave_Click
        Case "Print"
            mnuFilePrint_Click
        Case "Copy"
            mnuEditCopy_Click
        Case "Cut"
            mnuEditCut_Click
        Case "Paste"
            mnuEditPaste_Click
        Case "Bold"
            ActiveForm.rtfText.SelBold = Not ActiveForm.rtfText.SelBold
            Button.Value = IIf(ActiveForm.rtfText.SelBold, tbrPressed,_
                tbrUnpressed)
        Case "Italic"
            ActiveForm.rtfText.SelItalic = Not ActiveForm.rtfText._
                SelItalic
            Button.Value = IIf(ActiveForm.rtfText.SelItalic, tbrPressed,_
                tbrUnpressed)
        Case "Underline"
            ActiveForm.rtfText.SelUnderline = Not _
                ActiveForm.rtfText.SelUnderline
            Button.Value = IIf(ActiveForm.rtfText.SelUnderline,_
                tbrPressed,tbrUnpressed)
        Case "Align Left"
            ActiveForm.rtfText.SelAlignment = rtfLeft
        Case "Align Right"
            ActiveForm.rtfText.SelAlignment = rtfRight
        Case "Center"
            ActiveForm.rtfText.SelAlignment = rtfCenter
    End Select
End Sub
```

Adding A Toolbar To A Program Yourself

You can also add toolbars to already-existing programs; just follow these steps:

1. Use the Project|Components item to open the Components box, and select the Controls tab.

2. Click the Microsoft Windows Common Controls box, and click on OK to close the Components box.

3. Double-click the New Toolbar tool in the toolbox to add a new toolbar to your form now.

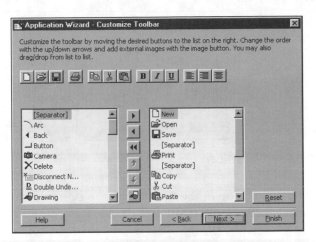

Figure 4.5   Designing a toolbar with the Application Wizard.

4. Right-click the toolbar now, and select the Properties item in the pop-up menu that appears, opening the button's property page, as shown in Figure 4.6.

5. Click the Buttons tab in the property page now, and click Insert Button to insert a new button into the toolbar.

6. Give the new button the caption you want, and set its **Key** property to a string of text you want to refer to the button with in code (in Figure 4.6, we set the new button's **Key** property to "First").

7. Add other buttons in the same way and close the property page.

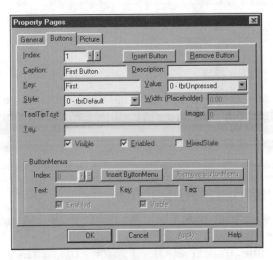

Figure 4.6   Setting a toolbar button's properties.

Figure 4.7   A form with a toolbar.

8. Double-click a button in the toolbar now to open the code window, displaying **Toolbar1_ButtonClick( )**:

```
Private Sub Toolbar1_ButtonClick(ByVal Button As MSComCtlLib.Button)
...
End Sub
```

9. Add the code you want to **Toolbar1_ButtonClick( )**. You do this with a **Select Case** statement, selecting on the buttons' **Key** property:

```
Private Sub Toolbar1_ButtonClick(ByVal Button As MSComCtlLib.Button)
    Select Case Button.Key
        Case "First"
            MsgBox "You clicked the first button."
        Case "Second"
            MsgBox "You clicked the second button."
        Case "Third"
            MsgBox "You clicked the third button."
    End Select

End Sub
```

And that's it—now we've added a toolbar to a program; when the user clicks a key in the toolbar, our program will handle it. The result appears in Figure 4.7.

Adding Status Bars To Forms

You've finished your program, and it's ready to go to market—but suddenly the project director calls and asks why there's so many message boxes popping up all the time. You explain that you have to give the user feedback on the file downloading process—after all, downloading the 200MB initialization file from the Internet takes some time, and you like to update the user on the process every time a kilobyte of data has been read.

"What about using the status bar?" the project director asks.

Hmm, you think—what *about* using the status bar?

The easiest way to put a status bar in a form is to design your program with the Application Wizard, and the result of that process appears earlier in Figure 4.2. However, you can also add status bars to a program yourself with these steps:

1. Use the Project|Components item to open the Components box, and select the Controls tab.

2. Click the Microsoft Windows Common Controls box, and click on OK to close the Components box.

3. Double-click the New Status Bar tool in the toolbox to add a new status bar to your form now.

4. Right-click the status bar, and select the Properties item in the pop-up menu that appears, opening the button's property page, as shown in Figure 4.8.

5. Status bars are organized into *panels*, and each panel can display separate text. To add the panels you want to the status bar, use the Insert Panel button. Close the property page.

6. Now you can set the text in the panels from code. You do that with the status bar's **Panels** collection. The first panel in the status bar is **Panels(1)**, the second **Panels(2)**, and so on. For example, to set the text in the first panel to "Status: OK", you would use this code:

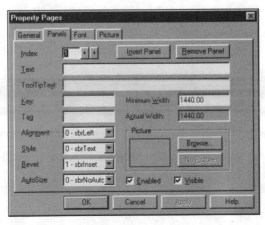

Figure 4.8   Adding panels to a status bar.

```
Private Sub Command1_Click ()
    StatusBar1.Panels(1).Text = "Status: OK"
End Sub
```

The result appears in Figure 4.9—now we're using status bars in our programs.

Referring To The Current Form

You've written a terrific subroutine to change a form's color to red

```
Sub ColorWindow(FormToColor As Form)
    FormToColor.BackColor = RGB(255, 0, 0)
End Sub
```

and you want to color all the forms in your project when the user clicks a button. That's easy to do using the **Me** keyword, which refers to the current object. Here, for example, is how we'd pass the current form to the **ColorWindow( )** subroutine:

```
Private Sub Command1_Click()
    ColorWindow Me
End Sub
```

That is, **Me** is an implicit variable, always available, and stands for the current object, which comes in handy when you want to pass the current object to a procedure.

TIP: *The **Me** keyword is also very useful in class modules where more than one instance of a class can occur, because it always refers to the current instance.*

Figure 4.9   A new status bar in a program.

Redrawing Form Contents

You've written some code to draw an "x" across a form like this:

```
Private Sub Command1_Click()
    Line (0, 0)-(ScaleWidth, ScaleHeight)
    Line (0, ScaleHeight)-(ScaleWidth, 0)
End Sub
```

You try it out and it looks perfect—but then the boss walks past and you mini-mize your program for a second to go back to that word-processing program so you'll look busy. When you maximize the x program again, the x is gone—what happened?

One of the biggest headaches for Windows programmers is refreshing the win-dow when required, because that involves redrawing the entire form's con-tents. To make matters worse, this is a common occurrence, because in Windows, the user is always covering and uncovering windows, minimizing and maximizing them, and changing their size, all of which means that your program has to keep redrawing itself.

In C or C++ programs, you have to write all the redrawing code yourself; for-tunately, there is an easy fix in Visual Basic (and that's one of the things that made Visual Basic so popular in the first place)—you just use the **AutoReDraw** property. You've probably already used the **AutoReDraw** property, but we include it here for reference. When you set this property to True, as shown in Figure 4.10, the graphics displayed in the form are stored and redisplayed when needed. All the window refreshes are done for you.

Now when you minimize and then maximize your x program, the x reappears as it should. Problem solved!

Setting Control Tab Order

Another call from the Testing Department. They've been going over your pro-gram with a fine-tooth comb and asking about the keyboard interface.

What does that mean? you ask.

They explain that theoretically, according to Microsoft, users should be able to run all Windows programs with the keyboard alone.

But that was archaic years ago, you say.

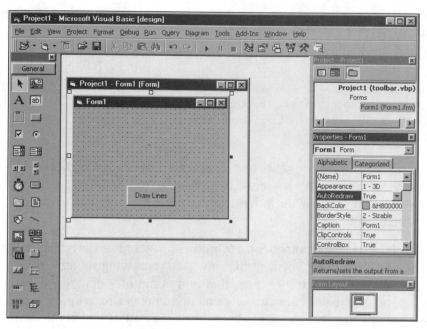

Figure 4.10   Setting AutoReDraw to True.

Add it to your program, they say.

In Visual Basic, you can make controls accessible to the keyboard by setting their *tab order*. The user can move around from control to control, highlighting the currently selected control, using the Tab key. But it's up to you to set the order in which the focus moves from control to control, and even whether or not a control can be reached with the Tab key.

To set the tab order of the controls in your program, follow these steps:

1. Select a control whose tab order you want to set with the mouse, as shown in Figure 4.11.

2. Next, make sure the control's **TabStop** property is set to True, as shown in Figure 4.11. If this property is False, the user cannot reach the control using the Tab key.

3. Now set the control's position in the tab order by setting its **TabIndex** property. The first control in the tab order has a **TabIndex** of 0, the next a **TabIndex** of 1, and so on.

4. When you run the program, the first control is highlighted; when the user presses the Tab key, the focus moves to the second control in the tab order, when he presses Tab again, the focus moves to the third control, and so on.

That's all it takes—now you're giving your program a keyboard interface.

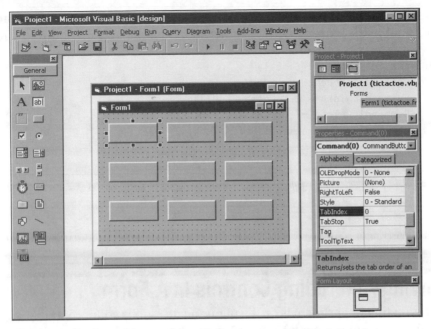

Figure 4.11   Setting a control's TabIndex property to set its tab order.

Moving And Sizing Controls From Code

Sometimes it's necessary to move or resize the controls in a form as a program is running, but for some reason, many Visual Basic programmers think you can only do that at design time. In fact, you can do it at runtime easily.

All controls have these properties available at design time or runtime to set their location and dimensions:

- **Top**—The y coordinate of the top left of the control.
- **Left**—The x coordinate of the top left of the control.
- **Width**—The width of the control.
- **Height**—The height of the control.

You can change all these settings interactively to move or resize a control in a form. Note that all measurements are in twips (1/1440 of an inch) by default, and that the origin (0, 0) in a form is at upper left.

You can also use a control's **Move()** method to move a control to a new location:

```
object.Move left, [top, [width, [height]]]
```

Here's an example—in this case, when the user clicks a button, **Command1**, we double the button's width and height, and move it 500 twips to the left:

```
Private Sub Command1_Click()
    Const intIncrement = 500
    Command1.Width = 2 * Command1.Width
    Command1.Height = 2 * Command1.Height
    Command1.Move (Command1.Left + intIncrement)
End Sub
```

*TIP: One way of creating simple animation is to use an Image control to display an image and use its **Move()** method to move it around a form.*

Showing And Hiding Controls In A Form

The Testing Department is on the phone again—does your program really *need* 120 buttons in the main form? After all, that's exactly what menus were designed for: to hide controls not needed, getting them out of the user's way. (In fact, that's usually a good way to determine if a control item should be in a menu or on the main form: you use menus to make options available to the user at all times, while keeping them out of the way.)

However, let's say you really don't want to put your control items into menus— you can still use buttons if you hide the ones that don't apply at a particular time, showing them when appropriate. Hiding and showing controls in a form as needed can produce dramatic effects at times.

Showing and hiding controls is easy: just use the control's **Visible** property. Setting this property to True displays the control; setting it to False hides it. Here's an example where we make a button disappear (probably much to the user's surprise) when the user clicks it:

```
Private Sub Command1_Click()
    Command1.Visible = False
End Sub
```

Measurements In Forms

The default measurement units for forms are twips, but the project design board says they want the data-entry forms you're designing to look like real 3×5 cards on the screen. Can you convert from twips to inches in Visual Basic? Yes, you can, and we'll take a look at that and other measurement issues here.

You can get the dimensions of a form's client area with these properties:

- **ScaleWidth**—The width of the client area.
- **ScaleHeight**—The height of the client area.
- **ScaleLeft**—The horizontal coordinate of upper left of client area.
- **ScaleTop**—The vertical coordinate of upper left of client area.

And you can get the overall dimensions of the form using these proportics:

- **Width**—The width of the form.
- **Height**—The height of the form.
- **Left**—The horizontal coordinate of upper left of the form
- **Top**—The vertical coordinate of upper left of the form

You can also use the **ScaleMode** property to set a form's coordinate system units—you don't have to use twips. Here are the possible values for **ScaleMode**:

- *0*—User-defined
- *1*—Twips (1/1440ths of an inch)
- *2*—Points (1/72nds of an inch)
- *3*—Pixels
- *4*—Characters (120 twips horizontally, 240 twips vertically)
- *5*—Inches
- *6*—Millimeters
- *7*—Centimeters

User-Defined Coordinates

To make life easier for yourself, you can set up a *user-defined coordinate system*: just set the **ScaleWidth** and **ScaleHeight** properties yourself. For example, if you want to plot data on a 1000x1000 grid, just set **ScaleWidth** and **ScaleHeight** to 1000. To draw a scatter plot of your data, then, you could use **PSet( )** to set individual pixels directly. If one of the points to graph was (233, 599), you could draw that dot this way: **PSet(233, 599)**.

Working With Multiple Forms

You've designed your program and it's a beauty: an introductory form to welcome the user, a data-entry form to get data from the user, a summary form to
display the data analysis results, a logon form to connect to the Internet—it's
all there.

Suddenly it occurs to you—aren't Visual Basic projects organized into modules and forms? How does the code in one form reach the code in another—
that is, how can the code in the analysis module read what the user has entered
in the data-entry form? It's time to take a look at working with multiple forms.

For example, let's say that your introductory form looks something like that in
Figure 4.12.

When the user clicks the Show Form2 button, the program should display
Form2 on the screen—and place the text "Welcome to Visual Basic" in the
text box in **Form2** as well, as shown in Figure 4.13. To be able to do that, we'll
need to reach one form from another in code.

Create a new Visual Basic project now. This project has one default form,
Form1. To add another form, **Form2**, just select the Add Form item in the
Project menu; click on OK in the Add Form dialog box that appears to accept
the default new form. In addition, add a new text box, **Text1**, to the new form,
Form2.

In addition, add a command button to **Form1** and give it the caption "Show
Form2" and open the code for that button now:

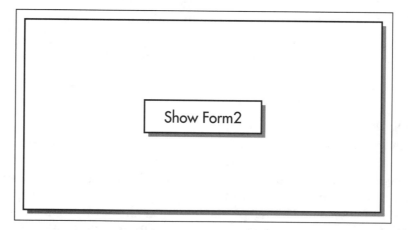

Figure 4.12   A single form that lets the user display another form.

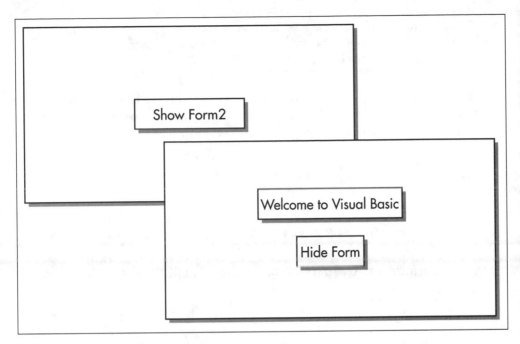

Figure 4.13   A multiform program.

```
Private Sub Command1_Click ()

End Sub
```

When the user clicks the Show Form2 button, we will show **Form2**, which we do with **Form2**'s **Show( )** method:

```
Private Sub Command1_Click()
    Form2.Show
...
End Sub
```

Next, to place the text "Welcome to Visual Basic" in the text box, **Text1**, in **Form2**, we need to use that text box's fully qualified name: Form2.Text1, indicating that the text box we want is in **Form2**. We can use that text box's **Text** property this way to set the text in the box:

```
Private Sub Command1_Click()
    Form2.Show
    Form2.Text1.Text = "Hello from Visual Basic"
End Sub
```

TIP: *One useful property that controls have is the **Parent** property. Controls are really child windows of the form they're in, so if you wanted to set the background color of the form that **Text1** is in and don't know that form's name, you can use the **Text1.Parent.BackColor** property.*

That completes the code for the Show Form2 button. **Form2** has a button labeled Hide Form, and we can implement that by hiding **Form2** in that button's event handler procedure:

```
Private Sub Command1_Click()
    Hide
End Sub
```

> ***Warning!*** *If you hide all windows in a Visual Basic program that has no **Main()** procedure in a module, the program will end.*

And that's it—we've written a program that handles multiple forms.

TIP: *You can also make variables global in a Visual Basic project by declaring them at the module level and using the **Public** keyword. The code in all forms has access to global variables (but in general, you should limit the number of global variables you use so the global space remains uncluttered and you don't get conflicts and unintended side effects with variables of the same name).*

Loading, Showing, And Hiding Forms

There are times when you might want to work with a form before displaying it on the screen to initialize it (with graphics and so on), in which case you can load the form into memory using the **Load** statement.

TIP: *You don't need to load or unload forms to show or hide them—the loading and unloading processes are automatic. You usually load forms explicitly only to work on them before displaying them, as Visual Basic recommends if you want to work with a form before showing it. However, it actually turns out that you don't really need to use **Load** even then, because referring to a form makes Visual Basic load it automatically. This means you don't have to load forms to use the **Show()** or **Hide()** methods with them.*

To actually show the form on the screen, then, you use the **Show()** method. Here's an example in which we load a new form, **Form2**, and then show it:

```
Private Sub Command1_Click()
    Load Form2
    Form2.Show
End Sub
```

TIP: *If you load an MDI child window without having loaded its associated MDI frame, the MDI frame is also loaded automatically.*

After displaying a form, you can hide it with the **Hide()** method and unload it (although that's not necessary) with the **Unload** statement. You usually unload forms if you have a lot of them and are concerned about memory usage. Here's an example in which we hide **Form2** and then unload it:

```
Private Sub Command2_Click()
    Form2.Hide
    Unload Form2
End Sub
```

Setting The Startup Form

Well, the program is complete, and you've saved writing the best for last: the opening form in which you greet the user. Unfortunately, that greeting form is **Form249**, and when you actually test the program, Visual Basic pops **Form1**, which is the Import File dialog box, onto the screen first. How can you make the program start with Form249?

You can set the startup form following these steps:

1. Select the Project|Properties item.

2. Select the General tab in the Project Properties box that opens, as shown in Figure 4.14.

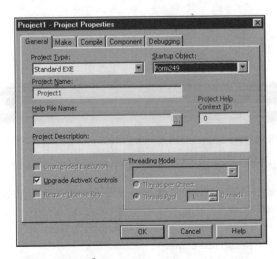

Figure 4.14   Setting the startup form.

3. Set the form you want as the startup form in the Startup Object box, as also shown in Figure 4.14.

That's it—now the program will display the form you've selected first when the program runs.

Creating Forms In Code

You've added a handy calculator form to your financial planning program—but you find that many users have several calculations open at once and want to open *multiple* calculators. How do you create and display new forms like that in Visual Basic?

New forms are simply new objects in Visual Basic. To declare a new form based on a form you already have, say Form1, you just use **Dim**:

```
Private Sub NewForm_Click()
    Dim NewForm As Form1
...
End Sub
```

Next, you create the new form with the **New** keyword:

```
Private Sub NewForm_Click()
    Dim NewForm As Form1
    Set NewForm = New Form1
...
End Sub
```

Finally, you show the new form:

```
Private Sub NewForm_Click()
    Dim NewForm As Form1
    Set NewForm = New Form1
    NewForm.Show
End Sub
```

Calling this subroutine will add as many new forms as you want to a program.

Note that we do not keep track of the new form's name (**NewForm** is a local variable in **NewForm_Click()**, and you can't use it after returning from that procedure); you might want to save the new forms in an array so you can close them under program control.

Using the code, we create new forms, as shown in Figure 4.15.

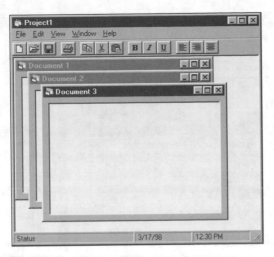

Figure 4.15   Creating and displaying new forms.

Using The Multiple Document Interface

You've written a new editor program, and it's a great success. But then you start getting calls from the Field Testing Department: users want to open more than one document at a time. Just how do you do that?

You use MDI forms. MDI frame windows can display multiple child windows inside them; in fact, the Visual Basic IDE itself is an MDI frame window.

For example, if you already have a program based on a single form, Form1, and you want to make that into an MDI child window inside an MDI frame, follow these steps:

1. Add a new MDI form to the project using the Project|Add MDI Form item.

2. Set the **MDIChild** property of the form you want to use as the MDI child form (Form1 here) to True, as shown in Figure 4.16.

3. Run the program; the form you've made into the MDI child form appears in the MDI form, as shown in Figure 4.17.

TIP: In Visual Basic, you can use all kinds of forms as MDI children in an MDI form, as long as their **MDIChild** property is set to True. You can also use **Show()** and **Hide()** on those windows to manage them as you like.

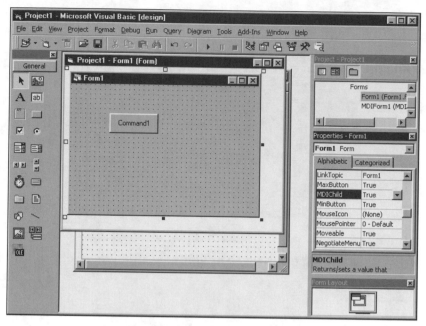

Figure 4.16   Setting a form's MDIChild property to True.

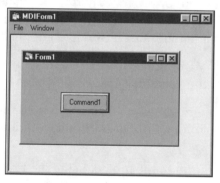

Figure 4.17   Creating an MDI child form

Arranging MDI Child Windows

So you've made your program an MDI program, just as the users asked. However, the Testing Department is back on the phone, and they think it would be nice if you could provide some way of arranging the MDI children in the main MDI form so it looks "tidy."

You could arrange the MDI child forms with their **Left**, **Top**, **Width**, and **Height** properties, but there's an easier way—you can use the MDI form method **Arrange()**.

For example, if you add a menu item to an MDI form named, say, "Arrange All," you can use the **Arrange()** method to arrange all the windows in the form in a cascade this way:

```
Private Sub ArrangeAll_Click()
    Me.Arrange vbCascade
End Sub
```

Using this method results in the cascade of MDI children seen in Figure 4.18.

The possible values to pass to **Arrange()** to specify the way you want to arrange MDI children appear in Table 4.1.

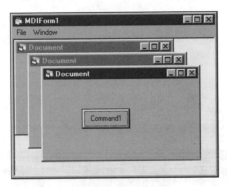

Figure 4.18   Arranging MDI child forms.

Table 4.1   Ways of arranging MDI child windows.

Constant	Value	Does This
vbCascade	0	Cascades all nonminimized MDI child windows
vbTileHorizontal	1	Tiles all nonminimized MDI child forms horizontally
vbTileVertical	2	Tiles all nonminimized MDI child forms vertically
vbArrangeIcons	3	Arranges icons for minimized MDI child forms

Opening New MDI Child Windows

Now that you've supported MDI, your program's users want to actually open multiple documents—how can you allow them to do that?

You can do this one of two ways: first, you can create all the forms you want to use at design time and set their **Visible** properties to False so they don't appear when the program starts. When you want to show or hide them, you can use **Show( )** or **Hide( )**.

You can also create new forms as needed—see "Creating Forms In Code" earlier in this chapter. For example, here we create and display a new MDI child form (assuming **Form1**'s **MDIChild** property is set to True), as well as setting its caption:

```
Private Sub NewWindow_Click ()
    Dim NewForm As Form1
    Set NewForm = New Form1
    NewForm.Caption = "Document"
    NewForm.Show
End Sub
```

(If you want to display text in these new child forms, you might use a rich text box to cover the form's client area when you design them.)

We're adding forms this way in Figure 4.19.

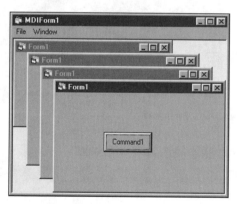

Figure 4.19   Creating new MDI children from code.

Arrays Of Forms

Now that you've written your MDI program, you suddenly have a lot of windows to manage. The user wants to open 20 documents at the same time—how can you keep track of all that? Wouldn't it be nice if you could use arrays of forms in Visual Basic and just refer to each form with one single array index?

You can do that in Visual Basic (in fact, you can create arrays of many types of objects, excluding such objects that there can only be one of, like the application object, **App**). You create an array of forms just as you would create an array of any other kind of object; here, we're creating an array of Form1 objects, because that's the type of form we'll use as MDI children in an MDI program:

```
Dim Forms(1 To 20) As Form1
```

If we declare this array, **Forms( )**, as a form-level array in the MDI form, we can refer to that array in all procedures in the MDI form. For example, we might want to create and display a new MDI child form in a procedure named **NewWindow_Click( )**:

```
Private Sub NewWindow_Click()


End Sub
```

Next, we set up a static variable to hold the total number of MDI child forms, **NumberForms**, and increment that variable now that we're adding a new form:

```
Private Sub NewWindow_Click()
    Static NumberForms
    NumberForms = NumberForms + 1
...
End Sub
```

Now, we create a new form and add it to the form array:

```
Private Sub NewWindow_Click()
    Static NumberForms
    NumberForms = NumberForms + 1
    Set Forms(NumberForms) = New Form1
...
End Sub
```

Throughout the rest of the program, now, we're able to refer to the new form as a member of the form array; here, for example, we set its caption and show it, referring to it with an index value in the form array:

```
Private Sub NewWindow_Click()
    Static NumberForms
    NumberForms = NumberForms + 1
    Set Forms(NumberForms) = New Form1
    Forms(NumberForms).Caption = "Document" & Str(NumberForms)
    Forms(NumberForms).Show
End Sub
```

Coordinating Data Between MDI Child Forms (Document Views)

Your new word-processor program is almost done—just one more refinement to add. You want to allow the user to open multiple *views* into the same document. A view is just a window into a document, and if a document has multiple views open, the user can scroll around in different parts of the same document at the same time. You've been able to open the same document in several view windows now—but what if the user starts typing into one view? All the other views should also be updated with the new text as well. How do you keep all the open views of the same document coordinated?

We'll see how this works now. In this example, the MDI child windows will be based on a form, **Form1**, in which we've placed a text box. The user can open as many MDI child windows as they like with the New item in the Window menu. When they type in one MDI child's text box, however, we should mirror any such changes in the other MDI children's text boxes as well. This is shown in Figure 4.20, where the text appears simultaneously in both MDI children while the user types into one.

We start by adding a new module to the program with the Project|Add Module item so that we can set up a global array of forms, **Forms**, and an array index variable, **NumberForms**, in that module:

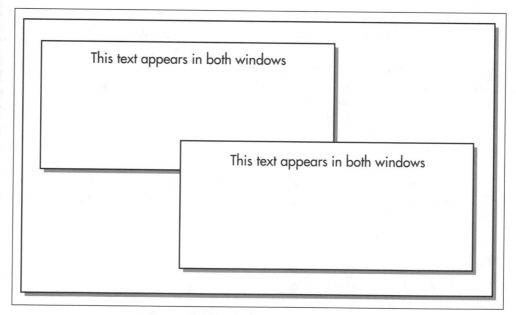

Figure 4.20   Coordinating MDI children.

```
Public Forms(1 To 20) As Form1
Public NumberForms As Integer
```

Next, we add a Window menu to the MDI form. We also add new forms to that array of forms when the user creates such new forms by adding this code to the MDI form's New item in the Window menu:

```
Private Sub NewWindow_Click()
    NumberForms = NumberForms + 1
    Set Forms(NumberForms) = New Form1
    Forms(NumberForms).Caption = "Document" & Str(NumberForms)
    Forms(NumberForms).Show
End Sub
```

Now the **Forms** array holds the MDI children in our program.

When the user types text into the text box displayed in an MDI child, we want to update all the other MDI children as well, making them display the same text. When you type into a text box, a **Change** event occurs, and we'll add code to that event's handler function to update all the other MDI children:

```
Private Sub Text1_Change()

End Sub
```

Here, we store the text in the just-changed text box and, in this simple example, just loop over all MDI children, updating them to match the changed text box:

```
Private Sub Text1_Change()
    Dim Text As String
    Text = Text1.Text
    For intLoopIndex = 1 To NumberForms
        Forms(intLoopIndex).Text1.Text = Text
    Next intLoopIndex
End Sub
```

Now when you change the text in one child, the text in all children is updated. In this way, we can support multiple views into the same document.

Creating Dialog Boxes

It's time to ask the user for some feedback, and you don't want to use the Visual Basic input box because that can only accept one line of text. Besides, you don't like the way it looks (it's not a great favorite among Visual Basic programmers, perhaps for that reason). Looks like you'll have to use a dialog box. How do they work in Visual Basic?

To add a dialog box to a project, select the Project|Add Form item. You can add a simple form and make it into a dialog box, but Visual Basic already has a predefined dialog box form, named Dialog, so select that in the Add Form box and click Open.

TIP: *To learn more about adding predefined forms to a project, see "Using Visual Basic Predefined Forms, Menus, And Projects" in Chapter 2.*

This adds a new dialog box to the project, as shown in Figure 4.21.

This dialog box comes with an OK and Cancel button, and its **BorderStyle** property is already set to 3, which creates a fixed dialog-style border with only one control button: a close button.

We add a text box, Text1, to the dialog box, as also shown in Figure 4.21. Next, we declare a **Public** string, **Feedback**, in the dialog box's (General) section; this string will hold the text that the user gives us as feedback:

```
Public Feedback As String
```

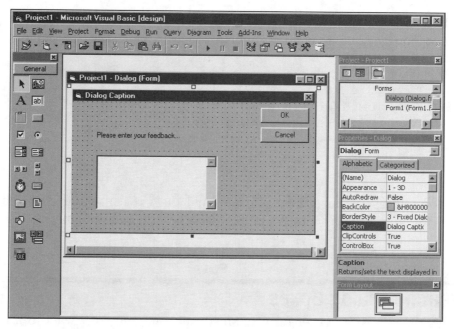

Figure 4.21   A new dialog box.

When the dialog box opens, we can initialize **Feedback** to the empty string:

```
Private Sub Form_Load()
    Feedback = ""
End Sub
```

If the user clicks the Cancel button, we want to leave the text in **Feedback** as the empty string and just hide the dialog box:

```
Private Sub CancelButton_Click()
    Hide
End Sub
```

If the user clicks OK, on the other hand, we fill the **Feedback** string with what the user has typed into the text box, and then hide the dialog box:

```
Private Sub OKButton_Click()
    Feedback = Text1.Text
    Hide
End Sub
```

That completes the dialog box. In the program's main form, we can show that dialog box when required this way—note that we pass a value of 1 to the **Show()** method, which displays our dialog box as *modal*. Modal means that the user must dismiss the dialog box before continuing on with the rest of the program (the default value passed to **Show()** is 0, which displays windows in a non-modal way):

```
Private Sub Command1_Click()
    Dialog.Show 1
    ...
End Sub
```

Next, we can display the feedback that the user has given us, if any, by examining the dialog's **Feedback** string this way:

```
Private Sub Command1_Click()
    Dialog.Show 1
    Text1.Text = Dialog.Feedback
End Sub
```

And that's it—now we are supporting dialog boxes, as shown in Figure 4.22.

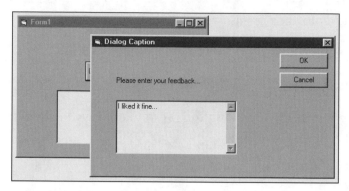

Figure 4.22   Using a newly created dialog box.

TIP: One good rule for constructing dialog boxes: always add a Cancel button so that if users open the dialog box by mistake, they can close it without consequences.

All About Message Boxes And Input Boxes

Visual Basic provides two ways of displaying message boxes and input dialog boxes: using **MsgBox()** and **InputBox()**. We'll cover their syntax in the following subsections.

The **MsgBox()** Function

You use **MsgBox()** to display a message to the user and get a return value corresponding to one of the buttons in the message box. Here's the syntax:

```
MsgBox(prompt[, buttons] [, title] [, helpfile, context])
```

The *prompt* argument holds the string displayed as the message in the dialog box. (The maximum length of *prompt* is approximately 1,024 characters.)

TIP: If prompt is made up of more than one line, you can separate the lines using a carriage return character (**Chr(13)**), a linefeed character (**Chr(10)**), or both (**Chr(13) & Chr(10)**) between each line.

The *buttons* argument specifies what to put into the message box, as specified in Table 4.2. The default value for *buttons* is 0.

The *title* parameter holds the string displayed in the title bar of the dialog box. (If you don't specify *title*, the application name is placed in the title bar.)

The *helpfile* argument is a string that identifies the Help file to use to provide context-sensitive Help for the dialog box.

Table 4.2   MsgBox() constants.

Constant	Value	Description
vbOKOnly	0	Display OK button only
vbOKCancel	1	Display OK and Cancel buttons
vbAbortRetryIgnore	2	Display Abort, Retry, and Ignore buttons
vbYesNoCancel	3	Display Yes, No, and Cancel buttons
vbYesNo	4	Display Yes and No buttons
vbRetryCancel	5	Display Retry and Cancel buttons
vbCritical	16	Display Critical Message icon
vbQuestion	32	Display Warning Query icon
vbExclamation	48	Display Warning Message icon
vbInformation	64	Display Information Message icon
vbDefaultButton1	0	First button is default
vbDefaultButton2	256	Second button is default
vbDefaultButton3	512	Third button is default
vbDefaultButton4	768	Fourth button is default
vbApplicationModal	0	Application modal; the user must respond to the message box before continuing work in the current application.
vbSystemModal	4096	System modal; all applications are suspended until the user responds to the message box.
vbMsgBoxHelpButton	10384	Adds Help button to the message box
VbMsgBoxSetForeground	65536	Specifies the message box window as the foreground window
vbMsgBoxRight	524288	Text is right-aligned
vbMsgBoxRtlReading	1048576	Specifies text should appear as right-to-left reading on Hebrew and Arabic systems

The *context* argument is the Help context number assigned to the appropriate Help topic.

The possible return values from **MsgBox( )** appear in Table 4.3.

The **InputBox()** Function

You can use the **InputBox( )** function to get a string of text from the user. Here's the syntax for this function:

```
InputBox(prompt[, title] [, default] [, xpos] [, ypos] [, helpfile,
context])
```

Table 4.3   MsgBox() return values.

Constant	Value	Description
vbOK	1	OK
vbCancel	2	Cancel
vbAbort	3	Abort
vbRetry	4	Retry
vbIgnore	5	Ignore
vbYes	6	Yes
vbNo	7	No

The *prompt* argument is a string displayed as the message in the dialog box.

The *title* argument is a string displayed in the title bar of the dialog box. (If you don't specify the *title*, the application name is placed in the title bar.)

The *default* argument is a string displayed in the text box as the default response if no other input is provided.

The *xpos* argument is a number that specifies (in twips) the horizontal distance of the left edge of the dialog box from the left edge of the screen.

The *ypos* argument is a number that specifies (in twips) the vertical distance of the upper edge of the dialog box from the top of the screen.

The *helpfile* argument is a string that identifies the Help file to use to provide context-sensitive Help for the dialog box.

The *context* argument is the Help context number assigned to the appropriate Help topic.

The **InputBox()** function returns the string the user entered.

Passing Forms To Procedures

You can pass forms to procedures just as you would any object. Here, we've set up a subroutine, **ColorWindowWhite()**, to turn the background color of a form to white:

```
Sub ColorWindowWhite(FormToColor As Form)

End Sub
```

In this case, we can simply refer to the form passed to this subroutine by the name we've given the passed parameter, **FormToColor**:

```
Sub ColorWindowWhite(FormToColor As Form)
    FormToColor.BackColor = RGB(255, 255, 255)
End Sub
```

Now you can pass a form to the **ColorWindowWhite()** subroutine easily:

```
Private Sub Command1_Click()
    ColorWindowWhite Me
End Sub
```

And that's all it takes to pass a form to a procedure.

Minimizing/Maximizing And Enabling/Disabling Forms From Code

To exert a little more control over the windows in your programs, you can set the **WindowState** property to maximize or minimize them. Here's how you set that property, and what those settings mean:

- *0*—Normal
- *1*—Minimized
- *2*—Maximized

Here's an example, where we minimize a form when the user clicks a button:

```
Private Sub Command1_Click()
    WindowState = 1
End Sub
```

You can also set the **Enabled** property to enable or disable a window (when it's disabled, it will only beep if the user tries to give it the focus). You set the **Enabled** property to True to enable a window and to False to disable it.

Chapter 5

Visual Basic Menus

If you need an immediate solution to:	See page:
Using The Visual Basic Application Wizard To Set Up Your Menus	157
What Item Goes In What Menu?	163
Adding A Menu To A Form	165
Modifying And Deleting Menu Items	168
Adding A Menu Separator	169
Adding Access Characters	170
Adding Shortcut Keys	171
Creating Submenus	173
Creating Immediate ("Bang") Menus	175
Using The Visual Basic Predefined Menus	176
Adding A Checkmark To A Menu Item	178
Disabling (Graying Out) Menu Items	180
Handling MDI Form And MDI Child Menus	181
Adding A List Of Open Windows To An MDI Form's Window Menu	182
Making Menus And Menu Items Visible Or Invisible	184
Creating And Displaying Pop-Up Menus	184
Adding And Deleting Menu Items At Runtime	187
Adding Bitmaps To Menus	190
Using The Registry To Store A Most Recently Used (MRU) Files List	192

In Depth

Everyone who uses Windows knows about menus—they're those clever controls that hide away lists of items until you want to make a selection, like the Visual Basic File menu, which appears in Figure 5.1. And, in fact, that's the design philosophy behind menus: rather than presenting the user with all possible controls at once, menus hide their items until needed. Imagine a program with 50 buttons all over it—Save File, Save File As, Insert Object, Paste Special, and so on—you'd hardly have space for anything else. That's why menus are so popular: they present their controls in drop-down windows, ready to use when needed.

In this chapter, we're going to take a look at using menus in Visual Basic. We'll start with an overview of designing your menu system, including some considerations that Microsoft has developed. Then we'll go to this chapter's Immediate Solutions, seeing how to use the Visual Basic Menu Editor to create and

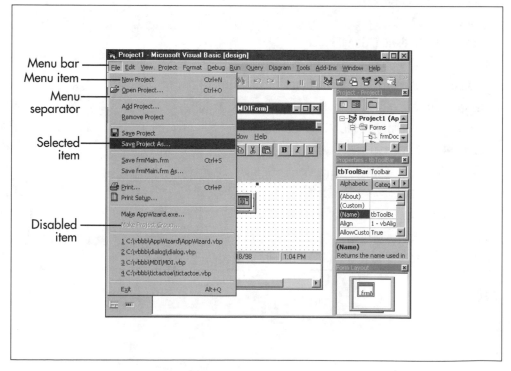

Figure 5.1   The Visual Basic File menu.

modify menus. We'll also see how to modify menus and the items they include from code, when a program is running. And, of course, we'll see some special topics, like how to create a Most Recently Used (MRU) list of files and how to use Windows functions to add bitmaps to menu items.

We'll start our overview on Visual Basic menus now by taking a look at the parts of a menu.

Menu Design Considerations

Every Windows programmer is familiar with the parts of a menu; for reference, they appear in Figure 5.1. The menu names in a program appear in the menu bar—usually just under the title bar—and when the user selects a menu, that menu opens, like the File menu in Figure 5.1.

Each menu usually contains items arranged in a vertical list. These items are often grouped into functional groups with menu separators, or thin horizontal rules, as shown in Figure 5.1. When the user selects a menu item (from the keyboard or with the mouse), that item appears highlighted; pressing Enter or releasing the mouse button opens that item.

Menu items can also be disabled (also called "grayed out"), as shown in Figure 5.1. A disabled item is not accessible to the user and does nothing if selected.

TIP: *If your program presents the user with a lot of disabled menu items, the user may feel locked out and frustrated. To avoid such situations, many programs add or remove menu items from menus at runtime, and we'll see how to do that in this chapter.*

Access Characters And Shortcuts

Ideally, each item should have a unique *access character* for users who choose commands with keyboards. The user reaches the menu or menu item by pressing Alt key and the *access character*. The access character should be the first letter of the menu title, unless another letter offers a stronger link; no two menus or menu items should use the same access character.

Shortcuts are also useful to the user; these keys are faster than access characters in that the user only needs to enter a shortcut to execute the corresponding menu item. For example, the New Project shortcut in Figure 5.1 is Ctrl+N.

Note also that an ellipsis (…) should follow names of menu items that display a dialog box (Save As…, Preferences…, etc.) when selected. In addition, if you have menus in the menu bar that execute a command immediately instead of opening a menu, you should append an exclamation point to the menu's name, such as Collate!

Designing Your Menus

A popular aspect of Windows is that it gives the user a common interface, no matter what program they're using, and users have come to expect that. In fact, if it's hard to learn a new, nonstandard Windows program, the user may well turn to a Windows-compliant alternative, so it's a good idea to stick with the Windows standards.

Most programs have a File menu first (at left) in the menu bar, followed by other menus, like a View menu, a Tools menu, and so on, followed by a Help menu, which usually appears last (and often at the extreme right in the menu bar). Users expect to find certain standard items in particular menus; for a list of these items, see "What Item Goes In What Menu?" in this chapter.

Microsoft recommends that you keep your menu item names short. For one thing, if you want to release your application internationally, the length of words tends to increase approximately 30 percent in foreign versions, and you may not have enough space to list all of your menu items. Microsoft also recommends that you use the **mnu** prefix in code for menus, like **mnuFile**, and menu items, like **mnuFileOpen**.

That completes our overview—it's time to turn to the Immediate Solutions.

Immediate Solutions

Using The Visual Basic Application Wizard To Set Up Your Menus

Probably the easiest way to get a substantial menu system going in your program is to design that program with the Visual Basic Application Wizard. The menu-designing window that appears when you build an application with the Application Wizard appears in Figure 5.2.

You can arrange, add, or remove menu items with the click of a mouse. The Application Wizard isn't for everyone, but it can create a very complete menu system, as shown in Figure 5.3, where the File menu in the created application is open.

When you design your menu system with the Application Wizard, there's a tremendous amount of menu support already built in, and all you have to do is modify the menu-handling routines you want. The menu-handling section of a typical Application Wizard program appears in Listing 5.1. It's a little long, but it's worth it to take the time to go through to understand what kind of support is in these programs and if the Application Wizard is for you. Note that although many menu-handler procedures already have code in them, many also have "ToDo" comments, which are placeholders for you to add your own code.

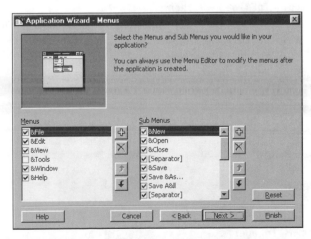

Figure 5.2   Using the Application Wizard to design a menu system.

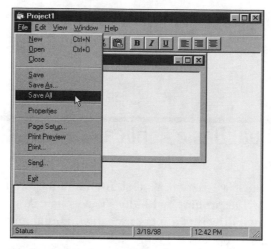

Figure 5.3   An Application Wizard–designed program's menu system.

Listing 5.1   The menu-handling section of an Application Wizard–designed program.

```
Private Sub mnuHelpAbout_Click()
    MsgBox "Version " & App.Major & "." & App.Minor & "." & App.Revision
End Sub


Private Sub mnuHelpSearchForHelpOn_Click()
    Dim nRet As Integer

    'if there is no helpfile for this project display a message to the
    'user you can set the HelpFile for your application in the
    'Project Properties dialog
    If Len(App.HelpFile) = 0 Then
        MsgBox "Unable to display Help Contents. There is no Help_
            associated with this project.", vbInformation, Me.Caption
    Else
        On Error Resume Next
        nRet = OSWinHelp(Me.hwnd, App.HelpFile, 261, 0)
        If Err Then
            MsgBox Err.Description
        End If
    End If

End Sub


Private Sub mnuHelpContents_Click()
    Dim nRet As Integer
```

```
'if there is no helpfile for this project display a message to the
'user you can set the HelpFile for your application in the
'Project Properties dialog
If Len(App.HelpFile) = 0 Then
    MsgBox "Unable to display Help Contents. There is no Help_
        associated with this project.", vbInformation, Me.Caption
Else
    On Error Resume Next
    nRet = OSWinHelp(Me.hwnd, App.HelpFile, 3, 0)
    If Err Then
        MsgBox Err.Description
    End If
End If

End Sub


Private Sub mnuWindowArrangeIcons_Click()
    Me.Arrange vbArrangeIcons
End Sub

Private Sub mnuWindowTileVertical_Click()
    Me.Arrange vbTileVertical
End Sub

Private Sub mnuWindowTileHorizontal_Click()
    Me.Arrange vbTileHorizontal
End Sub

Private Sub mnuWindowCascade_Click()
    Me.Arrange vbCascade
End Sub

Private Sub mnuWindowNewWindow_Click()
    LoadNewDoc
End Sub

Private Sub mnuViewWebBrowser_Click()
    'ToDo: Add 'mnuViewWebBrowser_Click' code.
    MsgBox "Add 'mnuViewWebBrowser_Click' code."
End Sub

Private Sub mnuViewOptions_Click()
    'ToDo: Add 'mnuViewOptions_Click' code.
    MsgBox "Add 'mnuViewOptions_Click' code."
End Sub
```

```vb
Private Sub mnuViewRefresh_Click()
    'ToDo: Add 'mnuViewRefresh_Click' code.
    MsgBox "Add 'mnuViewRefresh_Click' code."
End Sub


Private Sub mnuViewStatusBar_Click()
    mnuViewStatusBar.Checked = Not mnuViewStatusBar.Checked
    sbStatusBar.Visible = mnuViewStatusBar.Checked
End Sub


Private Sub mnuViewToolbar_Click()
    mnuViewToolbar.Checked = Not mnuViewToolbar.Checked
    tbToolBar.Visible = mnuViewToolbar.Checked
End Sub


Private Sub mnuEditPasteSpecial_Click()
    'ToDo: Add 'mnuEditPasteSpecial_Click' code.
    MsgBox "Add 'mnuEditPasteSpecial_Click' code."
End Sub


Private Sub mnuEditPaste_Click()
    On Error Resume Next
    ActiveForm.rtfText.SelRTF = Clipboard.GetText

End Sub


Private Sub mnuEditCopy_Click()
    On Error Resume Next
    Clipboard.SetText ActiveForm.rtfText.SelRTF

End Sub


Private Sub mnuEditCut_Click()
    On Error Resume Next
    Clipboard.SetText ActiveForm.rtfText.SelRTF
    ActiveForm.rtfText.SelText = vbNullString

End Sub


Private Sub mnuEditUndo_Click()
    'ToDo: Add 'mnuEditUndo_Click' code.
    MsgBox "Add 'mnuEditUndo_Click' code."
End Sub
```

```
Private Sub mnuFileExit_Click()
    'unload the form
    Unload Me

End Sub

Private Sub mnuFileSend_Click()
    'ToDo: Add 'mnuFileSend_Click' code.
    MsgBox "Add 'mnuFileSend_Click' code."
End Sub

Private Sub mnuFilePrint_Click()
    On Error Resume Next
    If ActiveForm Is Nothing Then Exit Sub

    With dlgCommonDialog
        .DialogTitle = "Print"
        .CancelError = True
        .Flags = cdlPDReturnDC + cdlPDNoPageNums
        If ActiveForm.rtfText.SelLength = 0 Then
            .Flags = .Flags + cdlPDAllPages
        Else
            .Flags = .Flags + cdlPDSelection
        End If
        .ShowPrinter
        If Err <> MSComDlg.cdlCancel Then
            ActiveForm.rtfText.SelPrint .hdc
        End If
    End With

End Sub

Private Sub mnuFilePrintPreview_Click()
    'ToDo: Add 'mnuFilePrintPreview_Click' code.
    MsgBox "Add 'mnuFilePrintPreview_Click' code."
End Sub

Private Sub mnuFilePageSetup_Click()
    On Error Resume Next
    With dlgCommonDialog
        .DialogTitle = "Page Setup"
        .CancelError = True
        .ShowPrinter
    End With

End Sub
```

```
Private Sub mnuFileProperties_Click()
    'ToDo: Add 'mnuFileProperties_Click' code.
    MsgBox "Add 'mnuFileProperties_Click' code."
End Sub

Private Sub mnuFileSaveAll_Click()
    'ToDo: Add 'mnuFileSaveAll_Click' code.
    MsgBox "Add 'mnuFileSaveAll_Click' code."
End Sub

Private Sub mnuFileSaveAs_Click()
    Dim sFile As String

    If ActiveForm Is Nothing Then Exit Sub

    With dlgCommonDialog
        .DialogTitle = "Save As"
        .CancelError = False
        'ToDo: set the flags and attributes of the common dialog control
        .Filter = "All Files (*.*)|*.*"
        .ShowSave
        If Len(.FileName) = 0 Then
            Exit Sub
        End If
        sFile = .FileName
    End With
    ActiveForm.Caption = sFile
    ActiveForm.rtfText.SaveFile sFile

End Sub

Private Sub mnuFileSave_Click()
    Dim sFile As String
    If Left$(ActiveForm.Caption, 8) = "Document" Then
        With dlgCommonDialog
            .DialogTitle = "Save"
            .CancelError = False
            'ToDo: set the flags and attributes of the common dialog
            'control
            .Filter = "All Files (*.*)|*.*"
            .ShowSave
            If Len(.FileName) = 0 Then
                Exit Sub
            End If
            sFile = .FileName
        End With
        ActiveForm.rtfText.SaveFile sFile
```

```
      Else
          sFile = ActiveForm.Caption
          ActiveForm.rtfText.SaveFile sFile
      End If

End Sub

Private Sub mnuFileClose_Click()
    'ToDo: Add 'mnuFileClose_Click' code.
    MsgBox "Add 'mnuFileClose_Click' code."
End Sub

Private Sub mnuFileOpen_Click()
    Dim sFile As String

    If ActiveForm Is Nothing Then LoadNewDoc

    With dlgCommonDialog
        .DialogTitle = "Open"
        .CancelError = False
        'ToDo: set the flags and attributes of the common dialog control
        .Filter = "All Files (*.*)|*.*"
        .ShowOpen
        If Len(.FileName) = 0 Then
            Exit Sub
        End If
        sFile = .FileName
    End With
    ActiveForm.rtfText.LoadFile sFile
    ActiveForm.Caption = sFile

End Sub

Private Sub mnuFileNew_Click()
    LoadNewDoc
End Sub
```

What Item Goes In What Menu?

The Testing Department gives you a call to ask why the Paste item in your new application is in the View menu. You ask if they had a different menu in mind, and they mention something about the Edit menu. How can you avoid such calls? With the following lists.

Users expect to find certain standard items in certain menus if your program is going to support those items. To start us off, here's the kind of item you might find in the File menu (note that not all programs will use all these menus):

- New
- Open
- Close
- Close All
- Save
- Save As
- Save All
- Properties
- Templates
- Page Setup
- Print Preview
- Print
- Print Using
- Send
- Update
- Exit

*TIP: Even in programs that don't handle files, it's not uncommon to see a File menu for one reason—that's where the user expects the Exit item. Don't forget to add an Exit item to your menu system (you can end a Visual Basic program using the **End** statement, so this menu item is easy to implement).*

The Edit menu usually holds items like these:

- Undo
- Redo
- Cut
- Copy
- Paste
- Paste Using
- Paste Special
- Clear
- Select All

- Find

- Replace

- Bookmark

- Insert Object (unless you have a separate Insert menu)

The View menu has items like these:

- Toolbar

- Status Bar

- Refresh

- Options

The Window menu has items like these:

- New Window

- Cascade

- Tile Windows

- Arrange All

- Split

- List Of Windows

The Help menu has items like these:

- Help

- Help Index

- Help Table of Contents

- Search for Help On

- Web Support

- About

Adding A Menu To A Form

The design process is complete—it's time to start adding menus to your new program. But when you sit down and start looking for the Menu tool in the toolbox, you find that there isn't one. Just how do you add a menu to a form?

You use the Visual Basic Menu Editor. You'll get a basic introduction to the Menu Editor here, and we'll use it throughout this chapter. To add a menu to a form, select that form (that is, click on it), and open the Menu Editor by selecting the Menu Editor in the Tools menu. Or, you can select its icon in the toolbar (which has the tool tip "Menu Editor"). The Visual Basic Menu Editor appears in Figure 5.4.

Creating A New Menu

To create a new menu, you only have to provide two essential items: the caption of the menu and its name. The **Caption** property holds the title of the menu, such as File, and the **Name** property holds the name you'll use for that menu in code, such as **mnuFile**.

Fill in the **Caption** and **Name** properties for your new menu now. Congratulations—you've created a new menu. Now it's time to add items to the new menu.

Creating A New Menu Item

We can add a new menu item, say, New, to the File menu we've just created. To do so, click the Next button in the Menu Editor, moving the highlighted bar in the box at the bottom of the Menu Editor down one line. If you just entered new **Caption** and **Name** values and left it at that, you'd create a new menu, not a new menu item. So click the right-pointing arrow button in the Menu Editor now to indent the next item four spaces in the box at the bottom of the Menu Editor. Now enter the **Caption** ("New") and **Name**, ("mnuFileNew") values for the new menu item.

The menu item you've just created appears in the Menu Editor below the File menu item and indented, like this:

```
File
....New
```

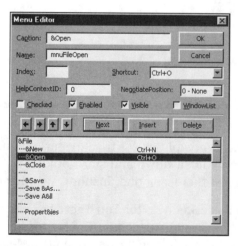

Figure 5.4   The Visual Basic Menu Editor.

This means that we now have a File menu with one item in it—New.

That's how your menu system is displayed in the Menu Editor: as a series of indented items. For example, here's how a File menu with New and Open items, followed by an Edit menu with three items, Cut, Copy, and Paste, would look in the Menu Editor:

```
File
....New
....Open
Edit
....Cut
....Copy
....Paste
```

Here's how to create a new menu system in the Menu Editor, step-by-step:

1. Enter the first menu's **Caption** and **Name**.
2. Click the Next button (or press Enter).
3. Click the right arrow to indent one level, making this next entry a menu item.
4. Enter the menu item's **Caption** and **Name**.
5. Click the Next button (or press Enter).
6. Repeat Steps 4 and 5 for all the items in the first menu.
7. Click the Next button (or press Enter).
8. Click the left arrow to outdent, making this next entry a menu.
9. Enter the next menu's **Caption** and **Name**.
10. Click the right arrow to indent one level, making this next entry a menu item.
11. Repeat Steps 4 and 5 for the items in this new menu.
12. Repeat Steps 7 through 11 for the rest of the menus in the program.
13. Click on OK to close the Menu Editor.
14. Edit the code.

You edit the code for menu items just as you do for other controls—click the menu item in the form under design (opening the item's menu if necessary). This opens the menu item's event handler, like this:

```
Private Sub mnuFileNew_Click()

End Sub
```

Just add the code you want to execute when the user chooses this menu item to the event handler procedure:

```
Private Sub mnuFileNew_Click()
    LoadNewDoc
End Sub
```

And that's it—now you've added a menu system to your program.

Modifying And Deleting Menu Items

You think the program is perfect, but the users are complaining that they don't like having the Save As item in the Edit menu and want to move it to the File menu. Is that possible?

Yes, using the Menu Editor. You can rearrange, add, or remove items in your menu with the Menu Editor, so open that tool now (as shown in Figure 5.4).

Inserting Or Deleting Items In A Menu System

To add a new item to a menu, or a new menu to the menu system, select an item in the Menu Editor, and click the Insert button. This inserts a new, empty entry into the menu just before the item you selected:

```
File
....New
....Open
....
Edit
....Cut
....Copy
....Paste
```

Now just enter the new item's **Caption** and **Name** properties, and you're all set.

To remove a menu or menu item, just select that menu or item and click the Delete button.

Rearranging Items In A Menu System

You can use the four arrow buttons in the Menu Editor to move items up and down, as well as indent or outdent (that is, remove one level of indenting) menu items. Here's what the arrows do:

- *Right arrow*—Indents a menu item.
- *Left arrow*—Outdents a menu item.

- *Up arrow*—Moves the currently selected item up one level.
- *Down arrow*—Moves the currently selected item down one level.

For example, to move the Save As item from the Edit menu to the File menu, just select that item and keep clicking the up arrow button until the Save As item is positioned as you want it in the File menu.

Adding A Menu Separator

Menus themselves allow you ways to group commands by function (File, Edit, and so on). Often within a menu, however, it helps the user to group menu *items* by function (Print, Print Preview, Page Setup, and so on). You do that with *menu separators*.

A menu separator is a horizontal rule that really only has one purpose—to divide menu items into groups (refer back to Figure 5.1). And using the Menu Editor, you can add separators to your menus.

To add a menu separator, select an item in the Menu Editor and click Insert to create a new item just before the item you selected. To make this new item a menu separator, just give use a hyphen (-) for its **Caption** property. You must give all menu items a name—even if they don't do anything—so give it a dummy **Name** property value as well, such as **mnuSeparator**.

When you run the program, you'll see the menu separators in place, as in the menu in Figure 5.5. Now we're adding menu item separators to our menus.

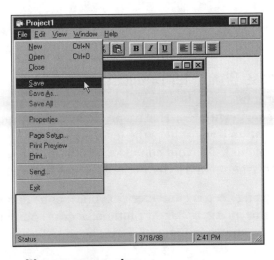

Figure 5.5   A menu with menu separators.

Adding Access Characters

The Testing Department's calling again: They like the menus you've added to your program, but there's the keyboard access issue. Theoretically, they say, users should be able to use the keyboard for everything.

It's time to add access characters to your program. When the user presses the Alt key and an access character, the menu item corresponding to that access character is selected. How do you associate an access character with a menu or menu item? It's easy—just place an ampersand (&) in front of the character you want to make into the access character in that menu or item's caption.

For example, if you had this menu system

```
File
....New
....Open
Edit
....Cut
....Copy
....Paste
```

you could make a letter in all menus or menu items into access characters by placing an ampersand in front of it:

```
&File
....&New
....&Open
&Edit
....&Cut
....C&opy
....&Paste
```

Avoiding Access Character Duplication

Note in the previous example that we have two items—Cut and Copy—in the Edit menu that begin with "C". That's a problem, because an access character must be unique at its level (where the level is the menu bar for menus and a menu for menu items). To avoid confusion (both to the user and to Visual Basic), we make "o", the second letter in Copy, the access character for that item.

The result of adding access characters to your menus at design time appears in the Menu Editor in Figure 5.6. At runtime, access characters appear underlined in menus, as shown in Figure 5.7.

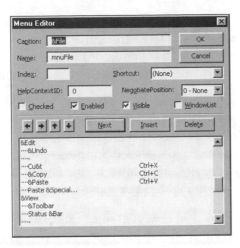

Figure 5.6   Adding access characters.

To use an access key, users first open the menu in which the item they want to
select appears (possibly using an access key, like Alt+F for the File menu),
then they press the Alt key and the access key.

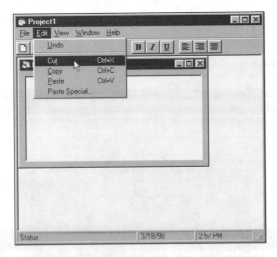

Figure 5.7   Access characters are underlined.

Adding Shortcut Keys

One of the most powerful aspects of menus are *shortcut keys*—single keys or
key combinations that let the user execute a menu command immediately
(without having to open the menu the command is in, as you must do with

access keys). You usually use function keys (although many PCs now go up to F16, it's best to limit yourself to F1 through F10) or Ctrl key combinations for shortcut keys. For example, the standard shortcut key for Select All is Ctrl+A, and entering that shortcut selects all the text in a document.

Giving a menu item a shortcut key is very easy in the Menu Editor. Just open the Menu Editor, select the item you want to give a shortcut key to (such as the File menu's New item in Figure 5.8) and select the shortcut key you want to use in the Menu Editor box labeled Shortcut. (Note that to open the Menu Editor, the form you're designing must be the active window in Visual Basic, not the code window.) In Figure 5.8, we give the New item the shortcut Ctrl+N.

That's all it takes—now run the program, as shown in Figure 5.9. You can see the Ctrl+N at the right in the menu item named New—we've installed our menu shortcut.

Shortcut Key Standards

Windows conventions now include a set of standard shortcut keys that are supposed to apply across most Windows applications. Here are the most common shortcut keys (be very careful when using these key combinations for other purposes; your users may expect the standard response):

- *Ctrl+A*—Select All
- *Ctrl+B*—Bold
- *Ctrl+C*—Copy
- *Ctrl+F*—Find
- *Ctrl+G*—Go To

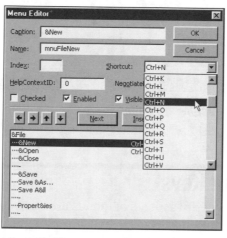

Figure 5.8   Setting a shortcut key.

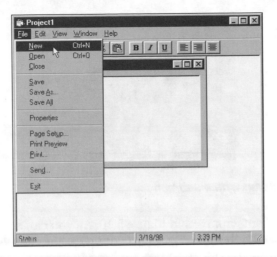

Figure 5.9   Shortcut key in a program's menu.

- *Ctrl+H*—Replace
- *Ctrl+I*—Italic
- *Ctrl+J*—Justify
- *Ctrl+N*—New
- *Ctrl+O*—Open
- *Ctrl+P*—Print
- *Ctrl+Q*—Quit
- *Ctrl+S*—Save
- *Ctrl+U*—Underline
- *Ctrl+V*—Paste
- *Ctrl+W*—Close
- *Ctrl+X*—Cut
- *Ctrl+Z*—Undo
- *F1*—Help

Creating Submenus

The email is in—and it's more praise for your program, *AmazingWingDings* (Deluxe version). It's gratifying to read the great reviews—but one user asks if you couldn't place the Red, Green, and Blue color selections in the Edit menu into a *submenu*. What are submenus, and how can you create them?

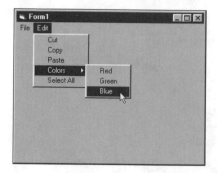

Figure 5.10   A program with a submenu.

What the user wants appears in Figure 5.10. As you can see in that figure, the Colors item in the Edit menu has a small arrow at the right. This indicates that there's a submenu attached to this menu item. Selecting the menu item opens the submenu, as also shown in Figure 5.10. As you can see, submenus appear as menus attached to menus.

Submenus let you organize your menu system in a compact way, and adding them to a program is simple. For example, let's say you started this way, with a Red, Green, and Blue menu item in the Edit menu:

```
Edit
....Cut
....Copy
....Paste
....Red
....Green
....Blue
....Select All
```

To put those items in a submenu, we first add a name for the submenu—say, Colors:

```
Edit
....Cut
....Copy
....Paste
....Colors
....Red
....Green
....Blue
....Select All
```

All that's left is to indent (using the right arrow in the Menu Editor) the items that should go into that submenu (note that they must appear just under the submenu's name):

```
Edit
....Cut
....Copy
....Paste
....Colors
........Red
........Green
........Blue
....Select All
```

That's it—close the Menu Editor.

You add code to submenu items in the same way that you add code to menu items—just click them to open the corresponding event-handling function and add the code you want, as we've done here to report the user's color selection:

```
Private Sub mnuEditColorsBlue_Click()
    MsgBox ("You selected Blue")
End Sub

Private Sub mnuEditColorsGreen_Click()
    MsgBox ("You selected Green")
End Sub

Private Sub mnuEditColorsRed_Click()
    MsgBox ("You selected Red")
```

Creating Immediate ("Bang") Menus

Sometimes you'll see immediate menus (also called "bang" menus) in menu bars. These are special menus that don't open—when you merely click them in the menu bar, they execute their associated command. The name of these menus is followed with an exclamation mark (!) like this: Download! When you click the Download! item in the menu bar, the downloading process starts at once, without opening a menu at all.

Now that toolbars are so common, one sees fewer immediate menus (that is, toolbars act very much like immediate menus are supposed to work), but some

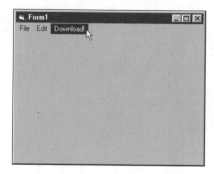

Figure 5.11   Selecting an immediate menu.

programmers still use them And because they're easy to create, we'll cover them here.

To create an immediate menu, just add a menu, such as Download! (don't forget to add exclamation point on the end of "Download" in the **Caption** property, but not in the **Name** property), and don't give it any menu items. Instead, place the code you want to run in the **Click** event handler for the menu itself:

```
Private Sub mnuDownload_Click()
    MsgBox ("Downloading from the Internet...")
End Sub
```

That's all you need. Now when the user selects the Download! menu, this code will be executed. We're about to execute the Download! immediate menu in Figure 5.11. Note that there is no menu opening, even though the Download! item in the menu bar is selected.

Using The
Visual Basic
Predefined
Menus

Using The Visual Basic Predefined Menus

You can use the Visual Component Manager to add a predefined menu to a form (note that not all versions of Visual Basic come with the Visual Component Manager). As you can see in the Visual Component Manager's Visual Basic|Templates|Menus folder, as shown in Figure 5.12, six predefined menus are available. These menus include a File menu, an Edit menu, a Help menu, a Window menu, and so on. To add one of these menus to a form, just select the form and double-click the menu in the Visual Component Manager.

For example, we can add a predefined File menu to a form this way. The result appears in Figure 5.13.

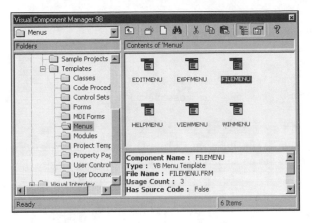

Figure 5.12 Selecting a predefined menu.

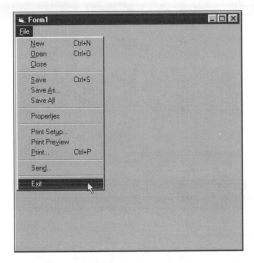

Figure 5.13 Using a predefined menu.

Adding a predefined menu also adds code to the form. For example, here's the skeletal code that's added when you add a predefined File menu:

```
Private Sub mnuFileNew_Click()
  MsgBox "New File Code goes here!"
End Sub

Private Sub mnuFileOpen_Click()
  MsgBox "Open Code goes here!"
End Sub
```

```
Private Sub mnuFilePrint_Click()
  MsgBox "Print Code goes here!"
End Sub

Private Sub mnuFilePrintPreview_Click()
  MsgBox "Print Preview Code goes here!"
End Sub

Private Sub mnuFilePrintSetup_Click()
  MsgBox "Print Setup Code goes here!"
End Sub

Private Sub mnuFileProperties_Click()
  MsgBox "Properties Code goes here!"
End Sub

Private Sub mnuFileSave_Click()
  MsgBox "Save File Code goes here!"
End Sub

Private Sub mnuFileSaveAll_Click()
  MsgBox "Save All Code goes here!"
End Sub

Private Sub mnuFileSaveAs_Click()
  MsgBox "Save As Code goes here!"
End Sub

Private Sub mnuFileSend_Click()
  MsgBox "Send Code goes here!"
End Sub
```

TIP: *If you don't have the Visual Component Manager, you can add a form with a predefined menu to a project. Select Project|Add Form, click the Existing tab, and open the Menus folder to find the possible menu forms to add to your project.*

Adding A Checkmark To A Menu Item

When you want to toggle an option in a program, such as Insert mode for entering text, it's easy to add or remove checkmarks in front of menu items.

Displaying a checkmark gives visual feedback to the user about the toggle state of the option, and there's two ways to add checkmarks to menu items: at design time and at runtime.

Adding Checkmarks At Design Time

To add a checkmark to a menu item at design time, you simply select the Checked box in the Menu Editor, as shown in Figure 5.14, where we add a checkmark to the Edit menu's Insert item.

Now when the Edit menu is first displayed, the Insert item will appear checked.

Adding Checkmarks At Runtime

You can also set checkmarks at runtime using a menu item's **Checked** property. For example, here's how we toggle the Insert item's checkmark each time the user selects that item; setting **Checked** to True places a checkmark in front of the item, and to False removes that checkmark:

```
Private Sub mnuEditInsert_Click()
    Static blnChecked As Boolean
    blnChecked = Not blnChecked
    mnuEditInsert.Checked = blnChecked
End Sub
```

Running this code toggles a checkmark in front of the Insert item, as shown in Figure 5.15.

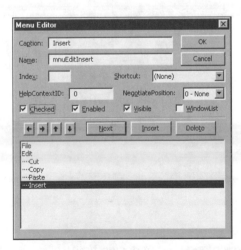

Figure 5.14   Adding a checkmark to a menu item at design time.

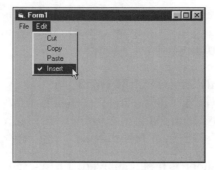

Figure 5.15   Adding a checkmark to a menu item at runtime.

Disabling (Graying Out) Menu Items

To indicate to the user that a menu item is not available at a particular time (such as Copy when there is no selected text), you can disable a menu item (also called "graying it out"). And you can do this at design time or runtime.

Disabling Menu Items At Design Time

To disable a menu item at design time, just deselect the Enabled box in the Menu Editor, as shown in Figure 5.16, where we disable the Insert menu item.

Now when the Edit menu is first shown, the Insert item will be disabled.

Figure 5.16   Disabling a menu item at design time.

Disabling Menu Items At Runtime

You can also disable (and enable) menu items at runtime using the item's **Enabled** property. You set this property to True to enable a menu item and to False when you want to disable an item.

For example, here's how we disable the Edit menu's Insert item when the user clicks it (note that in this program there is then no way for the user to enable it again):

```
Private Sub mnuEditInsert_Click()
    mnuEditInsert.Enabled = False
End Sub
```

Figure 5.17 shows the result—we've disabled the Insert menu item.

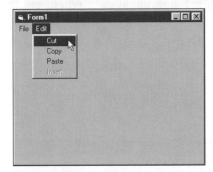

Figure 5.17   Disabling a menu item at runtime.

Handling MDI Form And MDI Child Menus

You've created your new program, the *SuperWizardTextEditor*, and made it an MDI program. But now there's a call from the Testing Department—users are getting confused. Why is the Edit menu still visible when no documents are open to edit? Can you fix this?

Yes you can. Visual Basic lets you specify two menus in an MDI program, one for the MDI form and one for the MDI child form (and more if you have several types of MDI child forms). If the MDI form has a menu and the MDI child form has no menu, the MDI form's menu is active at all times.

If, on the other hand, the MDI child form *has* a menu, that menu *takes over* the MDI form's menu system any time one or more of those child forms is open. What this means in practice is that you give the MDI form a rudimentary menu system (typically just File and Help menus) and save the full menu system (like File, Edit, View, Insert, Format, Tools, Window, Help, and so on) for the child windows to ensure the full menu system is on display only when documents are open and those menus apply.

For example, you might add just this simple menu system to the MDI form in an MDI program. Note that you should, at a minimum, give the user some way to open a new or existing document, and you should provide access to Help:

```
File
....New
....Open
Help
....Contents
```

Here's an example of a full menu system you might then give to the MDI child form, which will take over the main MDI form's menu system when a child form is open:

```
File
....New
....Open
....Save
....Save As
Edit
....Cut
....Copy
....Paste
Tools
....Graphics Editor
....Charts Editor
....Exporter
Help
....Contents
```

TIP: If the user closes all documents at any time, the MDI form's menu system becomes active again—it's only when MDI child forms are open that their menus take over the main menu system.

Adding A List Of Open Windows To An MDI Form's Window Menu

You might have noticed that Window menus in professional MDI programs include a list of open MDI child windows, and you can select which child is active by selecting from this list. You can add that to your program by adding all the code yourself, but there's an easier way—you can set a menu's **WindowList** property.

Setting a menu's **WindowList** property to True adds a list of windows to that menu, and you can set the **WindowList** property in the Menu Editor simply by selecting a checkbox, as shown in Figure 5.18.

Now when the program runs, the menu you added a window list to will indeed display a list of open windows, separated from the rest of the menu items with a menu separator, as shown in Figure 5.19.

You've added a touch of professionalism to your program with a single mouse click.

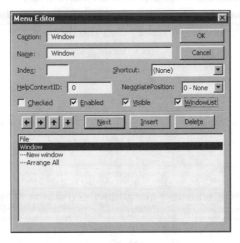

Figure 5.18   Adding a window list to a Window menu.

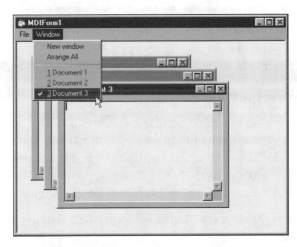

Figure 5.19   Our window list is active.

Making Menus
And Menu
Items Visible Or
Invisible

Making Menus And Menu Items Visible Or Invisible

The Field Testing Department is on the phone again. Someone there doesn't like the look of the 30 disabled menu items in the Edit menu. You explain that those items just don't apply in most cases, so they should be disabled. The Field Testing people suggest you just remove those items from the Edit menu until they can be used. How does that work?

Like other Visual Basic controls, menus and menu items have a **Visible** property, and you can set that property to True to make a menu or menu item visible, and to False to make it invisible (and so remove it from a menu bar or menu).

For example, you might have an item in the File menu: "Connect to the Internet", which is inappropriate in a computer that has no way to connect to the Internet. You can make that item disappear from the File menu by setting its **Visible** property to False, as we do here after checking some hypothetical variable **blnCanConnect**:

```
If blnCanConnect Then
    mnuFileInternet.Visible = True
Else
    mnuFileInternet.Visible = False
End If
```

Making menus and menu items visible or invisible is often a better alternative to displaying menus with too many disabled items (which can frustrate the user and make a program seem inaccessible).

Creating And
Displaying
Pop-Up Menus

Creating And Displaying Pop-Up Menus

Pop-up menus—those menus that appear when you right-click a form—have become very popular these days, and we can add them to Visual Basic programs.

Creating A Pop-up Menu

To create a new pop-up menu, just use the Menu Editor as shown in Figure 5.20, where we create a new menu named Popup (you can use whatever caption you want for the menu; the caption does not appear when the popup menu appears—only the items in the menu appear). The menu has two items in it: Message (displays a message box) and Beep (beeps).

Note that we set this menu's **Visible** property to False to make sure we don't display it in the menu bar.

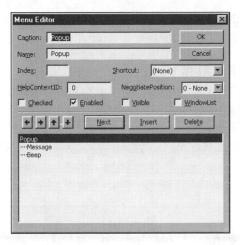

Figure 5.20   Designing a pop-up menu.

We've created our pop-up menu now—but it doesn't appear in the menu bar. How can we add code to the two items in that menu?

You reach those two items, **mnuPopupMessage** and **mnuPopupBeep**, in the code window. Double-click the form now to open the code window. The left drop-down box in the code window lists all the objects in the form, so find **mnuPopupMessage** and **mnuPopupBeep** and add event-handling functions to their **Click** events:

```
Private Sub mnuPopupBeep_Click()

End Sub

Private Sub mnuPopupMessage_Click()

End Sub
```

Here, we'll just make the Beep item beep and the Message item display a message box acknowledging the user's action:

```
Private Sub mnuPopupBeep_Click()
    Beep
End Sub

Private Sub mnuPopupMessage_Click()
    MsgBox ("You selected the Message item")
End Sub
```

That completes the design of the pop-up menu—but how do we display it when the user right-clicks the form?

Displaying A Pop-Up Menu

We want to check for right mouse button events, so add a **MouseDown** event handler to our program using the code window now:

```
Private Sub Form_MouseDown(Button As Integer, Shift As Integer,_
    X As Single,Y As Single)

End Sub
```

You can tell which mouse button went down by comparing the **Button** argument to these predefined Visual Basic constants:

- **vbLeftButton** = 1

- **vbRightButton** = 2

- **vbMiddleButton** = 4

This means we check for the right mouse button:

```
Private Sub Form_MouseDown(Button As Integer, Shift As Integer,_
    X As Single, Y As Single)
    If Button = vbRightButton Then
...
    End If
End Sub
```

If the right mouse button did go down, we display the pop-up menu with the **PopupMenu** method:

```
[object.]PopupMenu menuname [, flags [,x [, y [, boldcommand ]]]]
```

Here, *menuname* is the name of the menu to open, the possible values for the *flags* parameter appear in Table 5.1, *x* and *y* indicate a position for the menu, and *boldcommand* is the name of the one (but no more than one) menu item you want to appear bold. Here's how we use **PopupMenu**:

```
Private Sub Form_MouseDown(Button As Integer, Shift As Integer,_
    X As Single, Y As Single)
    If Button = vbRightButton Then
        PopupMenu Popup
    End If
End Sub
```

Table 5.1   Pop-UpMenu constants.

Constant	Does This
vbPopupMenuLeftAlign	Default. The specified *x* location defines the left edge of the pop-up menu.
vbPopupMenuCenterAlign	The pop-up menu is centered around the specified *x* location.
vbPopupMenuRightAlign	The specified *x* location defines the right edge of the pop-up menu.
vbPopupMenuLeftButton	Default. The pop-up menu is displayed when the user clicks a menu item with the left mouse button only.
vbPopupMenuRightButton	The pop-up menu is displayed when the user clicks a menu item with either the right or left mouse button.

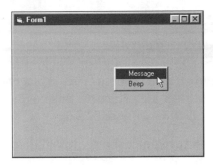

Figure 5.21   Our pop-up menu at work.

That's it—the result appears in Figure 5.21. Now we're using pop-up menus in Visual Basic.

Adding And Deleting Menu Items At Runtime

*Adding And
Deleting Menu
Items At
Runtime*

We've all seen menus that change as a program runs, and that can be a sophisticated effect. It's also impressive if the menu can change in response to user input (for example, adding a new item with the caption "Create *Progname*.exe", where *Progname* is the name given the program). You can add this capability to your program in Visual Basic.

Here, we'll just add new items—Item 1, Item 2, and so on—to the File menu with the user clicks a button. We start by designing our menu system, giving it a File menu with two items: New and Items, as you can see in Figure 5.22.

The Items item is actually a placeholder for the items we'll add to the File menu. Make this item into a control array by giving it an index, 0, in the Index

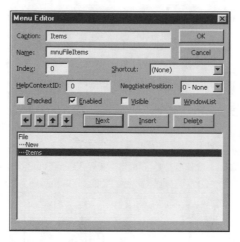

Figure 5.22   Designing an extendable menu.

box, as shown in Figure 5.22. This item is just a placeholder—we don't want it to be visible before the user adds items to this menu—so set its **Visible** property to False, as also shown in Figure 5.22.

Now add a button to the program, and give it a **Click** event-handling function:

```
Private Sub Command1_Click()

End Sub
```

We'll keep track of the items in the File menu with a variable named **intItemCount**, which we increment each time the button is clicked:

```
Private Sub Command1_Click()
    Static intItemCount
    intItemCount = intItemCount + 1
...
End Sub
```

To add a new item to the Items control array, we use **Load()**:

```
Private Sub Command1_Click()
    Static intItemCount
    intItemCount = intItemCount + 1
    Load mnuFileItems(intItemCount)
...
End Sub
```

Finally, we set the caption of the item to indicate what its item number is, and make it visible:

```
Private Sub Command1_Click()
    Static intItemCount
    intItemCount = intItemCount + 1
    Load mnuFileItems(intItemCount)
    mnuFileItems(intItemCount).Caption = "Item " & intItemCount
    mnuFileItems(intItemCount).Visible = True
End Sub
```

You can also add a **Click** event handler to the Items menu item (because it's not visible in the menu bar, find **mnuFileItems** in the code window and add the event handler to it there). This event handler is passed the index of the clicked item in the control array, so we can indicate to the user which item he has clicked:

```
Private Sub mnuFileItems_Click(Index As Integer)
    MsgBox ("You clicked item " + Str(Index))
End Sub
```

That's it—now the File menu can grow as you like, as shown in Figure 5.23.

To remove items from the menu, just use **Unload()** statement like this (and make sure you adjust the total item count):

```
Unload mnuFileItems(intItemCount)
```

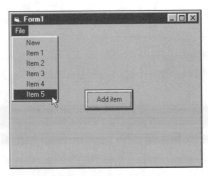

Figure 5.23   Adding items to a menu at runtime.

Adding Bitmaps To Menus

You can even add bitmaps to Visual Basic menu items, although you can't use Visual Basic directly to do that. To see how to do that, we'll create an example that will load in a small bitmap file, image.bmp, and display it in a menu item.

This is going to take some Windows work, which we'll introduce later in the book (if you don't understand what's going on, it will become clear later). First, create a new project and give Form1 a File menu with one item in it. Add a Picture control, **Picture1**, to the form, setting that control's **Visible** property to False, and its **AutoRedraw** property to True. We'll use that control to load in the image file when the form loads:

```
Private Sub Form_Load()
    Picture1.Picture = LoadPicture(App.Path & "\image.bmp")
...
End Sub
```

To insert a bitmap into a menu item, we'll need a handle to a bitmap. We have access to the image in the Picture control, so we create a device context with the Windows **CreateCompatibleDC( )** function, and an empty bitmap with the Windows **CreateCompatibleBitmap( )** function (note that all the Windows functions we used must be declared before being used—we'll see more about this later in the book):

```
Private Sub Form_Load()
    Picture1.Picture = LoadPicture(App.Path & "\image.bmp")

    Dim dcMemory As Long
    Dim hMemoryBitmap As Long
    dcMemory = CreateCompatibleDC(Picture1.hdc)
    hMemoryBitmap = CreateCompatibleBitmap(Picture1.hdc, 60, 30)
...
End Sub
```

Next, we select (that is, install) the new bitmap into the device context using **SelectObject**:

```
Private Sub Form_Load()
    Picture1.Picture = LoadPicture(App.Path & "\image.bmp")

    Dim dcMemory As Long
    Dim hMemoryBitmap As Long
    dcMemory = CreateCompatibleDC(Picture1.hdc)
    hMemoryBitmap = CreateCompatibleBitmap(Picture1.hdc, 60, 30)
```

```
    Dim pObject As Long
    pObject = SelectObject(dcMemory, hMemoryBitmap)
...
End Sub
```

Now that we've created our new device context and installed a bitmap, we can copy the image from the Picture control's device context to the new device context this way using the Windows **BitBlt()** function:

```
Private Sub Form_Load()
    Picture1.Picture = LoadPicture(App.Path & "\image.bmp")

    Dim dcMemory As Long
    Dim hMemoryBitmap As Long
    dcMemory = CreateCompatibleDC(Picture1.hdc)
    hMemoryBitmap = CreateCompatibleBitmap(Picture1.hdc, 60, 30)

    Dim pObject As Long
    pObject = SelectObject(dcMemory, hMemoryBitmap)

    dummy = BitBlt(dcMemory, 0, 0, 60, 30, Picture1.hdc, 0, 0, &HCC0020)
    dummy = SelectObject(dcMemory, pObject)
...
End Sub
```

Finally, we use the Windows **ModifyMenu()** function to modify the menu, installing our new bitmap:

```
Private Sub Form_Load()
    Picture1.Picture = LoadPicture(App.Path & "\image.bmp")

    Dim dcMemory As Long
    Dim hMemoryBitmap As Long
    dcMemory = CreateCompatibleDC(Picture1.hdc)
    hMemoryBitmap = CreateCompatibleBitmap(Picture1.hdc, 60, 30)

    Dim pObject As Long
    pObject = SelectObject(dcMemory, hMemoryBitmap)

    dummy = BitBlt(dcMemory, 0, 0, 60, 30, Picture1.hdc, 0, 0, &HCC0020)
    dummy = SelectObject(dcMemory, pObject)

    dummy = ModifyMenu(GetSubMenu(GetMenu(Me.hwnd), 0), 0, &H404, 0,_
        hMemoryBitmap)
End Sub
```

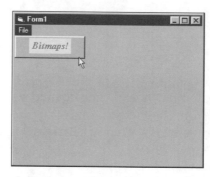

Figure 5.24   Using bitmapped menu items.

The result appears in Figure 5.24, where you can see our bitmap in the File menu.

The listing for this form appears in is locate in the bitmap folder on this book's accompaning CD-ROM. (Note that all the Windows functions we used must be declared before being used—we'll see more about this later in the book.)

Using The Registry To Store A Most Recently Used (MRU) Files List

Using The
Registry To
Store A Most
Recently Used
(MRU) Files List

Your program's users love your new application—but there's always something new in the Suggestions box. Today's suggestion asks whether you can add a Most Recently Used (MRU) list of files to the File menu. These lists are appended to the end of the File menu and let the user select recently opened files easily. In fact, the Visual Basic IDE has an MRU list, as you can see in Figure 5.25.

In this example, we'll support a very short MRU list—just one item—but the idea is easily extendable. Create a new Visual Basic project now named "mru", and give Form1 a File menu with two items in it: Open (" mnuOpen") and MRU ("mnuMRU"). Make the MRU item a control array by setting its **Index** property to 0 in the Menu Editor, and make it invisible by deselecting the **Visible** box in the Menu Editor so we can use it as a placeholder.

This example uses the Visual Basic **GetSetting()** and **SetSetting()** functions to access the Windows Registry. We'll see how to use these functions in depth later in this book, but for now, we use **GetSetting()** when Form1 is first loaded to see if we've saved a file name for the MRU list in the Registry's Settings/Doc1 section (here, we'll use the application's name as its Registry key, and we get that name from **App.Title**):

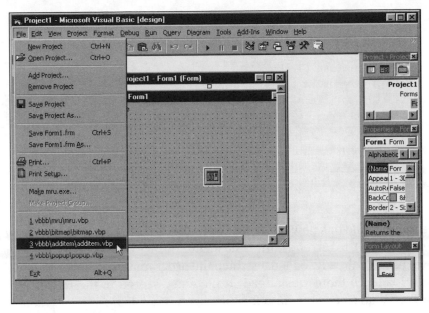

Figure 5.25   The Visual Basic MRU list.

```
Private Sub Form_Load()
    Dim FileName As String
    FileName = GetSetting(App.Title, "Settings", "Doc1")
```

If we have saved a file name in the Registry, we should place it in the File menu, and we do that by loading a new menu item in the **mnuMRU** array, setting its caption to the file name, and making it visible this way:

```
Private Sub Form_Load()
    Dim FileName As String
    FileName = GetSetting(App.Title, "Settings", "Doc1")

    If FileName <> "" Then
        Load mnuMRU(1)
        mnuMRU(1).Caption = FileName
        mnuMRU(1).Visible = True
    End If
End Sub
```

That solves the case where we've stored a file name for the MRU list in the registry—but how do we store those names there in the first place? We do that when the user selects the Open item in the File menu. To get the file name from the user, we'll use an Open Common Dialog box, so add a Common Dialog control named **dlgCommonDialog** to the form now (if you don't know how to do that, see Chapter 17, which discusses file handling) and get a file name to open from the user this way:

```
Private Sub mnuOpen_Click()
    With dlgCommonDialog
        .DialogTitle = "Open"
        .CancelError = False
        .Filter = "All Files (*.*)|*.*"
        .ShowOpen
        If Len(.FileName) = 0 Then
            Exit Sub
        End If
```

We want to add this newly opened file to the MRU list, so we load a new item, **mnuMRU(1)**, to the end of the File menu. But we only want to load that item if we haven't already loaded it (which the program would have done when the form loaded if there was already a file name stored in the Registry). Here's how we load a new item into the File menu if needed:

```
Private Sub mnuOpen_Click()
    With dlgCommonDialog
        .DialogTitle = "Open"
        .CancelError = False
        .Filter = "All Files (*.*)|*.*"
        .ShowOpen
        If Len(.FileName) = 0 Then
            Exit Sub
        End If

        If GetSetting(App.Title, "Settings", "Doc1") = "" Then
            Load mnuMRU(1)
        End If
```

Now that the new MRU item is loaded, we set its caption to the file name the user has just opened, make it visible, and store the new file name in the Registry for next time:

```
With dlgCommonDialog
        .DialogTitle = "Open"
        .CancelError = False
        .Filter = "All Files (*.*)|*.*"
        .ShowOpen
        If Len(.FileName) = 0 Then
            Exit Sub
        End If
```

```
        If GetSetting(App.Title, "Settings", "Doc1") = "" Then
            Load mnuMRU(1)
        End If

        mnuMRU(1).Caption = .FileName
        mnuMRU(1).Visible = True
        SaveSetting App.Title, "Settings", "Doc1", .FileName
    End With
End Sub
```

That's it—now we're supporting an MRU list, as you can see in Figure 5.26.

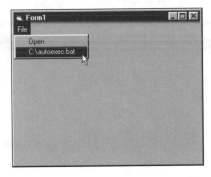

Figure 5.26   Supporting an MRU list.

Chapter 6

Text Boxes And Rich Text Boxes

If you need an immediate solution to:	See page:
Creating Multiline, Word-Wrap Text Boxes	200
Aligning Text In Text Boxes	200
Adding Scroll Bars To Text Boxes	201
Making A Text Box Read-Only	202
Accessing Text In A Text Box	203
Selecting And Replacing Text In A Text Box	204
Copying Or Getting Selected Text To Or From The Clipboard	204
Creating A Password Control	205
Controlling Input In A Text Box	206
Adding An RTF Box To A Form	207
Accessing Text In A Rich Text Box	208
Selecting Text In Rich Text Boxes	208
Using Bold, Italic, Underline, And Strikethru	209
Indenting Text In Rich Text Boxes	211
Setting Fonts And Font Sizes In Rich Text Boxes	212
Using Bullets In Rich Text Boxes	214
Aligning Text In A Rich Text Box	216
Setting Text Color In RTF Boxes	216
Moving The Insertion Point In RTF Boxes	217
Adding Superscripts And Subscripts In Rich Text Boxes	219
Setting The Mouse Pointer In Text Boxes And Rich Text Boxes	220
Searching For (And Replacing) Text In RTF Boxes	221
Saving RTF Files From Rich Text Boxes	222
Reading RTF Files Into A Rich Text Box	223
Printing From A Rich Text Box	223

In Depth

In this chapter, we're going to start working with Visual Basic controls—in this case, text boxes and rich text boxes. Every Windows user is familiar with text boxes. They're exactly what their name implies: box-like controls in which you can enter text. Text boxes can be multiline, have scroll bars, be read-only, and have many other attributes, as we'll see in this chapter. Not every Windows user is familiar with rich text boxes, on the other hand. Rich text boxes (also known as *RTF boxes*) support not only plain text, but also Rich Text Format (RTF) text.

RTF text supports a variety of formats. For example, you can color text in a rich text box, underline it, bold it, or make it italic. You can select fonts and font sizes, as well as write the text out to disk or read it back in. RTF boxes can also hold a great amount of data, unlike standard text boxes, which are limited to 64K characters.

RTF text was designed to be a step beyond plain text, and because many word processors let you save text in that format, it can provide a link between different types of word processors. Using RTF boxes, you can also create your own simple word processors, and that's exactly what the Visual Basic Application Wizard does if you create an application with it. You'll find that the child windows in an Application Wizard program have a rich text box stretched across them, ready for the user to put to work.

How do you create text boxes and RTF boxes? As with other Visual Basic controls, you use the toolbox, as shown in Figure 6.1. In that figure, the Text Box tool is the second tool down on the right, and the RTF Box tool (which you add to a project with the Project|Components box's Controls tab) appears at lower right.

Use Of Text Boxes And RTF Boxes In Windows Programs

In Windows programs, text boxes and RTF boxes are used to handle text-based data, and not to let the user enter commands. When Windows first appeared, DOS-oriented programmers used to use text boxes to accept text-based commands from the user, but Microsoft considers that an abuse of the Windows user interface. The user is supposed to issue commands to a program with

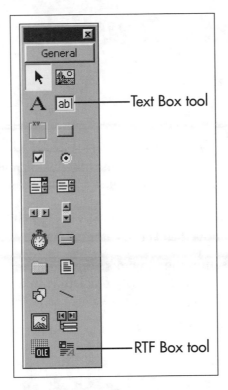

Text Box tool

RTF Box tool

Figure 6.1   The Text Box and RTF Box tools.

standard Windows controls like menu items, command buttons, radio buttons, toolbars, and so forth, not by typing command syntax into a text box. Text boxes and RTF boxes can certainly hold data that commands require for execution, but those controls are not usually intended to hold the commands themselves.

With all that in mind, then, let's start working with text boxes and RTF boxes. These are two of the most fundamental controls in Windows, and two of the most fun to work with. We'll cover text boxes first in the Immediate Solutions and then turn to rich text boxes.

Immediate Solutions

Creating Multiline, Word-Wrap Text Boxes

You've got a text box all set up for user feedback, and it can hold about 60 characters of text. Surely that's enough, you think. But when you start actually reading the users' comments, you find that they're all favorable, but truncated ("I loved your program! In fact, let me say that I never saw a"). Maybe it's worthwhile to allow the user to enter more text.

You can do that by setting the text box's **MultiLine** property to True, converting a text box into a multiline text box, complete with word wrap. The result appears in Figure 6.2. Now your program's users can type in line after line of text.

Note that you can also add scroll bars to multiline text boxes. (See "Adding Scroll Bars To Text Boxes" later in this chapter.)

Figure 6.2   Creating a multiline text box.

Aligning Text In Text Boxes

The Aesthetic Design Department has sent you a memo. Your new program meets its requirements for design standards, except for one thing: all the text boxes in your program are stacked one on top of the other, and the Aesthetic Design Department thinks it would be terrific if you display the text in those boxes as centered, not left-justified.

Well, you seem to remember that text boxes have an **Alignment** property, so you set it to Centered at design time in all the text boxes (there are three

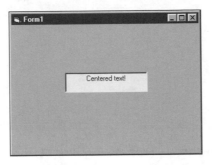

Figure 6.3   Aligning text in a text box.

possibilities: 0 for left-justified, 1 for right-justified, and 2 for centered). You run your program—and the text you enter ends up being left-justified. The **Alignment** property doesn't seem to work. What's wrong?

You need to set the text boxes' **MultiLine** property to True before text alignment will work; that's one of the quirks of text boxes. When you set the **MultiLine** property to True, everything works as it should, as you see in Figure 6.3.

Adding Scroll Bars To Text Boxes

Now that you're using multiline text boxes, it would be even better if you could add scroll bars to let the user enter even more text. If your program's users are going to be entering a lot of text into text boxes, you can avoid the need for huge text boxes by adding scroll bars.

Using the **ScrollBars** property, there are four ways to add scroll bars to a text box. Here are the settings you use for the **ScrollBars** property, and the type of scroll bars each setting displays:

- *0*—None
- *1*—Horizontal
- *2*—Vertical
- *3*—Both

Note that in order for the scroll bars to actually appear, the text box's **MultiLine** property must be True. After you install scroll bars in a text box, the result appears as in Figure 6.4. Now the user can enter much more text simply by scrolling appropriately.

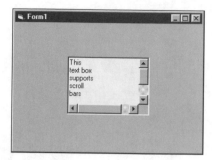

Figure 6.4   Using scroll bars in a text box.

TIP: *Although text boxes can hold up to 64K characters, that may be too much for you to conveniently handle, and you may want to limit the maximum number of characters a text box can hold. You do that by setting the text box's **MaxLength** property to the maximum number of characters you want the user to be able to enter (the default value for **MaxLength** is 0, which actually means 64K characters).*

Making A Text Box Read-Only

There are times when you want to make text boxes read-only. For example, you might have written a calculator program in which you let the user enter operands in text boxes and display the result in another text box. The result text box should be read-only so that the user doesn't enter text there by mistake. Here's how you do that.

Locking A Text Box

You use the **Locked** property to make a text box read-only. Setting this property to True means that the user cannot enter text into the text box except under your program's control, like this:

```
Private Sub Command1_Click()
    Text1.Text = "This box is locked."
End Sub
```

An example of a locked text box appears in Figure 6.5 (note that users can't tell if a text box is locked until they try to enter text in it!)

Disabling A Text Box

You can also disable a text box by setting its **Enabled** property to False. However, although this means the user can't enter text into the text box, it also means the text in the box appears grayed. Disabling is better done to indicate that the control is inaccessible.

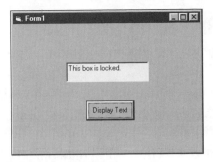

Figure 6.5   *A locked text box.*

Using Labels Instead Of Text Boxes

Another alternative to using read-only text boxes is to display read-only text in label controls. (Label controls can hold as much text as a text box.) You can change the text in a label control from code using the label's **Caption** property.

Accessing Text In A Text Box

Java, C++, Visual Basic—a programmer has to switch between a lot of languages these days. So how do you set the text in a text box again? Is there a **SetText( )** method?

No, you use the **Text** property like this:

```
Private Sub Command1_Click()
Text1.Text = "Hello from Visual Basic"
End Sub
```

When the user clicks the command button **Command1**, the text "Hello from Visual Basic" appears in the text box, as shown in Figure 6.6.

Figure 6.6   *Setting a text box's text.*

Selecting And Replacing Text In A Text Box

To work with part of the text in a text box, you select the text you want using three properties:

- **SelLength**—Returns or sets the number of characters selected.
- **SelStart**—Returns or sets the starting point of selected text. If no text is selected, **SelStart** indicates the position of the insertion point.
- **SelText**—Returns or sets the string containing the currently selected text. If no characters are selected, **SelText** consists of a zero-length string ("").

For example, here's how we select all the text in a text box and replace it with "Welcome to Visual Basic" (which we could have done just as easily by assigning that string to the **Text** property, of course). Note the use of **Len()** to get the length of the text currently in the text box:

```
Private Sub Command1_Click()
    Text1.SelStart = 0
    Text1.SelLength = Len(Text1.Text)
    Text1.SelText = "Welcome to Visual Basic"
End Sub
```

That's how it works when you want to select some text: you specify the beginning of the selected text in **SelStart**, the end in **SelLength**, and refer to the text with the **SelText** property.

Note that text selected under program control this way does *not* appear highlighted in the text box.

The **HideSelection** Property

While on the topic of text selection, we might note the **HideSelection** property, which, when True, turns off text-selection highlighting when your program loses the focus.

Copying Or Getting Selected Text To Or From The Clipboard

After entering their new novels into your program, users were surprised that they couldn't copy them to the Clipboard and paste them into other applications. How can you support the Clipboard with text in a text box?

You can copy selected text to the Clipboard using **SetText**:

```
Clipboard.SetText text, [format]
```

Here, *text* is the text you want to place into the Clipboard, and *format* has these possible values:

- **vbCFLink**—&HBF00; DDE conversation information
- **vbCFRTF**—&HBF01; Rich Text Format
- **vbCFText**—1 (the default); Text

You can get text from the clipboard using the **GetText()** function this way

```
Clipboard.GetText([format])
```

where *format* can be taken from the earlier list of possible format types.

Here's an example to make this clearer; in this case, we place all the text in text box **Text1** into the clipboard:

```
Private Sub Command1_Click()
    Clipboard.SetText Text1.Text
...
End Sub
```

Then we read the text back and display it in a new text box, **Text2**:

```
Private Sub Command1_Click()
    Clipboard.SetText Text1.Text
    Text2.Text = Clipboard.GetText
End Sub
```

TIP: *Text boxes already allow the user to use these shortcuts to work with the Clipboard: Ctrl+C to copy selected text, Ctrl+V to paste text from the clipboard, and Ctrl+X to cut selected text.*

Creating A Password Control

It's time to heighten security. Users of your new *SuperSpecialDataBase* program are worried about the low security of your program, so you decide to add a little security with password controls. Visual Basic will help out.

To convert a standard text box into a password box, you just assign some character (usually an asterisk [*]) to the text box's **PasswordChar** property.

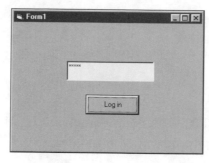

Figure 6.7   Creating a password control.

After that, your program can read the text in the text box, but only the password character will appear on the screen each time the user types a character, as shown in Figure 6.7.

TIP: You may be concerned that someone can copy the text in a password control and paste it into a word processor to read it, but in fact, Clipboard-handling from the text box is disabled if you are using a password character.

> **WARNING!   A note about security: don't trust the password control too far, because there may be some security loopholes in it that someone out there can exploit. I once wrote an article that included a tiny program to encrypt data in a minimum-security way just to get readers started and got a letter full of angry satisfaction from a code-breaking expert who told me it had taken him "only" five days (with full-time access to a supercomputer) to break a file encoded with my program.**

Controlling Input In A Text Box

The Testing Department is on the phone—there's a bug in your program. The users are getting runtime errors. Don't panic, you say; you'll be right down.

You ask the users to duplicate what caused the problem, and you find that they're trying to add two numbers with your program: 15553 and 955Z. What's 955Z? you ask. A typo, they say. Is there any way you can restrict user input so this doesn't happen?

Yes, you can. Just use the **KeyPress** event and check the **KeyAscii** parameter, which is the ANSI (*not* ASCII, despite its name) code for the just-struck key. Let's make this clearer with an example; here's how you would restrict users to only typing digits into **Text1**; all non-digits are simply discarded:

```
Private Sub Text1_KeyPress(KeyAscii As Integer)
    If KeyAscii < Asc("0") Or KeyAscii > Asc("9") Then
        KeyAscii = 0
    End If
End Sub
```

Besides the **KeyPress**, text boxes support the **KeyUp** and **KeyDown** events, although the **KeyPress** event is easiest to use, because you get the character code of the typed character passed to you immediately. In the **KeyUp** and **KeyDown** events, you are passed a virtual key code you have to translate into a character, after checking to see if the Shift key was down and so on. You can also use the text box's **Change** event, which occurs when there's a change in the text box's text.

Adding An RTF Box To A Form

So you've decided to make the move from text boxes to rich text boxes, and you turn to the toolbox. Wait a minute—where's the Rich Text Box tool in the toolbox? The answer is that it's not there until you add it.

To add a rich text box to a form, follow these steps:

1. Select the Project|Components menu item.

2. Click the Controls tab in the Components box.

3. Find and select the Microsoft Rich Textbox Control box, and click on OK to close the Components box.

4. The rich text control now appears in the toolbox (at lower right in Figure 6.1), and you can use it to add rich text boxes to your forms, as shown in Figure 6.8.

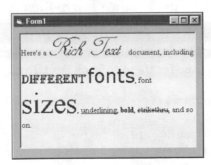

Figure 6.8   Displaying rich text in a rich text box.

TIP: *What these steps really accomplish is to add the Richtx32.ocx file to your program, and you'll need to distribute that file with your program if you use rich text boxes.*

Accessing Text In A Rich Text Box

To access text in a rich text box, you can use two properties: **Text** and **TextRTF**. As their names imply, **Text** holds the text in a rich text box in plain text format (like a text box), and **TextRTF** holds the text in Rich Text Format.

Here's an example where we read the text in **RichTextBox1** without any RTF codes and display that text as plain text in **RichTextBox2**:

```
Private Sub Command1_Click()
    RichTextBox2.Text = RichTextBox1.Text
End Sub
```

Here's the same operation where we transfer the text including all RTF codes— that is, here we're transferring rich text from one rich text box to another:

```
Private Sub Command1_Click()
    RichTextBox2.TextRTF = RichTextBox1.TextRTF
End Sub
```

Selecting Text In Rich Text Boxes

Rich text boxes support the **SetText** property just like standard text boxes. However, **SetText** only works with plain text. You can set the start and end of plain-text selection with the **SelStart** and **SelLength** properties.

If you want to work with RTF-selected text, on the other hand, use the **SelRTF** property. For example, here's how we select the first 10 characters in **RichTextBox1** and transfer them to **RichTextBox2** using **SelRTF**:

```
Private Sub Command1_Click()
    RichTextBox1.SelStart = 0
    RichTextBox1.SelLength = 10
    RichTextBox2.TextRTF = RichTextBox1.SelRTF
End Sub
```

The **Span** Method

Besides the **SelRTF** property, you can use the **Span( )** method to select text based on a set of characters:

```
RichTextBox.Span characterset, [forward, [negate]]
```

The *characterset* parameter is a string that specifies the set of characters to look for. The *forward* parameter determines which direction the insertion point moves. The *negate* parameter specifies whether the characters in *characterset* define the set of target characters or are excluded from the set of target characters.

You use **Span( )** to extend a selection from the current insertion point based on a set of specified characters. This method searches the text in the rich text box (forwards or backwards as you've specified) and extends the text selection to include (or exclude, if you've so specified) as many of the characters you've specified in the character set that it can find. For example, to select the text from the current insertion point to the end of the sentence, use **Span(".?!")**, which works for sentences ending in periods, question marks, or exclamation marks.

Here's an example where we use **Span( )** to find the word "underlined" and underline it:

```
Private Sub Command1_Click()
    RichTextBox1.Text = "This rich text box supports underlined, bold, _
        italic, and strikethru text."

    RichTextBox1.SelStart = RichTextBox1.Find("underlined")
    RichTextBox1.Span ("underlined")
    RichTextBox1.SelUnderline = True
End Sub
```

Using Bold, Italic, Underline, And Strikethru

To make text bold, italic, underlined, or strikethru, you use the **SelBold**, **SelItalic**, **SelUnderline**, and **SelStrikethru** properties. These properties work on selected RTF text only, so you have to select the text whose format you want to change.

To make this clearer, here's an example where we set the underline, bold, italic, and strikethru properties of text. We start by placing some text into a rich text box:

```
Private Sub Command1_Click()
    RichTextBox1.Text = "This rich text box supports underlined, bold,_
        italic, and strikethru text."
...
```

Next, we'll underline the word "underlined" in the text. We start by finding that word using the rich text box **Find( )** method:

```
Private Sub Command1_Click()
    RichTextBox1.Text = "This rich text box supports underlined, bold,_
        italic, and strikethru text."

    RichTextBox1.SelStart = RichTextBox1.Find("underlined")
...
```

We then use **Span( )** to select the word "underlined":

```
Private Sub Command1_Click()
    RichTextBox1.Text = "This rich text box supports underlined, bold,_
        italic, and strikethru text."

    RichTextBox1.SelStart = RichTextBox1.Find("underlined")
    RichTextBox1.Span ("underlined")
...
```

Finally, we underline the selected text by setting the rich text box's **SelUnderline** property to True:

```
Private Sub Command1_Click()
    RichTextBox1.Text = "This rich text box supports underlined, bold,_
        italic, and strikethru text."

    RichTextBox1.SelStart = RichTextBox1.Find("underlined")
    RichTextBox1.Span ("underlined")
    RichTextBox1.SelUnderline = True
...
```

And we can do the same to demonstrate bold, italic, and strikethru text:

```
Private Sub Command1_Click()
    RichTextBox1.Text = "This rich text box supports underlined, bold,_
        italic, and strikethru text."

    RichTextBox1.SelStart = RichTextBox1.Find("underlined")
    RichTextBox1.Span ("underlined")
    RichTextBox1.SelUnderline = True
```

```
    RichTextBox1.SelStart = 0
    RichTextBox1.SelStart = RichTextBox1.Find("bold")
    RichTextBox1.Span ("bold")
    RichTextBox1.SelBold = True

    RichTextBox1.SelStart = 0
    RichTextBox1.SelStart = RichTextBox1.Find("italic")
    RichTextBox1.Span ("italic")
    RichTextBox1.SelItalic = True

    RichTextBox1.SelStart = 0
    RichTextBox1.SelStart = RichTextBox1.Find("strikethru")
    RichTextBox1.Span ("strikethru")
    RichTextBox1.SelStrikeThru = True
End Sub
```

Running this program yields the results you see in Figure 6.9.

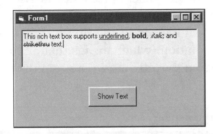

Figure 6.9   Setting rich text properties.

Indenting Text In Rich Text Boxes

One of the aspects of word processors that users have gotten used to is the ability to indent text, and rich text boxes (which are designed to be RTF word processors in a control) have this capability. To indent paragraph-by-paragraph, you use these properties (you set them to numeric values to indicate the indentation amount, using the measurement units of the underlying form, which is usually twips):

- **SelIndent**—Indents the first line of the paragraph

- **SelHangingIndent**—Indents all other lines of the paragraph with respect to **SelIndent**

- **SelRightIndent**—Sets the right indentation of the paragraph

Figure 6.10   Indenting a paragraph of text.

To use these properties on a paragraph of text, you either select the paragraph (using **SelStart** and **SelLength**, or **Span()**), or simply place the insertion point in the paragraph (you can move the insertion point under program control with the **UpTo()** method).

Here's an example: When the user places the insertion point in a paragraph of text and clicks a button, **Command1**, we can indent the paragraph 500 twips. We can then *outdent* all lines after the first by 250 twips with respect to the overall 500-twip indentation (which means that all lines after the first will be indented 250 twips from the left margin) and set the right indent to 100 twips:

```
Private Sub Command1_Click()
    RichTextBox1.SelIndent = 500
    RichTextBox1.SelHangingIndent = -250
    RichTextBox1.SelRightIndent = 100
End Sub
```

Running this code on a paragraph of text yields the result you see in Figure 6.10. Now we're indenting individual paragraphs in rich text controls.

Besides working paragraph-by-paragraph, you can set the right margin for the whole rich text at once with the **RightMargin** property. Just assign this property the new value you want for the right margin, and you're set.

Setting Fonts And Font Sizes In Rich Text Boxes

Another call from the Field Testing Department. It seems that the users want to use different *fonts* in your word-processor program. Well, some people are never satisfied—but rich text boxes can help here, too.

To set a selection's font, you just set the **SelFontName** to the new font name (for example, Arial or Times New Roman). To set a selection's font size, you just set the **SelFontSize** property. That's all it takes.

Here's an example. In this case, we'll display the text "This rich text box supports fonts like Arial and Courier in different sizes." in a rich text box, and format the words "Arial" and "Courier" in those fonts, and in different font sizes.

We start by placing that text in a rich text box:

```
Private Sub Command1_Click()
    RichTextBox1.Text = "This rich text box supports fonts like Arial and_
        Courier in different sizes."
...
```

Next, we select the word "Arial":

```
Private Sub Command1_Click()
    RichTextBox1.Text = "This rich text box supports fonts like Arial and_
        Courier in different sizes."

    RichTextBox1.SelStart = RichTextBox1.Find("Arial")
    RichTextBox1.Span ("Arial")
...
```

Then we display that word in Arial font, with a 24-point size:

```
Private Sub Command1_Click()
    RichTextBox1.Text = "This rich text box supports fonts like Arial and_
        Courier in different sizes."

    RichTextBox1.SelStart = RichTextBox1.Find("Arial")
    RichTextBox1.Span ("Arial")
    RichTextBox1.SelFontName = "Arial"
    RichTextBox1.SelFontSize = 24
...
```

We do the same for the word "Courier", displaying it in 18-point size:

```
Private Sub Command1_Click()
    RichTextBox1.Text = "This rich text box supports fonts like Arial and_
        Courier in different sizes."

    RichTextBox1.SelStart = RichTextBox1.Find("Arial")
    RichTextBox1.Span ("Arial")
```

```
        RichTextBox1.SelFontName = "Arial"
        RichTextBox1.SelFontSize = 24

        RichTextBox1.SelStart = 0
        RichTextBox1.SelStart = RichTextBox1.Find("Courier")
        RichTextBox1.Span ("Courier")
        RichTextBox1.SelFontName = "Courier"
        RichTextBox1.SelFontSize = 18
End Sub
```

The result appears in Figure 6.11.

Being able to set the font and font size of individual text selections instead of working with all the text at once in a rich text box is a very powerful capability.

Figure 6.11   Setting fonts and font sizes.

Using Bullets In Rich Text Boxes

Rich text boxes support *bullets*, those black dots that appear in lists of items that you want to set off in text. Putting a bullet in front of each item gives the list a snappy appearance and helps the reader assimilate the information quickly.

To set bullets, you use the **SelBullet** and **BulletIndent** properties. The **SelBullet** property displays a bullet in front of the paragraph in which the current selection is; the **BulletIndent** property indicates how much you want the bullet to be indented from the left.

TIP: *It's a good idea to set the bullet indentation, because if you don't, the bullet will appear right in front of the first character in the paragraph you're bulleting, which can look awkward.*

Let's make this clearer with an example. We start by placing some text in a rich text box:

```
Private Sub Command1_Click()
    RichTextBox1.Text = "This rich text box shows how to use bullets _
        and indent bulleted text."
...
```

We set the indentation for this paragraph to 200 twips:

```
Private Sub Command1_Click()
    RichTextBox1.Text = "This rich text box shows how to use bullets _
        and indent bulleted text."
    RichTextBox1.SelIndent = 200
...
```

Next, we set the bullet's indent to 90 twips, so it's set off from the rest of the text. We set that indent with the **BulletIndent** property:

```
Private Sub Command1_Click()
    RichTextBox1.Text = "This rich text box shows how to use bullets _
        and indent bulleted text."
    RichTextBox1.SelIndent = 200
    RichTextBox1.BulletIndent = 90
...
```

Finally, we add the bullet with the **SelBullet** property:

```
Private Sub Command1_Click()
    RichTextBox1.Text = "This rich text box shows how to use bullets _
        and indent bulleted text."
    RichTextBox1.SelIndent = 200
    RichTextBox1.BulletIndent = 90
    RichTextBox1.SelBullet = True
End Sub
```

That's it—the result appears in Figure 6.12.

Figure 6.12   Adding a bullet to text in a rich text box.

Aligning Text In A Rich Text Box

You can set the alignment of text in a rich text box paragraph-by-paragraph using the **SelAlignment** property. You just select the paragraph you want to align, or place the insertion point in that paragraph, and set the **SelAlignment** property to one of the following values:

- **rtfLeft**—0(the default); the paragraph is aligned along the left margin.
- **rtfRight**—1; the paragraph is aligned along the right margin.
- **rtfCenter**—2; the paragraph is centered between the left and right margins.

Being able to align text paragraph-by-paragraph like this is much more powerful than the simple **Alignment** property of a standard text box, which aligns all the text at the same time.

Setting Text Color In RTF Boxes

Another call from the Testing Department—now the users want to use different text *colors* in your word-processing program. Can you do that? Yes, you can, using the **SelColor** property.

To set colors in a rich text box, you just make a selection and set the rich text box's **SelColor** property using the **RGB( )** function. You pass three values (each ranging from 0 to 255) to the **RGB( )** function for the three color values: red, green, and blue.

Here's an example to make this clearer. We display the text "This rich text box supports font colors like red and blue and green." in a rich text box, and color the word "red" red, "blue" blue, and "green" green. Here's how that example looks in code:

```
Private Sub Command1_Click()
    RichTextBox1.Text = "This rich text box supports font colors like _
        red and blue and green."

    RichTextBox1.SelStart = RichTextBox1.Find("red")
    RichTextBox1.Span ("red")
    RichTextBox1.SelColor = RGB(255, 0, 0)

    RichTextBox1.SelStart = 0
    RichTextBox1.SelStart = RichTextBox1.Find("green")
    RichTextBox1.Span ("green")
    RichTextBox1.SelColor = RGB(0, 255, 0)

    RichTextBox1.SelStart = 0
    RichTextBox1.SelStart = RichTextBox1.Find("blue")
    RichTextBox1.Span ("blue")
    RichTextBox1.SelColor = RGB(0, 0, 255)
End Sub
```

This program produces the display you see in Figure 6.13. (Although it only appears in black and white in this book, the word red is red, and so on!)

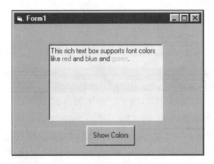

Figure 6.13   Coloring text in a rich text box.

Moving The Insertion Point In RTF Boxes

Using the **UpTo( )** method, you can move the insertion point around in a rich text box. This method moves the insertion point up to (but not including) a character or set of characters. Moving the insertion point yourself can be a powerful technique in a rich text box—for example, you can move the insertion point to a section of text the user is searching for. Here's how the **UpTo( )** method works:

RichTextBox.UpTo(*characterset, forward, negate*)

The *characterset* parameter is a string that specifies the set of characters to look for. The *forward* parameter determines which direction the insertion point moves. The *negate* parameter specifies whether the characters in *characterset* define the set of target characters or are excluded from the set of target characters.

This is made easier to understand with an example, so let's put together an example now. Here, we'll display the text "Click the button to move the insertion point here: *", and when the user clicks a button, we'll move the insertion point right up to the asterisk (*).

We begin by displaying that text in a rich text box when the form loads:

```
Private Sub Form_Load()
    RichTextBox1.Text = "Click the button to move the insertion point _
        here: *"
End Sub
```

Next, when the user clicks a button, we can move the insertion point up to the asterisk in the text this way (note, of course, that you can search for multi-character text as well as single characters):

```
Private Sub Command1_Click()
    RichTextBox1.UpTo ("*")
...
End Sub
```

That's not quite good enough, though. Because we've clicked the command button, the button now has the focus, which means the blinking insertion point in the rich text box isn't visible at all. To make sure the insertion point in the rich text box reappears, we give the focus back to the rich text box. This program appears in Figure 6.14. Now we're handling the insertion point.

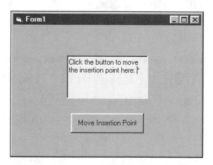

Figure 6.14   Moving the insertion point in a rich text box.

```
Private Sub Command1_Click()
    RichTextBox1.UpTo ("*")
    RichTextBox1.SetFocus
End Sub
```

Adding Superscripts And Subscripts In Rich Text Boxes

Uh oh—the users of your new word-processing program, *SuperDuperTextPro*, are demanding more text-formatting power. Your program has become so popular that the staff physicists are starting to use it, but they want to use superscripts and subscripts in text. Can you add that?

Yes, with the rich text box **SelCharOffset** property. You use this property to make a selection a superscript or subscript—if you set this value to a positive value, you get a superscript, and if you set it to a negative value, you get a subscript. (All measurements use the measurement units of the underlying form, such as twips.)

Let's see an example. Here we can display a simple quadratic equation using this text

```
X12 + 2X1 + 1 = 0
```

where we'll make the 1s subscripts and the first 2 a superscript. We start by displaying that text in a rich text box:

```
Private Sub Form_Load()
    RichTextBox1.Text = "X12 + 2X1 + 1 = 0"
End Sub
```

Next, we select the characters we want and set the **SelCharOffset** property to positive or negative twip values to create superscripts and subscripts:

```
Private Sub Command1_Click()
    RichTextBox1.UpTo ("1")
    RichTextBox1.Span ("1")
    RichTextBox1.SelCharOffset = -60

    RichTextBox1.UpTo ("2")
    RichTextBox1.Span ("2")
    RichTextBox1.SelCharOffset = 40
```

```
    RichTextBox1.UpTo ("1")
    RichTextBox1.Span ("1")
    RichTextBox1.SelCharOffset = -60
End Sub
```

That's it—the result of this code appears in Figure 6.15. Now even the physicists will be happy.

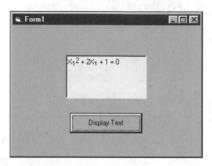

Figure 6.15   Using superscripts and subscripts in a rich text box.

Setting The Mouse Pointer In Text Boxes And Rich Text Boxes

You can set the mouse pointer when it travels over a text box or rich text box. Just set the **Mousepointer** property to one of the values in Table 6.1.

Table 6.1   Mouse pointer options.

Constant	Value	Description
rtfDefault	0	(Default) Shape determined by the object
rtfArrow	1	Arrow
rtfCross	2	Cross (cross-hair pointer)
rtfIbeam	3	I beam
rtfIcon	4	Icon (small square within a square)
rtfSize	5	Size (four-pointed arrow pointing north, south, east, and west)
rtfSizeNESW	6	Size NE SW (double arrow pointing northeast and southwest)
rtfSizeNS	7	Size N S (double arrow pointing north and south)
rtfSizeNWSE	8	Size NW, SE
rtfSizeEW	9	Size E W (double arrow pointing east and west)

(continued)

Table 6.1   Mouse pointer options (continued).

Constant	Value	Description
rtfUpArrow	10	Up arrow
rtfHourglass	11	Hourglass (wait)
rtfNoDrop	12	No drop
rtfArrowHourglass	13	Arrow and hourglass
rtfArrowQuestion	14	Arrow and question mark
rtfSizeAll	15	Size all
rtfCustom	99	Custom icon specified by the **MouseIcon** property

Searching For (And Replacing) Text In RTF Boxes

The users of your popular new word processor, *SuperDuperTextPro*, are still not satisfied. They find it inconvenient to search through 300-page documents for a particular word. Can you add search capability to your program? Better yet, they ask, how about search and replace?

Any word processor of any value will let the user search for text, and rich text boxes do that with the **Find()** method. For example, if we placed this text in a rich text box:

```
Private Sub Form_Load()
    RichTextBox1.Text = "Here is some text."
End Sub
```

Next, we could search for the word "some" this way with **Find()**:

```
Private Sub Command1_Click()
    RichTextBox1.Find ("some")
...
End Sub
```

After you find an item, it becomes the new selection. So, if we wanted to replace the word "some" with, say, "the", we could do that this way:

```
Private Sub Command1_Click()
    RichTextBox1.Find ("some")
    RichTextBox1.SelRTF = "the"
End Sub
```

In this way, we search for the word "some" in the text and replace it with "the", as shown in Figure 6.16.

Figure 6.16   Searching for and replacing text.

Saving RTF Files From Rich Text Boxes

You've gotten feedback from a user of your word processor, *SuperDuperTextPro*, and it seems she's written a 600-page novel with the program and now finds there's no way to save it to disk. Can you help? She will keep her computer on until she hears from you.

You use the **SaveFile()** method to save the text in a rich text box to disk, and doing that is really easy—you just use **SaveFile()** this way:

```
RichTextBox.SaveFile(pathname, [filetype])
```

You can save text as plain or RTF text; the settings for *filetype* are as follows:

- **rtfRTF**—0(the default) ; the RichTextBox control saves its contents as an RTF file.

- **rtfText**—1; the RichTextBox control saves its contents as a text file.

Here's an example where we display some text in a rich text box:

```
Private Sub Form_Load()
    RichTextBox1.Text = "This is the text in the file."
End Sub
```

Next, we save that text to a file this way:

```
Private Sub Command1_Click()
    RichTextBox1.SaveFile ("c:\data.txt")
End Sub
```

And that's all it takes. Now we've written RTF to a file.

TIP: *Many word processors, like Microsoft Word, support RTF files, so you can now write text formatted files that such word processors can read in and use.*

Reading RTF Files Into A Rich Text Box

You can write files to disk from a rich text box with **SaveFile( )**; how can you read files back in? You use **LoadFile( )**.

Like **SaveFile( )**, **LoadFile( )** is very easy to use:

```
RichTextBox.LoadFile pathname, [filetype]
```

And you can load in plain text or RTF text files; the settings for *filetype* are as follows:

- **rtfRTF**—0(The default); the RichTextBox control saves its contents as an RTF file.

- **rtfText**—1; the RichTextBox control saves its contents as a text file.

Here's an example where we load in the file we wrote in the last topic on saving files, data.txt:

```
Private Sub Command1_Click()
    RichTextBox1.LoadFile "c:\data.txt"
End Sub
```

That's all there is to it—it's that easy to load in files.

Printing From A Rich Text Box

You can print from a rich text box using the **SelPrint( )** method and the Visual Basic Printer object. The only thing to remember here is that you should first initialize the printer by printing a string of zero length or similar operation.

Here's how we print the last two words in the text "Printing this text..."; first, we display that text in the rich text box:

```
Private Sub Form_Load()
    RichTextBox1.Text = "Printing this text..."
End Sub
```

Next, we select the last two words:

```
Private Sub Command1_Click()
    RichTextBox1.Find ("this text...")
    RichTextBox1.SelLength = Len("this text...")
...
```

Finally, we print them. Note that we have to pass the handle of the device context with which we want to print to **SelPrint( )**, and here, that's the Printer object's device context, **Printer.hDC**:

```
Private Sub Command1_Click()
    RichTextBox1.Find ("this text...")
    RichTextBox1.SelLength = Len("this text...")
    Printer.NewPage
    RichTextBox1.SelPrint (Printer.hDC)
End Sub
```

Chapter 7

Command Buttons, Checkboxes, And Option Buttons

If you need an immediate solution to:	See page:
Setting A Button's Caption	229
Setting A Button's Background Color	229
Setting Button Text Color	230
Setting Button Fonts	231
Reacting To Button Clicks	232
Creating Button Control Arrays	233
Resetting The Focus After A Button Click	234
Giving Buttons Access Characters	235
Setting Button Tab Order	236
Disabling Buttons	236
Showing And Hiding Buttons	237
Adding Tool Tips To Buttons	238
Resizing And Moving Buttons From Code	239
Adding A Picture To A Button	239
Adding A Down Picture To A Button	241
Adding Buttons At Runtime	242
Passing Buttons To Procedures	243
Handling Button Releases	244
Making A Command Button Into A Cancel Button	244
Getting A Checkbox's State	245
Setting A Checkbox's State	245
Grouping Option Buttons Together	246

(continued)

If you need an immediate solution to:	See page:
Getting An Option Button's State	247
Setting An Option Button's State	247
Using Graphical Checkboxes And Radio Buttons	248
Using Checkboxes And Option Buttons Together	249

In Depth

In this chapter, we're going to take a look at what are arguably the most popular controls in Visual Basic: buttons. These include command buttons, checkboxes, and option buttons.

Command buttons—the plain buttons that you simply click and release—are the most common type of buttons. These are the buttons you see everywhere in Visual Basic applications. They are usually just rounded, rectangular, gray buttons with a caption.

Checkboxes are also familiar controls. You click a checkbox to select it and click it again to deselect it. When you select a checkbox, a checkmark appears in it, indicating that the box is indeed selected.

Option buttons, also called radio buttons, are like checkboxes in that you select and deselect them. However, they are round, whereas checkboxes are square, and you usually use option buttons together in groups. In fact, that's the functional difference between checkboxes and option buttons: checkboxes can work independently, but option buttons are intended to work in groups. When you select one option button in a group, the others are automatically deselected. For example, you might use checkboxes to select trimmings on a sandwich (of which there can be more than one), whereas you might use option buttons to let the user select one of a set of exclusive options, like the current day of the week.

You use tools in the toolbox to add command buttons, checkboxes, and option buttons to a form. In the toolbox in Figure 7.1, the Command Button tool is third down on the right, the Checkbox tool is fourth down on the left, and the Option Button tool is fourth down on the right.

How This Chapter Works

Because the three different types of buttons have many similar characteristics, it makes sense to cover them in the same chapter. In fact, the three types of buttons have so many properties and methods in common that when covering such topics, we'll refer to command buttons, checkboxes, and option buttons collectively as *buttons*.

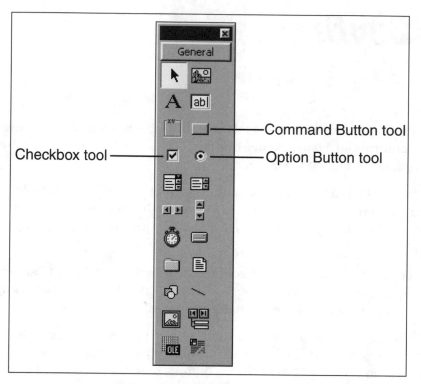

Checkbox tool ——————

—————— Command Button tool

—————— Option Button tool

Figure 7.1   The Command Button tool, the Checkbox tool, and the Option Button tool.

For example, all three controls have a **Caption** property, so when we cover how to set captions in those controls, we'll refer to them collectively as buttons. The title of that topic, then, is "Setting A Button's Caption." If we're covering something that refers to one type of button exclusively, I'll indicate that in the title of the topic, for example, "Grouping Option Buttons Together." In this way, we'll be able to address both what all the buttons have in common and what makes them useful independently.

That's all the introduction we need—we'll turn to the Immediate Solutions now.

Immediate Solutions

Setting A Button's Caption

You use a button's **Caption** property to set its caption. This property is available at both design time and runtime.

After you add a button to a form, you set its caption by placing the appropriate text in the **Caption** property in the Properties window. You can also change the button's caption at runtime, of course. As an example, we'll use our tic-tac-toe program from Chapter 1:

```
Private Sub Form_Load()
    xNow = True
End Sub

Private Sub Command_Click(Index As Integer)
    If xNow Then
        Command(Index).Caption = "x"
    Else
        Command(Index).Caption = "o"
    End If

    xNow = Not xNow

End Sub
```

TIP: *It's useful to be able to change the captions of buttons. For example, if a command button's caption reads Connect To Internet, then when you're connected you could change the button's caption to Disconnect From Internet, and disconnect from the Internet when the button is clicked.*

Setting A Button's Background Color

You've got your program running at last, but now the Aesthetic Design Department is on the phone. The "emergency" window in your program is colored red—why not the Panic button in the middle of that window also?

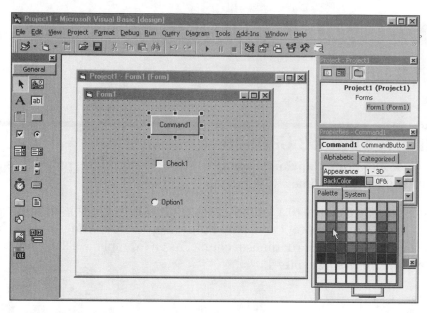

Figure 7.2   Setting a button's background color.

So, how do you do that? You can use the button's **BackColor** property, as shown in Figure 7.2. Note that you also have to set the button's **Style** property to **Graphical** (which has a numeric value of 1). We'll see more about graphical buttons later in this chapter. Here, we're setting the background color of a button at design time, and two sets of colors are available: a set of standard Visual Basic control colors (like "Button Face," "Button Shadow," and so on), and a palette of colors.

You can also set the button's **BackColor** property at runtime, setting it to a value using the **RGB()** function, which takes three parameters (0 to 255) for the red, green, and blue color values you want to set. Here, we change the color of a graphical button to red:

```
Command1.BackColor = RGB(255, 0, 0)
```

Setting Button
Text Color

Setting Button Text Color

You've got your graphic design program working at last. But wouldn't it be a nice touch if you could set the captions in the color-selection buttons to match the colors the buttons correspond to? For example, the button with the red text lets the user select red as the drawing color, the button with the green

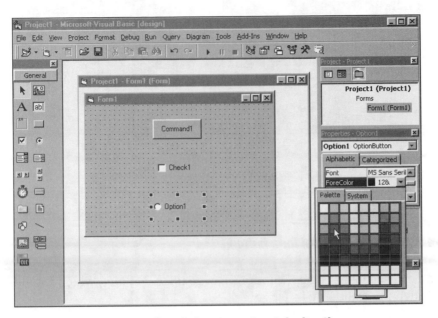

Figure 7.3   Setting a button's ForeColor property at design time.

text lets the user select green, and so on. You can set the color of a button's caption using the button's **ForeColor** property.

Interestingly, only checkboxes and option buttons have a **ForeColor** property; command buttons do not.

You set a button's **ForeColor** property at design time, as in Figure 7.3, or at runtime like this:

```
Private Sub Check1_Click()
    Check1.ForeColor = RGB(255, 0, 0)
End Sub
```

Setting Button Fonts

You've written an adventure-type game for your grandfather, but he's emailed to let you know he can't read the "tiny text" in the buttons. He likes to run his screen in super high-resolution mode. Can you fix that?

Yes you can. All you have to do is to make the font size in the buttons' captions larger. To do that, you use the button's **Font** property. Selecting the Font item in the Properties window opens the Font dialog box shown in Figure 7.4. As

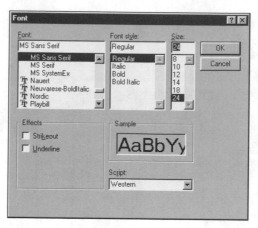

Figure 7.4   Selecting a font for a button.

you can see in that figure, captions can go up to 24 point, which should be big enough for grandfather.

Notice that there are number of options in the Font dialog box in Figure 7.4, which means that you can't set a single property at runtime to set a button's font. Instead, you can use the following properties:

- **FontBold**

- **FontItalic**

- **FontName**

- **FontSize**

- **FontStrikethru**

- **FontUnderline**

You also have direct access to the button's Font object, so you can set those properties by referring to them as, for example, **Option1.Font.Bold**, **Option1.Font.Italic**, and so on.

Reacting To
Button Clicks

Reacting To Button Clicks

For completeness, we'll include this one here: You respond to button clicks with the button's **Click** event. To add a **Click** event handler, just double-click the button at design time, which adds a subroutine like this one:

```
Private Sub Command1_Click()

End Sub
```

Place the code you want to execute when the button is clicked in this subroutine:

```
Private Sub Command1_Click()
    MsgBox "You clicked the command button!"
End Sub
```

All three buttons have a **Click** event—they wouldn't be much use otherwise—and option buttons also have a double-click event, **DblClick**. If you double-click a checkbox, you select and then deselect it (or deselect and then select it), so you're back to where you started. If you double-click an option button, however, you select it, no matter what its original state, and cause a **DblClick** event.

Creating Button Control Arrays

You've decided that your new game program really does need 144 buttons in the main form, arranged in a grid of 12×12. But what a pain it is to write 144 subroutines to handle the click event for each of them! Isn't there a better way?

There is. You use a control array and one event handler function (the control array index of the button that was clicked is passed to the event handler, so you can tell which button you need to respond to). To create a control array, just give two controls of the same type the same name (in the **Name** property); when you do, Visual Basic will ask if you want to create a control array, as in Figure 7.5.

When you create an event handler subroutine for a button in the control array, Visual Basic will automatically pass the index of the control in the control array to that subroutine:

```
Private Sub GamePiece_Click(Index As Integer)

End Sub
```

Figure 7.5   Creating a control array.

You can then refer to the control that caused the event as a member of an array, using the index passed to the subroutine:

```
Private Sub GamePiece_Click(Index As Integer)
    GamePiece(Index).Caption = "You clicked me!"
End Sub
```

TIP: *When you add controls to a control array, the first one has Index 0, the next has Index 1, and so on. You can change the index of each control with its **Index** property, rearranging the controls in the control array as you like.*

You can also create a control array with just one control—just set that control's **Index** property to 0. Later, you can add more controls to the array at runtime if you like, using the **Load** statement (see "Adding Buttons At Runtime" later in this chapter).

Resetting The Focus After A Button Click

When you click a button, the input focus is transferred to the button—and in some cases, you don't want that to happen. For example, say you've got a word-processor program based on a rich text box control, and you have a button labeled "Search" in the program. When the user clicks the button, then we can search for target text in the rich text box using that box's **UpTo( )** method—but the focus remains on the button the user clicked. When the user starts typing again, nothing appears in the rich text box control because the focus is still on the button. How do you transfer the focus back to the rich text box?

You do that with the control's **SetFocus( )** method, which is something you frequently do in real programs after button clicks. Here's how it might look in code:

```
Private Sub Command1_Click()
    RichTextBox1.UpTo (gstrStringToFind)
    RichTextBox1.SetFocus
End Sub
```

Now, when the user clicks the button and starts typing again, the focus will be back on the rich text box, as it should be. Note that you can set the control that has the focus when a form first appears by setting the control's **Default** property to True (only one control on a form may have that property set to True).

TIP: *Buttons also have two events—**GotFocus** and **LostFocus**—that can tell you when your button has gotten or lost the focus.*

Giving Buttons Access Characters

The Testing Department is on the phone again. Everyone loves your new program, *SuperDuperTextPro*, but as usual there are "one or two little things." And, as usual, one of those things is *keyboard access*. Ideally, they say, the user should be able to use programs entirely from the keyboard, without the mouse at all. Well, you say, the button's tab order was set correctly (see the next topic). But, they say, what about giving your buttons access characters?

You know you can give menu items access characters—those underlined characters in a menu item that the user can reach with the Alt key. Can you add them to buttons?

Yes, you can, and in the same way as you do with menu items. Just place an ampersand (&) in front of the character in the button's caption that you want to make into the access character for that button (and make sure that the access character is unique among all the access characters available at one time). As an example, we've given the buttons in Figure 7.6 access characters—note the ampersand in the **Caption** property in the Properties window.

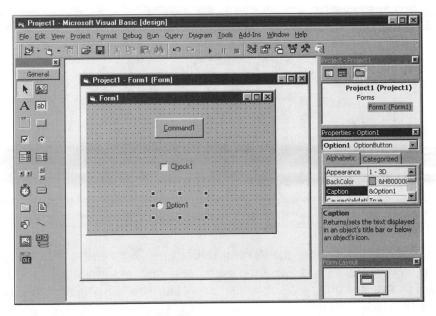

Figure 7.6   Setting access characters.

Setting Button Tab Order

To make your buttons more accessible from the keyboard—especially if you've got a lot of them—you can use the **TabStop**, **TabIndex**, and **Default** properties. Here's what those properties do:

- **TabStop** indicates if this button can accept the focus when the user tabs to it.
- **TabIndex** is the index of the current button in the tab order (starts at 0).
- **Default** is True for one control on a form only; that control will have the focus when the form first appears (by default, so to speak, the default control is the control with **TabIndex** 0).

When the user presses the Tab key, the focus moves from button to button, ascending through the tab order.

You can arrange the tab order for your buttons with the **TabIndex** property. For example, in Figure 7.7 the first button, at upper left, has the focus (you can tell because its border is thickened). Pressing the Tab key will move the focus to the next button, and the next, then to the next row, and so on.

TIP: Another use of tab order is in text-entry forms. If, for example, you have 10 text boxes in a row that need to be filled out, the user can enter text in the first one, press the Tab key to move to the next one, enter text there, press Tab again to move to the next text box, and so on. Thoughtfully setting the tab order in such a case can make text-oriented forms much easier on your users.

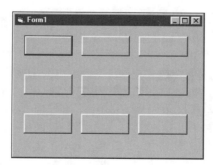

Figure 7.7   Using tab-enabled buttons.

Disabling Buttons

Another problem from the Testing Department concerning your program, *SuperDuperTextPro*. It seems the users are sometimes pressing your Connect To The Internet button twice by mistake, confusing the program and causing crashes. Can you stop that from happening?

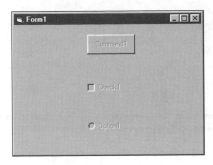

Figure 7.8   Disabling buttons in a form.

Yes, you can—you can disable the button by setting its **Enabled** property to False when it's inappropriate to use that button. For example, we've disabled all the buttons in Figure 7.8. When a button is disabled, it is inaccessible to the user (and it can't accept the focus).

You can also disable buttons at runtime, of course, like this:

```
Private Sub Command1_Click()
    Command1.Enabled = False
End Sub
```

---

*TIP: If you set a button's **Style** property to **Graphical (Style = 1**), you can set the button's **DisabledPicture** property to a picture, such as from an image file. And when the button is disabled, that image will appear in the button. That can be very useful to reinforce the fact that the button is disabled—you might have a big X appear, for example.*

Showing And Hiding Buttons

In the last topic, we saw that we can disable buttons using the **Enabled** property. However, it's an inefficient use of space (and frustrating to the user) to display a lot of disabled buttons. If you have to disable a lot of buttons, you should hide them.

To make a button disappear, just set its **Visible** property to False. To make it reappear, set the **Visible** property to True. You can set this property at either design time or runtime. Here's how to make a button disappear when you click it (and probably startle the user!):

```
Private Sub Command1_Click()
    Command1.Visible = False
End Sub
```

TIP: *If your program shows and hides buttons, you can rearrange the visible buttons to hide any gaps using the buttons' **Move** method (the **Move** method is discussed in "Resizing And Moving Buttons From Code" later in this chapter).*

Adding Tool Tips To Buttons

Your new word processor, *SuperDuperTextPro*, is a winner, but the User Interface Testing Department has a request—can you add *tool tips* to the buttons in your program? What's a tool tip, you ask? They say that it's one of those small yellow boxes with explanatory text that appears when you let the mouse cursor rest above an object on the screen. "Of course I can add *those*," you say—but can you really?

Yes you can, using the **ToolTipText** property for the buttons. You just place the text you want to appear in the tool tip into the **ToolTipText** property to create a tool tip for the button, and you're all set. For example, we've added a tool tip to the command button in Figure 7.9.

You can also set tool tip text at runtime, using the **ToolTipText** property this way in code:

```
Private Sub Command1_Click()
    Command1.ToolTipText = "You already clicked me!"
End Sub
```

If your buttons change functions as your program runs, changing the buttons' tool tip text can be very helpful to your program's users.

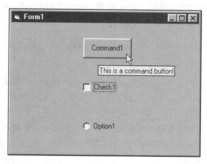

Figure 7.9   A button's tool tip.

Resizing And Moving Buttons From Code

Your new April Fool's program has an Exit button, but it moves around and resizes itself, making it a moving target for the user to try to hit. Your coworkers think it's hilarious and they love it. Your boss hates it and asks to see you in his cubicle to discuss time management—immediately.

How do you move buttons and resize them in code? You use the **Top**, **Left**, **Height**, and **Width** properties, or the **Move** method. Here's what those properties hold:

- **Left** holds the horizontal coordinate of the upper left of the button.

- **Top** holds the vertical coordinate of the upper left of the button.

- **Height** holds the button's height.

- **Width** holds the button's width.

(When setting these properties, remember that the default measurement units in Visual Basic are twips, and that the default coordinate system's origin is at upper left in a form.)

And here's how you use the **Move** method:

```
Button.Move left, [top, [width, [height]]]
```

Let's see an example; here, we move a command button 500 twips to the right when the user clicks it:

```
Private Sub Command1_Click()
    Const iIncrement = 500
    Command1.Move Command1.Left + iIncrement
End Sub
```

Adding A Picture To A Button

Your boss (who's been angling for a promotion) wants the company logo to appear in all the buttons in your program. Before you start looking for a new job, take a look at the Visual Basic **Picture** property.

Using the **Picture** property, you can load an image into a button—just click the button with the ellipsis (...) in the **Picture** property's entry in the Properties window and indicate an image file in the Load Picture dialog box that opens. That's not all, however—you also have to set the button's **Style** property to

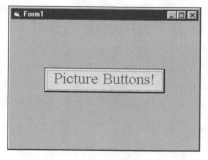

Figure 7.10   Adding a picture to a button.

Graphical (which has a numeric value of 1). We've loaded an image into a command button in Figure 7.10.

When you set checkboxes and option buttons to graphical style, they actually look just like graphical command buttons. The only difference is that when you click a graphical checkbox or option button, as shown in Figure 7.11, they stay clicked until you click them again (and option buttons still function in groups, of course).

You can also set the **Picture** property at runtime—but don't try setting it directly to the name of a file. You can only load Visual Basic Picture objects into the **Picture** property; such objects are returned by the **LoadPicture()** function like this:

```
Private Sub Command1_Click()
    Command1.Picture = LoadPicture("c:\vbbb\picturebuttons\image.bmp")
End Sub
```

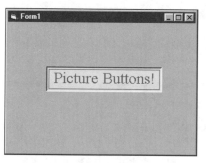

Figure 7.11   A graphical checkbox.

Adding A Down Picture To A Button

Besides adding a simple image to a button, you can add an image that is displayed when the button is down. This is more useful with checkboxes and option buttons—which stay down when clicked—than it is with command buttons.

Using the **DownPicture** property, you can load an image into a button—just click the button with the ellipsis (...) in the **DownPicture** property's entry in the Properties window, and indicate an image file in the Load Picture dialog box that opens.

You also have to set the button's **Style** property to **Graphical** (which has a numeric value of 1). For example, we've loaded a down image into a command button in Figure 7.12.

You can also set the **DownPicture** property at runtime using the **LoadPicture()** function:

```
Private Sub Check1_Click()
    Check1.DownPicture = LoadPicture("c:\vbbb\picturebuttons\image2.bmp")
End Sub
```

TIP: *You can also add an image to be displayed in a graphical button when it's disabled by using the* **DisabledPicture** *property.*

Figure 7.12   Adding a down picture to a graphical checkbox.

Adding Buttons At Runtime

Your new program lets the user add options to customize things, and you want to display a new button for each option. Is there a way to add buttons to a Visual Basic program at runtime?

Yes, there is. You can use the **Load** statement to load new buttons if they're part of a control array. To see how this works, add a new button to a form, giving it the name, say, "Command". To make it the first member of a control array, set its **Index** property to 0. Now when the user clicks this button, we can add a new button of the same type to the form with **Load**. Here, we load **Command(1)**, because **Command(0)** is already on the form:

```
Private Sub Command_Click(Index As Integer)
    Load Command(1)
...
End Sub
```

The new button is a copy of the original one—which includes the original button's position—so we move the new button so it doesn't cover the original one:

```
Private Sub Command_Click(Index As Integer)
    Load Command(1)
    Command(1).Move 0, 0
...
End Sub
```

Finally, we make the new button visible by setting its **Visible** property to True:

```
Private Sub Command_Click(Index As Integer)
    Load Command(1)
    Command(1).Move 0, 0
    Command(1).Visible = True
End Sub
```

And that's it—we've added a new button to the program at runtime.

TIP: You can also remove buttons at runtime by unloading them with **Unload**.

Passing Buttons To Procedures

You've got 200 buttons in your new program, and each one has to be initialized with a long series of code statements. Is there some easy way to organize this process? There is. You can pass the buttons to a procedure and place the initialization code in that procedure.

Here's an example. We can set a button's caption by passing it to a subroutine named **SetCaption( )** like this:

```
Private Sub Command1_Click()
    SetCaption Command1
End Sub
```

In the **SetCaption( )** procedure, you just declare the button as a parameter; we'll name that parameter **Button** and make it of type **Control**:

```
Private Sub SetCaption(Button As Control)

End Sub
```

Now we can refer to the passed button as we would any parameter passed to a procedure, like this:

```
Private Sub SetCaption(Button As Control)
    Button.Caption = "You clicked me!"
End Sub
```

The result appears in Figure 7.13—when you click the command button, the **SetCaption( )** subroutine changes its caption, as shown.

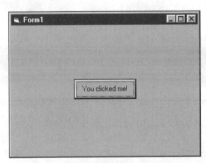

Figure 7.13   Passing a button to a procedure to change its caption.

Handling Button Releases

You can tell when a button's been pushed using its **Click** event, but can you tell when it's been released? Yes, using the **MouseUp** event. In fact, buttons support the **MouseDown**, **MouseMove**, **MouseUp**, **KeyDown**, **KeyPress**, and **KeyUp** events.

To determine when a button's been released, you can just use its **MouseUp** event this way:

```
Private Sub Command1_MouseUp(Button As Integer, Shift As Integer,_
    X As Single, Y As Single)
    MsgBox "You released the button."
End Sub
```

This can be useful if you want the user to complete some action that has two parts; for example, you can use **MouseDown** to begin changing (for example, incrementing or decrementing) a setting of some kind in realtime, giving the user interactive visual feedback, and you can use **MouseUp** to freeze the setting when the user releases the button.

Making A Command Button Into A Cancel Button

When you're designing dialog boxes, you usually include an OK button and a Cancel button. In fact, you can skip the OK button if you have other ways of letting the user select options (for example, a Finish button or a Yes button), but a Cancel button is just about required in dialog boxes. You should always have a Cancel button to let the user close the dialog box in case he has opened it by mistake or changed his mind.

Command buttons do have a **Cancel** property, and Microsoft recommends that you set it to True if you are making a command button into a Cancel button. Only one button can be a Cancel button in a form.

However, there doesn't seem to be much utility in making a command button into a Cancel button. There's nothing special about that button, really—it won't automatically close a dialog box, for example—except for one thing: when the user hits the Esc key, the Cancel button is automatically clicked. Using the Esc key is one way users have of closing dialog boxes, but it's not a very compelling reason to have a separate **Cancel** property for buttons.

Tellingly, the Cancel button in the predefined dialog box that comes with Visual Basic (you can add it when you select Project|Add Form) does not have its **Cancel** property set to True.

Getting A Checkbox's State

You've added all the checkboxes you need to your new program, *WinBigSuperCasino*, and you've connected those checkboxes to **Click** event handlers. But now there's a problem—when the users set the current amount of money they want to bet, you need to check if they've exceeded the limit they've set for themselves. But they set their limit by clicking another checkbox. How can you determine which one they've checked?

You can see if a checkbox is checked by examining its **Value** property (Visual Basic does have a **Checked** property, but that's only for menu items, a fact that has confused more than one programmer). Here are the possible **Value** settings for checkboxes:

- *0*—Unchecked
- *1*—Checked
- *2*—Grayed

Here's an example; in this case, we will change a command button's caption if a checkbox, **Check1**, is checked, but not otherwise:

```
Private Sub Command1_Click()
    If Check1.Value = 1 Then
        Command1.Caption = "The check mark is checked"
    End If
End Sub
```

Setting A Checkbox's State

Your new program, *SuperSandwichesToGoRightNow*, is just about ready, but there's one hitch. You use checkboxes to indicate what items are in a sandwich (cheese, lettuce, tomato, and more) to let users custom-build their sandwiches, but you also have a number of specialty sandwiches with preset ingredients. When the user selects one of those already-built sandwiches, how do you set the ingredients checkboxes to show what's in them?

You can set a checkbox's state by setting its **Value** property to one of the following:

- *0*—Unchecked
- *1*—Checked
- *2*—Grayed

Here's an example; In this case, we check a checkbox, **Check1**, from code:

```
Private Sub Command1_Click()
    Check1.Value = 1
End Sub
```

Here's another example that uses the Visual Basic **Choose( )** function to toggle a checkbox's state each time the user clicks the command button **Command1**:

```
Private Sub Command1_Click()
    Check1.Value = Choose(Check1.Value + 1, 1, 0)
End Sub
```

Grouping Option Buttons Together

Grouping Option Buttons Together

When you add option buttons to a form, they are automatically coordinated so that only one option button can be selected at a time. If the user selects a new option button, all the other options buttons are automatically deselected. But there are times when that's not convenient. For example, you may have two sets of options buttons: days of the week and day of the month. You want the user to be able to select one option button in each list. How do you group option buttons together into different groups on the same form?

You can use the frame control to group option buttons together (and, in fact, you can also use Picture Box controls). Just draw a frame for each group of option buttons you want on a form and add the option buttons to the frames (in the usual way—just select the Option Button tool and draw the option buttons in the frames). Each frame of option buttons will act as its own group, and the user can select one option button in either group, as shown in Figure 7.14.

For organizational purposes, and if appropriate, you might consider making the option buttons in each group into a control array, which can make handling multiple controls easier.

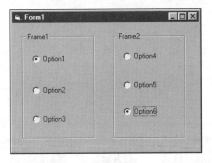

Figure 7.14   Grouping option buttons together using frames.

Getting An Option Button's State

You can check if an option button is selected or not with the **Value** property. Unlike checkboxes, which have three settings for the **Value** property (corresponding to checked, not checked, and grayed), option buttons' **Value** property only has two settings: True if the button is selected, and False if not.

Here's an example showing how to see whether or not an option button is selected. In this case, we display a message in a message box that indicates if an option button, **Option1**, is selected:

```
Private Sub Command1_Click()
    If Option1.Value Then
        MsgBox "The option button is selected."
    Else
        MsgBox "The option button is not selected."
    End If
End Sub
```

And that's all there is to it.

Setting An Option Button's State

Besides examining an option button's state, you can also set it using the **Value** property. The **Value** property can take two values: True or False.

Here's an example. In this case, we just set an option button, **Option1**, to its selected state by setting its **Value** property to True:

```
Private Sub Command1_Click()
    Option1.Value = True
End Sub
```

And that's all it takes.

Using Graphical Checkboxes And Radio Buttons

The Aesthetic Design Department is on the phone again. Your new program is fine, but it lacks a certain pizzazz. You say, *Pizzazz?* They say, how about using something better than option buttons? Something more *graphical*.

As it happens, Visual Basic can help out here, because it does support graphical—that is, image-oriented—buttons. You add an image to a button by connecting an image (as from an image file) to its **Picture** property. When you're working with checkboxes and option buttons, you should also set the button's **DownPicture** property to specify what image it should display when selected (in other words, when the button is "down").

Graphical checkboxes and option buttons look like image-bearing command buttons, not standard checkboxes and option buttons. The only way you tell them apart from command buttons when the program runs is that checkboxes and option buttons, when clicked, stay clicked (and, of course, option buttons still function in groups).

To see how this works, we set the **Picture** and **DownPicture** properties of a set of option buttons to image files (using the Picture and DownPicture entries in the Properties window). We also must set the **Style** property of the option buttons to 1 to make them graphical buttons, and then run the program. As you can see in Figure 7.15, the option buttons now display images: one when the button is selected and another (as in the top button in Figure 7.15) when the button is selected.

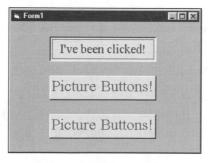

Figure 7.15   Using graphical option buttons.

You can also add images to buttons in code using the Visual Basic **LoadPicture( )** function. For example, here's how we load in a new down picture for **Option1** when the user clicks it:

```
Private Sub Option1_Click(Index As Integer)
    Option1.DownPicture = LoadPicture("c:\vbbb\picturebuttons\image.bmp")
End Sub
```

Using Checkboxes And Option Buttons Together

Your new assignment: to create a program for the SuperDuper Excelsior Tours travel agency. It wants to present users with a list of four tour packages they can choose from and to list the destination cities in each tour. But SuperDuper also wants to let users customize their tours to some extent, so they should be able to add or remove cities from a tour package.

Sounds like a job for Visual Basic. In fact, it sounds like a job for both option buttons and checkboxes, because this is just how they are intended to work together: the option buttons let you select one (and only one) option from a list, and the checkboxes display which item or items (that is, one or more than one) correspond to that option. And because checkboxes are interactive controls, users can use them to set the items they want.

To actually write the program the travel agency wants, we add two frames to a form, as shown in Figure 7.16, giving the first frame the caption "Tour" and the second frame the caption "Cities". In addition, add the option buttons and checkboxes you see in Figure 7.16.

When the user clicks Package 1, corresponding to the first tour package, we can indicate what cities are in this tour by setting the appropriate checkboxes:

Figure 7.16   The tour packages program.

```
Private Sub Option1_Click()
    Check1.Value = 1
    Check2.Value = 0
    Check3.Value = 1
    Check4.Value = 0
End Sub
```

And that's how the program works; we can do the same for the other option buttons now:

```
Private Sub Option2_Click()
    Check1.Value = 0
    Check2.Value = 1
    Check3.Value = 0
    Check4.Value = 1
End Sub

Private Sub Option3_Click()
    Check1.Value = 1
    Check2.Value = 1
    Check3.Value = 0
    Check4.Value = 0
End Sub

Private Sub Option4_Click()
    Check1.Value = 1
    Check2.Value = 1
    Check3.Value = 1
    Check4.Value = 1
End Sub
```

And that's it—now run the program as shown in Figure 7.16. When you click one option button, the corresponding tour's cities are displayed in the checkboxes; when you click another option button, that tour's cities are displayed.

This program, then, offers a good example of how the unique capabilities of option buttons and checkboxes may be integrated into the same program. The complete code for the form in Figure 7.16, tourpackages.frm, is located in the tourpackages folder on this book's accompaning CD-ROM.

Chapter 8

List Boxes And Combo Boxes

If you need an immediate solution to:	See page:
Adding Items To A List Box	254
Referring To Items In A List Box By Index	255
Responding To List Box Events	256
Removing Items From A List Box	257
Sorting A List Box	258
Determining How Many Items Are In A List Box	259
Determining If A List Box Item Is Selected	259
Using Multiselect List Boxes	261
Making List Boxes Scroll Horizontally	263
Using Checkmarks In A List Box	264
Clearing A List Box	264
Creating Simple Combo Boxes, Drop-Down Combo Boxes, And Drop-Down List Combo Boxes	265
Adding Items To A Combo Box	266
Responding To Combo Box Selections	267
Removing Items From A Combo Box	269
Getting The Current Selection In A Combo Box	270
Sorting A Combo Box	271
Clearing A Combo Box	272
Locking A Combo Box	272
Getting The Number Of Items In A Combo Box	273
Setting The Topmost Item In A List Box Or Combo Box	274
Adding Numeric Data To Items In A List Box Or Combo Box	275
Determining Where An Item Was Added In A Sorted List Box Or Combo Box	276
Using Images In Combo Boxes	277

In Depth

In this chapter, we're going to take a look at two popular Visual Basic controls: list boxes and combo boxes. These controls present the user with a list of items that the user can select from, and every Windows user is familiar with them.

List boxes do just what their name implies: display a list of items. The user can make a selection from that list, and Visual Basic will inform our program what's going on. Because list boxes can use scroll bars if a list gets too long, these controls are very useful to present long lists of items in a way that doesn't take up too much space.

Combo boxes are list boxes combined with text boxes. With combo boxes, you can give users the option of selecting from a list (usually a drop-down list activated when users click the downwards-pointing arrow at right in a combo box) or typing their selections directly into the text box part of the combo box.

List boxes and combo boxes share many properties, so it makes sense to look at them in the same chapter. The reason they share so many properties is that the basis of working with list boxes and combo boxes is item selection. For example, if your program lists various books for sale, you can present their titles in a list; clicking a book's name can display more information about the selected book. If you want to let the user set font size in a program, you might present font sizes in a combo box, and when the user selects a font size, the program can then read the selected size from the combo box.

Both list boxes and combo boxes are controls intrinsic to Visual Basic (in other words, you don't have to add them). You add list boxes to a form with the List Box tool, which is fifth down on the right in the toolbox in Figure 8.1, and combo boxes with the Combo Box tool, which is the fifth tool down on the left in the toolbox. There's nothing special about these controls here—you just add them as usual with the tools in the toolbox.

In overview, here's how you work with both list boxes and combo boxes: To add or delete items in one of these controls, use the **AddItem** or **RemoveItem** methods. You can use the **List**, **ListCount**, and **ListIndex** properties to enable a user to access items in the control (or you can add items to the list by using the **List** property at design time). When the user makes a selection, you can determine which item was selected with the **ListIndex** or **Text** properties.

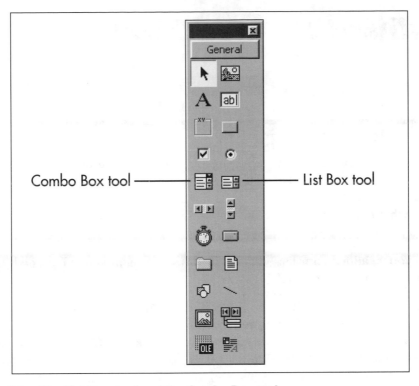

Combo Box tool ——————————————— List Box tool

Figure 8.1   The List Box tool and the Combo Box tool.

Both list boxes and combo boxes have **Click** and **DblClick** events, and the way you use these events depends on how you've defined your user interface (in other words, does clicking an item to select it in one of these controls launch an action, or does the user have to double-click the item?). It's important to realize that a combo box really is a text box and a list box—the **Click** events only work for the list part of a combo box. When the user makes changes to the text box part of the combo box by typing into that text box, a **Change** event (as is usual for text boxes) is triggered.

That's how you use the list box events: **Click** when the user clicks the list box, and **DblClick** when the user double-clicks it. For combo boxes, it's a little more complex: **Click** when the user clicks an item, **DblClick** when the user double-clicks an item (the **Style** of the combo box must be set to **Simple**, **Style = 1**, for the **DblClick** event to work), and **Change** when the user enters text. Note in particular that when the user makes a selection in a combo box's list box that changes the text in the text box, a **Change** event is *not* triggered; the **Change** event only occurs when the user types text into the combo box.

That's all the overview we need—we'll turn to the Immediate Solutions now.

Immediate Solutions

Adding Items To A List Box

The Testing Department is calling again, and they're telling you to get rid of all the beautiful buttons that you've placed on the main form of your program. But, you say, it's a program that lets the user buy computer parts. We have to list what computer parts are available. That's just it, they say, a list should go in a list box.

So you've added your list box, and now it's staring at you: a blank white box. How do you add items to the list box?

You can add items to a list box at either design time or at runtime. At design time, you can use the **List** property, which is a very handy array of the items in the list box; and at runtime, you can use both the **List** property and the **AddItem( )** method. Here's how you use the **List** property in code (keep in mind that you can get or set items in the list box with the **List** array):

```
ListBox.List(index) [= string]
```

How do you keep track of the total number of items in a list box? You use the **ListCount** property; that is, if you loop over the **List** array, you'll use **ListCount** as the maximum value to loop to.

At design time, you can add items directly to your list box by typing them into the **List** property in the Properties window. Selecting the **List** property displays a drop-down list (which is appropriate considering you're filling a list box), and you can type item after item into the list box that way.

At runtime, you can either use the indexed **List** property as detailed previously, or the **AddItem( )** method this way:

```
Private Sub Form_Load()
    List1.AddItem ("Item 1")
    List1.AddItem ("Item 2")
    List1.AddItem ("Item 3")
    List1.AddItem ("Item 4")
End Sub
```

Running this code gives us the list box in Figure 8.2.

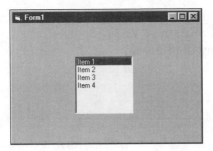

Figure 8.2   Placing items in a list box.

We should note that when you place items in a list box, they are stored by index, and you can refer to them by their index with the **List** property. See the next topic for more details.

Referring To Items In A List Box By Index

When you add items to a list box, each item is given an *index*, and you can refer to the item in the list box using this index (for example, you can get the item's text by using the **List** property: **List(*index*)**). The first item added to a list box gets the index 0, the next index 1, and so on.

When the user selects an item in a list box, you can get the selected item's index with the list box's **ListIndex** property. Let's see an example to make this clear. Here, we might just add four items, Item 0 to Item 3, to a list box this way with **AddItem( )**:

```
Private Sub Form_Load()
    List1.AddItem ("Item 0")
    List1.AddItem ("Item 1")
    List1.AddItem ("Item 2")
    List1.AddItem ("Item 3")
End Sub
```

This code places the four items into the list box with indexes 0 through 3 like this:

```
List(0) = "Item 0"
List(1) = "Item 1"
List(2) = "Item 2"
List(3) = "Item 3"
```

Now we can refer to the items in the list box by index using the **List** property as **List(0)**, **List(1)**, and so on. When the user clicks the list, causing a **Click** event, we can display the item number the user clicked with the **ListIndex** property, which holds the index of the currently selected item:

```
Private Sub List1_Click()
    MsgBox "You clicked item " & Str(List1.ListIndex)
End Sub
```

You can also change an item's index with its **Index** property like this:

```
List(index).Index = 3
```

In addition, you can sort items in a list box—see "Sorting A List Box" later in this chapter.

Responding To List Box Events

Now you've created your new list box, and it's a beauty. The boss is very pleased with it when you show your new program at the company's expo. The boss clicks the list box with the mouse—and nothing happens. The boss asks, Didn't you connect that list box to code? Oh, you think.

Click And DblClick

You use two main events with list boxes: **Click** and **DblClick**. How you actually use them is up to you, because different programs have different needs. For example, if a list box sets a new font that doesn't become active until a font chooser dialog box is closed, it's fine to respond to the **Click** event to display a sample of the font the user has selected in a text box. On the other hand, if you display the names of programs to launch in a text box, you should probably launch a program only after a user double-clicks it in the list box to avoid mistakes.

You use the **Click** event just as you use the **Click** event in a button, with a **Click** event handler. Here, we display the item in the list box the user has clicked, using the **ListIndex** property (you can get the selected item's text with **List1.List(ListIndex)** or with **List1.Text**):

```
Private Sub List1_Click()
    MsgBox "You clicked item " & Str(List1.ListIndex)
End Sub
```

And displaying the selected item is the same for **DblClick**—you just add a **DblClick** handler with the code you want:

```
Private Sub List1_DblClick()
    MsgBox "You clicked item " & Str(List1.ListIndex)
End Sub
```

Note, by the way, that a **DblClick** event also triggers the **Click** event, because to double-click an item, you must first click it.

Multiselect List Boxes

List boxes can also be multiselect list boxes (see "Using Multiselect List Boxes" later in this chapter), which means the user can select a number of items in the list box. If your list box is a multiselect box, you can determine which items the user has selected by using the **Selected** property this way:

```
For intLoopIndex = 0 To List1.ListCount - 1
    If List1.Selected(intLoopIndex) Then
...
    End If
Next intLoopIndex
```

*Removing Items
From A List Box*

Removing Items From A List Box

The Testing Department is calling again—how about letting the users customize your program? You ask, what do you mean? Well, they say, let's give the user some way of removing the 50 fine French cooking tips from the list box.

You can remove items from a list box at design time simply by deleting them in the **List** property. At runtime, you use the **RemoveItem()** method. Here's an example; in this case, we add four items, Items 0 through 3 to a list box:

```
Private Sub Form_Load()
    List1.AddItem ("Item 0")
    List1.AddItem ("Item 1")
    List1.AddItem ("Item 2")
    List1.AddItem ("Item 3")
End Sub
```

Item 0 has index 0 in the list box, Item 1 has index 1, and so on. To remove, say, Item 1 when the user clicks a command button, we can use **RemoveItem** and pass it the item's index:

```
Private Sub Command1_Click()
    List1.RemoveItem 1
End Sub
```

Running the program and clicking the button gives the result shown in Figure 8.3. Now we're able to remove items from a list box.

TIP: *You should note that removing an item from a list box changes the indexes of the remaining items. After you remove Item 1 in the preceding example, Item 2 now gets index 1 and Item 3 gets index 2. If you want to change those indexes back to their original values, set the items' **Index** properties.*

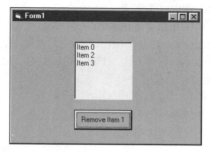

Figure 8.3   Removing an item from a list box.

Sorting A List Box

You're very proud of your new program's list box, which lists *all* the classical music recordings available for the last 40 years. But the Testing Department isn't so happy. They ask, Can't you *alphabetize* that list?

You can alphabetize the items in a list box by setting its **Sorted** property to True (it's False by default) at design time or runtime. That's all it takes. (In fact, I've known lazy programmers who sorted arrays of text by placing the text into a hidden list box and then read it back to save writing the code for the string comparisons!)

TIP: *You should know, however, that sorting a list box can change the indexes of the items in that list box (unless they were already in alphabetical order). After the sorting is finished, the first item in the newly sorted list has index 0, the next index 1, and so on. If you want to change the indexes of the items back to their original values, you can set their **Index** properties.*

Determining How Many Items Are In A List Box

You want to loop over the items in your list box to find out if a particular item is in the list, but you need to know how many items are in the list box in order to set up the loop. How can you set up the loop?

You can use the **ListCount** property to determine how many items are in a list box. When setting up loops over the items in a list box, you should note that **ListCount** is the total number of items in a list, whereas index values start at 0, not 1. This means that if you're looping over indices, you should loop to **ListCount - 1**, not **ListCount**.

Let's see an example. Here, we'll search a list box to see if it has an item whose caption is "Item 1". First, we set up the loop over the indexes of the items in the list box:

```
Private Sub Command1_Click()
    Dim intLoopIndex As Integer
    For intLoopIndex = 0 To List1.ListCount - 1
...
    Next intLoopIndex
End Sub
```

Then we check the caption of each item, checking for the caption "Item 1", and report if we find that item:

```
Private Sub Command1_Click()
    Dim intLoopIndex As Integer
    For intLoopIndex = 0 To List1.ListCount - 1
        If List1.List(intLoopIndex) = "Item 1" Then
            MsgBox "Found item 1!"
        End If
    Next intLoopIndex
End Sub
```

Determining If A List Box Item Is Selected

The big point of list boxes is to let the user make selections, of course, and there are a number of properties to handle that process. Here's an overview.

You get the index of the selected item in a list box with the **ListIndex** property. If no item is selected, **ListIndex** will be –1.

You can get the text of a list's selected item as **List1.Text** or **List1**.**List(List1.ListIndex)**.

You can use a list box's **Selected** array to determine if individual items in the list box are selected or not. Let's see an example to see how that works; in this case, we'll loop over the elements in the list box until we find the selected one.

We start by loading items into the list box when the form loads:

```
Private Sub Form_Load ()
    List1.AddItem ("Item 0")
    List1.AddItem ("Item 1")
    List1.AddItem ("Item 2")
    List1.AddItem ("Item 3")
    List1.AddItem ("Item 4")
    List1.AddItem ("Item 5")
    List1.AddItem ("Item 6")
    List1.AddItem ("Item 7")
End Sub
```

When the user clicks a command button, we can indicate which item is selected in the list box by displaying that item's caption in a message box. We just loop over all the items in the list box:

```
Private Sub Command1_Click ()
    Dim intLoopIndex
    For intLoopIndex = 0 To List1.ListCount - 1
...
    Next intLoopIndex
End Sub
```

And we check the **Selected** array for each item to find the selected item:

```
Private Sub Command1_Click ()
    Dim intLoopIndex
    For intLoopIndex = 0 To List1.ListCount - 1
        If List1.Selected(intLoopIndex) Then
            MsgBox "You selected " & List1.List(intLoopIndex)
        End If
    Next intLoopIndex
End Sub
```

Note that list boxes can support multiple selections if you set their **MultiSelect** property to True. See the next topic in this chapter to see how to handle selections in multiselect list boxes.

Using Multiselect List Boxes

Everyone's very pleased with your new program to sell classical music CDs—except for the Sales Department. Why, they want to know, can the user only buy one CD at a time? Well, you explain, the program uses a list box to display the list of CDs, and when the user makes a selection, the program orders that CD. They ask, How about using a multiselect list box? So what's that?

A multiselect list box allows the user to select a number of items at one time. You make a list box into a multiselect list box with the **MultiSelect** property. The user can then select multiple items using the Shift and Ctrl keys. Here are the possible settings for **MultiSelect**:

- *0*—Multiple selection isn't allowed (this is the default).
- *1*—Simple multiple selection. A mouse click or pressing the spacebar selects or deselects an item in the list. (Arrow keys move the focus.)
- *2*—Extended multiple selection. Pressing the Shift key and clicking the mouse or pressing the Shift key and one of the arrow keys extends the selection from the previously selected item to the current item. Pressing the Ctrl key and clicking the mouse selects or deselects an item in the list.

---

*TIP: The **DblClick** event isn't very useful with multiselect list boxes, because when you click the list box a second time, every item but the one you've clicked is deselected. In addition, a **Click** event is generated each time the user selects a new item, and you might want to wait until all selections are made before taking action. This is why you often use a command button to initiate action after a user selects items in a multiselect list box. Take a look at the following example to see how this works.*

Let's see an example of a multiselect list box at work. In this case, we'll have two list boxes, **List1** and **List2**, as well as a command button displaying an arrow (here, we'll just give a button the caption "—>" to display the arrow). Set **List1**'s **MultiSelect** property to 1. When the user selects a number of items in **List1** and clicks the button with an arrow, we'll copy the selected items in **List1** to **List2**, as in Figure 8.4.

We start by loading items into **List1** when the form loads:

```
Private Sub Form_Load ()
    List1.AddItem ("Item 0")
    List1.AddItem ("Item 1")
    List1.AddItem ("Item 2")
    List1.AddItem ("Item 3")
    List1.AddItem ("Item 4")
    List1.AddItem ("Item 5")
```

```
      List1.AddItem ("Item 6")
      List1.AddItem ("Item 7")
End Sub
```

Next, when the user clicks the command button to indicate he has made all the selections he wants, we loop over the list this way:

```
Private Sub Command1_Click ()
    Dim intLoopIndex
    For intLoopIndex = 0 To List1.ListCount - 1
    ...
    Next intLoopIndex
End Sub
```

In the loop, we see which items were selected and move them to the other list box, **List2**:

```
Private Sub Command1_Click ()
    Dim intLoopIndex
    For intLoopIndex = 0 To List1.ListCount - 1
        If List1.Selected(intLoopIndex) Then
            List2.AddItem List1.List(intLoopIndex)
        End If
    Next intLoopIndex
End Sub
```

The result appears in Figure 8.4, where we're letting the user make multiple selections using the mouse, Shift, and Ctrl keys.

Note that we looped over every item in the list box to see if it was selected or not—is this necessary? Aren't there **SelStart** and **SelLength** properties for the list box as there are for text boxes? Those properties don't exist for list boxes, because the selected items in a multiselect list box may not be contiguous, which also means that we do indeed have to loop over all items in the list box, checking each one individually to see if it's been selected.

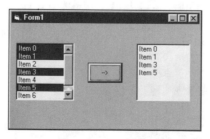

Figure 8.4   Selecting multiple items in a multiselect list box.

Making List Boxes Scroll Horizontally

It's a pity that there's so little vertical space for the list box in your new program's layout—the user can only view 4 of the more than 40 items in the list box at once. Can't you make a list box work horizontally instead of vertically?

Yes you can, if you break up the list into *columns* using the **Columns** property. When that property is set to 0, the default, the list box presents just a vertical list to the user. When you set the **Columns** property to another value, the list box displays its items in that number of columns instead.

Let's see an example—can multiselect list boxes also be multicolumn list boxes? They sure can; take a look at Figure 8.5.

In this example, we've just set **List1**'s **Columns** property to 2 and used the same code we developed for our multiselect example, which transfers selected items from **List1** to **List2** when the user clicks the command button (if you've made **List1** large, you might have to make it smaller before it will display the items in a number of columns rather than one large column):

```
Private Sub Command1_Click ()
    Dim intLoopIndex
    For intLoopIndex = 0 To List1.ListCount - 1
        If List1.Selected(intLoopIndex) Then
            List2.AddItem List1.List(intLoopIndex)
        End If
    Next intLoopIndex
End Sub
```

Now the user can select multiple items from the columns in **List1** and transfer them to **List2** at the click of a button.

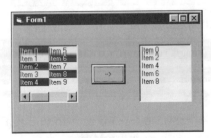

Figure 8.5   A multiselect multicolumn list box.

Using Checkmarks In A List Box

The Aesthetic Design Department has sent you a memo. People are so tired, they write, of standard list boxes. Can't you punch them up a little in your program, *SuperDuperTextPro*? Suppressing your immediate response, which is to tell the Aesthetic Design Department just what you think of them in rather direct terms, you give the problem a little thought. Well, you decide, I could use those new checkmark list boxes.

When you use checkmark list boxes, selected items appear with a checkmark in front of them. You can make a list box into a checkmark list box with its **Style** property, which can take these values:

- *0*—Standard list box (the default)
- *1*—Checkmark list box

For example, the list box in Figure 8.6 has its **Style** property set to 1, making it a checkmark list box.

TIP: By default, checkmark list boxes can support multiple selections; the **MultiSelect** property of these list boxes must be set to 0.

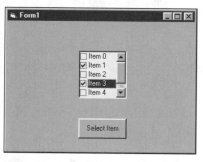

Figure 8.6   Using checkmark list boxes.

Clearing A List Box

It's time to load new items into a list box—do you really have to clear the old items out one at a time with **RemoveItem**?

You can use the **Clear** method to clear a list box. Nothing could be easier (so be careful—there's no "undelete" function here!). You just use clear like this: *List*.**Clear**.

Here's how that looks in code; in this case, we're clearing a list box, **List1**, when the user clicks a command button:

```
Private Sub Command1_Click()
    List1.Clear
End Sub
```

Creating Simple Combo Boxes, Drop-Down Combo Boxes, And Drop-Down List Combo Boxes

Combo boxes are those controls that usually display a text box and a drop-down list. In fact, you might think there is only one kind of combo box, but there are really *three* types, and you select which type you want with the combo box's **Style** property. The default type of combo box is probably what you think of when you think of combo boxes, because, as mentioned, it is made up of a text box and a drop-down list. However, you can also have combo boxes where the list doesn't drop down (the list is always open, and you have to make sure to provide space for it when you add the combo box to your form) and combo boxes where the user can only select from the list.

Here are the settings for the combo box **Style** property:

- **VbComboDropDown**—0; drop-down combo box. Includes a drop-down list and a text box. The user can select from the list or type in the text box. (This the default.)

- **VbComboSimple**—1; simple combo box. Includes a text box and a list, which doesn't drop down. The user can select from the list or type in the text box. The size of a simple combo box includes both the edit and list portions. By default, a simple combo box is sized so that none of the list is displayed. Increase the **Height** property to display more of the list.

- **VbComboDrop-DownList**—2; drop-down list. This style allows a selection only from the drop-down list. This is a good one to keep in mind when you want to restrict the user's input; however, if you want to use this one, you should also consider simple list boxes. The selected item appears in the (read-only) text box.

Adding Items To A Combo Box

You've added a new combo box to your program, and it looks great. When you run it, however, all you see is "Combo1" in it. How do you add items to your combo box?

A combo box is a combination of a text box and a list box, so at design time, you can change the text in the text box part by changing the **Text** property. You change the items in the list box part with the **List** property (this item opens a drop-down list when you click it in the Properties window) at design time.

At runtime, you can add items to a combo box using the **AddItem( )** method, which adds items to the list box part. You can also add items to the list box using the **List** property, which is an indexed array of items in the list box. If you want to set text in the text box, set the combo box's **Text** property.

Here's an example; in this case, we add four items to a combo box's list:

```
Private Sub Form_Load()
    Combo1.AddItem ("Item 0")
    Combo1.AddItem ("Item 1")
    Combo1.AddItem ("Item 2")
    Combo1.AddItem ("Item 3")
End Sub
```

You can also add items to the list with the **List** property. Here we create a fifth item and give it a caption this way:

```
Private Sub Form_Load()
    Combo1.AddItem ("Item 0")
    Combo1.AddItem ("Item 1")
    Combo1.AddItem ("Item 2")
    Combo1.AddItem ("Item 3")
    Combo1.List(4) = "Item 4"
End Sub
```

That's it—the result appears in Figure 8.7.

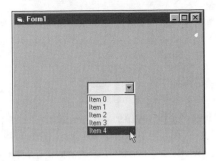

Figure 8.7   A newly filled combo box.

Responding To Combo Box Selections

So you've installed a new combo box in your program, *SuperDuperTextPro*, to let the user select new text font sizes, and the combo box is staring at you— just a blank box. How do you connect it to your code?

Combo boxes are combinations of text boxes and list boxes, and that combination means that there are two sets of input events: **Change** events when the user types into the text box and **Click** or **DblClick** when the user uses the mouse. Note that, unlike standard list boxes, you cannot make multiple selections in a combo box's list box.

Change Events

When the user changes the text in a combo box, a **Change** event occurs, just as it does when the user types in a standard text box. You can read the new text in the text box with the **Text** property. For example, here's how we display the new text in the combo box every time the user changes that text by typing:

```
Private Sub Form_Load()
    Combo1.AddItem ("Item 0")
    Combo1.AddItem ("Item 1")
    Combo1.AddItem ("Item 2")
    Combo1.AddItem ("Item 3")
End Sub

Private Sub Combo1_Change()
    MsgBox "New text is: " & Combo1.Text
End Sub
```

TIP: *Here's a fact that takes many programmers by surprise: no **Change** event occurs when you use the mouse to select an item in a combo box's list, even if doing so changes the text in the combo's text box. The only event that occurs is **Click** (or **DblClick**) when the user uses the mouse.*

Click Events

You can also get **Click** events when the user makes a selection in the list box using the mouse. You can determine which item the user clicked using the combo's **ListIndex** property (which holds the index of the clicked item) or get that item's text using the **Text** property, because when you click an item, it is made the new selected item in the text box. Here's an example using the **ListIndex** property; in this case, we report to the user which item in the combo box he has clicked:

```
Private Sub Form_Load()
    Combo1.AddItem ("Item 0")
    Combo1.AddItem ("Item 1")
    Combo1.AddItem ("Item 2")
    Combo1.AddItem ("Item 3")
End Sub

Private Sub Combo1_Click()
    MsgBox "You clicked item " & Str(Combo1.ListIndex)
End Sub
```

DblClick Events

You might expect that where there are **Click** events there are **DblClick** events, and that's true—but for simple combo boxes only (**Style = VbComboSimple**, where **VbComboSimple** is a Visual Basic constant that equals 1). When you click an item in the list part of a combo box once, the list closes, so it's impossible to double-click an item—except in simple combo boxes, where the list stays open at all times.

For simple combo boxes, then, we can support the **DblClick** event this way:

```
Private Sub Form_Load()
    Combo1.AddItem ("Item 0")
    Combo1.AddItem ("Item 1")
    Combo1.AddItem ("Item 2")
    Combo1.AddItem ("Item 3")
End Sub

Private Sub Combo1_DblClick()
    MsgBox "You double clicked item " & Str(Combo1.ListIndex)
End Sub
```

Removing Items From A Combo Box

Just as with list boxes, you can remove items from combo boxes using the **RemoveItem( )** method. You just pass the index of the item you want to remove from the combo box's list to **RemoveItem( )**.

Here's an example. In this case, we can add four items to a combo box, Items 0 through 3, when the combo box's form loads:

```
Private Sub Form_Load()
    Combo1.AddItem ("Item 0")
    Combo1.AddItem ("Item 1")
    Combo1.AddItem ("Item 2")
    Combo1.AddItem ("Item 3")
End Sub
```

Next, we remove Item 1 in the list this way:

```
Private Sub Command1_Click()
    Combo1.RemoveItem 1
End Sub
```

And that's it—now Item 1 is gone (see Figure 8.8).

TIP: You should note that removing an item from a combo box changes the indexes of the remaining items. After you remove Item 1 in the preceding example, Item 2 now gets Index 1 and Item 3 gets Index 2. If you want to change those indexes back to their original values, set the items' **Index** properties.

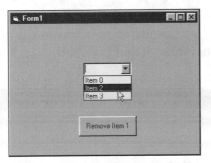

Figure 8.8   *Removing an item from a combo box.*

Getting The Current Selection In A Combo Box

When you make a selection in a combo box, that new selection appears in the combo box's text box, so it's easy to get the current selection—you just use the combo box's **Text** property.

For example, say we've added these items to a combo box:

```
Private Sub Form_Load()
    Combo1.AddItem ("Item 0")
    Combo1.AddItem ("Item 1")
    Combo1.AddItem ("Item 2")
    Combo1.AddItem ("Item 3")
End Sub
```

Then, when the user clicks a command button, we can get the text of the current selection in the combo box this way, using the **Text** property.

```
Private Sub Command1_Click()
    MsgBox "New text is: " & Combo1.Text
End Sub
```

That's the way to do it—when you need to know what the current selection in a combo box is, you can use the **Text** property.

You can also get the currently selected item's index in the combo box's list using the **ListIndex** property. If no selection is made (for instance, when the form first loads and the combo's text box is empty), this property will return –1. If the user has altered the selection by typing into the text box (in other words, so the selected item no longer matches the item the combo box's list), **ListIndex** will also be –1. And if the user opens the combo box's list and then clicks outside that list without making a selection, **ListIndex** is set to –1.

Here's an example in which we display the index of the currently selected item using **ListIndex**. First, we fill the combo box with items:

```
Private Sub Form_Load()
    Combo1.AddItem ("Item 0")
    Combo1.AddItem ("Item 1")
    Combo1.AddItem ("Item 2")
    Combo1.AddItem ("Item 3")
End Sub
```

Then we can display the index of the current selection when the user clicks a command button using **ListIndex** this way:

```
Private Sub Command1_Click()
    MsgBox Str(Combo1.ListIndex)
End Sub
```

TIP: *If you want to restrict the user's input to items from the combo box's list, set the combo box's **Style** property to **VbComboDrop-DownList**, a predefined Visual Basic constant whose value is 2. In this style of combo boxes, the user cannot type into the text part of the control.*

Sorting A Combo Box

You've been newly commissioned to write the guidebook to the local zoo with Visual Basic, and everything looks great—except for one thing. The program features a combo box with a list of animals that the user can select to learn more about each animal, and it would be great if you could make that list appear in alphabetical order. The zoo, however, keeps adding and trading animals all the time. Still, it's no problem, because you can leave the work up to the combo box itself if you set its **Sorted** property to True (the default is False).

For example, say we set the **Sorted** property to True for a combo box, **Combo1**. Now it doesn't matter in what order you add items to that combo box

```
Private Sub Form_Load()
    Combo1.AddItem ("zebra")
    Combo1.AddItem ("tiger")
    Combo1.AddItem ("hamster")
    Combo1.AddItem ("aardvark")
End Sub
```

because all the items will be sorted automatically. The sorted combo box appears in Figure 8.9. Now you'll be able to handle the animals from aardvark to zebra automatically.

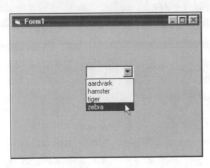

Figure 8.9   Sorting the items in a combo box.

---

*TIP: You should know, however, that sorting a combo box can change the indexes of the items in that combo box (unless they were already in alphabetical order). After the sorting is finished, the first item in the newly sorted combo list has Index 0, the next Index 1, and so on. If you want to change the indexes of the items back to their original values, you can set their **Index** properties.*

Clearing A Combo Box

It's time to put new items into a combo box—but does that mean you have to delete all the current items there one by one with **RemoveItem( )**?

No, you can clear a whole combo box at once with the **Clear( )** method. Here's an example. First, we add items to a combo box:

```
Private Sub Form_Load()
    Combo1.AddItem ("Item 0")
    Combo1.AddItem ("Item 1")
    Combo1.AddItem ("Item 2")
    Combo1.AddItem ("Item 3")
End Sub
```

Then we can clear the combo box when the user clicks a command button:

```
Private Sub Command1_Click()
    Combo1.Clear
End Sub
```

Note that there is no "unclear" method! Once you remove the items from a combo box, they're gone until you expressly add them again.

Locking A Combo Box

You can *lock* a combo box by setting its **Locked** property to True. When locked, the user cannot enter text in the combo's text box and cannot make selections from the combo's list (although if the list is drop-down, it will still open). However, when programmers think of "locking" a combo box, it's not usually the **Locked** property that they want.

The more common operation is to restrict the user's ability to enter text in a combo box so that he must instead select one of the items in the combo's list. You can make sure that the user can't enter text in the combo box's text box by setting the combo box's **Style** property to **VbComboDrop-DownList**. Here are the settings for the combo box **Style** property:

- **VbComboDropDown**—0; drop-down combo box. Includes a drop-down list and a text box. The user can select from the list or type in the text box. (This is the default.)

- **VbComboSimple**—1; simple combo box. Includes a text box and a list, which doesn't drop down. The user can select from the list or type in the text box. The size of a simple combo box includes both the cdit and list portions. By default, a simple combo box is sized so that none of the list is displayed; size the combo box to display more of the list.

- **VbComboDrop-DownList**—2; drop-down list. This style allows a selection only from the drop-down list. This is a good one to keep in mind when you want to restrict the user's input, but if you want to use this one, you should also consider simple list boxes.

Besides locking or setting the **Style** property of a combo box, you can also disable a combo box, of course, by setting its **Enabled** property to False; however, this grays out the control and makes it completely inaccessible. Another option is to make the combo box disappear by setting its **Visible** property to False (setting the **Visible** property to True makes the combo box reappear).

Getting The Number Of Items In A Combo Box

You're trying to bend over backwards to make your program user-friendly and have let the user add items to the main combo box. But now you need to see if he has added a particular item to the combo box. How do you find out how many items there are in the combo box currently so you can set up your loop?

You can use a combo box's **ListCount** property to determine how many items are in the combo box's list. Let's see how to use **ListCount** in an example. Here, we'll search the items in a combo box for one particular item with the caption "Item 1", and if we find it, we'll display a message box.

We start by setting up our loop over the indexes of all the items in the combo box this way (note that we subtract 1 from **ListCount** because indices are zero-based):

```
Private Sub Command1_Click()
    Dim intLoopIndex As Integer
    For intLoopIndex = 0 To Combo1.ListCount - 1
...
```

```
        Next intLoopIndex
End Sub
```

Then we search the indexed **List** property for the item we want and, if we find it, report that fact to the user:

```
Private Sub Command1_Click()
    Dim intLoopIndex As Integer
    For intLoopIndex = 0 To Combo1.ListCount - 1
        If Combo1.List(intLoopIndex) = "Item 1" Then
            MsgBox "Found item 1!"
        End If
    Next intLoopIndex
End Sub
```

Setting The Topmost Item In A List Box Or Combo Box

One of the properties of list and combo boxes, the **TopIndex** property, has fooled a lot of programmers, because according to Microsoft, this property lets you set the topmost item in a list box or combo box's list. However, what that seems to mean is not exactly how it works.

When you set a list box or combo box's **TopIndex** property to some value, the items in the list are *not* reordered (if you want to reorder them, use the items' **Index** properties or the control's **Sorted** property). What **TopIndex** does is to set the topmost *visible* item in the list in those cases where not all items in the list are visible (in other words, if the list has scroll bars on the side).

Let's see an example. Here we place some items into a simple combo box (in other words, a simple combo box has its list permanently open and its **Style** property is set to **VbComboSimple**, whose value is 1):

```
Private Sub Form_Load()
    Combo1.AddItem ("Item 0")
    Combo1.AddItem ("Item 1")
    Combo1.AddItem ("Item 2")
    Combo1.AddItem ("Item 3")
End Sub
```

When the user clicks a command button, we can make Item 2 topmost in the visible portion of the list:

```
Private Sub Command1_Click()
    Combo1.TopIndex = 2
End Sub
```

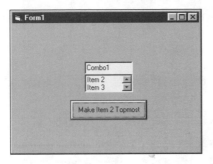

Figure 8.10   Making an item topmost.

The result appears in Figure 8.10. When you click the button, the list scrolls automatically so Item 2 is the topmost visible item (note that this scrolling operation only occurs if not all items in the list are visible at once).

---

*TIP: The reason for **TopIndex**'s existence is to make life easier for users when they are working with long lists. Each time they reopen a list, it's a pain to have to scroll down to the former location just to be able to select the following item. For this reason, programs often "remember" the last-selected item in a list and make that topmost when the list is opened again.*

Adding Numeric Data To Items In A List Box Or Combo Box

You've been asked to write the employee phone directory program and place a combo box with all the employee's names in the middle of a form. Now how do you connect phone numbers to the names?

You can use a list box's or combo box's **ItemData** array to hold **Long** integers, because that array is indexed in the same way as the control's items themselves are indexed. That is, you can store numeric data for Item 5 in the list or combo box in **ItemData(5)**.

Let's see an example to make this easier. Here, we add four items to a combo box when its form loads:

```
Private Sub Form_Load()
    Combo1.AddItem ("Item 0")
    Combo1.AddItem ("Item 1")
    Combo1.AddItem ("Item 2")
    Combo1.AddItem ("Item 3")
    ...
```

Next, we add numeric data to each item in the combo box:

```
Private Sub Form_Load()
    Combo1.AddItem ("Item 0")
    Combo1.AddItem ("Item 1")
    Combo1.AddItem ("Item 2")
    Combo1.AddItem ("Item 3")

    Combo1.ItemData(0) = 0
    Combo1.ItemData(1) = 111
    Combo1.ItemData(2) = 222
    Combo1.ItemData(3) = 333
End Sub
```

Now when the user clicks an item in the combo box, we can indicate what that item's numeric data is with a message box:

```
Private Sub Combo1_Click()
    MsgBox "Data for the clicked item is: " & _
        Str(Combo1.ItemData(Combo1.ListIndex))
End Sub
```

In this way, you're able to store more than just text for list or combo box items.

TIP: *Associating simple numbers with your list or combo box items isn't enough? What if you have more data? Try using the* **ItemData** *value as an index into an array of data structures instead.*

Determining Where An Item Was Added In A Sorted List Box Or Combo Box

You're letting the user customize a combo box by adding items to the combo box, and in code, you place data into the **ItemData** array for this item after it's been added. But there's a problem—this is a *sorted* combo box (or list box), which means you don't know the item's actual index when it's added, and you therefore don't know its index in the **ItemData** array. How can you find out where the item was placed in the sorted combo box?

You can use the control's **NewIndex** property to determine the index of the most recently added item to the control. For example, let's say that the user can add items to a sorted combo box by placing the text of the new item in a text box and clicking a command button:

```
Private Sub Command1_Click()
    Combo1.AddItem (Text1.Text)
End Sub
```

The index of the new item in the sorted list is now in the **NewIndex** property, so we can add data to the new item's entry in the **ItemData** array (if you don't know what this array does, see the previous topic) and display that data in a message box this way:

```
Private Sub Command2_Click()
    Combo1.ItemData(Combo1.NewIndex) = 10000
    MsgBox "Data for the new item is: " & _
        Str(Combo1.ItemData(Combo1.NewIndex))
End Sub
```

Using Images In Combo Boxes

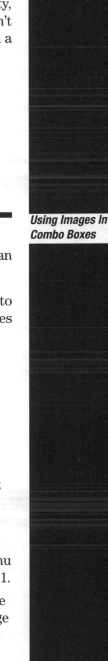

Using Images In Combo Boxes

We've seen in this book that you can add images to menus and to buttons. Can you add images to combo boxes? Yes, you can, using *image combo* boxes.

Image combo boxes are one of the Windows common controls, so you have to add those controls to your project. Here's how you install image combo boxes step-by-step:

1. Select the Project|Components menu item.
2. Select the Controls tab in the Components box that opens.
3. Click the Microsoft Windows Common Controls item in the Components box now, and click on OK to close the Components box, adding the common controls to the toolbox.
4. Draw a new image combo box in your program.
5. To store the images for the image combo box, you'll need an image list control (another of the Windows common controls), so add one of those to your program as well by drawing it on your form (the control will not appear at runtime).
6. Right-click the image list control now, and select Properties in the menu that appears in order to open the property pages, as shown in Figure 8.11.
7. Click the Images tab in the image list's property pages now, and use the Insert Picture button to insert all the images you want to use in the image list, as also shown in Figure 8.11 (where we're using solid colors for each image).
8. Close the image list property page by on clicking OK.

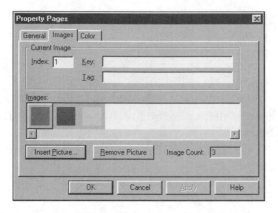

Figure 8.11   The Images tab of the image list property pages.

9. Right-click the image combo control now and select the Properties item in the menu that opens.

10. We need to connect the image list, **ImageList1**, to the image combo box, so click the General tab in the image combo property pages and select ImageList1 in the ImageList box, as shown in Figure 8.12.

11. Close the image combo property pages by clicking on OK.

12. Now add the items to the image combo, **ImageCombo1**, in code. To add those items to the image combo box, you actually add ComboItem objects to that control. To do that, you can use the image combo's **ComboItems** collection's **Add** method. This method takes the index of the item to add, a key (which is a unique text string that identifies the item), the caption of the item if any, and the index of the item's picture in the associated image list control:

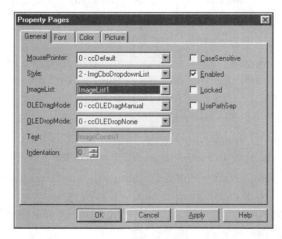

Figure 8.12   The General tab of the image combo property pages.

```
Private Sub Form_Load()
    ImageCombo1.ComboItems.Add 1, "key1", "Item 1", 1
    ImageCombo1.ComboItems.Add 2, "key2", "Item 2", 2
    ImageCombo1.ComboItems.Add 3, "key3", "Item 3", 3
End Sub
```

And that's it. Now when you run the program, the combo box displays images, as shown in Figure 8.13. Now we're using images in combo boxes.

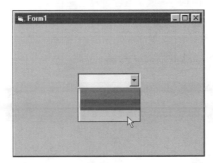

Figure 8.13   A combo box displaying images.

Chapter 9

Scroll Bars And Sliders

If you need an immediate solution to:	See page:
Adding Horizontal Or Vertical Scroll Bars To A Form	286
Setting Scroll Bars' Minimum And Maximum Values	286
Setting Up Scroll Bar Clicks (Large Changes)	287
Setting Up Scroll Bar Arrow Clicks (Small Changes)	288
Getting A Scroll Bar's Current Value	289
Handling Scroll Bar Events	289
Handling Continuous Scroll Bar Events	291
Showing And Hiding Scroll Bars	292
Coordinating Scroll Bar Pairs	293
Adding Scroll Bars To Text Boxes	293
Creating And Using Flat Scroll Bars	294
Customizing Flat Scroll Bar Arrows	295
Creating Slider Controls	296
Setting A Slider's Orientation	297
Setting A Slider's Range	298
Setting Up Slider Groove Clicks	298
Adding Ticks To A Slider	299
Setting A Slider's Tick Style	300
Getting A Slider's Current Value	301
Handling Slider Events	301
Handling Continuous Slider Events	302
Handling Slider Selections	303
Clearing A Selection In A Slider	306

(continued)

If you need an immediate solution to:	*See page:*
Creating An Updown Control	307
Setting An Updown Control's Minimum And Maximum	308
Handling Updown Events	308

In Depth

In this chapter, we're going to take a look at those controls that scroll and slide in Visual Basic. The controls we'll cover here are scroll bars, sliders, flat scroll bars, and updown controls, shown in Figure 9.1. Every Windows user is familiar with scroll bars. If computers had wall-sized displays, we might not need scroll bars, but as it is, scroll bars help control what parts of your program's data are visible at any one time. For example, you can place a large document in a text box, only part of which is visible at once. Using scroll bars, you can manipulate the document, moving through it as you like. You manipulate that document by dragging the small box in the scroll bar, which is called the scroll bar's thumb. A relatively new control is the flat scroll bar, which functions just like a normal scroll bar, except that it can appear flat, rather than three-dimensional.

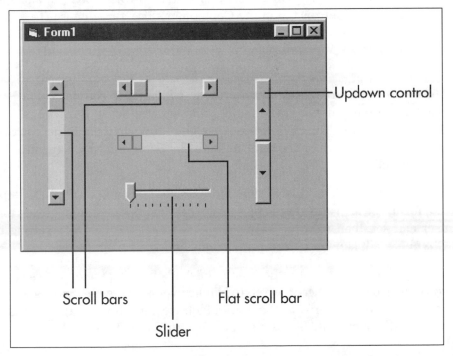

Figure 9.1   Scroll bars, a flat scroll bar, a slider, and an updown control.

A new control for some Windows user is the *slider* control, which appears at the bottom of Figure 9.1. Using the mouse, you can drag the knob in a slider control much the way you'd work the volume control on a stereo. You use slider controls to let the user make a selection from a range of values in a convenient way. For example, you may use a slider control to resize an image rather than asking the user to type in twip values.

The updown control is also new to many users. This control consists of two buttons, one pointing up and one pointing down, as you see at right in Figure 9.1. Updowns actually work much like the arrow buttons in scroll bars, because each time you click them, the setting of the control changes. You use updowns to let the user increment or decrement a setting.

Adding Scroll Bars And Sliders To A Program

Standard scroll bars are intrinsic controls in Visual Basic, which means that they appear in the toolbox as soon as you start Visual Basic. You'll find both the Vertical and the Horizontal Scroll Bar tools in the toolbox; to add those controls to a form, just paint them as you need them in that form.

You add the other controls in this chapter with the Project|Components menu item (click the Controls tab in the Components box that opens). To add flat scroll bars, you select the Microsoft Flat Scrollbar Control item; to add sliders, you select the Microsoft Windows Common Controls item; and to add the updown control, you click the Microsoft Windows Common Controls-2 item.

The toolbox tools for these controls appear in Figure 9.2. The Horizontal Scroll Bar tool is fourth down in the middle, the Vertical Scroll Bar tool is fourth down on the right. The Updown tool is eighth down in the middle, the Slider tool is eleventh down on the right, and the Flat Scroll Bar tool is twelfth down in the middle.

In overview, these controls work in more or less the same way: you add them to a form, use **Min** and **Max** properties to set the possible range of values the user can set, then read the **Value** property to get the control's setting in a **Change** event handler to interpret actions undertaken by the user.

Change events occur after the user is finished changing the control's setting; you can also use the **Scroll** event to handle events as the user works with the control, as we'll see in this chapter. In fact, we'll see how all this works and more in the Immediate Solutions, and we'll turn to that now.

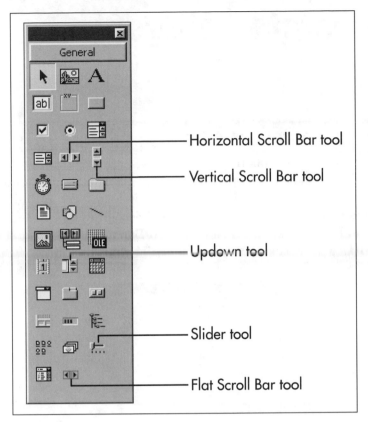

Horizontal Scroll Bar tool

Vertical Scroll Bar tool

Updown tool

Slider tool

Flat Scroll Bar tool

Figure 9.2   The Horizontal Scroll Bar, Vertical Scroll Bar, Updown, Slider, and Flat Scroll Bar tools.

Immediate Solutions

Adding Horizontal Or Vertical Scroll Bars To A Form

Many programmers think that there is one Scroll Bar tool that you add to a form and then set its orientation—vertical or horizontal. In fact, those are two different controls, as you see in the toolbox in Figure 9.2. To add a horizontal scroll bar to a form, you use the Horizontal Scroll Bar tool, and to add a vertical scroll bar, you use the Vertical Scroll Bar tool. A horizontal scroll bar, **HScroll1**, and a vertical scroll bar, **VScroll1**, appear in Figure 9.3.

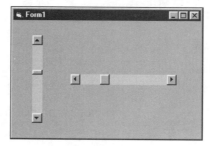

Figure 9.3   A horizontal and a vertical scroll bar.

Setting Scroll Bars' Minimum And Maximum Values

The Testing Department is calling again. The Field Testing Unit loves the new program you've written to help them record in-the-field performance of the company's products, but there's just one problem: performance is measured on a scale of 1 to 100, and the scroll bars in your program seem to go from 0 to 32767. It's been very hard for the users of your program to operate with only 1/32 of the whole scroll bar. Can you rescale it?

Yes, you can. After you place a scroll bar in a program, the first thing to do is to set its range of possible values, which by default is 0 to 32767. The minimum value a scroll bar can be set to is stored in its **Min** property, and the maximum value in the **Max** property. You can set the **Min** and **Max** properties for scroll bars at design time or at runtime; here's how we change those properties in a vertical scroll bar:

```
Private Sub Form_Load()
    VScroll1.Min = 1
    VScroll1.Max = 100
End Sub
```

Setting Up Scroll Bar Clicks (Large Changes)

The Testing Department is calling again. The scroll bars you've added to your program, *SuperDuperTextPro*, look terrific. But why doesn't anything happen when the user clicks the scroll bar itself, in the area between the thumb (the scroll box) and an arrow button? You ask, *should* something happen? They say, yes.

When the user clicks the scroll bar itself, not the thumb and not an arrow button, the thumb should move in that direction by the amount set by the scroll bar's **LargeChange** property (see also the next topic, which deals with the **SmallChange** property). For example, if you've set the scroll bar's range to be 1 to 100, a reasonable **LargeChange** setting would be 10. You can set the **LargeChange** property at design time or at runtime.

Here's an example where we set the **LargeChange** property for two scroll bars, a horizontal one and a vertical one:

```
Private Sub Form_Load()
    VScroll1.Min = 1
    VScroll1.Max = 100
    VScroll1.LargeChange = 10

    HScroll1.Min = 1
    HScroll1.Max = 100
    HScroll1.LargeChange = 10
End Sub
```

Now when the user clicks the scroll bar between the thumb and arrow buttons, the scroll bar's value will increase or decrease by 10.

Note that on some occasions, you should change the **LargeChange** property while a program is running. For example, if you let the user scroll through a document with this property, setting it to 1, and the user loads in a 30,000-line document, it might be wise to change the value of this property, such as making the large change, say, 5 percent of the total, or 1,500 lines.

Setting Up Scroll Bar Arrow Clicks (Small Changes)

As far as the user is concerned, there are three ways to change the setting of a scroll bar: by moving the thumb (the scroll box), by clicking the area of the scroll bar between the thumb and an arrow button, and by clicking an arrow button. When the user clicks an arrow button, the thumb moves by an amount stored in the **SmallChange** property (see also the previous topic, which deals with the **LargeChange** property).

I've known someone who thought the **SmallChange** property was a joke because its name can be interpreted humorously, but it exists all right. When the user clicks a scroll bar's arrow, the setting of the scroll bar is incremented or decremented (depending on which arrow was clicked) by the value in the **SmallChange** property.

You can set a scroll bar's **SmallChange** property at design time or at runtime. Here we set the **SmallChange** property for two scroll bars, a horizontal one and a vertical one:

```
Private Sub Form_Load()
    VScroll1.Min = 1
    VScroll1.Max = 100
    VScroll1.SmallChange = 1

    HScroll1.Min = 1
    HScroll1.Max = 100
    HScroll1.SmallChange = 1
End Sub
```

Now when the user clicks the arrow buttons, the setting of the scroll bar will change by 1.

Note that on some occasions, you should change the **SmallChange** property while a program is running. For example, if you let the user scroll through a document with this property, setting it to 1, and the user loads in a 30,000-line document, it might be wise to change the value of this property to, say, something like 1 percent of the total, or 300 lines.

TIP: This is one of those values that you should test yourself, because it's part of your program's feel. I know of a graphics program that scrolls exactly one pixel at a time when you click the arrow buttons in the scroll bars next to an image. Such a thing is annoying and gives users the impression that your program is unresponsive and hard to use.

Getting A Scroll Bar's Current Value

You've added the scroll bars you need to a program and set their **Min**, **Max**, **SmallChange**, and **LargeChange** properties, but you'd like to add one more touch. When your program first displays the scroll bars, you'd like them to display a default value, which is right in the middle of their range. How do you set the setting of a scroll bar?

You use the **Value** property to set a scroll bar's setting. You can set this value at either design time or runtime, and you can set it to read a scroll bar's setting while the program is running. The **Value** property holds values that can be in the range spanned by the values in the **Min** and **Max** properties.

Here's an example. In this case, we're setting up two scroll bars, a horizontal one and a vertical one, and placing the thumb of each scroll bar in the center of the range when the scroll bar first appears by setting the **Value** properties this way:

```
Private Sub Form_Load()
    VScroll1.Min = 1
    VScroll1.Max = 100
    VScroll1.LargeChange = 10
    VScroll1.SmallChange = 1
    VScroll1.Value = 50

    HScroll1.Min = 1
    HScroll1.Max = 100
    HScroll1.LargeChange = 10
    HScroll1.SmallChange = 1
    HScroll1.Value = 50
End Sub
```

When the user makes a change in a scroll bar, you get the new setting from the **Value** property when the **Change** event is triggered (see the next topic).

Handling Scroll Bar Events

You've added the scroll bars the Testing Department wanted. You've set the scroll bars' **Min**, **Max**, **SmallChange**, and **LargeChange** properties. Now how do you add the scroll bars to your program's code?

When the user changes the setting in a scroll bar, a **Change** event occurs, and you can react to those changes with an event handler attached to that event. For example, you may use scroll bars to move other controls around on the form (using those controls' **Move** method), and when the user changes a scroll bar's setting, you'll be informed of the new value in the **Change** event handler.

Let's look at an example. We start by adding two scroll bars—a horizontal scroll bar, **HScroll1**, and a vertical scroll bar, **VScroll1**—to a form. We set those controls' **Min**, **Max**, **SmallChange**, **LargeChange**, and **Value** properties when the form loads:

```
Private Sub Form_Load()
    VScroll1.Min = 1
    VScroll1.Max = 100
    VScroll1.LargeChange = 10
    VScroll1.SmallChange = 1
    VScroll1.Value = 50

    HScroll1.Min = 1
    HScroll1.Max = 100
    HScroll1.LargeChange = 10
    HScroll1.SmallChange = 1
    HScroll1.Value = 50
End Sub
```

Now when the user changes the setting in a scroll bar, we can report the new setting in a text box, **Text1**, simply by using the new setting in the **Value** property. This looks like the following code. Now we're handling scroll bar events, as shown in Figure 9.4.

```
Private Sub HScroll1_Change()
    Text1.Text = "Horizontal setting: " & Str(HScroll1.Value)
End Sub

Private Sub VScroll1_Change()
    Text1.Text = "Vertical setting: " & Str(VScroll1.Value)
End Sub
```

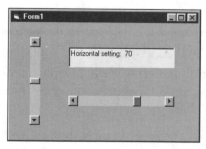

Figure 9.4   Working with scroll bars.

Handling Continuous Scroll Bar Events

You can use the **Change** event to catch the user's scrolling actions, but there's another one that's a lot better for many uses: the **Scroll** event. When you use the **Change** event, nothing happens until users are done with their scrolling actions. After the action is completed, the **Change** event is triggered, and you find out what happened. With the **Scroll** event, on the other hand, you get continuous updates as the action is happening. This means that you can update the screen immediately to show users the results of their scrolling actions. It's very useful to be able to update the screen as the user scrolls, especially in cases where you're scrolling a long document. Imagine trying to scroll 25 pages at a time, only to have to stop scrolling before the screen was updated.

Here's an example showing how to use the **Scroll** event; fundamentally, using this event is the same as using the **Change** event (unless you have an action that should only be performed after the user is done scrolling, in which case you should stick to the **Change** event). We start the example by adding two scroll bars, a horizontal scroll bar (**HScroll1**) and a vertical scroll bar (**VScroll1**), to a form. We set those controls' **Min**, **Max**, **SmallChange**, **LargeChange**, and **Value** properties when the form loads:

```
Private Sub Form_Load()
    VScroll1.Min = 1
    VScroll1.Max = 100
    VScroll1.LargeChange = 10
    VScroll1.SmallChange = 1
    VScroll1.Value = 50

    HScroll1.Min = 1
    HScroll1.Max = 100
    HScroll1.LargeChange = 10
    HScroll1.SmallChange = 1
    HScroll1.Value = 50
End Sub
```

Next, we just add code to the two scroll bar's **Scroll** events to display the new setting in a text box, **Text1**:

```
Private Sub HScroll1_Scroll()
    Text1.Text = "Horizontal setting: " & Str(HScroll1.Value)
End Sub

Private Sub VScroll1_Scroll()
    Text1.Text = "Vertical setting: " & Str(VScroll1.Value)
End Sub
```

With this code, the text box is *continuously* updated with the setting of the scroll bars as users manipulate them. This is in sharp contrast to using the **Change** event, which only occurs when users are finished with their scrolling actions.

Showing And Hiding Scroll Bars

Unlike other controls, there are well-defined times when scroll bars should disappear from your program. If the object you're scrolling can be entirely visible, there is no need for scroll bars, and you should remove them. (Another option is to disable them by setting their **Enabled** property to False. Disabled scroll bars appear gray and don't display a thumb.)

You can make a scroll bar disappear by setting its **Visible** property to False, and you can make it reappear by setting that property to True. Here's an example. In this case, we add two scroll bars to a form—a horizontal scroll bar and a vertical scroll bar—and initialize them when the form loads:

```
Private Sub Form_Load()
    VScroll1.Min = 1
    VScroll1.Max = 100
    VScroll1.LargeChange = 10
    VScroll1.SmallChange = 1
    VScroll1.Value = 50

    HScroll1.Min = 1
    HScroll1.Max = 100
    HScroll1.LargeChange = 10
    HScroll1.SmallChange = 1
    HScroll1.Value = 50
End Sub
```

When the user clicks a command button, we can hide both scroll bars simply by setting their **Visible** properties to False:

```
Private Sub Command1_Click()
    HScroll1.Visible = False
    VScroll1.Visible = False
End Sub
```

And that's it—now we can hide and show scroll bars at will. As mentioned, you usually hide scroll bars (or disable them) when the object they scroll is entirely visible and the scroll bars are no longer needed.

Coordinating Scroll Bar Pairs

The Testing Department is calling again. The two scroll bars you've added to your *SuperDuperWinBigCasino* game look great, but there's one problem: A pair of scroll bars straddle the user's view of the roulette table in *SuperDuperWinBigCasino*, but when you scroll one, the other doesn't move to match it. Can you fix that?

It's common to have two scroll bars that perform the same scrolling action— one on either side of an image you're scrolling, for example. The user should be able to scroll either scroll bar and have the other one match.

Keeping scroll bars coordinated is easy. All you have to do is make sure that when one scroll bar has a **Change** event, you update the other scroll bar's **Value** property. For example, say we have two vertical scroll bars, **VScroll1** and **VScroll2**, that straddle an object they're in charge of scrolling. You can update **VScroll2** when **VScroll1** changes this way:

```
Private Sub VScroll1_Change()
    VScroll2.Value = VScroll1.Value
End Sub
```

And you can update **VScroll1** when **VScroll2** changes:

```
Private Sub VScroll2_Change()
    VScroll1.Value = VScroll2.Value
End Sub
```

That's all there is to it. Now the scroll bars are coordinated.

Adding Scroll Bars To Text Boxes

How do you add scroll bars to text boxes? You use the text box's **ScrollBars** property instead of using actual scroll bar controls, but we include this topic here anyway because this is a natural chapter to turn to with this question.

First, make sure you set the text box's **MultiLine** property to True, because only multiline text boxes support scroll bars. Next, decide what kind of scroll bars you want on the text box: horizontal, vertical, or both, and set the **ScrollBars** property to match. That property can take these values:

- **VbSBNone**—0; no scroll bars (the default)
- **VbHorizontal**—1; horizontal

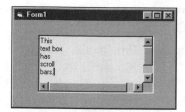

Figure 9.5   Adding scroll bars to a text box.

- **VbVertical**—2; vertical
- **VbBoth**—3; both vertical and horizontal

For example, we've added both horizontal and vertical scroll bars to the text box in Figure 9.5.

Creating And Using Flat Scroll Bars

A relatively new control is the flat scroll bar control. This control can function just like any other scroll bar, except that it appears flat, not 3D.

To add flat scroll bars to a form, follow these steps:

1. Select the Project|Components menu item, and click the Controls tab in the Components box that opens.

2. Select the Microsoft Windows Common Controls-2 item.

3. Close the Components box by clicking on OK.

4. The Flat Scroll Bar tool appears in the toolbox at this point. Add a flat scroll bar to your form in the usual way.

5. Set the flat scroll bar's **Min**, **Max**, **SmallChange**, and **LargeChange** values as you want them.

6. Add the code you want to the scroll bar event you want, **Change** or **Scroll**. For example, here we add code to a flat scroll bar's **Change** event, updating a text box with the setting of the scroll bar when the user is finished scrolling it:

```
Private Sub FlatScrollBar1_Change()
    Text1.Text = "Scroll bar's value: " & _
        Str(FlatScrollBar1.Value)
End Sub
```

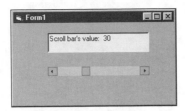

Figure 9.6   Adding a flat scroll bar to a program.

Run the program now, as shown in Figure 9.6. As you can see in that figure, the flat scroll bar does indeed appear flat, but it functions like any other scroll bar when the user scrolls it.

Unlike standard scroll bars, you can change the orientation of a flat scroll bar with its **Orientation** property. The **Orientation** property can take these values:

- **fsbVertical**—0; vertical scroll bar
- **fsbHorizontal**—1; horizontal scroll bar

---

*TIP: You can actually make a flat scroll bar appear 3D by setting its **Appearance** property. This property can take these values: **fsb3D** (whose value is 0), **fsbFlat** (value 1), and **fsbTrack3D** (value 2).*

Customizing Flat Scroll Bar Arrows

Flat scroll bars have one advantage over standard scroll bars: you can disable either arrow button selectively in a flat scroll bar using the **Arrows** property. You set the **Arrows** property to one of these values:

- **fsbBoth**—0; enable both arrows
- **fsbLeftUp**—1; enable left/up arrow
- **fsbRightDown**—2; enable right/down arrow

For example, we set the flat scroll bar's **Arrows** property to **fsbLeftUp** at design time in Figure 9.7, which means the right button is disabled.

You can also work with the **Arrows** property in code like this, where we enable both arrow buttons:

```
Private Sub Command2_Click()
    FlatScrollBar1.Arrows = fsbBoth
End Sub
```

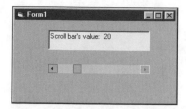

Figure 9.7   Disabling the right arrow button in a flat scroll bar.

Creating Slider Controls

The Aesthetic Design Department is on the phone again. They've heard about slider controls in Visual Basic and like their look. Is there any way you can add them to your program, *SuperDuperTextPro*?

Adding a slider to a program is easy; just follow these steps:

1. Select the Project|Components menu item, and click the Controls tab in the Components box that opens.

2. Select the Microsoft Windows Common Controls item.

3. Close the Components box by clicking on OK.

4. The Slider tool appears in the toolbox at this point. Add a slider to your form in the usual way.

5. Set the slider's **Orientation** property to **ccOrientationHorizontal** (value 0, the default) or **ccOrientationVertical** (value 1) to specify the orientation you want.

6. Set the slider's **Min**, **Max**, **SmallChange**, and **LargeChange** values as you want them.

7. Set the slider's **TickFrequency** property to the number of units between tics on the slider's scale.

8. Add the code you want to the slider event you want, **Change** or **Scroll**. For example, here we add code to a slider's **Change** event, setting the blue color of a text box, **Text1**, to match the slider's setting, using the Visual Basic **RGB** function:

```
Private Sub Form_Load()
    Slider1.Max = 255
    Slider1.Min = 0
End Sub
```

```
Private Sub Slider1_Click()
    Text1.BackColor = RGB(0, 0, Slider1.Value)
End Sub
```

Running this program yields the result you see in Figure 9.8. Now we're using sliders in Visual Basic.

Figure 9.8   Adding a slider to a program.

Setting A Slider's Orientation

Like scroll bars, sliders can be horizontal or vertical, but unlike scroll bars, horizontal and vertical sliders are not two different controls. Instead, you set a slider's **Orientation** property to make it horizontal or vertical.

You can set the **Orientation** at design time or run-time; this property takes these values:

- **ccOrientationHorizontal** (value 0, the default) orients the slider horizontally.

- **ccOrientationVertical** (value 1) orients the slider vertically.

Can you change a slider's orientation in code? You certainly can. In this example, we make a slider's orientation vertical when the user clicks a button:

```
Private Sub Command1_Click()
    Slider1.Orientation = ccOrientationVertical
End Sub
```

*TIP: Besides reorienting sliders, you can move them around a form using their **Move** method.*

Setting A Slider's Range

You've added a new slider to your environment control program to let users set the temperature they want in their homes, but now they have a complaint. Why does the slider return values of up to 32,767 degrees?

It's time to reset the slider's range of possible values, and you use the **Min** (default value 0) and **Max** (default value 10) properties to do that. You can set a slider's range at design time or runtime.

For example, here's how we set a slider's range to a more reasonable span of temperatures:

```
Private Sub Form_Load()
    Slider1.Max = 90
    Slider1.Min = 50
End Sub
```

After setting the **Min** and **Max** properties, you'll probably want to set the slider's *tick frequency* so the ticks on the slider's scale look appropriate for the new range (see "Adding Ticks to a Slider" in this chapter).

Setting Up Slider Groove Clicks

Besides dragging the knob along the groove in a slider, you can click the groove itself to move the knob (just as you can click the area of a scroll bar between the thumb and arrow buttons). The amount the knob moves each time the user clicks the groove is set with the slider's **LargeChange** property (just as it is in scroll bars). The default value for this property is 5.

You can set the **LargeChange** property at design time or runtime. For example, here's how we set a slider's **LargeChange** property to 5 when the form containing the slider first loads:

```
Private Sub Form_Load()
    Slider1.Max = 255
    Slider1.Min = 0
    Slider1.LargeChange = 5
End Sub
```

If you change a slider's range of possible values (in other words, the **Min** and **Max** properties), keep in mind that you might also have to change the **LargeChange** property as well. For example, if you change the possible range of slider values from 0 to 32767 to 1 to 100 but leave **LargeChange** at 4096, there's going to be a problem when the user clicks the slider's groove.

TIP: *Sliders also have a **SmallChange** property, but this seems to be one of the mystery properties you run across occasionally in Visual Basic, because there just is no way to use it in a slider. (Even looking it up in the Visual Basic documentation reveals nothing—it's undocumented, although it appears in the Properties window.) When you click a slider's groove, the slider moves by the **LargeChange** amount, but there aren't any arrow buttons in sliders to cause **SmallChange** events.*

Adding Ticks To A Slider

The Aesthetic Design Department is on the phone. The slider you've added to the program looks good, but what's that thick black bar underneath it? You explain that sliders use tick marks to make it easier to move the knob to the approximate position that the user wants. In this case, the slider's possible values extend from 0 to 32767, and you've just added a tick mark for each unit on that scale. That would give you 32,767 tick marks, they say. Right, you say. Maybe it's time to reset the **TickFrequency** property.

To set the number of tick marks in a slider's scale, you actually set the distance between ticks with the **TickFrequency** property. For example, if your slider's scale goes from 0 to 100, a good value for the slider's **TickFrequency** might be 10 (although this depends on the slider's width or height, of course— a **TickFrequency** of 5 might be better for a long slider).

You can set this property at design time or runtime. For example, here's how we set the tick frequency in a slider to 10 units:

```
Private Sub Form_Load()
    Slider1.Max = 255
    Slider1.Min = 0
    Slider1.TickFrequency = 10
End Sub
```

The result of this code appears in Figure 9.9.

TIP: *To make the tick marks come out evenly spaced, you should set the **TickFrequency** value so that the equation (**Max** - **Min**) / **TickFrequency** comes out to be a whole number with no remainder. To find out how many ticks there are in a slider, use its **GetNumTicks()** method.*

Figure 9.9   Setting tick frequency in a slider control.

Setting A Slider's Tick Style

The Aesthetic Design Department is on the phone again. Your multimedia program is great, but wouldn't it be better if the sliders had tick marks on *both* sides? Well, you think, *is* that possible?

It is. You can set a slider's **TickStyle** property to **sldBoth** to place tick marks on both sides of a slider. In fact, you can place ticks on one side, both sides, or no sides of a slider. Here are the possible values of the **TickStyle** property:

- **sldBottomRight**—0; ticks on bottom or right only
- **sldTopLeft**—1; ticks on top or left only
- **sldBoth**—2; ticks on both sides
- **sldNoTicks**—3; no ticks

For example, we've set **TickStyle** to **sldBoth** in the slider that appears in Figure 9.10.

You can also set the **TickStyle** property in code. Here, we set **TickStyle** to **sldNoTicks** when a slider loads:

```
Private Sub Form_Load()
    Slider1.Max = 100
    Slider1.Min = 0
    Slider1.LargeChange = 5
```

Figure 9.10   A slider with ticks on both sides.

```
    Slider1.TickFrequency = 10
    Slider1.TickStyle = sldNoTicks
End Sub
```

Getting A Slider's Current Value

Now that you've added a new slider control to your program, how exactly can you determine that control's setting? As with scroll bars, you use the slider's **Value** property.

The **Value** property is the slider's fundamental property. You can get or set the **Value** property at design time or runtime. For example, here's how we set a slider to a value of 125, halfway through its range of 0 to 250 (when you set a slider's **Value** in code, the knob in the slider moves to match):

```
Private Sub Form_Load()
    Slider1.Max = 250
    Slider1.Min = 0
    Slider1.LargeChange = 5
    Slider1.TickFrequency = 25
    Slider1.Value = 125
End Sub
```

To work with the **Value** property when the user moves the slider's knob, see the next two topics.

Handling Slider Events

You've added the new slider to your program, and it looks fine. But how do you connect it to your code? How can you make sure that the slider events are handled properly when the user uses it?

Like scroll bars, sliders have a **Change** event (and like scroll bars, they also have a **Scroll** event to handle continuous changes—see the next topic in this chapter). You make use of the **Change** event to catch the user's slider actions.

An example will make this clearer; here, we set up a slider when the form loads, setting its **Min**, **Max**, and other properties:

```
Private Sub Form_Load()
    Slider1.Max = 250
    Slider1.Min = 0
```

```
      Slider1.LargeChange = 5
      Slider1.TickFrequency = 25
End Sub
```

When the user is done moving the slider's knob, a **Change** event occurs, which you can catch in a **Change** event handler:

```
Private Sub Slider1_Change()

End Sub
```

For example, we can display the current setting of the slider in a text box this way, using the slider's **Value** property:

```
Private Sub Slider1_Change()
    Text1.Text = "Slider's position: " & Str(Slider1.Value)
End Sub
```

The result of this code appears in Figure 9.11. When the user moves the slider's knob, the slider's new setting appears in the text box. Now you're handling slider events.

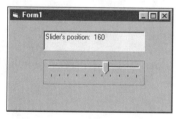

Figure 9.11   Handling slider events.

Handling Continuous Slider Events

Although sliders have a **Change** event, the **Scroll** event might be a better choice when working with a slider. The **Change** event only occurs when users complete their slider actions, but **Scroll** events occur as users move the slider's knob. In other words, the **Change** event lets you know what *happened*, whereas the **Scroll** event lets you know what's *happening*.

Here's an example. We set up a slider, **Slider1**, when the form containing that slider loads, like this:

```
Private Sub Form_Load()
    Slider1.Max = 250
```

```
        Slider1.Min = 0
        Slider1.LargeChange = 5
        Slider1.TickFrequency = 25
End Sub
```

Then we can catch slider actions by setting up an event handler for the **Scroll** event:

```
Private Sub Slider1_Scroll()

End Sub
```

In this case, we'll just display the slider's new setting in a text box, **Text1**:

```
Private Sub Slider1_Scroll()
    Text1.Text = "Slider's position: " & Str(Slider1.Value)
End Sub
```

Note that unlike code using the **Change** event, this code updates the text box with the slider's new setting as the slider moves.

TIP: *Of course, the **Scroll** event is not appropriate for all cases. For example, if you have an action that needs a firm setting before getting started, it might be better to use the **Change** event. However, providing visual feedback to users as they move a slider using **Scroll** can prove very useful.*

Handling Slider Selections

Using the Shift key, you can select a range of values in a slider. From the users' point of view, the process goes like this: they move the slider's knob to the beginning of the selection they want to make in a slider and press the Shift key. Then they move the knob to the end of the range they want to select and release the Shift key. When the Shift key is released, the selection appears in the slider as a blue band.

This capability of sliders is useful when you want to specify a range—for example, you might want to set the tolerable level of music volume to a certain range. To let a slider select a range, you must first set the **SelectRange** property to True (when it's False, the slider will not support range selection). Here are the two properties you use when selecting ranges in sliders:

- **SelLength** returns or sets the length of a selected range in a slider control.
- **SelStart** returns or sets the start of a selected range in a slider control.

However, setting the range when the user uses the Shift key is up to you. Let's see how that can work in a simple example. We'll need some way of determining if the Shift key is up or down in this example, so we set up a form-wide Boolean variable, **blnShiftUp**, in the (General) declarations area of the form:

```
Dim blnShiftUp As Boolean
```

And we set that variable to True when the form loads:

```
Private Sub Form_Load()
    Slider1.Max = 250
    Slider1.Min = 0
    Slider1.LargeChange = 5
    Slider1.TickFrequency = 25
    blnShiftUp = True
End Sub
```

When users move the knob to the beginning of the range they want to select and press the Shift key, we can catch that in the **KeyDown** event handler for the slider; here, we check if the **Shift** argument is 1, which means the Shift key is down:

```
Private Sub Slider1_KeyDown(KeyCode As Integer, Shift As Integer)

    If Shift = 1 And blnShiftUp Then
    ...
    End If

End Sub
```

(The **Shift** argument in **KeyUp** and **KeyDown** event handlers is a bit field, with the least-significant bits corresponding to the Shift key [bit 0], the Ctrl key [bit 1], and the Alt key [bit 2]. These bits correspond to the values 1, 2, and 4, respectively.)

If the Shift key is down, we set the flag **blnShiftUp** to False; we set the start of the selection, **SelStart**, to the current slider position; and we set the length of the selection, **SelLength**, to 0. (Note that it's necessary to set the length of the selection to 0 in case the user starts further selections after finishing with the current one):

```
Private Sub Slider1_KeyDown(KeyCode As Integer, Shift As Integer)

    If Shift = 1 And blnShiftUp Then
        blnShiftUp = False
```

```
        Slider1.SelStart = Slider1.Value
        Slider1.SelLength = 0
    End If

End Sub
```

Now when a key goes up, we check to make sure the Shift key is up in the **KeyUp** event handler:

```
Private Sub Slider1_KeyUp(KeyCode As Integer, Shift As Integer)

    If Shift = 0 Then
...
    End If

End Sub
```

If the Shift key is indeed up, we set the Boolean flag **blnShiftUp** to True, place the selection length in **SelLength** (note that we use the Visual Basic absolute value, **Abs( )**, function here to find the selection length, because the user may have moved the slider's knob to a lower, not higher, setting), and set the **SelStart** property to the current value of the slider if that value is less than the current **SelStart**:

```
Private Sub Slider1_KeyUp(KeyCode As Integer, Shift As Integer)

    If Shift = 0 Then

        blnShiftUp = True
        Slider1.SelLength = Abs(Slider1.Value - Slider1.SelStart)
        If Slider1.Value < Slider1.SelStart Then
            Slider1.SelStart = Slider1.Value
        End If
...
```

Finally, we can display the length of the new selection in a text box this way:

```
Private Sub Slider1_KeyUp(KeyCode As Integer, Shift As Integer)

    If Shift = 0 Then

        blnShiftUp = True
        Slider1.SelLength = Abs(Slider1.Value - Slider1.SelStart)
        If Slider1.Value < Slider1.SelStart Then
            Slider1.SelStart = Slider1.Value
        End If
```

```
        Text1.Text = "Selection length: " & Str(Slider1.SelLength)
    End If

End Sub
```

And that's it. When you run this program and make a selection with the slider, the length of that selection appears in the text box, as in Figure 9.12.

Figure 9.12   Selecting a range in a slider.

Clearing A Selection In A Slider

Besides setting selections in sliders, you can also clear them with the **ClearSel** method. For example, here's how we might set up a selection in a slider when the form holding that slider loads:

```
Private Sub Form_Load()
    Slider1.Max = 250
    Slider1.Min = 0
    Slider1.LargeChange = 5
    Slider1.TickFrequency = 25
    Slider1.SelStart = 30
    Slider1.SelLength = 10
End Sub
```

And here's how we can clear that selection when the user clicks a command button:

```
Private Sub Command1_Click()
    Slider1.ClearSel
End Sub
```

That's all there is to it.

Creating An Updown Control

The testing department is on the phone again, with an issue about the Print dialog box in your program, *SuperDuperTextPro*. Why is there a scroll bar next to the Number Of Copies To Print box in the Print dialog box? Well, you say, that's in case the user wants to increment or decrement the number of copies to print. There's a better control than a scroll bar for that, they say—what about using an *updown* control?

What's an updown control? It's a control made up of two buttons next to each other, and each button holds an arrow (each pointing away from the other button). You can use an updown when values should be incremented and decremented, and you want to give the user an easy way to do that.

Adding an updown control to a program is easy; just follow these steps:

1. Select the Project|Components menu item, and click the Controls tab in the Components box that opens.
2. Select the Microsoft Windows Common Controls-2 item.
3. Close the Components box by clicking on OK.
4. The Updown tool appears in the toolbox at this point. Add an updown to your form in the usual way.
5. Set the updown's **Orientation** property as you want it: **cc2OrientationVertical** (the default) or **cc2OrientationHorizontal**.
6. Set the updown's **Min** and **Max** values as you want them.
7. Add the code you want to the updown's event you want to work with (**Change**, **UpClick**, or **DownClick**). For example, here we add code to report the setting of the updown control in a text box when the user changes it in the updown's **Change** event:

```
Private Sub UpDown1_Change()
Text1.Text = "New setting: " & Str(UpDown1.Value)
End Sub
```

The result of this code appears in Figure 9.13.

TIP: *Updown controls can have buddy controls that are clicked when you click the updown. To make a control an updown's "buddy," place that control's name in the updown's **BuddyControl** property, and set the updown's **SyncBuddy** property to True. This will align the updown next to the buddy property; for example, if you make an updown the buddy of a command button, that command button is clicked each time the user clicks the updown's up/right arrow. Or, you can increment or decrement a value in a text box by making an updown the buddy of the text box, setting the updown's **SyncBuddy** property to True, and setting the updown's **Min** and **Max** properties to the minimum and maximum value you want the user to be able to increment and decrement to in the text box.*

Figure 9.13   Using an updown control.

Setting An Updown Control's Minimum And Maximum

The default maximum value for an updown control is 10, and the default minimum is 0. How can you change those?

Just set the updown's **Max** and **Min** properties as you want them. For example, here's how we set those properties in an updown when it loads:

```
Private Sub Form_Load()
    UpDown1.Min = 0
    UpDown1.Max = 100
End Sub
```

That's all there is to it. To handle the updown control's events, take a look at the next topic.

Handling Updown Events

You've added an updown control to your program—but how do you connect it to your code? There are three main events you can use: the **Change** event, the **UpClick** event, and the **DownClick** event.

The **Change** event occurs when the user clicks either of the two buttons in the updown. Here's an example; we can report the new setting of an updown when the user clicks a button by catching that action in a **Change** event handler:

```
Private Sub UpDown1_Change()
...
End Sub
```

We can display the updown's new value in a text box, **Text1**, this way, using the updown's **Value** property:

```
Private Sub UpDown1_Change()
    Text1.Text = "New setting: " & Str(UpDown1.Value)
End Sub
```

Besides the **Change** event, you can also attach event handlers to the updown's **UpClick** and **DownClick** events to handle Up/Right button clicks and Down/Left button clicks. Being able to work with the individual buttons this way makes the updown a more versatile control.

Chapter 10

Picture Boxes And Image Controls

If you need an immediate solution to:	See page:
Adding A Picture Box To A Form	315
Setting Or Getting The Picture In A Picture Box	316
Adjusting Picture Box Size To Contents	317
Aligning A Picture Box In A Form	317
Handling Picture Box Events (And Creating Image Maps)	318
Picture Box Animation	320
Grouping Other Controls In A Picture Box	322
Using A Picture Box In An MDI Form	322
Drawing Lines And Circles In A Picture Box	323
Using Image Lists With Picture Boxes	326
Adding Text To A Picture Box	327
Formatting Text In A Picture Box	329
Clearing A Picture Box	330
Accessing Individual Pixels In A Picture Box	331
Copying Pictures To And Pasting Pictures From The Clipboard	332
Stretching And Flipping Images In A Picture Box	333
Printing A Picture	335
Using Picture Box Handles	336
Setting Measurement Scales In A Picture Box	337
Saving Pictures To Disk	338
Adding An Image Control To A Form	338
Stretching An Image In An Image Control	339

In Depth

In this chapter, we're going to take an in-depth look at two popular Visual Basic controls: image controls and picture boxes. In fact, this will be our introduction to a very popular Visual Basic topic, working with graphics, because picture boxes let you do far more with images than just display them.

The two controls we'll work with in this chapter appear in Figure 10.1. We'll take a closer look at these two controls now.

Image Controls

You use image controls to do just what the name implies: display images. This control is a very simple one that doesn't take up many program resources: it's just there to display (and stretch, if you wish) images. If that's all you want to do, use an image control. You load a picture into an image control's **Picture** property (either at design time or using **LoadPicture( )** at runtime).

TIP: *You should also know that if you just want to display a picture as a sort of backdrop for your program, Form objects themselves have a* **Picture** *property that you can load images into without the need for image controls or picture boxes.*

Image controls are very accommodating—they resize themselves automatically to fit the image you're placing in them. On the other hand, if you don't want the image control to change size, set its **Stretch** property to True. Doing so means that the image, not the control, will be resized when loaded to fit the control. Another advantage of the image control over the picture box is that it

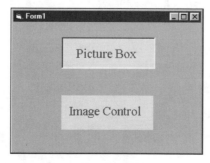

Figure 10.1   A picture box and an image control.

repaints itself faster than picture boxes. Image boxes can't do a lot of things that picture boxes can do, however, such as act as containers for other controls.

Both image controls and picture boxes are intrinsic controls in Visual Basic, which means they appear in the toolbox when you start the program. The Image Control tool is tenth down on the left in the toolbox in Figure 10.2.

Picture Boxes

Picture boxes are more complete controls than image controls. Just as the rich text control provides a sort of word-processor-in-a-control, so the picture box does for graphics in Visual Basic. You can load images into a picture box, save images to disk, draw with some rudimentary graphics methods, print images, work pixel by pixel, set an image's scale, and more. Besides graphics handling, the picture box can also act as a container for other controls—and besides toolbars and status bars, it's the only control that can appear by itself in an MDI form.

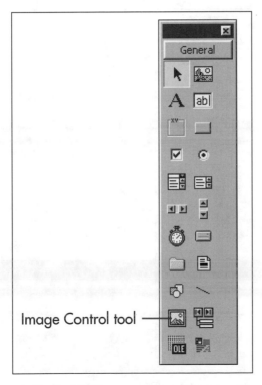

Figure 10.2   The Image Control tool.

As with image controls, you load pictures into a picture box's **Picture** property, and you can do that at design time or runtime (at runtime you use the **LoadPicture( )** method). When you load an image into a picture box, the picture box does not resize itself by default to fit that image as the image control does—but it will if you set its **AutoSize** property to True. The picture box has a 3D border by default, so it doesn't look like an image control—unless you set its **BorderStyle** property to 0 for no border (instead of 1, the default). In other words, you can make a picture box look and behave just like an image control if you wish, but keep in mind that picture boxes use a lot more memory and processor time, so if you just want to display an image, stick with image controls.

Like image controls, picture boxes are intrinsic controls in Visual Basic; the Picture Box tool is at right in the first row of tools in Figure 10.3.

That's all the overview we need for these two popular controls. It's time to start working with them directly in the Immediate Solutions.

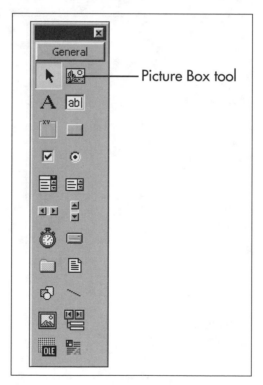

Figure 10.3   The Picture Box tool.

Immediate Solutions

Adding A Picture Box To A Form

You've decided that you need a picture box in your program. How do you add one? Adding a picture box is simple; just follow these steps:

1. Select the Picture Box tool in the toolbox, and double-click it to add a picture box to your form, or click it once and draw the picture box where you want it on the form.

2. If you want the picture box to resize itself to fit the picture you'll load into it, set its **AutoSize** property to True. If you don't want a border on the control, set its **BorderStyle** property to None (0).

3. If you want the picture box's contents to be refreshed when needed (for example, in case another window obscuring the picture box is removed), set its **AutoRedraw** property to True.

4. Load the image you want to display into the picture box using its **Picture** property. Click that property in the Properties window and click the button with an ellipsis (...) in it to open the Load Picture dialog box. At runtime, you can load a picture using **LoadPicture( )** like this:

```
Private Sub Command1_Click()
    Picture1.Picture = LoadPicture _
        ("c:\vbbb\picturesandimages\image.bmp")
End Sub
```

We've loaded an image into the picture box in Figure 10.4 following the preceding steps. Now the picture box is ready to go. That's all there is to it.

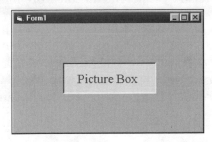

Figure 10.4   A picture box in a form.

Setting Or Getting The Picture In A Picture Box

You've added a new picture box to your form, and it looks fine—except for one thing: it's completely blank. How do you add images to a picture box again?

You use the **Picture** property. A picture box is very versatile and can display images from bitmap (.bmp), icon (.ico), metafile (.wmf), JPEG (.jpg), or GIF (.gif) files—just load the file's name into the **Picture** property.

At design time, click that property in the Properties window and click the button with an ellipsis (...) in it to open the Load Picture dialog box. Specify the file you want to load into the picture box, and click on OK.

At runtime, you can use **LoadPicture( )** to load in a picture like this, where we load in an image when the user clicks a command button:

```
Private Sub Command1_Click()
    Picture1.Picture = LoadPicture("c:\vbbb\picturesandimages\image.bmp")
End Sub
```

TIP: *Besides **LoadPicture()**, Visual Basic also supports **LoadResPicture()**, which lets you load pictures from resource files. Using **LoadResPicture()** is useful for localizing a Visual Basic application—the resources are isolated in one resource file, and there is no need to access the source code or recompile the application.*

If you want to get the picture in a picture box, you also use the **Picture** property. For example, here we copy the picture from **Picture1** to **Picture2** when the user clicks a command button:

```
Private Sub Command1_Click()
    Picture2.Picture = Picture1.Picture
End Sub
```

The **Picture** property is very useful in Visual Basic because it provides such an easy way of handling images, as you can see in the preceding two code snippets. With the **Picture** property, you can store images and transfer them between controls.

Besides the **Picture** property, picture boxes also have an **Image** property. The **Image** property is actually the handle to the image's bitmap in the picture box and as such is very useful when working with Windows calls directly. You can also assign images from an **Image** property to a **Picture** property like this:

```
Private Sub Command1_Click()
    Picture2.Picture = Picture1.Image
End Sub
```

Adjusting Picture Box Size To Contents

You've displayed the image of the company's Illustrious Founder in a picture box in your new program—but the picture box was a little small, and you can only see most of the I.F.'s forehead. There's some email waiting for you from the president's office, and you think you know what it says. How can you make sure picture boxes readjust themselves to fit the picture they're displaying?

When you load a picture into a picture control, it does not readjust itself to fit the picture (although image controls do)—at least, not by default. Picture boxes will resize themselves to fit their contents if you set their **AutoSize** properties to True. If **AutoSize** is set to True, you don't have to worry about resizing the picture box, even if you load images into the picture box at runtime. This saves a lot of fiddling with the picture box's **Left**, **Top**, **Width**, and **Height** properties.

Aligning A Picture Box In A Form

Picture boxes are special controls in that they can *contain* other controls (in Visual Basic terms, picture boxes are container controls). In fact, if you place option buttons inside a picture box (just draw them inside the picture box), those option buttons act together as a group.

Besides grouping option buttons together, the original idea here was to provide Visual Basic programmers a (rather rudimentary) way of creating toolbars and status bars in their programs. That's been superceded now by the toolbar and status bar controls, of course.

To let you create toolbars or status bars, picture boxes have an **Align** property. You use this property to place the picture box at top, bottom, or on a side of a form. Here are the possible values for **Align**:

- *0*—Align none
- *2*—Align bottom
- *3*—Align left
- *4*—Align right

For example, we've aligned the picture box in Figure 10.5 to the top of the form, giving it a few buttons, and we've set its **BackColor** property to deep blue to make a rudimentary toolbar.

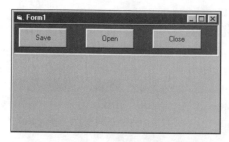

Figure 10.5   Creating a toolbar with an aligned picture box.

Handling Picture Box Events (And Creating Image Maps)

The New Products Department is on the phone; they want you to design a program to welcome new employees to the company. The program should display a picture of the main plant, and when the new employee clicks part of that image, "it should sort of zoom in on it." Can you do something like that in Visual Basic?

Responding to targeted mouse clicks in an image means creating an *image map*, and you can create one with a picture box. Picture boxes have **Click** events (and even **DblClick** events), of course, but **Click** event handlers only tell you that the picture box was clicked, not where it was clicked:

```
Private Sub Picture1_Click()

End Sub
```

The **Click** event is useful if you want to use picture boxes as sort of image-bearing buttons (although buttons can also display images now). However, if you want to know where in a picture box the user clicked the mouse, use **MouseDown**. (Besides the full range of mouse events, picture boxes also support key events like **KeyDown**, **KeyPress**, and so on.)

Creating An Image Map

Here's an example where we create an image map. We'll need to know the exact locations of the various hotspots in the image that do something when clicked, and it's easy to find their dimensions and location by using a simple graphics program like the Windows Paint program.

Note, however, that programs like Windows Paint will measure your image in pixels, and if you want to use pixel measurements, not twips, you must set the picture box's **ScaleMode** property to **vbPixels**, like this:

```
Private Sub Form_Load()
    Picture1.ScaleMode = vbPixels
End Sub
```

We'll use the image you see in the picture box in Figure 10.6 as our image map and report to users when they click either word, "Picture" or "Box".

In the **MouseDown** event handler, we're passed the location of the mouse click as (X, Y), and we check to see if the mouse went down on either word in the image:

```
Private Sub Picture1_MouseDown(Button As Integer, Shift As Integer, _
    X As Single, Y As Single)
    If X > 16 And X < 83 And Y > 11 And Y < 36 Then
...
    End If

    If X > 83 And X < 125 And Y > 11 And Y < 36 Then
...
    End If
End Sub
```

If the user did click one or the other word, we can report that to the user this way:

```
Private Sub Picture1_MouseDown(Button As Integer, Shift As Integer, _
    X As Single, Y As Single)
    If X > 16 And X < 83 And Y > 11 And Y < 36 Then
        MsgBox "You clicked the word ""Picture"""
    End If

    If X > 83 And X < 125 And Y > 11 And Y < 36 Then
        MsgBox "You clicked the word ""Box"""
    End If
End Sub
```

The result appears in Figure 10.6—now we're creating image maps in Visual Basic.

One more note here—image controls also have **MouseDown** events, so if you're just creating an image map, you should consider an image control because they use far fewer system resources.

TIP: *Other picture box events that can be useful include the **Resize**, **Change**, and **Paint** events.*

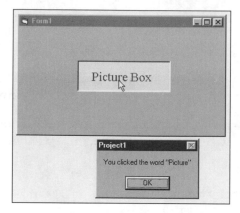

Figure 10.6   Creating an image map with a picture box.

Picture Box Animation

One easy way to support graphics animation in Visual Basic is to use a picture box. For example, you may have a control array of picture boxes, only one of which is visible at any one time. You can then make the others appear (at the same location) by setting the first picture box's **Visible** property to False, the next one's **Visible** property to True, and so on, cycling through the picture boxes.

That method is *very* wasteful of memory, however; if you're going to use picture boxes to support animation, a better idea is to use one picture box and keep changing its **Picture** property to display successive frames of an animation. You can store the images themselves in an image list control.

To add an image list control, follow these steps:

1. Select the Project|Components menu item.
2. Select the Controls tab in the Components box.
3. Select the Microsoft Windows Common Controls item in the Components box and click on OK to close that box.
4. Add a new image list control to your program using the Image List tool in the toolbox.
5. Right-click the new image list control and select the Properties item in the menu that opens.
6. Click the Images tab in the Property Pages box that opens, and load the images you want to use in the image list using the Insert Picture button.
7. Close the Property Pages box by clicking on OK.

All that remains is to add the code you need. For example, here we've added a timer control, **Timer1**, to the program, set its Enabled property to False, and set its **Interval** property to 1000 (the **Interval** property is measured in milliseconds, 1/1000s of a second), which means the **Timer1_Timer( )** event handler will be called once a second.

For the purposes of this example, we will just switch back and forth between two images in the picture box. These two images are the first two images in an image list, **ImageList1**. To switch back and forth, we use a static Boolean flag named **blnImage1** like this (for more information on using image lists, see Chapter 16):

```
Private Sub Timer1_Timer()
    Static blnImage1 As Boolean

    If blnImage1 Then
        Picture1.Picture = ImageList1.ListImages(1).Picture
    Else
        Picture1.Picture = ImageList1.ListImages(2).Picture
    End If
...
```

At the end of **Timer1_Timer( )**, we toggle the **blnImage1** flag this way:

```
Private Sub Timer1_Timer()
    Static blnImage1 As Boolean

    If blnImage1 Then
        Picture1.Picture = ImageList1.ListImages(1).Picture
    Else
        Picture1.Picture = ImageList1.ListImages(2).Picture
    End If

    blnImage1 = Not blnImage1
End Sub
```

And that's all we need—now we're supporting a rudimentary animation using picture boxes.

Grouping Other Controls In A Picture Box

The Aesthetic Design Department is on the phone again. They like the new option buttons you've added to your program, but wouldn't it be nice if you could display pictures behind each group of option buttons?

You can do that with picture boxes. Picture boxes are container controls, which means they can contain other controls. You usually use this capability to group option buttons together, because those controls work as a group (you can also group option buttons together by form or frame control).

The important thing here is to make sure that you paint the option buttons in the target picture box; don't just double-click the Option Button tool. Only when an option button is drawn entirely inside a picture box from the start is it associated with that picture box.

For example, we've added nine option buttons to two picture boxes in the form in Figure 10.7. As you can see in that figure, we can click option buttons in the two groups independently—they function as separate groups.

Picture boxes can also contain other controls, of course, like command buttons (see "Aligning A Picture Box In A Form" earlier in this chapter to see how to create rudimentary toolbars and status bars this way) or checkboxes.

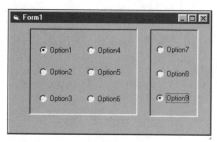

Figure 10.7   Grouping option buttons with picture boxes.

Using A Picture Box In An MDI Form

Another special use of picture boxes is to draw toolbars or status bars in an MDI form. This method has been superceded by the toolbar and status bar controls, but it used to be the way you could add those items to MDI forms.

For example, to add a Picture Box toolbar to an MDI form (only controls that support the **Align** property may be added to MDI forms), you just draw that control in the MDI form. Visual Basic will align the picture box with the top of the client area of the MDI form by default, but you can align it at bottom or on either side as well. Here are the possible values for the picture box's **Align** property:

- *0*—Align none
- *1*—Align top
- *2*—Align bottom
- *3*—Align left
- *4*—Align right

As an example, we've added a picture box to the MDI form in Figure 10.8 and placed a few command buttons in that picture box to create a rudimentary toolbar. As you can see in that figure, the MDI form draws a border at the bottom of the new toolbar automatically.

Although this used to be the way to create toolbars and status bars in MDI forms, it's now better to use the controls specifically designed for this purpose, the toolbar and status bar controls.

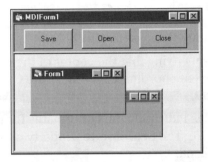

Figure 10.8   Using a picture box to create a toolbar in an MDI form.

Drawing Lines And Circles In A Picture Box

The Testing Department is on the phone again. The new picture box-based image map you've put in your program is terrific, but can you draw a box around the hotspots in the map as the user clicks them? That would make things much clearer.

Visual Basic can help out here because picture boxes give you some rudimentary graphics-drawing capabilities that you can make use of in code. In particular, you can draw lines and circles, and set points to particular colors in picture boxes using the following methods (note, by the way, that you can also use all the following methods with forms as well as picture boxes).

Some of the following methods make use of **CurrentX** and **CurrentY**; these are properties that you can set in a picture box. For example, if you omit the first set of coordinates when using the **Line( )** method, Visual Basic draws the line from the location (**CurrentX, CurrentY**).

You may want to specify measurements to the graphics methods using pixels, not the default twips, and you can change the measurements in a picture box to pixels by setting its **ScaleMode** property this way:

```
Private Sub Form_Load()
    Picture1.ScaleMode = vbPixels
End Sub
```

We'll start working with the drawing methods of picture boxes now, starting with the **Circle( )** method.

Drawing Circles

You use the **Circle( )** method to draw circles:

```
PictureBox.Circle [Step] (x, y), radius, [color, start, end, aspect]
```

Here are the arguments you pass to **Circle( )**:

- **Step**—Keyword specifying that the center of the circle, ellipse, or arc is relative to the current coordinates given by the **CurrentX** and **CurrentY** properties of *object*.

- *x, y*—**Single** values indicating the coordinates for the center point of the circle, ellipse, or arc. The **ScaleMode** property of *object* determines the units of measure used.

- *radius*—**Single** value indicating the radius of the circle, ellipse, or arc. The **ScaleMode** property of *object* determines the unit of measure used.

- *color*—**Long** integer value indicating the RGB color of the circle's outline. If omitted, the value of the **ForeColor** property is used. You can use the **RGB** function or **QBColor** function to specify the color.

- *start, end*—Single-precision values. When an arc or a partial circle or ellipse is drawn, *start* and *end* specify (in radians) the beginning and end positions of the arc. The range for both is -2 pi radians to 2 pi radians. The default value for *start* is 0 radians; the default for *end* is 2 * pi radians.

- *aspect*—Single-precision value indicating the aspect ratio of the circle. The default value is 1.0, which yields a perfect (nonelliptical) circle on any screen.

As an example, we draw a circle in a picture box with this code:

```
Private Sub Command1_Click()
    Picture1.Circle (80, 70), 50
End Sub
```

The result of this code appears in Figure 10.9. If there were an image already in the picture box, the circle would appear drawn on top of it.

Drawing Lines

You use the **Line( )** method to draw lines:

```
PictureBox.Line [Step] (x1, y1) [Step] (x2, y2), [color], [B][F]
```

Here are the arguments you pass to **Line( )**:

- **Step**—Keyword specifying that the starting point coordinates are relative to the current graphics position given by the **CurrentX** and **CurrentY** properties.

- *x1*, *y1*—**Single** values indicating the coordinates of the starting point for the line or rectangle. The **ScaleMode** property determines the unit of measure used. If omitted, the line begins at the position indicated by **CurrentX** and **CurrentY**.

- **Step**—Keyword specifying that the end-point coordinates are relative to the line starting point.

- *x2*, *y2*—**Single** values indicating the coordinates of the end point for the line being drawn.

- *color*—**Long** integer value indicating the RGB color used to draw the line. If omitted, the **ForeColor** property setting is used. You can use the **RGB** function or **QBColor** function to specify the color.

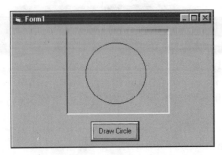

Figure 10.9   Drawing a circle in a picture box.

- **B**—If included, causes a box to be drawn using the coordinates to specify opposite corners of the box.

- **F**—If the **B** option is used, the **F** option specifies that the box is filled with the same color used to draw the box. You cannot use **F** without **B**. If **B** is used without **F**, the box is filled with the current **FillColor** and **FillStyle**. The default value for **FillStyle** is transparent.

Setting Points

You use **PSet( )** to set points in a picture box:

```
PictureBox.PSet [Step] (x, y), [color]
```

Here are the arguments you pass to **PSet( )**:

- **Step**—Keyword specifying that the coordinates are relative to the current graphics position given by the **CurrentX** and **CurrentY** properties.

- *x, y*—**Single** values indicating the horizontal (x-axis) and vertical (y-axis) coordinates of the point to set.

- *color*—**Long** integer value indicating the RGB color specified for point. If omitted, the current **ForeColor** property setting is used. You can use the **RGB** function or **QBColor** function to specify the color.

TIP: *In a picture box, you set the color of figures with the **ForeColor** property and the fill color with the **FillColor** property.*

TIP: *If you want your images to persist (in other words, be redrawn automatically when needed), set the picture box's **AutoRedraw** property to True.*

Using Image Lists With Picture Boxes

When handling images, it's often useful to use *image lists*. An image list is an invisible control whose only purpose is to hold images. A common thing to do is to load images into an image list and then when they're all loaded (and stored in memory, not on the disk), place them rapidly into picture boxes as needed.

We'll see how to use an image list with picture boxes here. To add an image list control to a program, just follow these steps:

1. Select the Project|Components menu item.
2. Select the Controls tab in the Components box.

3. Select the Microsoft Windows Common Controls item in the Components box and click on OK to close that box.

4. Add a new image list control to your program using the Image List tool in the toolbox.

5. Right-click the new image list control, and select the Properties item in the menu that opens.

6. Click the Images tab in the Property Pages box that opens, and load the images you want to use in the image list using the Insert Picture button.

7. Close the Property Pages box by clicking on OK.

Now you're free to load images from the image list into a picture box. To reach the actual images, you can use the image lists' **ListImages** array of ImageList objects; there's one such object for each image in the image list, and you can reach it with the image list's **Picture** property.

For example, here's how we load Image 1 (image lists are 1-based, not 0-based) into **Picture1** when the user clicks **Command1**, Image 2 when the user clicks **Command2**, and Image 3 when the user clicks **Command3**:

```
Private Sub Command1_Click()
        Picture1.Picture = ImageList1.ListImages(1).Picture
End Sub
Private Sub Command2_Click()
        Picture1.Picture = ImageList1.ListImages(2).Picture
End Sub
Private Sub Command3_Click()
        Picture1.Picture = ImageList1.ListImages(3).Picture
End Sub
```

Loading all your images into memory and storing them with an image list can be a valuable asset when working with multiple images and picture boxes this way.

Adding Text To A Picture Box

Besides drawing figures, picture boxes support drawing text as well. This can come in very handy to label the parts of a figure in a picture box.

You draw text in a picture box with its **Print** method, passing that method the text you want to print. Where does that text appear? It appears at the location set by the picture box's **CurrentX** and **CurrentY** properties—that is, at

(**CurrentX**, **CurrentY**) in the picture box (with respect to the upper left corner of the picture box).

Keep in mind that picture boxes use twips (1/1440s of an inch) as their default measurement unit. You can change that to, say, pixels by setting the picture box's **ScaleMode** property to **vbPixels**:

```
Private Sub Form_Load()
    Picture1.ScaleMode = vbPixels
...
```

Then we can specify an absolute location at which to display text:

```
Private Sub Form_Load()
    Picture1.ScaleMode = vbPixels
    Picture1.CurrentX = 25
    Picture1.CurrentY = 20
...
```

Finally, we print the text in the picture box with the **Print** method; here, we just print the text "Text in a picture box!":

```
Private Sub Form_Load()
    Picture1.ScaleMode = vbPixels
    Picture1.CurrentX = 25
    Picture1.CurrentY = 20
    Picture1.Print ("Text in a picture box!")
End Sub
```

Make sure the picture box's **AutoRedraw** property is set to True, which it needs to be for the picture box to display text. The results of the preceding code appear in Figure 10.10. Now we're displaying text in picture boxes.

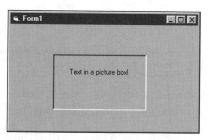

Figure 10.10 Printing text in a picture box.

Formatting Text In A Picture Box

The Aesthetic Design Department is calling. The text your program uses to label images in picture boxes is fine, but how about making it, say, **bold** and *italic* to emphasize what's going on? You think, *can* you do that?

Yes, you can. You can format text in a picture box using the **FontBold**, **FontItalic**, **FontStrikethru**, and **FontUnderline** properties. Each of those properties does just what it says: when you set a property to True, that property applies the next time you use the **Print** method in the picture box.

You can also format the placement of text using the **CurrentX** and **CurrentY** properties; setting these properties sets the location where text will next appear when you use the **Print** method. In addition, you can determine the height and width of a string of text with the **TextHeight** and **TextWidth** methods.

Here's an example. First, set the picture box's **AutoRedraw** property to True, which you need to display text. Next, we set the measurement units in a picture box to pixels, set the **CurrentX** and **CurrentY** properties, and print a plain string of text:

```
Private Sub Form_Load()
    Picture1.ScaleMode = vbPixels
    Picture1.CurrentX = 25
    Picture1.CurrentY = 20
    Picture1.Print ("Text in a picture box!")
...
```

Next, we skip to the next line using **TextHeight( )**, set **FontUnderline** to True, and print some underlined text:

```
Private Sub Form_Load()
    Picture1.ScaleMode = vbPixels
    Picture1.CurrentX = 25
    Picture1.CurrentY = 20
    Picture1.Print ("Text in a picture box!")
    Picture1.CurrentX = 25
    Picture1.CurrentY = Picture1.CurrentY + Picture1.TextHeight("ABCDEFG")
    Picture1.FontUnderline = True
    Picture1.Print ("Underlined text.")
...
```

Finally, we set **FontBold** to True as well, skip to the next line, and print bold underlined text:

```
Private Sub Form_Load()
    Picture1.ScaleMode = vbPixels
    Picture1.CurrentX = 25
    Picture1.CurrentY = 20
    Picture1.Print ("Text in a picture box!")
    Picture1.CurrentX = 25
    Picture1.CurrentY = Picture1.CurrentY + Picture1.TextHeight("ABCDEFG")
    Picture1.FontUnderline = True
    Picture1.Print ("Underlined text.")
    Picture1.CurrentX = 25
    Picture1.CurrentY = Picture1.CurrentY + Picture1.TextHeight("ABCDEFG")
    Picture1.FontBold = True
    Picture1.Print ("Bold underlined text.")
End Sub
```

Running this code yields the result shown in Figure 10.11, where the picture box displays formatted text. It's no rich text box, but you can use the text capabilities of a picture box to display labels and call-outs for graphics.

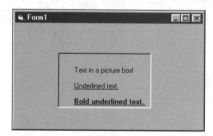

Figure 10.11   Formatting text in a picture box.

Clearing A Picture Box

How can you clear the current image in a picture box and start over? You use the **Cls** method. Here's an example that clears a picture box when the user clicks a command button:

```
Private Sub Command1_Click()
    Picture1.Cls
End Sub
```

*TIP: The name **Cls** comes from the original DOS days, when it stood for "clear screen." That command was adopted in Microsoft Basic, and from there became a part of Visual Basic, even though it's no longer intended to clear the screen.*

Accessing Individual Pixels In A Picture Box

The Testing Department is calling. Wouldn't it be better to let users select new colors in your *SuperDuperTextPro* program by just clicking the new color they want in a picture box instead of asking them to type in new color values? Hmm, you think, how do you do that?

You can use the **Point** method to determine the color of a pixel in a picture box. This method returns the red, green, and blue colors in one **Long** integer.

Let's see an example to make this clear. Here, we'll let the user click one picture box, **Picture1**, to set the color in another, **Picture2**, using the **MouseDown** event:

```
Private Sub Picture1_MouseDown(Button As Integer, Shift As Integer, _
    X As Single, Y As Single)

End Sub
```

When the user clicks a pixel in **Picture1**, we'll set the background color of **Picture2** to the same color, and we get that color using the **Point** method:

```
Private Sub Picture1_MouseDown(Button As Integer, Shift As Integer, _
    X As Single, Y As Single)
    Picture2.BackColor = Picture1.Point(X, Y)
End Sub
```

The result of this code appears in Figure 10.12. When the user clicks a point in the top picture box, the program sets the background color of the bottom picture box to the same color.

TIP: *Besides getting a pixel with the **Point** method, you can also set individual pixels with the **PSet** method. See "Drawing Lines And Circles In A Picture Box" earlier in this chapter.*

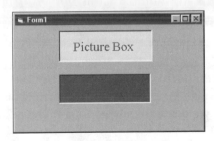

Figure 10.12   Using the Point method to get a point's color.

Copying Pictures To And Pasting Pictures From The Clipboard

The users love your new graphics program, *SuperDuperGraphics4U*, but would like to *export* the images they create to other programs. How can you do that?

You can copy the images to the Clipboard, letting the user paste them into other programs. To place data in the Clipboard, you use **SetData( )**, and to retrieve data from the Clipboard, you use **GetData( )**.

An example will make this clearer. Here, we'll paste a picture from **Picture1** to **Picture2** using two buttons: **Command1** and **Command2**. When users click **Command1**, we'll copy the picture from **Picture1** to the Clipboard; when they click **Command2**, we'll paste the picture to **Picture2**.

To place the image in **Picture1** into the Clipboard, we use **SetData( )**:

```
Clipboard.SetData data, [format]
```

Here are the possible values for the *format* parameter for images:

- **vbCFBitmap**—2; bitmap (.bmp) file
- **vbCFMetafile**—3; metafile (.wmf) file
- **vbCFDIB**—8; device-independent bitmap (.dib) file
- **vbCFPalette**—9; color palette

If you omit the format parameter, Visual Basic will determine the correct format, so we'll just copy the picture from **Picture1.Picture** to the Clipboard this way:

```
Private Sub Command1_Click()
    Clipboard.SetData Picture1.Picture
End Sub
```

To paste the picture, use **GetData( )**:

```
Clipboard.GetData ([format])
```

The format parameter here is the same as for **SetData( )**, and as before, if you don't specify the format, Visual Basic will determine it. So when the user clicks the second button, we paste the image into **Picture2** this way:

```
Private Sub Command2_Click()
    Picture2.Picture = Clipboard.GetData()
End Sub
```

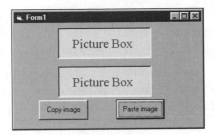

Figure 10.13   Copying a picture to and pasting it from the Clipboard.

That's all it takes. When you run the program and click the Copy and then the Paste button, the image is copied to the Clipboard and then pasted into the second picture box, as shown in Figure 10.13. The program is a success. Now we're using the Clipboard with picture boxes.

Stretching And Flipping Images In A Picture Box

You can gain a lot more control over how images are displayed in picture boxes using the **PaintPicture** method:

```
PictureBox.PaintPicture picture, x1, y1, [width1, height1, [x2, y2, _
    [width2, height2, [opcode]]]]
```

Using this method, you can stretch or flip images in a picture box. Here's what the arguments passed to **PaintPicture** mean:

- *picture*—The source of the graphic to be drawn onto the object; should be a **Picture** property.

- *x1, y1*—Single-precision values indicating the destination coordinates (x-axis and y-axis) on the object for the picture to be drawn. The **ScaleMode** property of the object determines the unit of measure used.

- *width1*—Single-precision value indicating the destination width of the picture. The **ScaleMode** property of the object determines the unit of measure used. If the destination width is larger or smaller than the source width (*width2*), the picture is stretched or compressed to fit. If omitted, the source width is used.

- *height1*—Single-precision value indicating the destination height of the picture. The **ScaleMode** property of the object determines the unit of measure used. If the destination height is larger or smaller than the source height (*height2*), the picture is stretched or compressed to fit. If omitted, the source height is used.

- *x2, y2*—Single-precision values indicating the coordinates (x-axis and y-axis) of a clipping region within the picture. The **ScaleMode** property of the object determines the unit of measure used. If omitted, 0 is assumed.

- *width2*—Single-precision value indicating the source width of a clipping region within the picture. The **ScaleMode** property of the object determines the unit of measure used. If omitted, the entire source width is used.

- *height2*—Single-precision value indicating the source height of a clipping region within the picture. The **ScaleMode** property of the object determines the unit of measure used. If omitted, the entire source height is used.

- *opcode*—**Long** value or code that is used only with bitmaps. It defines a bit-wise operation (such as **vbMergeCopy**) that is performed on the picture as it is drawn on the object.

You can flip a bitmap horizontally or vertically by using negative values for the destination height (*height1*) and/or the destination width (*width1*). For example, here's how we flip the image in **Picture1** horizontally and display it in **Picture2** (keep in mind that to draw from the **Form_Load** event, you have to set the form's **AutoRedraw** property to True):

```
Private Sub Form_Load()
    Picture2.PaintPicture Picture1.Picture, Picture1.ScaleWidth, 0, _
        -1 * Picture1.ScaleWidth, Picture1.ScaleHeight
    Picture2.Height = Picture1.Height
End Sub
```

The results of the preceding code appear in Figure 10.14. Now we're flipping images in picture boxes.

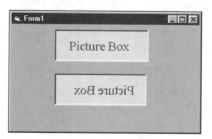

Figure 10.14   Flipping an image in a picture box.

Printing A Picture

Can you print the image in a picture box out on the printer? You sure can, using the **PaintPicture** method. To print on the printer, you just use the Visual Basic Printer object this way with **PaintPicture**:

```
Printer.PaintPicture picture, x1, y1, [width1, height1, [x2, y2, _
    [width2, height2, [opcode]]]]
```

Here's what the arguments passed to **PaintPicture** mean:

- *picture*—The source of the graphic to be drawn onto the object (for example, **Picture1.Picture**).

- *x1, y1*—Single-precision values indicating the destination coordinates (x-axis and y-axis) on the object for the picture to be drawn. The **ScaleMode** property of the object determines the unit of measure used.

- *width1*—Single-precision value indicating the destination width of the picture. The **ScaleMode** property of the object determines the unit of measure used. If the destination width is larger or smaller than the source width (*width2*), the picture is stretched or compressed to fit. If omitted, the source width is used.

- *height1*—Single-precision value indicating the destination height of the picture. The **ScaleMode** property of the object determines the unit of measure used. If the destination height is larger or smaller than the source height (*height2*), the picture is stretched or compressed to fit. If omitted, the source height is used.

- *x2, y2*—Single-precision values indicating the coordinates (x-axis and y-axis) of a clipping region within the picture (drawing operations outside the clipping region are ignored). The **ScaleMode** property of the object determines the unit of measure used. If omitted, 0 is assumed.

- *width2*—Single-precision value indicating the source width of a clipping region within the picture. The **ScaleMode** property of the object determines the unit of measure used. If omitted, the entire source width is used.

- *height2*—Single-precision value indicating the source height of a clipping region within the picture. The **ScaleMode** property of the object determines the unit of measure used. If omitted, the entire source height is used.

- *opcode*—**Long** value or code that is used only with bitmaps. It defines a bit-wise operation (such as **vbMergeCopy**) that is performed on the picture as it is drawn on the object.

For example, here's how to print the picture in **Picture1** on the printer:

```
Private Sub Command1_Click()
    Printer.PaintPicture Picture1.Picture, 0, 0
End Sub
```

That's all there is to it—the **PaintPicture** method is extraordinarily powerful. Note that before printing a picture, you may want to display a Print dialog box (see the next chapter).

Using Picture Box Handles

You can gain even more control over what's going on in a picture box by using the various Windows handles available for that control together with direct Windows API calls. Here are the picture box handle properties:

- **hDC**—Handle to the picture box's device context
- **hWnd**—Handle to the picture box's window
- **Image**—Handle to the picture box's bitmap
- **Handle**—Different handle types depending on the picture's **Type** property (for example, **Picture1.Picture.Type**) as follows:
  - **Type = 1**—An **HBITMAP** handle
  - **Type = 2**—An **HMETAFILE** handle
  - **Type = 3**—An **HICON** or an **HCURSOR** handle
  - **Type = 4**—An **HENHMETAFILE** handle

For example, here we use the **hDC** property of a picture box to create a compatible bitmap and device context matching the picture box, using the Windows API functions **CreateCompatibleDC( )** and **CreateCompatibleBitmap( )** (these and all Windows API functions must also be declared in the program, as we'll see in Chapter 23):

```
Private Sub Form_Load()
    Picture1.Picture = LoadPicture("image.bmp")

    Dim dcMemory As Long
    Dim hMemoryBitmap As Long
    dcMemory = CreateCompatibleDC(Picture1.hdc)
    hMemoryBitmap = CreateCompatibleBitmap(Picture1.hdc, 60, 30)
End Sub
```

Setting Measurement Scales In A Picture Box

Picture boxes have a number of scale properties, and perhaps the most popular one is **ScaleMode**, which sets the units of measurement in a picture box. Here are the possible values for **ScaleMode** (note that when you set the scale mode of a picture box, all measurements are in those new units, including coordinates passed to your program, like mouse-down locations):

- **vbUser**—0; indicates that one or more of the **ScalcHcight**, **ScaleWidth**, **ScaleLeft**, and **ScaleTop** properties are set to custom values
- **vbTwips**—1(the default); Twip (1440 twips per logical inch; 567 twips per logical centimeter)
- **vbPoints**—2; point (72 points per logical inch)
- **vbPixels**—3; pixel (smallest unit of monitor or printer resolution)
- **vbCharacters**—4; character (horizontal equals 120 twips per unit; vertical equals 240 twips per unit)
- **vbInches**—5; inch
- **vbMillimeters**—6; millimeter
- **vbCentimeters**—7; centimeter
- **vbHimetric**—8; hiMetric
- **vbContainerPosition**—9; units used by the control's container to determine the control's position
- **vbContainerSize**—10; units used by the control's container to determine the control's size

For example, in our image map example, we set the scale mode to pixels:

```
Private Sub Form_Load()
    Picture1.ScaleMode = vbPixels
End Sub
```

Then we could use pixel dimensions in the **MouseDown** event:

```
Private Sub Picture1_MouseDown(Button As Integer, Shift As Integer, X As _
    Single, Y As Single)
    If X > 16 And X < 83 And Y > 11 And Y < 36 Then
        MsgBox "You clicked the word ""Picture"""
    End If

    If X > 83 And X < 125 And Y > 11 And Y < 36 Then
        MsgBox "You clicked the word ""Box"""
    End If
End Sub
```

If you set the scale mode to **vbUser**, you can define your own units by setting the dimensions of the picture box using the **ScaleLeft**, **ScaleTop**, **ScaleWidth**, and **ScaleHeight** properties. This can be very useful if you're plotting points and want to use a picture box as a graph.

---

*TIP: The **ScaleWidth** and **ScaleHeight** properties of a picture box hold the image's actual dimensions (in units determined by the **ScaleMode** property), not the **Width** and **Height** properties, which hold the control's width and height (including the border).*

Saving Pictures To Disk

We already know you can load pictures into a picture box with the **LoadPicture** function. Can you save them to disk?

Yes, you can, using **SavePicture**. Here's how that statement works:

```
SavePicture picture, stringexpression
```

Here's what the parameters for **SavePicture** mean:

- **picture**—Picture or image control from which the graphics file is to be created
- **stringexpression**—File name of the graphics file to save

SavePicture only saves images in BMP, WMF, and ICO formats (depending on the file type the image came from originally); if the image came from a GIF or JPEG file, it's saved in BMP format. Graphics in an **Image** property are always saved as bitmap (.bmp) files no matter what their original format.

Here's an example where we save the image from **Picture1** to a file, C:\image.bmp, when the user clicks a button:

```
Private Sub Command1_Click()
    SavePicture Picture1.Picture, "c:\image.bmp"
End Sub
```

Adding An Image Control To A Form

You've got 200 picture boxes in your program, and suddenly the Testing Department is on the line: your program is causing users' computers to run out of memory.

No problem here, you say. They say, that's because not everyone has 128MB of RAM like you do—it's time to decrease your program's memory consumption.

One way of using fewer system resources is to use fewer picture boxes. As we've seen in this chapter, picture boxes are powerful controls—and with that power comes lots of overhead. If you're just going to be displaying images, use image controls instead. The image control uses fewer system resources and repaints faster than a picture box (however, it supports only a subset of the picture box properties, events, and methods).

To install an image control, just use the Image Control tool in the toolbox. After adding the image control to your form, just set its **Picture** property to the image file you want to display. By default, image controls shape themselves to the image you display; if you want to stretch the image to fit the image control and not the other way around, set the image control's **Stretch** property to True (the default is False).

As an example, we've placed an (unstretched) image in the image control in Figure 10.15.

Figure 10.15   Using an image control.

Stretching An Image In An Image Control

You can stretch (or flip) an image in a picture box using the **PaintPicture** method, but you can't use **PaintPicture** with image controls. Is there still some way of producing interesting graphics effects in an image control?

You can use the image control's **Stretch** property. By default, image controls shape themselves to fit the images inside them (after all, their primary purpose is to display images), but if you set the **Stretch** property to True (the default is False), the image control will stretch the image to fit the control.

As an example, we're stretching an image in the image control in Figure 10.16.

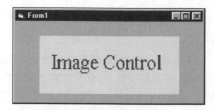

Figure 10.16   Stretching an image in an image control.

You can also stretch an image in an image control by resizing the control (using its **Width** and **Height** properties) at runtime as long as the control's **Stretch** property is True.

Chapter 11

Windows Common Dialogs

If you need an immediate solution to:	See page:
Creating And Displaying A Windows Common Dialog	345
Setting A Common Dialog's Title	346
Did The User Click OK Or Cancel?	347
Using A Color Dialog Box	348
Setting Color Dialog Flags	350
Using The Open And Save As Dialogs	350
Setting Open And Save As Flags	352
Getting The File Name In Open, Save As Dialogs	354
Setting Maximum File Name Size In Open And Save As Dialog Boxes	354
Setting Default File Extensions	355
Set Or Get The Initial Directory	355
Setting File Types (Filters) In Open, Save As Dialogs	356
Using A Font Dialog Box	358
Setting Font Dialog Flags	360
Setting **Max** And **Min** Font Sizes	361
Using The Print Dialog Box	363
Setting Print Dialog Flags	365
Setting The Minimum And Maximum Pages To Print	366
Setting Page Orientation	367
Showing Windows Help From A Visual Basic Program	368

In Depth

In this chapter, we're going to examine the Windows Common Dialogs, which provide a powerful and professional set of dialog boxes for interacting with the user. Microsoft created the Common Dialogs to promote a common user interface across all Windows programs, and in fact the Common Dialogs do work well—and they make programming easier for the programmer. Having a common user interface across all Windows programs is valuable for the user, because it simplifies tasks. For the programmer, the Common Dialogs means that we have a powerful set of dialog boxes ready for us to use, without having to create them ourselves. From both ends of the spectrum, then, the Windows Common Dialogs may be considered a success.

The Common Dialog control can display five different dialog boxes—Open A File, Save A File, Set A Color, Set A Font, and Print A Document.

The Common Dialog Control

The Common Dialogs are all part of one control: the Common Dialog control. You add that control to a program with the Visual Basic Project|Components menu item. Click the Controls tab in the Components box that opens, and select the entry labeled Microsoft Common Dialog Control, then click on OK to close the Components box. You add a Common Dialog control to a form in the usual way—just double-click the Common Dialog tool in the toolbox, or select it and paint the control on the form. The Common Dialog tool appears as the eleventh tool down on the right in the Visual Basic toolbox in Figure 11.1. The Common Dialog control will appear as a nonresizable icon on your form and is not visible at runtime.

You use the control's **Action** property to display a dialog box or, equivalently, these methods:

- **ShowOpen**—Show Open dialog box
- **ShowSave**—Show Save As dialog box
- **ShowColor**—Show Color dialog box
- **ShowFont**—Show Font dialog box
- **ShowPrinter**—Show Print or Print Options dialog box

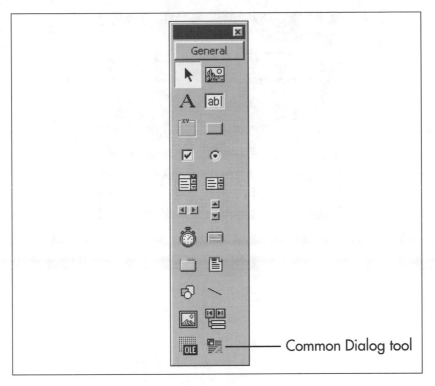

Common Dialog tool

Figure 11.1   The Common Dialog tool.

Besides these dialog boxes, you can also display Windows Help:

• **ShowHelp**—Invokes the Windows Help engine

The Common Dialog control automatically provides context-sensitive Help on the interface of the dialog boxes. You invoke context-sensitive Help by clicking the Help button labeled What's This in the title bar, then clicking the item for which you want more information. In addition, you can right-click the item for which you want more information, then select the What's This command in the displayed context menu.

TIP: *We might also note, by the way, that there is no way currently to specify where a dialog box is displayed; that might change in some future release.*

As an example, the Font dialog box appears in Figure 11.2.

That's really all the overview we need. We're ready to start the Immediate Solutions now.

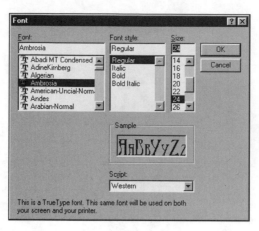

Figure 11.2   The Font dialog box.

Immediate Solutions

Creating And Displaying A Windows Common Dialog

The Testing Department is calling again. Your program, *SuperDuperTextPro*, is great, but why is the File Save As dialog box the size of a postage stamp? And why is it colored purple? Shouldn't it match the uniform kind of dialog box that other Windows programs use?

To make your dialog boxes look just like the dialog boxes other programs use (and add professionalism to your program), you can use the Windows Common Dialogs, which are wrapped up in the Windows Common Dialog control. The Common Dialog control can display five different dialog boxes—Open A File, Save A File, Set A Color, Set A Font, and Print A Document, and you can also display Windows Help.

Adding a Windows Common Dialog control to your program is easy: just follow these steps:

1. Select the Project|Components menu item.
2. Select the Controls tab in the Components box that opens.
3. Select the entry labeled Microsoft Common Dialog Control, then click on OK to close the Components box.
4. Add a Common Dialog control to a form in the usual way—just double-click the Common Dialog tool in the toolbox, or select it and paint the control on the form. (The Common Dialog tool appears as the eleventh tool down on the right in the Visual Basic toolbox in Figure 11.1.)
5. Add the code you want to open the dialog box and make use of values the user sets.

To display various dialog boxes, you use these Common Dialog methods (for example, **CommonDialog1.ShowColor**):

- **ShowOpen**—Show Open dialog box
- **ShowSave**—Show Save As dialog box
- **ShowColor**—Show Color dialog box
- **ShowFont**—Show Font dialog box

- **ShowPrinter**—Show Print or Print Options dialog box
- **ShowHelp**—Invokes the Windows Help engine

You can also set the Common Dialog's **Action** property to do the same thing (and in fact, that's the way you used to display Common Dialogs until recent Visual Basic releases). Microsoft says that using the preceding methods "adds functionality," but in fact, the two ways of displaying dialog boxes are equivalent at this writing (although using methods like **ShowHelp** instead of **Action = 6** makes code a little clearer). Here are the values you can place in the **Action** property:

- *0*—No action
- *1*—Displays the Open dialog box
- *2*—Displays the Save As dialog box
- *3*—Displays the Color dialog box
- *4*—Displays the Font dialog box
- *5*—Displays the Print dialog box
- *6*—Runs winhelp32.exe

Now that you've added a Common Dialog control to your program, refer to the individual topics in this chapter for the dialog box you want to work with to see how to retrieve values from the user.

---

*TIP: Before displaying the Font and Help dialog boxes, you need to set the Common Dialogs control's **Flags** property or nothing will appear. See "Setting Color Dialog Flags," "Setting Open and Save As Flags," "Setting Font Dialog Flags," and "Setting Print Dialog Flags" later in this chapter.*

Setting A Common Dialog's Title

The Aesthetic Design Department is calling again: can't you change the text in the title bar of those dialog boxes? How about changing the title of the Open dialog box from "Open" to "Select A File To Open"?

Although some programmers may question the wisdom of changing a Common Dialog's title, you can do it using the **DialogTitle** property. As an example, here we're changing the title of an Open dialog box to "Select a file to open" (see Figure 11.3):

```
Private Sub Command1_Click()
    CommonDialog1.DialogTitle = "Select a file to open"
    CommonDialog1.ShowOpen
End Sub
```

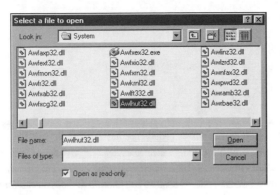

Figure 11.3   Our dialog box with revised title.

Warning!   Note that this property, DialogTitle, does not work for the Color, Font, and Print dialog boxes.

Did The User Click OK Or Cancel?

You've displayed your dialog box, and the user has dismissed it. But did the user click the OK or the Cancel button? Should you take action or not?

You can check which button the user has selected by examining the various properties of the dialog box control—for example, when the user clicks Cancel in a File Open dialog box, the **FileName** property returns an empty string, "".

However, Visual Basic provides a more systematic way of checking which button was clicked. You can set the Common Dialog **CancelError** property to True to create a special, nonharmful, and trappable error, error number 32755 (Visual Basic constant **cdlCancel**), when the user clicks the Cancel button.

To trap this error if you've set the **CancelError** property to True, use **On Error GoTo**, and place the label control at the end of the procedure:

```
Private Sub Command1_Click()
    On Error GoTo Cancel
...
Cancel:
End Sub
```

Then you can show the dialog box and take action, assuming the user clicked on OK. If, on the other hand, the user clicked Cancel, control will go to the end of the procedure and exit harmlessly:

```
Private Sub Command1_Click()
    On Error GoTo Cancel
    CommonDialog1.ShowColor
    Text1.BackColor = CommonDialog1.Color
Cancel:
End Sub
```

TIP: *If you have enabled other trappable errors in your procedure (the **On Error GoTo** statement in the preceding code does not affect code outside the procedure it's defined in), check to make sure that the error you're expecting when the user clicks Cancel does in fact have the number **cdlCancel**. You can do this by checking the **Err** object's **Number** property. Note also that Common Dialog controls can return errors besides **cdlCancel**—such as **cdlHelp** when the Help system failed to work properly, or **cdlFonts** if no fonts exist—and you might check for those separately.*

Using A Color Dialog Box

The Aesthetic Design Department is calling again. Wouldn't it be nice if you let the user select the color of the controls in your program? Yes, you say, but.... Great, they say, and hang up.

To let the user select colors, you use the Color dialog box, and you display that dialog box with the Common Dialog method **ShowColor**. To retrieve the color the user selected, you use the dialog box's **Color** property. There are special flags you can set for the Color dialog box—see the next topic for more information.

Let's see an example. When the user clicks a button, we'll display a Color dialog box and let the user select the background color of a text box. Add a Common Dialog control to a form and set its **CancelError** property to True so that clicking Cancel will cause a **cdlCancel** error. Next, we trap that error this way:

```
Private Sub Command1_Click()
    On Error GoTo Cancel
    ...
Cancel:
End Sub
```

Now we use the Common Dialog control's **ShowColor** method to show the color dialog:

```
Private Sub Command1_Click()
    On Error GoTo Cancel
    CommonDialog1.ShowColor
```

```
...
Cancel:
End Sub
```

When control returns from the dialog box, we use the **Color** property to set the text box's background color to the color the user has selected:

```
Private Sub Command1_Click()
    On Error GoTo Cancel
    CommonDialog1.ShowColor
    Text1.BackColor = CommonDialog1.Color
Cancel:
End Sub
```

That's it—when you run the program and click the button, the Color dialog box appears, as in Figure 11.4.

When the user selects a color and clicks on OK, the program sets the text box's background color to the newly selected color, as shown in Figure 11.5.

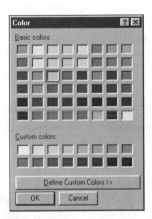

Figure 11.4   The Color dialog box.

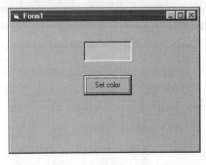

Figure 11.5   Setting a control's color with the Color dialog box.

Now we're using the Color dialog box. The listing for the preceding program is located in the colordialog folder on this book's accompanying CD-ROM.

Setting Color Dialog Flags

There are a number of options you can set before displaying a Color dialog box, and you set them in the **Flags** property of the Common Dialog control. Here are the possible values:

- **cdlCCRGBInit**—1; sets the initial color value for the dialog box
- **cdCClFullOpen**—2; entire dialog box is displayed, including the Define Custom Colors section
- **cdlCCPreventFullOpen**—4; disables the Define Custom Colors command button and prevents the user from defining custom colors
- **cdlCCHelpButton**—8; causes the dialog box to display a Help button

You can set more than one flag for a dialog box using the **Or** operator. For example:

```
CommonDialog1.Flags = &H10& Or &H200&
```

(Note that although this shows what we're doing numerically, it's usually better to use constants to make the code more readable.) Adding the desired constant values produces the same result.

Using The Open And Save As Dialogs

Probably the most common use of the Common Dialog control is to display File Open and File Save As dialog boxes, and you display those dialog boxes with the Common Dialog control's **ShowOpen** and **ShowSave** methods. These methods need no arguments passed to them—to set various options, you set the Common Dialog control's **Flags** property (see the next topic), such as overwriting existing files and so on.

You can also set the **Filter** property so the dialog box displays only certain types of files, such as text files. See "Setting File Types (Filters) In Open, Save As Dialogs" a little later in this chapter.

To find out what file the user wants to work with, you check the Common Dialog's **FileName** property after the user clicks on OK in the dialog box.

That property holds the fully qualified (that is, with path) name of the file to open. If you just want the file's name, use the **FileTitle** property.

Let's see an example. In this case, we'll let the user select a file to open, and then display the file's name and path in a message box.

Start by adding a Common Dialog control to a form, then set the control's **CancelError** property to True so we can check if the user clicked Cancel. To check that, we use **On Error GoTo**:

```
Private Sub Command1_Click()
    On Error GoTo Cancel
...
Cancel:
End Sub
```

Then we display the Open dialog box:

```
Private Sub Command1_Click()
    On Error GoTo Cancel
    CommonDialog1.ShowOpen
...
Cancel:
End Sub
```

Finally, assuming the user clicked on OK, we can display the name of the file they selected in a message box using the **FileName** property:

```
Private Sub Command1_Click()
    On Error GoTo Cancel
    CommonDialog1.ShowOpen
    MsgBox "File to open: " & CommonDialog1.FileName
Cancel:
End Sub
```

When you run this code and click the button, the Open dialog box appears, as in Figure 11.6.

If you make a file selection and click on OK, the Open dialog box closes and the program displays the name of the file you selected, along with its path, in a message box. Our program is a success; the code for this program is located in the opendialog folder on this book's accompanying CD-ROM.

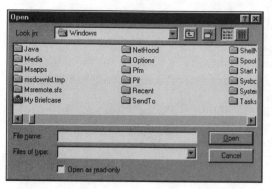

Figure 11.6   The Open dialog box.

Setting Open And Save As Flags

You can set a wide variety of options when you display File Open and File Save As dialog boxes by setting the Common Dialog control's **Flags** property. Here are the possible settings:

- **cdlOFNAllowMultiselect**—&H200; specifies that the File Name list box allows multiple selections.

- **cdlOFNCreatePrompt**—&H2000; the user can select more than one file at runtime by pressing the Shift key and using the up arrow and down arrow keys to select the desired files. When this is done, the **FileName** property returns a string containing the names of all selected files. The names in the string are delimited by spaces.

- **cdlOFNCreatePrompt**—&H2000; specifies that the dialog box prompts the user to create a file that doesn't currently exist. This flag automatically sets the **cdlOFNPathMustExist** and **cdlOFNFileMustExist** flags.

- **cdlOFNExplorer**—&H80000; displays the Explorer-like Open A File dialog box template. Works with Windows 95 and Windows NT 4.

- **cdlOFNExtensionDifferent**—&H400; indicates that the extension of the returned file name is different from the extension specified by the **DefaultExt** property. This flag isn't set if the **DefaultExt** property is **Null**, if the extensions match, or if the file has no extension. This flag value can be checked upon closing the dialog box. This can be useful if you want to track the kind of file the user wants to open.

- **cdlOFNFileMustExist**—&H1000; specifies that the user can enter only names of existing files in the File Name text box. If this flag is set and the user enters an invalid file name, a warning is displayed. This flag automatically sets the **cdlOFNPathMustExist** flag.

- **cdlOFNHelpButton**—&H10; causes the dialog box to display the Help button.
- **cdlOFNHideReadOnly**—&H4; hides the Read Only checkbox.
- **cdlOFNLongNames**—&H200000; enables the use of long file names.
- **cdlOFNNoChangeDir**—&H8; forces the dialog box to set the current directory to what it was when the dialog box was opened.
- **cdlOFNNoDereferenceLinks**—&H100000; disables the use of shell links (also known as shortcuts). By default, choosing a shell link causes it to be interpreted by the shell.
- **cdlOFNNoLongNames**—&H40000; disables long file names.
- **cdlOFNNoReadOnlyReturn**—&H8000; specifies that the returned file won't have the Read Only attribute set and won't be in a write-protected directory.
- **cdlOFNNoValidate**—&H100; specifies that the Common Dialog allows invalid characters in the returned file name.
- **cdlOFNOverwritePrompt**—&H2; causes the Save As dialog box to generate a message box if the selected file already exists. The user must confirm whether to overwrite the file.
- **cdlOFNPathMustExist**—&H800; specifies that the user can enter only valid paths. If this flag is set and the user enters an invalid path, a warning message is displayed.
- **cdlOFNReadOnly**—&H1; causes the Read Only checkbox to be initially checked when the dialog box is created. This flag also indicates the state of the Read Only checkbox when the dialog box is closed.
- **cdlOFNShareAware**—&H4000; specifies that sharing violation errors will be ignored.

You can set more than one flag for a dialog box using the **Or** operator. For example:

```
CommonDialog1.Flags = &H10& Or &H200&
```

(Although this shows what we're doing numerically, it's usually better to use constants to make your code more readable.) Adding the desired constant values produces the same result.

Getting The File Name In Open, Save As Dialogs

Now that you've used the Common Dialog control's **ShowOpen** or **ShowSave** to display an Open or Save As dialog box, how do you get the file name the user has specified? You do that using one of two properties after the user clicks on the OK button:

- **FileName**—Holds the file name the user selected, with the file's full path.
- **FileTitle**—Holds just the file's name, without the path.

Here's an example where we've set a Common Dialog control's **CancelError** property to True so Visual Basic will create a trappable **cdlCancel** error if the user clicks the Cancel button, show a File Open dialog box, and display the name and path of the file the user selected in a message box:

```
Private Sub Command1_Click()
    On Error GoTo Cancel
    CommonDialog1.ShowOpen
    MsgBox "File to open: " & CommonDialog1.FileName
Cancel:
End Sub
```

You can set the **Filter** property so the dialog box displays only certain types of files, such as text files. The **Flags** property can be used to change various elements on the dialog box, as well as to prompt the user when certain actions may occur, such as overwriting a file. See "Setting File Types (Filters) In Open, Save As Dialogs" for more on filters. For more on flags, see "Setting Color Dialog Flags," "Setting Open and Save As Flags," "Setting Font Dialog Flags," and "Setting Print Dialog Flags" later in this chapter.

Setting Maximum File Name Size In Open And Save As Dialog Boxes

You can use the Common Dialog control's **MaxFileSize** property to set—not the maximum file size you can open, but the maximum *file name* size. You set this property to a number of bytes as follows, where we're restricting the file name and path to fit into 100 bytes:

```
CommonDialog1.MaxFileSize = 100
```

This is useful if you're passing file names to other programs that can't use names longer than a certain length.

TIP: *When using the **cdlOFNAllowMultiselect** flag, you may want to increase the value in the **MaxFileSize**
property to allow enough memory for the selected file names.*

Setting Default File Extensions

Like many Windows programs, you can make your programs set the default
extension for the types of files you want to save (for example, .txt) if the user
doesn't specify one. You specify a default extension with the Common Dialog
control's **DefaultExt** property.

An example will make this clearer. Here, we set the default extension of our
files to save to "txt" by setting the **DefaultExt** property:

```
Private Sub Command1_Click()
    On Error GoTo Cancel
    CommonDialog1.DefaultExt = "txt"
    CommonDialog1.ShowSave
    MsgBox "File to save: " & CommonDialog1.FileName
Cancel:
End Sub
```

Let's say the user just types a file name without an extension, such as
"phonebook", in the Save As dialog box; the dialog box will then report the
actual name of the file to save as phonebook.txt. If, on the other hand, the user
specifies a file extension, that extension is preserved.

Set Or Get The Initial Directory

The Testing Department is calling again: users of your program, *SuperDuper-
TextPro*, are complaining. When they want to save many files to their favorite
directory, C:\poetry\roses\are\red\violets\are\blue, they have to open folder after
folder each time to get back to that directory. Can't you let them set a default
directory to save files to?

You can, using the Common Dialog control's **InitDir** property. For example,
here's how we set the initial directory to C:\windows when we open files using
the Open dialog box:

```
Private Sub Command1_Click()
    On Error GoTo Cancel
    CommonDialog1.InitDir = "c:\windows"
```

```
        CommonDialog1.ShowOpen
        MsgBox "File to open: " & CommonDialog1.FileName
Cancel:
End Sub
```

Running this code results in the Open dialog box you see in Figure 11.7.

Setting the initial directory like this can make multiple opens or saves much easier, which is very considerate to the user (and I know of some Microsoft software that could benefit by doing this).

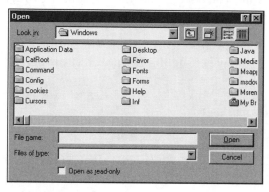

Figure 11.7   Setting an initial directory.

Setting File Types (Filters) In Open, Save As Dialogs

The Testing Department is calling again. Your program, *SuperDuper-Graphics4U*, only works with graphics files, but somehow users are trying to open text (.txt) files—and crashing the program. Is there some way you can clue them in as to allowed file types when they open files?

Yes—you can set the Common Dialog control's **Filter** property to indicate the allowed file types and extensions in a drop-down list box in the Open and Save As dialog boxes. (To see an example of such a drop-down list box, use Visual Basic's Save Project As menu item in the File menu; this list box gives two file extension types: *.vbp and all files, *.*.)

To set up the **Filter** string, you separate prompts to the user—for example, "Text files (*.txt)"—with upright characters ("|", also called the *pipe* symbol) from the file specifications to Visual Basic ("*.txt"). (Don't add extra spaces around the uprights, because if you do, they'll be displayed along with the rest of the file extension information.)

This is obviously one of those things made easier with an example (in fact, I always forget how to set up file filter strings unless I can work from an example), so let's see one now. Here, we'll let the user select from three options: text files (*.txt), image files (*.jpg, *.gif), and all files (*.*). We set the **Filter** string this way in that case; look closely at the following string and you'll be able to see how to set up this string for yourself. (Here we've also set the Common Dialog control's **CancelError** property to True to create a trappable error if the user clicks the Cancel button):

```
Private Sub Command1_Click()
    On Error GoTo Cancel
    CommonDialog1.Filter = "Text files (*.txt)|*.txt|Image files _
        (*.jpg, *.gif)|*.jpg;*.gif|All files (*.*)|*.*"
    CommonDialog1.ShowOpen
    MsgBox "File to open: " & CommonDialog1.FileName
Cancel:
End Sub
```

Note in particular that when you have two file extensions for one file type—as we do for image files (*.jpg, *.gif)—you surround the file extensions with a semicolon (;) and enclose them in parentheses.

The result of this code appears in Figure 11.8. Here, we're letting the user select from our three types of files: text files (*.txt), image files (*.jpg, *.gif), and all files (*.*).

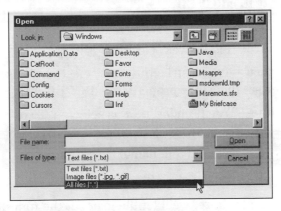

Figure 11.8   Setting file extension types in dialog boxes.

Using A Font Dialog Box

The Testing Department is calling again. Your new word processor, *SuperDuperTextPro*, is great, but why can't the users select the font they want to use? You ask, should they be able to do that? The Testing Department says, take a look at the Font dialog box.

You use the Common Dialog control's **ShowFont** method to show a Font dialog box. Note that before you use the **ShowFont** method, you must set the **Flags** property of the Common Dialog control to one of three constants to indicate if you want to display screen fonts, printer fonts, or both. The possible values are as follows:

- **cdlCFScreenFonts**—&H1; show screen fonts
- **cdlCFPrinterFonts**—&H2; show printer fonts
- **cdlCFBoth**—&H3; show both types of fonts

If you don't set one of these in the **Flags** property, a message box is displayed advising the user that "There are no fonts installed", which will probably cause them to panic. To see more possible settings for the **Flags** property, take a look at the next topic in this chapter.

When the user dismisses the Font dialog box by clicking on OK, you can determine their font selections using these properties of the Common Dialog control:

- **Color**—The selected color. To use this property, you must first set the **Flags** property to **cdlCFEffects**.
- **FontBold**—True if bold was selected.
- **FontItalic**—True if italic was selected.
- **FontStrikethru**—True if strikethru was selected. To use this property, you must first set the **Flags** property to **cdlCFEffects**.
- **FontUnderline**—True if underline was selected. To use this property, you must first set the **Flags** property to **cdlCFEffects**.
- **FontName**—The selected font name.
- **FontSize**—The selected font size.

Let's see an example. Here, we'll let the user set the font, font size, and font styles (like underline and bold) in a text box. We start by setting the Common Dialog control's **CancelError** property to True so clicking the Cancel button causes a trappable error:

```
Private Sub Command1_Click()
    On Error GoTo Cancel
...
Cancel:
End Sub
```

Next, we set the **Flags** property and show the Font dialog box:

```
Private Sub Command1_Click()
    On Error GoTo Cancel
    CommonDialog1.Flags = cdlCFBoth Or cdlCFEffects
    CommonDialog1.ShowFont
...
Cancel:
End Sub
```

Finally, we set the text box's properties to match what the user set in the Font dialog box:

```
Private Sub Command1_Click()
    On Error GoTo Cancel
    CommonDialog1.Flags = cdlCFBoth Or cdlCFEffects
    CommonDialog1.ShowFont

    Text1.FontName = CommonDialog1.FontName
    Text1.FontBold = CommonDialog1.FontBold
    Text1.FontItalic = CommonDialog1.FontItalic
    Text1.FontUnderline = CommonDialog1.FontUnderline
    Text1.FontSize = CommonDialog1.FontSize
    Text1.FontName = CommonDialog1.FontName
Cancel:
End Sub
```

Now when you run this program and click the button, the Font dialog box appears, as in Figure 11.9.

When you select the font options you want and click on OK, those options are installed in the text box, **Text1**, as shown in Figure 11.10.

That's it—now we're using Font dialog boxes. The listing for this program, fontdialog.frm, is located in the fontdialog folder on this book's accompanying CD-ROM.

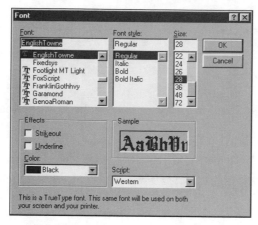

Figure 11.9   The Font dialog box.

Figure 11.10   Setting fonts and font styles with the Font dialog box.

Setting Font Dialog Flags

You can set a wide variety of options when using Font dialog boxes by using the Common Dialog control's **Flags** property. Here are the possible values to use with that property:

- **cdlCFANSIOnly**—&H400; specifies that the dialog box allows only a selection of the fonts that use the Windows character set. If this flag is set, the user won't be able to select a font that contains only symbols.

- **cdlCFApply**—&H200; enables the Apply button on the dialog box.

- **cdlCFBoth**—&H3; causes the dialog box to list the available printer and screen fonts. The **hDC** property identifies the device context associated with the printer.

- **cdlCFEffects**—&H100; specifies that the dialog box enables strikethru, underline, and color effects.

- **cdlCFFixedPitchOnly**—&H4000; specifies that the dialog box selects only fixed-pitch fonts.
- **cdlCFForceFontExist**—&H10000; specifies that an error message box is displayed if the user attempts to select a font or style that doesn't exist.
- **cdlCFHelpButton**—&H4; causes the dialog box to display a Help button.
- **cdlCFLimitSize**—&H2000; specifies that the dialog box selects only font sizes within the range specified by the **Min** and **Max** properties.
- **cdlCFNoFaceSel**—&H80000; no font name was selected.
- **cdlCFNoSimulations**—&H1000; specifies that the dialog box doesn't allow graphic device interface (GDI) font simulations.
- **cdlCFNoSizeSel**—&H200000; no font size was selected.
- **cdlCFNoStyleSel**—&H100000; no style was selected.
- **cdlCFNoVectorFonts**—&H800; specifies that the dialog box doesn't allow vector-font selections.
- **cdlCFPrinterFonts**—&H2; causes the dialog box to list only the fonts supported by the printer, specified by the **hDC** property.
- **cdlCFScalableOnly**—&H20000; specifies that the dialog box allows only the selection of fonts that can be scaled.
- **cdlCFScreenFonts**—&H1; causes the dialog box to list only the screen fonts supported by the system.
- **cdlCFTTOnly**—&H40000; specifies that the dialog box allows only the selection of TrueType fonts.
- **cdlCFWYSIWYG**—&H8000; specifies that the dialog box allows only the selection of fonts that are available on both the printer and on screen. If this flag is set, the **cdlCFBoth** and **cdlCFScalableOnly** flags should also be set.

You can set more than one flag for a dialog box using the **Or** operator. For example:

```
CommonDialog1.Flags = &H10& Or &H200&
```

Adding the desired constant values produces the same result.

Setting **Max** And **Min** Font Sizes

Setting Max And Min Font Sizes

The Testing Department is calling again. Now users are setting the font size in your program, *SuperDuperTextPro*, to 3 points—and then complaining they can't read what they've typed. Can you limit the allowed font range?

Yes, you can, using the Common Dialog control's **Min** and **Max** properties. When you want to make these properties active with a Font dialog box, you must first add the **cdlCFLimitSize** flag to the Common Dialog control's **Flags** property. Then you're free to restrict the possible range of font sizes.

Here's an example. We set the Common Dialog's **CancelError** property to True to catch Cancel button clicks, then set the **Flags** property of the Common Dialog control to display both screen fonts and printer fonts, and set the **cdlCFLimitSize** flag:

```
Private Sub Command1_Click()
    On Error GoTo Cancel
    CommonDialog1.Flags = cdlCFBoth Or cdlCFLimitSize
...
```

Then we set the minimum and maximum font sizes we want to allow, measured in points:

```
Private Sub Command1_Click()
    On Error GoTo Cancel
    CommonDialog1.Flags = cdlCFBoth Or cdlCFLimitSize
    CommonDialog1.Min = 12
    CommonDialog1.Max = 24
...
```

Finally, we show the Font dialog box, and then make use of the newly set font size:

```
Private Sub Command1_Click()
    On Error GoTo Cancel
    CommonDialog1.Flags = cdlCFBoth Or cdlCFLimitSize
    CommonDialog1.Min = 12
    CommonDialog1.Max = 24
    CommonDialog1.ShowFont
    Text1.FontName = CommonDialog1.FontSize
Cancel:
End Sub
```

That's all we need—the result of this code appears in Figure 11.11, where, as you can see, we've restricted the range of font sizes from 12 to 24 points in the Font dialog box.

TIP: *Note that because the font size is entered in a combo box in a Font dialog box, the user can enter a value outside the allowed range in the text box part of the combo. If they do and click on OK, however, an error message box appears saying the font size must be in the **Min** to **Max** range.*

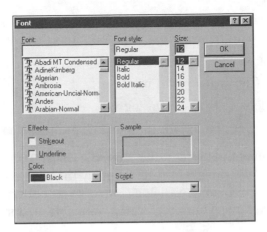

Figure 11.11   Restricting font size range in a Font dialog box.

Using The Print Dialog Box

The Testing Department is calling again. The Print button you've placed in your word processor, *SuperDuperTextPro*, is very nice, but it doesn't let the user set the number of copies of a document they want to print. You can't do that with a button, you explain. Right, they say—use a Print dialog box.

You show the Print dialog box with the Common Dialog control's **ShowPrinter** method. If you know your document's length, you can set the minimum and maximum pages to print in the Common Dialog control's **Min** and **Max** properties; setting these properties enables the From and To page range text boxes in the Print dialog box (see "Setting The Minimum And Maximum Pages To Print" later in this chapter). You can also set the Common Dialog control's **Flags** property to select various options here—see the next topic in this chapter.

This dialog box does *not* send data to the printer; instead, it lets the user specify how he wants data printed. Printing is up to you.

How do you print? If you've set the **PrinterDefault** property to True, you can use the **Printer** object to print data (the user can change the default printer from the Printer dialog box, setting a new default printer in the Windows registry or win.ini, but that new printer automatically becomes the one referred to by the **Printer** object). For example, you can print the picture in a picture box using the **Printer** object this way: **Printer.PaintPicture Picture1.Picture, 0, 0**. Otherwise, you must use Windows functions to print to the device represented by the **hDC** (a device context handle) property.

After the user clicks on OK, you can read these properties from the Common Dialog control to determine what printer options they've selected:

- **Copies**—The number of copies to print
- **FromPage**—The page to start printing
- **ToPage**—The page to stop printing
- **hDC**—The device context for the selected printer

Let's see an example. In this case, we'll use the Visual Basic **PrintForm** method to print a copy of the current form as many times as the user specifies. We start by setting the Common Dialog control's **CancelError** property to True so we can catch Cancel button clicks as trappable errors:

```
Private Sub Command1_Click()
    On Error GoTo Cancel
...
Cancel:
End Sub
```

Then we set the **PrinterDefault** property to True and show the Print dialog box:

```
Private Sub Command1_Click()
    On Error GoTo Cancel
    CommonDialog1.PrinterDefault = True
    CommonDialog1.ShowPrinter
...
Cancel:
End Sub
```

All that's left is to loop over the number of copies the user has requested (as returned in the **Copies** property) and call **PrintForm** each time:

```
Private Sub Command1_Click()
    Dim intLoopIndex As Integer

    On Error GoTo Cancel
    CommonDialog1.PrinterDefault = True
    CommonDialog1.ShowPrinter
    For intLoopIndex = 1 To CommonDialog1.Copies
        PrintForm
    Next intLoopIndex

Cancel:
End Sub
```

That's it—when the user clicks **Command1**, the program displays the Print dialog box; the user can set the number of copies to print and when they click on OK, Visual Basic displays a dialog box with the text "Printing..." momentarily, and the print job starts.

Our Print dialog box example is a success—the code for this program is located in the printerdialog folder on this book's accompanying CD-ROM.

Setting Print Dialog Flags

You can set a number of options in the Common Dialog control's **Flags** property when working with the Print dialog box:

- **cdlPDAllPages**—&H0; returns or sets the state of the All Pages option button.
- **cdlPDCollate**—&H10; returns or sets the state of the Collate checkbox.
- **cdlPDDisablePrintToFile**—&H80000; disables the Print To File checkbox.
- **cdlPDHelpButton**—&H800; causes the dialog box to display the Help button.
- **cdlPDHidePrintToFile**—&H100000; hides the Print To File checkbox.
- **cdlPDNoPageNums**—&H8; disables the Pages option button and the associated edit control.
- **cdlPDNoSelection**—&H4; disables the Selection option button.
- **cdlPDNoWarning**—&H80; prevents a warning message from being displayed when there is no default printer.
- **cdlPDPageNums**—&H2; returns or sets the state of the Pages option button.
- **cdlPDPrintSetup**—&H40; causes the system to display the Print Setup dialog box rather than the Print dialog box.
- **cdlPDPrintToFile**—&H20; returns or sets the state of the Print To File checkbox.
- **cdlPDReturnDC**—&H100; returns a device context for the printer selection made in the dialog box. The device context is returned in the dialog box's **hDC** property.
- **cdlPDReturnDefault**—&H400; returns the default printer name.
- **cdlPDReturnIC**—&H200; returns an information context for the printer selection made in the dialog box. An information context provides a fast

way to get information about the device without creating a device context. The information context is returned in the dialog box's **hDC** property.

- **cdlPDSelection**—&H1; returns or sets the state of the Selection option button. If neither **cdlPDPageNums** nor **cdlPDSelection** is specified, the All option button is in the selected state.

- **cdlPDUseDevModeCopies**—&H40000; if a printer driver doesn't support multiple copies, setting this flag disables the Number Of Copies control in the Print dialog box. If a driver does support multiple copies, setting this flag indicates that the dialog box stores the requested number of copies in the **Copies** property.

You can set more than one flag for a dialog box using the **Or** operator. For example:

```
CommonDialog1.Flags = &H10& Or &H200&
```

Adding the desired constant values produces the same result.

Setting The Minimum And Maximum Pages To Print

When displaying a Print dialog box, you can set the minimum and maximum allowed values for the print range (in other words, the From and To pages to print) using the **Min** and **Max** properties of the Common Dialog control. The **Min** property sets the smallest number the user can specify in the From text box. The **Max** property sets the largest number the user can specify in the To text box. For example, here we restrict the possible pages to print to a maximum of 10, in the range 0 to 9:

```
Private Sub Command1_Click()
    Dim intLoopIndex As Integer

    On Error GoTo Cancel
    CommonDialog1.PrinterDefault = True
    CommonDialog1.Min = 0
    CommonDialog1.Max = 9
    CommonDialog1.ShowPrinter
    For intLoopIndex = 1 To CommonDialog1.Copies
        PrintForm
    Next intLoopIndex

Cancel:
End Sub
```

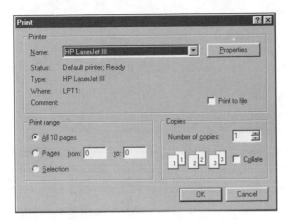

Figure 11.12   Setting print range in a Print dialog box.

Now when the Print dialog box appears, you can see that in the Print Range box, at lower left in Figure 11.12, one option button says "All 10 Pages". That is, we've set a maximum total of 10 pages for our document. The actual page range is from 0 to 9.

TIP: *If the user enters a number outside the allowed From and To range and clicks on OK, an error message box will appear letting them know what the allowed range is.*

Setting Page Orientation

When printing, you can set the page orientation—portrait (upright) or landscape (sideways)—with the Common Dialog control's **Orientation** property. This setting is communicated to the printer automatically, but note that not all printers will be able to set a document's orientation.

Here are the possible values for the **Orientation** property:

- **cdlPortrait**—1; documents are printed with the top at the narrow side of the paper (the default).

- **cdlLandScape**—2; documents are printed with the top at the wide side of the paper.

Here's an example. In this case, we're setting the printer's **Orientation** property to landscape:

```
Private Sub Command1_Click()
    Dim intLoopIndex As Integer
```

```
On Error GoTo Cancel
CommonDialog1.PrinterDefault = True
CommonDialog1.Orientation = cdlLandscape
CommonDialog1.ShowPrinter
For intLoopIndex = 1 To CommonDialog1.Copies
    PrintForm
Next intLoopIndex

Cancel:
End Sub
```

*Showing
Windows Help
From A Visual
Basic Program*

Showing Windows Help From A Visual Basic Program

You can display a Windows Help file (.hlp) with the Common Dialog control's **ShowHelp** method. To use this method, you first set the Common Dialog control's **HelpCommand** property to one of the following settings, and the **HelpFile** property to the actual name of the Help file to open.

Here are the possible settings for **HelpCommand**:

- **cdlHelpCommand**—&H102&; executes a Help macro.

- **cdlHelpContents**—&H3&; displays the Help contents topic as defined by the Contents option in the **[OPTION]** section of the HPJ file. This constant doesn't work for Help files created with Microsoft Help Workshop Version 4.0X. Instead, you use the value &HB to get the same effect.

- **cdlHelpContext**—&H1&; displays Help for a particular context. When using this setting, you must also specify a context using the **HelpContext** property.

- **cdlHelpContextPopup**—&H8&; displays in a pop-up window a particular Help topic identified by a context number defined in the **[MAP]** section of the HPJ file.

- **cdlHelpForceFile**—&H9&; ensures WinHelp displays the correct Help file. If the correct Help file is currently displayed, no action occurs. If the incorrect Help file is displayed, WinHelp opens the correct file.

- **cdlHelpHelpOnHelp**—&H4&; displays Help for using the Help application itself.

- **cdlHelpIndex**—&H3&; displays the index of the specified Help file. An application should use this value only for a Help file with a single index.

- **cdlHelpKey**—&H101&; displays Help for a particular keyword. When using this setting, you must also specify a keyword using the **HelpKey** property.

- **cdlHelpPartialKey**—&H105&; displays the topic found in the keyword list that matches the keyword passed in the **dwData** parameter if there is one exact match.

- **cdlHelpQuit**—&H2&; notifies the Help application that the specified Help file is no longer in use.

- **cdlHelpSetContents**—&H5&; determines which contents topic is displayed when a user presses the F1 key.

- **cdlHelpSetIndex**—&H5&; sets the context specified by the **HelpContext** property as the current index for the Help file specified by the **HelpFile** property. This index remains current until the user accesses a different Help file. Use this value only for Help files with more than one index.

Often, you want to open a Help file to its contents page, and so you'd set the **HelpCommand** property to the **cdlHelpContents** constant. Be careful, however, that constant doesn't work with some Help files (those constructed with the Microsoft Help Workshop Version 4.0X), so check if **ShowHelp** works properly before releasing your program. The **cdlHelpContents** constant works with fewer Help files than you might think—in fact, it won't open the main Windows Help file itself, windows.hlp, correctly. Instead, you must use a special value, &HB:

```
Private Sub Command1_Click()
    CommonDialog1.HelpCommand = &HB
    CommonDialog1.HelpFile = "c:\windows\help\windows.hlp"
    CommonDialog1.ShowHelp
End Sub
```

The result of this code appears in Figure 11.13. Here, we're opening the Windows main Help file to its contents page.

Our **ShowHelp** example is a success. The code for this example is located in the helpdialog folder on this book's accompanying CD-ROM.

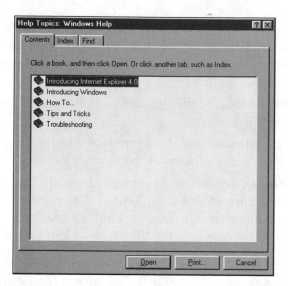

Figure 11.13   Opening Windows Help from a Visual Basic program.

Chapter 12

The Chart And Grid Controls

If you need an immediate solution to:	See page:
Adding A Chart Control To A Program	375
Adding Data To A Chart Control	376
Working With A Multiple Data Series	379
Setting Chart And Axis Titles And Chart Colors	382
Creating Pie Charts	382
Creating 2D And 3D Line Charts	384
Creating 2D And 3D Area Charts	385
Creating 2D And 3D Bar Charts	387
Creating 2D And 3D Step Charts	388
Creating 2D And 3D Combination Charts	390
Adding A Flex Grid Control To A Program	392
Working With Data In A Flex Grid Control	393
Typing Data Into A Flex Grid	397
Setting Flex Grid Grid Lines And Border Styles	400
Labeling Rows And Columns In A Flex Grid	400
Formatting Flex Grid Cells	401
Sorting A Flex Grid Control	401
Dragging Columns In A Flex Grid Control	402
Connecting A Flex Grid To A Database	403

In Depth

In this chapter, we're going to work with two types of Visual Basic controls: chart and grid controls. You use these controls to display data—for example, a chart of a data set can make it come alive in a unique way. Like most Visual Basic controls, both of these control types can be filled with data in two ways: under program control or from a database. In this chapter, we'll get familiar with charts and grids and placing data in them ourselves; when we discuss the Visual Basic's data-bound controls later in this book, we'll see how to make the connection to databases.

The Chart Control

The Visual Basic chart control takes a little getting used to—and it's changed significantly over time—but when you get the hang of it, you can create dramatic effects. For making your data visible, there's little better than an effective graph. Here are the types of charts you can create using the Visual Basic chart control:

- 2D or 3D bar chart
- 2D or 3D line chart
- 2D or 3D area chart
- 2D or 3D step chart
- 2D or 3D combination chart
- 2D pie chart
- 2D XY chart

As we'll see, there are several ways of working with the data in a chart control; that data is stored in a data grid, and we're responsible for filling that grid. To create a simple graph, such as a line chart showing wheat production over time, you fill the data grid with a one-dimensional array. If you want to display a graph of a *series* of data sets in the same chart, such as a line chart with three lines showing wheat, soybean, and rye production over time, you use a two-dimensional array (with three columns in this case). We'll see how this works in the Immediate Solutions.

To add a chart control to your program, open the Components dialog box by selecting Project|Components, click the Controls tab, select the Microsoft Chart

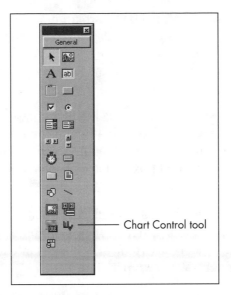

Chart Control tool

Figure 12.1   The Chart Control tool.

Control entry, and click on OK to close the Components dialog box. The Chart Control tool appears as the eleventh tool down on the right in Figure 12.1.

The chart control takes care of many programming concerns automatically—such as scaling the axes or setting colors—although you can override those settings if you wish.

Grid Controls

Grid controls display data in a table-like form, with rows and columns of cells. In fact, you can use grids to do just that: display tables of data. You can also use them to display spreadsheets.

Visual Basic has a number of grid controls: the data grid control, the flex grid control, and the hierarchical flex grid control. We'll take a look at the flex grid control here and save the data grid control for our discussion of data-bound controls (in fact, flex grids can connect to databases just as data grid controls can, but they present the database's data in read-only format).

Like charts, grids give you a way of displaying data. Whereas charts present data in graphical format, grids appear like spreadsheets (and, in fact, if you want to create a spreadsheet in Visual Basic, you use a grid). A grid presents the user with a two-dimensional array of individual cells. You can make the cells in the grid active just as you'd expect in a spreadsheet; for example, you can keep a running sum at the bottom of columns of data.

One thing that takes many Visual Basic programmers by surprise is that there's no automatic way for users to enter data in a grid control (that is, it doesn't function as a grid of text boxes). When you display a grid, it seems that users should be able to just type the data they want into the grid, but that's not the way it works.

Grid controls can hold data in each cell when you put it there, but the user can't simply enter that data—you have to add the code to do that. We'll see how to fix this with a moveable text box in this chapter—when the user types into a cell, we'll move the text box to that cell and make it appear that the user is typing directly into the cell.

The flex grid control is often used to display database data in read-only format. It also features the ability to rearrange its columns under user control, as we'll see, as well as the ability to display images in each cell instead of just text. Each cell supports word wrap and formatting.

To add a flex grid control to your program, open the Components dialog box by selecting Project|Components, click the Controls tab, select the Microsoft FlexGrid Control entry, then click on OK to close the Components dialog box. The Flex Grid Control tool is the twelfth tool down on the left in Figure 12.2.

That's it for our overview of charts and grids—it's time to turn to the Immediate Solutions.

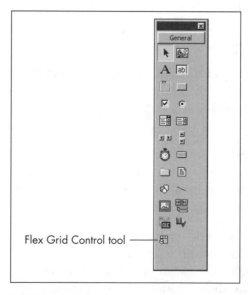

Flex Grid Control tool

Figure 12.2   The Flex Grid Control tool.

Immediate Solutions

Adding A Chart Control To A Program

The Testing Department is calling again. Your new program, *SuperDuperData-Crunch*, is great, but why does it display the data as a long stream of numbers in a text box? Well, you ask, what else would you suggest? They say, how about a chart?

It's time to add a Microsoft chart control to your program, and doing that is easy—just follow these steps:

1. Select the Project|Components menu item.

2. Select the Controls tab in the Components box that opens.

3. Select the Microsoft Chart Control entry in the Components box, and click on OK to close the Components box.

4. Draw a new chart control on your form.

To select the type of chart you want, you set the chart control's **ChartType** property. Here are the possible settings for that property:

- **VtChChartType3dBar**—3D bar chart

- **VtChChartType2dBar**—2D bar chart

- **VtChChartType3dLine**—3D line chart

- **VtChChartType2dLine**—2D line chart

- **VtChChartType3dArea**—3D area chart

- **VtChChartType2dArea**—2D area chart

- **VtChChartType3dStep**—3D step chart

- **VtChChartType2dStep**—2D step chart

- **VtChChartType3dCombination**—3D combination chart

- **VtChChartType2dCombination**—2D combination chart

- **VtChChartType2dPie**—2D pie chart

- **VtChChartType2dXY**—2D XY chart

TIP: Note that the **ChartType** property actually appears with a small initial letter, **chartType**, in the current build of Visual Basic, although when you check the Visual Basic documentation, it has a large initial letter, **ChartType**. Because Visual Basic corrects capitalization automatically, you can type this property in either way, but it's an oddity you might note.

Now that you've added a new chart control to your program, it's time to fill it with data. There are several ways of doing so, and they can get pretty involved. See the next topic in this chapter for the details.

Adding Data To A Chart Control

You've added a chart control to your form, and it's displaying data—but it's not your data. How do you fix that?

When you add a chart control to a form, it displays random data (which is good if you want to change chart types and see what the possibilities look like). That's fine as far as it goes, but now it's time to enter your own data in that chart. There are several ways of doing so, and we'll look at them here.

Using The **ChartData** Property

As mentioned in this chapter's overview, the data in a chart control is stored in an internal data grid (in fact, it's stored in a Visual Basic data grid control, one of the data-bound controls, inside the chart control). Probably the quickest way of filling a chart control is by filling that data grid directly, and we can access the data grid directly with the chart control's **ChartData** property.

You can either get or set the data grid in a chart control with this property, because it refers directly to an array of variants. Let's take a look at an example. Here, we'll just create a simple bar chart (**ChartType = VtChChartType2dBar**, the default).

Start by adding a new chart control, **MSChart1** (that's the default name Visual Basic will give it) to your program. Next, we declare an array of variants to hold our data:

```
Private Sub Form_Load()

    Dim X(1 To 5) As Variant
    . . .
```

The first entry in the array is a label that will appear on the x-axis; we'll just label it "Data":

```
Private Sub Form_Load()

    Dim X(1 To 5) As Variant
    X(1) = "Data"
...
```

Next, we add the data itself we want to display:

```
Private Sub Form_Load()

    Dim X(1 To 5) As Variant
    X(1) = "Data"
    X(2) = 1
    X(3) = 2
    X(4) = 3
    X(5) = 4
...
```

Finally, we install the array in **MSChart1** using the **ChartData** property:

```
Private Sub Form_Load()

    Dim X(1 To 5) As Variant
    X(1) = "Data"
    X(2) = 1
    X(3) = 2
    X(4) = 3
    X(5) = 4

    MSChart1.ChartData = X

End Sub
```

That's it. Now run the program as you see in Figure 12.3. We've created our first simple chart.

The code for this program is located in the chart folder on this book's accompanying CD-ROM.

Another way of installing data in a chart is to use the **Data** property.

Using The **Data** Property

You can also use the chart control's **Data** property to enter data. To use the **Data** property to fill the chart control's data grid, you set the row and column you want to place data in using the chart control's **Row** and **Column** properties,

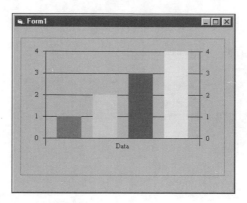

Figure 12.3   Creating a simple chart.

and then you just set the **Data** property to the value you want at that location, like this: **MSChart1.Data = 5**. Note that because we're not passing an array to the chart control here, you must give that control the proper dimensions of the array you're setting up, which means you must set the **RowCount** and **ColumnCount** properties.

If you're just entering sequential data points, you can set the chart control's **AutoIncrement** property to True, and then enter the sequential points into the **Data** property, one after another:

```
Private Sub Form_Load()
    MSChart1.Data = 1
    MSChart1.Data = 2
    MSChart1.Data = 3
    MSChart1.Data = 4
...
```

The **Data** property can only take numeric data, so to set the text that will appear on the x-axis for our data, we use the **RowLabel** property to label row 1 like this:

```
Private Sub Form_Load()
    MSChart1.Data = 1
    MSChart1.Data = 2
    MSChart1.Data = 3
    MSChart1.Data = 4
    MSChart1.Row = 1
    MSChart1.RowLabel = "Data"
End Sub
```

And that's it—this code produces the same result you see in Figure 12.3.

Using The **SetData** Method

You can use the data grid **SetData** method to place data in the chart control. Here's how you use **SetData**:

```
DataGrid.SetData (row, column, dataPoint, nullFlag)
```

Here's what the various arguments you pass to **SetData** mean:

- *row*—Identifies the row containing the data point value
- *column*—Identifies the column containing the data point value
- *dataPoint*—Holds the data value (a **Double** value)
- *nullFlag*—Indicates whether or not the data point value is a null

All the data in our simple chart is in the same row, so we fill the data grid in the chart control using **SetData** this way (note that we access the data grid with the chart control's **DataGrid** property here):

```
Private Sub Form_Load()

MSChart1.DataGrid.SetData 1, 1, 1, False
MSChart1.DataGrid.SetData 1, 2, 2, False
MSChart1.DataGrid.SetData 1, 3, 3, False
MSChart1.DataGrid.SetData 1, 4, 4, False

MSChart1.Row = 1
MSChart1.RowLabel = "Data"

End Sub
```

This code produces the same result as before, shown in Figure 12.3.

Working With A Multiple Data Series

The Testing Department is calling again. Your graph of total imported wheat by month looks very nice, but now that the company has diversified, you need to show the imports of rice, corn, wheat, lentils, and rye all on the same chart. Can you do that?

You certainly can, using a data *series*. When you fill the chart control's data grid, you just add a new column for each crop, and a new line will appear in your graph. How does that work? Let's see an example.

Here, we'll graph rice, corn, wheat, lentils, and rye imports for the months of January and February. Each set of data, rice, corn, wheat, lentils, and rye makes up a series, and each column in the data grid will hold the data for one series. We add a new row to make a new x-axis point for each item in the series. In this example, we'll have two rows, one for January and one for February, and five columns, one each for rice, corn, wheat, lentils, and rye.

In fact, we add one row to hold row labels and one column to hold column labels. The row labels (January and February) will appear on the x-axis, and the column labels (rice, corn, wheat, lentils, and rye) will appear in the chart's *legend* so the user can figure out what all the different-color lines (the data series) in the chart mean. Here's the way the data grid will be set up when we're done:

	Rice	Corn	Lentils	Wheat	Rye
January	2	3	4	5	6
February	4	6	8	10	12

Here's how that looks in code:

```
Private Sub Form_Load()

Dim X(1 To 3, 1 To 6) As Variant

X(1, 2) = "Rice"
X(1, 3) = "Corn"
X(1, 4) = "Lentils"
X(1, 5) = "Wheat"
X(1, 6) = "Rye"

X(2, 1) = "January"
X(2, 2) = 2
X(2, 3) = 3
X(2, 4) = 4
X(2, 5) = 5
X(2, 6) = 6

X(3, 1) = "February"
X(3, 2) = 4
X(3, 3) = 6
X(3, 4) = 8
X(3, 5) = 10
X(3, 6) = 12

MSChart1.ChartData = X

End Sub
```

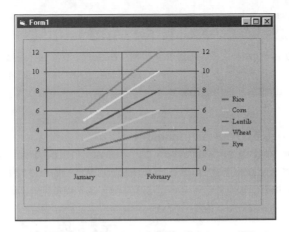

Figure 12.4   A 2D line chart with a data series.

When you set the chart control's **ChartType** property to **VtChChartType2dLine** and the **ShowLegend** property to True so the legend is displayed, the result appears as shown in Figure 12.4. You can see the various data series represented there, and the legend at right explains what each line means.

You can also use a data series with 3D graphs—setting **ChartType** to **VtChChartType3dStep** creates the 3D step chart in Figure 12.5.

The code for this example is located in the chartseries folder on this book's accompanying CD-ROM.

TIP: *To draw the sum of various series in a chart, you can open the chart control's property pages, click the Chart tab, and in the Chart Options box, click the Stack Series item. This will stack the series one on top of the other, which can be convenient if you want to look at a sum of various series.*

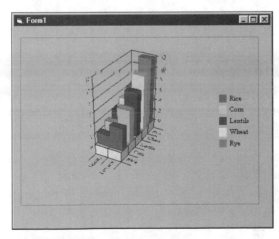

Figure 12.5   A 3D step chart with a data series.

Setting Chart And Axis Titles And Chart Colors

In the previous topic, we've seen how to create row labels and use a legend in a chart. However, there's much more here—you can also set a chart's title, as well as give titles to the entire x- and y-axes.

To set a chart's titles, you can open the chart control's property pages, and you do that at design time by right-clicking the chart control and selecting Properties in the menu that appears. You can then click the Text tab in the property pages and set the text for the chart's title, as well as the titles of the two axes. If you click the Fonts tab, you can set the fonts used in those titles.

As an example, we've added axis titles to the chart in Figure 12.6.

You can also set the colors used in a series in a chart in the property pages—just click the Series Color tab in the property pages, and you can set the color used for each series (that is, each column in the data grid).

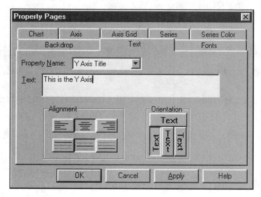

Figure 12.6   Setting axis titles.

Creating Pie Charts

The Testing Department is calling again: bar charts are nice, but how about some pie charts in your new program, *SuperDuperDataCrunch*? You think, How do you do that?

You set the chart control's **ChartType** property to **VtChChartType2dPie**. The chart control will display as many pie charts as you set up rows in the data grid (minus one row for the use of labels). For example, we'll set up two pie charts here, January and February, each with five pie slices, rice, corn, lentils, wheat, and rye:

```
Private Sub Form_Load()

Dim X(1 To 3, 1 To 6) As Variant

X(1, 2) = "Rice"
X(1, 3) = "Corn"
X(1, 4) = "Lentils"
X(1, 5) = "Wheat"
X(1, 6) = "Rye"


X(2, 1) = "January"
X(2, 2) = 2
X(2, 3) = 3
X(2, 4) = 4
X(2, 5) = 5
X(2, 6) = 6


X(3, 1) = "February"
X(3, 2) = 4
X(3, 3) = 6
X(3, 4) = 8
X(3, 5) = 10
X(3, 6) = 12


MSChart1.ChartData = X

End Sub
```

The result appears in Figure 12.7. Now we're creating pie charts in Visual Basic.

TIP: You can also select a pie slice to make it stand out.

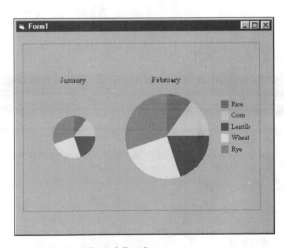

Figure 12.7   Two pie charts in Visual Basic.

Creating 2D And 3D Line Charts

How can you create a 2D or a 3D line chart? You set the Microsoft chart control's **ChartType** property to **VtChChartType2dLine** or **VtChChartType3dLine**.

Here's an example where we create a 2D line chart in the chart control **MSChart1** and a 3D line chart in **MSChart2**. First, we set up the data we'll use in the chart controls' data grids:

```
Private Sub Form_Load()

Dim X(1 To 3, 1 To 6) As Variant

X(1, 2) = "Rice"
X(1, 3) = "Corn"
X(1, 4) = "Lentils"
X(1, 5) = "Wheat"
X(1, 6) = "Rye"

X(2, 1) = "January"
X(2, 2) = 6
X(2, 3) = 5
X(2, 4) = 4
X(2, 5) = 3
X(2, 6) = 2

X(3, 1) = "February"
X(3, 2) = 12
X(3, 3) = 10
X(3, 4) = 8
X(3, 5) = 6
X(3, 6) = 4

MSChart1.ChartData = X
MSChart2.ChartData = X
...
```

Then we set the **ChartType** property:

```
Private Sub Form_Load()

Dim X(1 To 3, 1 To 6) As Variant

...
MSChart1.ChartData = X
MSChart2.ChartData = X
```

```
MSChart1.chartType = VtChChartType2dLine
MSChart2.chartType = VtChChartType3dLine

End Sub
```

And that's it—the result of this code appears in Figure 12.8.

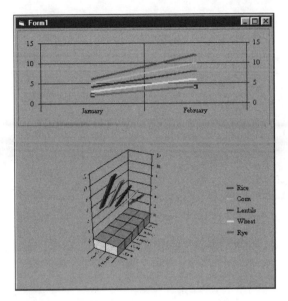

Figure 12.8   A 2D and 3D line chart.

Creating 2D And 3D Area Charts

An area chart displays data in a series as *areas*. How can you create a 2D or a 3D area chart? You set the Microsoft chart control's **ChartType** property to **VtChChartType2dArea** or **VtChChartType3dArea**.

Here's an example where we create a 2D area chart in the chart control **MSChart1** and a 3D area chart in **MSChart2**. First, we set up the data we'll use in the chart controls' data grids:

```
Private Sub Form_Load()

Dim X(1 To 3, 1 To 6) As Variant

X(1, 2) = "Rice"
X(1, 3) = "Corn"
X(1, 4) = "Lentils"
```

```
X(1, 5) = "Wheat"
X(1, 6) = "Rye"

X(2, 1) = "January"
X(2, 2) = 2
X(2, 3) = 3
X(2, 4) = 4
X(2, 5) = 5
X(2, 6) = 6

X(3, 1) = "February"
X(3, 2) = 4
X(3, 3) = 6
X(3, 4) = 8
X(3, 5) = 10
X(3, 6) = 12

MSChart1.ChartData = X
MSChart2.ChartData = X
...
```

Then we set the **ChartType** property:

```
Private Sub Form_Load()

Dim X(1 To 3, 1 To 6) As Variant

...
MSChart1.ChartData = X
MSChart2.ChartData = X

MSChart1.chartType = VtChChartType2dArea
MSChart2.chartType = VtChChartType3dArea

End Sub
```

And that's it—the result of this code appears in Figure 12.9. Now we're drawing 2D and 3D area charts.

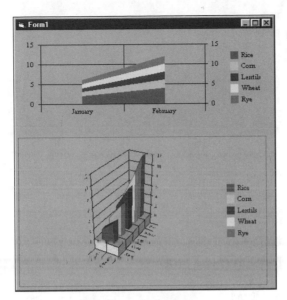

Figure 12.9   A 2D and 3D area chart in Visual Basic.

Creating 2D And 3D Bar Charts

Bar charts, also called *histograms*, just present their data using bars that match the respective data values. How can you create a 2D or a 3D bar chart? You set the Microsoft chart control's **ChartType** property to **VtChChartType2dBar** or **VtChChartType3dBar**.

Here's an example where we create a 2D bar chart in the chart control **MSChart1** and a 3D bar chart in **MSChart2**. First, we set up the data we'll use in the chart controls' data grids:

```
Private Sub Form_Load()

Dim X(1 TO 3, 1 TO 6) As Variant

X(1, 2) = "Rice"
X(1, 3) = "Corn"
X(1, 4) = "Lentils"
X(1, 5) = "Wheat"
X(1, 6) = "Rye"

X(2, 1) = "January"
X(2, 2) = 4
X(2, 3) = 6
```

```
X(2, 4) = 8
X(2, 5) = 10
X(2, 6) = 12

X(3, 1) = "February"
X(3, 2) = 2
X(3, 3) = 3
X(3, 4) = 4
X(3, 5) = 5
X(3, 6) = 6

MSChart1.ChartData = X
MSChart2.ChartData = X
...
```

Then we set the **ChartType** property:

```
Private Sub Form_Load()

Dim X(1 To 3, 1 To 6) As Variant

...
MSChart1.ChartData = X
MSChart2.ChartData = X

MSChart1.chartType = VtChChartType2dBar
MSChart2.chartType = VtChChartType3dBar

End Sub
```

And that's it—the result of this code appears in Figure 12.10. Note that the data rows in the 2D chart's series are presented side by side.

Creating 2D And 3D Step Charts

Step charts present their data using bars as a series of steps. How can you create a 2D or a 3D step chart? You set the Microsoft chart control's **ChartType** property to **VtChChartType2dStep** or **VtChChartType3dStep**.

Here's an example where we create a 2D step chart in the chart control **MSChart1** and a 3D step chart in **MSChart2**. First, we set up the data we'll use in the chart controls' data grids:

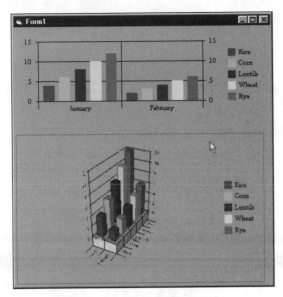

Figure 12.10   A 2D and a 3D bar chart in Visual Basic.

```
Private Sub Form_Load()

Dim X(1 To 3, 1 To 6) As Variant

X(1, 2) = "Rice"
X(1, 3) = "Corn"
X(1, 4) = "Lentils"
X(1, 5) = "Wheat"
X(1, 6) = "Rye"

X(2, 1) = "January"
X(2, 2) = 4
X(2, 3) = 6
X(2, 4) = 8
X(2, 5) = 10
X(2, 6) = 12

X(3, 1) = "February"
X(3, 2) = 2
X(3, 3) = 3
X(3, 4) = 4
X(3, 5) = 5
X(3, 6) = 6

MSChart1.ChartData = X
MSChart2.ChartData = X
...
```

Then we set the **ChartType** property:

```
Private Sub Form_Load()

Dim X(1 To 3, 1 To 6) As Variant

...
MSChart1.ChartData = X
MSChart2.ChartData = X

MSChart1.chartType = VtChChartType2dStep
MSChart2.chartType = VtChChartType3dStep

End Sub
```

And that's it—the result of this code appears in Figure 12.11. Note that the data rows in the 2D chart's series are presented side by side.

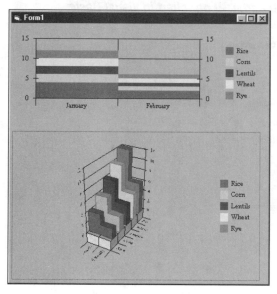

Figure 12.11   A 2D and a 3D step chart in Visual Basic.

Creating 2D And 3D Combination Charts

Combination charts present their data as bars whose height matches relative data values. How can you create a 2D or a 3D combination chart? You set the Microsoft chart control's **ChartType** property to **VtChChartType2d-Combination** or **VtChChartType3dCombination**.

Here's an example where we create a 2D combination chart in the chart control **MSChart1** and a 3D combination chart in **MSChart2**. First, we set up the data we'll use in the chart controls' data grids:

```
Private Sub Form_Load()

Dim X(1 To 3, 1 To 6) As Variant

X(1, 2) = "Rice"
X(1, 3) = "Corn"
X(1, 4) = "Lentils"
X(1, 5) = "Wheat"
X(1, 6) = "Rye"

X(2, 1) = "January"
X(2, 2) = 4
X(2, 3) = 6
X(2, 4) = 8
X(2, 5) = 10
X(2, 6) = 12

X(3, 1) = "February"
X(3, 2) = 2
X(3, 3) = 3
X(3, 4) = 4
X(3, 5) = 5
X(3, 6) = 6

MSChart1.ChartData = X
MSChart2.ChartData = X
...
```

Then we set the **ChartType** property:

```
Private Sub Form_Load()

Dim X(1 To 3, 1 To 6) As Variant

...
MSChart1.ChartData = X
MSChart2.ChartData = X

MSChart1.chartType = VtChChartType2dCombination
MSChart2.chartType = VtChChartType3dCombination

End Sub
```

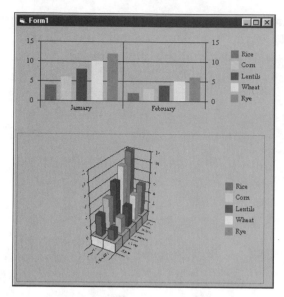

Figure 12.12   A 2D and a 3D combination chart in Visual Basic.

And that's it—the result of this code appears in Figure 12.12. Note that the data rows in the 2D chart's series are presented side by side.

Adding A Flex Grid Control To A Program

The Program Design Department is calling. Can you whip up a program to display a few tables of data? No problem, you say, I'll use the Microsoft flex grid control. They ask, and how about spreadsheets? You say, no problem—flex grids can handle that too.

You can add a flex grid to a Visual Basic project easily; just follow these steps:

1. Select the Project|Components menu item.
2. Click the Controls tab in the Components dialog box.
3. Select the Microsoft FlexGrid Control entry in the Components dialog box.
4. Close the Components dialog box by clicking on OK. This displays the Flex Grid Control tool in the toolbox.
5. Add a flex grid control to your form in the usual way for Visual Basic controls, using the Flex Grid Control tool.
6. Set the flex grid's **Rows** and **Cols** properties to the number of rows and columns you want in your flex grid. You can also customize your flex

grid by setting such properties as **BorderStyle**, **ForeColor**, **BackColor**, and so on.

This gives you a blank flex grid control in your program; the next step is to fill it with data. To start doing that, take a look at the next topic in this chapter.

TIP: *When you insert a flex grid, you can also connect it to a database. To do this, you create a new data control (it's an intrinsic Visual Basic control and appears in the toolbox when you start Visual Basic), connect that control to the database (by setting its **DatabaseName** and **RecordSource** properties), then set the flex grid's **DataSource** property to the name of the data control. We'll see more about connecting to a database when we discuss the data-bound Visual Basic controls. (See "Connecting A Flex Grid To A Database" later in this chapter.)*

Working With Data In A Flex Grid Control

You're writing your new program, *SuperDuperDataCrunch*, and it's time to write the code for the spreadsheet part. You can use a flex grid control here—but how do you insert and work with the data in a flex grid? To see how this works, we'll build a small spreadsheet example program that adds a column of numbers. This will show how to insert and access data in a flex grid, as well as how to handle text insertion direct from the user in a rudimentary way (we'll see a better method in the next topic in this chapter). Several flex grid properties will help us here:

- **Row**—The current row in a flex grid
- **Col**—The current column in a flex grid
- **Rows**—The total number of rows
- **Cols**—The total number of columns
- **Text**—The text in the cell at (**Row, Col**)

We start by adding a flex grid to a form; give it 7 rows in the **Rows** property and 7 columns in the **Cols** property. We'll begin by labeling the column heads with letters and the row heads with numbers, just as you would see in any spreadsheet program.

Flex grids have **FixedCols** and **FixedRows** properties, which set the header columns and rows in the flex grid. These columns and rows are meant to label the other columns and rows, and they appear in gray by default (the other cells are white by default). Both **FixedCols** and **FixedRows** are set to 1 by default.

We'll add a column of numbers here, so we can also place labels in the first column of cells, "Item 1" to "Item 6", and a label at the bottom, "Total", to indicate that the bottom row holds the total of the six above. These labels are

	A	B	C	D	E	F
1	Item 1	10				
2	Item 2	5				
3	Item 3	18				
4	Item 4	2				
5	Item 5	15				
6	Total	50				

Figure 12.13   Designing a spreadsheet.

not necessary, of course, but we'll add them to show that you can use text as well as numbers in a flex grid. These labels will appear in column 1 of the flex grid, and users can place the data they want to add in column 2. The running sum appears at the bottom of column 2, as shown in Figure 12.13.

To set text in a flex grid cell, you set the **Row** and **Col** properties to that location and then place the text in the flex grid's **Text** property. Here's how we set up the row and column labels in **MSFlexGrid1** when the form loads:

```
Sub Form_Load()
    Dim Items(6) As String
    Dim intLoopIndex As Integer

    Items(1) = "Item 1"
    Items(2) = "Item 2"
    Items(3) = "Item 3"
    Items(4) = "Item 4"
    Items(5) = "Item 5"
    Items(6) = "Total"

    For intLoopIndex = 1 To MSFlexGrid1.Rows - 1
        MSFlexGrid1.Col = 0
        MSFlexGrid1.Row = intLoopIndex
        MSFlexGrid1.Text = Str(intLoopIndex)
        MSFlexGrid1.Col = 1
        MSFlexGrid1.Text = Items(intLoopIndex)
    Next intLoopIndex
```

```
    MSFlexGrid1.Row = 0
    For intLoopIndex = 1 To MSFlexGrid1.Cols - 1
        MSFlexGrid1.Col = intLoopIndex
        MSFlexGrid1.Text = Chr(Asc("A") - 1 + intLoopIndex)
    Next intLoopIndex

    MSFlexGrid1.Row = 1
    MSFlexGrid1.Col = 1

End Sub
```

The rows and labels appear as in Figure 12.14.

We've set up the labels as we want them—but what about reading data when the user types it? We can use the flex grid's **KeyPress** event for that:

```
Sub MSFlexGrid1_KeyPress(KeyAscii As Integer)

End Sub
```

If the user enters numbers in the cells of column 2, we'll add those values together in a running sum that appears at the bottom of that column, just as in a real spreadsheet program. To enter a number in a cell, the user can click the flex grid, which sets the grid's **Row** and **Col** properties. Then, when the user types, we can add that text to the cell:

```
Sub MSFlexGrid1_KeyPress(KeyAscii As Integer)

    MSFlexGrid1.Text = MSFlexGrid1.Text + Chr$(KeyAscii)
    ...
End Sub
```

This represents one way of letting the user enter text into a grid, but notice that we'd have to handle all the editing and deleting functions ourselves this way; see the next topic in this chapter to see how to use a text box together with a flex grid for data entry.

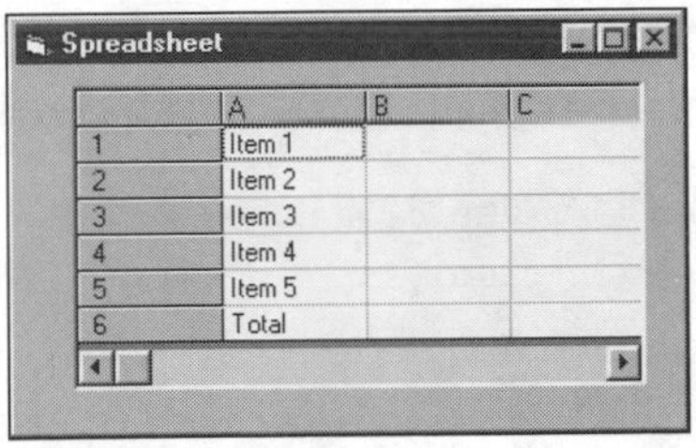

Figure 12.14   The flex grid spreadsheet program.

Now that the user has changed the data in the spreadsheet, we add the numbers in column 2 this way:

```
Sub MSFlexGrid1_KeyPress(KeyAscii As Integer)
    Dim intRowIndex As Integer
    Dim Sum As Integer

    MSFlexGrid1.Text = MSFlexGrid1.Text + Chr$(KeyAscii)

    MSFlexGrid1.Col = 2
    Sum = 0

    For intRowIndex = 1 To MSFlexGrid1.Rows - 2
        MSFlexGrid1.Row = intRowIndex
        Sum = Sum + Val(MSFlexGrid1.Text)
    Next intRowIndex
    ...
```

Note that each time you set the **Row** and **Col** properties to a new cell, that cell gets the focus. Because we want to place the sum of column 2 at the bottom of that column, that's a problem. When we place the sum there, as users type the digits of the current number they're entering, the focus would keep moving to the bottom of the column. To avoid that, we save the current row and column and restore them when we're done displaying the sum:

```
Sub MSFlexGrid1_KeyPress(KeyAscii As Integer)
    Dim intRowIndex As Integer
    Dim Sum As Integer

    MSFlexGrid1.Text = MSFlexGrid1.Text + Chr$(KeyAscii)
    OldRow = MSFlexGrid1.Row
    OldCol = MSFlexGrid1.Col
    MSFlexGrid1.Col = 2
    Sum = 0

    For intRowIndex = 1 To MSFlexGrid1.Rows - 2
        MSFlexGrid1.Row = intRowIndex
        Sum = Sum + Val(MSFlexGrid1.Text)
    Next intRowIndex

    MSFlexGrid1.Row = MSFlexGrid1.Rows - 1
    MSFlexGrid1.Text = Str(Sum)
    MSFlexGrid1.Row = OldRow
    MSFlexGrid1.Col = OldCol
End Sub
```

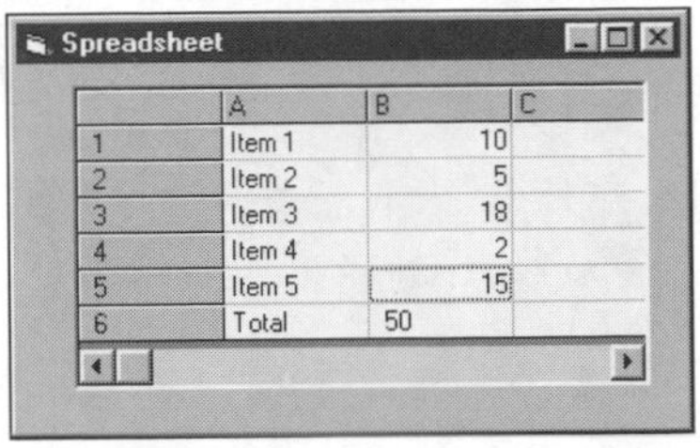

Figure 12.15 Adding numbers in the flex grid spreadsheet program.

And that's it. Now the user can type numbers into the spreadsheet, and we'll display the running sum, as shown in Figure 12.15. We've created a spreadsheet program using a flex grid control.

The code for this example is located in the spreadsheet folder on this book's accompanying CD-ROM. Note that in this case we had to handle text entry ourselves, and we didn't let the user delete characters or perform other edits like cut and paste. We can do that if we use a text box for character entry, and we'll see how to do that in the next topic.

Typing Data Into A Flex Grid

In the previous topic, we saw how to work with data in a flex grid and how to use the **KeyPress** event to support rudimentary text entry. Microsoft, however, suggests you use a text box for text entry in a flex grid—but how are you supposed to do that?

The way you do it is to keep the text box invisible until the user selects a cell, then move the text box to that cell, size it to match the cell, and make it appear. When the user is done typing and clicks another cell, you transfer the text to the current cell and make the text box disappear.

Why Microsoft didn't build this into flex grids is anybody's guess—perhaps because many flex grids are not supposed to support text entry, and that functionality would just take up memory. However, we can do it ourselves.

To see how this works, add a text box to a form, and set its **Visible** property to False so it starts off hidden. Then add a flex grid to the form and give it, say, 10 columns and 10 rows. We can label the columns with letters and the rows with numbers, as is standard in spreadsheets (note that we use the Visual Basic **Chr** and **Asc** functions to set up the letters, and that we enter the text directly into the flex grid using its **TextArray** property):

```
Sub Form_Load()
    Dim intLoopIndex As Integer

    For intLoopIndex = MSFlexGrid1.FixedRows To MSFlexGrid1.Rows - 1
        MSFlexGrid1.TextArray(MSFlexGrid1.Cols * intLoopIndex) =_
            intLoopIndex
    Next

    For intLoopIndex = MSFlexGrid1.FixedCols To MSFlexGrid1.Cols - 1
        MSFlexGrid1.TextArray(intLoopIndex) = Chr(Asc("A") +_
            intLoopIndex - 1)
    Next
End Sub
```

To select a cell, the user can click it with the mouse. When the user starts typing, we can add the text to the text box this way:

```
Sub MSFlexGrid1_KeyPress(KeyAscii As Integer)

    Text1.Text = Text1.Text & Chr(KeyAscii)
    Text1.SelStart = 1
    ...
```

We also move the text box to cover the current cell and shape it to match that cell using the flex grid's **CellLeft**, **CellTop**, **CellWidth**, and **CellHeight** properties:

```
Sub MSFlexGrid1_KeyPress(KeyAscii As Integer)

    Text1.Text = Text1.Text & Chr(KeyAscii)
    Text1.SelStart = 1

    Text1.Move MSFlexGrid1.CellLeft + MSFlexGrid1.Left,_
        MSFlexGrid1.CellTop + MSFlexGrid1.Top, MSFlexGrid1.CellWidth,_
        MSFlexGrid1.CellHeight
    ...
End Sub
```

Finally, we make the text box visible and give it the focus:

```
Sub MSFlexGrid1_KeyPress(KeyAscii As Integer)

    Text1.Text = Text1.Text & Chr(KeyAscii)
    Text1.SelStart = 1

    Text1.Move MSFlexGrid1.CellLeft + MSFlexGrid1.Left,_
        MSFlexGrid1.CellTop + MSFlexGrid1.Top, MSFlexGrid1.CellWidth,_
        MSFlexGrid1.CellHeight
```

```
    Text1.Visible = True
    Text1.SetFocus

End Sub
```

When the user clicks another cell, a **LeaveCell** event is generated, and we can take advantage of that event to transfer the text from the text box to the current cell and hide the text box. Note that if the text box is not visible—in other words, the user is just moving around in the flex grid—we do not want to transfer the text from the text box to the current cell, and so we exit the procedure in that case:

```
Sub MSFlexGrid1_LeaveCell()
    If Text1.Visible = False Then
        Exit Sub
    End If
...
```

Otherwise, we transfer the text from the text box to the current cell, clear the text box, and hide it:

```
Sub MSFlexGrid1_LeaveCell()
    If Text1.Visible = False Then
        Exit Sub
    End If
    MSFlexGrid1.Text = Text1
    Text1.Visible = False
    Text1.Text = ""
End Sub
```

And that's it. Now users can use the text box to enter text in a way that makes it look as though they're entering text directly into the flex grid, as shown in Figure 12.16. The code for this example is located in the flex folder on this book's accompanying CD-ROM.

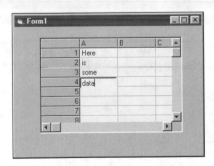

Figure 12.16   Using a text box for flex grid data entry.

Setting Flex Grid Grid Lines And Border Styles

You can set what types of grid lines a flex grid uses with the **GridLines** property. These can be set at design time or runtime to the following values:

- **flexGridNone**
- **flexGridFlat**
- **flexGridInset**
- **flexGridRaised**

You can set the grid line width with the **GridLineWidth** property.

In addition, you can set the **BorderStyle** property to show a border around the whole control, or no border at all:

- **flexBorderNone**
- **flexBorderSingle**

Labeling Rows And Columns In A Flex Grid

The usual convention in spreadsheets is to label the top row with letters and the first column with numbers. Here's some code to do just that (note that we use the Visual Basic **Chr** and **Asc** functions to set up the letters and enter text directly into the flex grid using its **TextArray** property, which holds the grid's text in array form):

```
Sub Form_Load()
    Dim intLoopIndex As Integer

    For intLoopIndex = MSFlexGrid1.FixedRows To MSFlexGrid1.Rows - 1
        MSFlexGrid1.TextArray(MSFlexGrid1.Cols * intLoopIndex) = _
            intLoopIndex
    Next

    For intLoopIndex = MSFlexGrid1.FixedCols To MSFlexGrid1.Cols - 1
        MSFlexGrid1.TextArray(intLoopIndex) = Chr(Asc("A") + _
            intLoopIndex - 1)
    Next
End Sub
```

*TIP: The columns and rows you label in a flex grid are usually colored gray; you set the number of label columns and rows with the **FixedCols** and **FixedRows** properties.*

Formatting Flex Grid Cells

The Aesthetic Design Department is calling again. Can't you use *italics* in that spreadsheet? Hmm, you think—*can* you?

Yes, you can: flex grid cells support formatting, including word wrap. You can format text using these properties of flex grids:

- **CellFontBold**
- **CellFontItalic**
- **CellFontName**
- **CellFontUnderline**
- **CellFontStrikethrough**
- **CellFontSize**

Besides the preceding properties, you can size cells as you like using the **CellWidth** and **RowHeight** properties.

Sorting A Flex Grid Control

The Testing Department is calling again. Your new program, *SuperDuperData-Crunch*, is terrific, but why can't the user sort the data in your spreadsheet? Sounds like a lot of work, you think.

Actually, it's easy. You just use the flex grid's **Sort** property (available only at runtime). For example, to sort a flex grid according to the values in column 1 when the user clicks a button, add this code to your program (setting **Sort** to 1 sorts the flex grid on ascending values):

```
Private Sub Command1_Click()
    MSFlexGrid1.Col = 1
    MSFlexGrid1.Sort = 1
End Sub
```

TIP: *Note that when the user clicks a column, that column becomes the new default column in the **Col** property, so if you want to let the user click a column and sort based on the values in that column, omit the **MSFlexGrid1.Col = 1** in the preceding code.*

Dragging Columns In A Flex Grid Control

One of the attractive aspects of flex grids is that you can use drag-and-drop with them to let users rearrange the flex grid as they like. To see how this works, we'll write an example here that lets users drag and move columns around in a flex grid.

When the user presses the mouse button to start the drag operation, we store the column where the mouse went down in a form-wide variable named, say, **intDragColumn** in the **MouseDown** event. This event is stored in the flex grid's **MouseCol** property:

```
Private Sub MSFlexGrid1_MouseDown(Button As Integer, Shift As Integer, _
    X As Single, Y As Single)

    intDragColumn = MSFlexGrid1.MouseCol
...
```

We also add that variable, **intDragColumn**, to the (General) declaration area of the form:

```
Dim intDragColumn As Integer
```

Then we start the drag and drop operation for the column in the flex grid:

```
Private Sub MSFlexGrid1_MouseDown(Button As Integer, Shift As Integer, _
    X As Single, Y As Single)

    intDragColumn = MSFlexGrid1.MouseCol
    MSFlexGrid1.Drag 1

End Sub
```

Finally, when the user drags the column to a new location and drops it, we can catch that in the **DragDrop** event. In that events handler's procedure, we move the column to its new location—the current mouse column—using the **ColPosition** property:

```
Private Sub MSFlexGrid1_DragDrop(Source As VB.Control, X As Single, _
    Y As Single)

    MSFlexGrid1.ColPosition(intDragColumn) = MSFlexGrid1.MouseCol

End Sub
```

Figure 12.17   Dragging a column in a flex grid.

And that's it. Now the user can drag and rearrange the columns in our flex grid. To see how this works, we display a database in our flex grid, as shown in Figure 12.17. To see how to do that, take a look at the next topic in this chapter where we use a Visual Basic data control (here, the database we use is the Nwind.mdb database, which comes with Visual Basic). When the user drags a column in our program, a special mouse pointer appears, as shown also in Figure 12.17.

The code for this example is located in the dragged folder on this book's accompanying CD-ROM (note that to run this example, you must set the data control's **DatabaseName** to the Nwind.mdb file on your computer, including the correct path).

Connecting A Flex Grid To A Database

We'll work with databases later in this book, but because flex grids are often used with databases, we'll take a look at how to connect a database to a flex grid here. To connect a database to a flex grid, follow these steps:

1. Add a data control, **Data1**, to your form (the data control is an intrinsic control in Visual Basic and appears in the toolbox when you start Visual Basic).

2. Set the data control's **DatabaseName** property to the database file you want to use. This can also be done at runtime, but if you do so, be sure to call the data control's Refresh method to update that control. In code, the process goes something like this, where we use the Visual Basic **App** object's **Path** property to get the application's path (assuming the database file is stored at the same path as the application):

```
Data1.DatabaseName = App.Path & "\Nwind.mdb"
  Data1.Refresh
```

3. Set **Data1**'s **RecordSource** property to the table in the database you want to work with.

4. Set the flex grid's **DataSource** property to the data control's name, which is **Data1** here.

For example, we display the Nwind.mdb database that comes with Visual Basic in a flex grid in Figure 12.18. (There's a lot more about data-bound controls later in this book; this is just an appetizer.)

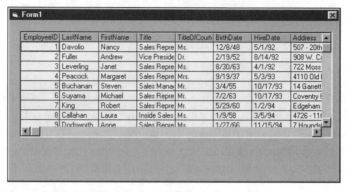

Figure 12.18   Opening a database in a flex grid.

Chapter 13

The Timer And Serial Communications Controls

If you need an immediate solution to:	See page:
Adding A Timer Control To A Program	412
Initializing A Timer Control	412
Handling **Timer** Events	413
Formatting Times And Dates	413
Creating A Clock Program	415
Creating A Stopwatch	416
Creating An Alarm Clock	417
Creating Animation Using The Timer Control	419
Adding A Communications Control To A Program	421
Setting Up The Receive And Transmit Buffers	422
Opening The Serial Port	423
Working With A Modem	423
Reading Data With The Communications Control	424
Sending Data With The Communications Control	425
Setting Up Communications Handshaking	425
Handling Communications Events	426
Closing The Serial Port	427
Adding A MonthView Control To Your Program	428
Getting Dates From A MonthView Control	428
Adding A DateTimePicker Control To Your Program	429
Using A DateTimePicker Control	430

In Depth

In this chapter, we're going to cover the timer and communication controls that come with Visual Basic. In particular, we'll cover the timer control, the serial port communications control, and two controls that exist mostly for convenience: the MonthView control and the DateTimePicker control. Let's get an overview of these controls first.

The Timer Control

You use a timer control when you want to execute code at specific intervals. To use a timer, you add a timer control to your program (timers are one of the intrinsic controls that appear in the toolbox when you start Visual Basic) and set its **Interval** property. From then on, while the timer is enabled, it creates **Timer** events, which are handled in an event handling procedure, like **Timer1_Timer( )**. You place the code you want executed each interval in that procedure.

To add a timer to your program, use the Timer Control tool in the toolbox, which is the seventh tool down on the left in Figure 13.1.

Timer Control tool ———

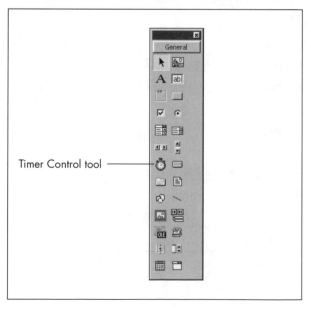

Figure 13.1   The Timer Control tool.

We should note, however, that there are a few issues about using the **Interval** property. Although measured in milliseconds (1/1000s of a second), **Timer** events cannot actually occur faster than 18.2 times a second (this is the period of the computer's timer interrupt). The interval can be set to values between 0 (in which case nothing happens) and 64,767, which means that even the longest interval can't be much longer than 1 minute (about 64.8 seconds). Of course, you can design your code to wait for several intervals to pass before doing anything.

You shouldn't count on a timer too closely if your task execution is dependent on exact intervals; if the system is busy executing long loops, intensive calculations, or drive, network, or port access (in which case software routinely disables the timer interrupt), your application may not get **Timer** events as often as the **Interval** property specifies. That is to say, **Timer** events are not guaranteed to happen exactly on time. If you need to be sure, your software should check the system clock when it needs to (using, for example, the Visual Basic **Time$** function), rather than try to keep track of time internally.

Another point here has to do with Windows programming philosophy. Using a timer can easily pull programmers back to thinking in terms of sequential programming (as in the DOS days), rather than event-oriented programming. When you use a timer, your code has a lot of control and can get a lot of execution time, because your code is called each time the timer ticks. However, that doesn't mean you should set a timer interval short and put in all kinds of loops. Remember that Windows is built around user events, not programs that are designed to retain control for long periods of time. Other programs will probably be running at the same time as yours, so it's considerate not to use timers simply to wrest control from the environment.

With all that said, though, the timer is a uniquely powerful control, and we'll put it to use in this chapter.

The Communications Control

You use the Microsoft communications control to support serial port—that is, modem—communications. If you want to write your own modem package, this is where you start. You can use the communications control to do everything from dialing phone numbers to creating a full-fledged terminal program.

To add this control to your program, select the Project|Components menu item, click the Controls tab in the Components dialog box that opens, select the Microsoft Comm Control entry, and click on OK to close the Components dialog box. Doing so adds this control to the toolbox, as shown in Figure 13.2; the Communications Control tool is the eleventh tool down on the right.

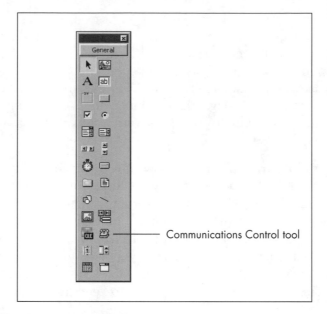

Communications Control tool

Figure 13.2   The Communications Control tool.

When you use the communications control, you use a serial port in your computer. The mouse is usually connected to COM1, and the modem is usually connected to COM2. You set baud rate, parity, and so on, and then call another computer by issuing commands to your modem. After the connection is made, you can exchange data with the other computer.

Receiving And Transmitting

When a serial port is opened, your program creates receive and transmit buffers. To work with these buffers, the communications control supports a number of properties that can be set at design time using the control's property pages.

The **InBufferSize** and **OutBufferSize** properties hold the size of the input and output buffers, and the **RThreshold** and **SThreshold** properties set or return the number of characters that are received into the receive and transmit buffers before the **OnComm** event is fired (this event is used to monitor changes in communications states). We'll see these and other such properties in this chapter.

To establish a connection, you set the communications control's **CommPort** property to the serial port's number (usually 2), the **Settings** property to the protocol settings you want (for example, "9600,N,8,1"), and set the **PortOpen** property to True. To start dialing, you send the appropriate commands to your modem.

Sending Data

To actually send data, you use the **Output** property. You can either send data to your modem or to the other computer. For example, here's how you dial a phone number, by sending an "ATDT" string to your modem (that string is part of the standard Hayes-compatible command set used with modems; **vbCr** is a Visual Basic constant standing for the ASCII code for carriage return/line feed):

```
MSComm1.Output = "ATDT 555-1234" & vbCr
```

You can also send data this way, as we'll see in this chapter:

```
MSComm1.Output = "Here's some text!"
```

Reading Data

You read data when an **OnComm** event occurs. In the **OnComm** event handler, you use the **CommEvent** property to determine what happened. For example, when **CommEvent** is equal to **comEvReceive**, we've received data and can use the **Input** property. Here we fill a buffer with data that the communications control has received:

```
Private Static Sub MSComm1_OnComm()

    Select Case MSComm1.CommEvent
        Case comEvReceive
            Dim Buffer As Variant
            Buffer = MSComm1.Input
...
```

Setting the **InputLen** property to some value means you'll get that number of bytes when you use the **Input** property (if those bytes are available). Setting **InputLen** to 0 makes the communications control read the entire contents of the receive buffer when you use **Input**. The **EOFEnable** property is used to indicate when an End Of File (**EOF**) character is found in the data input. If you set this property to True, it makes data input stop (and the **OnComm** event fire) when the **EOF** is encountered.

Finally, as each byte of data is received, the **InBufferCount** property is incremented by 1 (you use the **InBufferCount** property to get the number of bytes in the receive buffer). You can also clear the receive buffer by setting the value of this property to 0. You can monitor the number of bytes in the transmit buffer by using the **OutBufferCount** property. You can clear the transmit buffer by setting this value to 0.

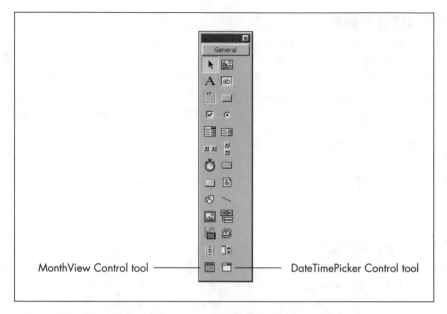

MonthView Control tool ———————————————— DateTimePicker Control tool

Figure 13.3   The MonthView Control and the DateTimePicker Control tools.

We'll see all about the communications control, such as how to support hand-shaking and how to hang up, in this chapter.

The MonthView And DateTimePicker Controls

We'll also cover two more controls in this chapter—the MonthView and DateTimePicker controls (see Figure 13.3). These controls really exist just to make life a little easier for the user, and they're not all that complex.

In particular, the MonthView control displays a calendar of the current month and lets the user scroll to other months as well. The user can select a date—or range of sequential dates—in MonthView controls.

The DateTimePicker control allows the user to specify a date or time, as its name implies. DateTimePickers can display a MonthView as a drop-down control, or the current time together with an updown control to let users select the time they want. The control's **UpDown** property determines which mode the control is in. When **UpDown** is False, the control is in drop-down calendar mode (that's the default). When the **UpDown** property is True, the DateTimePicker is in time format mode.

To add these controls to your program, select the Project|Components menu item, click the Controls tab in the Components dialog box that opens, select the Microsoft Windows Common Controls-2 entry, and click OK to close the

Components dialog box. This adds both these controls to the toolbox, as shown in Figure 13.3. The MonthView Control tool is the thirteenth tool down on the left in Figure 13.3, and the DateTimePicker Control tool is the tool just to the right of the MonthView Control tool.

That's it for our overview—it's time to turn to the Immediate Solutions.

Immediate Solutions

Adding A Timer Control To A Program

The Testing Department is calling again. The users of your new program, *SuperDuperDataCrunch*, turn out to be real clock-watchers. In fact, they'd like your program to display a clock so they don't get neck strain by looking up at the wall every now and then. Can you add a clock to your program?

You can, using the timer control. You add a timer control to your program just as you would any other intrinsic control—you just click the Timer Control tool and draw the timer on your form. The timer control is invisible when the program runs, so the size and location of the control don't matter too much.

Now that you've added a timer, how do you get it running? See the next topic.

Initializing A Timer Control

Now that you've installed a timer control in your program—how do you get it started? You use these two properties:

- **Enabled** determines whether or not the timer creates **Timer** events.
- **Interval** sets the number of milliseconds between **Timer** events.

When you place a timer in your program, you can set its **Enabled** property to False, which means no **Timer** events will occur. When you want to start the timer, you can set **Enabled** to True.

TIP: Note that a timer's **Enabled** property is different from other controls' **Enabled** properties; the timer's **Enabled** property makes **Timer** events occur or not, whereas other **Enabled** properties make controls accessible or inaccessible to the user.

The **Interval** property sets the interval between **Timer** events. Although measured in milliseconds (1/1000s of a second), **Timer** events cannot actually occur faster that 18.2 times a second. The interval can be between 0 (in which case nothing happens) and 64,767, which means that even the longest interval can't be much longer than 1 minute (about 64.8 seconds); however, you can design your code to wait for several intervals to pass before doing anything.

> **Warning!** If the system is busy, your application may not get Timer events as often as the Interval property specifies. That is, the interval is not guaranteed to elapse exactly on time. To be more sure of accuracy, the Timer event handler should check the system clock when needed.

Now that you've set up your timer as you want it, how do you use **Timer** events? See the next topic in this chapter for the details.

Handling **Timer** Events

Well, you've set your timer's **Interval** property and set its **Enabled** property to True. Presumably, your timer is doing something—but what?

The main event for timers is the **Timer** event, and double-clicking a timer at design time creates a handler function for that event:

```
Sub Timer1_Timer()

End Sub
```

All you need to do is to add the code you want executed to this procedure. For example, here we display the current time in a label named **Display** using the Visual Basic **Time$** function:

```
Sub Timer1_Timer()
    Display.Caption = Time$
End Sub
```

This code will be called as often as the timer's **Interval** property specifies (although note that **Timer** events are not guaranteed to occur—many other types of programs temporarily suspend the timer interrupt on occasion).

Formatting Times And Dates

When working with times and dates in Visual Basic, it's valuable knowing how to display them as strings. For example, you can use the Visual Basic **Time$** and **Date$** functions to get the time and date in string form, suitable for display:

```
Text1.Text = Time$
```

You can also use string comparisons here; for example, to check if the current time is past a time specified in string form, you can use code like this:

```
If (Time$ > AlarmSetting.Text) Then
...
End If
```

Besides **Time$** and **Date$**, you can use **Now**. This function refers to the current time in a numeric way, and you can use comparisons this way:

```
If (Now > AlarmTime) Then
...
End If
```

To display the current date and time using **Now**, you use the **Format$** function. For example, this use of **Format$** and **Now**:

```
Format$(Now, "dddd, mmmm d, yyy")
```

returns the string with the day of the week, the month, date, and year like this: "Friday, January 1, 2000". The different format strings and what they do appear in Table 13.1—and some examples appear in Table 13.2 to make all this clearer.

Table 13.1   Date and time format strings.

String	Description
d	The one- or two-digit day.
dd	The two-digit day. Single-digit day values are preceded by a zero.
ddd	The three-character day-of-week abbreviation.
dddd	The full day-of-week name.
h	The one- or two-digit hour in 12-hour format.
hh	The two-digit hour in 12-hour format. Single-digit values are preceded by a zero.
H	The one- or two-digit hour in 24-hour format.
HH	The two-digit hour in 24-hour format. Single-digit values are preceded by a zero.
m	The one- or two-digit minute.
mm	The two-digit minute. Single-digit values are preceded by a zero.
M	The one- or two-digit month number.
MM	The two-digit month number. Single-digit values are preceded by a zero.
MMM	The three-character month abbreviation.
MMMM	The full month name.
s	The one- or two-digit seconds.

(continued)

Table 13.1   Date and time format strings (continued).

String	Description
ss	The two-digit seconds. Single-digit values are proceeded by a zero.
AM/PM	The two-letter AM/PM abbreviation (that is, AM is displayed as "AM").
y	The one-digit year (that is, 1999 would be displayed as "9").
yy	The last two digits of the year (that is, 1999 would be displayed as "99").
yyyy	The full year (that is, 1999 would be displayed as "1999").

Table 13.2   Formatted date and time examples.

Format Expression	Result
Format$(Now, "m - d - yy")	"1-1-00"
Format$(Now, "m / d / yy")	"1 / 1 / 00"
Format$(Now, "mm - dd - yy")	"01 /01 / 00"
Format$(Now, "dddd, mmmm d, yyyy")	"Friday, January 1, 2000"
Format$(Now, "d mmm, yyyy")	"1 Jan, 2000"
Format$(Now, "hh:mm:ss mm/dd/yy")	"01:00:00 01/01/00"
Format$(Now, "hh:mm:ss AM/PM mm - dd- yy")	"01:00:00 AM 01-01-00"

Creating A Clock Program

Creating a clock in Visual Basic is easy with the timer control. To see how that works, just create a new project now and add a timer control, **Timer1**. Set the timer's **Interval** property to 1000 (that is, a thousand milliseconds, or one second).

Next, add a label that covers most of the form and give it a large font, like 48-point Courier New. We'll display the time in that label each time the timer ticks, so add the **Timer1_Tick()** event handler now:

```
Sub Timer1_Timer()

End Sub
```

All we have to do when there's a **Timer** event is to update the clock, and we use the Visual Basic **Time$** function to do that:

```
Sub Timer1_Timer()
    Display.Caption = Time$
End Sub
```

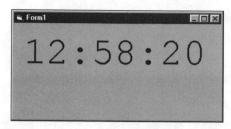

Figure 13.4 A clock created with the timer control.

That's all we need. Now the clock is functional, as shown in Figure 13.4.

The code for this example is located in the clock folder on this book's accompanying CD-ROM. If you want to create more than a simple clock—an alarm clock, for example—see the following topics in this chapter.

Creating A Stopwatch

The Testing Department is calling. Users are concerned about the time your *SuperDuperDataCrunch* program takes in execution—can you add a stopwatch to the program to convince them it's really pretty fast? You think, a stopwatch?

Building a stopwatch is valuable to see how to work with elapsed time instead of simply system time. To build a stopwatch program, create a new Visual Basic project now and add two buttons, labeled "Start" and "Stop", as well as a label control named **Display** (set the font in the label to something large, like 48-point Courier New). Also add a timer control, **Timer1**, and set its **Enabled** property to False so it doesn't do anything until the user clicks the Start button.

Now when the user clicks the Start button, **Command1**, we can store the current time using **Now** in a form-wide variable named **StartTime** (add **StartTime** to the (General) section of the form), and we can start the timer by setting its **Enabled** property to True:

```
Private Sub Command1_Click()
    StartTime = Now
    Timer1.Enabled = True
End Sub
```

When the user clicks the Stop button, **Command2**, we can stop the timer:

```
Private Sub Command2_Click()
    Timer1.Enabled = False
End Sub
```

Figure 13.5   A stopwatch created with the timer control.

Finally, in the **Timer** event, we just display the time that has elapsed from the starting time, and that time is just the difference between the current value of **Now** and the **StartTime** variable:

```
Sub Timer1_Timer()
    Display.Caption = Format$(Now - StartTime, "hh:mm:ss")
End Sub
```

That's it. The result of this code appears in Figure 13.5. Now we've created a stopwatch in Visual Basic. The code for this example is located in the stopwatch folder on this book's accompanying CD-ROM.

Creating An Alarm Clock

Your great-aunt is calling. Why can't you ever write a program that she can use? She doesn't use databases, spreadsheets, or word processors. You say, what else is there? She says, how about a nice alarm clock?

You can build an alarm clock using the timer control in Visual Basic. To see how to do that, create a new program now and add a timer, **Timer1**, to it, setting the timer's **Interval** property to 1000 (that is, 1 second). Add a label named **Display** and set the font in the label large enough to read easily (we'll use 48-point Courier New). We'll need some way of setting when the alarm should go off, so add a text box named **AlarmSetting**. We'll also need some way of turning the alarm on or off, so add two option buttons in a control array, **OnButton**; give **OnButton(1)** the caption "Alarm On" and **OnButton(2)** the caption "Alarm Off".

Now we're ready to write some code. Add a form-wide Boolean variable to the (General) section of the form named **AlarmOn**. We'll set this variable to True when the user clicks the Alarm On button:

```
Sub OnButton_Click(Index As Integer)
    If (Index = 1) Then
        AlarmOn = True
...
End Sub
```

and we'll set **AlarmOn** to False when the user clicks the Alarm Off button:

```
Sub OnButton_Click(Index As Integer)
    If (Index = 1) Then
        AlarmOn = True
    Else
        AlarmOn = False
    End If
End Sub
```

Now in the **Timer** event handler, we just check if the current time is past the setting in the **AlarmSetting** text box and if **AlarmOn** is True (notice that we can do a direct string comparison with **Time$** and **AlarmSetting.Text**):

```
Sub Timer1_Timer()
    If (Time$ > AlarmSetting.Text And AlarmOn) Then
...
End Sub
```

If the alarm is supposed to sound, we just use the Visual Basic **Beep** procedure, which will beep each time **Timer1_Timer()** is called (in other words, once a second) until the user turns the alarm off:

```
Sub Timer1_Timer()
    If (Time$ > AlarmSetting.Text And AlarmOn) Then
        Beep
    End If
...
End Sub
```

Finally, we just display the current time in the **Display** label:

```
Sub Timer1_Timer()
    If (Time$ > AlarmSetting.Text And AlarmOn) Then
        Beep
    End If
    Display.Caption = Time$
End Sub
```

As an added touch, you can restrict user input in the **AlarmSetting** text box to valid characters. Here's how you restrict user input in a text box—when you set the **KeyAscii** argument to 0, that cancels the struck key:

```
Sub AlarmSetting_KeyPress(KeyAscii As Integer)
    Dim Key As String
    Key = Chr$(KeyAscii)
    If ((Key < "0" Or Key > "9") And Key <> ":") Then
        Beep
        KeyAscii = 0
    End If
End Sub
```

And that's it—now we've got a functioning alarm clock, as shown in Figure 13.6. The code for this example is located in the alarm folder on this book's accompanying CD-ROM.

Figure 13.6   An alarm clock built on the timer control.

Creating Animation Using The Timer Control

A common use for the timer control is to create graphics animation, because the way you create animation is by displaying successive frames of the animation sequence at intervals. That's a good job for the timer control.

To see how this works, we'll create an example now. In this example, we'll just switch back and forth between two simple images, image1.bmp and image2.bmp, which are simply strips of solid color, red and blue.

To store those images in our program, add an image list control, **ImageList1**, now. You add image list controls with the Project|Components menu item; click the Controls tab in the Components dialog box that opens, select the Microsoft Windows Common Controls item, and click on OK to close the Components box.

Draw a new image list control, **ImageList1**, and right-click it, selecting Properties in the menu that opens. We click the Images tab in the image list's property pages, and we use the Insert Picture button to insert the two images in image1.bmp and image2.bmp into the image list.

Next, add a timer control, **Timer1**; set its **Interval** property to 1000 (in other words, 1 second), and set its **Enabled** property to False. Also add a command button, **Command1**, with the caption "Start Animation", and a picture box, **Picture1**, setting the picture box's **AutoSize** property to True so that it resizes itself to fit our images.

That's it—we're ready to write some code. We start the animation when the user clicks the Start Animation button by enabling the timer:

```
Private Sub Command1_Click()
    Timer1.Enabled = True
End Sub
```

We'll keep track of the current image with a Boolean variable named **blnImage1**; if this Boolean variable is True, we'll display the first image in the image list:

```
Private Sub Timer1_Timer()
    Static blnImage1 As Boolean

    If blnImage1 Then
        Picture1.Picture = ImageList1.ListImages(1).Picture
    ...
```

Otherwise, we'll display the second image in the image list:

```
Private Sub Timer1_Timer()
    Static blnImage1 As Boolean

    If blnImage1 Then
        Picture1.Picture = ImageList1.ListImages(1).Picture
    Else
        Picture1.Picture = ImageList1.ListImages(2).Picture
    End If
    ...
```

Finally, we toggle **blnImage1**:

```
Private Sub Timer1_Timer()
    Static blnImage1 As Boolean
```

```
If blnImage1 Then
    Picture1.Picture = ImageList1.ListImages(1).Picture
Else
    Picture1.Picture = ImageList1.ListImages(2).Picture
End If

blnImage1 = Not blnImage1

End Sub
```

And that's all we need. When you run the program and click the Start Animation button, shown in Figure 13.7, the animation starts: the picture box flashes red and blue images once a second. Our animation example is a success.

The code for this example is located in the coloranimation folder on this book's accompanying CD-ROM.

Figure 13.7   Graphics animation with the timer control in Visual Basic.

Adding A Communications Control To A Program

The Testing Department is calling. Wouldn't it be great if users of your program could call in directly to the company's bulletin board? Hmm, you think, how do you do that?

To support serial communications, you use the Microsoft communications control. Adding this control to your program is easy; just follow these steps:

1. Select the Project|Components menu item.

2. Click the Controls tab in the Components dialog box that opens.

3. Select the Microsoft Comm Control entry, and click on OK to close the Components dialog box.

4. Following the preceding steps adds this control to the toolbox; draw it on your program's form now. This control is invisible at runtime, so the control's size and location don't matter very much.

Now that you've added the control, how do you set it up and get it working? Take a look at those topics coming up in this chapter.

Setting Up The Receive And Transmit Buffers

When a port is opened, the program creates receive and transmit buffers. To manage these buffers, the communications control has a number of properties that you set at design time using the control's property pages. For example, it's probably not a good idea to have a communications event (an **OnComm** event) for every byte you read; instead, you can set the **RThreshold** property to the number of bytes you want to read before triggering that event. The communications control's buffer management properties are **InBufferSize**, **OutBufferSize**, **RThreshold**, **SThreshold**, **InputLen**, and **EOFEnable**.

InBufferSize And OutBufferSize

The **InBufferSize** and **OutBufferSize** properties indicate how much memory is allocated to the receive and transmit buffers. By default, **InBufferSize** is 1024 and **OutBufferSize** is 512, although you can set them as you like. If your buffer size is too small, you run the risk of overflowing the buffer (unless you use handshaking—see that topic later in this chapter).

RThreshold And SThreshold

The **RThreshold** and **SThreshold** properties set or return the number of bytes that are received into the receive and transmit buffers before the **OnComm** event is fired. The **OnComm** event is the important one for the communications control and is used to monitor changes in communications states. For example, when your program receives more than **RThreshold** bytes, an **OnComm** event occurs, and the control's **CommEvent** property will hold the value **comEvReceive**. (Setting the value for each of these properties to 0 prevents the **OnComm** event from occurring.)

InputLen And EOFEnable

You can read data in chunks of specific length by setting the **InputLen** property; this property sets how many bytes you want to read when you use the **Input** property. When you set this property to 0 (the default), the communications control will read the entire contents of the receive buffer when you use the **Input** property. The **EOFEnable** property is used to indicate when an End Of File (EOF) character is found while reading data. Setting this property to True makes data input stop when an **EOF** is found and triggers the **OnComm** event.

Opening The Serial Port

Before you can work with the serial port and call another computer, you have to open that port. There are three properties that you use with the communications control to do that:

- **CommPort** sets and returns the communications port number.

- **Settings** sets and returns the baud rate, parity, data bits, and stop bits as a string.

- **PortOpen** sets and returns the state of a communications port. Also opens and closes a port.

Here's an example where we open COM2, which is usually the modem port, setting it to 9600 bps, no parity, 8 data bits, and 1 stop bit.

```
MSComm1.CommPort = 2
MSComm1.Settings = "9600,N,8,1"
MSComm1.PortOpen = True
```

That's all there is to it. When you're ready to close the port again, set the **PortOpen** property to False.

TIP: *To close a connection with another computer, you usually do more than just set **PortOpen** to False. For example, if you're logged into a shell account on that computer, you should log off by sending the appropriate command (such as "logoff"), either by typing that command or having your program send it. To hang up, send your modem the "ATH" command, followed by carriage return, **vbCr**.*

Working With A Modem

To dial another computer, you send command strings to the modem. How do you do that? You can send standard Hayes-type commands to your modem using the communications control's **Output** property this way, where we're instructing the modem to dial a number:

```
MSComm1.Output = "ATDT 555-1234" & vbCr
```

In this case, the command "AT" starts the connection, "D" dials the number, and "T" specifies Touch-Tone—instead of pulse—dialing. Note that a carriage return character (**vbCr**) must be added when using text strings with **Output**. (You do not, however, need to add the return character when outputting byte arrays.)

If a command is successful, your modem will usually send back an "OK" result code, and you can look for that result with the **Input** property.

TIP: *For a list of Hayes-compatible commands, check your modem documentation—the complete list of commands your modem understands should be there.*

Reading Data With The Communications Control

You use the **Input** property to get data from a communication control's receive buffer. For example, if you wanted to retrieve data from the receive buffer and display it in a text box, you might use the following code:

```
Text1.Text = MSComm1.Input
```

To retrieve the entire contents of the receive buffer, you must first set the **InputLen** property to 0 at design time or runtime. Otherwise, you'll get the number of bytes specified in the **InputLen** property.

You can receive incoming data as either text or binary data by setting the **InputMode** property to either **comInputModeText** or **comInputModeBinary**. The data will be either formatted as string or as binary data in a byte array (the default is **comInputModeText**). Also, it's worth noting that when every byte of data is received, the **InBufferCount** property is incremented by 1, which means that you can get the total number of bytes waiting for you by checking this property.

TIP: *You can clear the receive buffer by setting the value of **InBufferCount** to 0.*

You usually use the **Input** property with the **CommEvent** property in the **OnComm** event handler (see "Handling Communications Events" later in this chapter). For example, here's how we read input data into a buffer in the **OnComm** event handler, after checking the **CommEvent** property to make sure we actually received data:

```
Private Static Sub MSComm1_OnComm()

    Select Case MSComm1.CommEvent
        Case comEvReceive
            Dim Buffer As Variant
            Buffer = MSComm1.Input
    . . .
```

Sending Data With The Communications Control

To send data with the communications control, you use the **Output** property—in fact, you use this property to send both data to another computer and commands to your modem. If you set this property to a string, the data is sent as text; if you set it to binary data (a binary array), that data is sent in binary format.

Here are some examples. In this case, we're directing the modem to dial a number using a Hayes-compatible modem command:

```
MSComm1.Output = "ATDT 555-1234" & vbCr
```

In this case, we're sending a text string to another computer:

```
MsComm1.Output = "Here's the text!" & vbCr
```

And here we're reading records from a file and sending them through the modem to another computer:

```
FileBuffer = Space$(BufferSize)
Get #1, , FileBuffer
MSComm1.Output = FileBuffer
```

TIP: *You can watch the number of bytes in the transmit buffer by using the **OutBufferCount** property, and you can clear the transmit buffer by setting this value to 0.*

Setting Up Communications Handshaking

Handshaking invokes a data-transmission protocol (which, for example, makes sure that data is not sent too fast or doesn't overflow the receive buffer). The communications control can handle several different types of handshaking.

In particular, you set the **Handshaking** property to the handshaking protocol you want to use; the default value is to have no handshaking (**Handshaking = comNone**). Here are the possible handshaking protocols you can use with the **Handshaking** protocol:

- **comNone**—0; no handshaking (the default)
- **comXOnXOff**—1; XOn/XOff handshaking
- **comRTS**—2; RTS/CTS (Request To Send/Clear To Send) handshaking
- **comRTSXOnXOff**—3; both Request To Send and XOn/XOff handshaking

Often the communications protocol itself handles handshaking, which means that setting this property to anything but **comNone** can result in conflicts.

*Warning!   Here's an important note: If you set Handshaking to either **comRTS** or **comRTSXOnXOff**, also set the **RTSEnabled** property to True. If you don't, you will be able to connect and send, but not receive, data.*

Handling Communications Events

To handle communications events (and errors), you use the **OnComm** event and the **CommEvent** property. The **OnComm** event is very useful, because you can keep track of just about everything going on with the communications control. In the **OnComm** event, you can determine what happened by checking the **CommEvent** property, which will hold one of these values:

- **comEvSend**—1; there are fewer than **SThreshold** number of characters in the transmit buffer.

- **comEvReceive**—2; received **RThreshold** number of characters. This event is generated continuously until you use the **Input** property to remove the data from the receive buffer.

- **comEvCTS**—3; change in Clear To Send line.

- **comEvDSR**—4; change in Data Set Ready line. This event is only fired when DSR changes from 1 to 0.

- **comEvCD**—5; change in Carrier Detect line.

- **comEvRing**—6; ring detected. Some universal asynchronous receiver-transmitters (UARTs) may not support this event.

- **comEvEOF**—7; End Of File (ASCII character 26) character received.

The **OnComm** event also occurs for the following errors (these values will be in the **CommEvent** property):

- **comEventBreak**—1001; Break Signal. A break signal was received.

- **comEventCTSTO**—1002; Clear To Send Timeout. The Clear To Send line was low for **CTSTimeout** number of milliseconds while trying to transmit a character.

- **comEventDSRTO**—1003; Data Set Ready Timeout. The Data Set Ready line was low for **DSRTimeout** number of milliseconds while trying to transmit a character.

- **comEventFrame**—1004; Framing Error. The hardware detected a framing error.

- **comEventOverrun**—1006; Port Overrun. A character was not read from the hardware before the next character arrived and was lost.
- **comEventCDTO**—1007; Carrier Detect Timeout. The Carrier Detect line was low for **CDTimeout** number of milliseconds while trying to transmit a character. Carrier Detect is also known as the *Receive Line Signal Detect (RLSD)*.
- **comEventRxOver**—1008; Receive Buffer Overflow. There is no room in the receive buffer.
- **comEventRxParity**—1009; Parity Error. The hardware detected a parity error in transmission.
- **comEventTxFull**—1010; Transmit Buffer Full. The transmit buffer was full while trying to queue a character.
- **comEventDCB**—1011; unexpected error retrieving Device Control Block (DCB) for the port.

Here's an example using **OnComm**. In this case, we check for a receive event, **CommEvent = comEvReceive**, and use the **Input** property to store the received data in a buffer:

```
Private Static Sub MSComm1_OnComm()

    Select Case MSComm1.CommEvent
        Case comEvReceive
            Dim Buffer As Variant
            Buffer = MSComm1.Input
...
```

Closing The Serial Port

To close a serial port, you set the **PortOpen** property to False. Note that although doing so closes the serial port, you usually do more than just close the serial port to close a connection with another computer. For example, if you're connected to a shell account on another computer, you should log out first, then send the Hayes-compatible "ATH" command to your modem to hang up before setting **PortOpen** to False.

Here's an example. When the user clicks **Command1**, we set up the serial port COM2 and dial a number:

```
Private Sub Command1_Click()
    MSComm1.CommPort = 2
```

```
        MSComm1.Settings = "9600,N,8,1"
        MSComm1.PortOpen = True

        MSComm1.Output = "ATDT 555-1234" & vbCr
End Sub
```

To hang up, we send the Hayes-compatible "ATH" command to the modem and set **PortOpen** to False to close the serial port:

```
Private Sub Command2_Click()
    MSComm1.Output = "ATH" & vbCr
    MSComm1.PortOpen = False
End Sub
```

Adding A MonthView Control To Your Program

The Testing Department is on the line again. Your financial planning program, *BigBucks4U*, is great, but what about displaying a calendar so the user can plan dates far into the future. You start thinking about the algorithm for determining the day of the week for any date throughout history—but there's a better way.

You can use a MonthView control. That control displays the current month and lets the user scroll through other months as well. Just think of it as a handy calendar, because that's what it's designed to be.

To add a MonthView control to your program, just follow these steps:

1. Select the Project|Components menu item.
2. Click the Controls tab in the Components dialog box that opens.
3. Select the Microsoft Windows Common Controls-2 entry, and click on OK to close the Components dialog box. This adds both the MonthView and DateTimePicker controls to the toolbox.
4. Just draw the control as you would any other control in your form.

Now that you've added this control, how do you use it? See the next topic.

Getting Dates From A MonthView Control

When the user clicks a date in a MonthView control, the control creates a **DateClick** event. We can take advantage of that event to display the date the user clicked in a text box, using the MonthView's **Day**, **Month**, and **Year** properties:

```
Private Sub MonthView1_DateClick(ByVal DateClicked As Date)
    Text1.Text = MonthView1.Month & "/" & MonthView1.Day & _
        "/" & MonthView1.Year
End Sub
```

In fact, we've done too much here. You can do the same thing with the MonthView's **Value** property, which holds the current date in mm/dd/yy format:

```
Private Sub MonthView1_DateClick(ByVal DateClicked As Date)
    Text1.Text = MonthView1.Value
End Sub
```

The result of this code appears in Figure 13.8 (the red circle indicates today's date).

Notice also that we are passed a Visual Basic **Date** object in this procedure, corresponding to the date the user clicked. You can use the **Format$( )** function as outlined earlier in this chapter to format the date held in that object in any way you wish.

The code for this example is located in the calendar folder on this book's accompanying CD-ROM.

TIP: *If you enable a MonthView's **MultiSelect** property by setting it to True, the user can select a number of dates in the MonthView (by using the Ctrl and Shift keys with the mouse). You can use the **SelStart** and **SelEnd** properties to determine the selected range.*

Figure 13.8   Reading a date from a clicked MonthView control.

Adding A DateTimePicker Control To Your Program

An easy way of letting the user select a date is to use a DateTimePicker control. The DateTimePicker control allows the user to specify a date or time.

DateTimePickers can display a MonthView as a drop-down control, or the current time with an updown control to let the user select the time they want.

In particular, the control's **UpDown** property determines which mode the control is in:

- **UpDown** = **False** means the control is in drop-down calendar mode (the default).

- **UpDown** = **True** means the DateTimePicker is in time format mode.

To add a DateTimePicker control to your program, just follow these steps:

1. Select the Project|Components menu item.

2. Click the Controls tab in the Components dialog box that opens.

3. Select the Microsoft Windows Common Controls-2 entry, and click on OK to close the Components dialog box. This adds both the MonthView and DateTimePicker controls to the toolbox.

4. Just draw the control as you would any other control in your form.

5. Set the **UpDown** property as discussed in the preceding list to select calendar mode or time format mode.

Now that you've added the control, how do you use it? See the next topic.

Using A
DateTimePicker
Control

Using A DateTimePicker Control

We'll see how to let the user select a time using a DateTimePicker control here. Just add a DateTimePicker to your program and set its **UpDown** property to True (which means we'll let the user set the time, not the date).

DateTimePicker controls have a **Change** event, and we'll make use of that event to catch new time settings as the user makes them. In this case, we'll just display the new time in a text box this way, using the DateTimePicker's **Value** property:

```
Private Sub DTPicker1_Change()
    Text1.Text = DTPicker1.Value
End Sub
```

That's all we need. Now the user can edit the hour, minute, and second of the time displayed in the DateTimePicker, and as soon as they make any change, we'll display the new value in the text box, as shown in Figure 13.9. Our DateTimePicker example is a success. The code for this example is located in the timepicker folder on this book's accompanying CD-ROM.

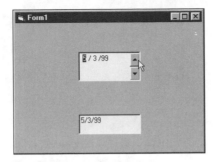

Figure 13.9   Using a DateTimePicker control.

Chapter 14

The Frame, Label, Shape, And Line Controls

If you need an immediate solution to:	See page:
Adding A Frame To A Program	439
Setting Frame Size And Location	440
Dragging And Dropping Controls	440
Grouping Controls In A Frame	442
Adding A Label To A Program	443
Using Labels Instead Of Text Boxes	444
Formatting Text In Labels	445
Aligning Text In Labels	446
Handling Label Control Events	446
Using Labels To Give Access Keys To Controls Without Captions	447
Adding A Shape Control To A Program	448
Drawing Rectangles	449
Drawing Squares	449
Drawing Ovals	450
Drawing Circles	450
Drawing Rounded Rectangles	451
Drawing Rounded Squares	451
Setting Shape Borders: Drawing Width, Dashes, And Dots	451
Filling Shapes	452
Drawing A Shape Without The IDE Grid	453
Moving Shapes At Runtime	454
Adding A Line Control To A Program	455
Drawing Thicker, Dotted, And Dashed Lines	456

(continued)

If you need an immediate solution to:	See page:
Drawing A Line Without The IDE Grid	456
Changing A Line Control At Runtime	457
Using Form Methods To Draw Lines	458
Using Form Methods To Draw Circles	459

In Depth

In this chapter, we're going to examine the controls you use to organize and label other controls in a form: the frame, label, shape, and line controls. You use the frame control to create a *frame*—a labeled box—in which you can place the following types of controls:

- Label controls to display noneditable text usually used to describe other controls or control groups
- Shape controls to draw circles and boxes in a form
- Line controls to draw lines

These controls are used primarily at design time, but they have their runtime uses as well, as we'll see. All these controls are intrinsic controls—that is, they appear in the toolbox when Visual Basic starts—and we'll take a closer look at all these controls now.

The Frame Control

You usually use the frame control to group controls together into a recognizable group. This control appears as a box with a label at upper left. You can make the controls in a frame into a functional group as well, such as when you group option buttons together. When you add option buttons to a frame, those buttons function in concert; when you click one, all the others are deselected. And those option buttons are separate from any other group of option buttons in the form.

The Frame Control tool appears as the third tool down on the left in the Visual Basic toolbox in Figure 14.1.

The Label Control

You use label controls to display text that you don't want the user to change directly. As their name implies, you can use these controls to display text that labels other parts of the form that don't have their own captions. For example, you might label a picture box something like "Current image", or a text box "New setting".

Despite their name, label controls are not static. You can change the text in a label at runtime by setting its **Caption** property, and in fact that's often a very

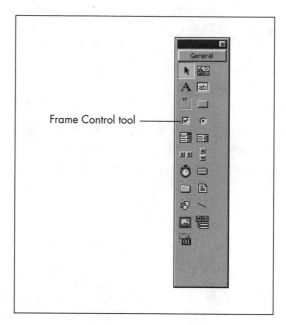

Frame Control tool

Figure 14.1   The Frame Control tool.

useful thing to do if you don't want the user to change that text. For example, we'll see how to build a stopwatch example in this chapter that displays the time in a label control. The label control in that example may be far from what you think of as a standard label, because the text in the label will change, and that text will be large—48 point. It's wise to remember that labels can indeed display any kind of text—you can even format, word wrap, or size a label to fit its text. All in all, labels are one of the most useful Visual Basic controls. They can even have **Click** events and access keys, as we'll see in this chapter.

The Label Control tool appears in the toolbox in Figure 14.2 as the second tool down on the left. Just about every Visual Basic programmer is familiar with this control, but we'll see some new label tricks in this chapter.

The Shape Control

The shape control is a graphical control. You can use this control to draw predefined colored and filled shapes, including rectangles, squares, ovals, circles, rounded rectangles, or rounded squares.

You use the shape control at design time to draw shapes in a form. There's no great programming complexity here—you just use this control as a design element to add rectangles, circles, and so on to your forms. In this way, the shape control is a little like the frame control; however, shapes can't act as

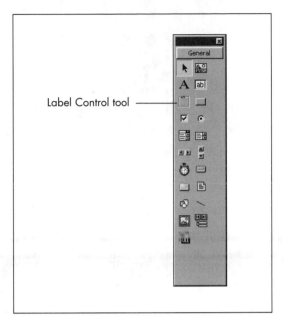

Label Control tool ———

Figure 14.2   The Label Control tool.

control containers (for example, you can't group option buttons together with shapes or move the controls inside them *en masse*). Still, shapes certainly come in more varieties than frames do.

Although shape controls are one of the Visual Basic intrinsic controls, Visual Basic programmers remain largely ignorant of them. That's too bad, because you can create some nice effects with shapes, as we'll see here.

The Shape Control tool appears in the Visual Basic toolbox in Figure 14.3 as the ninth tool down on the left.

The Line Control

Like the shape control, the line control is a graphical control. You use it to display horizontal, vertical, or diagonal lines in a form. You can use these controls at design time as a design element or at runtime to alter the original line you drew.

Drawing lines is easy—you just click the Line Control tool in the toolbox, press the mouse button when the cursor is at the line's start location on the form, and drag the mouse to the end position of the line. When you release the mouse, the line appears with sizing handles at each end that you can use to change the line as you like. You can also change a line at runtime by changing its **X1**, **X2**, **Y1**, and **Y2** properties.

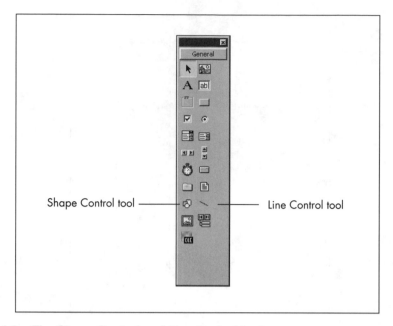

Shape Control tool —————————— Line Control tool

Figure 14.3   The Shape Control and Line Control tools.

You can draw lines with this control in forms, picture boxes, and frames. In fact, lines drawn with the line control stay visible even if its container's **AutoRedraw** property is set to False. (The line control even has its own **Visible** property, which means you can make lines appear and disappear.) The Line Control tool appears in the toolbox in Figure 14.3 as the ninth tool down on the right.

Form Drawing Methods

Besides using the preceding controls to draw lines and circles in forms, you can actually use methods built into the form to do much the same thing. Because this is a chapter about designing and organizing your controls on forms, we'll take a look at those methods as well.

That's it for the overview—it's time to turn to the Immediate Solutions.

Immediate Solutions

Adding A Frame To A Program

The Testing Department is calling again. Do you really need 200 buttons in your program? Of course, you say. They say, well, can you please organize them into groups? Hmm, you think, how do you do that?

You can use frames to group controls together in forms or picture boxes. To draw a frame, you just use the Frame Control tool in the toolbox as you would for any control. When you add a frame to a form or picture box, there are a few things you should know. To set the text that appears at upper left in a frame, you set the frame's **Caption** property (and you can change the caption at runtime by setting this property). You can make frames appear flat or 3D (the default) by setting their **Appearance** property. You can also give frames tool tips (the explanatory text that appears in a small yellow window when the mouse cursor rests over a control) by setting the **ToolTipText** property.

For example, we've given the left frame in Figure 14.4 the caption "Day of the week" and the tool tip "Enter the day here".

TIP: To group option buttons together in a frame, see "Grouping Controls In A Frame" later in this chapter.

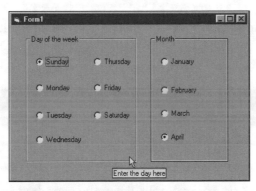

Figure 14.4   Organizing controls with frames.

Setting Frame Size And Location

Setting a frame's height and width is easy—just set the frame's **Height** and **Width** properties at design time or runtime. You can set the frame's location in its container (that is, a form or picture box) with its **Left** and **Top** properties, or by using its **Move** method.

TIP: The frame contains other controls, such as option buttons, they move with the frame.

For example, here's how you use a frame's **Move** method:

```
Private Sub Command1_Click()
      Frame1.Move Frame1.Left + 1000
End Sub
```

For more on dragging frames, take a look at the next topic.

Dragging And Dropping Controls

The Aesthetic Design Department is on the phone. The way you've set up your controls in your program is fine—but what if users want to move them around at runtime? Shouldn't they be able to do that?

You drag and drop frames just as you do any other control, and dragging frames also drags all the controls in that frame, so we'll take a look at how to drag controls now.

To start a drag operation, you use the control's **Drag** method:

```
Control.Drag action
```

Here, the *action* parameter can take these values:

- **vbCancel**—0; cancels drag operation
- **vbBeginDrag**—1; begins dragging *object*
- **vbEndDrag**—2; ends dragging and drops *object*

Let's see this at work. For example, when the user drags a frame, **Frame1**, in our program, we catch the **MouseDown** event first:

```
Private Sub Frame1_MouseDown(Button As Integer, Shift As Integer, X As _
      Single, Y As Single)

End Sub
```

When the control is dropped, we'll get the new mouse location at the upper left of the control. However, because the mouse was originally pressed at some location inside the control, and not at its upper left corner, we'll need to know that original mouse location before we move the control's upper left corner. We'll save that mouse location inside the control as (**intXoffset**, **intYoffset**):

```
Private Sub Frame1_MouseDown(Button As Integer, Shift As Integer, X As _
    Single, Y As Single)
    intXOffset = X
    intYOffset = Y
...
End Sub
```

Declare these new variables as form-wide variables in the (General) section of the form:

```
Dim intXOffset As Integer
Dim intYOffset As Integer
```

Then we start the drag operation of the control itself with the **Drag** method:

```
Private Sub Frame1_MouseDown(Button As Integer, Shift As Integer, X As _
    Single, Y As Single)
    intXOffset = X
    intYOffset = Y
    Frame1.Drag 1
End Sub
```

When the control is dropped on the form, we just move the upper left of the control to the mouse location minus the offset of the mouse in the control (this avoids making the control's upper left corner appear to jump to the mouse location). Doing so looks like this in code:

```
Private Sub Form_DragDrop(Source As Control, X As Single, Y As Single)
    Source.Move X - intXOffset, Y - intYOffset
End Sub
```

There's one more thing to consider here—users may just move the frame a little distance, in which case they are actually dropping the control on top of itself. In this case, the new mouse position we're passed is relative to the upper left of the control, so we have to add the **Left** and **Top** values to the mouse location to get form coordinates:

```
Private Sub Frame1_DragDrop(Source As Control, X As Single, Y As Single)
    Source.Move Source.Left + X - intXOffset, Source.Top + Y - intYOffset
End Sub
```

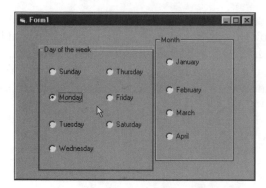

Figure 14.5   Dragging a frame control with all the controls in it.

That's it—when you run the program, you can drag **Frame1**, the left frame in Figure 14.5, as you like. Our drag and drop example is a success.

The code for this example is located in the dragdrop folder on this book's accompanying CD-ROM.

Grouping Controls In A Frame

The Testing Department is calling again. Using option buttons to let users specify months and days of the week is OK, but why can they only click one option button at a time? Shouldn't they be able to specify *both* day of the week *and* the month?

You can make option buttons function together in separate groups. Unless you set up a frame (or picture box) to hold the option buttons, however, they'll all be on the form, which means they'll be in the same group.

Warning!   If you draw a control outside the frame and then try to move it inside, the control will be on top of the frame, not in it, which means the control will not be grouped with other controls in the frame.

To group controls like option buttons, first draw the frame control, and then draw the controls inside the frame.

TIP: At design time, you can also align the controls in a frame. Just select multiple controls by holding down the Ctrl key, and use the Format menu to align the controls or set their spacing uniformly.

We already developed a good example of grouping controls in our chapter on option buttons and checkboxes, and we'll review it here. In that example, we

Figure 14.6   Grouping controls using frames.

created a tour package program that lets users select from one of four tour packages. When they clicked one of the four option buttons representing each of the four packages, a series of checkboxes in another frame are checked to indicate what cities are in that tour package, as shown in Figure 14.6.

As you can see in Figure 14.6, we've grouped the controls into two frames that have the captions "Tour" and "Cities". The option buttons and checkboxes each function as a control group; when the user selects a tour package by clicking an option button, the program displays the cities in that tour in the checkboxes. Because the option buttons function as a group, only one option button may be selected at a time.

The code for this example is located in the tourpackage folder on this book's accompanying CD-ROM.

Adding A Label To A Program

The Testing Department is calling again. What are all those text boxes in your new program, *SuperDuperDataCrunch*? You explain patiently that they are there to help users with financial planning and let them enter current value, interest rate, time period, taxable base, and so on. Well, they say, you better label those text boxes so users know what they are. Hmm, you think, *label* them?

You can label controls without a **Caption** property, like text boxes, with the label control. You simply use the Label Control tool in the toolbox to add a label to your form and set its **Caption** property to display the label you want. You can size the label as desired at design time using the sizing handles that appear around a label when you select it, or at runtime using its **Top**, **Left**, **Width**, and **Height** properties.

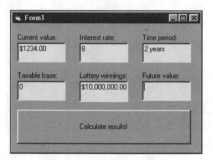

Figure 14.7   Labeling text boxes with label controls.

As an example, take a look at Figure 14.7. There, we've used labels to describe what value each of six text boxes are supposed to hold. In this way, labels can make your program a great deal easier to work with.

*Warning!   Don't forget that you can set labels' captions at runtime simply by changing their **Caption** property. In other words, labels can display text just like text boxes can, except that you can't edit it, and the text appears as though it's directly on the form. For more on this, see the next topic.*

Using Labels Instead Of Text Boxes

There are several advantages to using labels instead of text boxes in a Visual Basic program. Labels display read-only text (although you can make text boxes read-only by setting their **Locked** property to **True**), and they give the appearance of text directly on the form, which can look much better than a text box on occasion.

Let's see an example. In the stopwatch program we created in our chapter on timers, we used a label to display elapsed time. When the user clicked one button, we set a form-wide variable, **StartTime**, to the current time using the **Now** function, and we enabled a timer, **Timer1**:

```
Private Sub Command1_Click()
    StartTime = Now
    Timer1.Enabled = True
End Sub
```

When the user clicks another button, we stop the stopwatch by disabling the timer:

```
Private Sub Command2_Click()
    Timer1.Enabled = False
End Sub
```

In the **Timer1_Timer( )** subroutine, which is called by the timer every second, we display the elapsed time in a label named **Display**:

```
Sub Timer1_Timer()
    Display.Caption = Format$(Now - StartTime, "hh:mm:ss")
End Sub
```

You might think it odd to display time in a label, but we set the label's font size to 48 point (and its font to Courier New), which makes a very satisfactory display, as you can see in Figure 14.8.

In this way, we've used a label to display text instead of a text box, because the user can't edit the text in the label, and in this case the label looks like a more integral part of the program than a text box would. The code for this example is located in the stopwatch folder on this book's accompanying CD-ROM.

Figure 14.8   Displaying time in a label control.

Formatting Text In Labels

When you add labels to a form, you can make the label match the text's size or wrap as needed by setting these label control properties:

- **AutoSize** makes the label size itself to fit the text.

- **WordWrap** enables word wrap if lines of text are too long.

In addition, you can format the text in a label with these properties, making the text appear in any font or font size, or with attributes like bold or underline:

- **FontBold**

- **FontItalic**

- **FontName**
- **FontStrikeThru**
- **FontUnderline**

Keep in mind that you can use labels as a read-only text box, so formatting the text can be a very useful thing to do.

Aligning Text In Labels

As with text boxes, you can align text in labels. To do that, you just set the label's **Alignment** property at design time or runtime. Here are the possible values for the **Alignment** property:

- **VbLeftJustify**—0 (the default); text is left-aligned
- **VbRightJustify**—1; text is right-aligned
- **VbCenter**—2; text is centered

For example, if you're writing a calculator program and have a column of right-justified text boxes above a label that displays a running sum, you can also right-justify the label to match the controls above it.

Handling Label Control Events

Here's something that even experienced Visual Basic programmers often don't know: labels have events like **Click** and **DblClick** (although they don't have any keystroke-handling events). Using these events can be a good thing if you're using a label control as more than just a label—for example, to reset a setting of some kind.

Here's an example using the **DblClick** event. We developed a stopwatch program in our chapter on timers (Chapter 13) and displayed the elapsed time in a label named **Display** in that program. To make life easier for users, we can let them just double-click that label to reset the stopwatch to 00:00:00. Doing so is easy; we just add an event handle for the label's **DblClick** event:

```
Private Sub Display_DblClick()

End Sub
```

To reset the stopwatch, we just use the Visual Basic **Now** function to set the start time, held in a variable named **StartTime**, to the current time:

```
Private Sub Display_DblClick()
    StartTime = Now
End Sub
```

And that's it. Now when the user double-clicks the stopwatch's display, the stopwatch is reset to 00:00:00. We've made effective use of a label's **DblClick** event.

Using Labels To Give Access Keys To Controls Without Captions

The Testing Department is calling again. The old thorny issue of keyboard access has come up again. Theoretically, they say, users should be able to use your program, *SuperDuperDataCrunch*, with just the keyboard. Fine, you say, we can add access keys to all the button captions so the user can give the button the focus just by pressing Alt + the access key (just like menu items). Don't forget to do the same to all the text boxes, the testing department says. You think, how *do* you give an access key to a *text box*?

This is where a useful aspect of labels comes in handy. In fact, this aspect of the label control is built just to handle this problem. You can give access keys to controls with **Caption** properties just by placing an ampersand (&) in the caption in front of the letter you want to make the access key—but how can you do that if a control (like a text box) has no **Caption** property?

Here's the way you do it: you give the access key to a label control and then make sure the control you want to give the focus to with that access key is next in the tab order (that is, has the next highest **TabIndex** property value). Because labels cannot accept the focus themselves, this is a neat feature: when the user presses Alt + the access key, the label passes the focus on to the next control. In this way, you can give even controls without **Caption** properties access keys.

*Warning! When you use access keys, make sure you set the label's **UseMnemonic** property to True (the default), or the access key won't be enabled.*

As an example, we've given the two labels in Figure 14.9 access keys. When the user presses Alt + the access key above a text box, the focus is set to that text box, because those text boxes follow their individual labels in the tab order.

Now we're using access keys with text boxes.

Figure 14.9   Using access keys in labels to give the focus to text boxes.

Adding A Shape Control To A Program

The Aesthetic Design Department is calling again. Can't you jazz up the appearance of your program a little? How about something to give it a little *pizzazz*? Looking around, you happen to notice the *shape* control. OK, you say, no problem.

You use the shape control at design time to draw shapes on a form or picture box. The shapes you can draw are rectangles, squares, ovals, circles, rounded rectangles, and rounded squares.

At runtime, you can access and change the shape control's properties like **Left**, **Top**, **Width**, **Height**, **BackColor**, **FillStyle**, or **FillColor**, and use its methods, like **Move** or **Refresh**. However, shape controls have no events, so they can't respond directly to user actions like clicks.

You draw a shape using the Shape Control tool, which appears in the Visual Basic toolbox when Visual Basic starts. Just draw the shape as you want it (it starts as a rectangle). To set the shape's type (for example, a rectangle, square, oval, and so on), you set the control's **Shape** property to one of the following values:

- **VbShapeRectangle**—0 (the default); rectangle
- **VbShapeSquare**—1; square
- **VbShapeOval**—2; oval
- **VbShapeCircle**—3; circle
- **VbShapeRoundedRectangle**—4; rounded rectangle
- **VbShapeRoundedSquare**—5; rounded square

One important use of shape controls is to group other controls together. (Note, however, that shape controls can't act as true control containers in the way picture boxes or frames can. For example, you can't group option buttons together with shapes.) In Figure 14.10, we're using shape controls to group the buttons visually into two groups.

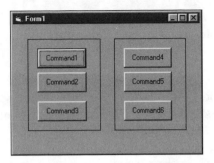

Figure 14.10 *Using the shape control to group other controls.*

You can also set the width of the shape's drawing line with the **BorderWidth** property and fill the shape using the **FillColor** and **FillStyle** properties. The **BorderStyle** property lets you select the style of the shape's drawing line, including using dots and dashes. For more on this control, see the other topics in this chapter.

Drawing Rectangles

How do you draw rectangles with the shape control? You start by clicking the Shape Control tool in the Visual Basic toolbox and drawing that control to match the size and location you want your new figure to have. To draw a rectangle, you simply set the control's **Shape** property to **VbShapeRectangle** (that's the default anyway).

That's all you have to do—the shape control is very easy to work with. Using the shape control, you can draw in both forms and picture boxes.

You can also set the width of the shape's drawing line with the **BorderWidth** property and fill the shape using the **FillColor** and **FillStyle** properties. The **BorderStyle** property lets you select the style of the shape's drawing line, including using dots and dashes.

Drawing Squares

How do you draw squares with the shape control? You start by clicking the Shape Control tool in the Visual Basic toolbox and drawing that control to match the size and location you want your new figure to have. To draw a square, you simply set the control's **Shape** property to **VbShapeSquare**.

That's all you have to do—the shape control is simple. Using the shape control, you can draw in both forms and picture boxes.

You can also set the width of the shape's drawing line with the **BorderWidth** property and fill the shape using the **FillColor** and **FillStyle** properties. The **BorderStyle** property lets you select the style of the shape's drawing line, including using dots and dashes. For more on this control, see the other topics in this chapter.

Drawing Ovals

To draw ovals with the shape control, you start by clicking the Shape Control tool in the Visual Basic toolbox and drawing that control to match the size and location you want your new figure to have. To draw an oval, you simply set the control's **Shape** property to **VbShapeOval**.

That's all you have to do—the shape control is very easy. Using the shape control, you can draw in both forms and picture boxes.

You can also set the width of the shape's drawing line with the **BorderWidth** property and fill the shape using the **FillColor** and **FillStyle** properties. The **BorderStyle** property lets you select the style of the shape's drawing line, including using dots and dashes. For more on this control, see the other topics in this chapter.

Drawing Circles

To draw circles, you start by clicking the Shape Control tool in the Visual Basic toolbox and drawing that control to match the size and location you want your new figure to have. To draw a circle, you simply set the control's **Shape** property to **VbShapeCircle**.

That's all you have to do—the shape control is very easy to work with. Using the shape control, you can draw in both forms and picture boxes.

You can also set the width of the shape's drawing line with the **BorderWidth** property and fill the shape using the **FillColor** and **FillStyle** properties. The **BorderStyle** property lets you select the style of the shape's drawing line, including using dots and dashes. For more on this control, see the other topics in this chapter.

Drawing Rounded Rectangles

Drawing Rounded Rectangles

How do you draw rounded rectangles with the shape control? You start by clicking the Shape Control tool in the Visual Basic toolbox and drawing that control to match the size and location you want your new figure to have. To draw a rounded rectangle, you simply set the control's **Shape** property to **VbShapeRoundedRectangle**.

That's all you have to do—this control is very easy. Using the shape control, you can draw in both forms and picture boxes.

You can also set the width of the shape's drawing line with the **BorderWidth** property, and fill the shape using the **FillColor** and **FillStyle** properties. The **BorderStyle** property lets you select the style of the shape's drawing line, including using dots and dashes. For more on this control, see the other topics in this chapter.

Drawing Rounded Squares

Drawing Rounded Squares

To draw rounded squares with the shape control, you start by clicking the Shape Control tool in the Visual Basic toolbox and drawing that control to match the size and location you want your new figure to have. To draw a rounded square, you simply set the control's **Shape** property to **VbShapeRoundedSquare**.

That's all you have to do. The shape control is easy. Using the shape control, you can draw in both forms and picture boxes.

You can also set the width of the shape's drawing line with the **BorderWidth** property and fill the shape using the **FillColor** and **FillStyle** properties. The **BorderStyle** property lets you select the style of the shape's drawing line, including using dots and dashes. For more on this control, see the other topics in this chapter.

Setting Shape Borders: Drawing Width, Dashes, And Dots

Setting Shape Borders: Drawing Width, Dashes, And Dots

The Aesthetic Design Department is on the line. Can't you do something about the shapes in your program? Maybe make them—dotted? You think, *dotted*?

Visual Basic can help here. Just set the shape control's **BorderStyle** property. Here are the possible values for the **BorderStyle** property:

- **vbTransparent**—0; transparent
- **vbBSSolid**—1 (the default); solid (the border is centered on the edge of the shape)
- **vbBSDash**—2; dash
- **vbBSDot**—3; dot
- **vbBSDashDot**—4; dash-dot
- **vbBSDashDotDot**—5; dash-dot-dot
- **vbBSInsideSolid**—6; inside solid (the outer edge of the border is the outer edge of the shape)

Using this property, you can adjust the border of your shape control as you want it.

Here's another way to customize a shape control: you can set the shape control's border width (in other words, the drawing line width) using the shape control's **BorderWidth** property. Just set that property to the new value you want for the border thickness (the default value is 1).

Filling Shapes

You can fill shape controls using the shape's **FillStyle** property with cross-hatching, diagonal lines, and other fill patterns. Here's a list of the possible values for the **FillStyle** property:

- **VbFSSolid**—0; solid
- **VbFSTransparent**—1 (the default); transparent
- **VbHorizontalLine**—2; horizontal line
- **VbVerticalLine**—3; vertical line
- **VbUpwardDiagonal**—4; upward diagonal
- **VbDownwardDiagonal**—5; downward diagonal
- **VbCross**—6; cross
- **VbDiagonalCross**—7; diagonal cross

You can see what each of these fill styles looks like in Figure 14.11. Note in particular the transparent fill style—which really just means that the shape control is not filled. That's usually the style you use when you draw shapes in a form to group controls together.

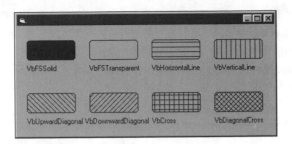

Figure 14.11   The Visual Basic fill styles.

TIP: To set the fill color in a shape control, you can use the **FillColor** property at both design time and runtime. To place a value in the **FillColor** property at runtime, use the Visual Basic **RGB** function like this, where we fill a shape with red: **Shape1.FillColor – RGB(255, 0, 0)**

Drawing A Shape Without The IDE Grid

When you draw shapes in the Visual Basic Integrated Development Environment (IDE), the boundaries of that control fall along the dotted grid you can see in forms. That grid can help in aligning controls and lines, but there are times when you want finer control.

To turn off the automatic alignment of controls to the grid as you draw them, follow these steps:

1. Select the Tools|Options menu item.
2. Click the General tab in the Options dialog box.
3. Deselect the box marked Align Controls To Grid.
4. Click on OK to close the Options dialog box.

That's it. Now you're free to draw controls as you want them and where you want them, without having your controls' boundaries fall on a grid line.

TIP: You can hide the grid by deselecting the Show Grid box in the Options dialog box, as well as reset its dimensions (the default size of each cell in the grid is 120x120 twips).

Moving Shapes At Runtime

Because shape controls are design elements, there are times you might want to move them around as a program runs, and you can do that with the control's **Move** method:

```
Shape.Move left, [top, [width, height]]
```

Besides using **Move**, you can change a shape's control **Top**, **Left**, **Width**, and **Height** properties. Let's see an example. Here, we'll just move four shape controls showing circles around at random in a form. To use random numbers in Visual Basic, we start with the **Randomize** statement when the form loads; this initializes the random number generator:

```
Private Sub Form_Load()
    Randomize
End Sub
```

Next, add four shape controls, **Shape1** to **Shape4**, showing circles, and a timer, **Timer1**, to the program, setting the timer **Interval** property to 1000 (in other words, 1 second), and adding a **Timer** event handler:

```
Private Sub Timer1_Timer()

End Sub
```

Now in **Timer1_Timer()**, we move the four circles around at random with the **Move** method:

```
Private Sub Timer1_Timer()
    Shape1.Move Shape1.Left + ScaleWidth * (Rnd - 0.5) / 50, Shape1.Top _
        + ScaleHeight * (Rnd - 0.5) / 50
    Shape2.Move Shape2.Left + ScaleWidth * (Rnd - 0.5) / 50, Shape2.Top _
        + ScaleHeight * (Rnd - 0.5) / 50
    Shape3.Move Shape3.Left + ScaleWidth * (Rnd - 0.5) / 50, Shape3.Top _
        + ScaleHeight * (Rnd - 0.5) / 50
    Shape4.Move Shape4.Left + ScaleWidth * (Rnd - 0.5) / 50, Shape4.Top _
        + ScaleHeight * (Rnd - 0.5) / 50
End Sub
```

And that's all it takes. The result of this code appears in Figure 14.12. When you run the program, the circles move around at random. The code for this example is located in the circles folder on this book's accompanying CD-ROM.

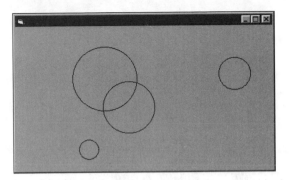

Figure 14.12   *Moving shape controls around at random.*

*TIP: Besides moving shapes, you can hide and show them by setting their **Visible** property to False and **True**, respectively.*

Adding A Line Control To A Program

The shape control offers a number of predefined shapes for visual design, but sometimes that's not enough (what if the Aesthetic Design Department were to start demanding octagons?). For other cases, there's the line control.

The line control does just as its name implies: it draws a line. You can draw lines at design time simply as you would any other control—just click the Line Control tool in the toolbox, press the mouse button at one end of the line you want, and drag the mouse to the other end.

The line control's primary properties are **X1**, **X2**, **Y1**, and **Y2**, and those values form the coordinates of the line segment: (**X1**, **Y1**) and (**X2**, **Y2**). You can even change those values at runtime to move or resize the line (line controls do not have a **Move** method).

You can also draw lines with this control in forms, picture boxes, and in frames. In fact, lines drawn with the line control stay visible even if its container's **AutoRedraw** property is set to **False** (unless its **Visible** property is set to False).

As an example, we've drawn a few lines in the form in Figure 14.13 using the line control.

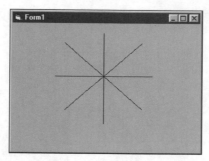

Figure 14.13   Lines drawn with the line control.

Drawing Thicker, Dotted, And Dashed Lines

Using the line control, you can select a line style with the **BorderStyle** property. Here are the possible values for the line control's **BorderStyle** property:

- **vbTransparent**—0; transparent
- **vbBSSolid**—1 (the default); solid
- **vbBSDash**—2; dash
- **vbBSDot**—3; dot
- **vbBSDashDot**—4; dash-dot
- **vbBSDashDotDot**—5; dash-dot-dot
- **vbBSInsideSolid**—6; inside solid

To set a line's width, you use the **BorderWidth** property (the default value is 1). It seems a little odd to call the line's style **BorderStyle** and its width **BorderWidth**—after all, what is the line a border to? However, those properties are named that way to be consistent with the shape control.

TIP: We might also note that the effect of setting the **BorderStyle** property depends on the setting of the **BorderWidth** property; if **BorderWidth** isn't 1 and **BorderStyle** isn't 0 or 6, Visual Basic sets **BorderStyle** to 1.

Drawing A Line Without The IDE Grid

When you draw lines in the Visual Basic Integrated Development Environment (IDE), those lines fall along the dotted grid you can see in forms. That grid can help in aligning controls and lines, but there are times when you want finer control.

To turn off the automatic alignment of controls to the grid as you draw them, follow these steps:

1. Select the Tools|Options menu item.
2. Click the General tab in the Options dialog box.
3. Deselect the box marked Align Controls To Grid.
4. Click on OK to close the Options dialog box.

That's it. Now you're free to draw controls as you want them and where you want them, without having your controls' boundaries fall on a grid line.

TIP: *You can hide the grid by deselecting the Show Grid box in the Options dialog box, as well as reset its dimensions (the default size of each cell in the grid is 120x120 twips).*

Changing A Line Control At Runtime

You can move Visual Basic controls at runtime—why not line controls? You can't use the **Move** method to move a line control at runtime, but you *can* move or resize it by altering its **X1**, **X2**, **Y1**, and **Y2** properties.

Let's see an example. In this case, we've added four random line controls to a form in a control array, **LineControl(0)** to **LineControl(3)**. When the user clicks a command button, **Command1**, we loop over all four lines and arrange them horizontally.

Here's what the code looks like (the measurements are in the Visual Basic default, twips, or 1/1440s of an inch):

```
Private Sub Command1_Click()
    Dim intLoopIndex As Integer

    For intLoopIndex = 0 To 3
        LineControl(intLoopIndex).X1 = 1000
        LineControl(intLoopIndex).X2 = 3500
        LineControl(intLoopIndex).Y1 = 1000 + 100 * intLoopIndex
        LineControl(intLoopIndex).Y2 = LineControl(intLoopIndex).Y1
    Next intLoopIndex

End Sub
```

The result of this code appears in Figure 14.14. Now we're moving lines around at runtime.

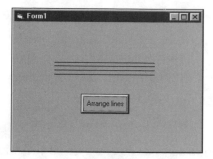

Figure 14.14   Changing line controls at runtime.

Using Form Methods To Draw Lines

We've seen how to draw lines with the line control—but you can use a form method, the **Line** method, to draw lines directly. The **Line** method can be an important part of graphic design (especially if you want to draw lines in a loop and don't want to create a dozen or more line controls), and because we're covering that topic in this chapter, we'll look at the line control here.

Here's how you use the **Line** method:

```
[Form.]Line [(x1, y1)]-(x2, y2)[, color]
```

Let's see an example. Here, we'll just draw four lines with the **Line** method when a form first loads. As with other graphic methods, to use this method in the **Form_Load( )** handler, you must set the form's **AutoRedraw** property to True.

Here's the code we add to the **Load** event, making use of the **Line** method:

```
Private Sub Form_Load()
    Dim intLoopIndex As Integer

    For intLoopIndex = 0 To 3
        Line (1000, 1000 + 400 * intLoopIndex)-(3500, 1000 + 400 _
        * intLoopIndex)
    Next intLoopIndex
End Sub
```

The result of the preceding code appears in Figure 14.15—you can see the four lines we've drawn there.

Figure 14.15   Drawing lines with the Line method.

TIP: The **Line** method is often a better choice than line controls if you have a large number of evenly spaced lines to draw, such as when you need to draw a grid or rules. Note, however, that if the user resizes the containing form, you might have to redraw those lines.

Using Form Methods To Draw Circles

We've seen that you can use the shape control to draw circles, but there is also a form method to do the same thing: the **Circle** method.

Here's how you use the **Circle** method:

```
[Form.]Circle (x, y), radius[, color]
```

For example, here's how we draw a few circles in a form using the **Circle** method (note that as with all graphics methods used in the **Form_Load()** event handler, you must set the form's **AutoRedraw** property to True here):

```
Private Sub Form_Load()

    Dim intLoopIndex As Integer

    For intLoopIndex = 1 To 4
        Circle (2300, 500 + 400 * intLoopIndex), 400 * intLoopIndex
    Next intLoopIndex

End Sub
```

Running this code yields the result you see in Figure 14.16. Now we're drawing circles using the form's **Circle** method.

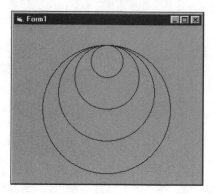

Figure 14.16   Drawing circles with the Circle method in a form.

Drawing Ellipses

You can also use the **Circle** method to draw ellipses. Here's how that works:

```
[Form.]Circle (x, y), radius, [color], [start], [end] [, aspect]
```

Here the *start* and *end* arguments are measured in radians (starting at 0 and coming full circle at 2 pi) and let you specify what angle to start and end drawing. This allows you to draw arcs.

The *aspect* argument specifies the ratio of the vertical to horizontal dimensions (*aspect* is a positive floating-point number). Large values for *aspect* produce ellipses stretched out along the vertical axis; small values for *aspect* produce ellipses stretched out along the horizontal axis. An ellipse has two radii—one horizontal x-radius and one vertical y-radius—and Visual Basic uses the *radius* argument as the longer axis. In other words, if *aspect* is less than 1, *radius* is the x-radius; if *aspect* is greater than or equal to 1, *radius* is the y-radius.

Also note that commas are necessary if you want to skip arguments. For example, here's how we draw a series of downward-pointing arcs, skipping the color argument:

```
Private Sub Form_Load()

    Dim intLoopIndex As Integer

    For intLoopIndex = 1 To 4
        Circle (2300, 500 + 400 * intLoopIndex), 400 * intLoopIndex, , _
                0, 3.1415
    Next intLoopIndex

End Sub
```

The result of this code appears in Figure 14.17.

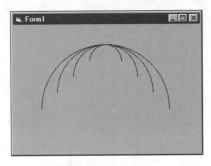

Figure 14.17   Drawing arcs with the Circle method in a form.

Chapter 15

Toolbars, Status Bars, Progress Bars, And Coolbars

If you need an immediate solution to:	See page:
Adding A Toolbar To A Form	469
Aligning Toolbars In A Form	470
Adding Buttons To A Toolbar	471
Handling Toolbar Buttons Clicks	471
Connecting Toolbar Buttons To Menu Items	473
Adding Separators To A Toolbar	474
Adding Images To Toolbar Buttons	475
Adding Check (Toggle) Buttons To A Toolbar	477
Creating Button Groups In A Toolbar	478
Adding Combo Boxes And Other Controls To A Toolbar	479
Setting Toolbar Button Tool Tips	481
Letting The User Customize The Toolbar	482
Adding Toolbar Buttons At Runtime	482
Adding A Status Bar To A Program	484
Aligning Status Bars In A Form	485
Adding Panels To A Status Bar	485
Displaying Text In A Status Bar	486
Displaying Time, Dates, And Key States In A Status Bar	487
Customizing A Status Bar Panel's Appearance	488
Displaying Images In A Status Bar	489
Handling Panel Clicks	490
Adding New Panels To A Status Bar At Runtime	490
Creating Simple Status Bars	491

(continued)

If you need an immediate solution to:	See page:
Adding A Progress Bar To A Form	491
Using A Progress Bar	492
Adding A Coolbar To A Form	493
Aligning Coolbars In A Form	494
Adding Bands To A Coolbar	494
Adding Controls To Coolbar Bands	495
Handling Coolbar Control Events	496

In Depth

In this chapter, we're going to take a look at the *bar* controls: toolbars, status bars, progress bars, and coolbars. All these controls have their uses in Visual Basic programs, and users are coming to expect them more and more. We'll start with an overview of these controls.

Toolbars

Every Windows user knows about toolbars: they're those bars at the top of a window (although they can appear other places as well) that are filled with buttons and, sometimes, other controls like combo bars.

Often, a toolbar contains buttons that correspond to items in an application's menu, providing an easy interface for the user to reach frequently used functions and commands. In this way, toolbars can make life a lot easier for the user. The user can also customize toolbars: double-clicking a toolbar at runtime opens the Customize Toolbar dialog box, which allows the user to hide, display, or rearrange toolbar buttons.

You create a toolbar by adding a toolbar control to a form, and to do that, you select the Project|Components menu item, then click the Controls tab in the Components dialog box, select the Microsoft Windows Common Controls item, and click on OK to close the Components dialog box. This adds the Toolbar Control tool to the Visual Basic toolbox, as shown in Figure 15.1; the Toolbar tool is the twelfth tool down on the left.

To add buttons to a toolbar, you add Button objects to its **Buttons** collection, usually by working with the toolbar's property pages. Each button can have text and/or an image, (supplied by an associated ImageList control). Set text with the **Caption** property and an image with the **Image** property for each Button object. At runtime, you can add or remove buttons from the **Buttons** collection using **Add** and **Remove** methods.

Status Bars

Status bars appear at the bottom of windows and usually hold several panels in which you can display text. The status bar is there to give feedback to the user on program operation, as well as other items like time of day or key states (such as the Caps Lock or the Ins key). Although status bars usually display

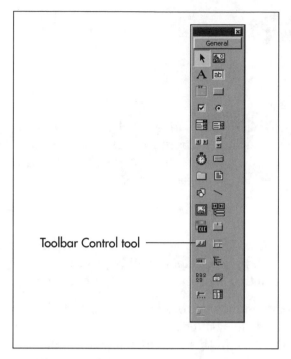

Toolbar Control tool

Figure 15.1   The Toolbar Control tool.

text in panels, there is a simple status bar style that makes the status bar function as one long panel, as we'll see.

Status bars are built around the **Panels** collection, which holds the panels in the status bar. Up to 16 Panel objects can be contained in the collection. Each object can display an image and text, as shown later in this chapter. You can change the text, images, or widths of any Panel object, using its **Text**, **Picture**, and **Width** properties. To add Panel objects at design time, right-click the status bar, and click Properties to display the Property Pages dialog box. (We'll cover the procedure in more detail later in the chapter.)

You add the Status Bar Control tool to the toolbox by following the same steps to add the Toolbar Control tool, because the status bar control is also part of the Microsoft Windows common controls. The Status Bar Control tool is the twelfth tool down on the right in Figure 15.2.

Progress Bars

Progress bars give the user some visual feedback on what's happening during a time-consuming operation. They present the user with a color bar that grows in the control to show how the operation is proceeding, usually from 0 to 100 percent. You can use a progress bar when an operation will take some time to

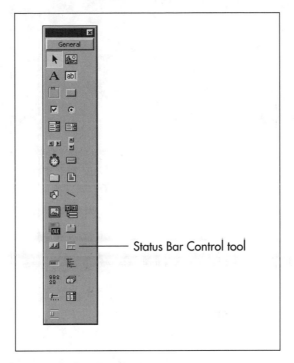

Status Bar Control tool

Figure 15.2   The Status Bar Control tool.

finish. The progress bar's **Value** property (not available at design time) determines how much of the control has been filled. The **Min** and **Max** properties set the limits of the control.

You add the Progress Bar Control tool to the toolbox by following the same steps to add the toolbar tool, because the progress bar control is also part of the Microsoft Windows common controls. The Progress Bar Control tool is the thirteenth tool down on the left in Figure 15.3.

Coolbars

Coolbars were first introduced in the Microsoft Internet Explorer, and they are toolbars that present controls in *bands*. Users can adjust these bands by dragging a *gripper*, which appears at left in a band. In this way, users can configure the coolbar by sliding the bands around as they want. One popular use of coolbars is to display toolbars in the bands of that coolbar, allowing users to move those toolbars around as they want.

The Coolbar Control tool is on the bottom, at left, in the Visual Basic toolbox in Figure 15.3. These controls can act just as toolbars do, as we'll see.

That's it for the overview—it's time to turn to the Immediate Solutions.

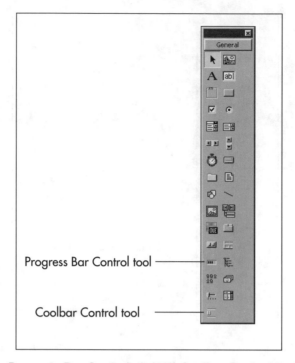

Progress Bar Control tool

Coolbar Control tool

Figure 15.3   The Progress Bar Control and the Coolbar Control tools.

Immediate Solutions

Adding A Toolbar To A Form

The Testing Department is calling again. Your program, *SuperDuperTextPro*, is wonderful—but what about putting in a toolbar? That would make things easier for the program's users, because they could click buttons in the toolbar instead of having to open menu items. So how do you add a toolbar to a form?

You use the toolbar control. In fact, probably the easiest way to add a toolbar to a program is to design that program with the Visual Basic Application Wizard. We'll take a look at what the Application Wizard has to offer us, and then add a toolbar to a program ourselves.

When you use the Application Wizard to create a program, that program gets a toolbar automatically. You can arrange and configure the toolbar with the Application Wizard Customize Toolbar dialog box, shown in Figure 15.4, which appears when you create a program with the Application Wizard.

The Application Wizard takes care of all the details for us. When you run the program it generates, you see a fully functional toolbar in that program, as shown in Figure 15.5.

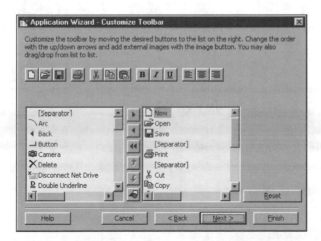

Figure 15.4   The Application Wizard Customize Toolbar dialog box.

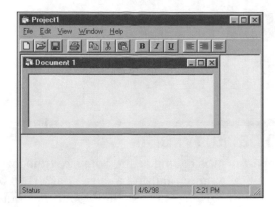

Figure 15.5   An Application Wizard program, complete with toolbar.

However, most programmers will want to add their own toolbars to their programs, and you create a toolbar by adding a toolbar control to a form. Here's how that works:

1. Select the Project|Components menu item.

2. Click the Controls tab in the Components dialog box.

3. Select the Microsoft Windows Common Controls item, and click on OK to close the Components dialog box.

This adds the Toolbar Control tool to the Visual Basic toolbox, as shown in Figure 15.1. To place a toolbar in your form, just double-click the Toolbar Control tool.

Now you've got a new toolbar—but how do you align it at the top of the window and add buttons to it? See the next couple of topics in this chapter.

Aligning Toolbars In A Form

Now that you've added a toolbar to your form, where does it go? By default, it aligns itself with the top of the client area of the form. You can set the alignment of the toolbar with its **Align** property, which can take these values:

- **vbAlignNone**—0
- **vbAlignTop**—1 (the default)
- **vbAlignBottom**—2
- **vbAlignLeft**—3
- **vbAlignRight**—4

Adding Buttons To A Toolbar

You've got your new toolbar in the form you want and aligned it correctly. How about adding some buttons?

You add buttons to a toolbar control at design time by right-clicking the control and clicking the Properties item in the menu that appears. When the toolbar's property pages open, click the Buttons tab, as shown in Figure 15.6.

You insert new buttons by clicking the Insert Button button (and remove them with the Remove Button button). When you add a new button to a toolbar, you can associate a picture or caption with it. For example, to give a button a caption, just fill in the Caption box in Figure 15.6.

Each button gets a new **Index** value, which will be passed to the **Click** event handler. You can also give each button a **Key** value, which is a string that you can use to identify the button.

When you're done, click on the OK button to close the toolbar's property pages. Now that you've installed buttons in your toolbar, how do you handle button clicks? Take a look at the next topic.

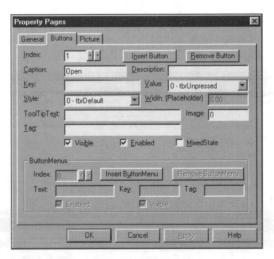

Figure 15.6   Adding new buttons to a toolbar.

Handling Toolbar Buttons Clicks

Now that you've set up your toolbar with the buttons you want, how can you make those buttons active? You do that with the toolbar control's **ButtonClick** event:

```
Private Sub Toolbar1_ButtonClick(ByVal Button As MSComCtlLib.Button)

End Sub
```

The button the user clicked is passed to us in this event handler procedure, and we can determine which button was clicked by checking either the button's **Index** or **Key** properties. For example, we can indicate to users which button they clicked with a message box and the **Index** property this way:

```
Private Sub Toolbar1_ButtonClick(ByVal Button As MSComCtlLib.Button)
    MsgBox "You clicked button " & Button.Index
End Sub
```

All buttons in a toolbar control have an **Index** value by default (this value is 1-based), so this code is ready to go. When the user clicks a button, we report which button the user has clicked, as shown in Figure 15.7.

Besides using the **Index** property, you can also give each button's **Key** property a text string (you do that at design time in the toolbar control's property pages). Then you use a **Select Case** statement to determine which button was clicked, like this:

```
Private Sub Toolbar1_ButtonClick(ByVal Button As MSComCtlLib.Button)
    Select Case Button.Key
        Case "OpenFile"
            OpenFile
        Case "SaveFile"
            SaveFile
        Case "CloseFile"
            CloseFile
    End Select
End Sub
```

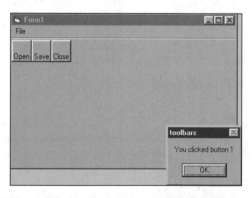

Figure 15.7   Determining which button the user has clicked.

The complete code for the preceding code where we use the **Index** property appears in the toolbars folder on this book's accompanying CD-ROM.

Connecting Toolbar Buttons To Menu Items

You often use buttons in a toolbar as shortcuts for menu items. How do you connect a toolbar button to a menu item? You just call the menu item's **Click** event handler when the button is clicked.

For example, if you have three items in the File menu, Open, Save, and Close, that you want to connect to toolbar buttons, you can set those buttons' **Key** properties to, say, "OpenFile", "SaveFile", and "CloseFile", testing for those button clicks this way:

```
Private Sub Toolbar1_ButtonClick(ByVal Button As MSComCtlLib.Button)
    Select Case Button.Key
        Case "OpenFile"
...
        Case "SaveFile"
...
        Case "CloseFile"
...
    End Select
End Sub
```

If one of those buttons were clicked, you simply call the associated menu item's **Click** event handler function directly:

```
Private Sub Toolbar1_ButtonClick(ByVal Button As MSComCtlLib.Button)
    Select Case Button.Key
        Case "OpenFile"
            mnuFileOpen_Click
        Case "SaveFile"
            mnuFileSave_Click
        Case "CloseFile"
            mnuFileClose_Click
    End Select
End Sub
```

And that's all it takes. Now we've connected toolbar buttons to menu items.

Adding Separators To A Toolbar

The Aesthetic Design Department is calling again. Can't you group the buttons in your toolbar into logical groups as you do with items in a menu?

You can, and just in the same way—by using *separators*. In menus, separators appear as solid lines, but in toolbars, separators just appear as blank spaces, setting groups of buttons apart.

Let's see an example. Insert a new button into a toolbar and set its **Style** property to **tbrSeparator**, as shown in Figure 15.8.

Now add other buttons, and click on OK to close the toolbar's property pages. When you do, you'll see that the separator puts some distance between the buttons, as shown in Figure 15.9.

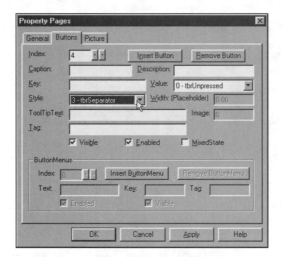

Figure 15.8   Adding a spacer to a toolbar.

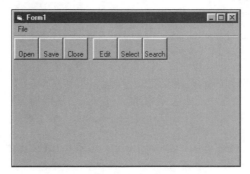

Figure 15.9   Using a separator in a toolbar.

TIP: *Although toolbar separators just look like blank space, they count as buttons, which means that they have their own **Index** value. That means that you have to take separators into account when figuring a button's **Index** value in your toolbar in order to handle it when it's clicked.*

Adding Images To Toolbar Buttons

The Aesthetic Design Department is calling. Your new toolbar looks great, but it would look even better if you used images in the buttons and not text captions. How about it?

You can give toolbar buttons if you place those images into an image list control. Image lists are Windows common controls just as toolbars are, so add an image list to a program now.

To place the images you want in the buttons in the image list, follow these steps:

1. Right-click the image list control.
2. Select the Properties menu item.
3. Click the Images tab in the image control's property pages.
4. Click the Insert Picture button to insert the first image (you can browse through your hard disks and select the images you want).
5. Keep going until all the images have been added to the image control, then click on OK to close the property pages.

Now you need to associate the image control with the toolbar, and you do that in the toolbar's property pages; just follow these steps:

1. Right-click the toolbar and select the Properties item to open the toolbar's property pages, as shown in Figure 15.10.
2. Next, click the Buttons tab in the property pages, as shown in Figure 15.11.
3. Enter the index of the image in the image control you want to connect to the first button in the box labeled Image (image lists are 1-based).
4. Keep going for the other buttons, entering the image control indices of the images you want to connect to those buttons.
5. Click on OK to close the property pages.

When you run the program, the images appear in the toolbar.

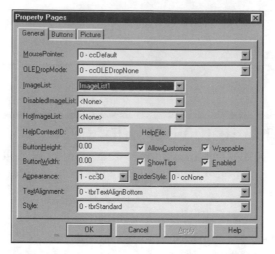

Figure 15.10   Adding images from an image control to a toolbar.

You can also connect an image control to a toolbar at runtime, using the toolbar's **ImageList** property:

```
Private Sub Command1_Click()
    Toolbar1.ImageList = ImageList1
End Sub
```

TIP: *Visual Basic comes with the standard bitmaps you'll find in Windows toolbars—just check the common\ graphics\bitmaps\offctlbr\small\color directory.*

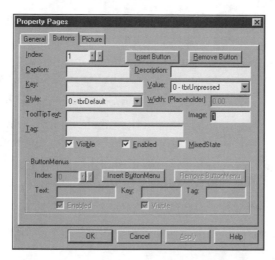

Figure 15.11   Connecting images from an image control to toolbar buttons.

Adding Check (Toggle) Buttons To A Toolbar

The Testing Department is calling again: The toolbar you've added to your program, *SuperDuperTextPro*, is terrific, but there's one problem. One of the menu items, the Insert item, displays a checkmark next to it when the user toggles that mode on. Can't you add a checkmark to the Insert button in the toolbar as well?

The way toolbars handle this problem instead of displaying checkmarks is to keep a button depressed once it's been pressed. In this way, you can show toggle states. Let's take a look at an example.

To make a toolbar button a "check" button, you must set its **Style** property to **tbrCheck**, and you do that in the toolbar's property pages. Right-click the toolbar now and select the Properties item to open the property pages. Click the Buttons tab in the property pages, as shown in Figure 15.12.

Select the button you want to work with, and set its style to **tbrCheck**, as shown in Figure 15.12. That's it. Now when the user clicks the button, it stays clicked, as shown in Figure 15.13, until the user clicks it again.

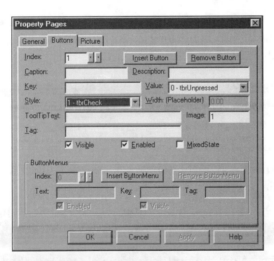

Figure 15.12   Making a toolbar button a check button.

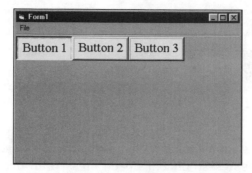

Figure 15.13   A check toolbar button at work.

Creating Button Groups In A Toolbar

You may notice in some toolbars that a set of buttons are mutually exclusive—for example, if your word processor lets you align text to the right, left, and center with buttons in a toolbar, only one of those styles can be active at once. When the user clicks one, the others should toggle off.

You can set up *groups* of mutually exclusive buttons in toolbars, just as you can with groups of option buttons (in fact, that's just what button groups in a toolbar resemble: a group of graphical [**Style = 1**] option buttons).

To create a button group, just follow these steps:

1. Open the toolbar's property pages by right-clicking the toolbar and selecting the Properties item.

2. Click the Buttons tab.

3. Select the button in the button group, and set its style to **tbrButtonGroup** in the Style box, as shown in Figure 15.14.

4. Repeat Step 3 for the other buttons in the button group.

5. Click on OK to close the property pages.

That's all it takes. Now the buttons you've placed together in a group will act together. When the user clicks one to select it, the others will toggle off (in other words, go back to their unselected position). Button groups can be very useful in a toolbar—any time option buttons would come in handy in a toolbar, just use a button group instead.

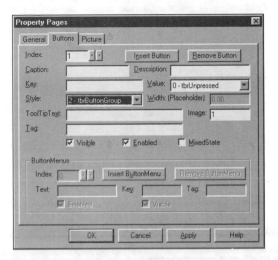

Figure 15.14   Creating a button group in a toolbar.

Adding Combo Boxes And Other Controls To A Toolbar

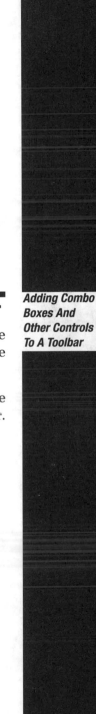

The Program Design Department is calling again. That shopping program you've written, *SuperDuperGroceryStore4U*, is nice, but what about listing the available groceries in a combo box in the toolbar. You wonder, how can you do that?

You can add combo boxes or other controls to a toolbar easily; just set aside space in the toolbar by setting a button's **Style** property to **tbrPlaceholder**. Here are the steps to follow to add a combo box to a toolbar:

1. Right-click the toolbar, and select Properties in the menu that appears.

2. Click the Buttons tab in the property pages that open, as shown in Figure 15.15.

3. Insert a new button where you want the combo box to go.

4. Set the new button's **Style** property to **tbrPlaceholder** in the box labeled Style. This means the button won't appear—there'll only be a blank space, and we'll place our combo box there.

5. Set the width of the space you want to leave for the combo box by entering a twip (1/1440s of an inch) value in the box labeled Width: (Placeholder), as shown in Figure 15.15.

6. Close the property pages by clicking on OK.

7. Click the Combo Box Control tool in the toolbox, and draw a new combo box in the new space in the toolbar.

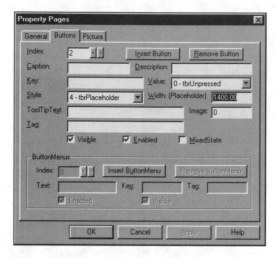

Figure 15.15   The toolbar property pages.

8. Add the items you want in the combo box in the Properties window's **List** property (or add items to the combo box at runtime).

9. Connect the code you want to the combo box. For example, here we respond to combo box clicks and text entry by displaying a message box:

```
Private Sub Combo1_Change()
    MsgBox "You entered " & Combo1.Text
End Sub

Private Sub Combo1_Click()
    MsgBox "You selected " & Combo1.Text
End Sub
```

That's all we need—now run the program, as shown in Figure 15.16.

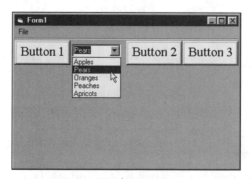

Figure 15.16   Adding a combo box to a toolbar.

When users make a selection with the combo box, we display a message box letting them know what they've selected. Our combo box toolbar example is a success.

The code for this example appears in the combotoolbar folder on this book's accompanying CD-ROM.

Setting Toolbar Button Tool Tips

Giving toolbar buttons tool tips (those small yellow windows that display explanatory text when the mouse cursor rests on the underlying control) is an easy process. All you need to do to give a button a tool tip is to set its **ToolTipText** property.

To set the **ToolTipText** property, right-click the toolbar and select the Properties item in the menu that opens. Click the Buttons tab and select the button you want to add the tool tip to. Place the tool tip text in the box labeled ToolTipText, as shown in Figure 15.17. Finally, close the property pages by clicking on OK. Now when you run the program, the button displays a tool tip, as shown in Figure 15.18.

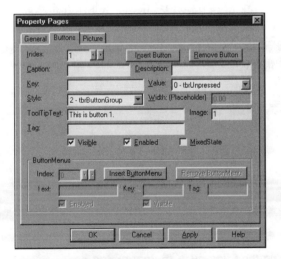

Figure 15.17   Setting a toolbar button's tool tip text.

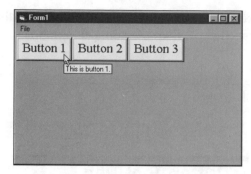

Figure 15.18   Toolbar buttons with tool tips.

Letting The User Customize The Toolbar

The Testing Department has sent you a memo. Some users of your new program, *SuperDuperTextPro*, want the Save button at left in the toolbar, but other users want the Create New Document button there. What can we do?

You can let the user customize the toolbar. Just set the **AllowCustomize** property to True (the default). When the user double-clicks the toolbar, the Customize Toolbar dialog box appears, as shown in Figure 15.19. Users can customize the toolbar as they like using that dialog box.

TIP: *If you allow your end user to reconfigure the toolbar control, you can save and restore the toolbar by using the **SaveToolbar** and **RestoreToolbar** methods.*

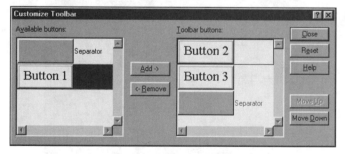

Figure 15.19   Using the Customize Toolbar dialog box.

Adding Toolbar Buttons At Runtime

How do you add buttons to a toolbar at runtime? It's possible to add menu items to menus, so it should be possible to add buttons to toolbars.

It is. To add a new button when the user clicks a button, we start by declaring a new Button object:

```
Private Sub Command1_Click()
    Dim Button1 As Button
...
End Sub
```

Next, we add a new button to the toolbar's **Buttons** collection, which is how it stores its buttons internally. As with all collections, the **Buttons** collection has an **Add** method, and we use it here:

```
Private Sub Command1_Click()
    Dim Button1 As Button
    Set Button1 = Toolbar1.Buttons.Add()
...
End Sub
```

Now we're free to set the button's style. Here, we make it a standard button by setting its **Style** property to **tbrDefault** (other options include **tbrButtonGroup**, **tbrSeparator**, **tbrCheck**, **tbrPlaceHolder**, and **tbrDropDown**):

```
Private Sub Command1_Click()
    Dim Button1 As Button
    Set Button1 = Toolbar1.Buttons.Add()
    Button1.Style = tbrDefault
...
End Sub
```

We can also give the new button a caption:

```
Private Sub Command1_Click()
    Dim Button1 As Button
    Set Button1 = Toolbar1.Buttons.Add()
    Button1.Style = tbrDefault
    Button1.Caption = "New button"
...
End Sub
```

Finally, we give the new button a tool tip:

```
Private Sub Command1_Click()
    Dim Button1 As Button
    Set Button1 = Toolbar1.Buttons.Add()
    Button1.Style = tbrDefault
```

```
      Button1.Caption = "New button"
      Button1.ToolTipText = "New button"
End Sub
```

And that's it—the new button is active. It's been added to the **Buttons** collection of the toolbar control, which means it has its own **Index** value. That **Index** value will be passed to the **ButtonClick** handler, and we can make use of the index this way (you can also set a button's key text from code by setting its **Key** property):

```
Private Sub Toolbar1_ButtonClick(ByVal Button As MSComCtlLib.Button)
      MsgBox "You clicked button " & Button.Index
End Sub
```

Adding A Status Bar To A Program

The Testing Department is calling again. Your new *SuperDuperDataCrunch* program looks good, but what about the status bar? You ask, what status bar? Exactly, they say.

How can you add a status bar to your program? You could design the program with the Visual Basic Application Wizard, which automatically adds a status bar (see "Adding A Toolbar To A Form" earlier in this chapter for more information). However, most programmers will want to add their own status bar to their programs, and you create a status bar by adding a status bar control to a form. Here's how that works:

1. Select the Project|Components menu item.

2. Click the Controls tab in the Components dialog box.

3. Select the Microsoft Windows Common Controls item, and click on OK to close the Components dialog box.

This adds the Status Bar Control tool to the Visual Basic toolbox, as shown in Figure 15.2. To place a status bar in your form, just double-click the Status Bar Control.

Now you've got a new status bar—but how do you align it at the top of the window and display text in it? See the next couple of topics in this chapter.

Aligning Status Bars In A Form

Now that you've added a status bar to your form, where does it go? By default, it aligns itself with the bottom of the client area of the form. You can set the alignment of the status bar with its **Align** property, which can take these values:

- **vbAlignNone**—0
- **vbAlignTop**—1 (the default)
- **vbAlignBottom**—2
- **vbAlignLeft**—3
- **vbAlignRight**—4

Adding Panels To A Status Bar

Now that you've added a status bar to your program, it's time to take the next step: adding panels to the status bar. The text in a status bar is displayed in those panels.

A status bar control has a **Panels** collection, and you add the panels you want to that collection. To do that at design time, follow these steps:

1. Right-click the status bar, and select the Properties item in the menu that opens.
2. Click the Panels tab in the property pages, as shown in Figure 15.20.
3. Click the Insert Panel button as many times as you want panels in your status bar.
4. Close the property pages by clicking on OK.

It's also easy to add a new status bar panel at runtime—just use the **Panels** collection's **Add** method. Here's an example where we add a panel to a status bar when the user clicks a command button:

```
Private Sub Command1_Click()
    Dim panel5 As Panel
    Set panel5 = StatusBar1.Panels.Add()
    Panel5.Text = "Status: OK"
End Sub
```

Now that you've added panels to the status bar, how do you display text in those panels? See the next topic.

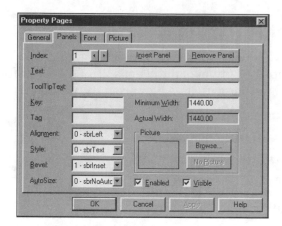

Figure 15.20   Adding a panel to a status bar.

Displaying Text In A Status Bar

You've added a new status bar to your program and added the panels you want to the status bar—but how do you display text? The status bar control you've added doesn't seem to have a **Text** property.

The text in a status bar is displayed in the status bar's panels (unless the status bar is a simple status bar—see "Creating Simple Status Bars" later in this chapter—in which case you use the status bar's **SimpleText** property). Displaying text in a status bar's panels is easy—just select the panel you want to work with as the index into the status bar's **Panels** collection, and use that panel's **Text** property.

Here's an example—in this case, we'll display the program status, "OK", in the first panel of the status bar (note that the **Panels** collection is 1-based) when the user clicks a command button, **Command1**:

```
Private Sub Command1_Click()
    StatusBar1.Panels(1).Text = "OK"
End Sub
```

That's it—the result of this code appears in Figure 15.21. Now we've displayed text in a status bar.

The code for this example is located in the statusbar folder on this book's accompanying CD-ROM.

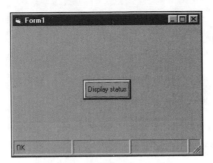

Figure 15.21 **Displaying text in a status bar control.**

Displaying Time, Dates, And Key States In A Status Bar

The Testing Department has sent you some email: the clock-watchers who use your *SuperDuperDataCrunch* program want a clock to watch. Can you add one to your program?

You can, and you can display it in the status bar. In fact, status bar controls are already set up to display common status items like key states and dates. To display one of those items, just right-click the status bar, select the Properties item in the menu that appears, click the Panels tab, select the panel you want to work with, and set the **Style** property in the box labeled Style to one of the following:

- **sbrText**—0 (the default); text and/or a bitmap. Displays text in the **Text** property.

- **sbrCaps**—1; Caps Lock key. Displays the letters "CAPS" in bold when Caps Lock is enabled, and dimmed when disabled.

- **sbrNum**—2; Num Lock key. Displays the letters "NUM" in bold when the Num Lock key is enabled, and dimmed when disabled.

- **sbrIns**—3; Insert key. Displays the letters "INS" in bold when the Insert key is enabled, and dimmed when disabled.

- **sbrScrl**—4; Scroll Lock key. Displays the letters "SCRL" in bold when Scroll Lock is enabled, and dimmed when disabled.

- **sbrTime**—5; time. Displays the current time in the system format.

- **sbrDate**—6; date. Displays the current date in the system format.

- **sbrKana**—7; Kana lock. Displays the letters "KANA" in bold when kana lock is enabled, and dimmed when disabled (this feature is enabled on Japanese operating systems only).

See Figure 15.22 for a status bar showing the time.

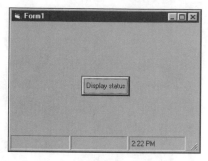

Figure 15.22   Displaying time in a status bar.

Customizing A Status Bar Panel's Appearance

You can customize the appearance of the panels in a status bar with the **Bevel**, **AutoSize**, and **Alignment** properties. The **Bevel** property specifies whether the panel will have an inset bevel (the default), raised, or none at all. Here's how you can set the **Bevel** property:

- **sbrNoBevel**—0; the Panel displays no bevel, and text looks like it is displayed right on the status bar.
- **sbrInset**—1; the Panel appears to be sunk into the status bar.
- **sbrRaised**—2; the Panel appears to be raised above the status bar.

The **AutoSize** property determines how a panel will resize itself when its container (usually a form) is resized by the user. Here are the settings for the **AutoSize** property:

- **sbrNoAutoSize**—0; None. No autosizing occurs. The width of the panel is always and exactly that specified by the **Width** property.
- **sbrSpring**—1; Spring. When the parent form resizes and there is extra space available, all panels with this setting divide the space and grow accordingly. (The panels' width never falls below that specified by the **MinWidth** property.)
- **sbrContents**—2; Content. The panel is resized to fit its contents.

The **Alignment** property indicates how the text or image in a panel will align in the panel. The settings for the **Alignment** property are as follows:

- **sbrLeft**—0; text appears left-justified and to the right of any bitmap.
- **sbrCenter**—1; text appears centered and to the right of any bitmap.
- **sbrRight**—2; text appears right-justified but to the left of any bitmap.

Displaying Images In A Status Bar

The Aesthetic Design Department is on the phone. How about adding a few images to the status bar? In fact, how about some animation for the user to watch while the program does other things? You think, is that possible?

Yes, it is, because status bar panels have a **Picture** property. To place an image in a status bar panel at design time, follow these steps:

1. Right-click the status bar, and select the Properties item in the menu that appears.
2. Click the Panels tab in the property pages that open.
3. Select the panel you want to work with.
4. Set the panel's **Picture** property by clicking the Browse button in the box labeled Picture. You can set this property with an image file on disk.
5. Close the property pages by clicking on OK.

That's it—now when you run the program, the image you've selected appears in the panel you've chosen, as shown in Figure 15.23.

You can also set a status bar panel's image at runtime. For example, here's how we set the image in the first panel of a status bar, using the image in a picture box when the user clicks a button (you can also use the **LoadPicture** function to load images in directly):

```
Private Sub Command1_Click()
    StatusBar1.Panels(1).Picture - Picture1.Picture
End Sub
```

TIP: *You can even create animation in a status bar panel; just set up a timer and place a succession of images in the panel's **Picture** property.*

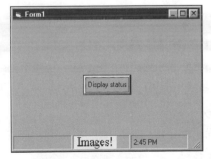

Figure 15.23   Displaying images in a status bar.

Handling Panel Clicks

Are status bars static controls? Or can they handle events? Status bars certainly can handle events, and the most common are **PanelClick** and **PanelDblClick**. The event handler procedures for those events are passed the panel that was clicked, as in this example:

```
Private Sub StatusBar1_PanelClick(ByVal Panel As MSComCtlLib.Panel)

End Sub
```

You can tell which panel was clicked by checking the **Panel** argument's **Index** or **Key** properties. For example, here's how we use the **Index** property to report to the user which panel was clicked:

```
Private Sub StatusBar1_PanelClick(ByVal Panel As MSComCtlLib.Panel)
    MsgBox "You clicked panel " & Panel.Index
End Sub
```

If you've set the **Key** properties of the panels in your status bar (the **Key** property holds a text string), you can set up a **Select Case** statement to see which panel was clicked and take the appropriate action:

```
Private Sub StatusBar1_PanelClick(ByVal Panel As MSComCtlLib.Panel)
    Select Case Panel.Key
        Case "Date"
            Panel.Text = Date$
        Case "Time"
            Panel.Text = Time$
    End Select
End Sub
```

Adding New Panels To A Status Bar At Runtime

It's easy to add a new status bar panel at runtime—just use the **Panels** collection's **Add** method. Here's an example where we add a panel to a status bar when the user clicks a command button:

```
Private Sub Command1_Click()
    Dim panel5 As Panel
    Set panel5 = StatusBar1.Panels.Add()
    Panel5.Text = "Status: OK"
End Sub
```

Creating Simple Status Bars

There's a way of using a status bar without using panels: by making the status bar a simple status bar. How do you make a status bar into a simple status bar? You set its **Style** property to **sbrSimple** (which equals 1; the other option is **sbrNormal**, which equals 0). Simple status bars have only one panel, and you set the text in that panel with the **SimpleText** property.

Here's an example; in this case, we just display the message "Status: OK" in the simple status bar when the user clicks a button:

```
Private Sub Command1_Click()
    StatusBar1.SimpleText = "Status: OK"
End Sub
```

The result of this code appears in Figure 15.24.

TIP: *One reason programmers used to use simple status bars was to show the progress of an operation by displaying a succession of dots (or other text) in the status bar's single long panel. However, you can use the progress bar control for that these days—see the next topic in this chapter.*

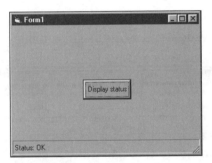

Figure 15.24   Using a simple status bar.

Adding A Progress Bar To A Form

The Testing Department is calling again. Why does downloading the 200MB data file your program requires take so long? Well, you explain, the Internet is like that. They ask, but can't you at least show the user what progress the downloading operation is making? You take a look at the Progress Bar Control tool in the Visual Basic toolbox. Sure, you say, no problem.

You can use progress bar controls to show the progress of a time-consuming operation. These controls display a colored band that can grow (or shrink) as time goes on. To add a progress bar to a form, follow these steps:

1. Select the Project|Components menu item.

2. Click the Controls tab in the Components dialog box.

3. Select the Microsoft Windows Common Controls item, and click on OK to close the Components dialog box. This adds the Progress Bar Control tool to the Visual Basic toolbox, as shown in Figure 15.3.

4. To place a progress bar in your form, just add it as you would any control, using the Progress Bar Control tool.

5. Set the progress bar's **Min** (default is 0) and **Max** (default is 100) properties as desired to match the range of the operation you're reporting on.

Now you've got a new progress bar in your form—but how do you use it? See the next topic.

Using A Progress Bar

Now that you've added a progress bar to your program and set its **Min** and **Max** properties, how do you actually use it to display data? You use a progress bar's **Value** property (available only at runtime) to specify how much of the progress bar is visible. As you might expect, setting **Value** to **Min** means none of the progress bar is visible, and setting it to **Max** means all of it is.

Let's see an example. In this case, we'll let the user click a button to display a progress bar whose bar lengthens from **Min** to **Max** in 10 seconds. Add a progress bar, command button, and a timer control to a form now. Set the timer's **Interval** property to 1000 (in other words, 1000 milliseconds, or 1 second). We'll leave the progress bar's **Min** property at 0 and its **Max** property at 100, the defaults.

When the form loads, we disable the timer and set the progress bar's **Value** to 0:

```
Private Sub Form_Load()
    Timer1.Enabled = False
    ProgressBar1.Value = 0
End Sub
```

When the user clicks the command button, we want to start the progress bar, so we enable the timer. We also set the progress bar back to 0 (even though we did that when the form loads, the user might want to restart the operation, which means he might click the button several times):

```
Private Sub Command1_Click()
    ProgressBar1.Value = 0
    Timer1.Enabled = True
End Sub
```

Finally, in the **Timer** event handler, **Timer1_Timer**, we add a value of 10 to the progress bar's **Value** property every second. We also check if we've filled the progress bar, and if so, disable the timer:

```
Private Sub Timer1_Timer()
    ProgressBar1.Value = ProgressBar1.Value + 10
    If ProgressBar1.Value >= 100 Then Timer1.Enabled = False
End Sub
```

That's all we need—now when the user clicks the command button, we start the progress bar in motion, and it goes from 0 to 100 in 10 seconds, as shown in Figure 15.25.

The code for this example is located in the progressbar folder on this book's accompanying CD-ROM.

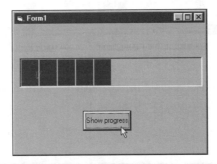

Figure 15.25 Using a progress bar.

Adding A Coolbar To A Form

Coolbars were first introduced in the Microsoft Internet Explorer, and they are toolbars that present controls in bands. The user can adjust these bands by dragging a gripper, which appears at left in a band. In this way, users can configure the coolbar by sliding the bands around as they want.

To add a coolbar control to a form, follow these steps:

1. Select the Project|Components menu item.

2. Click the Controls tab in the Components dialog box.

3. Select the Microsoft Windows Common Controls-3 item, and click on OK to close the Components dialog box. This adds the Coolbar Control tool to the Visual Basic toolbox, as shown in Figure 15.3.

4. To place a coolbar in your form, just add it as you would any control, using the Coolbar Control tool.

Now that you've added a coolbar to your form, maybe you'll need to align it in that form? See the next topic for the details.

Aligning
Coolbars In
A Form

Aligning Coolbars In A Form

Now that you've added a coolbar to your form, how do you align it to the top, bottom, or wherever you want to place it? You use the **Align** property, setting it to one of these values:

- **vbAlignNone**—0 (the default)
- **vbAlignTop**—1
- **vbAlignBottom**—2
- **vbAlignLeft**—3
- **vbAlignRight**—4

Now that you've added a coolbar to your form and set its alignment as you want, how do you add bands to that coolbar? See the next topic for the details.

Adding Bands
To A Coolbar

Adding Bands To A Coolbar

The controls in a coolbar are usually organized into bands (and note that those controls can themselves contain controls, as when you place toolbars in a band). To add a band to a coolbar, just follow these steps:

1. Right-click the coolbar and select the Properties item in the menu that appears.

2. Click the Bands tab in the coolbar's property pages, as shown in Figure 15.26.

3. Add new bands to the coolbar using the Insert Band button.

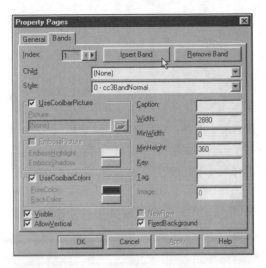

Figure 15.26   The coolbar property pages.

4. When finished, close the property pages by clicking on OK.

You can also add a band to a coolbar at runtime with its **Bands** collection, because that collection supports the usual collection methods **Add** and **Remove**. For example, here's how we add a new band to a coolbar at runtime:

```
Private Sub Command1_Click()
    Dim band5 As Band
    Set band5 = CoolBar1.Bands.Add()
End Sub
```

Now that you've added bands to a coolbar, how do you install controls in those bands? Take a look at the next topic to get the details.

Adding Controls To Coolbar Bands

You add controls to coolbar bands by setting the band's **Child** property. The **Child** property can only hold one child control, which you might think limits the power of coolbars, but in fact, that control can be a complete toolbar. If you fill a coolbar's bands with toolbar controls, users can arrange and slide those toolbars around as they like.

To add a control to a coolbar band, follow these steps:

1. Add the control (such as a toolbar) you want to place in a band to the coolbar by drawing it inside the coolbar.

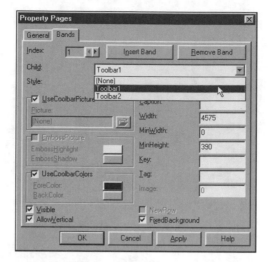

Figure 15.27   Adding a toolbar to a coolbar band.

2. Right-click the coolbar and select the Properties item in the menu that appears.

3. Click the Bands tab in the coolbar's property pages, as shown in Figure 15.27.

4. Select the band you want to work with.

5. Set the band's **Child** property to the control you want to add to that band, such as **Toolbar1** in Figure 15.27.

6. Close the coolbar's property pages by clicking on OK.

You can also set a band's **Child** property at runtime, as in this example where we set the control in the coolbar's first band to **Toolbar1**:

```
Private Sub Command1_Click()
    Set CoolBar1.Bands(1).Child = Toolbar1
End Sub
```

Handling Coolbar Control Events

You've set up the coolbar you want and placed a few toolbars in the various bands of that coolbar. Now how do you handle button clicks in those toolbars (or other controls you've place in a coolbar's bands)?

Handling events from controls in coolbar bands is easy—just connect event handlers to those controls as you normally would (in other words, if they weren't in a coolbar). Here's an example where we've added a toolbar, **Toolbar1**, to a coolbar. You can add buttons to the toolbar as you would normally—just open the toolbar's property pages and use the Insert Button button. To handle **Click** events for those button, you just double-click the toolbar's buttons at design time, which opens the matching **Click** event handler:

```
Private Sub Toolbar1_ButtonClick(ByVal Button As MSComCtlLib.Button)

End Sub
```

Then you just proceed as you would in a normal toolbar, such as adding this code where we indicate to users which button they've clicked:

```
Private Sub Toolbar1_ButtonClick(ByVal Button As MSComCtlLib.Button)
    MsgBox "You clicked button " & Button.Index

End Sub
```

Chapter 16

Image Lists, Tree Views, List Views, And Tab Strips

If you need an immediate solution to:	See page:
Adding An Image List To A Form	507
Adding Images To Image Lists	507
Using The Images In Image Lists	508
Setting Image Keys In An Image List	509
Adding A Tree View To A Form	510
Selecting Tree View Styles	511
Adding Nodes To A Tree View	511
Adding Subnodes To A Tree View	513
Adding Images To A Tree View	515
Expanding And Collapsing Nodes (And Setting Node Images To Match)	517
Handling Tree View Node Clicks	518
Adding A List View To A Form	518
Adding Items To A List View	520
Adding Icons To List View Items	522
Adding Small Icons To List View Items	523
Selecting The View Type In List Views	524
Adding Column Headers To A List View	525
Adding Column Fields To A List View	527
Handling List View Item Clicks	529
Handling List View Column Header Clicks	530
Adding A Tab Strip To A Form	531
Inserting Tabs Into A Tab Strip Control	532
Setting Tab Captions	533

(continued)

If you need an immediate solution to:	See page:
Setting Tab Images	534
Using A Tab Strip To Display Other Controls	535
Handling Tab Clicks	536

In Depth

In this chapter, we're going to take a look at image list controls and some of the controls that use image lists: tree views, list views, and tab strips. These controls are part of the Windows common controls package and are being used more and more frequently in Windows programs.

We'll get an overview of each control before tackling the programming issues. You add all the controls in this chapter to the Visual Basic toolbox by selecting the Project|Components menu item, clicking the Controls tab in the dialog box that opens, selecting the entry marked Windows Common Controls, and clicking on OK to close the Components dialog box.

Image Lists

Image list controls are invisible controls that serve one purpose: to hold images that are used by other controls. Usually, you add images to an image list control at design time, using the Insert Picture button in the control's property pages. You can also add images to an image list at runtime, using the **Add** method of its internal image collection, **ListImages**.

To use the images in the image list, you usually associate the image list with a Windows common control (which has an **ImageList** property). For each item in the common control, such as a tab in a tab strip control, you can then specify either an index into the image lists' **ListImages** collection or an image's key value to associate that image with the item.

You can also reach the images in an image list with the **ListImages** collection's **Picture** property. For example, if you wanted to use an image list with a control that's not a Windows common control, such as a picture box, you can assign the first image in the image control to that picture box this way:

```
Picture1.Picture = ImageList1.ListImages(1).Picture
```

The Image List Control tool appears in the Visual Basic toolbox in Figure 16.1 at bottom, on the right.

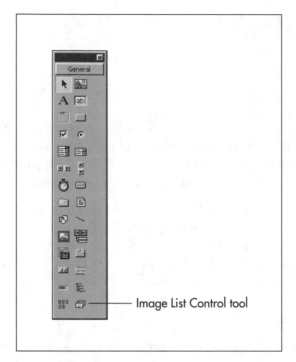

— Image List Control tool

Figure 16.1   The Image List Control tool.

Tree Views

If you've used the Windows Explorer, you're familiar with tree views. Tree views present data in a hierarchical way, such as the view of directories that appears in the tree view at left in the Windows Explorer, as shown in Figure 16.2.

Trees are composed of cascading branches of *nodes*, and each node usually consists of an image (set with the **Image** property) and a label (set with the **Text** property). Images for the nodes are supplied by an image list control associated with the tree view control.

A node can be expanded or collapsed, depending on whether or not the node has child nodes. At the topmost level are *root* nodes, and each root node can have any number of child nodes. Each node in a tree is actually a program-mable Node object, which belongs to the **Nodes** collection. As with other col-lections, each member of the collection has a unique **Index** and **Key** property that allows you to access the properties of the node.

The Tree View Control tool is the thirteenth tool down on the right in Figure 16.3.

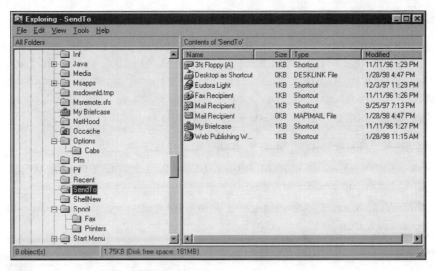

Figure 16.2   The Windows Explorer.

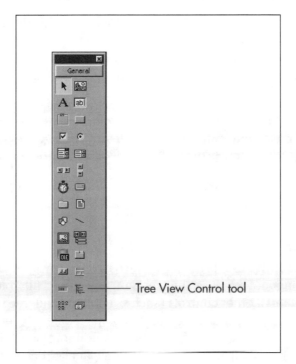

Figure 16.3   The Tree View Control tool.

List Views

The list view control displays, as its name implies, lists of items. You can see a list view at right in the Windows Explorer in Figure 16.2. There, the list view is displaying a list of files. Each item in a list view control is itself a ListItem object and can have both text and an image associated with it. The ListItem objects are stored in the list view's **ListItems** collection.

List views can display data in four different view modes:

- *Icon mode*—Can be manipulated with the mouse, allowing the user to drag and drop and rearrange objects.

- *SmallIcon mode*—Allows more ListItem objects to be viewed. Like the Icon view mode, objects can be rearranged by the user.

- *List mode*—Presents a sorted view of the ListItem objects.

- *Report mode*—Presents a sorted view, with sub-items, allowing extra information to be displayed.

The list view in the Windows Explorer in Figure 16.2 is displaying files in Report view mode (which is the only mode that has columns and column headers). In this mode, you add sub-items to each item, and the text in those sub-items will appear under the various column headings.

You usually associate two image list controls with a list view: one to hold the icons for the Icon view mode, and one to hold small icons for the other three modes. The size of the icons you use is determined by the image list control (the available sizes are 16×16, 32×32, 48×48, and Custom).

The List View Control tool is the fourteenth control down on the left in Figure 16.4.

Tab Strips

A tab strip control presents the user with a row (or rows) of tabs that acts like the dividers in a notebook or the labels on a group of file folders. Like an increasing number of other controls (such as coolbars and tree views), tab strips represent one of Microsoft's attempts to compact data into less and less of the screen (because there's getting to be more and more data). Using tab strips, the user can click a tab and see a whole new panel of data, like opening a file folder. In fact, we've already used tab strips in many parts of this book already to set Visual Basic options or to include ActiveX controls in our programs.

The most common use of tab strips today is to organize dialog boxes—often those dialog boxes that let the user set program options—into many different

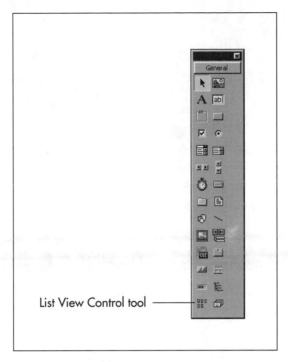

List View Control tool

Figure 16.4   The List View Control tool.

panels, all hidden from view except the current one the user has selected. In this way, you can pack a great deal into a small space in a dialog box and avoid the need for many dialog boxes.

From the programmer's point of view, a tab strip control consists of one or more Tab objects in a **Tabs** collection. At both design time and runtime, you can set the Tab object's appearance by setting properties, and at runtime, by invoking methods to add and remove Tab objects.

The Tab Strip Control tool appears as the eleventh tool down on the right in the Visual Basic toolbox in Figure 16.5.

That's it for the overview. It's time to turn to the Immediate Solutions.

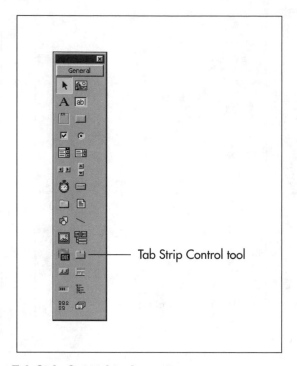

Tab Strip Control tool

Figure 16.5   The Tab Strip Control tool.

Immediate Solutions

Adding An Image List To A Form

To work with many Windows common controls, you need to use image lists. How do you add an image list control to a program? Just follow these steps:

1. Select the Project|Components menu item.

2. Click the Controls tab in the Components dialog box that opens.

3. Select the Windows Common Controls entry.

4. Close the Components dialog box by clicking on OK.

5. Double-click the Image List Control tool (see Figure 16.1 at bottom, on the right) to add an image list control to a form. This control is invisible at runtime, so its size and location don't make much difference.

Now that you've added an image list to a form, how do you add images to that image list? See the next topic.

Adding Images To Image Lists

To add images to an image list, you can use the image list's property pages at design time. Just right-click the image list and select the Properties item in the menu that opens. Next, click the Images tab in the property pages, as shown in Figure 16.6.

To insert images into the image list control, just use the Insert Picture button; clicking that button lets you search for image files on disk. Each successive image gets a new **Index** value, starting at 1 and counting up. If you wish, you can also give each image a **Key** value (a unique text string identifier) by entering text in the box labeled Key when you add an image.

When you're done adding images, close the property pages by clicking on OK.

You can also add images to an image list using the **ListImages** collection's **Add** method at runtime like this, where we give the image the key "tools":

```
ImageList1.ListImages.Add ,"tools", LoadPicture("c:\tools.bmp")
```

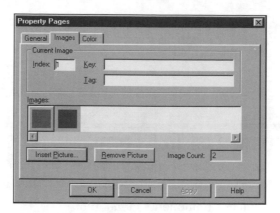

Figure 16.6   Adding images to an image list.

TIP: You should note that when the image list control is bound to another Windows common control, images of different sizes can be added to the control, but the size of the image displayed in the associated Windows common control will be constrained to the size of the first image added to the image list.

Using The Images In Image Lists

The Testing Department is calling again. The 40 picture boxes you have hidden in your program are taking up too much memory. Can't you do something else to store images?

You can. An image control can take up much less memory. Usually when you use an image control, you're storing images for a Windows common control. Those controls have an **ImageList** property, which you set to the name of the image list control you want to use (for example, **ImageList1**). From then on, you can associate the elements of the Windows common control with the images in the associated image list either by index or by key value.

However, you can also use image list controls with other controls, such as picture boxes. Here's an example taken from our earlier chapter on picture boxes that will create some graphics animation. We store images in an image list and swap them into a picture box in this example.

Add a timer control with its **Interval** property set to 1000 (that is, 1 second), setting its **Enabled** property to False; a picture box, **Picture1**, with its **AutoSize** property set to True; an image list control, **ImageList1**, adding two images to the image list control (we used image1.bmp and image2.bmp, which are just bands of blue and red, in this example); and a command button, **Command1**, labeled Start Animation.

When the user clicks the Start Animation button, we enable the timer:

```
Private Sub Command1_Click()
    Timer1.Enabled = True
End Sub
```

Then we toggle a Boolean variable, **blnImage1**, and alternate images from the image list control every second:

```
Private Sub Timer1_Timer()
    Static blnImage1 As Boolean

    If blnImage1 Then
        Picture1.Picture = ImageList1.ListImages(1).Picture
    Else
        Picture1.Picture = ImageList1.ListImages(2).Picture
    End If

    blnImage1 = Not blnImage1

End Sub
```

Note how we refer to the images in the image control, using the **ListImages** collection this way: **ImageList1.ListImages(1).Picture**.

That's all we need—the result appears in Figure 16.7. Now we're using the images in an image control. The code for this example is located in the coloranimation folder on this book's accompanying CD-ROM.

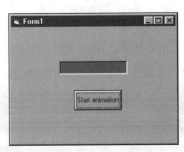

Figure 16.7   Using the images in an image control for animation.

Setting Image Keys In An Image List

When you add an image to an image list control, that image gets a new index value automatically. However, you can also refer to images with the **Key** property.

The key is a unique text string that identifies the image just as its index does, and in Windows common controls, you can refer to an image in an image list by either its index or key.

You set an image's key in the image list's property pages. For example, set an image's **Key** property to Image1 by entering that text in the Key field.

Adding A Tree View To A Form

The Testing Department is calling again. There sure is a lot of data in your new program, *SuperDuperDataCrunch*. Yes, you agree, there is. How about using a tree view instead? Hmm, you think, how does that work?

To add a tree view control to a form, follow these steps:

1. Select the Project|Components menu item.
2. Click the Controls tab in the Components dialog box that opens.
3. Select the Windows Common Controls item.
4. Click on OK to close the Components dialog box.
5. The preceding steps add the Tree View Control tool to the toolbox. Draw a tree view in the form as you want it.
6. Set the tree view's properties, and add the code you want.

When you first add a tree view control, there are only sample nodes visible in it, and nothing at runtime. You're responsible for adding the nodes and setting up their relationships, text, and images yourself. We'll do that in the topics that follow in this chapter, but for reference, we list the program we'll develop here, so you can refer back to it as you like.

Running this example program yields the results you see in Figure 16.8; as you can see, we let the user expand and collapse nodes in the tree view, have

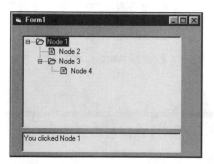

Figure 16.8   Using a tree view in a form.

associated both an image and text with each node, and report which node was clicked in a text box at the bottom on the form. This program has the following controls in it: an image list, **ImageList1**; a tree view control, **TreeView1**, with its **Style** property set to 7 (the default); and a text box, **Text1**.

The code for this example is located in the treeview folder on this book's accompanying CD-ROM.

Selecting Tree View Styles

There are many different styles for tree views—text nodes only, pictures and text nodes, showing or not showing the tree "lines" that connect nodes, showing or not showing the plus and minus symbols to expand or collapse nodes, and so on. You set the tree view's style using its **Style** property. Here are the possible values (we'll stick to the default, style 7, **tvwTreelinesPlusMinusPictureText**, in this chapter because that style offers the richest set of attributes):

- **tvwTextOnly**—0
- **tvwPictureText**—1
- **tvwPlusMinusText**—2
- **tvwPlusPictureText**—3
- **tvwTreelinesText**—4
- **tvwTreelinesPictureText**—5
- **tvwTreeLinesPlusMinusText**—6
- **tvwTreelinesPlusMinusPictureText**—7 (the default)

TIP: Note that you can set the tree view's style at design time or runtime, which means you can allow users to customize the tree view's appearance as they want.

Adding Nodes To A Tree View

The Testing Department is calling again. The tree view you've added to your program is fine, but why isn't there anything in it? Oops, you think, it's time to add some nodes.

You actually add Node objects to a tree view by adding them to the **Nodes** collection. How does this work? Let's see an example. Here, we'll add a node,

Node1, to a tree view, **TreeView1** (the tree view's **Style** property is set to **tvwTreelinesPlusMinusPictureText**, the default).

First, we declare that node:

```
Private Sub Form_Load()
    Dim Node1 As Node
...
```

Next, we add the node to the tree view using the **Nodes** collection's **Add** method (see the next topic for more information on this method):

```
Private Sub Form_Load()
    Dim Node1 As Node

    Set Node1 = TreeView1.Nodes.Add
...
```

Now we can refer to the node by name, **Node1**, as we set its text:

```
Private Sub Form_Load()
    Dim Node1 As Node

    Set Node1 = TreeView1.Nodes.Add
    Node1.Text = "Node 1"
...
```

We can also refer to the node as a member of the **Nodes** collection as here, where we set the node's **Key** property:

```
Private Sub Form_Load()
    Dim Node1 As Node

    Set Node1 = TreeView1.Nodes.Add
    Node1.Text = "Node 1"
    TreeView1.Nodes(1).Key = "Node 1"

End Sub
```

How does this look when you run it? You can see the result in Figure 16.9: not very spectacular with just one node. You can add other nodes by duplicating the preceding code and naming the new nodes **Node2**, **Node3**, and so on, but they'll all appear at the same level. Aren't trees supposed to have nodes that contain other nodes? They are, and we'll take a look at that in the next topic.

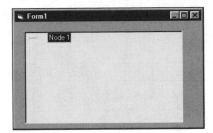

Figure 16.9   Placing a node in a tree view.

Adding Subnodes To A Tree View

The Testing Department is calling again. The new node you've put in your tree view is nice, but don't tree views usually display more than one node? What about other nodes and nodes that contain subnodes? Ok, you say, no problem.

When you add a new node to a tree view's **Nodes** collection using the **Add** method, you can specify how it is related to the nodes already there. Here's how you use the **Add** method in general:

```
Nodes.Add(relative, [relationship] [,key] [,text] [,image] [,selectedimage])
```

The *relative* argument is another node that you're relating the new node to with the relationship argument. Here are the possible values for *relationship*:

- **tvwLast**—1; the node is placed after all other nodes at the same level of the node named in *relative*.

- **tvwNext**—2; the node is placed after the node named in *relative*.

- **tvwPrevious**—3; the node is placed before the node named in *relative*.

- **tvwChild**—4; the node becomes a child node of the node named in *relative*.

Let's see an example. In this case, we'll set up the tree of text nodes, with one root node that has two nodes—and the second of those subnodes has a subnode itself.

In this example, we'll use a tree view control, **TreeView1**, (the tree view's **Style** property is set to **tvwTreelinesPlusMinusPictureText**, the default) and add four new nodes, **Node1** to **Node4**:

```
Private Sub Form_Load()
    Dim Node1, Node2, Node3, Node4 As Node
...
```

We add the first node like this using the **Nodes** collection's **Add** method:

```
Private Sub Form_Load()
    Dim Node1, Node2, Node3, Node4 As Node

    Set Node1 = TreeView1.Nodes.Add
    TreeView1.Nodes(1).Text = "Node 1"
    TreeView1.Nodes(1).Key = "Node 1"
    ...
```

Now we add two nodes, **Node2** and **Node3**, that are *child* nodes of the first node:

```
Private Sub Form_Load()
    Dim Node1, Node2, Node3, Node4 As Node

    Set Node1 = TreeView1.Nodes.Add
    TreeView1.Nodes(1).Text = "Node 1"
    TreeView1.Nodes(1).Key = "Node 1"

    Set Node2 = TreeView1.Nodes.Add("Node 1", tvwChild, "Node 2")
    TreeView1.Nodes(2).Text = "Node 2"
    TreeView1.Nodes(2).Key = "Node 2"

    Set Node3 = TreeView1.Nodes.Add("Node 1", tvwChild, "Node 3")
    TreeView1.Nodes(3).Text = "Node 3"
    TreeView1.Nodes(3).Key = "Node 3"
    ...
```

Finally, we add a fourth node, **Node4**, which is the child of **Node3**:

```
Private Sub Form_Load()
    Dim Node1, Node2, Node3, Node4 As Node

    Set Node1 = TreeView1.Nodes.Add
    TreeView1.Nodes(1).Text = "Node 1"
    TreeView1.Nodes(1).Key = "Node 1"

    Set Node2 = TreeView1.Nodes.Add("Node 1", tvwChild, "Node 2")
    TreeView1.Nodes(2).Text = "Node 2"
    TreeView1.Nodes(2).Key = "Node 2"

    Set Node3 = TreeView1.Nodes.Add("Node 1", tvwChild, "Node 3")
    TreeView1.Nodes(3).Text = "Node 3"
    TreeView1.Nodes(3).Key = "Node 3"
```

```
    Set Node4 = TreeView1.Nodes.Add("Node 3", tvwChild, "Node 4")
    TreeView1.Nodes(4).Text = "Node 4"
    TreeView1.Nodes(4).Key = "Node 4"

End Sub
```

And that's it—the result appears in Figure 16.10. Now we're adding nodes and subnodes to a tree view control.

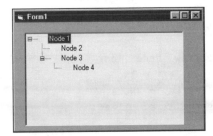

Figure 16.10   Nodes and subnodes in a tree view.

Adding Images To A Tree View

The Aesthetic Design Department is on the phone. About that tree view control in your program—can't you give each node an image? All the other Windows programs seem to do that. You look around, note that the tree view Node objects have an **Image** property, and say, no problem.

To add an image to a node in a tree view, you just have to set its **Image** property to an index or key in the tree view's associated image list control. Let's see an example. Here, we'll use an image list control, **ImageList1**, with two images taken from the Visual Basic common\graphics\bitmaps\outline directory: closed.bmp and leaf.bmp, which we add to the image list control with the **Key** properties "closed" and "leaf", respectively, as shown in Figure 16.11.

Now we can add those images to the nodes in a tree view control, **TreeView1**, by using the Node object's **Image** property, setting that property to the **Key** values for the various images:

```
Private Sub Form_Load()
    Dim Node1, Node2, Node3, Node4 As Node

    Set Node1 = TreeView1.Nodes.Add
    TreeView1.Nodes(1).Text = "Node 1"
    TreeView1.Nodes(1).Key = "Node 1"
```

```
    TreeView1.Nodes(1).Image = "closed"

Set Node2 = TreeView1.Nodes.Add("Node 1", tvwChild, "Node 2")
TreeView1.Nodes(2).Text = "Node 2"
TreeView1.Nodes(2).Key = "Node 2"
    TreeView1.Nodes(2).Image = "leaf"

Set Node3 = TreeView1.Nodes.Add("Node 1", tvwChild, "Node 3")
TreeView1.Nodes(3).Text = "Node 3"
TreeView1.Nodes(3).Key = "Node 3"
    TreeView1.Nodes(3).Image = "closed"

Set Node4 = TreeView1.Nodes.Add("Node 3", tvwChild, "Node 4")
TreeView1.Nodes(4).Text = "Node 4"
TreeView1.Nodes(4).Key = "Node 4"
    TreeView1.Nodes(4).Image = "leaf"
```

```
End Sub
```

The result appears in Figure 16.12—now we're adding images to tree view
nodes in Visual Basic.

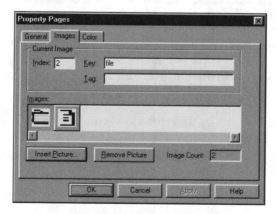

Figure 16.11   Adding images to an image list control.

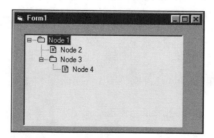

Figure 16.12   Using images in a tree view.

However, if you take a close look at Figure 16.12, you'll see that the folders there are closed, even when the node they represent is open. How can we change those images to an open folder when the user expands a node? For the details, see the next topic.

Expanding And Collapsing Nodes (And Setting Node Images To Match)

When the user clicks a plus or minus sign in a tree view to expand or contract a node, how can we make the node's image match? For example, when the node is closed, we can display a closed folder image, and when expanded, an open folder image. We'll take those images from the Visual Basic common\graphics\ bitmaps\outline directory: open.bmp and closed.bmp. Add those images to an image list, **ImageList1**, now, giving them the **Key** properties "open" and "closed". Next, connect the image list control to a tree view control, **TreeView1**, by setting that control's **ImageList** property to **ImageList1**.

When the user closes a node, the tree view control generates a **Collapse** event:

```
Private Sub TreeView1_Collapse(ByVal Node As MSComCtlLib.Node)

End Sub
```

In that event's handler, we can set the node's image to the closed folder by referring to that image by its key:

```
Private Sub TreeView1_Collapse(ByVal Node As MSComCtlLib.Node)
    Node.Image = "closed"
End Sub
```

Similarly, when the user expands a node, the tree view control generates an **Expand** event:

```
Private Sub TreeView1_Expand(ByVal Node As MSComCtlLib.Node)

End Sub
```

In that event's handler, we set the node's image to the open folder:

```
Private Sub TreeView1_Expand(ByVal Node As MSComCtlLib.Node)
    Node.Image = "open"
End Sub
```

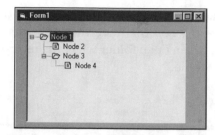

Figure 16.13   Expanded and collapsed node images in a tree view.

That's all it takes—now the nodes in this program display open and closed folders when they are expanded and collapsed, as shown in Figure 16.13.

TIP: *You can tell if a node is expanded or collapsed with its **Expanded** property.*

Handling Tree
View Node
Clicks

Handling Tree View Node Clicks

How do you know which node in a tree view the user clicked? You can use the **NodeClick** event:

```
Private Sub TreeView1_NodeClick(ByVal Node As MSComCtlLib.Node)

End Sub
```

For example, we can display the text in the node that the user has clicked in a text box, **Text1**, this way:

```
Private Sub TreeView1_NodeClick(ByVal Node As MSComCtlLib.Node)
    Text1.Text = "You clicked " & Node.Text
End Sub
```

The result of this code appears in Figure 16.14—when the user clicks a node, the program indicates which node was clicked in the text box at the bottom. Now we're handling tree view node clicks in Visual Basic.

Adding A List
View To A Form

Adding A List View To A Form

The Testing Department is calling again. When you list all files on disk in a text box in your *SuperDuperTextPro* program, doesn't that text box seem pretty

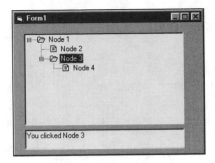

Figure 16.14 *Handling node clicks in a tree view.*

full? Of course, you say, there are hundreds of filenames to display. Try a list view control, they say.

To add a list view control to a form, follow these steps:

1. Select the Project|Components menu item.
2. Click the Controls tab in the Components dialog box that opens.
3. Select the Windows Common Controls item.
4. Click on OK to close the Components dialog box.
5. The preceding steps add the List View Control tool to the toolbox. Draw a list view in the form as you want it.
6. Set the list view's properties, and add the code you want.

After the list view is in your program, it's up to you to add items, images, and select what kind of view you want. There are four view types:

- *Icon mode*—Can be manipulated with the mouse, allowing the user to drag and drop and rearrange objects.

- *SmallIcon mode*—Allows more ListItem objects to be viewed. Like the icon view, objects can be rearranged by the user.

- *List mode*—Presents a sorted view of the ListItem objects.

- *Report mode*—Presents a sorted view, with sub-items allowing extra information to be displayed.

We'll set up the list view in the following topics in this chapter, creating the program listview, which is located on this book's accompanying CD-ROM. This program shows how to use a list view control and has the following controls in it: an image list control, **ImageList1**, that holds the images we'll use for the items in the list view; a list view control, **ListView1**, with its **ImageList** property set to **ImageList1**; a combo box, **Combo1**; and a text box, **Text1**.

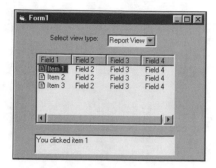

Figure 16.15   Using a list view in a program.

Running the program yields the result you see in Figure 16.15; we've added
four items to the list view in that program, and users can select what type of
view they want in the list view with the combo box. When the user clicks an
item in the list view, the program reports which item was clicked in a text box
at the bottom on the form. The code for this example is located in the listview
folder on this book's accompanying CD-ROM.

Adding Items To A List View

You add items to a list view's **ListItems** collection, using its **Add** method.
Each item you add is a ListItem object.

Let's see how this works in an example. In this case, we'll add three items to a
list view, **ListView1**. We start by declaring the first item, **ListItem1**, as a
ListItem object:

```
Private Sub Form_Load()
    Dim ListItem1 As ListItem
    ...
```

Next we add that item to the list view control with the **ListItems** collection's
Add method:

```
Private Sub Form_Load()
    Dim ListItem1 As ListItem
    Set ListItem1 = ListView1.ListItems.Add()
    ...
```

We can also give the new item some text to display in the list view:

```
Private Sub Form_Load()
    Dim ListItem1 As ListItem
    Set ListItem1 = ListView1.ListItems.Add()
    ListItem1.Text = "Item 1"
...
```

And we add the other two items in the same way:

```
Private Sub Form_Load()
    Dim ListItem1 As ListItem
    Set ListItem1 = ListView1.ListItems.Add()
    ListItem1.Text = "Item 1"

    Dim ListItem2 As ListItem
    Set ListItem2 = ListView1.ListItems.Add()
    ListItem2.Text = "Item 2"

    Dim ListItem3 As ListItem
    Set ListItem3 = ListView1.ListItems.Add()
    ListItem3.Text = "Item 3"

End Sub
```

We set the **ListView1** control's **View** property to **lvwList** (= 2) and run the program, yielding the result you see in Figure 16.16.

That's fine as far as it goes—but what about adding icons to list view items? We'll take a look at that in the next topic.

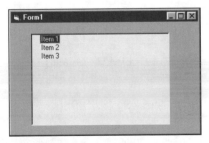

Figure 16.16   Adding items to a list view control.

Adding Icons To List View Items

The Aesthetic Design Department is on the phone. Your new list view control is fine, but what about adding icons to the items in that list view? Hmm, you think, how do you do that?

Each item in a list view is a ListItem object, and each such object has an **Icon** property. You set this property to an image's index or key in an image list control.

Let's see an example. We add a list view control, **ListView1**, to a form, as well as an image list, **ImageList1**. We add one image to the image list, new.bmp, which is in the Visual Basic common\graphics\bitmaps\offctlbr\large\color directory.

To connect the image list with the list view, right-click the list view at design time, and select the Properties item in the menu that appears. Click the Image Lists tab in the property pages, and select **ImageList1** in the box labeled Normal, then click on OK to close the property pages.

Now we can add the image in the image list to the items in a list view, using their **Icon** property like this:

```
Private Sub Form_Load()

    Dim ListItem1 As ListItem
    Set ListItem1 = ListView1.ListItems.Add()
    ListItem1.Text = "Item 1"
    ListItem1.Icon = 1

    Dim ListItem2 As ListItem
    Set ListItem2 = ListView1.ListItems.Add()
    ListItem2.Text = "Item 2"
    ListItem2.Icon = 1

    Dim ListItem3 As ListItem
    Set ListItem3 = ListView1.ListItems.Add()
    ListItem3.Text = "Item 3"
    ListItem3.Icon = 1

End Sub
```

Finally, we set the list view's **View** property to **lvwIcon** (= 0) and run the program. The result appears in Figure 16.17.

On the other hand, only the **lvwIcon** view uses icons this way—the other three list view control views use *small* icons. We'll see how to add small icons in the next topic.

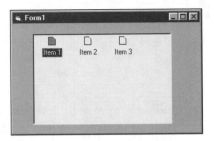

Figure 16.17   Displaying icons in a list view control.

Adding Small Icons To List View Items

You usually use two icons for each item in a list view, a normal icon and a small icon. Let's see how to add small icons now.

Each set of icons is stored in its own image list control, so we add a new image list control, **ImageList2**, to a program now to hold small icons (we'll use **ImageList1** to store the large icons and the actual list view control will be **ListView1**). In this example, we'll just place one image in **ImageList2**— leaf.bmp from the Visual Basic common\graphics\bitmap\outline directory.

To connect the image list with the list view, right-click the list view at design time, and select the Properties item in the menu that appears. Click the Image Lists tab in the property pages, and select **ImageList2** in the box labeled Small, then click on OK to close the property pages.

Now we can add the image we've stored as the small icon of all the list items:

```
Private Sub Form_Load()

    Dim ListItem1 As ListItem
    Set ListItem1 = ListView1.ListItems.Add()
    ListItem1.Text = "Item 1"
    ListItem1.Icon = 1
    ListItem1.SmallIcon = 1

    Dim ListItem2 As ListItem
    Set ListItem2 = ListView1.ListItems.Add()
    ListItem2.Text = "Item 2"
    ListItem2.Icon = 1
    ListItem2.SmallIcon = 1

    Dim ListItem3 As ListItem
    Set ListItem3 = ListView1.ListItems.Add()
```

```
        ListItem3.Text = "Item 3"
        ListItem3.Icon = 1
        ListItem3.SmallIcon = 1

End Sub
```

Finally, set the list view's **View** property to **lvwSmallIcon** (= 1) and run the program, as shown in Figure 16.18. You can see the icons we've selected for each item displayed in the list view in that figure. Our code is a success.

Figure 16.18   Using small icons in a list view.

Selecting The View Type In List Views

List view controls support four different *views*:

- **lvwIcon**—0; can be manipulated with the mouse, allowing the user to drag and drop and rearrange objects.

- **lvwSmallIcon**—1; allows more ListItem objects to be viewed. Like the icon view, objects can be rearranged by the user.

- **lvwList**—2; presents a sorted view of the ListItem objects.

- **lvwReport**—3; presents a sorted view, with sub-items, allowing extra information to be displayed.

You set the view type in a list view with its **View** property, which you can set at design time or runtime.

Let's see an example. Here, we'll display the various view types in a combo box, **Combo1**, and when the user selects one of them, we'll make that the current view type in the list view, **ListView1**.

When the form first loads, we place the view types in the combo box:

```
Private Sub Form_Load()

    With Combo1
        .AddItem "Icon View"
        .AddItem "Small Icon View"
        .AddItem "List View"
        .AddItem "Report View"
    End With

End Sub
```

Then when the user makes a selection in the combo box, we install the corresponding view in the list view:

```
Private Sub Combo1_Change()
    ListView1.View = Combo1.ListIndex
End Sub

Private Sub Combo1_Click()
    ListView1.View = Combo1.ListIndex
End Sub
```

The result appears in Figure 16.19. Although we can now select all four view types in a list view, note that we haven't implemented the last type, the report view, which displays a list of columns. We'll take a look at that starting with the next topic in this chapter.

Figure 16.19   Selecting view types in a list view control.

**Adding Column
Headers To A
List View**

Adding Column Headers To A List View

List views can display lists arranged in columns when you set their **View** property to **lvwReport**. We'll take a look at using the report view in this and the next topic. Here, we'll see how to add multiple columns to a list view control.

To add columns to a list view, you just need to add column headers, and you do that with the list view's **ColumnHeaders** collection. For example, here's how we add four columns to a list view, giving each column the caption "Field 1", "Field 2", and so on:

```
Private Sub Form_Load()
    Dim colHeader As ColumnHeader
    Dim intLoopIndex As Integer

    For intLoopIndex = 1 To 4
        Set colHeader = ListView1.ColumnHeaders.Add()
        colHeader.Text = "Field " & intLoopIndex
    Next intLoopIndex

End Sub
```

This code works fine, but each column appears in a default width, which might not be right for the size of your list view. To tailor the columns to your list view control, you can do something like this, where we set the columns' **Width** property:

```
Private Sub Form_Load()
    Dim colHeader As ColumnHeader
    Dim intLoopIndex As Integer

    For intLoopIndex = 1 To 4
        Set colHeader = ListView1.ColumnHeaders.Add()
        colHeader.Text = "Field " & intLoopIndex
        colHeader.Width = ListView1.Width / 4
    Next intLoopIndex

End Sub
```

After you set the **View** property of the list view control to **lvwReport**, the result of this code appears in Figure 16.20 (where we've added a few items to the list view control itself, Items 1 through 3, as well).

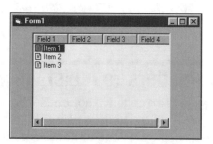

Figure 16.20   Supporting column headers in a list view.

Now that we're using columns in a list view, how do you add text for each column, item by item? We'll look into that next.

Adding Column Fields To A List View

You've set up a list view and added the items you want to it. Now you want to set the list view up to use columns by setting its **View** property to **lvwReport**. You've added headers to each column (see the previous topic in this chapter)—but how do you add text for each item in each column?

You use the **ListSubItems** collection's **Add** method to add column text to an item. Each ListItem object has a **ListSubItems** collection, and here's how you use that collection's **Add** method:

```
ListSubItems.Add [index] [,key] [,text] [,reporticon] [,tooltiptext]
```

For example, let's say that we add three items to a list view that has four columns. We can add text in each of the columns for each of the three items.

Here's how it works. The first column, or *field*, holds the item's text (set with its **Text** property). To add text for the following three columns of the first item (we'll display "Field 2" in field 2, "Field 3" in field 3, and so on), we use the **ListSubItems** collection's **Add** method this way:

```
Private Sub Form_Load()

    Dim colHeader As ColumnHeader
    Dim intLoopIndex As Integer

    For intLoopIndex = 1 To 4          'Label headers
        Set colHeader = ListView1.ColumnHeaders.Add()
        colHeader.Text = "Field " & intLoopIndex
        colHeader.Width = ListView1.Width / 4
    Next intLoopIndex

    Dim ListItem1 As ListItem
    Set ListItem1 = ListView1.ListItems.Add()
    ListItem1.Text = "Item 1"
    ListItem1.Icon = 1
    ListItem1.SmallIcon = 1
    ListView1.ListItems(1).ListSubItems.Add , , "Field 2"
    ListView1.ListItems(1).ListSubItems.Add , , "Field 3"
    ListView1.ListItems(1).ListSubItems.Add , , "Field 4"
    ...
```

And we do the same for the remaining two items:

```
Private Sub Form_Load()

    Dim colHeader As ColumnHeader
    Dim intLoopIndex As Integer

    For intLoopIndex = 1 To 4          'Label headers
        Set colHeader = ListView1.ColumnHeaders.Add()
        colHeader.Text = "Field " & intLoopIndex
        colHeader.Width = ListView1.Width / 4
    Next intLoopIndex

    Dim ListItem1 As ListItem
    Set ListItem1 = ListView1.ListItems.Add()
    ListItem1.Text = "Item 1"
    ListItem1.Icon = 1
    ListItem1.SmallIcon = 1
    ListView1.ListItems(1).ListSubItems.Add , , "Field 2"
    ListView1.ListItems(1).ListSubItems.Add , , "Field 3"
    ListView1.ListItems(1).ListSubItems.Add , , "Field 4"

    Dim ListItem2 As ListItem
    Set ListItem2 = ListView1.ListItems.Add()
    ListItem2.Text = "Item 2"
    ListItem2.Icon = 1
    ListItem2.SmallIcon = 1
    ListView1.ListItems(2).ListSubItems.Add , , "Field 2"
    ListView1.ListItems(2).ListSubItems.Add , , "Field 3"
    ListView1.ListItems(2).ListSubItems.Add , , "Field 4"

    Dim ListItem3 As ListItem
    Set ListItem3 = ListView1.ListItems.Add()
    ListItem3.Text = "Item 3"
    ListItem3.Icon = 1
    ListItem3.SmallIcon = 1
    ListView1.ListItems(3).ListSubItems.Add , , "Field 2"
    ListView1.ListItems(3).ListSubItems.Add , , "Field 3"
    ListView1.ListItems(3).ListSubItems.Add , , "Field 4"

End Sub
```

That's it—when you set **ListView1**'s **View** property to **lvwReport**, the preceding code gives us the results you see in Figure 16.21. Now we've added text to all the fields in our list view.

Figure 16.21   Adding column text to list view items.

Handling List View Item Clicks

Your list view is set up, and you've displayed the items you want in it in the view type you want. But now what? How do you let the user use that list view?

When the user clicks an item in a list view, the control generates an **ItemClick** event:

```
Private Sub ListView1_ItemClick(ByVal Item As MSComCtlLib.ListItem)

End Sub
```

The item that was clicked is passed to us as the argument named **Item**, and you can access its **Index** or **Key** properties to determine which item it is. As an example, here we display the item's index in a text box, **Text1**, when the user clicks it:

```
Private Sub ListView1_ItemClick(ByVal Item As MSComCtlLib.ListItem)
    Text1.Text = "You clicked item " & Item.Index
End Sub
```

Adding this code to a program gives us the results you see in Figure 16.22—when the user clicks an item, we report which item was clicked in the text box at bottom in that figure.

Besides item clicks, you can also handle column header clicks—see the next topic.

Figure 16.22   Handling list view clicks.

Handling List View Column Header Clicks

How do you know when the user clicks a column header in a list view? The control generates a **ColumnClick** event, which you can handle in its event handler:

```
Private Sub ListView1_ColumnClick(ByVal ColumnHeader As _
    MSComCtlLib.ColumnHeader)

End Sub
```

The column header the user clicked is passed to us as the **ColumnHeader** argument, and you can determine which column header was clicked with its **Index** property. For example, here we display which column the user has clicked with a message in a text box, **Text1**:

```
Private Sub ListView1_ColumnClick(ByVal ColumnHeader As _
    MSComCtlLib.ColumnHeader)
    Text1.Text = "You clicked column " & ColumnHeader.Index
End Sub
```

Now we can determine which column header the user clicked, as shown in Figure 16.23.

Figure 16.23   Determining which column was clicked in a list view.

Adding A Tab Strip To A Form

The Testing Department is calling again. There are just too many dialog boxes in your program. How can you fix that?

You can group the dialog boxes into one, using a tab strip; as the user selects tabs in the tab strip, you can display the contents that were separate dialog boxes in panels that appear when their tab is clicked. For an example of how this works, select the Project Properties item in the Visual Basic Project menu.

To add a tab strip control to a form, follow these steps:

1. Select the Project|Components menu item.
2. Click the Controls tab in the Components dialog box that opens.
3. Select the Windows Common Controls item.
4. Click on OK to close the Components dialog box.
5. The preceding steps add the Tab Strip Control tool to the toolbox. Draw a tab strip in the form as you want it.
6. Set the tab strip's properties, and add the code you want.

After you add a tab strip control to your program, it's up to you to tailor it the way you want it, by adding new tabs, text, and images to those tabs, and so on. We'll develop a tab strip example in the next topics in this chapter, and you can see that program at work in Figure 16.24. When the user clicks one of the three tabs in the program, we display a new panel of the tab strip control, each of which displays a picture box with a different color.

This example has these controls: a tab strip, **TabStrip1**; three picture boxes, **Picture1** through **Picture3**, which each hold a solid-color picture (and with their **AutoSize** property set to True); a text box, **Text1**, so we can report

Figure 16.24   Our tab strip example program at work.

which tab the user has clicked; and an image list control, **ImageList1**, which holds three images that we use in the tabs of the tab strip.

The code for this example is located in the tabstrip folder on this book's accompanying CD-ROM.

Inserting Tabs Into A Tab Strip Control

When you first add a tab strip control to a form, that control has one tab in it (and it can't have less than one—if you take that one tab out of the control, you'll find it back in place the next time you load the program into Visual Basic). How do you add others?

At design time, you use the tab strip's property pages. Just right-click the tab strip, select Properties from the menu that appears, and click the Tabs tab, as shown in Figure 16.25.

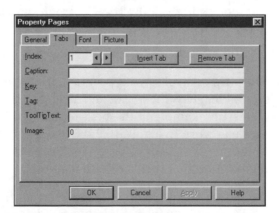

Figure 16.25   Adding tabs to a tab strip control.

You add new tabs by clicking the Insert Tab button, and at the same time you can set the tab's **Text**, **Key**, and other properties.

You can also add new tabs at runtime if you add them to the tab strip's **Tabs** property, using the **Add** method. For example, here's how we add two new tabs to a tab strip control and set their keys:

```
Private Sub Form_Load()
    Dim Tab2, Tab3 As MSComCtlLib.Tab

    Set Tab2 = TabStrip1.Tabs.Add()
    Tab2.Key = "Key2"

    Set Tab3 = TabStrip1.Tabs.Add()
    Tab3.Key = "key3"

End Sub
```

That's all there is to it. In the next topic, we'll take a look at adding text to the tabs.

Setting Tab Captions

Setting Tab Captions

You've added the tabs you want to your tab strip control—now how do you add text to those tabs?

At design time, you use the tab strip's property pages. Just right-click the tab strip, select Properties from the menu that appears, and click the Tabs tab, as shown in Figure 16.25. To enter the text for each tab, just select the tab you want to work on, and enter the text for that tab in the box labeled Caption, shown in Figure 16.25. That's all it takes.

You can also set a tab's **Caption** property at runtime. For example, here we set the captions of three tabs to "Tab 1", "Tab 2", and so on:

```
Private Sub Form_Load()
Dim Tab2, Tab3 As MSComCtlLib.Tab

Set Tab1 = TabStrip1.Tabs(1)
Tab1.Key = "Key1"
Tab1.Caption = "Tab 1"

Set Tab2 = TabStrip1.Tabs.Add()
Tab2.Key = "Key2"
Tab2.Caption = "Tab 2"
```

```
Set Tab3 = TabStrip1.Tabs.Add()
Tab3.Key = "key3"
Tab3.Caption = "Tab 3"
```

Adding this code to a program gives you the captions you see in Figure 16.26.

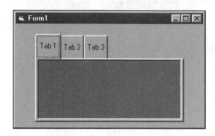

Figure 16.26   Making use of tab captions.

Setting Tab Images

The Aesthetic Design Department has sent you some email. How about adding some images to that tab strip control in your program? Hmm, you think, how does that work?

You can connect an image list control to a tab strip using the tab strip's **ImageList** property, and you can connect the images in that image list to the tabs in the tab strip. At design time, you use the tab strip's property pages. Just right-click the tab strip, select Properties from the menu that appears, and click the Tabs tab, as shown in Figure 16.25. Then select the tab you want to add an image to, and place the image's index or key in the image list into the box labeled Image, as shown in Figure 16.25. In addition, you must connect the image list to the tab strip control; select the General tab, shown in Figure 16.25, and enter the name of the image list control that holds the images you'll use (for example, **ImageList1**) in the box labeled ImageList.

You can also connect images to tabs at runtime. Let's see an example in code. Here, we add images displaying large numerals, 1, 2, and 3, as stored in an image list (**ImageList1**, which is connected to the tab strip with its **ImageList** property) to a tab strip's tabs this way:

```
Private Sub Form_Load()
Dim Tab2, Tab3 As MSComCtlLib.Tab

Set Tab1 = TabStrip1.Tabs(1)
Tab1.Key = "Key1"
Tab1.Caption = "Tab 1"
```

```
Tab1.Image = 1

Set Tab2 = TabStrip1.Tabs.Add()
Tab2.Key = "Key2"
Tab2.Caption = "Tab 2"
Tab2.Image = 2

Set Tab3 = TabStrip1.Tabs.Add()
Tab3.Key = "key3"
Tab3.Caption = "Tab 3"
Tab3.Image = 3
```

Now those numerals appear as images in the tabs in the tab strip, as shown in Figure 16.27.

Figure 16.27   Displaying images in a tab strip's tabs.

Using A Tab Strip To Display Other Controls

You usually use tab strips to display other controls. Let's see how this works with an example. Here, we'll use a tab strip to display three picture boxes.

After you've sized the tab strip control as you want it, you can move and size the picture boxes to cover the tab strip's *client area* (in other words, its display area). We do that for all three picture boxes like this, where we've placed them in a control array named **PictureControl** (we use a **With** statement because that's what you usually use here if you want to add other code to initialize the controls you're displaying):

```
For intLoopIndex = 0 To PictureControl.Count - 1
    With PictureControl(intLoopIndex)
        .Move TabStrip1.ClientLeft, TabStrip1.ClientTop,_
            TabStrip1.ClientWidth, TabStrip1.ClientHeight
    End With
Next intLoopIndex
```

This puts all the picture boxes on top of each other. How do you make sure only one is showing at a time? You set its **ZOrder** property to 0; for example, if we want to display the first picture box only, we'd use this code:

```
For intLoopIndex = 0 To PictureControl.Count - 1
    With PictureControl(intLoopIndex)
        .Move TabStrip1.ClientLeft, TabStrip1.ClientTop,_
            TabStrip1.ClientWidth, TabStrip1.ClientHeight
    End With
Next intLoopIndex
```

```
PictureControl(0).ZOrder 0
```

Now we've installed our picture boxes and displayed one on top. But how do we display the others when the user clicks a tab? We'll look into that in the next topic.

Handling Tab Clicks

When the user clicks a tab in a tab strip, the control creates a **Click** event:

```
Private Sub TabStrip1_Click()

End Sub
```

We can display the control that matches the clicked tab by setting its **ZOrder** to 0. For example, if we use the three picture boxes we added to a tab strip in the previous topic in this chapter, we can bring the selected picture box to the front this way:

```
Private Sub TabStrip1_Click()
    PictureControl(TabStrip1.SelectedItem.Index - 1).ZOrder 0
End Sub
```

We can also indicate which tab the user clicked in a text box:

```
Private Sub TabStrip1_Click()
    PictureControl(TabStrip1.SelectedItem.Index - 1).ZOrder 0
    Text1.Text = "You clicked tab " & Str$(TabStrip1.SelectedItem.Index)
End Sub
```

Adding this code to a program gives the results you see in Figure 16.28. Now we're letting the user click the tabs in a tab strip.

Figure 16.28   Clicking tabs in a tab strip.

Chapter 17

File Handling And File Controls

If you need an immediate solution to:	See page:
Using The Common Dialogs File Open And File Save As	544
Creating A File	546
Getting A File's Length	548
Opening A File	549
Writing To A Sequential File	550
Writing To A Random Access File	552
Writing To A Binary File	554
Reading From Sequential Files	554
Reading From Random Access Files	558
Reading From Binary Files	561
Accessing Any Record In A Random Access File	563
Closing A File	564
Saving Files From Rich Text Boxes	564
Opening Files In Rich Text Boxes	565
Saving Files From Picture Boxes	566
Opening Files In Picture Boxes	566
Using The Drive List Box Control	567
Using The Directory List Box Control	568
Using The File List Box Control	569
Creating And Deleting Directories	572
Changing Directories	572
Copying A File	572
Moving A File	573

(continued)

If you need an immediate solution to:	See page:
Deleting A File	574
When Was A File Created? Last Modified? Last Accessed?	574
Creating A TextStream	575
Opening A TextStream	576
Writing To A TextStream	577
Reading From A TextStream	578
Closing A TextStream	578

In Depth

This chapter focuses on file handling and using the file controls in Visual Basic. Here, we'll see how to:

- Use the Common Dialogs File Open and File Save As (you can find more information on this topic in Chapter 11).

- Create a file

- Open a file

- Read from a file

- Write to a file

- Close a file

- Read and write files with rich text boxes

- Use the file controls like the directory list box and drive list box

- Determine a file's creation date, last modified date, and more

- Move and copy files

- Use the TextStream object

There are three main ways to access files in Visual Basic: as sequential files, as random access files, and as binary files (you set the way you'll treat a file when you open it). We'll get an overview of these types of files before turning to the Immediate Solutions.

Sequential Access Files

Sequential files are like tape cassettes—you read data from them in a sequential manner. If you want data at the end of the file, you have to read all the intervening data first. Sequential files are often organized into text strings in Visual Basic. Here are the Visual Basic statements and functions you use with sequential files (the # symbol refers to an open file, as we'll see):

- **Open**
- **Line Input #**
- **Print #**
- **Write #**
- **Input$**

- **Input #**
- **Close**

In addition, Visual Basic supports TextStream objects to make working with sequential files easier, as we'll see later in this chapter. Here are the major TextStream methods:

- **Read**
- **ReadAll**
- **ReadLine**
- **Write**
- **WriteBlankLines**
- **WriteLine**
- **Close**

When do you use sequential files? If you've got a text file full of variable-length strings, you usually treat that file as sequential. You can also use sequential files to store binary-format items like numbers.

Random Access Files

If sequential files are like cassettes, random access files are more like CDs. Random files are organized into records (usually of the same length), and you can read a particular record without having to read all the intervening data—you can move to that record in a file directly, just as you can move to a CD track.

Here are the Visual Basic statements and functions you use with random access files:

- **Type...End Type** (to create and format records)
- **Open**
- **Put #**
- **Len**
- **Seek**
- **LOC**
- **Get #**
- **Close**

When do you use random access files? If you want to create your own database files, formatted as you want them, you'd organize them into records. In fact, any file that you want to organize into records is best formatted as a random access file.

Binary Files

Binary files are simply unformatted binary data, and Visual Basic does not interpret (such as looking for text strings) or organize the contents (into records) of such files at all. These files are just bytes to Visual Basic, and the statements and functions you usually use with these files include the following:

- **Open**
- **Get**
- **Put**
- **Seek**
- **Close**

Binary files include EXE files, graphics files, and so on.

The FileSystemObject

Besides the preceding file types, Visual Basic includes the FileSystemObject for easy file manipulation on disk. This object includes a number of methods for copying, moving, and deleting files such as these:

- **GetFile**
- **CopyFile**
- **DeleteFile**
- **MoveFile**
- **FileExists**
- **CreateFolder**
- **CreateTextFile**
- **OpenTextFile**

In fact, you use the FileSystemObject to create TextStream objects (with methods like **CreateTextFile** and **OpenTextFile**). We'll see more about this topic later in this chapter.

That's it for the overview of files and file handling. It's time to turn to the Immediate Solutions.

Immediate Solutions

Using The Common Dialogs File Open And File Save As

The usual way to start working with files is to get a file name from the user using the Common Dialogs File Open or File Save As. We've covered these dialogs in depth in Chapter 11, but we'll provide a quick overview here.

You display the File Open and File Save As dialog boxes with the Common Dialog control's **ShowOpen** and **ShowSave** methods. These methods need no arguments passed to them—to set various options, you set the Common Dialog control's **Flags** property (see Chapter 11). You can also set the **Filter** property so the dialog box displays only certain types of files, such as text files.

To find out what file the user wants to work with, you check the Common Dialog's **FileName** property after the user clicks on OK in the dialog box. That property holds the fully qualified (that is, with the path) name of the file to open. If you just want the file's name, use the **FileTitle** property.

Here's an example. In this case, we'll let the user select a file to open, and then display the file's name and path in a message box.

Add a Common Dialog control to a form and set the control's **CancelError** property to True so we can check if the user clicked the Cancel button. To check that, we use **On Error GoTo**:

```
Private Sub Command1_Click()
    On Error GoTo Cancel
    ...
Cancel:
End Sub
```

Then we display the Open dialog box:

```
Private Sub Command1_Click()
    On Error GoTo Cancel
    CommonDialog1.ShowOpen
    ...
Cancel:
End Sub
```

Finally, assuming the user clicked OK, we display the name of the file the user selected in a message box using the **FileName** property:

```
Private Sub Command1_Click()
    On Error GoTo Cancel
    CommonDialog1.ShowOpen
    MsgBox "File to open: " & CommonDialog1.FileName
Cancel:
End Sub
```

When you run this code and click the button, the Open dialog box appears, as in Figure 17.1.

If you make a file selection and click on OK, the Open dialog box closes and the program displays the name of the file you selected, and its path, in a message box, as shown in Figure 17.2.

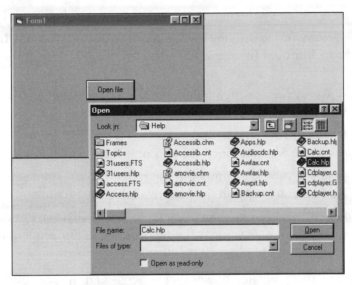

Figure 17.1   The Open dialog box.

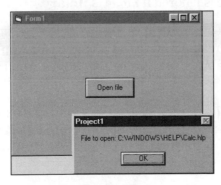

Figure 17.2   Getting a file to open from the user.

Creating A File

The Testing Department is on the phone again. Your new *SuperDuperTextPro* word-processing program is great, but shouldn't it offer users some way to save their text in a file? Hmm, you think, could be a good idea.

So how do you create a file in Visual Basic? The standard way is to use the **Open** statement (we'll see another way when we work with TextStream objects later in this chapter). Here's how the **Open** statement works:

```
Open pathname For mode [Access access] [lock] As [#]filenumber [Len=reclength]
```

Here are what the various arguments mean:

- *pathname*—A file name (may include directory or folder, and drive).
- *mode*—A keyword specifying the file mode: **Append**, **Binary**, **Input**, **Output**, or **Random** (if unspecified, the file is opened for **Random** access).
- *access*—A keyword specifying the operations permitted on the open file: **Read**, **Write**, or **Read Write**.
- *lock*—A keyword specifying the operations restricted on the open file by other processes: **Shared**, **Lock Read**, **Lock Write**, and **Lock Read Write**.
- *filenumber*—A valid file number in the range 1 to 511, inclusive. Use the **FreeFile** function to obtain the next available file number.
- *reclength*—A number less than or equal to 32,767 (bytes). For files opened for random access, this value is the record length. For sequential files, this value is the number of characters buffered.

If the file is already opened by another process and the specified type of access is not allowed, the **Open** operation fails and an error occurs. Also note that the **Len** clause is ignored if *mode* is **Binary**.

So how do you create a file with **Open**? If the file specified by *pathname* doesn't exist, it is created when a file is opened for **Append**, **Binary**, **Output**, or **Random** modes. After you've created the file, you refer to it using the file number.

Let's see an example. Here, we'll let users write the text in a text box, **Text1**, to a file on disk, file.txt, when they press a button. Because file operations are prone to error (we might run into missing diskettes, locked files, and so on), we start by checking for errors:

```
Private Sub Command1_Click()
    On Error GoTo FileError
```

```
...
FileError:
    MsgBox "File Error!"
End Sub
```

Next, we create file.txt as file #1:

```
Private Sub Command1_Click()
    On Error GoTo FileError
    Open "c:\file.txt" For Output As #1
...
FileError:
    MsgBox "File Error!"
End Sub
```

Now we write the text in **Text1** to the file with the **Print #** method:

```
Private Sub Command1_Click()
    On Error GoTo FileError
    Open "c:\file.txt" For Output As #1
    Print #1, Text1.Text
...
FileError:
    MsgBox "File Error!"
End Sub
```

And finally we close the file:

```
Private Sub Command1_Click()
    On Error GoTo FileError
    Open "c:\file.txt" For Output As #1
    Print #1, Text1.Text
    Close #1
    Exit Sub

FileError:
    MsgBox "File Error!"
End Sub
```

When you add a text box, **Text1**, to the form, and a command button, **Command1**, labeled "Write text to file", and run the program, you see the display much like that in Figure 17.3. When you click the command button, the new file is created and written.

Figure 17.3   Writing text to a file.

TIP: We should note that each open file needs its own unique file number; you can use the **FreeFile** function to return the next available free file number. You use **FreeFile** like this: **FreeFile[(rangenumber)]**. Here, the optional rangenumber argument is a variant that specifies the range from which the next free file number is to be returned. Pass a 0 (default) to return a file number in the range 1 to 255. Specify a 1 to return a file number in the range 256 to 511.

Getting A File's Length

When you start reading files in code, it can help to know the file's length (for one thing, it can tell you how many bytes to read in). There are two ways to determine file length, the **FileLen** and the **LOF** functions.

The **FileLen** Function

The **FileLen** function returns the length of a file (in bytes) on disk. Here's an example in which we report the size of a file, file.txt, in a message box using **FileLen**:

```
Private Sub Command1_Click()
    MsgBox "The file.txt file is" & Str(FileLen("c:\file.txt")) & _
        " bytes long."
End Sub
```

Running this code gives a result such as you see in Figure 17.4.

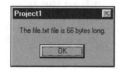

Figure 17.4   Reporting a file's length.

The **LOF** Function

The **LOF** function returns the length of a file (in bytes) opened with the **Open** statement. You pass the **LOF** function an open file number. Here's an example in which we report the length of a file we've just written, using the **LOF** function:

```
Private Sub Command1_Click()
    On Error GoTo FileError
    Open "c:\file.txt" For Output As #1
    Print #1, Text1.Text
    MsgBox "The file is" & Str(LOF(1)) & " bytes long."
    Close #1
    Exit Sub

FileError:
    MsgBox "File Error!"
End Sub
```

Opening A File

How do you open a file in Visual Basic? You use the **Open** statement. Here's how the **Open** statement works:

```
Open pathname For mode [Access access] [lock] As [#]filenumber [Len=reclength]
```

Here are what the various arguments mean:

- *pathname*—A file name (may include directory or folder, and drive).
- *mode*—A keyword specifying the file mode: **Append**, **Binary**, **Input**, **Output**, or **Random** (if unspecified, the file is opened for **Random** access).
- *access*—A keyword specifying the operations permitted on the open file: **Read**, **Write**, or **Read Write**.
- *lock*—A keyword specifying the operations restricted on the open file by other processes: **Shared**, **Lock Read**, **Lock Write**, and **Lock Read Write**.
- *filenumber*—A valid file number in the range 1 to 511, inclusive. Use the **FreeFile** function to obtain the next available file number.
- *reclength*—Number less than or equal to 32,767 (bytes). For files opened for random access, this value is the record length. For sequential files, this value is the number of characters buffered.

If the file is already opened by another process and the specified type of access is not allowed, the **Open** operation fails and an error occurs. Also note that the **Len** clause is ignored if *mode* is **Binary**. If the file specified by *pathname* doesn't exist, it is created when a file is opened for **Append**, **Binary**, **Output**, or **Random** modes. If you open an existing file for **Output**, it is overwritten; if you open it for **Append**, new data is added to the end of the file. After you've created the file, you refer to it using the file number.

For example, here we open a file named file.txt and write the contents of a text box, **Text1**, to that file:

```
Private Sub Command1_Click()
    On Error GoTo FileError
    Open "c:\file.txt" For Output As #1
    Print #1, Text1.Text
    Close #1
    Exit Sub

FileError:
    MsgBox "File Error!"
End Sub
```

Writing To A Sequential File

Sequential files are often text strings in Visual Basic, but they can also be combinations of text and numbers. You usually use these standard statements to write to sequential files in Visual Basic (we'll also see how to use the TextStream methods later in this chapter):

```
Print # number, expressionlist
Write # number, expressionlist
```

Here, *number* is an open file number and *expressionlist* is a list of variables to write, separated by commas. Let's take a look at some examples.

The **Print #** Statement

If you want to store your data in text format, use **Print #**. As an example, we'll store the text in a text box to a file named file.txt using **Print #**. We start by checking for errors:

```
Private Sub Command1_Click()
    On Error GoTo FileError
    ...
FileError:
    MsgBox "File Error!"
End Sub
```

Then we open a file for output:

```
Private Sub Command1_Click()
    On Error GoTo FileError
    Open "c:\file.txt" For Output As #1
...
FileError:
    MsgBox "File Error!"
End Sub
```

Then we print the text in a text box, **Text1**, to the file:

```
Private Sub Command1_Click()
    On Error GoTo FileError
    Open "c:\file.txt" For Output As #1
    Print #1, Text1.Text
...
FileError:
    MsgBox "File Error!"
End Sub
```

Finally we close the file:

```
Private Sub Command1_Click()
    On Error GoTo FileError
    Open "c:\file.txt" For Output As #1
    Print #1, Text1.Text
    Close #1
    Exit Sub

FileError:
    MsgBox "File Error!"
End Sub
```

And that's it—now the user can write the contents of a text box out to disk. The code for this is located in the filewrite folder on this book's accompanying CD-ROM.

The **Write #** Statement

You can also use the **Write #** statement to write text and other types of data to a file. You use this statement with a file number and a comma-delimited list of the variables you want to write to that file. For example, here we open a file, data.dat, and write two numbers that the user has entered in the text boxes **Text1** and **Text2** to that file:

```
Private Sub Command1_Click()
    Open "c:\data.dat" For Output As #1
    Write #1, Val(Text1.Text), Val(Text2.Text)
    Close #1
End Sub
```

To see how to read those values back in, take a look at "Reading From Sequential Files" coming up in this chapter.

Writing To A Random Access File

You usually write records to random access files using the **Put** statement:

```
Put [#]filenumber, [recnumber], varname
```

Here, *filenumber* is the number of a file to write to, *recnumber* is the number of the record to write (you set the record size when you open the file), and *varname* is the name of the variable that holds the data to write to the file.

To work with records in a random access file, you define a record type first. For example, here we define a new type named **Record** in a module (you can only define types in modules; to add a new module to a program, use the Project menu's Add Module item):

```
Type Record
    Name As String * 50
    Number As String * 50
End Type
```

Note that we use fixed-length strings here to make all our records the same size.

Now in a program, we can set up an array of such records in the (General) part of a form, as well as an integer to keep track of the total number of records:

```
Dim WriteData(1 To 50) As Record
Dim TotalRecords As Integer
```

In this example, we'll just have one record, which we fill from the text boxes **Text1** and **Text2** when the user clicks a button:

```
Private Sub Command1_Click()
    WriteData(1).Name = Text1.Text
```

```
        WriteData(1).Number = Text2.Text
        TotalRecords = 1
...
```

Next, we create a file to store our record(s) in—note that we set the size of each record in the file with the **Len** keyword:

```
Private Sub Command1_Click()
    WriteData(1).Name = Text1.Text
    WriteData(1).Number = Text2.Text
    TotalRecords = 1

    On Error GoTo FileError
    Open "c:\records.dat" For Random As #1 Len = Len(WriteData(1))
...
FileError:
    MsgBox "File Error!"
End Sub
```

Finally, we use the **Put** statement to write the data to the file. We only have one record here, but if we had a number of records, we could loop like this:

```
Private Sub Command1_Click()
    WriteData(1).Name = Text1.Text
    WriteData(1).Number = Text2.Text
    TotalRecords = 1

    On Error GoTo FileError
    Open "c:\records.dat" For Random As #1 Len = Len(WriteData(1))
    For loop_index = 1 To TotalRecords
        Put #1, , WriteData(loop_index)
    Next loop_index
    Close #1
    Exit Sub


FileError:
    MsgBox "File Error!"

End Sub
```

And that's it—we've written our data file. To see how to read records back in, see "Reading From Random Access Files" later in this chapter.

Writing To A Binary File

You usually write records to binary files using the **Put** statement:

```
Put [#]filenumber, [recnumber], varname
```

Here, *filenumber* is the number of a file to write to, *recnumber* is the number of the record to write for random files and the byte at which to start writing for binary files, and *varname* is the name of the variable that holds the data to write to the file.

Here's an example showing how to use **Put** to write a floating point number the user has entered in a text box, **Text1**, to a file—note that we open that file in **Binary** mode and don't use a record number with **Put** here:

```
Private Sub Command1_Click()
    Dim varOutput As Double
    varOutput = Val(Text1.Text)

    On Error GoTo FileError
    Open "c:\binary.dat" For Binary As #1
    Put #1, , varOutput
    Close #1
    Exit Sub

FileError:
    MsgBox "File Error!"
End Sub
```

To see how to read the binary data back in, see "Reading from Binary Files" later in this chapter.

Reading From Sequential Files

To read from sequential file, you can use these standard statements (we'll see how to use TextStream methods later in this chapter):

```
Input # number, expressionlist
Line Input # number, string
Input$ (numberbytes, [#] number)
```

Here, *number* is a file number, *expressionlist* is a list of variables the data will be stored in, *string* is a string variable to store data in, and *numberbytes* is the number of bytes you want to read. Let's see some examples.

The **Input #** Statement

You can use the **Input #** statement to read text and numbers from a sequential file. For example, if we write two integers the user has entered in **Text1** and **Text2** to a file, data.dat, this way using **Write #** when the user clicks **Command1**:

```
Private Sub Command1_Click()
    Open "c:\data.dat" For Output As #1
    Write #1, Val(Text1.Text), Val(Text2.Text)
    Close #1
End Sub
```

then we can read those integers back using **Input #** this way when the user clicks **Command2**:

```
Private Sub Command2_Click()
    Dim int1, int2 As Integer

    Open "c:\data.dat" For Input As #1
    Input #1, int1, int2
    Text3.Text = Str(int1)
    Text4.Text = Str(int2)
    Close #1

End Sub
```

The result appears in Figure 17.5. When the user enters two integers in the text boxes and clicks the Write Data button, we write them to disk. When the

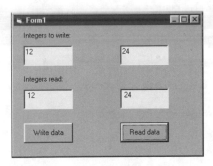

Figure 17.5   Using Write # and Input # to save and restore integers.

user clicks the Read data button, we read them back using **Input #**. In that way, we're able to write and read a sequential file. The code for this example is located in the filedata folder on this book's accompanying CD-ROM.

The **Line Input** Statement

Using the **Line Input** statement, you can read lines (text strings that end with a carriage return or carriage return/line feed pair) from a file. For example, say we had this set of lines, each separated by a carriage return/line feed pair in a file named file.txt:

```
Here is some
multi-line text
that we
will read in...
```

When the user clicks a button, we can read in the preceding text line by line with **Line Input**. First, we open the file:

```
Private Sub Command1_Click()

    On Error GoTo FileError
    Open "c:\file.txt" For Input As #1
...
FileError:
    MsgBox "File Error!"
End Sub
```

Now we need some way of looping over all the lines in the file—but how do we know when we've reached the end of the file? We use the Visual Basic **EOF** (End Of File) function, which returns True when we reach the end of the file:

```
Private Sub Command1_Click()

    On Error GoTo FileError
    Open "c:\file.txt" For Input As #1
    Do Until EOF(1)
...
    Loop

    Exit Sub

FileError:
    MsgBox "File Error!"
End Sub
```

Next we use **Line Input** to read lines of text from the file and append them to a multiline text box (that is, a text box with its **MultiLine** property set to True), **Text1**, along with a carriage return line feed pair this way:

```
Private Sub Command1_Click()
    Dim NewLine As String

    On Error GoTo FileError
    Open "c:\file.txt" For Input As #1
    Do Until EOF(1)
        Line Input #1, NewLine
        Text1.Text = Text1.Text + NewLine + vbCrLf
    Loop

    Exit Sub

FileError:
    MsgBox "File Error!"
End Sub
```

The result of this code appears in Figure 17.6. When the user clicks the command button, we read in the file.txt file line by line using **Line Input** and display it in the text box.

The code for this is located in the fileread folder on this book's accompanying CD-ROM.

The **Input$** Statement

The **Input$** statement lets you read in a string of a specified length. It might seem odd to have to know the strings' lengths before reading them in, but **Input$** does have one very useful aspect: if you use it together with the **LOF** (Length Of File) function, you can read in a whole text file at once.

Figure 17.6   Reading text with Line Input.

For example, here's how we read in the file from the previous example, file.txt, all at once, without having to work line by line:

```
Private Sub Command1_Click()
    Dim NewLine As String

    On Error GoTo FileError
    Open "c:\file.txt" For Input As #1

    Text1.Text = Input$(LOF(1), #1)

    Exit Sub

FileError:
    MsgBox "File Error!"
End Sub
```

This example produces the same result as the previous example that uses **Line Input**.

Reading From Random Access Files

The Testing Department is on the phone. Your new program, *SuperDuperData-Crunch*, is great for writing data to disk, but shouldn't you let the user read that data back in? Hmm, you think, good idea.

You use **Get** to read records from a random access file:

```
Get [#]filenumber, [recnumber], varname
```

Here, *filenumber* is the number of a file to read from, *recnumber* is the number of the record to read, and *varname* is the name of the variable that should receive the read-in data.

Let's see an example. Earlier in this chapter, we saw how to write records to a random access file. We set up a new type named **Record** in a module:

```
Type Record
    Name As String * 50
    Number As String * 50
End Type
```

Then we set up two formwide arrays of records, **WriteData** and **ReadData**, and an integer named **TotalRecords** to keep track of how many records are total (these variables are stored in the (General) section of the form):

```
Dim WriteData(1 To 50) As Record
Dim ReadData(1 To 50) As Record
Dim TotalRecords As Integer
```

When the user clicked a command button, we read the text from two text boxes, **Text1** and **Text2**, placed that text in the first record of the **WriteData** array, and wrote that record out to a file named records.dat with the **Put** statement:

```
Private Sub Command1_Click()
    WriteData(1).Name = Text1.Text
    WriteData(1).Number = Text2.Text
    TotalRecords = 1

    On Error GoTo FileError
    Open "c:\records.dat" For Random As #1 Len = Len(WriteData(1))
    For intLoopIndex  = 1 To TotalRecords
        Put #1, , WriteData(intLoopIndex )
    Next intLoopIndex
    Close #1
    Exit Sub

FileError:
    MsgBox "File Error!"

End Sub
```

Now we'll see how to read that record back in. First, we open the file records.dat for random access, setting the record size to the length of each array element:

```
Private Sub Command2_Click()

    Open "c:\records.dat" For Random As #1 Len = Len(ReadData(1))
...
```

Then we use **Get** to read in the records:

```
Private Sub Command2_Click()
    Dim intLoopIndex As Integer

    Open "c:\records.dat" For Random As #1 Len = Len(ReadData(1))
```

```
For intLoopIndex = 1 To LOF(1) / Len(ReadData(1))
    Get #1, , ReadData(intLoopIndex)
Next intLoopIndex
```

Next, we loop over all the records in the file (although we use **LOF(1) / Len(ReadData(1))** to determine the number of records in the file, we could also loop until the **EOF** function is True):

```
Private Sub Command2_Click()
    Dim intLoopIndex As Integer

    Open "c:\records.dat" For Random As #1 Len = Len(ReadData(1))

    For intLoopIndex = 1 To LOF(1) / Len(ReadData(1))
...
    Next intLoopIndex
...
```

Then we close the file and display the **Name** and **Number** fields of the first (and only) record in two new text boxes, **Text3** and **Text4**:

```
Private Sub Command2_Click()
    Dim intLoopIndex As Integer

    Open "c:\records.dat" For Random As #1 Len = Len(ReadData(1))

    For intLoopIndex = 1 To LOF(1) / Len(ReadData(1))
        Get #1, , ReadData(intLoopIndex)
    Next intLoopIndex

    Close #1

    Text3.Text = ReadData(1).Name
    Text4.Text = ReadData(1).Number

    Exit Sub

FileError:
    MsgBox "File Error!"
End Sub
```

When you run this program, as shown in Figure 17.7, the user can enter data into the two text boxes at left, click the Write To File button to write the data to a record in a file, then click the Read From File button to read the data back in and display that text in the two text boxes at right.

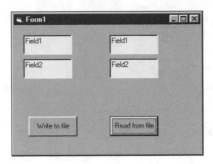

Figure 17.7   Writing and reading records to and from a random access file.

You can see the result in Figure 17.7. Now we're reading records from random access files in Visual Basic.

The code for this example is located in the filerecord folder on this book's accompanying CD-ROM.

Reading From Binary Files

How do you read raw data from files that have been opened in **Binary** format with the **Open** statement? You usually use **Get** to read data from a binary file (although you can use **Input #** as well—see the previous topic on reading from sequential files):

```
Get [#]filenumber, [recnumber], varname
```

Here, *filenumber* is the number of a file to read from, *recnumber* is the number of the record to read for random files and the byte at which to start reading for binary files, and *varname* is the name of the variable that will hold the read-in data.

Let's see an example. In this case, we first write some binary data—such as a floating point number—to a file, and then we'll read it back in. Here, we let the user enter a **Double** value in a text box, which we read in when the user clicks a command button, **Command1**:

```
Private Sub Command1_Click()
    Dim varOutput As Double
    varOutput = Val(Text1.Text)
    ...
```

Then we write that number out to a binary file, binary.dat (making it a binary file by opening it in **Binary** mode):

```
Private Sub Command1_Click()
    Dim varOutput As Double
    varOutput = Val(Text1.Text)

    On Error GoTo FileError
    Open "c:\binary.dat" For Binary As #1
    Put #1, , varOutput
    Close #1
    Exit Sub

FileError:
    MsgBox "File Error!"
End Sub
```

Now it's up to us to read that number back in as binary data when the user clicks a new button, **Command2**. We start by opening the file again:

```
Private Sub Command2_Click()

    On Error GoTo FileError
    Open "c:\binary.dat" For Binary As #1
...
FileError:
    MsgBox "File Error!"
End Sub
```

Next, we use **Get** to read in the number and store it in a new variable, **varInput**:

```
Private Sub Command2_Click()
    Dim varInput As Double

    On Error GoTo FileError
    Open "c:\binary.dat" For Binary As #1
    Get #1, , varInput
...
FileError:
    MsgBox "File Error!"

End Sub
```

Finally, we display the newly read-in variable in a text box, **Text2**, and close the file:

```
Private Sub Command2_Click()
    Dim varInput As Double

    On Error GoTo FileError
    Open "c:\binary.dat" For Binary As #1
    Get #1, , varInput
    Text2.Text = Str(varInput)
    Close #1
    Exit Sub

FileError:
    MsgBox "File Error!"

End Sub
```

The result appears in Figure 17.8, where we write the number 3.1415 out to disk in the file binary.dat and then read it in again. Now we're working with binary files in Visual Basic.

The code for this example is located in the filebinary folder on this book's accompanying CD-ROM.

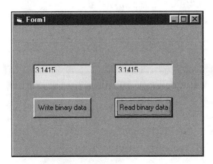

Figure 17.8   Writing and reading binary data.

Accessing Any Record In A Random Access File

When you've set up a file to hold records (by creating it in **Random** mode with the **Open** statement and passing the length of the records you want to open), you can use **Get** to access any record in the file by record number:

```
Get #1, recordnumber, variablename
```

In this case, we're reading record number *recordnumber* from file 1 and placing the data read into a variable named *variablename*. In the same way, you can write any record with **Put**:

```
Put #1, recordnumber, variablename
```

Using **Get** and **Put** in this way, you can read and write any record in the file.

TIP: Besides **Get** and **Put**, you can use the **Seek** function to set the position at which a record will next be read or written in a file—called the read/write position—and the **LOC** function to determine the current read/write position.

Closing A File

Closing A File

How do you close a file in Visual Basic? It's simple—you just use the **Close** statement:

```
Private Sub Command1_Click()
    On Error GoTo FileError
    Open "c:\file.txt" For Output As #1
    Print #1, Text1.Text
    Close #1
    Exit Sub

FileError:
    MsgBox "File Error!"
End Sub
```

Closing a file writes all its data out to disk.

TIP: If you want to close all files your application has open, just use the **Close** statement without any arguments.

---

*Saving Files
From Rich
Text Boxes*

Saving Files From Rich Text Boxes

You can use the **SaveFile( )** method to save the text in a rich text box to disk, and doing that is really easy—you just use **SaveFile( )** this way:

```
RichTextBox.SaveFile(pathname, [filetype])
```

You can save text as plain or RTF text; the settings for *filetype* are as follows:

- **rtfRTF**—0 (the default); the rich text box control saves its contents as an RTF file.

- **rtfText**—1; the rich text box control saves its contents as a text file.

Here's an example where we display some text in a rich text box:

```
Private Sub Form_Load()
    RichTextBox1.Text = "This is the text in the file."
End Sub
```

Next, we save that text to a file this way:

```
Private Sub Command1_Click()
    RichTextBox1.SaveFile ("c:\data.txt")
End Sub
```

And that's all it takes—now we've written RTF to a file. For more information on rich text boxes, see Chapter 6.

TIP: *Many word processors, like Microsoft Word, support RTF files, so you can now write text formatted files that such word processors can read in and use.*

Opening Files In Rich Text Boxes

You can write files to disk from a rich text box with **SaveFile( )**; how can you read files back in? You use **LoadFile( )**. Like **SaveFile( )**, **LoadFile( )** is very easy to use:

```
RichTextBox.LoadFile pathname, [filetype]
```

And you can load in plain text or RTF text files; the settings for *filetype* are as follows:

- **rtfRTF**—0 (the default); the rich text box control saves its contents as an RTF file.

- **rtfText**—1; the rich text box control saves its contents as a text file.

Here's an example where we load in the file we wrote in the last topic on saving files, data.txt:

```
Private Sub Command1_Click()
    RichTextBox1.LoadFile "c:\data.txt"
End Sub
```

That's all there is to it—it's that easy to load in files. For more information on rich text boxes, see Chapter 6.

Saving Files
From Picture
Boxes

Saving Files From Picture Boxes

Can you save the images in picture boxes to disk files? Yes, you can, using **SavePicture**. Here's how that statement works:

```
SavePicture picture, stringexpression
```

Here's what the arguments in that statement mean:

- *picture*—Picture or image control from which the graphics file is to be created

- *stringexpression*—File name of the graphics file to save

Note that **SavePicture** only saves images in BMP, WMF, and ICO formats (depending on the file type the image came from originally); if the image came from a GIF or JPEG file, it's saved in BMP format. Graphics in an **Image** property are always saved as bitmap (BMP) files no matter what their original format.

Here's an example where we save the image from **Picture1** to a file, \image.bmp, when the user clicks a button:

```
Private Sub Command1_Click()
    SavePicture Picture1.Picture, "c:\image.bmp"
End Sub
```

Opening Files In
Picture Boxes

Opening Files In Picture Boxes

How do you open image files in a picture box? You use the **Picture** property. A picture box is very versatile and can display images from bitmap (.bmp), icon (.ico), metafile (.wmf), JPEG (.jpg), or GIF (.gif) files—just load the file's name into the **Picture** property.

You can use **LoadPicture()** to load in a picture like this, where we load in an image when the user clicks a command button:

```
Private Sub Command1_Click()
    Picture1.Picture = LoadPicture("c:\vbbb\picturesandimages\image.bmp")
End Sub
```

Using The Drive List Box Control

Usually you use the Common Dialogs File Open and File Save As to get file names and file paths from the user, but sometimes that just won't do. For example, you have a program where you want to let the user select files but don't want to use dialog boxes. In that and similar cases, you can use the Visual Basic file controls: the drive list box, the directory list box, and the file list box. These controls are intrinsic to Visual Basic (that is, they appear in the toolbox when you start Visual Basic).

The Drive List Box Control tool appears as the seventh tool down on the right in the Visual Basic toolbox in Figure 17.9. Use this tool to draw a drive list box in a form, as shown at upper left in Figure 17.10.

You get the currently selected drive in a drive list box by using its **Drive** property, and when the user changes the drive in that control, a **Change** event is

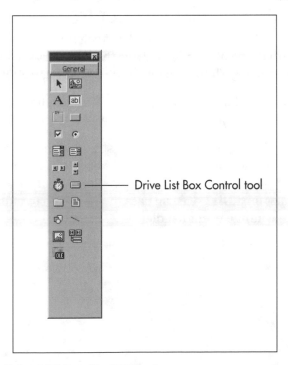

Figure 17.9   The Drive List Box Control tool.

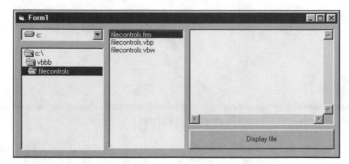

Figure 17.10   A program with a drive list box.

generated. Here's an example—when the user selects a new drive, we pass that new drive on to a directory list box, **Dir1**, using that drive as the new root directory in **Dir1**:

```
Sub Drive1_Change()
    Dir1.Path = Drive1.Drive
End Sub
```

Using The
Directory List
Box Control

Using The Directory List Box Control

The directory list box control displays directories as a hierarchical set of folders. This control is one of the file controls that are intrinsic to Visual Basic; its tool appears as the eighth tool down on the left in Figure 17.11.

To add a directory list box to a form, just use its tool in the toolbox. We've added a directory list box to the program in Figure 17.10 (see earlier), at lower left.

The important property of the directory list box is the **Path** property, which holds the path of the current directory. When the user changes the current path, a **Change** event is generated. For example, when the user makes a change in a directory list box, **Dir1**, we can pass the new path to a file list box, **File1**, this way in the **Change** event handler:

```
Sub Dir1_Change()
    File1.Path = Dir1.Path
End Sub
```

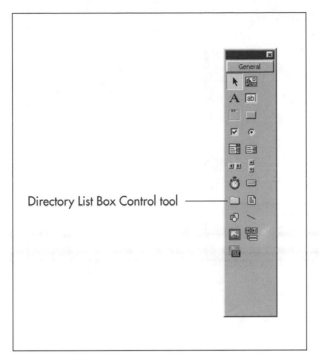

Directory List Box Control tool —

Figure 17.11   The Directory List Box Control tool.

Using The File List Box Control

The file list box control lets you display the files in a directory as a list of names. This control's tool appears as the eighth tool down on the right in Figure 17.12. To add this control to a form, just draw it as you want it with its tool in the toolbox.

The important properties of the file list box are the **Path** and **FileName** properties. Let's see an example using the drive, directory, and file list boxes. When the user selects a file and clicks a button labeled Display File, or double-clicks the file's name in the file list box, we'll display the contents of the selected file in a text box.

We start by adding the controls we'll need: a drive list box, **Drive1**; a directory list box, **Dir1**; a file list box, **File1**; a command button, **Command1**, which is labeled Display File; and a text box with its **MultiLine** property set to True and its **Scrollbars** property set to **Both** (if the file you are displaying is too long for a text box, use a rich text box).

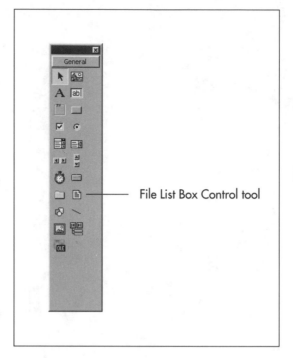

Figure 17.12   The File List Box Control tool.

When the user changes the drive, we pass that new drive to the directory list box as the new directory in **Drive1_Change( )**:

```
Sub Drive1_Change()
    Dir1.Path = Drive1.Drive
End Sub
```

When the user changes the directory, we pass that new path to the file list box in **Dir1_Change( )**:

```
Sub Dir1_Change()
    File1.Path = Dir1.Path
End Sub
```

When the user clicks the button, we want to display the contents of the selected file in the text box, and we'll do that in the command button's **Click** event handler, **Command1_Click( )**. We'll also call the button's **Click** event handler to let the user open a file by double-clicking it in the file control:

```
Sub File1_DblClick()
    Command1_Click
End Sub
```

When the user wants to open a file, we put together the file's name and path this way:

```
Sub Command1_Click()
    Dim FileName As String
    On Error GoTo FileError
    If (Right$(Dir1.Path, 1) = "\") Then
        FileName = File1.Path & File1.FileName
    Else
        FileName = File1.Path & "\" & File1.FileName
    End If
...
```

Then we simply open the file and display it in the text box, **Text1**:

```
Sub Command1_Click()
    Dim FileName As String
    On Error GoTo FileError
    If (Right$(Dir1.Path, 1) = "\") Then
        FileName = File1.Path & File1.FileName
    Else
        FileName = File1.Path & "\" & File1.FileName
    End If

    Open FileName For Input As #1
    Text1.Text = Input$(LOF(1), #1)
    Close #1
    Exit Sub

FileError:
    MsgBox "File Error!"
End Sub
```

That's it—when you run the program, the user can use the file controls to open a file, as shown in Figure 17.13. Now we're using the Visual Basic file controls.

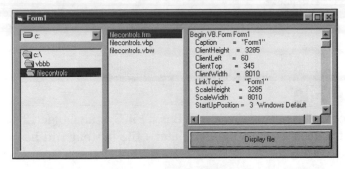

Figure 17.13   Displaying a file using the Visual Basic file controls.

The code for this example is located in the filecontrols folder on this book's accompanying CD-ROM.

Creating And Deleting Directories

You can create a new directory with the **MkDir** statement and remove a directory with the **RmDir** statement. For example, here's how we create a new directory, C:\data, using **MkDir** when the user clicks a command button, **Command1** (if the directory already exists, Visual Basic generates an error):

```
Private Sub Command1_Click()
    MkDir "c:\data"
End Sub
```

Here's another example. We remove the same directory using **RmDir** when the user clicks another command button, **Command2**:

```
Private Sub Command2_Click()
    RmDir "c:\data"
End Sub
```

Changing Directories

To change the default directory (that is, the directory where Visual Basic will look for the files you want to work with if you don't specify a path), use **ChDir**. Here's an example where we change the default directory to C:\windows using **ChDir** when the user clicks a command button, **Command1**:

```
Private Sub Command1_Click()
    ChDir "c:\windows"
End Sub
```

Copying A File

You can copy files using the Visual Basic FileSystemObject. This object provides you with access to the computer's file system and has methods like **CopyFile** to copy a file:

```
FileSystemObject.CopyFile source, destination[, overwrite]
```

Here, *source* is the source file name (including path), *destination* is the destination file name (also including path), and *overwrite* is a Boolean that, if True, means you want to overwrite the destination file if it already exists. You can use wildcards (in other words, the asterisk [*]).

CopyFile solves a tedious problem for the programmer—if all you want to do is copy a file, why should you have to write all the code specifically to do that? You don't, using **CopyFile**. Here's an example where we copy a file, file.txt, to file2.txt. Notice that we must first create a FileSystemObject:

```
Private Sub Command1_Click()
    Dim FileSystemObject As Object
    Set FileSystemObject = CreateObject("Scripting.FileSystemObject")
    FileSystemObject.CopyFile "c:\file.txt", "c:\file2.txt"
End Sub
```

You can also do the same thing with the Visual Basic FileObject, where we use **GetFile** to get a FileObject object and then use the FileObject's **Copy** method:

```
Private Sub Command1_Click()
    Dim FileSystemObject, FileObject As Object
    Set FileSystemObject = CreateObject("Scripting.FileSystemObject")
    Set FileObject = FileSystemObject.GetFile("c:\file.txt")
    FileObject.Copy "c:\file2.txt"
End Sub
```

Moving A File

The Visual Basic FileSystemObject lets you move a file from one directory to another using its **MoveFile** method. This method takes only two arguments, the source and destination paths. Here's an example where we move a file, file.txt, from the C: to the D: drive; note that we must first create a FileSystemObject:

```
Private Sub Command1_Click()
    Dim FileSystemObject As Object
    Set FileSystemObject = CreateObject("Scripting.FileSystemObject")
    FileSystemObject.MoveFile "c:\file.txt", "d:\file.txt"
End Sub
```

You can also do the same thing with the Visual Basic FileObject, where we use **GetFile** to get a FileObject and then use the FileObject's **Move** method:

```
Private Sub Command1_Click()
    Dim FileSystemObject, FileObject As Object
    Set FileSystemObject = CreateObject("Scripting.FileSystemObject")
    Set FileObject = FileSystemObject.GetFile("c:\file.txt")
    FileObject.Move "d:\file.txt"
End Sub
```

Deleting A File

The Visual Basic FileSystemObject lets you delete a file using its **DeleteFile** method:

```
FileSystemObject.DeleteFile filespec [,force]
```

Here, *filespec* is the file you want to delete, and *force* is a Boolean that, if True, means you want to delete read-only files as well. Let's see an example. Here, we delete a file, file.txt, from the C: drive; note that we must first create a FileSystemObject:

```
Private Sub Command1_Click()
    Dim FileSystemObject As Object
    Set FileSystemObject = CreateObject("Scripting.FileSystemObject")
    FileSystemObject.DeleteFile "c:\file.txt"
End Sub
```

You can also do the same thing with the Visual Basic FileObject, where we use **GetFile** to get a FileObject and then use the FileObject's **Delete** method:

```
Private Sub Command1_Click()
    Dim FileSystemObject, FileObject As Object
    Set FileSystemObject = CreateObject("Scripting.FileSystemObject")
    Set FileObject = FileSystemObject.GetFile("c:\file.txt")
    FileObject.Delete
End Sub
```

When Was A File Created? Last Modified? Last Accessed?

You can use Visual Basic FileObject to determine when a file was created, last modified, and last accessed. The properties that are important here are **DateCreated**, **DateLastModified**, and **DateLastAccessed**.

Let's see an example. Here, we use a multiline (that is, **MultiLine = True**) text box, **Text1**, to display when a file, file.dat, was created, last modified, and last accessed. First, we get a FileObect for that file:

```
Private Sub Command1_Click()
    Dim FileSystemObject, FileObject As Object
    Set FileSystemObject = CreateObject("Scripting.FileSystemObject")
    Set FileObject = FileSystemObject.GetFile("c:\file.dat")
...
```

The we display the file's created, last modified, and last accessed dates in the text box:

```
Private Sub Command1_Click()
    Dim FileSystemObject, FileObject As Object
    Set FileSystemObject = CreateObject("Scripting.FileSystemObject")
    Set FileObject = FileSystemObject.GetFile("c:\file.dat")
    Text1.Text = "c:\file.dat:" & vbCrLf & "was created " & _
        FileObject.DateCreated & vbCrLf & "was last modified: " & _
        FileObject.DateLastModified & vbCrLf & "was last accessed: " & _
        FileObject.DateLastAccessed & vbCrLf
End Sub
```

The result of this code appears in Figure 17.14. Using the FileObject, you can find out quite a bit of information about a file.

Figure 17.14   Displaying a file's creation, last modified, and last accessed dates.

Creating A TextStream

Creating A TextStream

You can use TextStream objects to work with text files in Visual Basic. We'll see how to work with TextStream objects in the next few topics in this chapter. For example, you create a text stream with the **CreateTextFile** method:

```
FileSystemObject.CreateTextFile(filename[, overwrite[, unicode]])
```

Here's what the arguments we pass to **CreateTextFile** mean:

- *filename*—String which identifies the file to create.

- *overwrite*—Boolean value that indicates if an existing file can be overwritten. The value is True if the file can be overwritten; False if it can't be overwritten. If omitted, existing files are not overwritten.

- *unicode*—Boolean value that indicates whether the file is created as a Unicode or an ASCII file. The value is True if the file is created as a Unicode file; False if it's created as an ASCII file. If omitted, an ASCII file is assumed.

Here's an example where we create a TextStream object corresponding to a file named file.txt:

```
Private Sub Command1_Click()
    Dim FileSystemObject, TextStream As Object

    Set FileSystemObject = CreateObject("Scripting.FileSystemObject")
    Set TextStream = FileSystemObject.CreateTextFile("c:\file.txt", True)
End Sub
```

Now that we've created a TextStream, we can write to it, as we'll see later in this chapter.

Opening A TextStream

To open a TextStream, you use the FileSystemObject's **OpenTextFile** method:

```
FileSystemObject.OpenTextFile(filename[, iomode[, create[, format]]])
```

Here are what the arguments to **OpenTextFile** mean:

- *filename*—The file to open.

- *iomode*—Indicates input/output mode. Can be one of two constants, either **ForReading** or **ForAppending**.

- *create*—Boolean value that indicates whether a new file can be created if the specified file doesn't exist. The value is True if a new file is created; False if it isn't created. The default is False.

- *format*—One of three values used to indicate the format of the opened file. If omitted, the file is opened as ASCII.

Here's an example where we open a TextStream object corresponding to a file named file.txt:

```
Private Sub Command2_Click()
    Dim FileSystemObject, TextStream As Object

    Set FileSystemObject = CreateObject("Scripting.FileSystemObject")
    Set TextStream = FileSystemObject.OpenTextFile("c:\file.txt")
End Sub
```

After you've opened a TextStream object, you can read from it, as we'll see later in this chapter.

Writing To A TextStream

To write to a TextStream object, you use one of these methods:

```
Write(string)
WriteLine([string])
```

Here's an example where we create a file named file.txt and write a string, "Here is some text!" to that file. First, we create a new TextStream:

```
Private Sub Command1_Click()
    Dim FileSystemObject, TextStream As Object

    Set FileSystemObject = CreateObject("Scripting.FileSystemObject")
    Set TextStream = FileSystemObject.CreateTextFile("c:\file.txt", True)
    ...
```

Then we write our line of text to the file and close that file:

```
Private Sub Command1_Click()
    Dim FileSystemObject, TextStream As Object

    Set FileSystemObject = CreateObject("Scripting.FileSystemObject")
    Set TextStream = FileSystemObject.CreateTextFile("c:\file.txt", True)

    TextStream.WriteLine ("Here is some text!")
    TextStream.Close
End Sub
```

Reading From A TextStream

To read from a TextStream object, you use one of these methods; note that the **Read** method lets you specify how many characters to read:

```
Read(numbercharacters)
ReadAll
ReadLine
```

Each of these methods returns the text read. Let's see an example. In this case, we'll open a file, file.txt, and read one line from it, displaying that line in a text box. First, we create a TextStream object for that file:

```
Private Sub Command1_Click()
    Dim FileSystemObject, TextStream As Object

    Set FileSystemObject = CreateObject("Scripting.FileSystemObject")
    Set TextStream = FileSystemObject.OpenTextFile("c:\file.txt")
...
```

Next, we use the **ReadLine** method to read a line from the file and display it in a text box, **Text1**, and close the TextStream:

```
Private Sub Command1_Click()
    Dim FileSystemObject, TextStream As Object

    Set FileSystemObject = CreateObject("Scripting.FileSystemObject")
    Set TextStream = FileSystemObject.OpenTextFile("c:\file.txt")

    Text1.Text = TextStream.ReadLine
    TextStream.Close
End Sub
```

Closing A TextStream

When you're finished working with a TextStream object, you close it using the **Close** method. In the following example, we write to a file, file.txt, using a TextStream object and then close that TextStream (and therefore the file) using **Close** (this method takes no arguments):

```
Private Sub Command1_Click()
    Dim FileSystemObject, TextStream As Object
```

```
     Set FileSystemObject = CreateObject("Scripting.FileSystemObject")
     Set TextStream = FileSystemObject.CreateTextFile("c:\file.txt", True)

     TextStream.WriteLine ("Here is some text!")
     TextStream.Close
End Sub
```

Chapter 18

Working With Graphics

If you need an immediate solution to:	See page:
Redrawing Graphics In Windows: **AutoRedraw** And **Paint**	584
Clearing The Drawing Area	585
Setting Colors	585
Drawing Text	588
Working With Fonts	589
Drawing Lines	591
Drawing Boxes	593
Drawing Circles	594
Drawing Ellipses	596
Drawing Arcs	597
Drawing Freehand With The Mouse	599
Filling Figures With Color	601
Filling Figures With Patterns	602
Setting Figure Drawing Style And Drawing Width	602
Drawing Points	604
Setting The Drawing Mode	604
Setting Drawing Scales	606
Using The Screen Object	608
Resizing Graphics When The Window Is Resized	608
Copying Pictures To And Pasting Pictures From The Clipboard	609
Printing Graphics	610
Layering Graphics With The **AutoRedraw** And **ClipControls** Properties	611

In Depth

This chapter is on one of the most popular topics in Visual Basic—graphics. Here, we'll cover drawing graphics in Visual Basic. (We won't, however, deal with handling bitmapped images until the next chapter.)

There's a great deal of graphics power in Visual Basic, and we'll see that power in this chapter. Here are some of the topics we'll cover:

- Drawing figures (boxes, circles, and so on)
- Filling figures with color
- Filling figures with patterns
- Setting the drawing mode (for example, XOR drawing)
- Setting the drawing width
- Setting the drawing style
- Using fonts
- Using the Screen object
- Using the Clipboard with graphics
- Printing graphics
- Resizing graphics
- Layering graphics

We've see some of these techniques before when we worked with picture boxes, but we'll expand that coverage in this chapter. And as a bonus, we'll see how to work with the structured graphics control that comes with the Internet Explorer, putting that control to work in Visual Basic.

Graphics Methods Vs. Graphics Controls

There are two principal ways of drawing graphics in Visual Basic: using graphics methods, such as the ones we'll see in this chapter, and using graphics controls (like the line and shape controls). Graphics methods work well in situations where using graphical controls requires too much work. For example, creating gridlines on a graph would require an array of line controls but only a small amount of code using the **Line** method. In addition, when you want an effect to appear temporarily, you can write a couple of lines of code for this temporary effect instead of using another control. Also, graphics methods offer some visual effects that are not available in the graphical controls. For example, you can only create arcs or paint individual pixels using the graphics methods.

All in all, the graphics methods we'll use in this chapter are usually preferred by programmers when they want to create graphics at runtime, and the graphics controls are preferred to create design elements at design time.

About Visual Basic Coordinates

Because we'll be drawing figures in forms and controls like picture boxes, we should know how measurements and coordinates are set up in those objects. Visual Basic coordinate systems have the origin (0, 0) at upper left and are specified as (x, y), where x is horizontal and y is vertical (note that y is positive in the *downwards* direction). When we draw graphics in Visual Basic, we'll be using this coordinate system.

> **Warning!** Bear in mind that the origin is at upper left (for forms, that's the upper left of the form's client area—the part that excludes borders, menu bars, and so on); that fact more than any other is responsible for confusing Visual Basic programmers when they start working with graphics.

The default unit of measurement in Visual Basic is twips (or 1/1440s of an inch). That unit was originally chosen to be small enough to be device-independent, but if you don't like working with twips, you can change to other measurement units like millimeters, inches, and so on, as we'll see in this chapter. You can also define your own measurement units, as we'll also see.

That's it for the overview of graphics. It's time to turn to our Immediate Solutions to start digging into the graphics power that Visual Basic has to offer.

Immediate Solutions

Redrawing Graphics In Windows: **AutoRedraw** And **Paint**

The Testing Department is on the phone. Did you test out your new program, *SuperDuperGraphicsPro*, in Windows? Of course, you say—why? Well, they say, when your program's window is uncovered, it doesn't redraw its displayed graphics automatically. Can you fix that?

One of Visual Basic's most popular aspects is that you can make a form or control redraw itself as needed by setting its **AutoRedraw** property to True. What really happens is that Visual Basic keeps an internal copy of your window's display and refreshes the screen from that copy as needed. This solves one of the biggest headaches of Windows programming in a neat way.

TIP: *You must also set a form's **AutoRedraw** property to True to make a form display graphics when you draw those graphics in the form's **Load** event handler. Note that **AutoRedraw** is set to False in forms by default.*

However, setting **AutoRedraw** to True can use a lot of system resources, notably memory, and you might not want to do so in all cases. If not, you can use the **Paint** event to redraw your graphics, because this event occurs every time a form or control like a picture box is drawn or redrawn. (Note that if you set **AutoRedraw** to False, you are responsible for handling refreshes of your program's appearance yourself.)

Here's an example. In this case, we draw a circle inscribed in the smaller dimension (width or height) of a form when the form is drawn:

```
Private Sub Form_Paint()
    Form1.Circle (ScaleWidth / 2, ScaleHeight / 2), _
        Switch(ScaleWidth >= ScaleHeight, ScaleHeight / 2, _
        ScaleWidth < ScaleHeight, ScaleWidth / 2)
End Sub
```

The result appears in Figure 18.1.

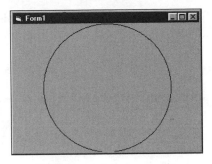

Figure 18.1   Drawing a circle using the Paint event.

Clearing The Drawing Area

One of the first things to learn about drawing graphics is how to clear the drawing area. You do that with the **Cls** method, which redraws the form or control in the current **BackColor**. Here's an example where we clear a picture box, **Picture1**, when the user clicks that picture box:

```
Private Sub Picture1_Click()
    Picture1.Cls
End Sub
```

Setting Colors

Here are some commonly used properties you can specify colors for and what they mean:

- **BackColor**—The background color of the control or form.
- **ForeColor**—The drawing color used to draw figures and text.
- **BorderColor**—The color of the border.
- **FillColor**—The color you want the figure filled in with.

To set color properties like these in Visual Basic, you need to know how to set colors in general. There are four ways to do that:

- Using the **RGB** function
- Using the **QBColor** function to choose one of 16 Microsoft QuickBasic colors
- Using one of the intrinsic Visual Basic color constants
- Entering a color value directly

We'll use the **RGB** function most often to specify colors. This function takes three colors values, 0 to 255, to specify the red, green, and blue values in the color you want like this: **RGB(*RRR*, *GGG*, *BBB*)**, where *RRR*, *GGG*, and *BBB* are the red, green, and blue color values, respectively.

Here are some examples showing how to use this function and the color created:

```
RGB(255, 0, 0)       'Red
RGB(0, 255, 0)       'Green
RGB(0, 0, 255)       'Blue
RGB(0, 0, 0)         'Black
RGB(255, 255, 255)   'White
RGB(128, 128, 128)   'Gray
```

The **QBColor** function returns one of these colors when you pass it the matching numbers, 0 to 15:

- Black—0
- Blue—1
- Green—2
- Cyan—3
- Red—4
- Magenta—5
- Yellow—6
- White—7
- Gray—8
- Light blue—9
- Light green—10
- Light cyan—11
- Light red—12
- Light magenta—13
- Light yellow—14
- Light white—15

You can also use one of the built-in Visual Basic color constants, like **vbRed**, to specify a color. The standard Visual Basic color constants appear in Table 18.1. If you dig hard enough, you can even find the colors Visual Basic uses for system objects; these values appear in Table 18.2.

Table 18.1   Visual Basic color constants.

Constant	Value	Description
vbBlack	&H0	Black
vbRed	&HFF	Red
vbGreen	&HFF00	Green
vbYellow	&HFFFF	Yellow
vbBlue	&HFF0000	Blue
vbMagenta	&HFF00FF	Magenta
vbCyan	&HFFFF00	Cyan
vbWhite	&HFFFFFF	White

Table 18.2   System color constants.

Constant	Value	Description
vbScrollBars	&H80000000	Scroll bar color
vbDesktop	&H80000001	Desktop color
vbActiveTitleBar	&H80000002	Color of the title bar for the active window
vbInactiveTitleBar	&H80000003	Color of the title bar for the inactive window
vbMenuBar	&H80000004	Menu background color
vbWindowBackground	&H80000005	Window background color
vbWindowFrame	&H80000006	Window frame color
vbMenuText	&H80000007	Color of text on menus
vbWindowText	&H80000008	Color of text in windows
vbTitleBarText	&H80000009	Color of text in caption, size box, and scroll arrow
vbActiveBorder	&H8000000A	Border color of active window
vbInactiveBorder	&H8000000B	Border color of inactive window
vbApplicationWorkspace	&H8000000C	Background color of multiple document interface (MDI) applications
vbHighlight	&H8000000D	Background color of items selected in a control
vbHighlightText	&H8000000E	Text color of items selected in a control
vbButtonFace	&H8000000F	Color of shading on the face of command buttons
vbButtonShadow	&H80000010	Color of shading on the edge of command buttons
vbGrayText	&H80000011	Grayed (disabled) text
vbButtonText	&H80000012	Text color on push buttons
vbInactiveCaptionText	&H80000013	Color of text in an inactive caption

(continued)

Table 18.2   System color constants (continued).

Constant	Value	Description
vb3DHighlight	&H80000014	Highlight color for 3D display elements
vb3DDKShadow	&H80000015	Darkest shadow color for 3D display elements
vb3DLight	&H80000016	Second lightest of the 3D colors after vb3Dhighlight
vb3DFace	&H8000000F	Color of text face
vb3Dshadow	&H80000010	Color of text shadow
vbInfoText	&H80000017	Color of text in tool tips

You can also specify colors as 4-byte integers directly, if you want to. The range for full RGB color is 0 to 16,777,215 (&HFFFFFF&).The high byte of a number in this range equals 0. The lower 3 bytes, from least to most significant byte, determine the amount of red, green, and blue. The red, green, and blue components are each represented by a number between 0 and 255 (&HFF). This means that you can specify a color as a hexadecimal number like this: **&HBBGGRR&**.

Drawing Text

You can display text in forms and picture boxes with the **Print** method:

```
[object.]Print [outputlist] [{ ; | , }]
```

The upper-left corner of the text you print appears at the location (**CurrentX**, **CurrentY**) (**CurrentX** and **CurrentY** are properties of forms or picture boxes). If you want to print multiple items on different lines, separate them with commas. If you want to print multiple items on the same line, separate them with semicolons.

Let's see an example. Here, we draw text starting at the center of both a form and a picture box, **Picture1** (note that to draw graphics from the **Form Load** event, you must set the form and picture box's **AutoRedraw** property to True):

```
Private Sub Form_Load()
    CurrentX = ScaleWidth / 2
    CurrentY = ScaleHeight / 2
    Print "Hello from Visual Basic"

Picture1.CurrentX = Picture1.ScaleWidth / 2
    Picture1.CurrentY = Picture1.ScaleHeight / 2
```

```
    Picture1.Print "Hello from Visual Basic"
End Sub
```

The result of the preceding code appears in Figure 18.2. Now we're printing text in forms and picture boxes (we'll print on the printer later in this chapter).

TIP: *You can format text when you print it to forms, picture boxes, or the Printer object by determining its width and height, and you do that with the **TextWidth** and **TextHeight** methods.*

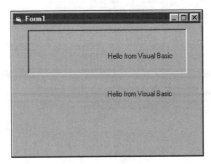

Figure 18.2   Drawing text in a form and picture box.

Working With Fonts

You have a lot of formatting options when working with text. In particular, you can use these font properties in forms and picture boxes:

- **FontBold**
- **FontItalic**
- **FontName**
- **FontSize**
- **FontStrikeThru**
- **FontTransparent**
- **FontUnderline**

For example, we set the font in a form to bold and the font size to 12 in a picture box this way (note that to draw graphics from the **Form Load** event, you must set the form and picture box's **AutoRedraw** property to True):

```
Private Sub Form_Load()
    CurrentX = ScaleWidth / 2
    CurrentY = ScaleHeight / 2
```

```
        FontBold = True
    Print "Hello from Visual Basic"

    Picture1.CurrentX = Picture1.ScaleWidth / 2
    Picture1.CurrentY = Picture1.ScaleHeight / 2
    Picture1.FontSize = 12
    Picture1.Print "Hello from Visual Basic"
End Sub
```

The result of this code appears in Figure 18.3.

The Font Object

You can also create a Font object that holds all the properties of a font; here are the Font object's properties (note that whereas the font property is **FontStrikeThru**, the Font object property is **StrikeThrough**, not **StrikeThru**):

- **Bold**
- **Italic**
- **Name**
- **Size**
- **StrikeThrough**
- **Underline**
- **Weight**

To create a Font object, you dimension it as a new object of type **StdFont**. For example, here's how we install 24-point Arial as the font in a text box, using a Font object:

```
Private Sub Command1_Click()
    Dim Font1 As New StdFont
    Font1.Size = 24
    Font1.Name = "Arial"
    Set Text1.Font = Font1
End Sub
```

Which Fonts Are Available?

You can also determine which fonts are available for either screen or printer by checking the **Fonts** property of the Visual Basic Printer and Screen objects. This property holds an array (0-based) of the available font's names (note that this collection is *not* a collection of Font objects).

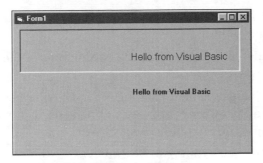

Figure 18.3   Setting font properties in Visual Basic.

Here's an example. To see all the fonts available on your display using Visual Basic, you can loop over all fonts in the Screen object—the total number of fonts is stored in the **FontCount** property—and display the font names in message boxes this way (note that this code may display a lot of message boxes):

```
Private Sub Command1_Click()
    Dim intLoopIndex As Integer

    For intLoopIndex = 0 To Screen.FontCount
        MsgBox Screen.Fonts(intLoopIndex)
    Next intLoopIndex
End Sub
```

TIP: *You can format text when you print it to forms, picture boxes, or the Printer object by determining its width and height, and you do that with the **TextWidth** and **TextHeight** methods.*

Drawing Lines

You draw lines in forms and picture boxes with the **Line** method:

```
object.Line [Step] (x1, y1) [Step] (x2, y2), [color], [B][F]
```

Here are the arguments you pass to **Line**:

- **Step**—Keyword specifying that the starting point coordinates are relative to the current graphics position given by the **CurrentX** and **CurrentY** properties.

- *x1*, *y1*—**Single** values indicating the coordinates of the starting point for the line or rectangle. The **ScaleMode** property determines the unit of measure used. If omitted, the line begins at the position indicated by **CurrentX** and **CurrentY**.

- **Step**—Keyword specifying that the end point coordinates are relative to the line starting point.

- *x2, y2*—**Single** values indicating the coordinates of the end point for the line being drawn.

- *color*—**Long** integer value indicating the RGB color used to draw the line. If omitted, the **ForeColor** property setting is used. You can use the **RGB** function or **QBColor** function to specify the color.

- **B**—If included, causes a box to be drawn using the coordinates to specify opposite corners of the box.

- **F**—If the **B** option is used, the **F** option specifies that the box is filled with the same color used to draw the box. You cannot use **F** without **B**. If **B** is used without **F**, the box is filled with the current **FillColor** and **FillStyle**. The default value for **FillStyle** is transparent.

Let's see an example. Here, we'll draw lines crisscrossing a form and a picture box, **Picture1**, when the user clicks a button:

```
Private Sub Command1_Click()
    Line (0, 0)-(ScaleWidth, ScaleHeight)
    Line (ScaleWidth, 0)-(0, ScaleHeight)

    Picture1.Line (0, 0)-(Picture1.ScaleWidth, Picture1.ScaleHeight)
    Picture1.Line (Picture1.ScaleWidth, 0)-(0, Picture1.ScaleHeight)
End Sub
```

The result of this code appears in Figure 18.4. Now we're drawing lines in forms and picture boxes.

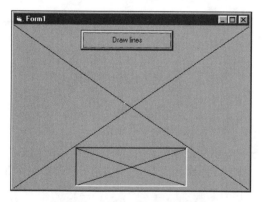

Figure 18.4   Drawing lines in forms and picture boxes.

Drawing Boxes

You draw boxes in forms and picture boxes with the **Line** method, using the **B** argument:

```
object.Line [Step] (x1, y1) [Step] (x2, y2), [color], [B][F]
```

Here are the arguments you pass to **Line**:

- **Step**—Keyword specifying that the starting point coordinates are relative to the current graphics position given by the **CurrentX** and **CurrentY** properties.

- *x1*, *y1*—**Single** values indicating the coordinates of the starting point for the line or rectangle. The **ScaleMode** property determines the unit of measure used. If omitted, the line begins at the position indicated by **CurrentX** and **CurrentY**.

- **Step**—Keyword specifying that the end point coordinates are relative to the line starting point.

- *x2*, *y2*—**Single** values indicating the coordinates of the end point for the line being drawn.

- *color*—**Long** integer value indicating the RGB color used to draw the line. If omitted, the **ForeColor** property setting is used. You can use the **RGB** function or **QBColor** function to specify the color.

- **B**—If included, causes a box to be drawn using the coordinates to specify opposite corners of the box.

- **F**—If the **B** option is used, the **F** option specifies that the box is filled with the same color used to draw the box. You cannot use **F** without **B**. If **B** is used without **F**, the box is filled with the current **FillColor** and **FillStyle**. The default value for **FillStyle** is transparent.

Let's see an example showing how to draw boxes in forms and picture boxes when the user clicks a command button. In this case, we'll draw a box in a form

```
Private Sub Command1_Click()

    Line (ScaleWidth / 4, ScaleHeight / 4)-(3 * ScaleWidth / 4, 3 * _
        ScaleHeight / 4), , B
...
```

and another box in a picture box:

```
Private Sub Command1_Click()
```

```
Line (ScaleWidth / 4, ScaleHeight / 4)-(3 * ScaleWidth / 4, 3 * _
    ScaleHeight / 4), , B
```

```
Picture1.Line (Picture1.ScaleWidth / 4, Picture1.ScaleHeight / 4)-_
    (3 * Picture1.ScaleWidth / 4, 3 * Picture1.ScaleHeight / 4), , B
```

```
End Sub
```

The result of this code appears in Figure 18.5. Now we're drawing boxes in
Visual Basic.

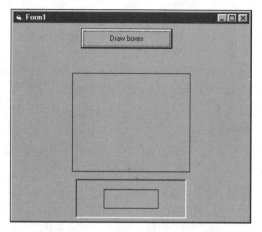

Figure 18.5   Drawing boxes in forms and picture boxes.

Drawing Circles

You use the **Circle** method to draw circles in forms and picture boxes:

```
object.Circle [Step] (x, y), radius, [color, [start, end, [aspect]]]
```

Here are the arguments you pass to **Circle**:

• **Step**—Keyword specifying that the center of the circle, ellipse, or arc is
relative to the current coordinates given by the **CurrentX** and **CurrentY**
properties of *object*.

• *x, y*—**Single** values indicating the coordinates for the center point of the
circle, ellipse, or arc. The **ScaleMode** property of *object* determines the
units of measure used.

• *radius*—**Single** value indicating the radius of the circle, ellipse, or arc.
The **ScaleMode** property of *object* determines the unit of measure used.

- *color*—**Long** integer value indicating the RGB color of the circle's outline. If omitted, the value of the **ForeColor** property is used. You can use the **RGB** function or **QBColor** function to specify the color.

- *start, end*—Single-precision values. When an arc or a partial circle or ellipse is drawn, *start* and *end* specify (in radians) the beginning and end positions of the arc. The range for both is –2 pi radians to 2 pi radians. The default value for *start* is 0 radians; the default for *end* is 2 * pi radians.

- *aspect*—Single-precision value indicating the aspect ratio of the circle. The default value is 1.0, which yields a perfect (nonelliptical) circle on any screen.

As an example, we draw the biggest circle possible in both a form and a picture box, **Picture1**, when the user clicks a command button, **Command1**, using this code, and using a **Switch** function to determine if the form's width or height is larger:

```
Private Sub Command1_Click()

    Circle (ScaleWidth / 2, ScaleHeight / 2), _
        Switch(ScaleWidth >= ScaleHeight, ScaleHeight / 2, _
        ScaleWidth < ScaleHeight, ScaleWidth / 2)

    Picture1.Circle (Picture1.ScaleWidth / 2, Picture1.ScaleHeight / 2), _
        Switch(Picture1.ScaleWidth >= Picture1.ScaleHeight, _
        Picture1.ScaleHeight / 2, Picture1.ScaleWidth < _
        Picture1.ScaleHeight, Picture1.ScaleWidth / 2)

End Sub
```

Running this code gives us the result you see in Figure 18.6.

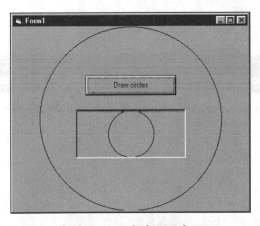

Figure 18.6   Drawing circles in forms and picture boxes.

The code for this example is located in the drawcircle folder on this book's accompanying CD-ROM.

Drawing Ellipses

You use the **Circle** method to draw ellipses in picture boxes and forms, setting the *aspect* argument to set the ellipse's aspect ratio:

```
object.Circle [Step] (x, y), radius, [color, [start, end, [aspect]]]
```

Here are the arguments you pass to **Circle**:

- **Step**—Keyword specifying that the center of the circle, ellipse, or arc is relative to the current coordinates given by the **CurrentX** and **CurrentY** properties of *object*.

- *x, y*—**Single** values indicating the coordinates for the center point of the circle, ellipse, or arc. The **ScaleMode** property of *object* determines the units of measure used.

- *radius*—**Single** value indicating the radius of the circle, ellipse, or arc. The **ScaleMode** property of *object* determines the unit of measure used.

- *color*—**Long** integer value indicating the RGB color of the circle's outline. If omitted, the value of the **ForeColor** property is used. You can use the **RGB** function or **QBColor** function to specify the color.

- *start, end*—Single-precision values. When an arc or a partial circle or ellipse is drawn, *start* and *end* specify (in radians) the beginning and end positions of the arc. The range for both is –2 pi radians to 2 pi radians. The default value for *start* is 0 radians; the default for *end* is 2 * pi radians.

- *aspect*—Single-precision value indicating the aspect ratio of the circle. The default value is 1.0, which yields a perfect (nonelliptical) circle on any screen.

Here's how it works: the aspect ratio is the ratio of the vertical to horizontal axes in the ellipse, and the length of the ellipse's major (that is, longer) axis is the value you specify in the *radius* argument. As an example, we draw an ellipse in both a form and a picture box, **Picture1**, with this code when the user clicks a command button, **Command1**. In this case, we use a vertical to horizontal ratio of 0.8 for both ellipses:

```
Private Sub Command1_Click()

    Circle (ScaleWidth / 2, ScaleHeight / 2), _
        Switch(ScaleWidth >= ScaleHeight, ScaleHeight / 2, _
        ScaleWidth < ScaleHeight, ScaleWidth / 2), , , , 0.8
```

```
    Picture1.Circle (Picture1.ScaleWidth / 2, Picture1.ScaleHeight / 2), _
        Switch(Picture1.ScaleWidth >= Picture1.ScaleHeight, _
        Picture1.ScaleHeight / 2, Picture1.ScaleWidth < _
        Picture1.ScaleHeight, Picture1.ScaleWidth / 2), , , , 0.8
```

End Sub

Running the preceding code gives you the result you see in Figure 18.7. The program is a success. Now we're drawing ellipses in Visual Basic.

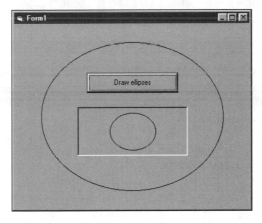

Figure 18.7   Drawing ellipses with Visual Basic.

Drawing Arcs

You use the **Circle** method to draw arcs, using the *start*, *end*, and *aspect* arguments:

object.Circle [Step] (*x, y*), *radius*, [*color*, [*start*, *end*, [*aspect*]]]

Here are the arguments you pass to **Circle**:

- **Step**—Keyword specifying that the center of the circle, ellipse, or arc is relative to the current coordinates given by the **CurrentX** and **CurrentY** properties of *object*.

- *x, y*—**Single** values indicating the coordinates for the center point of the circle, ellipse, or arc. The **ScaleMode** property of *object* determines the units of measure used.

- *radius*—**Single** value indicating the radius of the circle, ellipse, or arc. The **ScaleMode** property of *object* determines the unit of measure used.

- *color*—**Long** integer value indicating the RGB color of the circle's outline. If omitted, the value of the **ForeColor** property is used. You can use the **RGB** function or **QBColor** function to specify the color.

- *start, end*—Single-precision values. When an arc or a partial circle or ellipse is drawn, *start* and *end* specify (in radians) the beginning and end positions of the arc. The range for both is –2 pi radians to 2 pi radians. The default value for *start* is 0 radians; the default for *end* is 2 * pi radians.

- *aspect*—Single-precision value indicating the aspect ratio of the circle. The default value is 1.0, which yields a perfect (nonelliptical) circle on any screen.

In Visual Basic, an arc is part of an ellipse. To draw an arc, you proceed as though you were going to draw an ellipse, including specifying the origin, major radius (in the radius argument), color, and aspect ratio. Then you specify values for the beginning and end of the arc, in radians (in other words, radians go from 0 to 2 * pi for a full circle).

Let's see an example. In this case, we draw a convex arc in a form and a concave arc in a picture box, **Picture1**, when the user clicks a command button, **Command1**:

```
Private Sub Command1_Click()

    Circle (ScaleWidth / 2, ScaleHeight / 2), _
        Switch(ScaleWidth >= ScaleHeight, ScaleHeight / 2, _
        ScaleWidth < ScaleHeight, ScaleWidth / 2), , 0, 3.14, 0.8

    Picture1.Circle (Picture1.ScaleWidth / 2, Picture1.ScaleHeight / 2), _
        Switch(Picture1.ScaleWidth >= Picture1.ScaleHeight, _
        Picture1.ScaleHeight / 2, Picture1.ScaleWidth < _
        Picture1.ScaleHeight, Picture1.ScaleWidth / 2), , 3.14, 6.28, 0.8

End Sub
```

The result of this code appears in Figure 18.8. Now we're drawing arcs in Visual Basic.

The code for this example is located in the drawarcs folder on this book's accompanying CD-ROM.

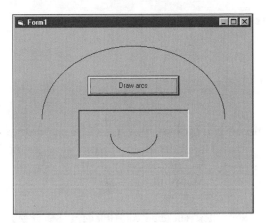

Figure 18.8 *Drawing ellipses in forms and picture boxes.*

Drawing Freehand With The Mouse

The Testing Department is on the phone. Your new program, *SuperDuper-GraphicsPro*, is fine, but how about letting the user draw freehand with the mouse? Hmm, you think, how does that work?

As the user moves the mouse, you can use the **Line** statement to connect the mouse locations passed to your program in the **MouseMove** event handler. Note that you are not passed every pixel the mouse travels over, so you must connect the dots, so to speak, rather than setting individual pixels as a lot of programmers think.

Here's an example where we draw freehand with the mouse. Because we should only draw after the mouse button has gone down, we set up a Boolean flag, **blnDrawFlag**, in the (General) part of the form:

```
Dim blnDrawFlag As Boolean
```

We set that flag to False when the form first loads:

```
Private Sub Form_Load()
    blnDrawFlag = False
End Sub
```

When the user presses the mouse button, we set the current drawing location (**CurrentX**, **CurrentY**) to the location of the mouse (so we don't start drawing from the origin of the form by mistake), and set **blnDrawFlag** to True in the **MouseDown** event handler:

```
Private Sub Form_MouseDown(Button As Integer, Shift As Integer, _
    X As Single, Y As Single)
    CurrentX = X
    CurrentY = Y
    blnDrawFlag = True
End Sub
```

When the user moves the mouse, we check if the **blnDrawFlag** is True in the **MouseMove** event, and if so, draw a line from the current drawing location to the current (X, Y) position (if you omit the first coordinate of a line, Visual Basic uses the current drawing location):

```
Private Sub Form_MouseDown(Button As Integer, Shift As Integer, _
    X As Single, Y As Single)
    If blnDrawFlag Then Line -(X, Y)
End Sub
```

When the mouse button goes up, we set **blnDrawFlag** to False in the **MouseUp** event:

```
Private Sub Form_MouseDown(Button As Integer, Shift As Integer, _
    X As Single, Y As Single)
    blnDrawFlag = False
End Sub
```

Running this program results in the kind of display you see in Figure 18.9, where we're letting the user draw with the mouse. Note that we've also changed the mouse cursor into a cross in this drawing example, by setting the form's **MousePointer** property to 2.

Now we're drawing freehand in Visual Basic. The code for this example is located in the drawfreehand folder on this book's accompanying CD-ROM.

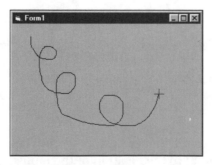

Figure 18.9   Drawing freehand with the mouse.

Filling Figures With Color

To fill figures with color, you can use the **FillColor** property of forms and picture boxes, along with the **FillStyle** property to set the type of fill you want.

Let's see an example. Here, we'll draw a circle and a box in a form in the default drawing color (black) and fill those figures with solid blue when the user clicks a button, **Command1**. First, we set the form's **FillColor** property to blue:

```
Private Sub Command1_Click()
    FillColor = RGB(0, 0, 255)
...
```

Then we specify we want figures colored in solidly by setting the **FillStyle** property to **vbSolid** (for more on **FillStyle**, see the next topic in this chapter):

```
Private Sub Command1_Click()
    FillColor = RGB(0, 0, 255)
    FillStyle = vbFSSolid
...
```

Finally we draw the box and the circle:

```
Private Sub Command1_Click()
    FillColor = RGB(0, 0, 255)
    FillStyle = vbFSSolid
    Line (0, 0)-(ScaleWidth / 2, ScaleHeight / 2), , B
    Circle (3 * ScaleWidth / 4, 3 * ScaleHeight / 4), ScaleHeight / 4
End Sub
```

That's it—now the preceding code will draw a box and a circle with a black border, filled in blue, as shown in Figure 18.10.

Figure 18.10   Filling figures with color.

TIP: *If you use the **F** argument when drawing boxes with the **Line** method, Visual Basic will use the color you specify for the box's drawing color (and if you didn't specify a color, it will use the current **ForeGround** color) instead of the **FillColor**.*

Filling Figures With Patterns

You can use the form and picture box **FillStyle** property to set the fill pattern in Visual Basic graphics. Here are the possibilities:

- **VbFSSolid**—0; solid
- **VbFSTransparent**—1 (the default); transparent
- **VbHorizontalLine**—2; horizontal line
- **VbVerticalLine**—3; vertical line
- **VbUpwardDiagonal**—4; upward diagonal
- **VbDownwardDiagonal**—5; downward diagonal
- **VbCross**—6; cross
- **VbDiagonalCross**—7; diagonal cross

Figure 18.11 shows what the fill patterns look like. The default, **VbFSTransparent**, means that by default figures are not filled in.

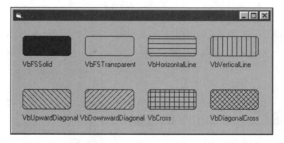

Figure 18.11   The Visual Basic fill patterns.

Setting Figure Drawing Style And Drawing Width

The Aesthetic Design Department is on the phone. Can't you do something about the graphics figures in your program? Maybe make them—dotted? You think, *dotted*?

Visual Basic can help: just set the **DrawStyle** property in forms or picture boxes. Here are the possible values for that property:

- **vbSolid**—1 (the default); solid (the border is centered on the edge of the shape)

- **vbDash**—2; dash

- **vbDot**—3; dot

- **vbDashDot**—4; dash-dot

- **vbDashDotDot**—5; dash-dot-dot

- **vbInvisible**—5; invisible

- **vbInsideSolid**—6; inside solid (the outer edge of the border is the outer edge of the figure)

You can also set the drawing width with the **DrawWidth** property.

Here's an example where we set the **DrawStyle** property to dashed and draw two figures in a form, a box and a circle:

```
Private Sub Command1_Click()
    DrawStyle = vbDash
    Line (0, 0)-(ScaleWidth / 2, ScaleHeight / 2), , B
    Circle (3 * ScaleWidth / 4, 3 * ScaleHeight / 4), ScaleHeight / 4
End Sub
```

The result of the preceding code appears in Figure 18.12.

TIP: *You cannot use different drawing styles if the drawing width is not set to 1.*

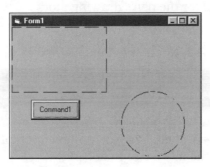

Figure 18.12   Drawing dashed figures.

Drawing Points

To draw individual points, you use **PSet** in forms and picture boxes like this:

```
object.PSet [Step] (x, y), [color]
```

Here are the arguments you pass to **PSet**:

- **Step**—Keyword specifying that the coordinates are relative to the current graphics position given by the **CurrentX** and **CurrentY** properties.

- *x, y*—**Single** values indicating the horizontal (x-axis) and vertical (y-axis) coordinates of the point to set.

- *color*—**Long** integer value indicating the RGB color specified for the point. If omitted, the current **ForeColor** property setting is used. You can use the **RGB** function or **QBColor** function to specify the color.

You can also use the **Point** method to retrieve the color of a point at a specific (x, y) location.

Setting The Drawing Mode

You draw with *pens* in Windows. Every drawing operation uses these pens. When you set the drawing width, you're really setting the width of the pen; when you set the drawing color, you're setting the color of the pen.

You can also use the **DrawMode** property to specify how the current pen interacts with the graphics it already finds in a form or picture box. Here are the possible settings for the pen's drawing mode:

- **vbBlackness**—1, Blackness

- **vbNotMergePen**—2, Not Merge Pen; inverse of setting 15 (Merge Pen)

- **vbMaskNotPen**—3, Mask Not Pen; combination of the colors common to the background color and the inverse of the pen

- **vbNotCopyPen**—4, Not Copy Pen; inverse of setting 13 (Copy Pen)

- **vbMaskPenNot**—5, Mask Pen Not; combination of the colors common to both the pen and the inverse of the display

- **vbInvert**—6, Invert; inverse of the display color

- **vbXorPen**—7, XOR Pen; combination of the colors in the pen and in the display color, but not in both

- **vbNotMaskPen**—8, Not Mask Pen; inverse of setting 9 (Mask Pen)

- **vbMaskPen**—9, Mask Pen; combination of the colors common to both the pen and the display
- **vbNotXorPen**—10, Not XOR Pen; inverse of setting 7 (XOR Pen)
- **vbNop**—11 Nop, No operation; output remains unchanged (in effect, this setting turns drawing off)
- **vbMergeNotPen**—12, Merge Not Pen; combination of the display color and the inverse of the pen color
- **vbCopyPen**—13, Copy Pen (the default); color specified by the **ForeColor** property
- **vbMergePenNot**—14, Merge Pen Not; combination of the pen color and the inverse of the display color
- **vbMergePen**—15, Merge Pen; combination of the pen color and the display color
- **vbWhiteness**—16, Whiteness

For example, we can set the pen to be an invert pen with this code and draw over some lines. The pen will invert the pixels it finds:

```
Private Sub Form_Load()
    Dim intLoopIndex As Integer

    For intLoopIndex = 1 To 9
        DrawWidth = intLoopIndex
        Line (0, intLoopIndex * ScaleHeight / 10) (ScaleWidth, _
            intLoopIndex * ScaleHeight / 10)
    Next intLoopIndex

    DrawMode = vbInvert
    DrawWidth = 10
    Line (0, 0)-(ScaleWidth, ScaleHeight)
    Line (0, ScaleHeight)-(ScaleWidth, 0)
End Sub
```

The result of this code appears in Figure 18.13; the two diagonal lines are drawn with the inverted pen.

TIP: *The XOR (exclusive OR) pen is a popular one, because when you draw with it twice in the same location, the display is restored to its original condition. This happens because if you XOR number A to number B twice, number B is restored. Programmers use this to draw figures they know they'll need to erase, such as when letting the user stretch a graphics figure with the mouse. In such a case, each figure you draw will have to be erased before you can draw the next one to give the illusion of stretching the figure. What programmers usually do is to draw the stretched figure with the XOR pen, and when it's time to erase it, they draw it again with the same pen, thereby restoring the screen.*

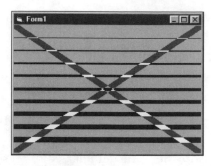

Figure 18.13   Drawing with the Invert pen.

The code for this example is located in the drawinvert folder on this book's accompanying CD-ROM.

Setting Drawing Scales

Forms and picture boxes have a number of scale properties, and perhaps the most popular one is **ScaleMode**, which sets the units of measurement in a picture box. Here are the possible values for **ScaleMode** (note that when you set the scale mode of a picture box, all measurements are in those new units, including coordinates passed to your program, like mouse down locations):

- **vbUser**—0; indicates that one or more of the **ScaleHeight**, **ScaleWidth**, **ScaleLeft**, and **ScaleTop** properties are set to custom values
- **vbTwips**—1 (the default); twip (1440 twips per logical inch; 567 twips per logical centimeter)
- **vbPoints**—2; point (72 points per logical inch)
- **vbPixels**—3; pixel (smallest unit of monitor or printer resolution)
- **vbCharacters**—4; character (horizontal equals 120 twips per unit; vertical equals 240 twips per unit)
- **vbInches**—5; inch
- **vbMillimeters**—6; millimeter
- **vbCentimeters**—7; centimeter
- **vbHimetric**—8; HiMetric
- **vbContainerPosition**—9; units used by the control's container to determine the control's position
- **vbContainerSize**—10; units used by the control's container to determine the control's size

For example, to report the mouse location in pixels in a form using two text boxes, **Text1** and **Text2**, we set the form's **ScaleMode** property to **vbPixels** when the form loads:

```
Private Sub Form_Load()
    ScaleMode = vbPixels
End Sub
```

This means that the X and Y values for the mouse location passed to us will be in pixels, so we can display those coordinates in the text boxes this way:

```
Private Sub Form_MouseMove(Button As Integer, Shift As Integer, X As _
    Single, Y As Single)
    Text1.Text = "Mouse x location (in pixels): " & Str(X)
    Text2.Text = "Mouse y location (in pixels): " & Str(Y)
End Sub
```

The result of the preceding code appears in Figure 18.14.

If you set the scale mode to **vbUser**, you can define your own units by setting the dimensions of the picture box using the **ScaleLeft**, **ScaleTop**, **ScaleWidth**, and **ScaleHeight** properties. This can be very useful if you're plotting points and want to use a picture box as a graph.

TIP: The **ScaleWidth** and **ScaleHeight** properties of a picture box hold the image's actual dimensions (in units determined by the **ScaleMode** property), not the **Width** and **Height** properties, which hold the control's width and height (including the border).

The code for this example is located in the pixelmouse folder on this book's accompanying CD-ROM.

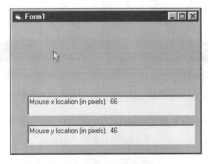

Figure 18.14   Displaying mouse location in pixels.

Using The Screen Object

The Visual Basic Screen object offers you a lot of information about the current display. Here are that object's properties:

- **TwipsPerPixelX**—Twips per pixel horizontally
- **TwipsPerPixelY**—Twips per pixel vertically
- **Height**—Screen height
- **Width**—Screen width
- **Fonts**—Collection of names of the available fonts
- **FontCount**—Total number of screen fonts available
- **ActiveControl**—Currently active control
- **ActiveForm**—Currently active form
- **MouseIcon**—Returns or sets a custom mouse icon
- **MousePointer**—Returns or sets a value indicating the type of mouse pointer displayed when the mouse is over a particular part of an object at runtime

Resizing Graphics When The Window Is Resized

The Testing Department is on the phone. When the user resizes your *Super-DuperGraphicsPro* program, the graphics in the program don't resize themselves. You ask, should they? They say, yes.

You can use the **Resize** event to catch window or picture box resizes. Let's see an example. Here, we add a new subroutine, **DrawBox**, to a form. This subroutine draws a rectangle in a form:

```
Private Sub DrawBox()
    Line (ScaleWidth / 4, ScaleHeight / 4)-(3 * ScaleWidth / 4, _
        3 * ScaleHeight / 4), , B
End Sub
```

We can call **DrawBox** in the **Load** event to draw the box the first time (set the form's **AutoRedraw** property to True to draw graphics in the **Form Load** event):

```
Private Sub Form_Load()
    DrawBox
End Sub
```

When the user resizes the form, we clear the form and redraw the box in the **Form Resize** event:

```
Private Sub Form_Resize()
    Cls
    DrawBox
End Sub
```

Now the program resizes its graphics to match the user's actions. The code for this example is located in the resizer folder on this book's accompanying CD-ROM.

Copying Pictures To And Pasting Pictures From The Clipboard

The users love your new graphics program, *SuperDuperGraphicsPro*, but would like to export the images they create to other programs. How can you do that?

You can copy the images to the Clipboard, letting the user paste them into other programs. To place data in the Clipboard, you use **SetData**, and to retrieve data from the Clipboard, you use **GetData**.

An example will make this clearer. Here, we'll paste a picture from **Picture1** to **Picture2** using two buttons, **Command1** and **Command2**. When the user clicks **Command1**, we'll copy the picture from **Picture1** to the Clipboard; when the user clicks **Command2**, we'll paste the picture to **Picture2**.

To place the image in **Picture1** into the Clipboard, we use **SetData**:

```
Clipboard.SetData data, [format]
```

Here are the possible values for the *format* parameter for images:

- **vbCFBitmap**—2; bitmap (BMP) files
- **vbCFMetafile**—3; metafile (WMF) files
- **vbCFDIB**—8; device-independent bitmap (DIB)
- **vbCFPalette**—9; color palette

If you omit the format parameter, Visual Basic will determine the correct format, so we'll just copy the picture from **Picture1.Picture** to the Clipboard this way:

```
Private Sub Command1_Click()
    Clipboard.SetData Picture1.Picture
End Sub
```

To paste the picture, use **GetData( )**:

```
Clipboard.GetData ([format])
```

The *format* parameter here is the same as for **SetData( )**, and as before, if you don't specify the format, Visual Basic will determine it, so when the user clicks the second button, we paste the image into **Picture2** this way:

```
Private Sub Command2_Click()
    Picture2.Picture = Clipboard.GetData()
End Sub
```

That's all it takes—when you run the program and click the Copy and then the Paste button, the image is copied to the Clipboard and then pasted into the second picture box. Now we're using the Clipboard with picture boxes.

Printing Graphics

Visual Basic has two ways of printing both text and graphics:

- Printing entire forms using the **PrintForm** method
- Printing with the Printer object and using graphical methods as well as the **NewPage** and **EndDoc** methods

The **PrintForm** Method

The **PrintForm** method sends an image of a given form to the printer, complete with menu bar, title bar, and so on. To print information from your application with **PrintForm**, you must first display that information on a form and then print that form with the **PrintForm** method like this:

```
[form.]PrintForm
```

If you omit the form name, Visual Basic prints the current form. Note that if a form contains graphics, those graphics print *only* if the form's **AutoRedraw** property is set to True.

The Printer Object

The Printer object represents the default printer and supports text and graphics methods like **Print**, **PSet**, **Line**, **PaintPicture**, and **Circle**. You use these methods on the Printer object just as you would on a form or picture box. The Printer object also has all the font properties we've seen earlier in this chapter.

When you finish placing the information on the Printer object, you use the **EndDoc** method to send the output to the printer. You can also print multiple-page documents by using the **NewPage** method on the Printer object.

TIP: *When applications close, they automatically use the **EndDoc** method to send any pending information on the Printer object.*

The **Printers** Collection

The **Printers** collection is an object that contains all the printers that are available, and each printer in the collection has a unique (0-based) index for identification. Let's see an example. Here, we select the first printer from the **Printers** collection to be the current printer by loading that printer into the Printer object:

```
Private Sub Command1_Click()
    Set Printer = Printers(0)
End Sub
```

Using the **Printers** collection in this way lets you print to printers other than the default.

Layering Graphics With The **AutoRedraw** And **ClipControls** Properties

When you create graphics in Visual Basic, bear in mind that graphical controls and labels, nongraphical controls, and graphics methods appear on different *layers*. The behavior of these layers depends on three things: the **AutoRedraw** property, the **ClipControls** property, and whether graphics methods appear inside or outside the **Paint** event. Usually the layers of a form or other container are as follows:

- *Front layer*—Nongraphical controls like command buttons, checkboxes, and file controls.
- *Middle layer*—Graphical controls and labels.
- *Back layer*—Drawing space for the form or container. This is where the results of graphics methods appear.

Anything in one layer covers anything in the layer behind it, so graphics you create with the graphical controls appear behind the other controls on the form, and all graphics you create with the graphics methods appear below all graphical and nongraphical controls. Combining settings for **AutoRedraw** and **ClipControls** and placing graphics methods inside or outside the **Paint** event affects layering and the performance of the application. You can find the effects created by different combinations of **AutoRedraw** and **ClipControls** and placement of graphics methods in Table 18.3.

*Table 18.3   Layering with **AutoRedraw** and **ClipControls**.*

AutoRedraw	ClipControls	Methods In/Out Paint Event	Description
True	True (default)	**Paint** event ignored	Normal layering.
True	False	**Paint** event ignored	Normal layering. Forms with many controls that do not overlap may paint faster because no clipping region is calculated or created.
False (default)	True (default)	In	Normal layering.
False	True	Out	Nongraphical controls in front. Graphics methods and graphical controls appear mixed in the middle and back layers. Not recommended by Microsoft.
False	False	In	Normal layering, affecting only pixels that were previously covered or that appear when resizing a form.
False	False	Out	Graphics methods and all controls appear mixed in the three layers. Not recommended by Microsoft.

Chapter 19

Working With Images

If you need an immediate solution to:	See page:
Adding Images To Controls	616
Adding Images To Forms	617
Using Image Controls	617
Using Picture Boxes	618
AutoSizing Picture Boxes	619
Loading Images In At Runtime	619
Clearing (Erasing) Images	621
Storing Images In Memory Using The Picture Object	621
Using Arrays Of Picture Objects	623
Adding Picture Clip Controls To A Program	623
Selecting Images In A Picture Clip Control Using Coordinates	625
Selecting Images In A Picture Clip Control Using Rows And Columns	629
Flipping Images	630
Stretching Images	632
Creating Image Animation	634
Handling Images Bit By Bit	635
Creating Grayscale Images	637
Lightening Images	640
Creating "Embossed" Images	642
Creating "Engraved" Images	644
Sweeping Images	645
Blurring Images	646
Freeing Memory Used By Graphics	647

In Depth

Visual Basic has quite an array of techniques for dealing with images. In this chapter, we'll work with bitmapped images in our programs, creating some powerful effects. We'll see how to load images in, display them in a variety of ways, including flipping them and stretching them, creating image effects, and saving them back to disk.

Images can be an asset to your program, enhancing the visual interface a great deal. We won't work on creating images here—instead, we'll work on reading them in, working on them, and displaying them from image files on disk.

There are a number of different image formats that you use today: bitmap (.bmp), GIF, JPEG, WMF (Windows metafile format), enhanced WMF, icon (.ico), compressed bitmap (.rle), and more. Visual Basic can handle all these formats.

However, you'll notice some anachronisms that have crept in over the years that indicate Visual Basic's historical development—for example, the picture clip control, which we'll see in this chapter, can only handle bitmaps with a maximum of 16 colors. This control is still a useful one, but it has largely been superseded by the more powerful image list control (which we cover in its own chapter in this book).

Picture Boxes Vs. Image Controls

The main controls that programmers use to display images are image controls and picture boxes. That's not to say there aren't other ways to display, of course: you can load images into many controls, like buttons, and even display them in forms, as we'll see in this chapter. However, when programmers think of displaying and working with images, they often think of picture boxes and image controls.

It's worth noting the difference between these controls. The image control really has one main purpose: to display images. If that's your goal, the image control is a good choice. On the other hand, picture boxes offer you a great deal more, if you need it. You can even think of picture boxes as mini-paint programs, because they include methods to let you draw text (on top of the current image in the picture box, which is good if you want to label elements in that image), draw circles, lines, boxes, and so on.

Note, however, that the added power of picture boxes comes with an added cost in terms of heavier use of system resources. If you don't need a picture box's added functionality, use an image control. For more on this topic, take a look at Chapter 10.

Image Effects: Working With Images Bit By Bit

In this chapter, we'll have some fun seeing how to work with images bit by bit. There are two main ways of doing that in Visual Basic: sticking with the Visual Basic methods, and using Windows methods directly.

We'll stick with the Visual Basic methods, which, although slower, are vastly easier to use and get the job done well. However, you should know that we'll take a look at the Windows way of doing things later in the book, in the chapter on connecting to Windows directly. (And you may have noticed our bitmapped menu item example in the chapter on menus works directly with Windows to create a bitmap object that it loads into a menu.)

We'll see quite a few image effects in this chapter: embossing images, engraving images, grayscale images, image lightening, blurring images, making an image seem to sweep from upper left to lower right, and more. All these effects are powerful techniques that you might not expect from Visual Basic.

That's it for the overview of images for the moment—it's time to turn to the Immediate Solutions.

Immediate Solutions

Adding Images To Controls

The Aesthetic Design Department is calling again. Can't you add some images to the controls in your program? That would make it look so much nicer.

These days, you *can* add images to many Visual Basic controls. For example, you can now display images in checkboxes, command buttons, and option buttons if you first set their **Style** property to **Graphical (Style = 1)**, then place the name of the image file you want to use in the control's **Picture** property. As an example, we display a bitmapped image in a command button in Figure 19.1.

At runtime, you can load a picture into the control's **Picture** property using the **LoadPicture** function:

```
Private Sub Command1_Click()
    Command1.Picture = LoadPicture("c:\image.bmp")
End Sub
```

Besides buttons, you can also display images in the Visual Basic image combo box—see Chapter 8. We also used a few advanced techniques to display an image in a menu item in Chapter 5.

The Windows common controls can also display images, including such controls as tree views, list views, and tab strips. There, you load the images you want into an image list control, and then connect that image list to the control using the control's **ImageList** property. For more information, see Chapter 16, and the chapters on the various Windows common controls.

Figure 19.1   Displaying an image in a button.

Adding Images To Forms

The Aesthetic Design Department is on the phone again. The form in your program looks pretty drab. How about spicing it up with an image of the company founder? Hmm, you wonder, how would you do that?

You can load an image into a form using the form's **Picture** property, both at design time or at runtime. As an example, we've placed an image in the form you see in Figure 19.2. Note that the controls on that form are layered on top of the form's image.

At runtime, you can use the **LoadPicture** function to read in an image and display it in a form like this:

```
Private Sub Command1_Click()
    Form1.Picture = LoadPicture("c:\image.bmp")
End Sub
```

The code for the example you see in Figure 19.2 is located in the imageform folder on this book's accompanying CD-ROM.

TIP: Note that if you just want to set the background color of a form to some uniform color, you should use the form's **BackColor** property instead of loading an image in.

Figure 19.2   Displaying an image in a form.

Using Image Controls

You use image controls to display images. Although that might seem obvious, it's usually the deciding factor in whether or not to use an image control or a picture box. Image controls are simple controls that don't use many system resources, whereas picture boxes are more powerful controls that do. When you just have an image to display, this is the control to use.

You load an image into an image control using its **Picture** property at design time or runtime. When you load an image in at runtime, use the **LoadPicture** function this way:

```
Private Sub Command1_Click()
    Image1.Picture = LoadPicture("c:\image.bmp")
End Sub
```

As you can see in the image control in Figure 19.3, image controls have no border by default, although you can add one using the **BorderStyle** property. In addition, image controls size themselves to the image they display automatically, unless you set their **Stretch** property to True, in which case they size the image to fit themselves.

Image controls support events like **Click**, **DblClick**, **MouseDown**, **MouseMove**, and **MouseUp**. However, they do not support all the events that picture boxes support, such as **Key** events. In general, you use image controls for one purpose only: to display an image (which can include stretching that image). Both image controls and picture boxes can read in images in all the popular formats: GIF, JPEG, BMP, and so on.

For a lot more information on image controls, take a look at Chapter 10.

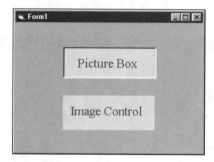

Figure 19.3   An image control and a picture box.

Using Picture Boxes

Picture boxes are like mini-paint programs. Not only can they display images—they can also create or modify them. You can use the built-in methods of picture boxes to draw text, ellipses, lines, boxes, and more, on top of the images they display.

You load an image into a picture box using its **Picture** property at design time or runtime. When you load an image in at runtime, use the **LoadPicture** function this way:

```
Private Sub Command1_Click()
    Picture1.Picture = LoadPicture("c:\image.bmp")
End Sub
```

As you can see in Figure 19.3, picture boxes display a border by default, although you can remove it with the control's **BorderStyle** property. By default, picture boxes display their images starting at the picture box's upper-left corner (leaving uncovered space at the lower-right blank), but you can change that by setting the **AutoSize** property to True. When you set **AutoSize** to True, the picture box sizes itself to fit its displayed image.

You can use a picture box's **PaintPicture** method to draw an image at different locations in a picture box, and even flip it as we'll see in this chapter. Both image controls and picture boxes can read in images in all the popular formats: GIF, JPEG, BMP, and so on.

For a lot more information on picture boxes, take a look at Chapter 10.

AutoSizing Picture Boxes

Image controls size themselves automatically to fit the image they're displaying—but picture boxes don't, by default. You can, however, make them resize themselves to fit the image they're displaying by setting the picture box's **AutoSize** property to True. You can set **AutoSize** to True either at design time or at runtime.

Loading Images In At Runtime

You know that you use the **Picture** property to load images into image controls and picture boxes, but how does that work at runtime? This code doesn't seem to work:

```
Private Sub Command1_Click()
    Image1.Picture = "c:\image.bmp"    'Error!
End Sub
```

You have to use the Visual Basic **LoadPicture** function here. That looks like this when we load an image into an image control:

```
Private Sub Command1_Click()
    Image1.Picture = LoadPicture("c:\image.bmp")
End Sub
```

Here's how we load that image into a picture box:

```
Private Sub Command1_Click()
    Picture1.Picture = LoadPicture("c:\image.bmp")
End Sub
```

You can also load an image into a Visual Basic Picture object. Let's see an example of how that works. First, we create a Picture object, **picObject1**:

```
Private Sub Command1_Click()
    Dim picObject1 As Picture
...
End Sub
```

Next, we load the image into that Picture object using **LoadPicture**:

```
Private Sub Command1_Click()
    Dim picObject1 As Picture
    Set picObject1 = LoadPicture("c:\image.bmp")
...
End Sub
```

Finally, we just set a picture box's **Picture** property to the Picture object, and that's it:

```
Private Sub Command1_Click()
    Dim picObject1 As Picture
    Set picObject1 = LoadPicture("c:\image.bmp")
    Set Picture1.Picture = picObject1
End Sub
```

If, on the other hand, you want to *save* an image to disk, use the picture box's **SavePicture** method.

Clearing (Erasing) Images

One of the handiest things to know about handling images is how to clear an image in a form or picture box. You use the **Cls** method (which originally stood for "Clear Screen") to do that (image controls don't have a **Cls** method).

For example, here's how we erase an image in a picture box when the user clicks that picture box:

```
Private Sub Picture1_Click()
    Picture1.Cls
End Sub
```

Storing Images In Memory Using The Picture Object

You want to load a number of images into your program, *SuperDuperGraphics-Pro*, and store them in the background, invisibly. How do you do that?

Visual Basic offers a number of ways of loading in images and storing them unobserved (all of them covered in this book, of course). You can use the image list control to store images, or the picture clip controls (picture clips are covered in this chapter). You can even load images into picture boxes and make those picture boxes invisible (by setting their **Visible** properties to False). And you can use Picture objects. In fact, in some ways, you can think of the Picture object as an invisible picture box that takes up far fewer system resources (although Picture objects don't have drawing methods like **Line** or **Circle**, like picture boxes). The Picture object supports bitmaps, GIF images, JPEG images, metafiles, and icons.

Let's see an example to show how the Picture object works. First, we create a Picture object, **picObject1**:

```
Private Sub Command1_Click()
    Dim picObject1 As Picture
    ...
End Sub
```

Then we load the image into that Picture object using **LoadPicture**:

```
Private Sub Command1_Click()
    Dim picObject1 As Picture
    Set picObject1 = LoadPicture("c:\image.bmp")
    ...
End Sub
```

Finally, we just set a picture box's **Picture** property to the Picture object, and that's it:

```
Private Sub Command1_Click()
    Dim picObject1 As Picture
    Set picObject1 = LoadPicture("c:\image.bmp")
    Set Picture1.Picture = picObject1
End Sub
```

You can also use the **Render** method to draw images with the Picture object (although **PaintPicture** is Microsoft's preferred method these days).

The **Render** Method

Here's how you use the **Render** method to draw images with the Picture object:

```
PictureObject.Render(hdc, xdest, ydest, destwid, desthgt, xsrc, ysrc, _
    srcwid, srchgt, wbounds)
```

Here are what the arguments for **Render** mean:

- *hdc*—The handle to the destination object's device context, such as **Picture1.hDC**.

- *xdest*—The x-coordinate of the upper-left corner of the drawing region in the destination object. This coordinate is in the scale units of the destination object.

- *ydest*—The y-coordinate of the upper-left corner of the drawing region in the destination object. This coordinate is in the scale units of the destination object.

- *destwid*—The width of the drawing region in the destination object, expressed in the scale units of the destination object.

- *desthgt*—The height of the drawing region in the destination object, expressed in the scale units of the destination object.

- *xsrc*—The x-coordinate of the upper-left corner of the drawing region in the source object. This coordinate is in HiMetric units.

- *ysrc*—The y-coordinate of the upper-left corner of the drawing region in the source object. This coordinate is in HiMetric units.

- *srcwid*—The width of the drawing region in the source object, expressed in HiMetric units.

- *srchgt*—The height of the drawing region in the source object, expressed in HiMetric units.

- *wbounds*—The bounds of a metafile. This argument should be passed a value of Null unless drawing to a metafile, in which case the argument is passed a user-defined type corresponding to a **RECTL** structure.

TIP: *Note that some of the arguments to **Render** must be in HiMetric units. Here's an important note: You can convert from one set of units to another using the Visual Basic **ScaleX** and **ScaleY** functions, so use those functions to convert from twips or pixels to HiMetric.*

Using Arrays Of Picture Objects

You can use an array of Picture objects to keep a series of graphics in memory without using a form that contains multiple picture box or image controls. This is good for creating animation sequences or other applications where rapid image changes are required.

Let's see an example. Here, we'll create an array of Picture objects and load images into them. We start by setting up an array of two Picture objects as a form-wide array:

```
Dim picObjects(1 To 2) As Picture
```

Then when the form loads, we read in two image files into the array:

```
Private Sub Form_Load()
    Set picObjects(1) = LoadPicture("c:\vbbb\pictureanimation\image1.bmp")
    Set picObjects(2) = LoadPicture("c:\vbbb\pictureanimation\image2.bmp")
End Sub
```

Now the images in the array will be available for use in our program (and we'll use them in a later topic in this chapter—see "Creating Image Animation").

Adding Picture Clip Controls To A Program

One way of storing images in a Visual Basic program is to use a picture clip control. This control stores a number of images as one large bitmap, and to get the image you want, you have to clip it out of that bitmap. If that sounds a little less convenient to you than using an image list control or array of Picture objects, you're right—it is. Picture clips were first made available long ago in Visual Basic and don't support all the convenience of more modern controls. However, programmers still use them, and we'll cover them here.

TIP: One excellent reason to use picture clip controls besides storing images is to edit existing images, because picture clip controls let you clip rectangular sections of image from exiting images.

To add a picture clip control to a program, follow these steps:

1. Select the Project|Components menu item.
2. Click the Controls tab in the Components dialog box.
3. Select the Microsoft PictureClip Control item.
4. Close the Components dialog box by clicking on OK.
5. This adds the Picture Clip Control's tool to the Visual Basic toolbox; that tool is at the bottom right in Figure 19.4. Use that tool to draw a picture clip control in your program; because the control is invisible at runtime, size and placement of the control don't matter.

Now we add an image that consists of three images added together to the picture clip control, as you can see in Figure 19.5. When you want to get a picture from a picture clip control, you specify the (x, y) coordinates of the bitmap section you want, and its height and width. You can also divide the image up into rows and columns, as we'll see in a few topics.

To put the picture clip control to work, see the next few topics in this chapter.

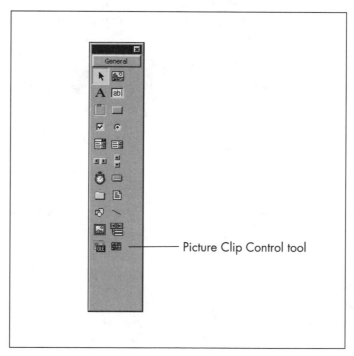
Picture Clip Control tool

Figure 19.4   The Picture Clip Control tool.

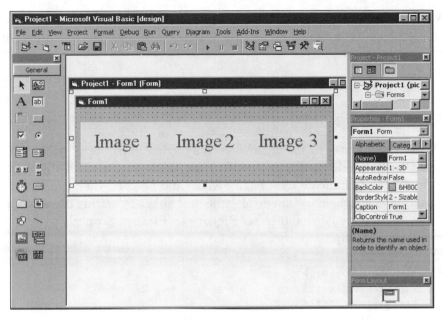

Figure 19.5   Adding a picture clip control to a program.

Selecting Images In A Picture Clip Control Using Coordinates

You've placed all the images you want to store into a picture clip control as one large bitmap. How can you get your images back out again?

There are two ways to get images out of a picture clip control (three, if you count accessing the whole bitmap with the control's **Picture** property): by specifying the image's coordinates in the whole bitmap, or by breaking the bitmap into rows and columns and accessing the image by row and column. After you specify an image, you can retrieve it using the picture clip's **Clip** property. We'll see how to use bitmap coordinates in this topic, and rows and columns in the next topic.

An example will make this clearer. Here, we'll use a picture clip control to hold the three images from the previous topic in this chapter, and flip through them when the user clicks a command button. We'll need a picture clip control, **PictureClip1**; a command button, **Command1**, labeled "Clip next image"; and a picture box, **Picture1**, to display the images in (set **Picture1**'s **AutoSize** property to True so it will resize itself to match the images).

We start by storing the dimensions of each of the three images in the entire bitmap as constants and storing the currently displayed image in an index, **intImageIndex**:

```
Const intImageWidth = 137
Const intImageHeight = 70
Dim intImageIndex As Integer
```

To use coordinates to specify images in a picture clip control, you use **ClipX** and **ClipY** to indicate the upper-left point of the image, and **ClipWidth** and **ClipHeight** to indicate the image's width and height. When the form in our example loads, then, we can display the first image by setting these properties to match that image, and then set **Picture1**'s **Picture** property to the picture clip control's **Clip** property:

```
Private Sub Form_Load()
    PictureClip1.ClipX = 0
    PictureClip1.ClipY = 0
    PictureClip1.ClipWidth = intImageWidth
    PictureClip1.ClipHeight = intImageHeight
    Picture1.Picture = PictureClip1.Clip
End Sub
```

Now the picture box displays the first image. When the user clicks the command button, Command1, we increment the image index, **intImageIndex**:

```
Private Sub Command1_Click()
    intImageIndex = intImageIndex + 1
    If intImageIndex >= 3 Then intImageIndex = 0
...
End Sub
```

Then we reset the **ClipX** property to point to the new image and display it in the picture box (note that we're just working with a strip of images here; if you were working with a grid of images, you'd also have to calculate **ClipY**):

```
Private Sub Command1_Click()
    intImageIndex = intImageIndex + 1
    If intImageIndex >= 3 Then intImageIndex = 0
    PictureClip1.ClipX = intImageIndex * intImageWidth
    Picture1.Picture = PictureClip1.Clip
End Sub
```

Figure 19.6   Using coordinates in a picture clip control to retrieve images.

That's all we need. Run the program now, as shown in Figure 19.6. When the user clicks the Clip Next Image button, the next image appears in the picture box. Our picture clip example is a success.

The code for this example, picclip.frm version 1 (version 2, which appears on the CD-ROM, will include the use of rows and columns and will be developed in the next topic), appears in Listing 19.1.

Listing 19.1   picclip.frm version 1

```
VERSION 6.00
Object = "{27395F88-0C0C-101B-A3C9-08002B2F49FB}#1.1#0"; "PICCLP32.OCX"
Begin VB.Form Form1
    Caption         =   "Form1"
    ClientHeight    =   2370
    ClientLeft      =   60
    ClientTop       =   345
    ClientWidth     =   4680
    LinkTopic       =   "Form1"
    ScaleHeight     =   2370
    ScaleWidth      =   4680
    StartUpPosition =   3   'Windows Default
    Begin VB.CommandButton Command2
        Caption         =   "Get next cell"
        Height          =   495
        Left            =   3120
        TabIndex        =   2
        Top             =   1560
        Width           =   1215
    End
    Begin VB.CommandButton Command1
        Caption         =   "Clip next image"
        Height          =   495
        Left            =   240
        TabIndex        =   1
        Top             =   1560
```

```
            Width              =     1215
        End
        Begin VB.PictureBox Picture1
            AutoSize           =     -1    'True
            Height             =     975
            Left               =     1200
            ScaleHeight        =     915
            ScaleWidth         =     2235
            TabIndex           =     0
            Top                =     240
            Width              =     2295
        End
        Begin PicClip.PictureClip PictureClip1
            Left               =     120
            Top                =     2040
            _ExtentX           =     10874
            _ExtentY           =     1852
            _Version           =     393216
            Picture            =     "picclip.frx":0000
        End
    End
Attribute VB_Name = "Form1"
Attribute VB_GlobalNameSpace = False
Attribute VB_Creatable = False
Attribute VB_PredeclaredId = True
Attribute VB_Exposed = False
Const intImageWidth = 137
Const intImageHeight = 70
Dim intImageIndex As Integer

Private Sub Command1_Click()
    intImageIndex = intImageIndex + 1
    If intImageIndex >= 3 Then intImageIndex = 0
    PictureClip1.ClipX = intImageIndex * intImageWidth
    Picture1.Picture = PictureClip1.Clip
End Sub

Private Sub Form_Load()
    PictureClip1.ClipX = 0
    PictureClip1.ClipY = 0
    PictureClip1.ClipWidth = intImageWidth
    PictureClip1.ClipHeight = intImageHeight
    Picture1.Picture = PictureClip1.Clip
End Sub
```

*Selecting
Images In A
Picture Clip
Control Using
Rows And
Columns*

Selecting Images In A Picture Clip Control Using Rows And Columns

In the previous topic, we saw how to select images in a picture clip control using coordinates in the single large bitmap that picture clip controls use to store images. You can also divide that bitmap up into rows and columns and access images that way.

In fact, using rows and columns is often much easier than using coordinates, because you don't have to figure things out using actual pixel values. Let's see an example. We'll just add some code to the picture clip control example we developed in the previous topic (picclip.frm). To start, we divide the picture clip control's bitmap into rows and columns with the **Rows** and **Columns** properties. Because there are three adjacent images in our bitmap (see Figure 19.5), we have one row and three columns, so we set the **Rows** and **Columns** properties this way when the form loads:

```
Private Sub Form_Load()
    PictureClip1.ClipX = 0
    PictureClip1.ClipY = 0
    PictureClip1.ClipWidth = intImageWidth
    PictureClip1.ClipHeight = intImageHeight
    PictureClip1.Rows = 1
    PictureClip1.Cols = 3
    Picture1.Picture = PictureClip1.Clip
End Sub
```

Now we add a new command button, **Command2**, to the form, and label it "Get next cell". When the user clicks this button, we can increment the image index, **intImageIndex**:

```
Private Sub Command2_Click()
    intImageIndex = intImageIndex + 1
    If intImageIndex >= 3 Then intImageIndex = 0
    ...
End Sub
```

Then we use the picture clip control's **GraphicCell** array to get the new image, placing that image in the picture control's **Picture** property:

```
Private Sub Command2_Click()
    intImageIndex = intImageIndex + 1
    If intImageIndex >= 3 Then intImageIndex = 0
```

```
        Picture1.Picture = PictureClip1.GraphicCell(intImageIndex)
End Sub
```

That's all we need—now the user can click the new button, Get Next Cell, to cycle through the images in the picture clip control, as shown in Figure 19.7. Our picture clip control example is a success.

The code for this example is located in the picclip folder on this book's accompanying CD-ROM.

Figure 19.7   Using rows and columns in a picture clip control to retrieve images.

Flipping Images

You can gain a lot of control over how images are displayed by the **PaintPicture** method, which lets you flip, translate, or resize images:

```
object.PaintPicture picture, x1, y1, [width1, height1, [x2, y2, [width2, _
    height2, [opcode]]]]
```

You can use this method to stretch or flip images in forms, picture boxes, and the Printer object. Here's what the arguments passed to **PaintPicture** mean:

- *picture*—The source of the graphic to be drawn onto the object; should be a **Picture** property.

- *x1*, *y1*—Single-precision values indicating the destination coordinates (x-axis and y-axis) on the object for the picture to be drawn. The **ScaleMode** property of the object determines the unit of measure used.

- *width1*—Single-precision value indicating the destination width of the picture. The **ScaleMode** property of the object determines the unit of measure used. If the destination width is larger or smaller than the source width (*width2*), the picture is stretched or compressed to fit. If omitted, the source width is used.

- *height1*—Single-precision value indicating the destination height of the picture. The **ScaleMode** property of the object determines the unit of measure used. If the destination height is larger or smaller than the source height (*height2*), the picture is stretched or compressed to fit. If omitted, the source height is used.

- *x2, y2*—Single-precision values indicating the coordinates (x-axis and y-axis) of a clipping region within the picture. The **ScaleMode** property of the object determines the unit of measure used. If omitted, 0 is assumed.

- *width2*—Single-precision value indicating the source width of a clipping region within the picture. The **ScaleMode** property of the object determines the unit of measure used. If omitted, the entire source width is used.

- *height2*—Single-precision value indicating the source height of a clipping region within the picture. The **ScaleMode** property of the object determines the unit of measure used. If omitted, the entire source height is used.

- *opcode*—**Long** value or code that is used only with bitmaps. It defines a bit-wise operation (such as **vbMergeCopy**) that is performed on the picture as it is drawn on the object.

You can flip a bitmap horizontally or vertically by using negative values for the destination height (*height1*) and/or the destination width (*width1*). Let's see an example. Here's how we flip the image in the current form horizontally and display it in **Picture2**:

```
Private Sub Form_Load()
    PaintPicture Picture. Picture1.ScaleWidth, 0, _
        -1 * ScaleWidth, ScaleHeight
End Sub
```

If we load the image we used in Figure 19.2 into a form and use the preceding code, we'll get the results you see in Figure 19.8. Now we're flipping images.

The code for this example appears in the imageflip folder on this book's accompanying CD-ROM.

Figure 19.8   Flipping an image in a form.

Stretching Images

The Aesthetic Design Department is calling. The image of the company founder you've put into your program looks fine, but why is it so *small*? Can't you enlarge it?

You can use the **PaintPicture** method to stretch images in forms, picture boxes, and the Printer object. Here's how that method works:

```
object.PaintPicture picture, x1, y1, [width1, height1, [x2, y2, [width2, _
    height2, [opcode]]]]
```

Here's what the arguments passed to **PaintPicture** mean:

- *picture*—The source of the graphic to be drawn onto the object; should be a **Picture** property.

- *x1*, *y1*—Single-precision values indicating the destination coordinates (x-axis and y-axis) on the object for the picture to be drawn. The **ScaleMode** property of the object determines the unit of measure used.

- *width1*—Single-precision value indicating the destination width of the picture. The **ScaleMode** property of the object determines the unit of measure used. If the destination width is larger or smaller than the source width (*width2*), the picture is stretched or compressed to fit. If omitted, the source width is used.

- *height1*—Single-precision value indicating the destination height of the picture. The **ScaleMode** property of the object determines the unit of measure used. If the destination height is larger or smaller than the source height (*height2*), the picture is stretched or compressed to fit. If omitted, the source height is used.

- *x2*, *y2*—Single-precision values indicating the coordinates (x-axis and y-axis) of a clipping region within the picture. The **ScaleMode** property of the object determines the unit of measure used. If omitted, 0 is assumed.

- *width2*—Single-precision value indicating the source width of a clipping region within the picture. The **ScaleMode** property of the object determines the unit of measure used. If omitted, the entire source width is used.

- *height2*—Single-precision value indicating the source height of a clipping region within the picture. The **ScaleMode** property of the object determines the unit of measure used. If omitted, the entire source height is used.

- *opcode*—**Long** value or code that is used only with bitmaps. It defines a bit-wise operation (such as **vbMergeCopy**) that is performed on the picture as it is drawn on the object.

For example, here's how we stretch an image to fill a picture box (here, the picture we're stretching is the picture that already is displayed in the picture box—we're just sizing it to fill the picture box by making its width and height the width and height of the picture box):

```
Private Sub Form_Load()
    Picture1.PaintPicture Picture1.Picture, 0, 0, Picture1.ScaleWidth,_
        Picture1.ScaleHeight
End Sub
```

In Figure 19.9, we're applying this code to the picture in the picture box.

What About Image Controls?

You can stretch (or flip) an image in a picture box, form, or the Printer object using the **PaintPicture** method, but you can't use **PaintPicture** with image controls. Is there still some way of producing interesting graphics effects in an image control?

You can use the image control **Stretch** property. By default, image controls shape themselves to fit the images inside them (after all, their primary purpose is to display images), but if you set the **Stretch** property to True (the default is False), the image control will stretch the image to fit the control. As an example, we're stretching an image in the image control in Figure 19.9.

You can also stretch an image in an image control by resizing the control (using its **Width** and **Height** properties) at runtime as long as the control's **Stretch** property is True. The code for the example is located in the imagestretch folder on this book's accompanying CD-ROM.

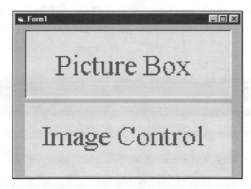

Figure 19.9   Stretching an image in an image control.

Creating Image Animation

One way to create image animation is to use a picture box and keep changing its **Picture** property to display successive frames of an animation. You can store the images themselves in the program, such as using an image list control or an array of Picture objects. We've seen how to create animation earlier in this book in our chapter on Visual Basic timers using image lists; here, we can do the same thing using an array of Picture objects.

We add a timer control, **Timer1**, to the program and set its **Interval** property to 1000 (the **Interval** property is measured in milliseconds, 1/1000s of a second), which means the **Timer1_Timer( )** event handler will be called once a second. We also add a picture box, **Picture1**, in which to display images and a command button, **Command1**, with the caption "Start animation" to start the animation.

For the purposes of this example, we will just switch back and forth between two images in the picture box. These two images are the two images in the Picture object array, **picObjects**, which we store in the form's (General) section:

```
Dim picObjects(1 To 2) As Picture
```

We load those images when the form first loads:

```
Private Sub Form_Load()
    Set picObjects(1) = LoadPicture("c:\vbbb\pictureanimation\image1.bmp")
    Set picObjects(2) = LoadPicture("c:\vbbb\pictureanimation\image2.bmp")
End Sub
```

To switch back and forth, we use a static Boolean flag named **blnImage1** like this, alternating between images in the Picture object array in **Timer1_Timer**:

```
Private Sub Timer1_Timer()
    Static blnImage1 As Boolean

    If blnImage1 Then
        Picture1.Picture = picObjects(1)
    Else
        Picture1.Picture = picObjects(2)
    End If
    ...
```

At the end of **Timer1_Timer**, we toggle the **blnImage1** flag this way:

```
Private Sub Timer1_Timer()
    Static blnImage1 As Boolean
```

```
    If blnImage1 Then
        Picture1.Picture = picObjects(1)
    Else
        Picture1.Picture = picObjects(2)
    End If

    blnImage1 = Not blnImage1
End Sub
```

All that's left is to start the animation when the user clicks the command button, and we do that like this, by enabling the timer:

```
Private Sub Command1_Click()
    Timer1.Enabled = True
End Sub
```

And that's all we need—now we're supporting animation using picture boxes and Picture object arrays. The result of this code appears in Figure 19.10.

The code for this example is located in the pictureanimation folder on this book's accompanying CD-ROM.

Figure 19.10   Image animation with a picture box.

Handling Images Bit By Bit

The Aesthetic Design Department is calling again. How about adding some special effects to the images in your program, *SuperDuperGraphicsPro*? Doesn't that mean working with images bit by bit, you ask? Probably, they say.

We can use Visual Basic methods to work bit by bit with images. Does that mean we'll actually use the **PSet** (sets a pixel) and **Point** (reads a pixel) methods to handle whole images? Exactly.

We'll see this in action over the next few topics. In this topic, we'll see how to read an image in from one picture box, **Picture1**, and write it out to another, **Picture2**, when the user clicks a command button, **Command1**. To be able to work pixel by pixel, set each picture box's **ScaleMode** property to **vbPixel (3)**.

We start by setting up an array, **Pixels**, to hold the colors of each pixel for an image up to 500×500 (to be more efficient, you can redimension your storage array with **ReDim** when you know the actual size of the image you're to work with) in the (General) declarations area of the form:

```
Const intUpperBoundX = 500
Const intUpperBoundY = 500
Dim Pixels(1 To intUpperBoundX, 1 To intUpperBoundY) As Long
```

The first task is to read the pixels in from **Picture1**, and we start by setting up loops over all the pixels in that image:

```
Private Sub Command1_Click()
    Dim x, y As Integer

    For x = 1 To intUpperBoundX
        For y = 1 To intUpperBoundY
...
        Next y
    Next x
```

Then we read each pixel from **Picture1** using the **Point** method and store the pixels in the **Pixels** array we've set up:

```
Private Sub Command1_Click()
    Dim x, y As Integer

    For x = 1 To intUpperBoundX
        For y = 1 To intUpperBoundY
            Pixels(x, y) = Picture1.Point(x, y)
        Next y
    Next x
```

Now we've stored the image in the **Pixels** array. To copy that image to **Picture2**, we just use that control's **PSet** method, pixel by pixel:

```
Private Sub Command1_Click()
    Dim x, y As Integer

    For x = 1 To intUpperBoundX
```

```
        For y = 1 To intUpperBoundY
            Pixels(x, y) = Picture1.Point(x, y)
        Next y
    Next x

    For x = 1 To intUpperBoundX
        For y = 1 To intUpperBoundY
            Picture2.PSet (x, y), Pixels(x, y)
        Next y
    Next x

End Sub
```

Does this work? It certainly does (although it might take a little time to execute), as you can see in Figure 19.11, where we copy the image in the top picture box (**Picture1**) to the bottom picture box (**Picture2**).

The code for this example is located in the imagecopy folder on this book's accompanying CD-ROM. Now that we've seen how to work with an image bit by bit, we'll see how to implement some image effects in the next few topics.

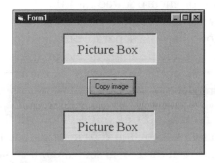

Figure 19.11   Copying an image bit by bit.

Creating Grayscale Images

We've seen how to work with images bit by bit in the previous topic. We'll augment that in this topic, where we see how to convert color images to grayscale images.

We do this by reading an image into a pixel array, then by converting each of those pixels to gray and writing the pixel array out to a new image. Let's see how this works. We'll convert the image in a picture box, **Picture1**, to grayscale, and display it in a new picture box, **Picture2**, when the user clicks a command button, **Command1**. To be able to work pixel by pixel, set each picture box's **ScaleMode** property to **vbPixel (3)**.

First, we set up storage space for the image in an array named **Pixels**, declared in the form's (General) section:

```
Const intUpperBoundX = 300
Const intUpperBoundY = 300
Dim Pixels(1 To intUpperBoundX, 1 To intUpperBoundY) As Long
```

When the user clicks the command button, we store the image in **Picture1** into the array **Pixels**:

```
Private Sub Command1_Click()
    Dim x, y As Integer

    For x = 1 To intUpperBoundX
        For y = 1 To intUpperBoundY
            Pixels(x, y) = Picture1.Point(x, y)
        Next y
    Next x
```

Now we're free to work with the image's pixels in a new loop (to be efficient, this new loop should be incorporated into the first loop where we read the pixels in, but here we'll use a new loop to make the image-handling process clear). In that new loop, we first separate out the color values (red, green, and blue) for each pixel. To create a grayscale image, you average those color values and then use the resulting average as the red, green, and blue color values in the new image.

The **Point** method returns a **Long** integer holding the red, green, and blue color values (which range from 0 to 255) in hexadecimal: **&HBBGGRR**. That means we can separate out the red, green, and blue color values, storing them as the bytes **bytRed**, **bytGreen**, and **bytBlue** this way:

```
Private Sub Command1_Click()
    Dim x, y As Integer
    Dim bytRed, bytGreen, bytBlue As Integer

    For x = 1 To intUpperBoundX
        For y = 1 To intUpperBoundY
            Pixels(x, y) = Picture1.Point(x, y)
        Next y
    Next x

    For x = 1 To intUpperBoundX
        For y = 1 To intUpperBoundY
            bytRed = Pixels(x, y) And &HFF
```

```
        bytGreen = ((Pixels(x, y) And &HFF00) / &H100) Mod &H100
        bytBlue = ((Pixels(x, y) And &HFF0000) / &H10000) Mod &H100
...
```

To convert each pixel to grayscale, we just average its color values. Finally, we display the new image in a second picture box, **Picture2**:

```
Private Sub Command1_Click()
    Dim x, y As Integer
    Dim bytRed, bytGreen, bytBlue, bytAverage As Integer
...
    For x = 1 To intUpperBoundX
        For y = 1 To intUpperBoundY
            bytRed = Pixels(x, y) And &HFF
            bytGreen = ((Pixels(x, y) And &HFF00) / &H100) Mod &H100
            bytBlue = ((Pixels(x, y) And &HFF0000) / &H10000) Mod &H100

            bytAverage = (bytRed + bytGreen + bytBlue) / 3
            Pixels(x, y) = RGB(bytAverage, bytAverage, bytAverage)
        Next y
    Next x

    For x = 1 To intUpperBoundX
        For y = 1 To intUpperBoundY
            Picture2.PSet (x, y), Pixels(x, y)
        Next y
    Next x

End Sub
```

The result of this code appears in Figure 19.12. Although the effect is not terribly obvious in a book with black-and-white images, we're converting an image from color to grayscale in that figure.

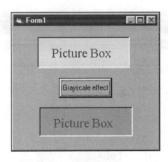

Figure 19.12   Converting an image to grayscale.

The code for this example is located in the imagegrayscale folder on this book's accompanying CD-ROM.

Lightening Images

The Testing Department is calling. Some of the users of your *SuperDuper-GraphicsPro* program are saying the images in that program are too dark—can you let them lighten them? Hmm, you think—how does that work?

You can lighten images by adding the same positive number to each color value (red, green, and blue) of each pixel. Let's see how this works in an example. Here, we'll take the image in a picture box, **Picture1**, and add a value specified by the user to each color value when the user clicks a command button, **Command1**, displaying the result in a second picture box, **Picture2**. To be able to work pixel by pixel, set each picture box's **ScaleMode** property to **vbPixel** (3). We'll also have a text box, **Text1**, that will hold the value the user wants to add to each color value to lighten it.

We start by setting up the storage we'll need for the image:

```
Const intUpperBoundX = 200
Const intUpperBoundY = 200
Dim Pixels(1 To intUpperBoundX, 1 To intUpperBoundY) As Long
```

Next, we place the value the user wants added to each color value in a new variable named **intAddOn** when the user clicks the command button:

```
Private Sub Command1_Click()
    Dim intAddOn As Integer

    intAddOn = Val(Text1.Text)
```

Now we read the image in **Picture1** into the array named **Pixels**:

```
Private Sub Command1_Click()
    Dim x, y, intAddOn As Integer

    intAddOn = Val(Text1.Text)

    For x = 1 To intUpperBoundX
        For y = 1 To intUpperBoundY
            Pixels(x, y) = Picture1.Point(x, y)
        Next y
    Next x
```

Next, we get the red, green, and blue color values for each pixel and add the value in **intAddOn** to those color values, making sure they don't go higher than 255 (of course, you can also darken images by subtracting values here, although you should make sure the resulting color values don't go below 0):

```
Private Sub Command1_Click()
    Dim x, y, intAddOn As Integer
    Dim bytRed, bytGreen, bytBlue As Integer
...
    For x = 1 To intUpperBoundX
        For y = 1 To intUpperBoundY
            bytRed = Pixels(x, y) And &HFF
            bytGreen = ((Pixels(x, y) And &HFF00) / &H100) Mod &H100
            bytBlue = ((Pixels(x, y) And &HFF0000) / &H10000) Mod &H100

            bytRed = bytRed + intAddOn
            If bytRed > 255 Then bytRed = 255
            bytGreen = bytGreen + intAddOn
            If bytGreen > 255 Then bytGreen = 255
            bytBlue = bytBlue + intAddOn
            If bytBlue > 255 Then bytBlue = 255

            Pixels(x, y) = RGB(bytRed, bytGreen, bytBlue)
        Next y
    Next x
End Sub
```

Finally, we just copy the new pixels to the second picture box, **Picture2**:

```
Private Sub Command1_Click()
    Dim x, y, intAddOn As Integer
    ...
    For x = 1 To intUpperBoundX
        For y = 1 To intUpperBoundY
            Picture2.PSet (x, y), Pixels(x, y)
        Next y
    Next x

End Sub
```

The result of this code appears in Figure 19.13. Now we're lightening images pixel by pixel in Visual Basic.

The code for this example is located in the imagelighten folder on this book's accompanying CD-ROM.

Figure 19.13   Lightening an image pixel by pixel.

Creating "Embossed" Images

You can create a striking visual effect by *embossing* an image, which makes it appear to be raised in 3D. Using the technique developed in the previous few topics, we can work pixel by pixel in an image to emboss it.

Let's see how this works in an example. Here, we'll take the image in a picture box, **Picture1**, and emboss the image in it when the user clicks a button, **Command1**, displaying the result in a second picture box, **Picture2**. To be able to work pixel by pixel, set each picture box's **ScaleMode** property to **vbPixel (3)**.

We start by storing the image in **Picture1** in an array named **Pixels**:

```
Const intUpperBoundX = 300
Const intUpperBoundY = 300
Dim Pixels(1 To intUpperBoundX, 1 To intUpperBoundY) As Long
Private Sub Command1_Click()
    Dim x, y As Integer

    For x = 1 To intUpperBoundX
        For y = 1 To intUpperBoundY
            Pixels(x, y) = Picture1.Point(x, y)
        Next y
    Next x
    ...
```

Now we'll emboss the image in the **Pixels** array. Embossing is the process of plotting the difference between a pixel and a pixel above and to the left of it; this difference is added to 128 to make the whole image appear gray. Here's one important note: when we're setting a pixel, we use both it and the pixel to the upper-left of it, which means that to avoid incorporating pixels we've already set, we will proceed from the bottom-right of the array, not the upper-left. Here's how that process looks in code:

```
Private Sub Command1_Click()
    Dim bytRed, bytGreen, bytBlue, bytAverage As Integer
...
    For x = intUpperBoundX To 2 Step -1
        For y = intUpperBoundY To 2 Step -1
            bytRed = ((Pixels(x - 1, y - 1) And &HFF) - (Pixels(x, y) And _
                &HFF)) + 128
            bytGreen = (((Pixels(x - 1, y - 1) And &HFF00) / &H100) Mod _
                &H100 - ((Pixels(x, y) And &HFF00) / &H100) Mod &H100) + 128
            bytBlue = (((Pixels(x - 1, y - 1) And &HFF0000) / &H1000) Mod _
                &H100 - ((Pixels(x, y) And &HFF0000) / &H10000) Mod &H100)_
                + 128

            bytAverage = (bytRed + bytGreen + bytBlue) / 3
            Pixels(x, y) = RGB(bytAverage, bytAverage, bytAverage)
        Next y
    Next x
End Sub
```

Note that we also average all the color values together so that the resulting image is a grayscale image. When we're done, we just copy the image to the second picture box, **Picture2**:

```
Private Sub Command1_Click()
    Dim bytRed, bytGreen, bytBlue, bytAverage As Integer
...
    For x = 1 To intUpperBoundX
        For y = 1 To intUpperBoundY
            Picture2.PSet (x - 2, y - 2), Pixels(x, y)
        Next y
    Next x

End Sub
```

Running this program gives the result you see in Figure 19.14. Now we're embossing images in Visual Basic.

The code for this example is located in the imageemboss folder on this book's accompanying CD-ROM.

Figure 19.14   Embossing an image pixel by pixel.

Creating "Engraved" Images

In the previous topic, we created embossed images by taking the difference between a pixel and the pixel to the upper-left of it and adding 128 to the result to create a grayscale image. We can also create *engraved* images by taking the difference between a pixel and the pixel to its *lower-right* and adding 128 to the result.

The code to create engraved images is the same as that to create embossed images, except that we work in the reverse direction and use the pixel to the lower-right, not the upper-left. Here's the new image effect loop:

```
For x = 2 To intUpperBoundX - 1
    For y = 2 To intUpperBoundY - 1
        bytRed = ((Pixels(x + 1, y + 1) And &HFF) - (Pixels(x, y) And _
            &HFF)) + 128
        bytGreen = (((Pixels(x + 1, y + 1) And &HFF00) / &H100) _
            Mod &H100 - ((Pixels(x, y) And &HFF00) / &H100) Mod &H100)_
            + 128
        bytBlue = (((Pixels(x + 1, y + 1) And &HFF0000) / &H10000)_
            Mod &H100 - ((Pixels(x, y) And &HFF0000) / &H10000) Mod_
            &H100) + 128

        bytAverage = (bytRed + bytGreen + bytBlue) / 3
        Pixels(x, y) = RGB(bytAverage, bytAverage, bytAverage)
    Next y
Next x
```

When you put this code to work, you see the result as in Figure 19.15. Now we're engraving images in Visual Basic. (To be able to work pixel by pixel, make sure you set each picture box's **ScaleMode** property to **vbPixel (3)**.)

Figure 19.15   Engraving images by working pixel by pixel.

The code for this example is located in the imageengrave folder on this book's accompanying CD-ROM.

Sweeping Images

When we created embossed and engraved images in the previous two topics, we were careful to set up our embossing or engraving loop so that when setting a pixel, we did not make use of other pixels that we had already set in the same loop. The reason for that is that we only wanted to plot the difference between adjacent pixels—that is, the difference between two pixels only—to create embossed or engraved images.

If we had not restricted our operation to two pixels we had not already worked on, and instead worked on pixels we had already set earlier, we could end up *propagating* a pixel's color values among several other pixels. That is, one pixel's setting could affect many other pixels.

In fact, there are times when you want to have that happen—for example, you might want to make an image appear as though it is sweeping from upper-left to lower-right, giving the illusion of motion. In that case, you'd copy pixels with the ones to the upper-left over and over, progressively blending them together to create the effect you see in Figure 19.16, where it looks as though the text has a fading trail of color behind it.

Seeing the code that gives us the image in Figure 19.16 will help make this effect easier to understand. As with the previous few topics in this chapter, we load the image in a picture box, **Picture1**, into an array named **Pixels**. Then we move from lower-right to upper-left, averaging each pixel with the one to the lower-right:

```
For x = intUpperBoundX - 1 To 1 Step -1
    For y = intUpperBoundY - 1 To 1 Step -1
```

```
                bytRed = Abs((Pixels(x + 1, y + 1) And &HFF) + (Pixels(x, y)_
                    And &HFF)) / 2
                bytGreen = Abs(((Pixels(x + 1, y + 1) And &HFF00) / &H100)_
                    Mod &H100 + ((Pixels(x, y) And &HFF00) / &H100) Mod_
                    &H100) / 2
                bytBlue = Abs(((Pixels(x + 1, y + 1) And &HFF0000) / &H10000) _
                    Mod &H100 + ((Pixels(x, y) And &HFF0000) / &H10000) Mod_
                    &H100) / 2
                Pixels(x, y) = RGB(bytRed, bytGreen, bytBlue)
            Next y
        Next x
```

That's all it takes—now we copy the image into the second picture box, **Picture2**. (To be able to work pixel by pixel, make sure you set each picture box's **ScaleMode** property to **vbPixel (3)**.) By combining successive pixels as we do in this example, we create the sweeping effect you see in Figure 19.16. Now we're creating complex images using image handling techniques.

The complete code for this example is located in the imagesweep folder on this book's accompanying CD-ROM.

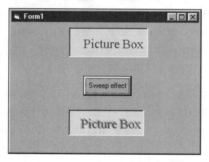

Figure 19.16   Sweeping an image by working pixel by pixel.

Blurring Images

The Aesthetic Design Department is calling again. If you're going to add image effects to your program, *SuperDuperGraphicsPro*, why not let the user *blur* images?

You can blur images by averaging pixels. To see how this works, we load the pixels from a picture box, **Picture1**, and blur them, then display the result in another picture box, **Picture2**. To be able to work pixel by pixel, set each picture box's **ScaleMode** property to **vbPixel** (3).

As with the code in the previous few topics in this chapter, we load the pixels from **Picture1** into an array named **Pixels**. To blur the pixels, you average them together; here, we just average each pixel with the next pixel to the right, but you can set up any blurring region you like (such as all eight pixels that surround the current pixel). This is the way our blurring process looks in code:

```
For x = 1 To intUpperBoundX - 1
    For y = 1 To intUpperBoundY
        bytRed = Abs((Pixels(x + 1, y) And &HFF) + (Pixels(x, y) _
            And &HFF)) / 2
        bytGreen = Abs(((Pixels(x + 1, y) And &HFF00) / &H100) Mod _
            &H100 + ((Pixels(x, y) And &HFF00) / &H100) Mod &H100) / 2
        bytBlue = Abs(((Pixels(x + 1, y) And &HFF0000) / &H10000) _
            Mod &H100 + ((Pixels(x, y) And &HFF0000) / &H10000)_
            Mod &H100) / 2
        Pixels(x, y) = RGB(bytRed, bytGreen, bytBlue)
    Next y
Next x
```

After the pixels have been blurred, we display the result in **Picture2**, as shown in Figure 19.17. As you can see, the blurring produced with this algorithm is slight; to blur the image more, you can apply the same algorithm again or increase the number of pixels over which you average.

The code for this example is located in the imageblur folder on this book's accompanying CD-ROM.

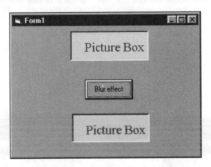

Figure 19.17   Blurring an image by working pixel by pixel.

Freeing Memory Used By Graphics

The Testing Department is calling again. Your program, *SuperDuperGraphics-Pro*, is using up a lot of memory. Is there any way to free some memory when you're not using it anymore?

Yes, there is. When you are no longer using a picture in the **Picture** property of a form, picture box, or image control, set the **Picture** property to the Visual Basic **Nothing** keyword to empty it:

```
Set Picture1.Picture = Nothing
```

In addition, if you use the **Image** property of a picture box or form, Visual Basic creates an **AutoRedraw** bitmap (this happens even if the **AutoRedraw** property for that form or picture box is False). When you've finished using the **Image** property, you can empty the memory used by that bitmap with the **Cls** method before you set **AutoRedraw** to False, as in this example:

```
Picture1.AutoRedraw = True
Picture1.Cls
Picture1.AutoRedraw = False
```

Chapter 20

Creating ActiveX Controls And Documents

If you need an immediate solution to:	See page:
Creating An ActiveX Control	653
Designing An ActiveX Control From Scratch	654
Giving ActiveX Controls Persistent Graphics	657
Basing An ActiveX Control On An Existing Visual Basic Control	657
Handling Constituent Control Events In An ActiveX Control	659
Adding Controls To An ActiveX Control (A Calculator ActiveX Control)	660
Testing An ActiveX Control	661
Creating A Visual Basic Project Group To Test An ActiveX Control	662
Registering An ActiveX Control	664
Using A Custom ActiveX Control In A Visual Basic Program	664
Adding A Property To An ActiveX Control	666
Making ActiveX Control Properties Persistent (PropertyBag Object)	671
Adding A Method To An ActiveX Control	674
Adding An Event To An ActiveX Control	678
Adding Design Time Property Pages	680
Creating An ActiveX Document	682
ActiveX Document DLLs Vs. EXEs	684
Adding Controls To An ActiveX Document (A Tic-Tac-Toe Example)	684
Handling Constituent Control Events In An ActiveX Document	689
Testing An ActiveX Document	690
Creating ActiveX Documents That Run Outside Visual Basic	690
Distributed Computing: ActiveX Documents And Integrated Browsers	691
Making ActiveX Document Properties Persistent (PropertyBag Object)	693

In Depth

ActiveX controls and ActiveX documents are two of the ActiveX components you can build with Visual Basic. In fact, the ActiveX part of Visual Basic has exploded in scope lately, along with many changes in terminology, and will surely do so again. We'll start this chapter with an overview of ActiveX and ActiveX controls and documents in particular.

All About ActiveX Components

The whole ActiveX field started originally to differentiate controls designed for Internet usage from general OLE (Object Linking and Embedding) controls. In time, however, all OLE controls have come to be referred to as ActiveX controls. In fact, the field has taken off so vigorously that now Visual Basic can build not just ActiveX controls in Visual Basic (you used to have to build ActiveX controls for use in Visual Basic in other programming packages, like Visual C++), but ActiveX *components*.

What is an ActiveX component? In programming terms, all ActiveX components are really OLE servers, but that doesn't help us understand what's going on. It's better to break things down and look at the three types of ActiveX components:

- ActiveX controls
- ActiveX documents
- Code components (OLE automation servers)

Let's take a look at these types now.

ActiveX Controls

We have seen ActiveX controls throughout the book—those are the controls you can add to the Visual Basic toolbox using the Components dialog box. You can add those controls to a Visual Basic program like any other control. You can also use ActiveX controls on the Internet, embedding them in your Web pages, as we'll see when we work on creating ActiveX controls. ActiveX controls can support properties, methods, and events.

Your ActiveX control can be built entirely from scratch (in other words, you're responsible for its appearance), it can be built on another control (such as a list box), or it can contain multiple existing controls (these ActiveX controls are said to contain *constituent* controls). Visual Basic ActiveX controls are based on the Visual Basic UserControl object. When you create an ActiveX control, you create a control class file with the extension .ctl. Visual Basic uses that file to create the actual control, which has the extension .ocx. After you register that control with Windows (you can use Windows utilities like regsvr32.exe to register a control, as we'll see in this chapter), the control will appear in the Visual Basic Components dialog box, ready for you to add to a program. You can also use these controls in Web pages.

ActiveX Documents

ActiveX documents are new to many programmers, but the idea is simple. Instead of restricting yourself to a single control in a Web page, now you can create the whole page. ActiveX documents can include as many controls as any other Visual Basic program, and as we'll see when we start creating ActiveX documents, the result is just like running a Visual Basic program in your Web browser or other application.

Visual Basic ActiveX documents are based on the Visual Basic UserDocument object. When you create an ActiveX document, you save it with the extension .dob. Visual Basic uses that DOB file to create the EXE or DLL file that holds the actual code for the ActiveX document. In addition, Visual Basic produces a specification file, with the extension .vbd, that describes the ActiveX document, and it's that file that you actually open in the host application, such as the Microsoft Internet Explorer. With ActiveX documents, you can let users save data (using the **PropertyBag** property); that data is stored in the VBD file.

Code Components

Code components were formerly called OLE automation servers. These objects let you use their code in other programs. For example, you might have a calculation routine that you *expose* in a code component; doing so makes that routine available to other programs. Code components can support properties and methods. We'll see more about code components in Chapter 27.

If you take a look at the kind of ActiveX components you can build with Visual Basic in the New Project window, you'll see all kinds:

- ActiveX document DLL, ActiveX EXE
- ActiveX control
- ActiveX EXE, ActiveX DLL (these are code components)

There's still quite a confusion of terms here—what's the difference between a DLL and EXE ActiveX component? Let's explore further.

In-Process Vs. Out-Of-Process Components

If an ActiveX component has been implemented as part of an executable file (EXE file), it is an *out-of-process* server and runs in its own process. If it has been implemented as a dynamic link library (DLL file), it is an *in-process* server and runs in the same process as the client application.

If your ActiveX component is an out-of-process server, it is an EXE file, and can run standalone. Applications that use in-process servers usually run faster than those that use out-of-process servers because the application doesn't have to cross process boundaries to use an object's properties, methods, and events.

There are a few reasons why you may want to create your ActiveX document as an in-process component (DLL file). The performance of an in-process component surpasses that of the same component compiled as an EXE. In addition, multiple programs accessing the same EXE can overwrite global data; that doesn't happen if they each have their own in-process server.

Which ActiveX Component Do I Want To Build?

With all the different types of ActiveX components to choose from, how do you decide which type of component you want to create? Take a look at this list:

- To build an invisible component that provides routines in code that you can call, build a code component (ActiveX EXE or an ActiveX DLL).

- To build a component that can run in the same process with your application, build an ActiveX DLL.

- To build a component that can serve multiple applications and can run on a remote computer, build an ActiveX EXE.

- To build a visible component that can be dropped into an application at design time, build an ActiveX control.

- To build a visible component that can take over an application window at runtime, build an ActiveX document.

That's it for the overview of ActiveX controls and documents for the moment—it's time to turn to the Immediate Solutions.

Immediate Solutions

Creating An ActiveX Control

The Testing Department is calling again. Wouldn't it be great if you built a new ActiveX control that displayed a digital clock? That control could be reused in many other programs. Hmm, you think, how do you create an ActiveX control?

Select the New Project menu item in the Visual Basic File menu to open the New Project dialog box, as shown in Figure 20.1.

Select the ActiveX Control item in the New Project dialog box and click on OK. This creates a new, empty ActiveX control, as shown in Figure 20.2.

Believe it or not, you've created your first ActiveX control, **UserControl1**. You can even run the control with the Run menu's Start item, which would display the control by launching the Microsoft Internet Explorer if you have it installed in your computer; however, there would be nothing to see because the control is empty.

The default name of the control is **Project1**, but we can change that to, say, **FirstControl**. To do that, select the Project1 Properties item in the Project menu, and type "FirstControl" into the Project Name box in the Project Properties dialog box, then click on OK. Also, save the project as firstcontrol.vbp. Instead of a FRM file, you save ActiveX controls in CTL files. Select the Save UserControl1 item in the file menu to save the control as firstcontrol.ctl. Here's what appears in that file on disk:

```
VERSION 6.00
Begin VB.UserControl UserControl1
   ClientHeight    =    3600
   ClientLeft      =    0
   ClientTop       =    0
   ClientWidth     =    4800
   ScaleHeight     =    3600
   ScaleWidth      =    4800
End
Attribute VB_Name = "UserControl1"
Attribute VB_GlobalNameSpace = False
Attribute VB_Creatable = True
Attribute VB_PredeclaredId = False
Attribute VB_Exposed = True
```

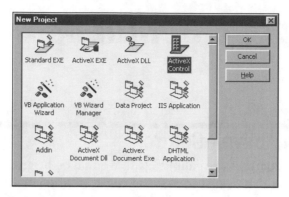

Figure 20.1   The New Project dialog box.

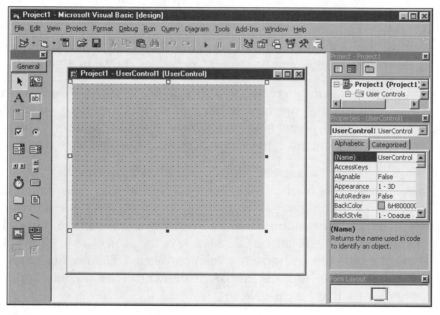

Figure 20.2   A new ActiveX control.

Now that we've seen how to create a new ActiveX control, it's time to make it do something. We'll see how that works in the next topic.

Designing An ActiveX Control From Scratch

The testing department is on the phone. Your new ActiveX control looks fine, but why doesn't it do anything? Should it? you ask. Yes, they say.

You can design the appearance of your ActiveX control entirely from scratch, creating an entirely new control, never seen before. In that case, you're responsible for creating the control's appearance from scratch. Later, you can add events to your control, as well as methods and properties, as we'll see later in this chapter.

To design the appearance of your entirely new control, you can use the Visual Basic graphics methods that the UserControl object supports, such as **Circle**, **Line**, **PSet**, **Print**, **Cls**, and **Point**. You can also display an image in the UserControl object by setting its **Picture** property.

Let's see an example. Here, we'll just draw two lines to crisscross an ActiveX control and draw a black box in the middle. Create a new ActiveX control now, and double-click it at design time to open the code window to the **UserControl_Initialize** function:

```
Private Sub UserControl_Initialize()

End Sub
```

This function is just like the **Form Load** procedure that we're familiar with. Set the control's **AutoRedraw** property to True so we can draw graphics from **UserControl_Initialize**, and then draw the lines to crisscross the control, using the **Line** method and **ScaleWidth** and **ScaleHeight** just as you would in a Visual Basic form:

```
Private Sub UserControl_Initialize()
    Line (0, 0)-(ScaleWidth, ScaleHeight)
    Line (0, ScaleHeight)-(ScaleWidth, 0)
...
End Sub
```

Next, we draw a filled-in black box in the center of the control this way:

```
Private Sub UserControl_Initialize()
    Line (0, 0)-(ScaleWidth, ScaleHeight)
    Line (0, ScaleHeight)-(ScaleWidth, 0)
    Line (ScaleWidth / 4, ScaleHeight / 4)-(3 * ScaleWidth / 4, _
        3 * ScaleHeight / 4), , BF
End Sub
```

Let's test this new ActiveX control now in the Microsoft Internet Explorer (assuming you have that browser installed). To do that, just select the Run menu's Start item now. Doing so opens the Project Properties dialog box, shown in Figure 20.3.

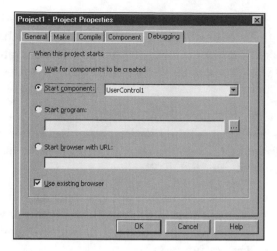

Figure 20.3   The Project Properties window.

Leave UserControl1 in the Start Component box, and make sure the Use Existing Browser box is clicked, then click on OK. This registers our control with Windows, creates a temporary HTML page with the control embedded in it, and starts the Internet Explorer, as you see in Figure 20.4.

You can see our new ActiveX control in Figure 20.4. Now we've created our first ActiveX control and designed its appearance from scratch. If we wanted to, we could add events, properties, and methods to this control (we'll see how to do so later in this chapter).

Here's the temporary HTML page that Visual Basic creates to display our ActiveX control; note that our control is registered with Windows and has its

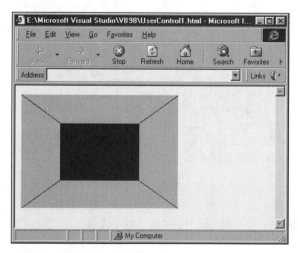

Figure 20.4   Our first ActiveX control.

own ID, so this page can use the HTML **<OBJECT>** tag to embed one of our controls in the page:

```
<HTML>
<BODY>
<OBJECT classid="clsid:B2A69D3B-D38C-11D1-8881-E45E08C10000">
</OBJECT>
</BODY>
</HTML>
```

Note, however, that when you select End in the Run menu, Visual Basic unregisters our control with Windows. To register it permanently, use a Windows utility like regsvr32.exe.

Giving ActiveX Controls Persistent Graphics

Giving ActiveX Controls Persistent Graphics

Visual Basic ActiveX controls are much like Visual Basic forms when it comes to graphics. If you want your control to be automatically redrawn when needed (such as when the program containing it needs to be redrawn), just set the control's **AutoRedraw** property to True, just as you would for a Visual Basic form or intrinsic control.

If you prefer not to set **AutoRedraw** to True (to save memory, for example), you can add your drawing code to the control's **Paint** event (just as you can with a Visual Basic form).

Basing An ActiveX Control On An Existing Visual Basic Control

Basing An ActiveX Control On An Existing Visual Basic Control

As we saw in the previous topic, you can design your ActiveX controls from scratch, creating the control's appearance yourself. However, you can also base your ActiveX on an existing Visual Basic control.

Let's see an example to make this clearer. In this case, we'll base an ActiveX control on a Visual Basic text box. Create a new ActiveX control now by selecting the ActiveX control item in the New Project dialog box. Now draw a text box, **Text1**, in the control (its size and position don't matter because we'll set that ourselves when the control runs); add this new text box just as you would any text box to a form—just use the Text Box tool. Now set the text box's **ScrollBars** property to **Both (3)**, and set its **MultiLine** property to True.

When the control is first displayed, we stretch the text box to cover the control this way in the ActiveX control **Initialize** event handler:

```
Private Sub UserControl_Initialize()
    Text1.Left = 0
    Text1.Top = 0
    Text1.Width = ScaleWidth
    Text1.Height = ScaleHeight
End Sub
```

That's it—now select the Start item in the Run menu, click on OK if the Project Properties dialog box appears (it only appears when you run the control for the first time) to open the control in the Internet Explorer, as shown in Figure 20.5. You can type text into the text box, as also shown in Figure 20.5.

As you can see in Figure 20.5, our ActiveX control displays a text box complete with scroll bars, ready for use. We've based our ActiveX control on an existing Visual Basic control.

Of course, as it stands, our ActiveX control is exactly like a Visual Basic text box, so it's hard to see why you'd make an ActiveX control out of it. However, you can tailor that control the way you want it—for example, you can do a lot of processing behind the scenes on the text in the text box (just as you could in any Visual Basic program). You can also change the way the control interacts with the user, as we'll see in the next topic.

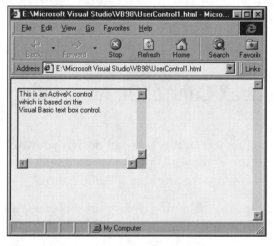

Figure 20.5   Basing an ActiveX control on a text box.

Handling Constituent Control Events In An ActiveX Control

The Aesthetic Design Department is calling. It's nearly Christmas and they've come up with a great idea for a new ActiveX control based on Visual Basic text box. This new Christmas text box control will not display the letter "L"— no "L", get it? Oh, you say. They ask, when can you have it ready?

The controls you use in an ActiveX control are called *constituent* controls, and you can handle events from those controls just as you would in a standard Visual Basic program. Let's see an example. Here, we'll set up the no "L" text box. Create a new ActiveX control by selecting the ActiveX Control item in the New Project dialog box. Now draw a text box, **Text1**, in the control (its size and position don't matter because we'll set that ourselves when the control runs); add this new text box just as you would any text box to a form— just use the Text Box tool. Now set the text box's **ScrollBars** property to **Both (3)**, and set its **MultiLine** property to True.

Add this code to the **Initialize** event handler to stretch the text box over the entire ActiveX control when the control first appears:

```
Private Sub UserControl_Initialize()
    Text1.Left = 0
    Text1.Top = 0
    Text1.Width = ScaleWidth
    Text1.Height = ScaleHeight
End Sub
```

Now add a **KeyPress** event handler to the text box in the same way as you would in a standard Visual Basic program (that is, using the drop-down list boxes in the code window):

```
Private Sub Text1_KeyPress(KeyAscii As Integer)

End Sub
```

Here, we'll just watch for the letter "L":

```
Private Sub Text1_KeyPress(KeyAscii As Integer)
    If KeyAscii = Asc("L") Then
...
    End If
End Sub
```

If the user does press the letter "L", we can cancel that letter by setting the **KeyAcsii** argument to 0, and we can also have the computer beep to indicate that we've canceled this letter:

```
Private Sub Text1_KeyPress(KeyAscii As Integer)
    If KeyAscii = Asc("L") Then
        KeyAscii = 0
        Beep
    End If
End Sub
```

And that's it—now this ActiveX control will display a text box, but it won't let the user type the letter "L". In this way, we've handled an event from a constituent control in our ActiveX control.

The code for this example is located in the activextextcontrol folder on this book's accompanying CD-ROM.

Adding Controls To An ActiveX Control (A Calculator ActiveX Control)

In the previous topics, we've seen how to design an ActiveX control's appearance from scratch and how to base an ActiveX control on a Visual Basic control (or other ActiveX controls). However, ActiveX controls frequently contain more than one constituent control. For example, what if you wanted to create a calculator ActiveX control? How would you design that control in Visual Basic?

Let's see how this works; here we'll create an ActiveX control that is really a calculator that the user can use to add numbers. Create a new ActiveX project now, giving it the project name "calculator" (use the Project1 Properties item in the Project menu to open the Project Properties dialog box and enter "calcuator" in the Project Name box). In addition, change the name of the control itself from **UserControl1** to **CalculatorControl** in the Properties window (just set the control's **Name** property). Now when we add this control to another program using the Components dialog box, this control will be listed as "calculator", and when we create controls of this type in that program, the first one will be called CalculatorControl1, the next CalculatorControl2, and so on.

To design the calculator, add these controls in a vertical line in the ActiveX control: a text box, **Text1**; a label with the caption "+"; another text box, **Text2**; a command button, **Command1**, with the caption "="; and a third text box, **Text3**. The result appears in Figure 20.6.

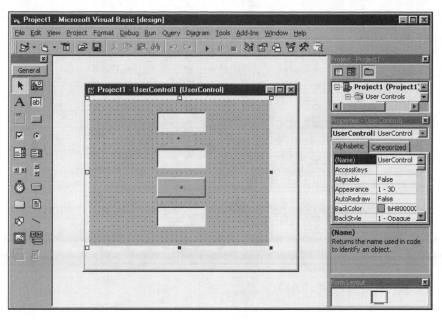

Figure 20.6   Designing the calculator ActiveX control.

Now double-click the command button to open its **Click** event handler:

```
Private Sub Command1_Click()

End Sub
```

When the user clicks the = button, we'll just add the two values in **Text1** and **Text2**, and place the sum in **Text3** at the bottom. That looks like this in code:

```
Private Sub Command1_Click()
    Text3.Text = Str(Val(Text1.Text) + Val(Text2.Text))
End Sub
```

And that's it—we've created a new calculator ActiveX control. How can we test it out? See the next topic.

Testing An ActiveX Control

You can test, and even debug, ActiveX controls in the Microsoft Internet Explorer, as long as you have version 3 or later. Just select the Start item in the Visual Basic Run menu to see the ActiveX control you're designing at work.

Let's see an example. Here, we'll run the ActiveX control we developed in the previous topic, the calculator control. To open this control in the Internet Explorer, select the Project menu's Calculator Properties item, opening the Project Properties dialog box, as shown in Figure 20.7. Click the Debugging tab now, as also shown in Figure 20.7.

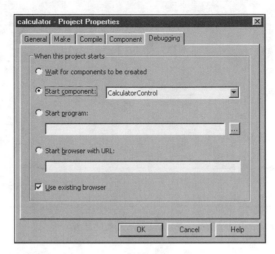

Figure 20.7   Setting Visual Basic debugging options.

Leave the entry CalculatorControl in the Start Component box, and make sure the Use Existing Browser box is clicked, then click on OK. To run the control, just select the Run menu's Start item now. This registers our control with Windows, creates a temporary HTML page with the control embedded in it, and starts the Internet Explorer, as you see in Figure 20.8.

That's it—now you can use the ActiveX control. In Figure 20.8, we're adding numbers with the calculator. Our calculator ActiveX control is a success.

Creating A Visual Basic Project Group To Test An ActiveX Control

In the previous topic, we saw how to test an ActiveX control in a Web browser, but you can use ActiveX controls in Visual Basic programs too. Can you test an ActiveX control in Visual Basic?

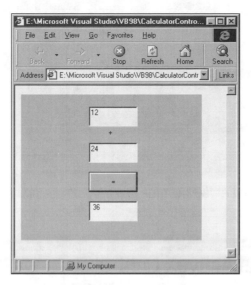

Figure 20.8   Testing the calculator control in the Internet Explorer.

Yes, you can, by creating a *project group*. How does that process work? As an example, we'll see how to add our calculator ActiveX control (developed in the last two topics) to a program group. Just follow these steps:

1. Create a new Visual Basic standard EXE project, Project1.

2. Select the Add Project item in the File menu.

3. Click the Existing tab in the Add Project dialog box, select the name of the ActiveX calculator project (we used activexcalculatorcontrol.vbp in the previous topic), and click on OK.

4. This adds the calculator ActiveX project to the current project and creates a program group. Select the Select Project Group As item in the File menu, accepting all default file names (although you can give those files the names you want), including the group file itself, group1.vbg.

5. Close the calculator project's window (that is, the window in which you design the calculator by adding text boxes and so on—its designer window); that makes the calculator ActiveX control available to us in the other project, and it will appear in the toolbox.

6. Add a new calculator control to Form1 of Project1.

7. Select the Run menu's Start item to start Project1.

Following these steps creates the running program you see in Figure 20.9. Now we're testing ActiveX controls in Visual Basic.

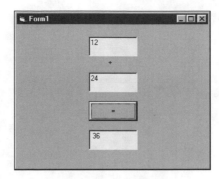

Figure 20.9   Testing an ActiveX control in a program group.

Registering An ActiveX Control

The Testing Department is calling again. It's all very well to be able to run ActiveX controls in a Visual Basic project group (see the previous topic), but wouldn't it be nice to let other users use those ActiveX controls too?

To install an ActiveX control in Windows, you must register it with Windows, and you can do that either with the setup program (such as the ones we'll create in Chapter 30), or with the Window regsvr32.exe utility. Let's see an example. Here, we'll see how to register an ActiveX control named, say, activex.ocx with Windows. First, use the File menu's Make activex.ocx menu item to create activex.ocx. Next, we'll use regsvr32.exe, which is usually found in the C:\windows\system directory, to register that control with Windows. Here's how to register our ActiveX control:

```
c:\windows\system>regsvr32 c:\vbbb\activex.ocx
```

After the ActiveX control is registered, it will appear in the Visual Basic Components dialog box (which you open with the Project menu's Components item), and you can add it to the Visual Basic toolbox.

Using A Custom ActiveX Control In A Visual Basic Program

Now that we've registered our Visual Basic control with Windows (see the previous topic), how do you add it to a form in a Visual Basic project? You add ActiveX controls that you build to Visual Basic projects just as you add any other ActiveX controls, such as the ones that come with Visual Basic.

Let's see an example. After we register the calculator ActiveX control that we've developed over the previous few topics, that control will appear in the Visual Basic Components dialog box. Start a new standard EXE project now and open the Visual Basic Components dialog box by selecting the Project|Components item. Next, click the Controls tab in the Components dialog box, as shown in Figure 20.10.

Click the entry labeled calculator ("calculator" was the name we gave to the project when we created this control) in the Components dialog box to add our calculator, and close that dialog box to add the calculator to the Visual Basic toolbox. Now draw a new calculator ActiveX control in the program's main form, creating the new control, **CalculatorControl1** (CalculatorControl was the name we gave to the UserControl object when we created this control), and run the program, as shown in Figure 20.11.

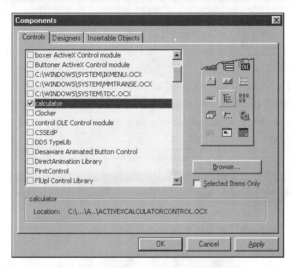

Figure 20.10   Our ActiveX control appears in the Components dialog box.

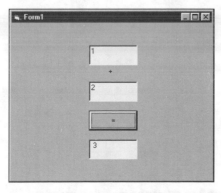

Figure 20.11   Running our ActiveX control in a Visual Basic program.

That's it—now we've created, registered, and added a functioning ActiveX control to a Visual Basic program.

Adding A Property To An ActiveX Control

When we add our new custom calculator ActiveX control to a Visual Basic program, as we did in the previous topic, you can see that the control already has quite a number of controls built into it, as shown in the Properties window in Figure 20.12. Besides that standard set of properties (called *ambient properties* and stored in AmbientProperties objects, which you get from the **Ambient** property), we can also add our own properties to an ActiveX control (stored in Extender objects, which you get from the **Extender** property).

Let's see an example. Here, we'll add two properties to the calculator ActiveX control, **Operand1** and **Operand2**, which will hold the text in the top two text boxes in the calculator, operand 1 and operand 2, which we add when the user clicks the = button. After we add those properties, you can access them in programs that make use of our ActiveX control just as you would any other ActiveX control's properties. Here's an example where we set operand 1 in the calculator after you add a calculator control, **CalculatorControl1**, to a standard Visual Basic program; as you can see, this is just like setting the text in a text box:

```
Private Sub Command1_Click()
    CalculatorControl1.Operand1 = 100/
End Sub
```

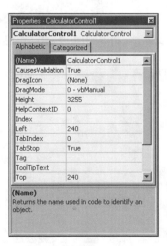

Figure 20.12   The Visual Basic Properties window.

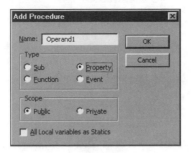

Figure 20.13   Adding a property to an ActiveX control.

To add the **Operand1** and **Operand2** properties to the calculator ActiveX project, open that project in Visual Basic, open the code window, and select the Add Procedure item in the Tools menu. This opens the Add Procedure box, as shown in Figure 20.13.

Put the name of the first property, **Operand1**, in the Name box, and select the option button labeled Property, then click on OK. Doing so creates two procedures, a **Let** and **Get** procedure for the property:

```
Public Property Get Operand1() As Variant

End Property

Public Property Let Operand1(ByVal vNewValue As Variant)

End Property
```

In the same way, add the **Operand2** property, creating the procedures for that property as well:

```
Public Property Get Operand2() As Variant

End Property

Public Property Let Operand2(ByVal vNewValue As Variant)

End Property
```

When **Operand1** is set in code or by Visual Basic, the **Operand1 Let** procedure is called; when other code or Visual Basic wants to retrieve the current value of **Operand1**, the **Operand1 Get** procedure is called. That means that we return the text in the two text boxes corresponding to the calculator's operands in the **Get** procedures:

```
Public Property Get Operand1() As Variant
    Operand1 = Text1.Text
End Property

Public Property Get Operand2() As Variant
    Operand2 = Text2.Text
End Property
```

And we set the text in the operand text boxes from the value passed to us in the **Let** procedures:

```
Public Property Let Operand1(ByVal vNewValue As Variant)
    Text1.Text = vNewValue
End Property

Public Property Let Operand2(ByVal vNewValue As Variant)
    Text2.Text = vNewValue
End Property
```

That's all it takes. Now when you create a control of this type in another Visual Basic program, you'll see that the new control has two new properties: **Operand1** and **Operand2**. You can set those properties in the Properties window at design time, as shown in Figure 20.14, or in code:

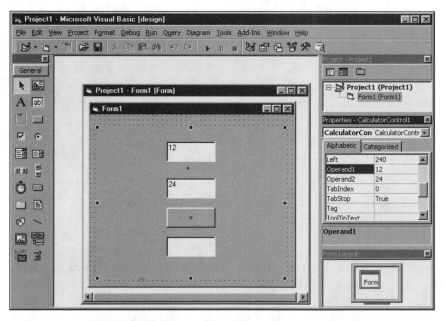

Figure 20.14   Setting a property to an ActiveX control.

```
Private Sub Command1_Click()
    CalculatorControl1.Operand1 = 100
End Sub
```

However, there is a problem. When you set the **Operand1** and **Operand2** properties at design time in a program that has a calculator control embedded in it and then run the program, nothing appears in the operand text boxes. Why not? It turns out that we have to make the properties persistent if we want to let the user set them at design time, and we'll look into that in the next topic.

The code for this example, activexcalculatorcontrol.ctl version 1 (version 2 will have persistent properties), appears in Listing 20.1.

TIP: *Another way to set up the **Let** and **Get** procedures for your properties in an ActiveX control is to use the ActiveX Control Interface Wizard in the Add-Ins menu (if that wizard does not appear in your Add-ins menu, select the Add-In Manager item in the Add-Ins menu and add the ActiveX Control Interface Wizard).*

Listing 20.1   activexcalculatorcontrol.ctl version 1

```
VERSION 6.00
Begin VB.UserControl CalculatorControl
    ClientHeight    =    3600
    ClientLeft      =    0
    ClientTop       =    0
    ClientWidth     =    4500
    ScaleHeight     =    3600
    ScaleWidth      =    4500
    Begin VB.TextBox Text2
        Height          =    495
        Left            =    1680
        TabIndex        =    4
        Top             =    1200
        Width           =    1215
    End
    Begin VB.CommandButton Command1
        Caption         =    "="
        Height          =    495
        Left            =    1680
        TabIndex        =    3
        Top             =    1920
        Width           =    1215
    End
    Begin VB.TextBox Text3
        Height          =    495
        Left            =    1680
```

```
              TabIndex        =    1
              Top             =    2640
              Width           =    1215
           End
           Begin VB.TextBox Text1
              Height          =    495
              Left            =    1680
              TabIndex        =    0
              Top             =    300
              Width           =    1215
           End
           Begin VB.Label Label1
              Caption         =    "+"
              Height          =    255
              Left            =    2160
              TabIndex        =    2
              Top             =    840
              Width           =    375
           End
        End
     End
     Attribute VB_Name = "CalculatorControl"
     Attribute VB_GlobalNameSpace = False
     Attribute VB_Creatable = True
     Attribute VB_PredeclaredId = False
     Attribute VB_Exposed = True
     Private Sub Command1_Click()
         Text3.Text = Str(Val(Text1.Text) + Val(Text2.Text))
     End Sub


     Public Property Get Operand1() As Variant
         Operand1 = Text1.Text
     End Property


     Public Property Let Operand1(ByVal vNewValue As Variant)
         Text1.Text = vNewValue
     End Property


     Public Property Get Operand2() As Variant
         Operand2 = Text2.Text
     End Property


     Public Property Let Operand2(ByVal vNewValue As Variant)
         Text2.Text = vNewValue
     End Property
```

Making ActiveX Control Properties Persistent (PropertyBag Object)

There's a way of storing property settings in ActiveX controls that uses the PropertyBag object. For example, if you want the property settings the user makes in your control at design time to apply when the program runs, you must make the properties *persistent*. A persistent property is one whose value is stored and restored as needed.

Let's see an example. Here, we'll make the **Operand1** and **Operand2** properties of the calculator ActiveX control we've developed in the previous few topics persistent. To do that, we first call the Visual Basic **PropertyChanged** procedure when **Operand1** or **Operand2** is changed in its **Let** procedure. You pass the name of the property that's been changed to **PropertyChanged** like this:

```
Public Property Let Operand1(ByVal vNewValue As Variant)
    Text1.Text = vNewValue
    PropertyChanged "Operand1"
End Property

Public Property Let Operand2(ByVal vNewValue As Variant)
    Text2.Text = vNewValue
    PropertyChanged "Operand2"
End Property
```

When you call **PropertyChanged**, the control creates a **WriteProperties** event, and you can write the new settings of properties to the PropertyBag object, which stores them on disk. Here's how you use **WriteProperty**:

```
UserControl.WriteProperty(propertyname, value [,default])
```

For example, to write the current settings of the calculator's operands, we add this code to the **WriteProperties** event handler:

```
Private Sub UserControl_WriteProperties(PropBag As PropertyBag)
    PropBag.WriteProperty "Operand1", Text1.Text
    PropBag.WriteProperty "Operand2", Text2.Text
End Sub
```

When the control needs to read its stored properties, it creates a **ReadProperties** event, and in that event's handler, we can use **ReadProperty**:

```
UserControl.ReadProperty(propertyname [,default])
```

Here's how we use **ReadProperty** to read stored properties:

```
Private Sub UserControl_ReadProperties(PropBag As PropertyBag)
    Text1.Text = PropBag.ReadProperty("Operand1")
    Text2.Text = PropBag.ReadProperty("Operand2")
End Sub
```

Now the **Operand1** and **Operand2** properties are persistent. The code for this example, activexcalculatorcontrol.ctl version 2, appears in Listing 20.2.

Besides the **WriteProperties** and **ReadProperties** events, user controls also have **Initialize** events that occur when the control is opened at design time and **Terminate** events that occur when you switch to runtime from design time (in other words, the design time—instance of the control is terminated).

Here's the order of events that occur when you switch from design time to runtime:

• **WriteProperties**

• **Terminate**

• **ReadProperties**

And here's the order of events that occur when you switch from runtime to design time:

• **Initialize**

• **ReadProperties**

Listing 20.2   activexcalculatorcontrol.ctl version 2

```
VERSION 6.00
Begin VB.UserControl CalculatorControl
    ClientHeight    =    3600
    ClientLeft      =    0
    ClientTop       =    0
    ClientWidth     =    4500
    ScaleHeight     =    3600
    ScaleWidth      =    4500
    Begin VB.TextBox Text2
        Height      =    495
        Left        =    1680
        TabIndex    =    4
        Top         =    1200
        Width       =    1215
    End
    Begin VB.CommandButton Command1
        Caption     =    "="
        Height      =    495
```

```
            Left            =    1680
            TabIndex        =    3
            Top             =    1920
            Width           =    1215
         End
         Begin VB.TextBox Text3
            Height          =    495
            Left            =    1680
            TabIndex        =    1
            Top             =    2640
            Width           =    1215
         End
         Begin VB.TextBox Text1
            Height          =    495
            Left            =    1680
            TabIndex        =    0
            Top             =    300
            Width           =    1215
         End
         Begin VB.Label Label1
            Caption         =    "+"
            Height          =    255
            Left            =    2160
            TabIndex        =    2
            Top             =    840
            Width           =    375
         End
      End
   End
Attribute VB_Name = "CalculatorControl"
Attribute VB_GlobalNameSpace = False
Attribute VB_Creatable = True
Attribute VB_PredeclaredId = False
Attribute VB_Exposed = True
Private Sub Command1_Click()
    Text3.Text = Str(Val(Text1.Text) + Val(Text2.Text))
End Sub

Public Property Get Operand1() As Variant
    Operand1 = Text1.Text
End Property

Public Property Let Operand1(ByVal vNewValue As Variant)
    Text1.Text = vNewValue
    PropertyChanged "Operand1"
End Property
```

```
Public Property Get Operand2() As Variant
    Operand2 = Text2.Text
End Property

Public Property Let Operand2(ByVal vNewValue As Variant)
    Text2.Text = vNewValue
    PropertyChanged "Operand2"
End Property
Private Sub UserControl_ReadProperties(PropBag As PropertyBag)
    Text1.Text = PropBag.ReadProperty("Operand1")
    Text2.Text = PropBag.ReadProperty("Operand2")
End Sub

Private Sub UserControl_WriteProperties(PropBag As PropertyBag)
    PropBag.WriteProperty "Operand1", Text1.Text
    PropBag.WriteProperty "Operand2", Text2.Text
End Sub
```

Adding A Method To An ActiveX Control

In the previous topic, we saw how to add a property to an ActiveX control—but how do you add a method? You add a method to an ActiveX control in much the same way you add a property—with the Tool menu's Add Procedure dialog box.

Let's see an example. In this case, we'll add a new method to the calculator ActiveX control that we've developed in the previous few topics: the **Calculate** method. When the control's **Calculate** method is called, we can add the values in the top two text boxes in the calculator and display the result in the bottom text box (just like clicking the equal (=) button in the calculator).

Open the calculator ActiveX project in Visual Basic now and open the code window as well. Next, select the Add Procedure item in the Tools menu, opening the Add Procedure dialog box, as shown in Figure 20.15. Give this new method the name **Calculate**.

Select the entry labeled Sub to make our new method a **Sub** procedure, and make sure the entry labeled Public in the Scope box is selected (making this method available outside the ActiveX control to container programs). Then click on OK to close the Add Procedure dialog box.

Following these steps creates a new procedure, **Calculate**, in the calculator ActiveX control:

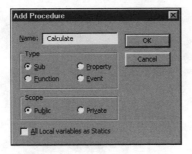

Figure 20.15   The Add Procedure dialog box.

```
Public Sub Calculate()

End Sub
```

If you have arguments you want passed to this method, just add them to the argument list between the parentheses as you would for any subroutine. In this case, we want to calculate the sum of the two operands now in **Text1** and **Text2** in this method, storing the sum in **Text3**, and we do that with this code:

```
Public Sub Calculate()
    Text3.Text = Str(Val(Text1.Text) + Val(Text2.Text))
End Sub
```

That's all we need; now create the calculator control and embed it in another program as, say, CalculatorControl1. When you do, you can use the control's **Calculate** method like this: **CalculatorControl1.Calculate**.

For example, we've added a new button with the caption Calculate to the project in Figure 20.16, and added this code to the command button's **Click** event:

```
Private Sub Command1_Click()
    CalculatorControl1.Calculate
End Sub
```

The result appears in Figure 20.16. When the user clicks the Calculate button, we execute the calculator ActiveX control's **Calculate** method. Our ActiveX method example is a success. The code for this example, activexcalculator-control.ctl version 3, appears in Listing 20.3.

TIP: Another way to set up methods in an ActiveX control is to use the ActiveX Control Interface Wizard in the Add-Ins menu (if that wizard does not appear in your Add-ins menu, select the Add-In Manager item in the Add-Ins menu and add the ActiveX Control Interface Wizard).

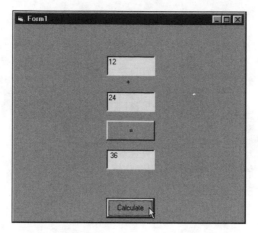

Figure 20.16   Calling a custom ActiveX control method.

Listing 20.3   activexcalculatorcontrol.ctl version 3

```
VERSION 6.00
Begin VB.UserControl CalculatorControl
    ClientHeight    =   3600
    ClientLeft      =   0
    ClientTop       =   0
    ClientWidth     =   4500
    ScaleHeight     =   3600
    ScaleWidth      =   4500
    Begin VB.TextBox Text2
        Height          =   495
        Left            =   1680
        TabIndex        =   4
        Top             =   1200
        Width           =   1215
    End
    Begin VB.CommandButton Command1
        Caption         =   "="
        Height          =   495
        Left            =   1680
        TabIndex        =   3
        Top             =   1920
        Width           =   1215
    End
    Begin VB.TextBox Text3
        Height          =   495
        Left            =   1680
        TabIndex        =   1
        Top             =   2640
```

```
            Width           =    1215
         End
         Begin VB.TextBox Text1
            Height          =    495
            Left            =    1680
            TabIndex        =    0
            Top             =    300
            Width           =    1215
         End
         Begin VB.Label Label1
            Caption         =    "+"
            Height          =    255
            Left            =    2160
            TabIndex        =    2
            Top             =    840
            Width           =    375
         End
      End
   End
Attribute VB_Name = "CalculatorControl"
Attribute VB_GlobalNameSpace = False
Attribute VB_Creatable = True
Attribute VB_PredeclaredId = False
Attribute VB_Exposed = True
Private Sub Command1_Click()
    Text3.Text = Str(Val(Text1.Text) + Val(Text2.Text))
End Sub


Public Property Get Operand1() As Variant
    Operand1 = Text1.Text
End Property


Public Property Let Operand1(ByVal vNewValue As Variant)
    Text1.Text = vNewValue
    PropertyChanged "Operand1"
End Property


Public Property Get Operand2() As Variant
    Operand2 = Text2.Text
End Property


Public Property Let Operand2(ByVal vNewValue As Variant)
    Text2.Text = vNewValue
    PropertyChanged "Operand2"
End Property
Private Sub UserControl_ReadProperties(PropBag As PropertyBag)
    Text1.Text = PropBag.ReadProperty("Operand1")
```

```
        Text2.Text = PropBag.ReadProperty("Operand2")
    End Sub

    Private Sub UserControl_WriteProperties(PropBag As PropertyBag)
        PropBag.WriteProperty "Operand1", Text1.Text
        PropBag.WriteProperty "Operand2", Text2.Text
    End Sub

    Public Sub Calculate()
        Text3.Text = Str(Val(Text1.Text) + Val(Text2.Text))
    End Sub
```

Adding An Event To An ActiveX Control

ActiveX controls can support events, of course, and the custom ActiveX controls you design with Visual Basic are no exception. You add events much like you add properties and methods—with the Add Procedure item in the Tools menu. After you create a new event, it's up to you to raise that event with the **RaiseEvent** method.

Let's see an example. Here, we'll add an event named **CalculatorClick** to the calculator ActiveX control we've developed in the previous few topics. When the user clicks the calculator control, this event, **CalculatorClick**, will occur.

To add this event to the calculator ActiveX control, open the calculator ActiveX project in Visual Basic, and open the code window as well. Next, select the Add Procedure item in the Tools menu to open the Add Procedure dialog box, as shown in Figure 20.17.

Type the name of this event, "CalculatorClick", into the Name box in the Add Procedure dialog box, select the option button labeled Event to indicate that

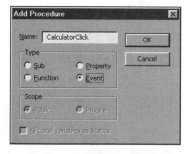

Figure 20.17   Adding an event to an ActiveX control.

we want to create a new event, and click OK. This creates the new event by declaring it in the ActiveX control's (General) section:

```
Public Event CalculatorClick()
```

If you want to add arguments to this event's handler procedures, just list them in the parentheses as you would for any procedure.

How do we make this new event active? It's up to us to raise this event when appropriate, using the **RaiseEvent** method. In this case, that's particularly easy—we'll just use the user control's **Click** event. Add a **Click** event handler to the calculator ActiveX control now:

```
Private Sub UserControl_Click ()

End Sub
```

This is the event handler that will be called when the calculator control is clicked, and we'll raise the **CalculatorClick** event here:

```
Private Sub UserControl_Click()
    RaiseEvent CalculatorClick
End Sub
```

TIP: *If your event supports arguments, you raise it and pass the arguments to it like this*

```
RaiseEvent eventname([argumentlist])
```

just as you would pass arguments to any procedure.

That's all we need. Now when you embed the calculator control in a Visual Basic program, you'll find that it has a **CalculatorClick** event that you can add text to:

```
Private Sub CalculatorControl1_CalculatorClick()
    CalculatorControl1.Calculate
End Sub
```

For example, we can call the calculator control's **Calculate** method when the user clicks that control, like this:

```
Private Sub CalculatorControl1_CalculatorClick()
    CalculatorControl1.Calculate
End Sub
```

In this way, we've added a new event to our ActiveX control. The code for the new version of the ActiveX calculator control is located in the activexcalculator-control folder on this book's accompanying CD-ROM.

TIP: Another way to set up events in an ActiveX control is to use the ActiveX Control Interface Wizard in the Add-Ins menu (if that wizard does not appear in your Add-Ins menu, select the Add-In Manager item in the Add-Ins menu and add the ActiveX Control Interface Wizard).

---

*Adding Design
Time Property
Pages*

Adding Design Time Property Pages

The Testing Department is calling again. Can't you add property pages to your new ActiveX control? The programmers who use your control are used to setting properties using property pages at design time.

You can add property pages to your control with the Visual Basic Property Page Wizard in the Add-Ins menu. If that wizard does not appear in your Add-ins menu, select the Add-In Manager item in the Add-Ins menu and add the Property Page Wizard. After you've added properties to an ActiveX control, you can use the Property Page Wizard to add property pages for those properties.

Let's see an example. Here, we'll add a set of property pages for our ActiveX calculator control that we've developed in the previous few topics. Start the Property Page Wizard by selecting that item in the Add-Ins menu now; a welcome screen will appear. Click the Next button until you get to the Select The Property Pages screen, as shown in Figure 20.18.

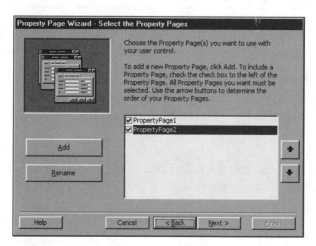

Figure 20.18   Creating property pages.

Here's where you set up the property pages your control will have. You can add property pages with the Add button and name them with the Rename button. In this case, the calculator control only has two properties, **Operand1** and **Operand2**, and we'll set up a separate property page for each, as shown in Figure 20.18.

Click Next to go to the next screen, Add Properties, as shown in Figure 20.19. Here you add properties from the list of all the available properties on the left to the property pages you've set up. Just click the tab matching the property page you want to add a property to, select the property in the list box at left, and click the right-pointing arrow button to add that property to the property page (or click the left-pointing arrow button to remove a button from a property page). In this way, you can organize which property appears on which page.

Finally, click Next to go to the Property Page Wizard's screen labeled Finished and click the Finish button. In this case, this creates two new property page documents, PropertyPage1.pag and PropertyPage2.pag, for your control, and adds them to your project. Save those files to disk and rebuild your control.

Now embed our ActiveX control in another program and open its property pages at design time, as shown in Figure 20.20. Now we're supporting property pages for custom ActiveX controls.

The code for the example property page files are located in the PropertyPage1 and PropertyPage2 folders on this book's accompanying CD-ROM.

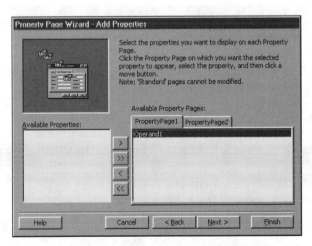

Figure 20.19   Adding properties to property pages.

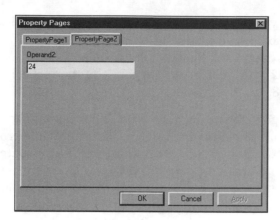

Figure 20.20   Our control's custom property pages

Creating An ActiveX Document

The Testing Department is calling again. The ActiveX controls you've been building are fine, but what about going on to the next step? How about creating an ActiveX *document*? You ask, why are ActiveX documents the next step? Because, they say, although ActiveX controls can appear in Web pages, ActiveX documents can *be* Web pages. That is, an entire Visual Basic form with all its controls can now appear in your Web browser or other application.

Let's see an example. To create a new ActiveX document, open the Visual Basic New Project dialog box, select the ActiveX document EXE entry, and click on OK (you can create either ActiveX document EXEs or DLLs—see the next topic for a discussion of the difference). This creates a new ActiveX document in Visual Basic, as shown in Figure 20.21.

To get our start with ActiveX documents, just double-click the document and add this code to the **Initialize** procedure that opens to draw a set of crisscrossing lines and a black box in the center of the document:

```
Private Sub UserDocument_Initialize()
    Line (0, 0)-(ScaleWidth, ScaleHeight)
    Line (0, ScaleHeight)-(ScaleWidth, 0)
    Line (ScaleWidth / 4, ScaleHeight / 4)-(3 * ScaleWidth / 4, _
        3 * ScaleHeight / 4), , BF
End Sub
```

This is the procedure that's run when the ActiveX document is first opened. Because we're drawing from the **Initialize** event handler, set the document's **AutoRedraw** property to True (just as you would for a form).

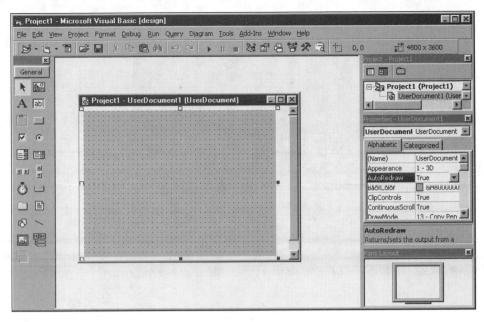

Figure 20.21   Creating a new ActiveX document.

Let's see our new ActiveX document at work in a Web browser (you can use ActiveX documents in other applications that support them, but Web browsers are particularly handy for testing ActiveX documents in an interactive way). Select the Project1 Properties item in the Project menu, and click the Debugging tab in the Project Properties dialog box that opens. Make sure that the option button labeled Start Component is selected (the start component should be given as **UserDocument1**) and the box labeled Use Existing Browser is checked. Then close the dialog box by clicking on OK, and run the document with the Start item in the Run menu.

Starting the document loads the document's specification, a VBD file, into the browser, which (if it supports ActiveX documents) runs the document's EXE file or adds the document's DLL file to its own process, as shown in Figure 20.22.

That's all there is to it. Now we've created our first ActiveX document. Still, not much is going on here yet. In the following topics, we'll develop our ActiveX documents further.

TIP: *Oh great, you're thinking, I've developed an extensive standard Visual Basic program based on forms, and now I've got to convert it into an ActiveX document? Visual Basic includes a wizard to help you in just this case: the ActiveX Document Migration Wizard. Just select that wizard in the Add-Ins menu (if the wizard does not appear in your Add-ins menu, select the Add-In Manager item in the Add-Ins menu and add the ActiveX Document Migration Wizard).*

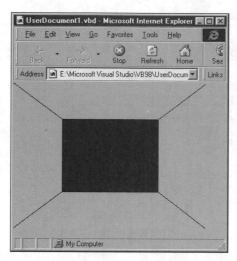

Figure 20.22   Opening our new ActiveX document in the Microsoft Internet Explorer.

ActiveX Document DLLs Vs. EXEs

You can create both ActiveX document EXEs and DLLs. Here's the difference: if an ActiveX document is written as an executable file (EXE file), it is an *out-of-process* server and runs in its own process; if it has been implemented as a dynamic link library (DLL file), it is an *in-process* server and runs in the same process as the client application.

Although ActiveX documents are usually built as EXE projects, the benefit of DLLs is that applications that use in-process servers usually run faster than those that use out-of-process servers because the application doesn't have to cross process boundaries to use an object's properties, methods, and events. In addition, the performance of an in-process component, or DLL file, surpasses that of the same component compiled as an EXE. Also, multiple programs accessing the same EXE can overwrite global data, but that doesn't happen if they each have their own in-process server.

Adding Controls To An ActiveX Document (A Tic-Tac-Toe Example)

The Testing Department is on the phone. The ActiveX document you've created is very nice, but why can't you do anything with it? Well, you say, I was just about to add controls to it and create a Web browser game.

Using ActiveX documents, you can display entire forms in Web browsers. To see this at work, we'll create a mini tic-tac-toe game. This game will let users click buttons to display alternate x's and o's (although it won't include the logic to actually play tic-tac-toe). Working with multiple controls in this way will demonstrate how to display entire programs as Web pages.

Create a new ActiveX document (EXE or DLL), and add nine command buttons to it arranged in a 3×3 grid in classic tic-tac-toe fashion. Give each button the same name, **Command**, clear each button's caption (that is, select the text in the caption and press the backspace key), and when Visual Basic asks if you want to create a control array, click Yes, because a control array will make the code shorter and easier to handle.

To alternate x's and o's as the user clicks buttons, we'll need a Boolean flag, which we'll call **blnXFlag**. If this flag is true, the next caption to set will be "x"; otherwise, "o". Add the declaration of **blnXFlag** to the (General) section:

```
Dim blnXFlag As Boolean
```

We also initalize **blnXFlag** to True when the document first loads by adding this code to the **Initialize** event handler:

```
Private Sub UserDocument_Initialize()
    blnXFlag = True
End Sub
```

Now when the user clicks a button, we alternate between setting the clicked buttons' captions to "x" and "o" this way:

```
Private Sub Command_Click(Index As Integer)
    If blnXFlag Then
        Command(Index).Caption = "x"
    Else
        Command(Index).Caption = "o"
    End If
    ...
End Sub
```

At the end of the code, we toggle the state of **blnXFlag** for the next time the user clicks a button:

```
Private Sub Command_Click(Index As Integer)
    If blnXFlag Then
        Command(Index).Caption = "x"
    Else
```

```
        Command(Index).Caption = "o"
    End If
    blnXFlag = Not blnXFlag
End Sub
```

Let's see our new ActiveX document game at work. Select the Project1 Properties item in the Project menu, and click the Debugging tab in the Project Properties dialog box that opens. Make sure that the option button labeled Start Component is selected (the start component should be given as **UserDocument1**), and the box labeled Use Existing Browser is checked. Then close the dialog box by clicking on OK, and run the game with the Start item in the Run menu.

The result appears in Figure 20.23. As you can see, our entire game appears in the Microsoft Internet Explorer. The user can alternate button captions just by clicking the buttons. Our ActiveX document example is a success.

We'll save the document as activextictactoe.dob (ActiveX documents have the extension .dob when saved in Visual Basic, just as form files have the extension .frm), and the project as activextictactoe.vbp. The default name for the document is UserDocument1, as you can see in the Visual Basic Properties window; if you want to use a different name for the document, set it in the Properties window. We'll change the document name to activextictactoedoc. When we create the VBD specification file for this document, then, that file will be activextictactoedoc.vbd, and that's the file to open in your Web browser

The code for this example, activextictactoedoc.dob version 1 (version 2 will support persistent data), appears in Listing 20.4.

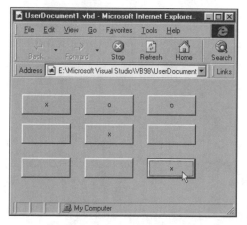

Figure 20.23   Our tic-tac-toe ActiveX document.

Listing 20.4   activextictactoedoc.dob version 1

```
VERSION 6.00
Begin VB.UserDocument activextictactoedoc
   AutoRedraw          =   -1  'True
   ClientHeight        =   2865
   ClientLeft          =   0
   ClientTop           =   0
   ClientWidth         =   4800
   HScrollSmallChange=   225
   ScaleHeight         =   2865
   ScaleWidth          =   4800
   VScrollSmallChange=   225
   Begin VB.CommandButton Command
      Height           =      495
      Index            =      8
      Left             =      3360
      TabIndex         =      8
      Top              =      1920
      Width            =      1215
   End
   Begin VB.CommandButton Command
      Height           =      495
      Index            =      7
      Left             =      3360
      TabIndex         =      7
      Top              =      1080
      Width            =      1215
   End
   Begin VB.CommandButton Command
      Height           =      495
      Index            =      6
      Left             =      3360
      TabIndex         =      6
      Top              =      360
      Width            =      1215
   End
   Begin VB.CommandButton Command
      Height           =      495
      Index            =      5
      Left             =      1800
      TabIndex         =      5
      Top              =      1920
      Width            =      1215
   End
```

```
      Begin VB.CommandButton Command
         Height          =   495
         Index           =   4
         Left            =   1800
         TabIndex        =   4
         Top             =   1080
         Width           =   1215
      End
      Begin VB.CommandButton Command
         Height          =   495
         Index           =   3
         Left            =   1800
         TabIndex        =   3
         Top             =   360
         Width           =   1215
      End
      Begin VB.CommandButton Command
         Height          =   495
         Index           =   2
         Left            =   240
         TabIndex        =   2
         Top             =   1920
         Width           =   1215
      End
      Begin VB.CommandButton Command
         Height          =   495
         Index           =   1
         Left            =   240
         TabIndex        =   1
         Top             =   1080
         Width           =   1215
      End
      Begin VB.CommandButton Command
         Height          =   495
         Index           =   0
         Left            =   240
         TabIndex        =   0
         Top             =   360
         Width           =   1215
      End
   End
End
Attribute VB_Name = "activextictactoedoc"
Attribute VB_GlobalNameSpace = False
Attribute VB_Creatable = True
Attribute VB_PredeclaredId = False
Attribute VB_Exposed = True
```

```
Option Explicit
Dim blnXFlag As Boolean

Private Sub Command_Click(Index As Integer)
    If blnXFlag Then
        Command(Index).Caption = "x"
    Else
        Command(Index).Caption = "o"
    End If
    blnXFlag = Not blnXFlag
End Sub

Private Sub UserDocument_Initialize()
    blnXFlag = True
End Sub
```

Handling Constituent Control Events In An ActiveX Document

After you add controls to an ActiveX document, how do you handle the events those controls create? That's the beauty of it all—you handle such events just as you would in a standard Visual Basic EXE program, so designing an ActiveX document is really just like designing a standard form in Visual Basic.

If you haven't already done so, take a look at the tic-tac-toe game we developed in the previous topic. There, we set up a control array of nine buttons and handled the button clicks just as you would in a standard Visual Basic form:

```
Private Sub Command_Click(Index As Integer)
    If blnXFlag Then
        Command(Index).Caption = "x"
    Else
        Command(Index).Caption = "o"
    End If
    blnXFlag = Not blnXFlag
End Sub
```

Microsoft has worked hard to make sure that creating ActiveX documents is as easy as creating standard Visual Basic EXE programs in the hopes that ActiveX documents will become popular, and the programmer is the winner.

Testing An ActiveX Document

To test an ActiveX document—and even debug it—while in the design process using your ActiveX document-supporting Web browser (such as the Microsoft Internet Explorer), just follow these steps:

1. Select the *ProjectName* Properties item in the Project menu (where *ProjectName* is the name of your project).

2. Click the Debugging tab in the Project Properties dialog box that opens.

3. Make sure that the option button labeled Start Component is selected (the start component should be given as the name of your document, such as **UserDocument1**).

4. To use your existing browser, make sure the box labeled Use Existing Browser is checked.

5. Close the dialog box by clicking on OK.

6. Start the document with the Start item in the Run menu.

When you follow these steps, Visual Basic creates a VBD file for your document and opens that file in your Web browser (VBD files hold the ActiveX document's specification and tell the browser where to find the document's EXE or DLL file).

Creating ActiveX Documents That Run Outside Visual Basic

The Testing Department is calling again. Your new ActiveX document is a winner, but how come you can only launch it from Visual Basic? Hmm, you say, I'll look into it.

ActiveX documents need either an EXE or a DLL file and a VBD file. (You select either EXE or DLL when you create the document—see "ActiveX Document DLLs Vs. EXEs," earlier in this chapter.) How do you create these files?

When you create an ActiveX document, you save it with the extension .dob. Visual Basic uses that DOB file to create the EXE or DLL file that holds the actual code for the ActiveX document. To create the EXE or DLL file, just select the Make *ProjectName*.exe item in the File menu (where *ProjectName* is your project's name).

In addition, Visual Basic produces the specification file, with the extension .vbd, that describes the ActiveX document, and it's that file that you actually

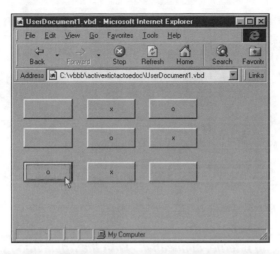

Figure 20.24   Displaying a VBD file in the Microsoft Internet Explorer.

open in the host application, such as the Microsoft Internet Explorer. To open the ActiveX document in the Internet Explorer, you just open the VBD file directly (use the File menu's Open item), as shown in Figure 20.24, where we've opened the VBD file for the tic-tac-toe document we developed in the previous few topics.

Distributed Computing: ActiveX Documents And Integrated Browsers

The Testing Department is calling. Now that the company's grown so huge (thanks to the success of your programs), we need to start using the Internet for the company reps in the field. Can't we download updated programs in a transparent way over the Internet? You think about ActiveX documents and say, no problem.

If you integrate a Web browser into a program, you can have that browser download ActiveX documents in a seamless way that makes those documents look like part of the program itself. In this way, users can download ActiveX documents filled with current data into a program in a way that seems transparent to them.

Let's see an example. Here, we'll add a Web browser to a program and use it to open the tic-tac-toe ActiveX document we've developed in the previous few topics. To create a program with a built-in Web browser, use the Visual Basic

Figure 20.25   Setting Internet connectivity with the Application Wizard.

Application Wizard. When the Application Wizard asks you about Internet connectivity, as shown in Figure 20.25, click the option button labeled Yes, and enter the URL of your document's VBD file (which can be on the Internet) in the startup URL box; here, we'll use the disk location of our VBD file, which is C:\vbbb\activextictactoedoc\activextictactoedoc.vbd. Then click the Finish button to create the program.

At design time, we can customize the program even more by changing the caption of the menu item that opens the game from "Web browser" to "Tic Tac Toe", and editing the browser form, **frmBrowser**, by removing the combo box that shows the URL and all the buttons. We can also stretch the Web browser control (**brwWebBrowser**) so it covers the whole **frmBrowser** form.

Customizing the browser form this way prevents it from appearing as a Web browser at all. Instead, it will look like a part of your program; the fact that it comes from the Internet is entirely transparent to the user. (You can also remove the form's title bar so the name of the displayed ActiveX document is not displayed, but we won't go that far here.)

Running this program and selecting the Tic Tac Toe menu item opens that ActiveX document in the program, as shown in Figure 20.26. The ActiveX document looks just like any other part of the program, which is the idea behind distributed computing.

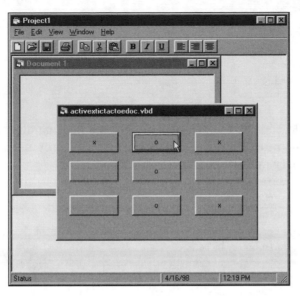

Figure 20.26   Opening an ActiveX document in a program with a Web browser.

Making ActiveX Document Properties Persistent (PropertyBag Object)

Just as with ActiveX controls, you can make the data in ActiveX documents *persistent*, which means the data is stored when you close the document and restored in the display when you open the document. How does this work? To make the data in an ActiveX document persistent, you use the **PropertyChanged** method as you do with ActiveX controls, and use the **ReadProperty** and **WriteProperty** methods.

Let's see an example to make this clearer. Here, we'll store the data in the tic-tac-toe ActiveX document game we've developed in the previous few topics. First, we notify the document that the game properties (that is, the captions of the buttons in the game) have changed by calling **PropertyChanged** when the user clicks a button (you can pass the name of the property that's changed to **PropertyChanged**, as we did when working with ActiveX controls earlier in this chapter, but here we'll just write all the captions in our control array when the user clicks a button to make the coding a little easier):

```
Private Sub Command_Click(Index As Integer)
    If blnXFlag Then
        Command(Index).Caption = "x"
```

```
        Else
            Command(Index).Caption = "o"
        End If
        blnXFlag = Not blnXFlag
        PropertyChanged
    End Sub
```

Next, we add code to the **WriteProperties** event handler to write the captions of the buttons to the PropertyBag object using that object's **WriteProperty** method:

```
Private Sub UserDocument_WriteProperties(PropBag As PropertyBag)
    Dim intLoopIndex As Integer

    For intLoopIndex = 0 To 8
        PropBag.WriteProperty "Command(" & Str(intLoopIndex) & ")", _
            Command(intLoopIndex).Caption
    Next intLoopIndex
End Sub
```

In addition, we read the property settings back in when needed in the **ReadProperties** event handler:

```
Private Sub UserDocument_ReadProperties(PropBag As PropertyBag)
    Dim intLoopIndex As Integer

    For intLoopIndex = 0 To 8
        Command(intLoopIndex).Caption = PropBag.ReadProperty("Command(" _
            & Str(intLoopIndex) & ")")
    Next intLoopIndex
End Sub
```

With this new code, the user can make changes to our ActiveX document when it's open in the Web browser and save those changes in the document (which, after all, is the purpose of documents—to save data).

The code for this new version of activextictactoedoc.dob is located in the activextictactoedoc folder on this book's accompanying CD-ROM.

Chapter 21

Visual Basic And The Internet: Web Browsing, Email, HTTP, FTP, And DHTML

If you need an immediate solution to:	See page:
Creating A Web Browser	699
Specifying URLs In A Web Browser	700
Adding Back And Forward Buttons To A Web Browser	704
Adding Refresh, Home, And Stop Buttons To A Web Browser	705
Creating DHTML Pages	706
Adding Text To DHTML Pages	709
Adding Images To DHTML Pages	710
Adding HTML Controls To DHTML Pages	712
Adding ActiveX Controls To DHTML Pages	713
Adding Tables To DHTML Pages	715
Adding Hyperlinks To DHTML Pages	716
Using MAPI Controls To Support Email	717
Sending Email From Visual Basic	721
Reading Email In Visual Basic	725
Using The Internet Transfer Control For FTP And HTTP Operations	727
Handling FTP Operations In Visual Basic	728
Handling HTTP Operations In Visual Basic	734

In Depth

In this chapter, we'll see how to create a Web browser, create a dynamic HTML page (DHTML), and work with email and the HTTP and FTP protocols. Not surprisingly, these are all hot topics in Visual Basic.

Creating A Web Browser

If you have the Microsoft Internet Explorer installed, you can build Web browsers using Visual Basic. Microsoft has packaged the Internet Explorer in a control, the WebBrowser control, and we'll be able to use that control to create a Web browser in this chapter that supports such browser functionality as Back, Forward, Home, Stop, and Refresh buttons. We'll also let the user specify what URL to navigate to with a combo box—as well as keeping track of recently visited URLs in that combo box.

Building a Web browser can be a worthwhile project in itself, but another popular use of the WebBrowser control is to add a Web browser to your existing program for added power. In fact, you can use the WebBrowser control to open ActiveX documents (as we did in Chapter 20) in a way that makes them look like a seamless part of the program—even though that document may have come from the Internet.

Creating A Dynamic HTML Page

Dynamic HTML is the new, although amorphous, Web page standard (that is, Netscape and Microsoft think of dynamic HTML as entirely different things). The Microsoft standard for DHTML makes all the tags in a Web page active elements in the sense that they have properties you can change at runtime, as well as events like **Click**. The DirectAnimation and DirectShow Internet Explorer packages are part of Microsoft DHTML as well.

Visual Basic can write dynamic HTML—in fact, you can now use Visual Basic as an HTML editor, adding text, images, hyperlinks, and tables. We'll see how to do that in this chapter. There's more here too. You can add ActiveX controls directly to your Web pages when designing them in the DHTML Designer. We'll see how to create Web pages using that designer and how to test them out in the Internet Explorer immediately, from Visual Basic.

Working With Email

Visual Basic includes support for working with email as well. That support is based on the Microsoft Exchange utility that's installed with Windows (and usually appears on the Windows desktop as the Inbox icon). In this chapter, we'll see how to connect Visual Basic to the Microsoft Exchange to handle email. To do that, we'll use the ActiveX MAPI controls (Messaging Applications Programming Interface) that come with Visual Basic.

To connect to the email system, you create a new MAPI session using the MAPISession control. When the session is created, you use the MAPIMessages control to work with individual messages. Note that these controls are interfaces to the Microsoft Exchange package, which means that we'll be using that package to send and receive email.

Using FTP

FTP (File Transfer Protocol) is a very popular Internet protocol for, as its name implies, transferring files. Visual Basic has good support for FTP work, and that support is contained in the Visual Basic Internet transfer control. That control has two approaches to working with FTP. You can use the **OpenURL** method to easily download a file from an FTP site. In addition, you can execute standard FTP commands with the control's **Execute** method. Using **Execute**, you can make use of the standard FTP commands like **CD**, **GET**, **CLOSE**, **QUIT**, **SEND**, and so on.

Using HTTP

HTTP (Hypertext Transfer Protocol) is the protocol on which the World Wide Web is based. As most programmers know, this is the protocol used for Web pages on the Internet. Because we're going to build a functioning Web browser in this chapter, you may wonder why we want to work with the HTTP protocol directly. The answer is that although Web browsers do indeed download and display Web pages, there's a lot more you can do with the HTTP protocol. When you download a file using the Internet transfer control's **OpenURL** method, you get access to the file's HTML directly, which is important if you want to interpret that HTML in a way different from how the Internet Explorer would. You can also use that control's **Execute** method to execute HTTP commands directly.

You can even write your own Web browser or use emerging Web languages like XML (Extended Markup Language). XML, intended to be a successor to HTML, allows you to create your own markup tags in a well-defined way, on a document-by-document basis. When reading those tags, it's up to the browser to interpret them, and you can write such XML browser programs in Visual Basic.

TIP: *Microsoft has made an XML parser available on its Web site in two versions: a Java version and a Visual C++ version. (Its URL keeps changing, though, so search the site for "XML parser".) This parser breaks XML documents down tag by tag in a way that makes reading XML documents more systematic. You can connect the Visual C++ version to Visual Basic if you place your Visual C++ code in a dynamic link library that Visual Basic can link in, but the Visual C++ parser is so complex to use that it may not be worth the bother. One aspect of the Microsoft parser is, however, very useful: it can tell you if an XML document meets the XML specification for being valid and well formed.*

Besides using the Internet transfer control's **OpenURL** method, you can also use the **Execute** method to execute such common HTTP commands as **GET**, **POST**, and **PUT**.

That's it for the overview of Visual Basic and the Internet for the moment—it's time to turn to our Immediate Solutions.

Immediate Solutions

Creating A Web Browser

The Testing Department is calling again. They need a new Web browser program right away. What's wrong with the old one? you ask. They say, it doesn't display the founder's picture. Oh, you say.

It's easy to build a Web browser in Visual Basic—you just use the Microsoft WebBrowser control. In this and the next few topics, we'll put together the functioning Web browser that you see in Figure 21.1. Our browser will support Back, Next, Home, Stop, and Refresh buttons, as you can see in that figure. In addition, the browser will have all the power of the Microsoft Internet Explorer (largely because it *is* the Internet Explorer; we use the WebBrowser control, which is the Internet Explorer in a control). To let the user navigate, we'll include a combo box, as you see in Figure 21.1. When the user types a new URL in the combo box and presses the Enter key, we'll navigate to that URL (and keep a record of the URLs we've been to in the combo box's drop-down list).

To create our Web browser, follow these steps:

1. Create a new standard Visual Basic project.
2. Select the Project|Components item.
3. Click the Controls tab in the Components dialog box.
4. Select the Microsoft Internet Controls and Microsoft Windows Common Controls entries, and click on OK to close the Components dialog box.
5. Add a WebBrowser control and a toolbar to the form, stretching the WebBrowser control, **WebBrowser1**, to fill the space under the toolbar.

Figure 21.1   Our Web browser.

6. Add five buttons to the toolbar (right-click the toolbar, select the Properties item, click the Buttons tab, and use the Insert Button button to add the buttons).

7. Give the buttons the same captions and **Key** properties: Back, Next, Home, Stop, and Refresh (for example, the button with the caption "Back" will also have its **Key** property set to Back so we can identify which button in the toolbar was clicked).

8. Add a combo box, **combo1**, to the end of the toolbar (draw the combo box in the toolbar to make sure it's part of the toolbar; don't double-click to create a combo box and then move it to the toolbar).

That sets up the Web browser—but how do we work with it in code? We'll take a look at that in the next few topics.

Specifying URLs In A Web Browser

Now that you've set up the controls we'll need in a Web browser (see the previous topic), how do you let the user navigate?

You use the WebBrowser control's **Navigate** method. Let's see this at work. For example, when our Web browser first loads, we can navigate to the Microsoft Web page this way (note that you can specify URLs with or without the "http://" part in the Internet Explorer, and although we omit it here, you can include that prefix if you prefer):

```
Private Sub Form_Load()
    WebBrowser1.Navigate "www.microsoft.com"
...
End Sub
```

We also want the user to be able to navigate to a new URL, and that's usually done with a combo box like the one we added to our Web browser in the previous topic, **combo1**. We start working with **combo1** by displaying the present URL and adding it to the combo box's drop-down list:

```
Private Sub Form_Load()
    WebBrowser1.Navigate "www.microsoft.com"
    Combo1.Text = "www.microsoft.com"
    Combo1.AddItem Combo1.Text
End Sub
```

Users can select past URLs from the combo box's drop-down list. When they do select a URL that way, a **Click** event is generated, and we can navigate to the newly selected URL this way:

```
Private Sub Combo1_Click()
    WebBrowser1.Navigate Combo1.Text
End Sub
```

In addition, users can type a new URL into the combo box and press Enter, just as they can in commercial browsers. When they press Enter, we can navigate to the new URL simply by calling the **Combo1_Click** event handler directly from the **KeyPress** event handler:

```
Private Sub Combo1_KeyPress(KeyAscii As Integer)
    If KeyAscii = vbKeyReturn Then
        Combo1_Click
    End If
End Sub
```

Finally, when the downloading process is complete, the WebBrowser control fires a **DownloadComplete** event, and we can display the present URL in the browser's title bar, just as any commercial browser might. To do that, we get the browser's present URL from its **LocationName** property:

```
Private Sub WebBrowser1_DownloadComplete()
    Me.Caption = WebBrowser1.LocationName
...
End Sub
```

In addition, we can add that URL to the top of the combo box's list this way:

```
Private Sub WebBrowser1_DownloadComplete()
    Me.Caption = WebBrowser1.LocationName
    Combo1.AddItem WebBrowser1.LocationURL, 0
End Sub
```

And that's it—now the user can navigate around using the combo box. However, we have yet to make all the buttons, such as Back, Forward, and Home, active, and we'll do that in the next two topics. The code for the browser, browser.frm version 1 (version 2, which is included on the accompanying CD-ROM, will include support for the browser buttons), appears in Listing 21.1.

TIP: *In our example, we made the Web browser navigate to the Microsoft home page when the browser is first opened. However, you can make the browser start with the user's home page (as recorded by the Internet Explorer) with the browser control's **GoHome** method.*

Listing 21.1   browser.frm version 1

```
VERSION 6.00
Object = "{EAB22ACO-30C1-11CF-A7EB-0000C05BAE0B}#1.1#0"; "SHDOCVW.DLL"
Object = "{6B7E6392-850A-101B-AFCO-4210102A8DA7}#2.0#0"; "MSCOMCTL.OCX"
Begin VB.Form Form1
   Caption         =   "Form1"
   ClientHeight    =   3195
   ClientLeft      =   60
   ClientTop       =   345
   ClientWidth     =   7560
   LinkTopic       =   "Form1"
   ScaleHeight     =   3195
   ScaleWidth      =   7560
   StartUpPosition =   3  'Windows Default
   Begin ComctlLib.Toolbar Toolbar1
      Align          =   1  'Align Top
      Height         =   630
      Left           =   0
      TabIndex       =   1
      Top            =   0
      Width          =   7560
      _ExtentX       =   13335
      _ExtentY       =   1111
      ButtonWidth    =   1164
      ButtonHeight   =   953
      Appearance     =   1
      _Version       =   393216
      BeginProperty Buttons {66833FE8-8583-11D1-B16A-00C0F0283628}
         NumButtons     =   6
         BeginProperty Button1 {66833FEA-8583-11D1-B16A-00C0F0283628}
            Caption        =   "Back"
            Key            =   "Back"
         EndProperty
         BeginProperty Button2 {66833FEA-8583-11D1-B16A-00C0F0283628}
            Caption        =   "Next"
            Key            =   "Next"
         EndProperty
         BeginProperty Button3 {66833FEA-8583-11D1-B16A-00C0F0283628}
            Caption        =   "Home"
            Key            =   "Home"
         EndProperty
         BeginProperty Button4 {66833FEA-8583-11D1-B16A-00C0F0283628}
            Caption        =   "Stop"
            Key            =   "Stop"
         EndProperty
```

```
        BeginProperty Button5 {66833FEA-8583-11D1-B16A-00C0F0283628}
            Caption         =     "Refresh"
            Key             =     "Refresh"
        EndProperty
        BeginProperty Button6 {66833FEA-8583-11D1-B16A-00C0F0283628}
            Style           =     4
            Object.Width            =     100
        EndProperty
    EndProperty
    Begin VB.ComboBox Combo1
        Height          =     315
        Left            =     3480
        TabIndex        =     2
        Top             =     120
        Width           =     3975
    End
End
Begin SHDocVwCtl.WebBrowser WebBrowser1
    Height          =     2295
    Left            =     120
    TabIndex        =     0
    Top             =     840
    Width           =     7335
    ExtentX         =     12938
    ExtentY         =     4048
    ViewMode        =     1
    Offline         =     0
    Silent          =     0
    RegisterAsBrowser=    0
    RegisterAsDropTarget=    1
    AutoArrange     =     -1   'True
    NoClientEdge    =     0    'False
    AlignLeft       =     0    'False
    ViewID          =     "{0057D0E0-3573-11CF-AE69-08002B2E1262}"
    Location        =     ""
End
End
Attribute VB_Name = "Form1"
Attribute VB_GlobalNameSpace = False
Attribute VB_Creatable = False
Attribute VB_PredeclaredId = True
Attribute VB_Exposed = False
Private Sub Form_Load()
    WebBrowser1.Navigate "www.microsoft.com"
    Combo1.Text = "www.microsoft.com"
    Combo1.AddItem Combo1.Text
End Sub
```

```
Private Sub WebBrowser1_DownloadComplete()
    Me.Caption = WebBrowser1.LocationName
    Combo1.AddItem WebBrowser1.LocationURL, 0
End Sub

Private Sub Combo1_Click()
    WebBrowser1.Navigate Combo1.Text
End Sub

Private Sub Combo1_KeyPress(KeyAscii As Integer)
    If KeyAscii = vbKeyReturn Then
        Combo1_Click
    End If
End Sub
```

*Adding Back
And Forward
Buttons To A
Web Browser*

Adding Back And Forward Buttons To A Web Browser

Now that we've set up a Web browser in which the user can navigate by typing URLs into the combo box (see the previous topic), we'll enable the Back and Forward buttons in the browser.

That's easier than you might expect—you just use the browser's **GoBack** or **GoForward** methods. We do that like this, where we determine which button in the toolbar has been clicked by checking the keys we've added to those buttons:

```
Private Sub Toolbar1_ButtonClick(ByVal Button As Button)
    Select Case Button.Key
        Case "Back"
            WebBrowser1.GoBack
        Case "Forward"
            WebBrowser1.GoForward
    End Select

End Sub
```

And that's all there is to it—now the user can navigate forwards and backwards in the browser's history. We've added Back and Forward buttons now, but the user also expects Refresh, Home, and Stop buttons in Web browsers, and we'll add those buttons next.

Adding Refresh, Home, And Stop Buttons To A Web Browser

In the previous few topics, we've set up a Web browser complete with combo box to let the user enter and select URLs, as well as a Back and Forward button to let the user navigate through the browser's history. However, we still have a few more buttons to implement: the Refresh, Home, and Stop buttons.

We can implement those buttons with the Web browser control's **Refresh**, **GoHome**, and **Stop** methods. We've given the Refresh, Home, and Stop buttons the keys "Refresh", "Home", and "Stop", so we just call the appropriate Web browser method when the matching button is clicked (note that if the user clicks the Stop button, we also update the current URL as displayed in the browser's title bar using the Web browser's **LocationName** property):

```
Private Sub Toolbar1_ButtonClick(ByVal Button As Button)
    Select Case Button.Key
        Case "Back"
            WebBrowser1.GoBack
        Case "Forward"
            WebBrowser1.GoForward
        Case "Refresh"
            WebBrowser1.Refresh
        Case "Home"
            WebBrowser1.GoHome
        Case "Stop"
            WebBrowser1.Stop
            Me.Caption = WebBrowser1.LocationName
    End Select
End Sub
```

Now the user can use the new buttons, Refresh, Home, and Stop. The code for the finished Web browser is located in the browser folder on this book's accompanying CD-ROM.

TIP: *You used to be able to specify the browser's search page in the Internet Explorer, but as of Internet Explorer version 4, you are taken to a page of Microsoft's choosing. If you still want to implement a Search button, however, just use the WebBrowser control's **GoSearch** method.*

Creating DHTML Pages

The Testing Department is on the phone. You may have heard of the company's Web site crash—they need to redesign the company Web page. From scratch. Can you do it? You start up Visual Basic—sure, you say, no problem.

You can use Visual Basic to design dynamic HTML pages. To do that, just select the Dynamic HTML Application item in the Visual Basic New Project dialog box. This opens the DHTML Page Designer you see in Figure 21.2.

In the following few topics, we'll see how to use the DHTML Page Designer to implement DHTML pages. In general, you add the elements you want in your page to the right window in the Page Designer, and it gives you an idea of how the page will look in the browser. The window on the left in the Page Designer shows the logical structure of the page by indicating which HTML elements are contained in other HTML elements. Using the Page Designer, then, you can get an idea of both how your page will look and how it's organized in HTML.

Note that you can use Visual Basic in the DHTML pages designed with Visual Basic. How is this possible? It's possible because what you're really creating is an ActiveX DLL project that will be loaded into the Internet Explorer when you open the Web page. This DLL runs in the Internet Explorer's process (and you have to place the DLL file for the project on your Web site so it can be downloaded). To make the needed DLL file, just select the Make *ProjectName*.dll item in the File menu.

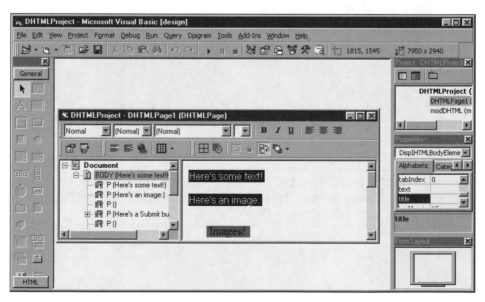

Figure 21.2   The Visual Basic DHTML Page Designer.

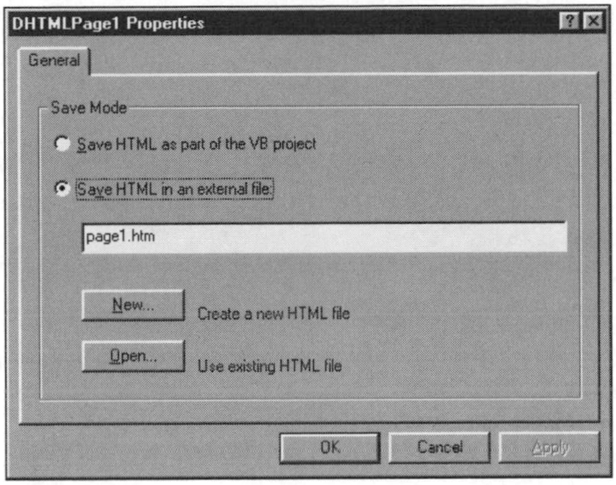

Figure 21.3   The DHTML Page Designer Properties dialog box.

You might just want to create an HTML Web page, without any DLL files at all, and you can do that too. Just don't add any code to the page; stick to standard HTML elements. Usually, the HTML page is stored in the Visual Basic project. To store it in a separate HTM file, click the DHTML Page Designer Properties icon at upper left in the DHTML Page Designer, opening the Properties dialog box, as shown in Figure 21.3.

Select the Save HTML in an external file option, and give an HTM file name to save your Web page as. To test the Web page, select the DHTMLProject Properties item in the Project menu, clicking the Debugging tab in the Properties pages that open. Make sure the Start Component option button is clicked and the start component is set to DHTMLPage1, then click on OK. Now select the Start item in the Run menu to open the Web page.

Now that we've started designing our DHTML Web page, we'll add text, images, tables, and other elements—including ActiveX controls—to the page in the next few topics. For reference, the Web page that we create, page1.htm, appears in Listing 21.2.

Listing 21.2   page1.htm

```
<HTML>
<HEAD>

<META content="text/html; charset=iso-8859-1" http-equiv=Content-Type>
<META content='"MSHTML 4.72.3007.2"' name=GENERATOR>
</HEAD>

<BODY>
<P>Here's some text!</P>
```

```
<P>Here's an image:</P>

<P> </P>

<P>Here's <INPUT id=SubmitButton1 name=SubmitButton1 style="LEFT: 17px;
POSITION: absolute; TOP: 170px; Z-INDEX: 103" type=submit
value=SubmitButton1>a
Submit button:
</P>
<P> </P>
<P><IMG id=Image1 name=Image1
src="c:\vbbb\dhtml\image1.bmp"
style="LEFT: 40px; POSITION: absolute; TOP: 107px; Z-INDEX: 100">
</P>
<P>
<OBJECT classid=CLSID:35053A22-8589-11D1-B16A-00C0F0283628 height=24
id=ProgressBar1
style="HEIGHT: 24px; LEFT: 127px; POSITION: absolute; TOP: 248px; WIDTH:
100px; Z-INDEX: 101"
width=100>
    <PARAM NAME="_ExtentX" VALUE="2646">
    <PARAM NAME="_ExtentY" VALUE="635">
    <PARAM NAME="_Version" VALUE="393216">
    <PARAM NAME="BorderStyle" VALUE="0">
    <PARAM NAME="Appearance" VALUE="1">
    <PARAM NAME="MousePointer" VALUE="0">
    <PARAM NAME="Enabled" VALUE="1">
    <PARAM NAME="OLEDropMode" VALUE="0">
    <PARAM NAME="Min" VALUE="0">
    <PARAM NAME="Max" VALUE="100">
    <PARAM NAME="Orientation" VALUE="0">
    <PARAM NAME="Scrolling" VALUE="0">
</OBJECT>
<INPUT id=Button1 name=Button1 style="LEFT: 26px; POSITION: absolute;
TOP:
248px; Z-INDEX: 102" type=button value="Click Me!">
</P>
<P>Here's an ActiveX control:</P>
<P align=center> </P>
<P>Here's a table:</P>
<P>
<TABLE border=1 id=Table1 name = Table1>

    <TR>
        <TD>This
        <TD>is
        <TD>a
```

```
    <TR>
        <TD>3x3
        <TD>HTML
        <TD>table
    <TR>
        <TD>ready
        <TD>to
        <TD>use.</TD></TR></TABLE></P>
<P>Here's a hyperlink:
<A href="http://www.microsoft.com"
id=Hyperlink11 name=Hyperlink1>Microsoft
</A>
</P>
</BODY>
</HTML>
```

Adding Text To DHTML Pages

Adding text to a DHTML page is easy: just click the right window in the DHTML Page Designer (which represents the way your page will look when it runs). Just use the mouse to place the blinking insertion point where you want the text to appear, and type the text you want there. For example, we've added the text "Here's some text!" in the Web page in the Page Designer in Figure 21.4.

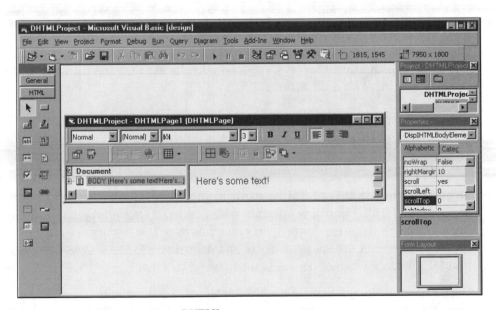

Figure 21.4   Adding text to a DHTML page.

Adding the text we've placed in our Web page adds this HTML to the Web page itself—note the Page Designer uses the **<P>** paragraph HTML tag for each paragraph of text:

```
<HTML>
<HEAD>

<META content="text/html; charset=iso-8859-1" http-equiv=Content-Type>
<META content='"MSHTML 4.72.3007.2"' name=GENERATOR>
</HEAD>

<BODY>
<P>Here's some text!</P>
```

You can format the text by selecting the text font, size, and style (bold, italic, or underlined) with the controls at the top of the Page Designer. Besides being able to format the text, you can also specify its alignment—right, center, or left—with the buttons in the Page Designer's toolbar.

TIP: You can break DHTML Web pages into sections using the **<SPAN>** and **<DIV>** tags, which you insert using buttons in the DHTML Page Designer toolbar. These HTML elements are especially important in DHTML because you can specify dynamic HTML styles and properties that apply specifically to **<SPAN>** or **<DIV>**.

Adding Images To DHTML Pages

The Aesthetic Design Department is calling again. Your new Web page is fine, but what about adding images? Can you do that? you ask. Sure, they say, that's half of what the Web is all about.

To add an image to a DHTML page in the Visual Basic DHTML Page Designer, you click the Image tool, which is the sixth tool down on the left in the Page Designer toolbox in Figure 21.5. Doing so adds an empty image to the page; move that image to the position you want and size it appropriately.

To add an image to this DHTML control, set its **src** property (the name of this and other DHTML control properties are intended to match the corresponding HTML tag attributes; this property matches the **<IMG>** tag's **src** attribute). In this case, we set the **src** property to an image on disk: file:/// C:/vbbb/dhtml/ image1.bmp, although of course you can use a URL here.

Here's how the image is added to the HTML of our Web page—note that the Page Designer sets the **<IMG>** tag's **position** attribute to **absolute**, which is how it can let you position the image anywhere you want in the Web page:

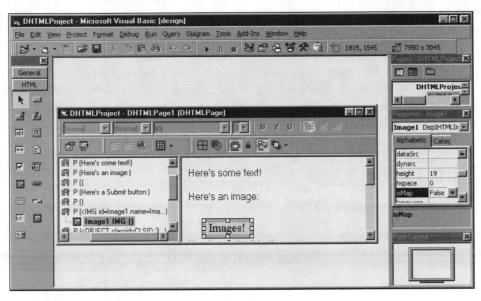

Figure 21.5   Adding an image to a DHTML Web page.

```
<HTML>
<HEAD>

<META content="text/html; charset=iso-8859-1" http-equiv=Content-Type>
<META content='"MSHTML 4.72.3007.2"' name=GENERATOR>
</HEAD>

<BODY>
<P>Here's some text!</P>

<P>Here's an image:</P>

<P> </P>

<P><IMG id=Image1 name=Image1
src="c:\vbbb\dhtml\image1.bmp"
style="LEFT: 40px; POSITION: absolute; TOP: 107px; Z-INDEX: 100">
</P>
```

Because we're using dynamic HTML, the image element is an active element: you can click it, for example, and add code to react to that click like this, where we display a message box indicating that the user clicked the image:

```
Private Function Image1_onclick() As Boolean
    MsgBox "You clicked the image!"
End Function
```

Adding HTML Controls To DHTML Pages

Using the Visual Basic DHTML Page Designer, you can add the standard HTML controls to a Web page: buttons, Submit buttons, Reset buttons, text fields, text areas, password fields, option buttons, checkboxes, select controls, file upload controls, hidden fields, and lists. As you can see, the whole HTML control set is here, and you can use these controls with Visual Basic just as you would in a standard form if you create the DLL file for your DHTML page (see "Creating DHTML Pages" earlier in this chapter), or with a scripting language such as VBScript or JavaScript.

Adding these controls to your Web page is just like adding them to a standard Visual Basic project. You just use the control's tool in the Page Designer's toolbox in the same way you'd use a tool in the Visual Basic toolbox. For example, we've added a Submit button to the DHTML Web page in Figure 21.6.

The code that the Page Designer adds to our Web page for the Submit button looks like this:

```
<HTML>
<HEAD>

<META content="text/html; charset=iso-8859-1" http-equiv=Content-Type>
<META content='"MSHTML 4.72.3007.2"' name=GENERATOR>
</HEAD>

<BODY>
<P>Here's some text!</P>

<P>Here's an image:</P>

<P> </P>
<P><IMG id=Image1 name=Image1
src="c:\vbbb\dhtml\image1.bmp"
style="LEFT: 40px; POSITION: absolute; TOP: 107px; Z-INDEX: 100">
</P>

<P> </P>
<P>Here's a Submit button:
<INPUT id=SubmitButton1 name=SubmitButton1 style="LEFT: 17px;
POSITION: absolute; TOP: 170px; Z-INDEX: 103" type=submit
value=SubmitButton1>
</P>
```

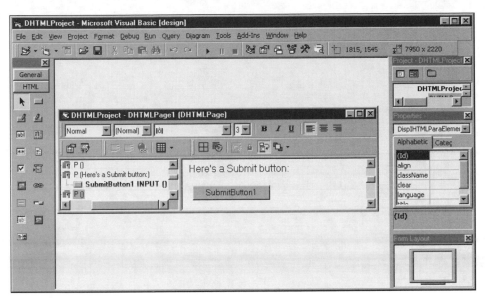

Figure 21.6   Adding a Submit button to a DHTML page.

To add code to the Submit button, you double-click it in the Page Designer just as you would when creating a standard Visual Basic. Doing so adds an event handler procedure to the page's code:

```
Private Function SubmitButton1_onclick() As Boolean

End Function
```

For example, here's how we display a message box when the user clicks the Submit button:

```
Private Function SubmitButton1_onclick() As Boolean
    MsgBox "You clicked the Submit button!"
End Function
```

Adding ActiveX Controls To DHTML Pages

You can add ActiveX controls to DHTML pages just as you can to standard Visual Basic projects—just use the Project|Components menu item to open the Components dialog box and select the ActiveX control you want to add. Then just add that control to the Web page as you would in any standard Visual Basic project.

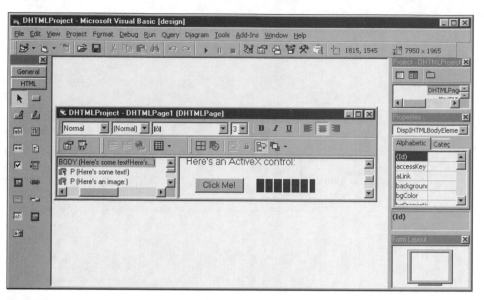

Figure 21.7   Adding ActiveX controls to DHTML pages.

For example, we add a standard HTML button and a progress bar ActiveX control to the Web page, as shown in Figure 21.7.

Here's the HTML code that the Page Designer adds to our Web page when we add those two new controls, the progress bar and the HTML button:

```
<P>Here's an ActiveX control:</P>
<OBJECT classid=CLSID:35053A22-8589-11D1-B16A-00C0F0283628 height=24
id=ProgressBar1
style="HEIGHT: 24px; LEFT: 127px; POSITION: absolute; TOP: 248px; WIDTH:
100px; Z-INDEX: 101"
width=100>
    <PARAM NAME="_ExtentX" VALUE="2646">
    <PARAM NAME="_ExtentY" VALUE="635">
    <PARAM NAME="_Version" VALUE="393216">
    <PARAM NAME="BorderStyle" VALUE="0">
    <PARAM NAME="Appearance" VALUE="1">
    <PARAM NAME="MousePointer" VALUE="0">
    <PARAM NAME="Enabled" VALUE="1">
    <PARAM NAME="OLEDropMode" VALUE="0">
    <PARAM NAME="Min" VALUE="0">
    <PARAM NAME="Max" VALUE="100">
    <PARAM NAME="Orientation" VALUE="0">
    <PARAM NAME="Scrolling" VALUE="0">
</OBJECT>
```

```
<INPUT id=Button1 name=Button1 style="LEFT: 26px; POSITION: absolute;
TOP:
248px; Z-INDEX: 102" type=button value="Click Me!">
```

Now we're free to use the HTML button to set the progress bar's value like this, just as you would in a standard Visual Basic project:

```
Private Function Button1_onclick() As Boolean
    ProgressBar1.Value = 20
End Function
```

Adding Tables To DHTML Pages

One popular HTML element is the table. Tables can present data in tabular form, but savvy HTML programmers use them for much more. They use tables to format the elements in a Web page, placing those elements at locations they want by inserting them into a table—for example, you can add sidebars and format image placement with hidden tables. Although the dynamic HTML **position** attribute helps you place HTML elements where you want them, that attribute is not yet supported by all browsers.

To add a table to a DHTML page, you use the Table Operation drop-down box that you see in Figure 21.8. To insert a table, use the Insert Table entry in that

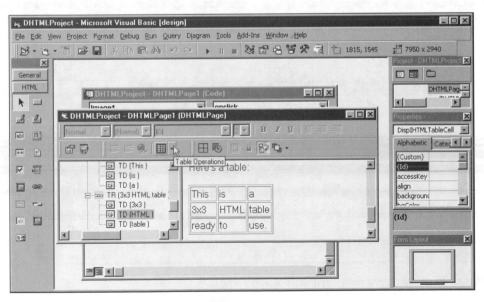

Figure 21.8   Adding a table to a DHTML page.

drop-down box. When you do, the Page Designer adds a 2×2 table to the page. To add a row, select the Insert Row entry in the Table Operation drop-down box; to add a column, select the Insert Column entry.

As an example, we've added a 3×3 table to our Web page, as shown in Figure 21.8. To add text to each cell in the table, just position the insertion point there with the mouse and type the text you want.

Adding Hyperlinks To DHTML Pages

To add a hyperlink to a DHTML page, you use the Hyperlink tool in the DHTML Page Designer's toolbox, which is the sixth tool down on the right in Figure 21.9. When you double-click the Hyperlink tool, a hyperlink object is added to the Web page with the caption Hyperlink1. Move that hyperlink to the location you want in the Web page, and change its caption to the text you want simply by changing the text in the hyperlink object directly (just click the hyperlink and type the text as you would in any word processor).

To set the hyperlink's target URL, right-click the hyperlink and select the Properties item in the menu that opens. Next, place the target URL in the box labeled link, as shown in Figure 21.10.

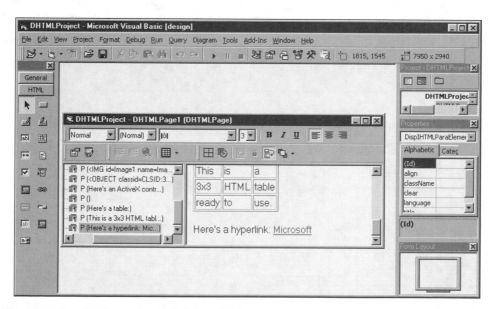

Figure 21.9   Adding a hyperlink to a Web page.

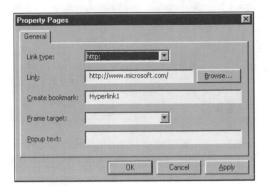

Figure 21.10   Setting hyperlink properties.

TIP: *Note that you can also set a frame as the target of a hyperlink, which means that the target URL will be loaded into the specified frame. See Figure 21.10.*

Here's the code that the Page Designer adds to our Web page for our hyperlink:

```
<P>Here's a hyperlink:
<A href="http://www.microsoft.com"
id=Hyperlink11 name=Hyperlink1>Microsoft
</A>
</P>
```

That's it—to run the Web page, select the DHTMLProject Properties item in the Project menu, clicking the Debugging tab in the Properties pages that open. Make sure the Start Component option button is clicked and the start component is set to DHTMLPage1, then click on OK. Now select the Start item in the Run menu to open the Web page, as shown in Figure 21.11. As you can see, our new Web page is a success.

Using MAPI Controls To Support Email

The testing department is calling again. How about adding email capabilities to your new program, *SuperDuperDataCrunch*? Why? you ask. If nothing else, they say, it can provide an automatic way for the user to register their new program. Hmm, you think—how do you add email to a program?

You use the MAPI (Messaging Applications Programming Interface) controls that come with Visual Basic.

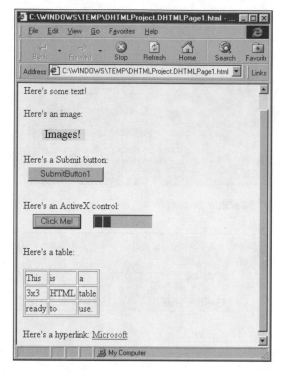

Figure 21.11   Our completed Web page.

Warning!   Note that if you want to run a program that uses the MAPI controls, make sure that you have the 32-bit MAPI DLLs installed properly or you may not be able to perform simple MAPI functions such as SignOn. For example, on Windows 95, you must install Mail during the operating system setup or install it separately from the control panel to correctly use MAPI functions or MAPI custom controls from Visual Basic. The Visual Basic email support is based on the Microsoft Exchange utility that's installed with Windows (and usually appears on the Windows desktop as the Inbox icon). If you want to use the MAPI controls, make sure your desktop Inbox is configured to send and receive email.

There are two MAPI controls, the MAPISession control and the MAPIMessages control. To add these controls to a program, follow these steps:

1. Select the Project|Components menu item.

2. Click the Controls tab in the Components dialog box that opens.

3. Select the entry labeled Microsoft MAPI Controls, and click on OK to close the Components dialog box.

4. Step 3 adds both the MAPISession control and the MAPIMessages control to the Visual Basic toolbox. You'll need to add one of each of those controls to your program to use email.

You use the MAPISession control to open a new MAPI session, which is the first step to sending or receiving email, and the MAPIMessages control lets you compose, send, and examine downloaded messages.

The MAPIMessages control is the primary control you use in your code (the MAPISession control is only used to connect to the Inbox). To work with the MAPIMessages control, you keep track of two buffers, the *read buffer* and the *compose buffer*.

The read buffer is made up of a set of messages read from a user's Inbox. The **MsgIndex** property is used to address individual messages within this set, starting with a value of 0 for the first message and incrementing by one for each message. You get the actual email's text from the control's **MsgNoteText** property.

Messages can be created or edited in the compose buffer. The compose buffer is automatically set as the active buffer when the **MsgIndex** property is set to –1.

The MAPIMessages control's message set is built with the **Fetch** method. This set includes all messages of type specified by the **FetchMsgType** property and is sorted as indicated by the **FetchSorted** property. (Previously read messages can be included or left out of the message set with the **FetchUnreadOnly** property.) Messages in the read buffer can't be altered by the user but can be copied to the compose buffer for alteration using the **Copy** method.

You can see an overview of the MAPIMessages control's methods in Table 21.1, and its properties appear in Table 21.2. We'll put this control to work in the following few topics.

Table 21.1 MAPIMessages control email methods.

Function	Method
Get email from Inbox	Fetch
Send email with Compose box	Send
Send email	Send
Save a message	Save
Copy a message for reply	Copy
Compose email	Compose
Reply to a message	Reply
Reply to all messages	ReplyAll
Forward a message	Forward
Delete a message	Delete

(continued)

Table 21.1   MAPIMessages control email methods (continued).

Function	Method
Show address book	Show
Show message details	Show
Resolve recipient name	ResolveName
Delete recipient	Delete
Delete attachment	Delete

Table 21.2   MAPIMessages control properties.

Property	Description
Action	Obsolete. Performs actions now performed by methods.
AddressCaption	Sets caption of the address book.
AddressEditFieldCount	Sets which address book edit controls to display.
AddressLabel	Sets appearance of "To" edit control in address book.
AddressModifiable	Sets whether address book can be modified by user.
AttachmentCount	Gets total number of attachments for current message.
AttachmentIndex	Sets currently indexed attachment.
AttachmentName	Sets name of the currently indexed attachment.
AttachmentPathName	Sets full path name of the currently indexed attachment.
AttachmentPosition	Sets position of indexed attachment in the message body.
AttachmentType	Sets type of currently indexed attachment.
FetchSorted	Sets message order when creating message set.
MsgConversationID	Sets the conversation thread identification value.
MsgCount	Gets the total number of messages in message set.
MsgDateReceived	Gets date on which current indexed message was received.
MsgID	Gets string identifier of current message.
MsgIndex	Sets index number of current message.
MsgNoteText	Text of current message.
MsgOrigAddress	Gets email address of originator of current message.
MsgOrigDisplayName	Gets originator's name for current message.
MsgRead	True or False depending on whether message has been read.
MsgReceiptRequested	Indicates if return receipt is requested for message.
MsgSent	Indicates if message has been sent to mail server.
MsgSubject	Message's subject.
MsgType	Sets type of current message.

Sending Email From Visual Basic

Now that you've added the MAPISession and MAPIMessages control to your program (see the previous topic), how do you use them to send email? Let's see an example. Create a new standard EXE project, and add the MAPISession and MAPIMessages controls **MAPISession1** and **MAPIMessages1**. Next add two command buttons, **Command1** and **Command2**, with the captions "Send email" and "Read email". We'll enable **Command1**, the Send Email button, in this topic, and **Command2**, the Read Email button, in the next topic. In addition, we'll need some place to display the email we've read, so add a text box, **Text1**, to the form, setting its **MultiLine** property to True and its **ScrollBars** property to **Both (3)**.

When users click **Command1**, they want to send email, and we let them do so by using the MAPIMessages control's **Compose** and **Send** methods. Our first task, however, is to start a new MAPI session, and we do that with the MAPISession control's **SignOn** method, after indicating that we don't want to download email by setting its **DownLoadMail** property to False:

```
Private Sub Command1_Click()

    MAPISession1.DownLoadMail = False
    MAPISession1.SignOn
...
```

After signing on to the Microsoft Exchange email system, we set the MAPIMessages control's **SessionID** to the MAPISession control's **SessionID** property to initialize **MAPIMessages1**:

```
Private Sub Command1_Click()

    MAPISession1.DownLoadMail = False
    MAPISession1.SignOn

    MAPIMessages1.SessionID = MAPISession1.SessionID
...
```

To compose a new email message, we have to set the **MAPIMessages1** control's **MsgIndex** property to –1 and call its **Compose** method:

```
Private Sub Command1_Click()

    MAPISession1.DownLoadMail = False
    MAPISession1.SignOn
```

```
    MAPIMessages1.SessionID = MAPISession1.SessionID
    MAPIMessages1.MsgIndex = -1
    MAPIMessages1.Compose
...
```

This code displays the Compose dialog box, as shown in Figure 21.12. Users can enter the email text and address they want to use in that dialog box and click the Send button (the Send button displays an envelope in Figure 21.12) to send their email.

When the user is done composing the email, we send it with the **MAPIMessages1** control's **Send** method and sign off the MAPI session using the **MAPISession1** control's **SignOff** method:

```
Private Sub Command1_Click()

    MAPISession1.DownLoadMail = False
    MAPISession1.SignOn

    MAPIMessages1.SessionID = MAPISession1.SessionID
    MAPIMessages1.MsgIndex = -1
    MAPIMessages1.Compose
    MAPIMessages1.Send True

    MAPISession1.SignOff
End Sub
```

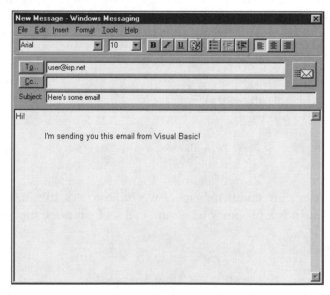

Figure 21.12   Composing an email message.

That's it—we've sent our email. What actually happens is that the program sends the new email message to the user's Outbox (which is also opened when you open the Inbox), and the Outbox is usually set to send email automatically. In fact, that's the way the Microsoft Exchange usually works: by logging into the mail server you've specified at regular intervals. When it logs in, it sends the mail waiting in the Outbox and reads any waiting email, placing it in the Inbox. (In fact, now that we've sent email, we'll see how to read that email in the next topic.)

The code for this example, email.frm version 1 (version 2, which is located on this book's accompanying CD-ROM, will let the user read email as well), appears in Listing 21.3.

Listing 21.3 email.frm version 1

```
VERSION 6.00
Object = "{20C62CAE-15DA-101B-B9A8-444553540000}#1.1#0"; "MSMAPI32.OCX"
Begin VB.Form Form1
   Caption         =   "Form1"
   ClientHeight    =   3405
   ClientLeft      =   60
   ClientTop       =   345
   ClientWidth     =   5970
   LinkTopic       =   "Form1"
   ScaleHeight     =   3405
   ScaleWidth      =   5970
   StartUpPosition =   3   'Windows Default
   Begin VB.TextBox Text1
      Height          =   2175
      Left            =   240
      MultiLine       =   -1   'True
      ScrollBars      =   3   'Both
      TabIndex        =   2
      Top             =   120
      Width           =   5415
   End
   Begin VB.CommandButton Command2
      Caption         =   "Read email"
      Height          =   495
      Left            =   360
      TabIndex        =   1
      Top             =   2520
      Width           =   1215
   End
   Begin MSMAPI.MAPISession MAPISession1
      Left            =   1440
      Top             =   1920
```

```
                    _ExtentX        =    1005
                    _ExtentY        =    1005
                    _Version        =    393216
                    DownloadMail    =    -1    'True
                    LogonUI         =    -1    'True
                    NewSession      =    0     'False
                End
                Begin MSMAPI.MAPIMessages MAPIMessages1
                    Left            =    2640
                    Top             =    1920
                    _ExtentX        =    1005
                    _ExtentY        =    1005
                    _Version        =    393216
                    AddressEditFieldCount=    1
                    AddressModifiable=    0     'False
                    AddressResolveUI=    0     'False
                    FetchSorted     =    0     'False
                    FetchUnreadOnly =    0     'False
                End
                Begin VB.CommandButton Command1
                    Caption         =    "Send email"
                    Height          =    495
                    Left            =    4320
                    TabIndex        =    0
                    Top             =    2520
                    Width           =    1215
                End
            End
            Attribute VB_Name = "Form1"
            Attribute VB_GlobalNameSpace = False
            Attribute VB_Creatable = False
            Attribute VB_PredeclaredId = True
            Attribute VB_Exposed = False
            Private Sub Command1_Click()

                MAPISession1.DownLoadMail = False
                MAPISession1.SignOn

                MAPIMessages1.SessionID = MAPISession1.SessionID
                MAPIMessages1.MsgIndex = -1
                MAPIMessages1.Compose
                MAPIMessages1.Send True

                MAPISession1.SignOff
            End Sub
```

```
Private Sub Command2_Click()
    MAPISession1.DownLoadMail = True
    MAPISession1.SignOn

    MAPIMessages1.SessionID = MAPISession1.SessionID
    MAPIMessages1.Fetch

    MAPIMessages1.MsgIndex = 0
    Text1.Text = MAPIMessages1.MsgNoteText

    MAPISession1.SignOff

End Sub
```

Reading Email In Visual Basic

Now that we've seen how to send email (see the previous topic), how do you read email? You set the MAPISession control's **DownLoadMail** property to True.

Let's see an example. In this case, we'll download any waiting email into the user's Inbox and then display the first message in a text box. We'll use the program we started in the previous topic and add the code we need to the Read Email button's event handler. First, we set the MAPISession control's **DownLoadMail** property to True, then we use that control's **SignOn** method to start the MAPI session and download any waiting email into the Inbox:

```
Private Sub Command2_Click()
    MAPISession1.DownLoadMail = True
    MAPISession1.SignOn
...
```

Now that the email is in the Inbox, how do we reach it? We use the MAPIMessages control's **Fetch** method to create a message set (you can find out how many messages are in the set with the **MsgCount** property). To do that, we first set the MAPIMessages control's **SessionID** property to the MAPISession control's **SessionID** property and then use **Fetch**:

```
Private Sub Command2_Click()
    MAPISession1.DownLoadMail = True
    MAPISession1.SignOn

    MAPIMessages1.SessionID = MAPISession1.SessionID
    MAPIMessages1.Fetch
...
```

Next, we display the text of the first email message now in the Inbox by setting the MAPIMessages control's **MsgIndex** to 0 and using the **MsgNoteText** property. (Note that in a real email program, you should check to make sure there really are messages waiting here, but in this case we assume there are because we just sent one using the Send Email button—note that if your system takes significant time to deliver email messages, you might have to alter this code.) Finally we sign off the MAPI session:

```
Private Sub Command2_Click()
    MAPISession1.DownLoadMail = True
    MAPISession1.SignOn

    MAPIMessages1.SessionID = MAPISession1.SessionID
    MAPIMessages1.Fetch

    MAPIMessages1.MsgIndex = 0
    Text1.Text = MAPIMessages1.MsgNoteText

    MAPISession1.SignOff

End Sub
```

And that's it—we can now receive email, as you see in Figure 21.13. Now we're sending and receiving email with Visual Basic.

The code for this example is located in the email folder on this book's accompanying CD-ROM.

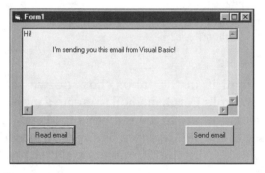

Figure 21.13   Receiving email.

Using The Internet Transfer Control For FTP And HTTP Operations

You use the Microsoft Internet transfer control to handle FTP and HTTP operations in Visual Basic. Using the HTTP protocol, you can connect to World Wide Web servers to retrieve HTML documents. With the FTP protocol, you can log on to FTP servers to download and upload files.

The **UserName** and **Password** properties allow you to log on to private servers that require authentication. Otherwise, you can connect to public FTP servers and download files. The common FTP commands, such as **CD** and **GET**, are supported through the **Execute** method. You can keep track of the Internet transfer control's operations with the **StillExecuting** property. If this property is True, the control is working on a transfer and will not respond to other actions.

The Internet transfer control performs asynchronous Internet transfers, so besides the **StillExecuting** property, Microsoft has given the control a **StateChanged** event. In this event's handler procedure, you are kept up-to-date on what's going on with the Internet transfer control:

```
Private Sub object_StateChanged(ByVal State As Integer)

End Sub
```

The *State* argument can take these values:

- **icNone**—0; no state to report.
- **icHostResolvingHost**—1; the control is looking up the IP address of the specified host computer.
- **icHostResolved**—2; the control successfully found the IP address of the specified host computer.
- **icConnecting**—3; the control is connecting to the host computer.
- **icConnected**—4; the control successfully connected to the host computer.
- **icRequesting**—5; the control is sending a request to the host computer.
- **icRequestSent**—6; the control successfully sent the request.
- **icReceivingResponse**—7; the control is receiving a response from the host computer.
- **icResponseReceived**—8; the control successfully received a response from the host computer.
- **icDisconnecting**—9; the control is disconnecting from the host computer.

- **icDisconnected**—10; the control successfully disconnected from the host computer.

- **icError**—11; an error occurred in communicating with the host computer.

- **icResponseCompleted**—12; the request has completed and all data has been received.

Note that when a request is finished, the *State* argument in the **StateChanged** event will be set to **icResponseCompleted**, and it's safe to execute another command with the Internet transfer control.

To add an Internet transfer control to a program, follow these steps:

1. Select the Project|Components menu item.

2. Click the Controls tab in the Components dialog box that opens.

3. Select the entry labeled Microsoft Internet Transfer Control.

4. Click on OK to close the Components dialog box to add the Microsoft Internet Transfer Control tool to the toolbox.

5. Double-click the Microsoft Internet Transfer Control tool to the toolbox and add that control to your form. This control is invisible at runtime, so its size and location are not important.

6. Add the code you want to use with the control to your program.

When you start an FTP or HTTP operation with the Internet transfer control, the control will connect to the Internet (using the user's system defaults) if the computer is not already connected.

TIP: *For a complete FTP file upload example, including using the **StateChanged** event, see our online application registration example in Chapter 30.*

Now that we've added an Internet transfer control to a program, we'll put that control to work in the next few topics.

Handling FTP Operations In Visual Basic

Handling FTP Operations In Visual Basic

There are two ways of handling FTP operations with the Microsoft Internet transfer control: using the **OpenUrl** method and using the **Execute** method. The **OpenUrl** method lets you download files and uses the FTP protocol if the URL you specify begins with ftp:// (for example, "ftp://ftp.microsoft.com/file.txt"); here's how you use **OpenUrl**:

```
InetControl.OpenUrl url [, datatype]
```

The *datatype* argument can either be **icString** (the default) for text data or **icByteArray** for binary data. If you use **icString**, **OpenUrl** returns a string; if you use **icByteArray**, **OpenUrl** returns a byte array.

The **Execute** method can execute FTP commands. Here's how you use **Execute**:

```
InetControl.Execute url, operation, data, requestHeaders
```

Here's what the arguments to **Execute** mean:

- *url*—String that specifies the URL to which the control should connect. If no URL is specified here, the URL specified in the **URL** property will be used.
- *operation*—String that specifies the type of operation to be executed.
- *data*—String that specifies the data for operations.
- *requestHeaders*—String that specifies additional headers to be sent from the remote server. The format for these is *header name: header value vbCrLf*.

The FTP commands that you can use with the Internet transfer control and what they do appear in Table 21.3.

After you've executed a GET FTP operation, you get the actual data received in the **StateChanged** event handler using **GetChunk**:

```
InetControl.GetChunk(size [,datatype] )
```

Here's what the arguments to **GetChunk** mean:

- *size*—A long numeric expression that determines the size of the chunk to be retrieved.
- *datatype*—An integer that specifies the data type of the retrieved chunk.

The settings for *datatype* are as follows:

- **icString**—0 (the default); retrieves data as string
- **icByteArray**—1; retrieves data as a byte array

TIP: For a complete FTP file upload example, including using the **StateChanged** event, see our online application registration example in Chapter 30.

Let's see an example. Here, we will take a look at the Microsoft Web site, listing the files in that site's root directory in a list box, **List1**. We'll fill that list box when the user clicks a button, **Command1**, labeled "Get directory". When the user clicks a button, **Command2**, labeled "Download file", or double-clicks

Table 21.3   FTP commands of the Internet transfer control's *Execute* method.

Command	Description
CD newdir	Changes directory (for example, **Execute** , "CD gifs\thegifs").
CDUP	Changes to parent directory. Identical to "CD ..".
DELETE file	Deletes specified file (for example, **Execute** , "DELETE old.dat").
DIR [newdir]	Searches current directory or directory specified. Use **GetChunk()** to get the data (for example, **Execute** , "DIR /gifs").
GET source target	Gets file "source" and creates a local file "target" (for example, **Execute** , "GET source.txt C:\target.txt").
LS	List. Same as **DIR**.
MKDIR newdir	Creates new directory newdir (for example, **Execute** , "MKDIR /newdir").
PUT source target	Copies local file "source" to remote computer as "target" (for example, **Execute** , "PUT C:\source.txt target.txt").
PWD	Print Working Directory (show the current path). Use **GetChunk()** method to get the data (for example, **Execute** , "PWD").
QUIT	Close the connection (for example, **Execute** , "QUIT").
RECV source target	Same as **GET**.
RENAME oldname newname	Renames a file (for example, **Execute** , "RENAME oldname.txt newname.txt").
RMDIR dirname	Remove directory (for example, **Execute** , "RMDIR dirname").
SEND source	Same as **PUT**.
SIZE filename	Gets the size of specified file (for example, **Execute** , "SIZE filename.txt").

the file's name in the list box, we'll download that file. If it's a text file, we'll display it in a text box, **Text1**; otherwise, we'll store it to disk. Set **Text1**'s **MultiLine** property to True and its **Scrollbars** property to **Both (3)**. Also, of course, add an Internet transfer control, **Inet1**, to the program.

We start when the user presses the Get Directory button, **Command1**. In this case, we want to list what files are in the Microsoft root FTP directory in our list box, **List1**. We'll use the **OpenUrl** method to get the directory listing of ftp.microsoft.com and place it into a string named **strDirString**:

```
Private Sub Command1_Click()
    Dim strDirString As String

    strDirString = Inet1.OpenUrl("ftp://ftp.microsoft.com")
...
```

What we actually get this way is a Web page (the directory document is a Web page to let Web browsers handle FTP transfers from ftp.microsoft.com) that looks something like this:

```
<!DOCTYPE HTML PUBLIC "-//IETF//DTD HTML//EN">
<HTML>
<HEAD>
<TITLE>FTP root at ftp.microsoft.com</TITLE>
</HEAD>
<BODY>
<H2>FTP root at ftp.microsoft.com</H2>
<HR>
<H4><PRE>
This is FTP.MICROSOFT.COM
 230-Please see the dirmap.txt file for
 230-more information. An alternate
 230-location for Windows NT Service
 230-Packs is located at:
 230-ftp://198.105.232.37/fixes/
</PRE></H4>
<HR>
<PRE>
03/13/98 10:09PM       Directory <A HREF="/bussys/"><B>bussys</B></A>
11/05/97 12:00AM       Directory <A HREF="/deskapps/"><B>deskapps</B></A>
12/12/97 12:00AM       Directory <A HREF="/developr/"><B>developr</B></A>
11/05/97 12:00AM          8,102 <A HREF="/dirmap.htm">dirmap.htm</A>
11/05/97 12:00AM          4,405 <A HREF="/dirmap.txt">dirmap.txt</A>
04/13/93 12:00AM            710 <A HREF="/DISCLAIM.TXT">DISCLAIM.TXT</A>
08/25/94 12:00AM            712 <A HREF="/disclaimer.txt">disclaimer.txt</A>
02/07/98 02:40AM       Directory <A HREF="/KBHelp/"><B>KBHelp</B></A>
04/21/98 10:38AM     10,040,111 <A HREF="/ls-lR.txt">ls-lR.txt</A>
04/21/98 10:38AM      1,930,148 <A HREF="/ls-lR.Z">ls-lR.Z</A>
04/21/98 10:38AM      1,031,623 <A HREF="/LS-LR.ZIP">LS-LR.ZIP</A>
02/18/98 10:07PM       Directory <A HREF="/MSCorp/"><B>MSCorp</B></A>
10/11/95 12:00AM       Directory <A HREF="/peropsys/"><B>peropsys</B></A>
10/30/97 12:00AM          7,873 <A HREF="/PRODUCT.TBL">PRODUCT.TBL</A>
03/17/98 04:28PM       Directory <A HREF="/Products/"><B>Products</B></A>
03/23/98 05:55PM       Directory <A HREF="/Services/"><B>Services</B></A>
12/09/97 12:00AM       Directory <A HREF="/Softlib/"><B>Softlib</B></A>
04/08/96 12:00AM       Directory <A HREF="/solutions/"><B>solutions</B></A>
</PRE>
<HR>
</BODY>
</HTML>
```

We have to pick the file names out of this Web page, omitting the directories, and add those file names to our list box, **List1**. Here's how we do that for the Microsoft site (note that this code is designed only for the directory format used in the Microsoft site):

```
Private Sub Command1_Click()
    Dim strDirString, strFileName As String
    Dim intStart, intEnd As Integer

    strDirString = Inet1.OpenUrl("ftp://ftp.microsoft.com")

    intStart = InStr(strDirString, """/")

    While (intStart <> 0)
        intEnd = InStr(intStart + 4, strDirString, """")
        strFileName = Mid(strDirString, intStart + 2, intEnd - _
            intStart - 2)
        If InStr(strFileName, "/") = 0 Then
            List1.AddItem strFileName
        End If
        intStart = InStr(intEnd + 4, strDirString, """/")
    Wend

End Sub
```

TIP: Note that we've kept this example short intentionally. If you want to get an FTP directory following the standard, formal FTP procedure, use **DIR** or **LS** followed by the Internet transfer control's **GetChunk** method.

At this point, then, we've listed all the files in the Microsoft root FTP directory in the list box **List1**. If the user double-clicks a file in the list box, we should download that file using the FTP protocol. If that file is a text file—which we determine by checking for the .txt extension—we can display the file in our text box, **Text1**, and we do that with the **OpenUrl** method this way:

```
Private Sub List1_DblClick()

    If InStr(List1.Text, ".txt") <> 0 Then
        Text1.Text = Inet1.OpenUrl("ftp://ftp.microsoft.com/" & _
            List1.Text)
    ...
```

On the other hand, if the file to download is not a text file, we'll store it to disk. First, we download that file into a byte array named **bytData** this way (note that we pass **OpenUrl** the **icByteArray** argument here to indicate we want a binary transfer):

```
Private Sub List1_DblClick()
    Dim bytData() As Byte

    If InStr(List1.Text, ".txt") <> 0 Then
        Text1.Text = Inet1.OpenUrl("ftp://ftp.microsoft.com/" & _
            List1.Text)
    Else
        bytData() = Inet1.OpenUrl("ftp://ftp.microsoft.com/" & _
            List1.Text, icByteArra
...
    End If
End Sub
```

When the transfer is complete, we've loaded the file into the byte array **bytData**, and we can write that file out to disk like this:

```
Private Sub List1_DblClick()
    Dim bytData() As Byte

    If InStr(List1.Text, ".txt") <> 0 Then
        Text1.Text = Inet1.OpenUrl("ftp://ftp.microsoft.com/" & _
            List1.Text)
    Else
        bytData() = Inet1.OpenUrl("ftp://ftp.microsoft.com/" & _
            List1.Text, icByteArray)
        Open "c:\vbbb\ftp\" & List1.Text For Binary Access Write As #1
        Put #1, , bytData()
        Close #1
        MsgBox "Download complete"
    End If
End Sub
```

Finally, because it might not be obvious to users that they can double-click a file's name in the list box to download it, we add a button, **Command2**, with the caption "Download file". When the user selects a file in the list box and clicks this button, we just call **List1_DblClick**:

```
Private Sub Command2_Click()
    List1_DblClick
End Sub
```

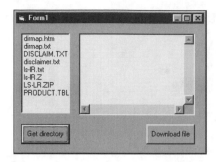

Figure 21.14   Getting a listing of ftp.microsoft.com's root directory.

That's it. Run the program now, as shown in Figure 21.14, and click the Get Directory button. Doing so lists the files (but not the subdirectories) in the root directory of ftp.microsoft.com.

When we double-click an entry in the list box in Figure 21.14, such as disclaimer.txt, the program downloads that file (note that the Microsoft site is swamped some times, and this operation may take some time), and because it's a text file, the program displays the file in the program's text box, as shown in Figure 21.15.

That's it—our FTP example is a success. The code for this example is located in the ftp folder on this book's accompanying CD-ROM.

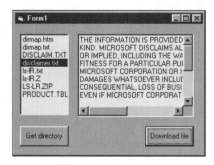

Figure 21.15   Downloading a text file from ftp.microsoft.com.

Handling HTTP Operations In Visual Basic

There are two ways of handling HTTP operations with the Microsoft Internet transfer control: using the **OpenUrl** method and using the **Execute** method. The **OpenUrl** method lets you download files and uses the HTTP protocol if the

URL you specify begins with http:// (for example, "http://www.microsoft.com"). Here's how you use **OpenUrl**:

```
InetControl.OpenUrl url [, datatype]
```

The *datatype* argument can either be **icString** (the default) for text data or **icByteArray** for binary data. If you use **icString**, **OpenUrl** returns a string; if you use **icByteArray**, **OpenUrl** returns a byte array.

The **Execute** method can execute HTTP commands. Here's how you use **Execute**:

```
InetControl.Execute url, operation, data, requestHeaders
```

The arguments for the **Execute** method are as follows:

- *url*—String that specifies the URL to which the control should connect. If no URL is specified here, the URL specified in the **URL** property will be used.
- *operation*—String that specifies the type of operation to be executed.
- *data*—String that specifies the data for operations.
- *requestHeaders*—String that specifies additional headers to be sent from the remote server. The format for these is *header name: header value vbCrLf*.

The HTTP commands that you can use with the Internet transfer control and what they do appear in Table 21.4.

Let's see an example. Add an Internet transfer control, **Inet1**, to a program, as well as a text box, **Text1**. We'll download the HTML of the Microsoft Visual Basic Web page using the HTTP protocol and display that page in the text box, so set **Text1**'s **MultiLine** property to True and its **Scrollbars** property to **Both (3)**. In addition, we can download a binary file—an image file, for example—

Table 21.4   HTTP commands of the Internet transfer control's **Execute** *method.*

Command	Description
GET	Gets the file named in URL (for example, **Execute** "http://www.server.com/index.htm", "GET")
HEAD	Gets headers of file given in URL property (for example, **Execute** , "HEAD")
POST	Provides additional data to support request to host (for example, **Execute** , "POST", strFormData)
PUT	Replaces data at URL (for example, **Execute** , "PUT", "new.htm")

using the HTTP protocol and store that image file on disk. To let the user perform these actions, add two buttons to the program: **Command1**, with the caption "Read HTML", and **Command2**, with the caption "Read binary".

When the user clicks **Command1**, the Read HTML button, we just download the raw HTML of the Microsoft Visual Basic Web page and display it in the text box **Text1** using the **OpenURL** method (note that by the time you read this, Microsoft may possibly have renamed this file):

```
Private Sub Command1_Click()
    Text1.Text = _
        Inet1.OpenURL("http://www.microsoft.com/vbasic/default.htm")
End Sub
```

When the user clicks **Command2**, the Read Binary button, we can read a binary file using the HTTP protocol. In this case, we'll read a GIF file from the Microsoft Web site, home.gif, which just displays the word "Microsoft". We load that image file into a byte array, **bytData**:

```
Private Sub Command2_Click()
    Dim bytData() As Byte

    bytData() = Inet1.OpenURL(_
    "http://www.microsoft.com/library/images/gifs/toolbar/home.gif", _
        icByteArray)
    ...
End Sub
```

All that's left is to write the file out to disk and to inform the user that the operation is complete, which we do with a message box:

```
Private Sub Command2_Click()
    Dim bytData() As Byte

    bytData() = Inet1.OpenURL(_
    "http://www.microsoft.com/library/images/gifs/toolbar/home.gif", _
        icByteArray)

    Open "c:\vbbb\http\home.gif" For Binary Access Write As #1
    Put #1, , bytData()
    Close #1

    MsgBox "home.gif downloaded"
End Sub
```

That's it. Run the program now, as shown in Figure 21.16. When you click the Read HTML button, the program downloads the Microsoft Visual Basic Web page and displays it in the text box, as shown in Figure 21.16. When you click the Read Binary button, the program downloads the home.gif file onto disk. Our http program is a success.

The code for this example is located in the http folder on this book's accompanying CD-ROM.

Figure 21.16   Downloading a Web page's HTML using the HTTP protocol.

Chapter 22

Multimedia

If you need an immediate solution to:	See page:
Using The Animation Control	742
Adding A Multimedia Control To A Program	743
Setting The Device Type And Opening The Device	744
Setting File Information And Opening Files	745
Setting A Multimedia Control's Time Format	746
Controlling The Multimedia Control From Code	747
Stopping And Pausing The Multimedia Control	749
Displaying The Multimedia Control's Status	750
Closing The Multimedia Control	753
Playing CDs From Your CD-ROM Drive	753
Playing WAV Files	755
Playing MID Files	757
Playing AVI Files	759
Playing MPG Files	761
Keeping Track Of Multimedia Command Execution Using Notification	763
Handling Multimedia Errors	764
Stepping A Multimedia Control Forward Or Backward Frame By Frame	769
Starting From And To In A Multimedia Control	770
Making The Multimedia Control Wait	770
Multimedia Without Multimedia Controls	771

In Depth

Multimedia has become a hot topic in recent years, and rightly so. Programs with interactive sound, images, and animations can be very effective—more so than static ones—and computers are increasingly well equipped to handle multimedia.

What do we mean by multimedia? For the purposes of this chapter, multimedia refers to supporting sound and animated images. There are endless devices and programs to work with multimedia, ranging from simple programs that can display simple animations to VCR and videodisc players and advanced MIDI devices. Visual Basic provides a great deal of multimedia support, and that support is wrapped up in the multimedia control. This chapter is about the multimedia control, although we'll also see a few additional techniques, such as using the animation control and interacting with Windows directly to support multimedia.

The Multimedia MCI Control

The multimedia MCI control we'll use in Visual Basic manages the recording and playback of multimedia files on Media Control Interface (MCI) devices. This control issues commands to devices like audio boards, MIDI sequencers, CD-ROM drives, audio CD players, videodisc players, videotape recorder/players, and more. The multimedia control also lets you play WAV and MID sound files and display video files like AVI and MPG.

The actual control displays a bar of buttons, as shown in Figure 22.1. The buttons are named Prev, Next, Play, Pause, Back, Step, Stop, Record, and Eject, in that order. As you can see, the multimedia control is designed to let the user control multimedia presentations, rather than present them itself.

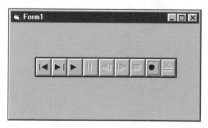

Figure 22.1   The Visual Basic multimedia control.

To use the multimedia control, your application should already have the MCI device open (and the appropriate buttons in the multimedia MCI control enabled) before the user chooses a button in the control. To make sure a device is open, you usually place the MCI **Open** command in the **Form_Load** event.

Using The Multimedia Control From Code

The multimedia control can be visible or invisible at runtime, and if it's invisible, you can use it in code. If the control is visible, the user can click buttons to operate the control; if the control is invisible, you can use it from your program's code by using its **Command** property to execute **Open**, **Play**, **Record**, **Close**, and other commands. In this way, you can play audio and display video (in controls like picture boxes) even though the user doesn't know you're using a multimedia control.

From code, you set various properties of the multimedia control, such as the time format the device uses, the file it is to open and play or record to, and other aspects, as we'll see in this chapter.

You can keep track of the multimedia control through two events, the **Done** event and the **StatusUpdate** event. The **Done** event is fired to indicate that various multimedia operations are completed (if you have set the control's **Notify** property to True), and the **StatusUpdate** property occurs when the status of the control changes (such as when the user clicks the Play button and the controls begins playback). The **Done** event handler is passed a notification code that you can check, and in the **StatusUpdate** event handler, you can check the control's **Mode** property to see if the control is playing, is paused, is stopped, and so forth. You can also redefine the buttons in a multimedia control in code if you want to by developing code for the control's button events, which occur when the user clicks a button.

TIP: *When you create and distribute applications that use the multimedia MCI control, you should install and register the appropriate files in the customer's Microsoft Windows System (or System32 directory). The Package and Deployment Wizard included with Visual Basic (see Chapter 30) provides tools to help you write setup programs that install your applications correctly.*

That's it for the overview of multimedia for the moment. It's time to turn to our Immediate Solutions.

Immediate Solutions

Using The Animation Control

Visual Basic comes with an animation control, and we'll start our multimedia operations by taking a look at this control. This control is smaller than the multimedia control and takes up fewer system resources, but it's very restricted. The animation control can only play AVI files, and those without sound at that. In addition, the animation control can display only uncompressed AVI files or AVI files that have been compressed using run-length encoding (RLE).

Warning!   *The animation control is pretty picky: if you try to load an AVI file into an animation control that includes sound data or that is in a format not supported by the control, an error (error 35752) is returned.*

This control is useful because you can play AVI files in it directly, without using another control (for example, the multimedia control uses a picture box to play animations). The control allows you to create buttons or other objects that display animations when clicked. For example, the File Copy progress bar in Windows 95 uses an animation control; as you've probably seen, pieces of paper "fly" from one folder to another while the copy operation is in progress, and that's supported with an animation control.

Here's how you add an animation control to a program:

1. Select the Project|Components menu item.
2. Click the Controls tab in the Components dialog box that opens.
3. Select the entry labeled Microsoft Windows Common Controls-2, and click on OK to close the Components dialog box.
4. The previous steps add the Animation Control tool to the Visual Basic toolbox; draw the control as you like in your program.

To display an AVI file, you use the control's **Open** method to open that file, passing the file name as the single argument to **Open**. After you've opened the file to play, you can use the **Play** method to play the file:

```
AnimationControl.Play ([varRepeatCount] [,varStartFrame] [,varEndFrame])
```

You can also set the control's **AutoPlay** property to True to make the control play the AVI file as soon as it opens that file. Here's an example in which we set **AutoPlay** to True for an animation control, **Animation1**:

```
Private Sub Command1_Click()
     Animation1.AutoPlay = True
...
End Sub
```

Then we open and play an AVI file, animation3.avi:

```
Private Sub Command1_Click()
     Animation1.AutoPlay = True
     Animation1.Open "animation3.avi"
End Sub
```

The animation control is relatively lightweight, so you can add it to your programs without taking up many system resources, but the limits of this control are severe. If you want to play AVI files with sound or other types of files, look into the multimedia control topics coming up in this chapter.

Adding A Multimedia Control To A Program

The Aesthetic Design Department is calling again. Users of your program, *SuperDuperDataCrunch*, get pretty tense around tax time while computing their taxes using that program. Wouldn't it be great if your program could play some soothing music in the background? Well, you say dubiously, if you really want to.

You can let your program play sounds (WAV files, MID files, or even the CD in the computer's CD drive) using the multimedia control, and we'll see how to add that control to a program now. Just follow these steps:

1. Select the Project|Components menu item.
2. Click the Controls tab in the Components dialog box that opens.
3. Select the entry labeled Microsoft Multimedia Control, and click on OK to close the Components dialog box.
4. The previous steps add the Multimedia Control tool to the Visual Basic toolbox; draw the control as you like in your program.
5. The multimedia control can be oriented horizontally or vertically—to orient it horizontally (the default), set the control's **Orientation** property to **mciOrientHorz (0)**; to orient it vertically, set it to

6. Set the control's **DeviceType**, **FileName**, and **TimeFormat** properties as needed—see the following topics in this chapter.

Now that you've added a multimedia control to your program, see the following few topics on how to configure and use it in code.

Setting The Device Type And Opening The Device

Now that you've added a multimedia control, how do you indicate what kind of multimedia device you want to open? And how do you open it? Does opening the device make the buttons in the multimedia control active?

You can use the control's **DeviceType** property to set the type of device you want to work with. You set this property when you're opening an actual device such as a CD drive, or when the name of the file you're working with (see the following topic, "Setting File Information") does not indicate the format of the multimedia data. Note that you do not need to set the **DeviceType** property when playing files in recognized file formats like WAV, MID, AVI, MPG, and so on.

Here are the different strings you can set the **DeviceType** property to, one for all the device types the multimedia control supports:

- AVIVideo
- CDAudio
- DAT
- DigitalVideo
- MMMovie
- Other
- Overlay
- Scanner
- Sequencer
- VCR
- Videodisc
- WaveAudio

You set the **DeviceType** property before opening the device with the **Open** command. To use the **Open** command, you set the multimedia control's **Command** property to **"Open"**.

Let's see an example. Here, we open a music CD in the computer's CD-ROM drive, connecting it to the multimedia control **MMControl1** when in the **Form_Load** event and then opening that device:

```
Private Sub Form_Load()
    MMControl1.TimeFormat = MCI_FORMAT_TMSF
    MMControl1.DeviceType = "CDAudio"
    MMControl1.Command = "Open"
End Sub
```

If there is a CD in the CD drive, the multimedia control's buttons become active after executing this code and the user can play the CD (if your version of Windows has AutoPlay enabled, you might have to hold down the shift key while inserting the CD to make sure the Windows CD player does not come up automatically).

Setting File Information And Opening Files

The Testing Department is calling again. The new multimedia control you've added to your program looks really fine—but how about that music you were going to play?

Besides physical devices like MIDI devices and CD players, the multimedia control can play files from disk, such as AVI, MPG, WAV, and MID files. If you want to play or record a file in a recognized multimedia format, you can specify the file name the control is to work with without specifying the device type in the **DeviceType** property (the control gets the data format from the file name's extension).

To specify which file you want to use with a multimedia control, you set that control's **FileName** property, and to open that file (and so make the multimedia control's buttons active so the user can play the file), you set the control's **Command** property to **"Open"**. Let's see an example. Here, we set the file to work with to C:\windows\media\ding.wav (which comes with Windows) and then open that file, making the buttons of the multimedia control, **MMControl1**, active:

```
Private Sub Form_Load()
    MMControl1.Notify = False
    MMControl1.Wait = True
    MMControl1.Shareable = False
```

```
     MMControl1.FileName = "C:\WINDOWS\MEDIA\DING.WAV"
     MMControl1.Command = "Open"
End Sub
```

When the multimedia control's buttons are active, users can work with the file—for example, to play the file, they click the Play button.

Setting A Multimedia Control's Time Format

Now that we're working with animations and sound playback, timing information becomes important, and we can set the time format (such as milliseconds) used in the multimedia control to specify timing information. In particular, the multimedia control supports these properties that access or send information in the current time format: **From**, **Length**, **Position**, **Start**, **To**, **TrackLength**, and **TrackPosition**.

To set the time format for a multimedia control, use the **TimeFormat** property; this property indicates the timing units used by the control. This property can take these values:

- **mciFormatMilliseconds**—0; milliseconds are stored as a 4-byte integer variable.

- **mciFormatHms**—1; hours, minutes, and seconds are packed into a 4-byte integer. From least significant byte to most significant byte, the individual data values are as follows: Hours/Minutes/Seconds/Unused.

- **mciFormatMsf**—2; minutes, seconds, and frames are packed into a 4-byte integer. From least significant byte to most significant byte, the individual data values are as follows: Minutes/ Seconds/ Frames/Unused.

- **mciFormatFrames**—3; frames are stored as a 4-byte integer variable.

- **mciFormatSmpte24**—4; 24-frame SMPTE packs the following values in a 4-byte variable from least significant byte to most significant byte: Hours/ Minutes/Seconds/ Frames. SMPTE (Society of Motion Picture and Television Engineers) time is an absolute time format expressed in hours, minutes, seconds, and frames. The standard SMPTE division types are 24, 25, and 30 frames per second.

- **mciFormatSmpte25**—5; 25-frame SMPTE packs data into the 4-byte variable in the same order as 24-frame SMPTE.

- **mciFormatSmpte30**—6; 30-frame SMPTE packs data into the 4-byte variable in the same order as 24-frame SMPTE.

- **mciFormatSmpte30Drop**—7; 30-drop-frame SMPTE packs data into the 4-byte variable in the same order as 24-frame SMPTE.

- **mciFormatBytes**—8; bytes are stored as a 4-byte integer variable.

- **mciFormatSamples**—9; samples are stored as a 4-byte integer variable.

- **mciFormatTmsf**—10; tracks, minutes, seconds, and frames are packed in the 4-byte variable from least significant byte to most significant byte: Tracks/Minutes/Seconds/Frames.

Warning!   As you might expect, not all formats are supported by every device. In practice, this means that if you try to set an invalid format, it is ignored.

Let's see an example. Here, we set the time format in a multimedia control that opens the file C:\windows\media\canyon.mid (which comes with Windows) to **mciFormatMilliseconds**:

```
Private Sub Form_Load()
    MMControl1.TimeFormat = mciFormatMilliseconds
    MMControl1.FileName = "c:\windows\media\canyon.mid"
    MMControl1.Command = "Open"
End Sub
```

Then we can report where we are in the MID file with the **StatusUpdate** event (see "Displaying the Multimedia Control's Status" later in this chapter) and the **Position** property, which holds the time that's elapsed from the beginning of the file, displaying that time in a label, **Label1**.

You should know that although we've set the time to milliseconds, it's actually only reported in tenths of a second (probably because the computer's **Timer** event can only occur 18.2 times a second), so we display the current time location in the MID file this way:

```
Private Sub MMControl1_StatusUpdate()
    Label1.Caption = Str(MMControl1.Position / 10)
End Sub
```

Controlling The Multimedia Control From Code

Controlling The Multimedia Control From Code

The multimedia control displays buttons for the user to control what's going on with a particular multimedia device, but there are times when you don't want the control to be visible. For example, you may want to play sounds under program control using the multimedia control, in which case you don't want your multimedia control to be visible. In such a case, you should issue commands to the control directly using its **Command** property.

TIP: *If you really just want to play sounds under program control, you can avoid the heavy drain on system resources by interfacing directly to Windows to play sounds instead of using a multimedia control. See "Multimedia Without Multimedia Controls" near the end of this chapter.*

Every action that you can perform with a multimedia control you can perform with the **Command** property. Here are the possible commands that you set (as text strings) in the **Command** property:

- **Open**—Opens a device using the **MCI_OPEN** command. Uses the **DeviceType** and/or **FileName** properties.

- **Close**—Closes a device using the **MCI_CLOSE** command.

- **Play**—Plays a device using the **MCI_PLAY** command. Can use the **From** and **To** properties if they are set.

- **Pause**—Pauses playing or recording using the **MCI_PAUSE** command. If executed while the device is paused, tries to resume playing or recording using the **MCI_RESUME** command.

- **Stop**—Stops playing or recording using the **MCI_STOP** command.

- **Back**—Steps backward using the **MCI_STEP** command. Uses the **Frames** property.

- **Step**—Steps forward using the **MCI_STEP** command. Uses the **Frames** property.

- **Prev**—Goes to the beginning of the current track using the **Seek** command. If executed within three seconds of the previous **Prev** command, it goes to the beginning of the previous track or to the beginning of the first track if at the first track.

- **Next**—Goes to the beginning of the next track (if at the last track, it goes to beginning of the last track) using the **Seek** command.

- **Seek**—If not playing, seeks a position using the **MCI_SEEK** command. If playing, continues playing from the given position using the **MCI_PLAY** command. Can use the **To** property if set.

- **Record**—Records using the **MCI_RECORD** command. Can use the **From** and **To** properties if they are set.

- **Eject**—Ejects media using the **MCI_SET** command.

- **Sound**—Plays a sound using the **MCI_SOUND** command. Uses the **FileName** property.

- **Save**—Saves an open file using the **MCI_SAVE** command. Uses the **FileName** property.

Let's see an example. Here, we open and play the file C:\windows\media\ding.wav (which comes with Windows) when a form loads, using the **Open** and **Play** commands:

```
Private Sub Form_Load()
    MMControl1.Notify = False
    MMControl1.Wait = True
    MMControl1.Shareable = False

    MMControl1.FileName = "C:\WINDOWS\MEDIA\DING.WAV"
    MMControl1.Command = "Open"
    MMControl1.Command = "Play"
End Sub
```

If you don't want the multimedia control in this code, **MMControl1**, to be visible, set its **Visible** property to False.

Stopping And Pausing The Multimedia Control

The Testing Department is calling again. Beethoven's Fifth Symphony is really fine, but does your program have to play it continuously? You explain that you like Beethoven. Fine, they say, add Stop and Pause buttons to your program.

Although the multimedia control has Stop and Pause buttons, those buttons won't be accessible if you're running the control from code and have made the control invisible. To stop the control, you can set its **Command** property to **"Stop"** this way:

```
Private Sub Stop_Click()
    MMControl1.Command = "Stop"
End Sub
```

To pause the control, you set the **Command** property to **"Pause"**:

```
Private Sub Pause_Click()
    MMControl1.Command = "Pause"
End Sub
```

Executing this line of code if the control is paused makes it try to resume again, but note that many devices don't support pause and resume. For example, if you're using the computer's CD-ROM drive to play music and try to pause it, you'll find that most drives stop and the multimedia control's **Mode** property (see the next topic in this chapter) will be set to **mciModeStop**, not **mciModePause**. If you try to resume the CD-ROM music with another **Pause** command, nothing will happen—you have to use the **Play** command to re-start playback.

Displaying The Multimedia Control's Status

The Testing Department is calling again. Your multimedia program, *SuperDuperSounds4U*, is terrific, but how about a control panel that shows the current operation—play, stop, pause, and so on? Hmm, you think, how can you do that?

You can use the **Mode** property to determine the current operation in a multimedia control. Here are the possible values for that property:

- **mciModeNotOpen**—524; device is not open
- **mciModeStop**—525; device is stopped
- **mciModePlay**—526; device is playing
- **mciModeRecord**—527; device is recording
- **mciModeSeek**—528; device is seeking
- **mciModePause**—529; device is paused
- **mciModeReady**—530; device is ready

As you can see, the **Mode** property tells you what's going on with the multimedia control—but when do you use the **Mode** property? You usually use that property in the multimedia control's **StatusUpdate** event handler. The **StatusUpdate** event occurs at regular intervals as specified in the **UpdateInterval** property (this property is set in milliseconds). You can take advantage of the **StatusUpdate** event to keep the user appraised of the status of multimedia operations.

Let's see an example. Here, we'll display the status of a multimedia control, **MMControl1**, in a label control, **Label1**. We start with a **Select Case** statement in the **StatusUpdate** event handler, which uses the control's **Mode** property as the selection criterion:

```
Private Sub MMControl1_StatusUpdate()
    Select Case MMControl1.Mode
...
    End Select

End Sub
```

Now we check for the various possible multimedia operations by setting up case statements for possible values of the **Mode** property:

```
Private Sub MMControl1_StatusUpdate()
    Select Case MMControl1.Mode

        Case mciModeReady

        Case mciModeStop

        Case mciModeSeek

        Case mciModePlay

        Case mciModeRecord

        Case mciModePause

    End Select

End Sub
```

Next we set up a string, **strMode**, to hold the current multimedia mode, and display that mode in a label control in the program, **Label1**, this way:

```
Private Sub MMControl1_StatusUpdate()
    Dim strMode As String
    strMode = ""

    Select Case MMControl1.Mode

        Case mciModeReady
            strMode = "Ready."

        Case mciModeStop
            strMode = "Stopped."

        Case mciModeSeek
            strMode = "Seeking."

        Case mciModePlay
            strMode = "Playing."

        Case mciModeRecord
            strMode = "Recording."
```

```
         Case mciModePause
             strMode = "Paused."

    End Select

    Label1.Caption = strMode

End Sub
```

Adding this code to a multimedia control program, such as the CD player program in Figure 22.2 (this program is developed later in this chapter), indicates to the user the current status of that control.

You can also display the time that's elapsed in the current operation. Let's see an example. Here, we set the time format in a multimedia control that opens the file C:\windows\media\canyon.mid (which comes with Windows) to **mciFormatMilliseconds**:

```
Private Sub Form_Load()
    MMControl1.TimeFormat = mciFormatMilliseconds
    MMControl1.FileName = "c:\windows\media\canyon.mid"
    MMControl1.Command = "Open"
End Sub
```

Then we can report where we are in the MID file with the **StatusUpdate** event and the **Position** property, which holds the time that's elapsed from the beginning of the file, displaying that time in a label, **Label1**. Although we've set the time to milliseconds, it's actually only reported in tenths of a second (probably because the computer's **Timer** event can only occur 18.2 times a second), so we display the current time in the MID file this way:

```
Private Sub MMControl1_StatusUpdate()
    Label1.Caption = Str(MMControl1.Position / 10)
End Sub
```

Figure 22.2   Showing the status of the multimedia control.

Closing The Multimedia Control

When you're finished with the multimedia control, you usually close it, typically in the **Form_Unload** event. Here, for example, we close the multimedia control when the form unloads using the **Close** command:

```
Private Sub Form_Unload (Cancel As Integer)
    MMControl1.Command = "Close"
End Sub
```

In fact, it's a good idea to execute a **Stop** command before closing the control, because closing the control does not necessarily stop operations like audio playback (for example, your CD will keep playing even if you exit your multimedia control CD player program, unless you explicitly stop the CD):

```
Private Sub Form_Unload (Cancel As Integer)
    MMControl1.Command = "Stop"
    MMControl1.Command = "Close"
End Sub
```

TIP: *If you're recording data with the multimedia control's **Record** command, you should use the **Save** command before closing the control to save the recorded data to disk (in the file whose name you've specified in the* **FileName** *property).*

Playing CDs From Your CD-ROM Drive

The Testing Department is calling again. Where's that program to play CDs from the user's CD-ROM drive? On its way, you say.

It's easy to create a program that will play music CDs in your computer's CD-ROM drive. Just add a multimedia control, **MMControl1**, to a form, and a label, **Label1**, which we'll use to display the player's current operation (for example, playing, stopped, and so on).

When the form loads, we just set the multimedia control's **DeviceType** property to **CDAudio** and open the device:

```
Private Sub Form_Load()
    MMControl1.DeviceType = "CDAudio"
    MMControl1.Command = "Open"
End Sub
```

That's all it takes. Now the user can play the CD in the computer's CD-ROM drive by using the buttons in the multimedia control.

Besides playing the CD, we can display what the multimedia control is doing in a label, **Label1**, by adding this code to the multimedia control's **StatusUpdate** event handler:

```
Private Sub MMControl1_StatusUpdate()
    Dim strMode As String
    strMode = ""

    Select Case MMControl1.Mode

        Case mciModeReady
            strMode = "Ready."

        Case mciModeStop
            strMode = "Stopped."

        Case mciModeSeek
            strMode = "Seeking."

        Case mciModePlay
            strMode = "Playing."

        Case mciModeRecord
            strMode = "Recording."

        Case mciModePause
            strMode = "Paused."

    End Select

    Label1.Caption = strMode

End Sub
```

Finally, we stop the CD (if it hasn't already been stopped) and close the multimedia control when the form is unloaded:

```
Private Sub Form_Unload(Cancel As Integer)
    MMControl1.Command = "Stop"
    MMControl1.Command = "Close"
End Sub
```

Figure 22.3   Our Visual Basic CD player.

---

*TIP: You can even eject a CD with the multimedia control's **Eject** command, if the CD drive supports that command.*

The program is ready to run—run it now as shown in Figure 22.3 (we've added a few more labels to hold captions like "CD Player" and so on in the program there). If you have loaded a music CD into your CD-ROM drive, you should be able to play that CD using the CD player program.

The code for this program is located in the cdplayer folder on this book's accompanying CD-ROM.

TIP: If you don't have a sound card in your computer (and so no speakers) but still want to play CDs with our CD player program, don't despair just yet—most modern CD-ROM drives come with an earphone jack in the front. Just plug your earphones right in.

Playing WAV Files

The Testing Department is calling again. How's that program that plays WAV sound files coming? Coming right up, you say.

It's easy to write a program to play WAV files using the multimedia control—just set the control's **FileName** property to the name of the file to open, and open it with the **Open** command. The multimedia control's buttons will become active at that point, and users can play the file as they like, or, if you've hidden the multimedia control, you can use its **Command** property to play the file with the **Play** command.

TIP: If you really just want to play sounds under program control, you can avoid the heavy drain on system resources by interfacing directly to Windows to play sounds instead of using a multimedia control. See "Multimedia Without Multimedia Controls" near the end of this chapter.

Let's see an example. Here, we set the file to work with to C:\windows\media\ ding.wav (which comes with Windows) and then open that file, making the buttons of the multimedia control, **MMControl1**, active when the form loads:

```
Private Sub Form_Load()
    MMControl1.FileName = "C:\WINDOWS\MEDIA\DING.WAV"
    MMControl1.Command = "Open"
End Sub
```

Now the user can play the WAV file using the multimedia control's buttons.

Besides playing the WAV file, we can display what the multimedia control is doing in a label, **Label1**, by adding this code to the multimedia control's **StatusUpdate** event handler:

```
Private Sub MMControl1_StatusUpdate()
    Dim strMode As String
    strMode = ""

    Select Case MMControl1.Mode

        Case mciModeReady
            strMode = "Ready."

        Case mciModeStop
            strMode = "Stopped."

        Case mciModeSeek
            strMode = "Seeking."

        Case mciModePlay
            strMode = "Playing."

        Case mciModeRecord
            strMode = "Recording."

        Case mciModePause
            strMode = "Paused."

    End Select

    Label1.Caption = strMode

End Sub
```

Finally, we stop playback (if it hasn't already been stopped), and close the multimedia control when the form is unloaded:

```
Private Sub Form_Unload(Cancel As Integer)
    MMControl1.Command = "Stop"
    MMControl1.Command = "Close"
End Sub
```

That's all we need. Now run the program as shown in Figure 22.4 (we've added a label to the program to display a caption). When you click the Play button, the WAV file will be played. Our program is a success.

The code for this example is located in the wavplayer folder on this book's accompanying CD-ROM.

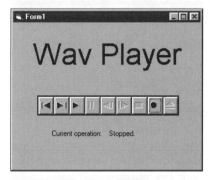

Figure 22.4   Playing WAV files from Visual Basic.

Playing MID Files

Can you play MID format sound files from Visual Basic? You sure can, using the multimedia control.

TIP: If you really just want to play sounds under program control, you can avoid the heavy drain on system resources by interfacing directly to Windows to play sounds instead of using a multimedia control. See "Multimedia Without Multimedia Controls" near the end of this chapter.

For example, we can play the C:\windows\media\canyon.mid file that comes with Windows. To do that, add a multimedia control, **MMControl1**, to a form, as well as a label, **Label1**, in which we can display the multimedia control's current operation (such as playing, stopped, and so on).

When the form first loads, we can open the canyon.mid file this way in the multimedia control:

```
Private Sub Form_Load()
    MMControl1.FileName = "c:\windows\media\canyon.mid"
    MMControl1.Command = "Open"
End Sub
```

Besides playing the MID file, we can display what the multimedia control is doing in a label, **Label1**, by adding this code to the multimedia control's **StatusUpdate** event handler:

```
Private Sub MMControl1_StatusUpdate()
    Dim strMode As String
    strMode = ""

    Select Case MMControl1.Mode

        Case mciModeReady
            strMode = "Ready."

        Case mciModeStop
            strMode = "Stopped."

        Case mciModeSeek
            strMode = "Seeking."

        Case mciModePlay
            strMode = "Playing."

        Case mciModeRecord
            strMode = "Recording."

        Case mciModePause
            strMode = "Paused."

    End Select

    Label1.Caption = strMode

End Sub
```

Finally, we stop playback (if it hasn't already been stopped) and close the multimedia control when the form is unloaded:

```
Private Sub Form_Unload(Cancel As Integer)
    MMControl1.Command = "Stop"
    MMControl1.Command = "Close"
End Sub
```

That's all we need. Now run the program as shown in Figure 22.5 (we've added a label to the program to display a caption). When you click the Play button, the MID file will be played. Our program works as we've designed it.

The code for this example is located in the midplayer folder on this book's accompanying CD-ROM.

Figure 22.5   Playing MID files from Visual Basic.

Playing AVI Files

The Testing Department is calling again. The company's glorious founder has made an inspirational speech, which they've been lucky enough to capture in an AVI file. Oh good, you say. They ask, can your program play that speech on demand?

You can play AVI files with the multimedia control. That control just displays a bar of control buttons, however—how can you display images? You can connect the multimedia control to a picture box control by setting the multimedia control's **hwdDisplay** property to the picture box's **hWnd** property (the **hWnd** property is a handle to the window that actually makes up the picture box's display).

Let's see how this works in an example. Here, we'll play the AVI file C:\windows\help\scroll.avi, which comes with Windows as one of the Windows tutorial animations—this one shows how to use scroll bars. Add a picture box, **Picture1**, to your form, as well as a multimedia control, **MMControl1**, and a label, **Label1**, in which we'll display the status of the multimedia control.

When the form first loads, we'll open scroll.avi and connect the multimedia control to the picture box **Picture1** this way:

```
Private Sub Form_Load()
    MMControl1.FileName = "C:\windows\help\scroll.avi"
    MMControl1.hWndDisplay = Picture1.hWnd
    MMControl1.Command = "Open"
End Sub
```

Now when users click the buttons in the multimedia control, they can play, stop, and restart the AVI file as they like. The animation appears in the picture box **Picture1**.

Besides playing the AVI file, we can display what the multimedia control is doing (for example, playing, stopped, and so on) in a label, **Label1**, by adding this code to the multimedia control's **StatusUpdate** event handler:

```
Private Sub MMControl1_StatusUpdate()
    Dim strMode As String
    strMode = ""

    Select Case MMControl1.Mode

        Case mciModeReady
            strMode = "Ready."

        Case mciModeStop
            strMode = "Stopped."

        Case mciModeSeek
            strMode = "Seeking."

        Case mciModePlay
            strMode = "Playing."

        Case mciModeRecord
            strMode = "Recording."

        Case mciModePause
            strMode = "Paused."

    End Select

    Label1.Caption = strMode

End Sub
```

Finally, we stop and close the multimedia control when the form is unloaded:

```
Private Sub Form_Unload(Cancel As Integer)
    MMControl1.Command = "Stop"
    MMControl1.Command = "Close"
End Sub
```

That's it—now run the program as shown in Figure 22.6. As you can see in that figure, the program plays the AVI in the picture box. Our multimedia animation example is a success.

The code for this example is located in the aviplayer folder on this book's accompanying CD-ROM.

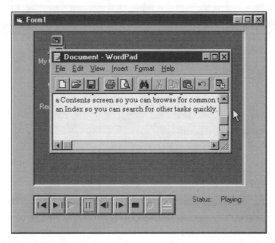

Figure 22.6   Playing AVI files with the multimedia control.

Playing MPG Files

The Testing Department is calling again. Your new program, *SuperDuperMultimedia4U*, is terrific—but how about playing MPG format files? No problem, you say.

You can play MPG format files with the multimedia control. How do you display the images in the MPG file? You connect the multimedia control to a picture box using the picture box's **hWnd** property, placing that handle in the multimedia control's **hWndDisplay** property. Opening the file itself makes the buttons in the multimedia control active.

Let's see an example; here, we'll play an MPG file named, say, demo.mpg. Add a multimedia control, **MMControl1**, to a program now, as well as a picture box, **Picture1**, in which we'll play demo.mpg. We also add a label, **Label1**, to display the multimedia control's status.

When the form loads, we load the multimedia control's **FileName** property with the name of the file we want to open:

```
Private Sub Form_Load()
    MMControl1.FileName = "c:\demo.mpg"
...
End Sub
```

Next we connect the picture box's **hWnd** property to the multimedia control's **hWndDisplay** property to connect the picture box to the multimedia control:

```
Private Sub Form_Load()
    MMControl1.FileName = "c:\demo.mpg"
    MMControl1.hWndDisplay = Picture1.hWnd
...
End Sub
```

Finally, we open the file, which enables the buttons in the multimedia control:

```
Private Sub Form_Load()
    MMControl1.FileName = "c:\demo.mpg"
    MMControl1.hWndDisplay = Picture1.hWnd
    MMControl1.Command = "Open"
End Sub
```

Now when users click the buttons in the multimedia control, they can play, stop, and restart the MPG file as they like. The animation appears in the picture box **Picture1**.

Besides playing the MPG file, we can display what the multimedia control is doing (for example, playing, stopped, and so forth) in a label, **Label1**, by adding this code to the multimedia control's **StatusUpdate** event handler:

```
Private Sub MMControl1_StatusUpdate()
    Dim strMode As String
    strMode = ""

    Select Case MMControl1.Mode

        Case mciModeReady
            strMode = "Ready."

        Case mciModeStop
            strMode = "Stopped."
```

```
        Case mciModeSeek
            strMode = "Seeking."

        Case mciModePlay
            strMode = "Playing."

        Case mciModeRecord
            strMode = "Recording."

        Case mciModePause
            strMode = "Paused."

    End Select

    Label1.Caption = strMode

End Sub
```

Finally, we stop and close the multimedia control when the form is unloaded:

```
Private Sub Form_Unload(Cancel As Integer)
    MMControl1.Command = "Stop"
    MMControl1.Command = "Close"
End Sub
```

That's it—multimedia controls can play files in this format just as they can play AVI files; our MPG player is a success. The code for this example is located in the mpgplayer folder on this book's accompanying CD-ROM.

Keeping Track Of Multimedia Command Execution Using Notification

You can gain more control over the multimedia control using the **Notify** property and the **Done** event. When you set a multimedia control's **Notify** property to True, you'll get notification when the control finishes executing commands. How does it notify you? It generates a **Done** event.

In fact, when you set **Notify** to True, your program is only supposed to be notified when the multimedia control is finished with the next command, but in fact, **Done** events appear to be generated for every command as long as **Notify** is True.

Let's see an example. Here, we add a multimedia control, **MMControl1**, to a program and set its **Notify** property to True when the form loads:

```
Private Sub Form_Load()
    MMControl1.FileName = "C:\WINDOWS\MEDIA\DING.WAV"
    MMControl1.Command = "Open"
    MMControl1.Notify = True
End Sub
```

When the control finishes executing a command, it fires a **Done** event, which we catch in an event handler procedure:

```
Private Sub MMControl1_Done(NotifyCode As Integer)

End Sub
```

Here, the event handler procedure is passed a notification code, **NotifyCode**, which can take these values:

- **mciSuccessful**—1; command completed successfully
- **mciSuperseded**—2; command was superseded by another command
- **mciAborted**—4; command was aborted by the user
- **mciFailure**—8; command failed

In this example, we just display a message box, indicating to the user that the multimedia command is finished:

```
Private Sub MMControl1_Done(NotifyCode As Integer)
    MsgBox "Finished the multimedia command."
End Sub
```

Using multimedia notification, you can coordinate your multimedia actions—for example, if you have two multimedia controls, you might not want to start playing sounds with one until the other is finished playing its own sounds.

Handling Multimedia Errors

Multimedia operations, which can involve working with files and physical devices, are inherently error-prone. To handle multimedia errors, you can use the **Error** and **ErrorMessages** properties. The multimedia control errors returned in the **Error** property and the error string IDs returned in the **ErrorMessages** property appear in Table 22.1.

Table 22.1   The multimedia control errors and error string IDs.

MCI Error Strings	MCI Error Numbers
MCIERR_BASE	256
MCIERR_INVALID_DEVICE_ID	257
MCIERR_UNRECOGNIZED_KEYWORD	259
MCIERR_UNRECOGNIZED_COMMAND	261
MCIERR_HARDWARE	262
MCIERR_INVALID_DEVICE_NAME	263
MCIERR_OUT_OF_MEMORY	264
MCIERR_DEVICE_OPEN	265
MCIERR_CANNOT_LOAD_DRIVER	266
MCIERR_MISSING_COMMAND_STRING	267
MCIERR_PARAM_OVERFLOW	268
MCIERR_MISSING_STRING_ARGUMENT	269
MCIERR_BAD_INTEGER	270
MCIERR_PARSER_INTERNAL	271
MCIERR_DRIVER_INTERNAL	272
MCIERR_MISSING_PARAMETER	273
MCIERR_UNSUPPORTED_FUNCTION	274
MCIERR_FILE_NOT_FOUND	275
MCIERR_DEVICE_NOT_READY	276
MCIERR_INTERNAL	277
MCIERR_DRIVER	278
MCIERR_CANNOT_USE_ALL	279
MCIERR_MULTIPLE	280
MCIERR_EXTENSION_NOT_FOUND	281
MCIERR_OUTOFRANGE	282
MCIERR_FLAGS_NOT_COMPATIBLE	283
MCIERR_FILE_NOT_SAVED	286
MCIERR_DEVICE_TYPE_REQUIRED	287
MCIERR_DEVICE_LOCKED	288
MCIERR_DUPLICATE_ALIAS	289
MCIERR_BAD_CONSTANT	290
MCIERR_MUST_USE_SHAREABLE	291

(continued)

Table 22.1 The multimedia control errors and error string IDs (continued).

MCI Error Strings	MCI Error Numbers
MCIERR_MISSING_DEVICE_NAME	292
MCIERR_BAD_TIME_FORMAT	293
MCIERR_NO_CLOSING_QUOTE	294
MCIERR_DUPLICATE_FLAGS	295
MCIERR_INVALID_FILE	296
MCIERR_NULL_PARAMETER_BLOCK	297
MCIERR_UNNAMED_RESOURCE	298
MCIERR_NEW_REQUIRES_ALIAS	299
MCIERR_NOTIFY_ON_AUTO_OPEN	300
MCIERR_NO_ELEMENT_ALLOWED	301
MCIERR_NONAPPLICABLE_FUNCTION	302
MCIERR_ILLEGAL_FOR_AUTO_OPEN	303
MCIERR_FILENAME_REQUIRED	304
MCIERR_EXTRA_CHARACTERS	305
MCIERR_DEVICE_NOT_INSTALLED	306
MCIERR_GET_CD	307
MCIERR_SET_CD	308
MCIERR_SET_DRIVE	309
MCIERR_DEVICE_LENGTH	310
MCIERR_DEVICE_ORD_LENGTH	311
MCIERR_NO_INTEGER	312
MCIERR_WAVE_OUTPUTSINUSE	320
MCIERR_WAVE_SETOUTPUTINUSE	321
MCIERR_WAVE_INPUTSINUSE	322
MCIERR_WAVE_SETINPUTINUSE	323
MCIERR_WAVE_OUTPUTUNSPECIFIED	324
MCIERR_WAVE_INPUTUNSPECIFIED	325
MCIERR_WAVE_OUTPUTSUNSUITABLE	326
MCIERR_WAVE_SETOUTPUTUNSUITABLE	327
MCIERR_WAVE_INPUTSUNSUITABLE	328
MCIERR_WAVE_SETINPUTUNSUITABLE	329
MCIERR_SEQ_DIV_INCOMPATIBLE	336

(continued)

Table 22.1 The multimedia control errors and error string IDs (continued).

MCI Error Strings	MCI Error Numbers
MCIERR_SEQ_PORT_INUSE	337
MCIERR_SEQ_PORT_NONEXISTENT	338
MCIERR_SEQ_PORT_MAPNODEVICE	339
MCIERR_SEQ_PORT_MISCERROR	340
MCIERR_SEQ_TIMER	341
MCIERR_SEQ_PORTUNSPECIFIED	342
MCIERR_SEQ_NOMIDIPRESENT	343
MCIERR_NO_WINDOW	346
MCIERR_CREATEWINDOW	347
MCIERR_FILE_READ	348
MCIERR_FILE_WRITE	349
MCIERR_CUSTOM_DRIVER_BASE	512

In addition, the multimedia control supports several trappable errors (which you can use with the Visual Basic **On Error GoTo** statement). These appear in Table 22.2.

Table 22.2 The multimedia control trappable errors.

Constant	Value	Description
mciInvalidProcedureCall	5	Invalid procedure call
mciInvalidPropertyValue	380	Invalid property value
mciSetNotSupported	383	Property is read-only
mciGetNotSupported	394	Property is write-only
mciInvalidObjectUse	425	Invalid object use
mciWrongClipboardFormat	461	Specified format doesn't match format of data
mciObjectLocked	672	DataObject formats list may not be cleared or expanded outside of the **OLEStartDrag** event
mciExpectedArgument	673	Expected at least one argument
mciRecursiveOleDrag	674	Illegal recursive invocation of OLE drag and drop
mciFormatNotByteArray	675	Non-intrinsic OLE drag-and-drop formats used with **SetData** require **Byte** array data; **GetData** may return more bytes than were given to **SetData**
mciDataNotSetForFormat	676	Requested data was not supplied to the DataObject during the **OLESetData** event

(continued)

Table 22.2   The multimedia control trappable errors (continued).

Constant	Value	Description
mciCantCreateButton	30001	Can't create button
mciCantCreateTimer	30002	Can't create timer resource
mciUnsupportedFunction	30004	Unsupported function

Let's see an example. Here, we set the **Notify** property of a multimedia control, **MMControl1**, to True, then open a WAV file:

```
Private Sub Form_Load()
    MMControl1.Notify = True
    MMControl1.FileName = "C:\WINDOWS\MEDIA\DING.WAV"
    MMControl1.Command = "Open"
...
End Sub
```

Then we add code to the **Done** event to display the error message for the current error, if there is one, using the **Error** and **ErrorMessage** properties:

```
Private Sub MMControl1_Done(NotifyCode As Integer)
    If MMControl1.Error <> 0 Then
        MsgBox MMControl1.ErrorMessage
    End If
End Sub
```

Now, if we execute an illegal command, we'll be notified of the fact. For example, we might try to eject the WAV file, which is an illegal multimedia operation:

```
Private Sub Form_Load()
    MMControl1.Notify = True
    MMControl1.FileName = "C:\WINDOWS\MEDIA\DING.WAV"
    MMControl1.Command = "Open"
    MMControl1.Command = "Eject"
End Sub
```

In this case, we get the error message you see in Figure 22.7.

Figure 22.7   A multimedia control error message.

Stepping A Multimedia Control Forward Or Backward Frame By Frame

The Testing Department is calling again. Your program that plays the inspirational speech by the company's founder is a big hit—but can't you let the user move through it frame by frame for more impact? Hmm, you think, how do you do that?

You can use the **Step** and **Back** multimedia control commands to step through animations frame by frame. Each time you use these commands, you move forward or back by the number of frames set in the **Frames** property (the default is 1). To check if a multimedia control is connected to a device that can step this way, check the **CanStep** property—if it's set to True, you can use the **Step** and **Back** commands.

Let's see an example. We might connect a multimedia control, **MMControl1**, to a picture box, **Picture1** this way so that it plays the file C:\windows\help\ scroll.avi (which comes with Windows):

```
Private Sub Form_Load()
    MMControl1.FileName = "C:\windows\help\scroll.avi"
    MMControl1.hWndDisplay = Picture1.hWnd
    MMControl1.Command = "Open"
End Sub
```

Now when the user clicks a command button, **Command1**, we will advance **MMControl1** by, say, five frames (after checking to make sure it can step):

```
Private Sub Command1_Click()
    If MMControl1.CanStep Then
        MMControl1.Frames = 5
        MMControl1.Command = "Step"
    End If
End Sub
```

When the user clicks another button, **Command2**, we can step back five frames:

```
Private Sub Command2_Click()
    If MMControl1.CanStep Then
        MMControl1.Frames = 5
        MMControl1.Command = "Back"
    End If
End Sub
```

That's it—now the user can step forwards and backwards in the animation.

Starting From And To In A Multimedia Control

The Testing Department is calling again. The sound file you play in the opening screen of your new program, *SuperDuperMultimedia4U*, is 10 minutes long. Yes, you say, but it's a good one. Can't you play just part of it? they ask.

You can specify the start and end point of play and record multimedia operations with the **From** and **To** properties. You set these properties in the same time format you've specified in the multimedia control's **TimeFormat** property (see "Setting a Multimedia Control's Time Format" earlier in this chapter).

Let's see an example. In this case, we'll just play the first 10 seconds of a MID file, C:\windows\media\canyon.mid, which comes with Windows. First, we open that file when the form first loads, using a multimedia control, **MMControl1**, and set the control's time format to **mciFormatMilliseconds**:

```
Private Sub Form_Load()
    MMControl1.TimeFormat = mciFormatMilliseconds
    MMControl1.FileName = "c:\windows\media\canyon.mid"
    MMControl1.Command = "Open"
End Sub
```

Now, when the user clicks a command button, **Command1**, we play the first 10 seconds of the file like this (although we've set the control's time format to **mciFormatMilliseconds**, times in this format are actually measured in tenths of a second, which means that we set to **From** property to 100 for 10 seconds):

```
Private Sub Command1_Click()
    MMControl1.From = 0
    MMControl1.To = 100
    MMControl1.Command = "Play"
End Sub
```

And that's it—now you can set the **To** and **From** locations in a multimedia file.

Making The Multimedia Control Wait

The Aesthetic Design Department is calling again. Users are flipping through your program too fast, not even waiting until the company's theme song finishes playing. Can't you do something about that?

You can set a multimedia control's **Wait** property to True (the default is False) if you want to make that control finish its current operation before continuing on to another. Note that this property is not available at design time.

Let's see an example; here, we open a file, C:\windows\media\canyon.mid, with a multimedia control, **MMControl1**, and set its **Wait** property to True:

```
Private Sub Form_Load()
    MMControl1.FileName = "c:\windows\media\canyon.mid"
    MMControl1.Command = "Open"
    MMControl1.Wait = True
End Sub
```

Now when the user performs an operation with the control, such as playing the file, the control will wait until that operation is complete before letting the user select another operation.

Multimedia Without Multimedia Controls

The Testing Department is calling again. The multimedia control in your program takes up more than 100K—can't you use something else? Hmm, you say, I'll look into it.

If you just want to play sounds, you can use the Windows API function **PlaySound**. Using this built-in function instead of a multimedia control can save you a lot of memory space. Let's see an example. Here, we'll play the Windows c:\windows\media\Tada.wav file (which comes with Windows) using **PlaySound**. First, we declare the **PlaySound** function in a program; here's how you use **PlaySound**:

```
Declare Function PlaySound Lib "winmm.dll" Alias "PlaySoundA" (ByVal _
    lpszName As String, ByVal hModule As Long, ByVal dwFlags As Long) _
    As Long
```

Declaring this function as a **Private** function lets us declare this in the (General) section of a form (without the **Private** keyword, we'd have to declare this function in a module):

```
Private Declare Function PlaySound Lib "winmm.dll" Alias _
    "PlaySoundA" (ByVal lpszName As String, ByVal hModule As Long, _
    ByVal dwFlags As Long) As Long
```

Now we can call **PlaySound** directly when the user clicks a command button, **Command1**; here, we pass it a value of &H20000 to indicate that we're reading the sound from a file and ignore the function's return value this way:

```
Private Sub Command1_Click()
    retVal = PlaySound("c:\windows\media\Tada.wav", 0&, &H20000)
End Sub
```

Here are the flags you can use in the **dwFlags** parameter of the **PlaySound** function:

- **SND_SYNC**—&H0 (the default); play the sound synchronously
- **SND_ASYNC**—&H1; play the sound asynchronously
- **SND_NODEFAULT**—&H2; silence is not the default, if sound is not found
- **SND_MEMORY**—&H4; lpszName points to a memory file
- **SND_ALIAS**—&H10000; name is a win.ini [sounds] entry
- **SND_FILENAME**—&H20000; name is a file name
- **SND_RESOURCE**—&H40004; name is a resource name or atom
- **SND_ALIAS_ID**—&H110000; name is a win.ini [sounds] entry identifier
- **SND_ALIAS_START**—0; must be > 4096 to keep strings in same section of resource file
- **SND_LOOP**—&H8; loop the sound until next **PlaySound**
- **SND_NOSTOP**—&H10; don't stop any currently playing sound
- **SND_NOWAIT**—&H2000; don't wait if the driver is busy

And that's it—now we're playing sounds without multimedia controls.

TIP: *For lots more information on interfacing directly to the Windows API, see the next chapter.*

Chapter 23

Connecting To The Windows API And Visual C++

If you need an immediate solution to:	See page:
Getting Or Creating A Device Context (Including The Whole Screen)	780
Drawing Lines In A Device Context	782
Drawing Ellipses In A Device Context	784
Drawing Rectangles In A Device Context	785
Setting Drawing Colors And Styles (Using Pens)	786
Setting Drawing Modes (ROP2)	788
Handling The Mouse Outside Your Program's Window	789
Copying Bitmaps Between Device Contexts Quickly	793
Capturing Images From The Screen	794
Getting A Window Handle For Any Window On The Screen	800
Getting A Window's Text	802
Playing Sounds With API Functions	804
Allocating Memory And Storing Data	805
Reading Data From Memory And Deallocating Memory	808
Making A Window Topmost	810
Determining Free And Total Disk Space	813
Determining The Windows Directory	814
Connecting To Visual C++	816

In Depth

This is our chapter on connecting Visual Basic directly to the Windows Application Programming Interface (API) and to Visual C++. There are literally thousands of functions and subroutines waiting for us to use in Windows, and we can reach them with the techniques in this chapter. With these Windows procedures, you can do things you just can't do in Visual Basic any other way. For example, we'll see how to draw anywhere on the screen (including outside our program's window), capture the screen, capture the mouse (so we get all mouse events even when the mouse is outside our window), play sounds directly, allocate and use memory, make fast bitmap copies, interrogate other windows about their contents, determine free space on a disk drive, make a window "topmost" (so it stays on top of all other windows), and much more.

We can connect to the Windows API because the procedures that make up that API are in dynamic link libraries in the windows\system directory, and we can call them directly from those DLLs. Here's a list of the core Windows DLLs of the kind we'll be using in this chapter:

- *Advapi32.dll*—Advanced API Services library supporting numerous APIs including many security and Registry calls
- *Comdlg32.dll*—Common Dialog API library
- *Gdi32.dll*—Graphics Device Interface API library
- *Kernel32.dll*—Core Windows 32-bit base API support
- *Lz32.dll*—32-bit compression routines
- *Mpr.dll*—Multiple Provider Router library
- *Netapi32.dll*—32-bit Network API library
- *Shell32.dll*—32-bit Shell API library
- *User32.dll*—Library for user interface routines
- *Version.dll*—Version library
- *Winmm.dll*—Windows Multimedia library

Besides connecting our code to the Windows API, we'll also see how to connect our code to Visual C++. In fact, that process works much like connecting to the Windows API, because in order to reach Visual C++ code, you place that code into a dynamic link library and then call it in the same way you call Windows API code.

So how do you actually connect code in a DLL to Visual Basic? We'll find out in the next section.

Declaring And Using DLL Procedures In Visual Basic

Let's say you want to play sounds directly, without using the Visual Basic multimedia control. You can do that with the Windows API **PlaySound** function. To inform Visual Basic where to find this function (it's stored in the winmm.dll dynamic link library), what arguments it takes, and what arguments it returns, you declare that function like this in the (General) declarations section of a form:

```
Private Declare Function PlaySound Lib "winmm.dll" Alias _
    "PlaySoundA" (ByVal lpszName As String, ByVal hModule As Long, _
    ByVal dwFlags As Long) As Long
```

Note that we've declared this function as *private* to be able to declare it in a form. If you omit the **Private** keyword, you must make declarations in a module. After you've declared the function, you're free to use it, like this where we play the file C:\windows\media\Tada.wav (which is one of the files that come with Windows):

```
Private Sub Command1_Click()
    retVal = PlaySound("c:\windows\media\Tada.wav", 0&, &H20000)
End Sub
```

There are a number of points to notice here; because most Windows procedures are functions, you have to provide a way to handle the return value, which we do by storing it in the **retVal** variable shown in the preceding code. We'll discard most of these return values, but Visual Basic will give you an error unless you handle functions as we've done in the preceding code. For subroutines, which do not return a value, you use the **Call** keyword like this:

```
Call MoveMemory(hMemoryPointer, outbuffer, DataLength)
```

Now look at the declaration we've made for **PlaySound**:

```
Private Declare Function PlaySound Lib "winmm.dll" Alias _
    "PlaySoundA" (ByVal lpszName As String, ByVal hModule As Long, _
    ByVal dwFlags As Long) As Long
```

This declaration comes from a file that comes with Visual Basic (in the Common\tools\winapi directory) named win32api.txt, which we'll see more about in a minute. Here, that declaration indicates to Visual Basic that this function is to be found in the winmm.dll file (which is in the windows\system directory).

The **Alias** clause, if there is one, gives the actual name of the Windows function. Here, what Visual Basic declares as **PlaySound** is actually the Windows function **PlaySoundA**. This function, **PlaySoundA**, uses ANSI text strings (as opposed to other versions of **PlaySound**, which can use other text formats like Unicode), which is what you need to work with Visual Basic. In general, you should use the Windows functions as declared in the win32api.txt file, because the designers of Visual Basic have already selected the functions that will work with Visual Basic in that file.

Handling C/C++ And Windows Data Types

Notice also that the **PlaySound** arguments that use Windows C/C++ Hungarian prefix notation (for instance, the prefix of the variable name *lpszName*, *lpsz*, means this variable is a long pointer to a zero-terminated string). You'll find a list of Hungarian notation prefixes in Table 23.1, which will let you unravel what the variable types in Windows API calls really are. The arguments to **PlaySound** are also passed with the **ByVal** keyword. What does this mean?

The standard Windows calling convention is actually the Pascal calling convention, which is not the same as the Visual Basic calling convention. When you pass a variable to a procedure in Visual Basic, Visual Basic usually passes a *reference* to the variable, and the called procedure then uses that reference to read (and possibly write) the value in the passed variable. That process is called *passing arguments by reference*. On the other hand, when you pass variables to the Windows API, you should often pass the variable's *value* directly, not a reference to the variable. That process is called *passing arguments by value*. You specify which way to pass variables using the **ByRef** and **ByVal** keywords.

As you can see, there are a few interface issues that we have to face when connecting to the Windows API. Take a look at the first argument in **PlaySound**: **lpszName**. This is a long C/C++ pointer to a zero-terminated string buffer—how do we construct one of those in Visual Basic, which doesn't even use pointers? It turns out that all we have to do is to pass a standard Visual Basic string for this argument, as we've done when we call **PlaySound** in Visual Basic:

```
retVal = PlaySound("c:\windows\media\Tada.wav", 0&, &H20000)
```

In fact, you can handle the C/C++ data types needed when you use the Windows API by using Visual Basic data types, as shown in Table 23.2. It may look

Table 23.1   Windows C/C++ Hungarian notation.

Prefix	Meaning
a	array
b	bool (int)
by	unsigned char (byte)
c	char
cb	count of bytes
cr	color reference value
cx, cy	short (count of x, y length)
dw	unsigned long (dword)
fn	function
h	handle
I	integer
m_	data member of a class
n	short or int
np	near pointer
p	pointer
l	long
lp	long pointer
s	string
sz	string terminated with a zero
tm	text metric
w	unsigned int (word)
x, y	short (x or y coordinate)

complex, but don't worry—we'll get practical experience passing variables using the conversions in Table 23.2 in the examples throughout this chapter. It's easier than you think—for example, when you need to pass a long integer variable to the Windows API, you just use a Visual Basic long variable, passing it by value.

Sometimes, a Windows API procedure takes an argument of a Windows-defined type. For example, the **MoveToEx** function, which moves the current drawing position (we'll see this function in this chapter), takes an argument of type **POINTAPI**:

```
Private Declare Function MoveToEx Lib "gdi32" (ByVal hdc As Long, ByVal x _
    As Long, ByVal y As Long, lpPoint As POINTAPI) As Long
```

Table 23.2   C/C++ and Visual Basic variable types.

C/C++ Type	Passed As
handle	ByVal Long
int	ByVal Integer
long	ByVal Long
lpint	ByRef Integer
lplong	ByRef Long
lpstr	ByVal String
lpsz	ByVal String
lpvoid	ByRef Any

You'll find the declarations of types like **POINTAPI** in the win32api.txt file, and you can copy them and put them in a module in your own program (data types need to be declared in a module):

```
Type POINTAPI
        x As Long
        y As Long
End Type
```

Now you're free to use that type in your Visual Basic programs like this:

```
Dim ptPoint As POINTAPI

ptPoint.x = 0
ptPoint.y = 0

lngRetVal = MoveToEx(intHandle, intX, intY, ptPoint)
```

In this way, you can handle the data types and data structures needed by Windows procedures. We'll get more experience with this throughout the chapter.

Now that we've gotten an overview of how to connect to the Windows API and Visual C++ through dynamic link libraries, the next question is, what's in those DLLs for us to use?

Note: Depending on your version of Windows, you may have to use longs for handles instead of integers. If you get overflows when assigning handles to integers, switch to longs.

What's Available In The Windows API?

You'll find the procedures, constants, and types used in the Windows API in the file win32api.txt. You can open that file in a text editor like the Windows WordPad and copy and paste the declarations you need into your Visual Basic program, as we'll do in this chapter. However, the win32api.txt file only includes the raw declarations for procedures, constants, and types, but it doesn't tell you what all the variables mean. To find reference information on the Windows API set, refer to the Microsoft Win32 Software Development Kit (SDK), which, depending on your version of Visual Basic, may be included on the Microsoft Developer Network Library CD.

You can also use the Visual Basic API Viewer add-in tool to work with win32api.txt. This tool appears in Visual Basic's Add-Ins menu (if it doesn't appear in your Add-Ins menu, you can add the API Viewer to Visual Basic with the Add-Ins menu's Add-In Manager item). You can open win32api.txt in the API Viewer, as shown in Figure 23.1.

The API Viewer makes it easy to work with the procedures in the Windows API and add them to your Visual Basic program. To add a declaration to your program, just select the procedure you want to add, set its declaration to **Public** or **Private** with the option buttons in the API Viewer, click the Add button to add it to the Selected Items box, and click the Insert button to add those items to your program.

That's it for the overview of connecting to Windows and Visual C++. We've seen how the process works in overview; now it's time to turn to our Immediate Solutions.

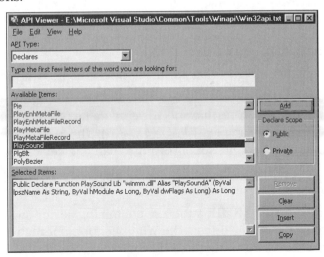

Figure 23.1   The Visual Basic API Viewer.

Immediate Solutions

Getting Or Creating A Device Context (Including The Whole Screen)

Before you can draw with the Windows API graphics functions, you need a device context. Visual Basic controls like picture boxes have an **hDC** property, which holds their device context, but you can also get device contexts for any window.

To get a device context for a window, you can use **GetDC**, which returns a handle to a device context, or 0 if unsuccessful:

```
Declare Function GetDC Lib "user32" Alias "GetDC" (ByVal hwnd As Long)_
    As Long
```

Here's the parameter for **GetDC:**

• *hwnd*—Handle to the window you want a device context for.

You can also get a device context for a particular device with the **CreateDC** function, which returns a handle to a device context, or 0 if unsuccessful:

```
Declare Function CreateDC Lib "gdi32" Alias "CreateDCA" (ByVal _
    lpszDriverName As String, ByVal lpszDeviceName As String, ByVal _
    lpszOutput As String, lpInitData As DEVMODE) As Long
```

Here are the parameters for **CreateDC:**

• *lpszDriverName*—String that specifies the file name (without extension) of the device driver (for example, "EPSON").

• *lpszDeviceName*—String that specifies the name of the specific device to be supported (for example, "EPSON LQ-80"). The *lpszDeviceName* parameter is used if the module supports more than one device.

• *lpszOutput*—String that specifies the file or device name for the physical output medium (file or output port).

• *lpInitData*—A **DEVMODE** structure containing device-specific initialization data for the device driver. The Windows **DocumentProperties** function retrieves this structure filled in for a given device. The *lpInitData* parameter must be NULL if the device driver is to use the default initialization (if any) specified by the user through the Control Panel.

This function, **CreateDC**, may seem a little abstract, but it has one very powerful use—you can get a device context for the entire screen using this function, which means you can then use Windows functions to draw anywhere in the screen. To get a device context for the screen, you declare the **DEVMODE** type, as declared in win32api.txt, in a module:

```
Type DEVMODE
        dmDeviceName As String * CCHDEVICENAME
        dmSpecVersion As Integer
        dmDriverVersion As Integer
        dmSize As Integer
        dmDriverExtra As Integer
        dmFields As Long
        dmOrientation As Integer
        dmPaperSize As Integer
        dmPaperLength As Integer
        dmPaperWidth As Integer
        dmScale As Integer
        dmCopies As Integer
        dmDefaultSource As Integer
        dmPrintQuality As Integer
        dmColor As Integer
        dmDuplex As Integer
        dmYResolution As Integer
        dmTTOption As Integer
        dmCollate As Integer
        dmFormName As String * CCHFORMNAME
        dmUnusedPadding As Integer
        dmBitsPerPel As Integer
        dmPelsWidth As Long
        dmPelsHeight As Long
        dmDisplayFlags As Long
        dmDisplayFrequency As Long
End Type
```

Next, you pass the string "DISPLAY" as the device type to **CreateDC** to get a device context for the entire screen, as we do here when a form loads:

```
Private Sub Form_Load()
    Dim devDevMode As DEVMODE
    Dim intHandleDisplay As Integer

    intHandleDisplay = CreateDC("DISPLAY", 0&, 0&, devDevMode)
End Sub
```

Now you can draw anywhere in the screen, using the screen device context and the Windows API drawing functions (see the next topics in this chapter).

---

*TIP: When you're done with a device context, you can delete it and reclaim its memory with the **DeleteDC** function.*

Drawing Lines In A Device Context

Now that you have a device context (see the previous topic), how do you draw in it? There are many, many drawing functions in the Windows API. For example, you can use the **LineTo** function to draw lines. This function draws a line from the current drawing position to the position you specify. You set the current drawing position with the **MoveToEx** function:

```
Declare Function MoveToEx Lib "gdi32" Alias "MoveToEx" (ByVal hdc As _
    Long, ByVal x As Long, ByVal y As Long, lpPoint As POINTAPI) As Long
```

Here's what the arguments to **MoveToEx** mean:

- *hdc*—The device context to draw in
- *x*—The x-coordinate of the new position
- *y*—The y-coordinate of the new position
- *lpPoint*—**POINTAPI** variable which will be filled with the old location

After setting the current drawing position, you use **LineTo** to draw a line to a new position:

```
Declare Function LineTo Lib "gdi32" (ByVal hdc As Long, ByVal x As _
    Long, ByVal y As Long) As Long
```

Here's what the arguments mean:

- *hdc*—The device context to draw in
- *x*—The x-coordinate of the end of the line
- *y*—The y-coordinate of the end of the line

Both **MoveToEx** and **LineTo** return non-zero values if successful.

Let's see an example. Here, we'll draw a line in a picture box. We start by adding a module to a program and declaring the **POINTAPI** type that **MoveToEx** needs:

```
Type POINTAPI
    x As Long
    y As Long
End Type
```

Next, we declare **MoveToEx** and **LineTo** as **Private** in the form's (General) section:

```
Private Declare Function MoveToEx Lib "gdi32" (ByVal hdc As Long, _
    ByVal x As Long, ByVal y As Long, lpPoint As POINTAPI) As Long

Private Declare Function LineTo Lib "gdi32" (ByVal hdc As Long, _
    ByVal x As Long, ByVal y As Long) As Long
```

Add a picture box to the form now, **Picture1**, and a command button, **Command1**; when the user clicks the command button, we can draw a line:

```
Private Sub Command1_Click()
    Dim ptPoint As POINTAPI

    retval = MoveToEx(Picture1.hdc, 20, 20, ptPoint)
    retval = LineTo(Picture1.hdc, 100, 50)
End Sub
```

The result of this code appears in Figure 23.2. Now we're drawing lines with the Windows API.

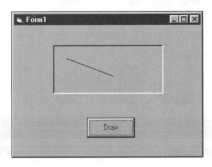

Figure 23.2   Drawing lines with the Windows API.

Drawing Ellipses In A Device Context

You draw ellipses in the Windows API with the **Ellipse** function:

```
Declare Function Ellipse Lib "gdi32" Alias "Ellipse" (ByVal hdc As _
    Long, ByVal X1 As Long, ByVal Y1 As Long, ByVal X2 As Long, ByVal _
    Y2 As Long) As Long
```

Here's what the arguments mean:

- *hdc*—The device context to draw in
- *X1*—The x-coordinate of the upper-left corner of the ellipse's bounding rectangle
- *Y1*—The y-coordinate of the upper-left corner of the ellipse's bounding rectangle
- *X2*—The x-coordinate of the lower-right corner of the ellipse's bounding rectangle
- *Y2*—The y-coordinate of the lower-right corner of the ellipse's bounding rectangle

Let's see an example. Here, we can draw an ellipse in a picture box's device context by declaring **Ellipse** as **Private** in a form:

```
Private Declare Function Ellipse Lib "gdi32" Alias "Ellipse" (ByVal hdc _
    As Long, ByVal X1 As Long, ByVal Y1 As Long, ByVal X2 As Long, _
    ByVal Y2 As Long) As Long
```

Then we draw the ellipse in a picture box, **Picture1**, when the user clicks a command button, **Command1**:

```
Private Sub Command1_Click()
    retval = Ellipse(Picture1.hdc, 10, 10, 160, 70)
End Sub
```

The result of this code appears in Figure 23.3. Now we're drawing ellipses with the Windows API functions.

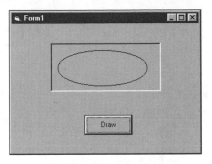

Figure 23.3   Drawing ellipses with the Windows API.

Drawing Rectangles In A Device Context

You draw rectangles in the Windows API with the **Rectangle** function:

```
Public Declare Function Rectangle Lib "gdi32" Alias "Rectangle" (ByVal _
    hdc As Long, ByVal X1 As Long, ByVal Y1 As Long, ByVal X2 As Long, _
    ByVal Y2 As Long) As Long
```

Here's what the arguments in this function mean:

- *hdc*—The device context to draw in
- *X1*—The x-coordinate of the upper-left corner of the rectangle
- *Y1*—The y-coordinate of the upper-left corner of the rectangle
- *X2*—The x-coordinate of the lower-right corner of the rectangle
- *Y2*—The y-coordinate of the lower-right corner of the rectangle

Let's see an example. Here, we'll draw a rectangle in a picture box, **Picture1**, when the user clicks a command button, **Command1**. We declare **Rectangle** in the form as **Private**:

```
Private Declare Function Rectangle Lib "gdi32" (ByVal hdc As Long, _
    ByVal X1 As Long, ByVal Y1 As Long, ByVal X2 As Long, ByVal Y2 As _
    Long) As Long
```

Then we're free to draw our rectangle, like this:

```
Private Sub Command1_Click()
    retval = Rectangle(Picture1.hdc, 10, 10, 160, 70)
End Sub
```

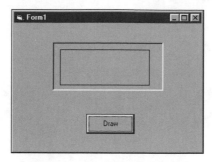

Figure 23.4   Drawing rectangles with the Windows API.

The result of this code appears in Figure 23.4. Now we're drawing rectangles with the Windows API functions.

Setting Drawing Colors And Styles (Using Pens)

The Aesthetic Design Department is on the phone. The figures you're drawing with the Windows API are nice, but what they really wanted was a dotted blue ellipse. Can you create one?

Yes, you can, using device context *pens*. A pen sets the drawing color and style for the device context it's loaded in. You create a pen with **CreatePen**:

```
Declare Function CreatePen Lib "gdi32" Alias "CreatePen" (ByVal_
    nPenStyle As Long, ByVal nWidth As Long, ByVal crColor As Long) _
    As Long
```

Here's what the arguments to this function mean:

- *nPenStyle*—The style for the pen. Here are the possibilities: **PS_SOLID (0)**, **PS_DASH (1)**, **PS_DOT (2)**, **PS_DASHDOT (3)**, **PS_DASHDOTDOT (4)**, **PS_NULL (5)**, **PS_INSIDEFRAME (6)**, **PS_USERSTYLE (7)**, **PS_ALTERNATE (8)**, and **PS_STYLE_MASK (&HF)**.
- *nWidth*—Specifies the width of the pen. Note that if this is not 1, the pen will draw solid lines only.
- *crColor*—An RGB color for the pen.

To install the new pen in a device context, you use the **SelectObject** function, which you use to install graphics objects like pens and brushes in device context:

```
Private Declare Function SelectObject Lib "gdi32" (ByVal hdc As Long, _
    ByVal hObject As Long) As Long
```

Here's what the arguments to that function mean:

- *hdc*—The device context to install the object in
- *hObject*—The handle to the object to install

This function returns the handle of the device context object you're replacing. Let's see an example in which we'll draw that dotted blue ellipse in a picture box, **Picture1**, when the user clicks a command button, **Command1**. We add the declarations we'll need in the program in the form's (General) section:

```
Private Declare Function CreatePen Lib "gdi32" (ByVal nPenStyle As Long, _
    ByVal nWidth As Long, ByVal crColor As Long) As Long
Private Const PS_SOLID = 0
Private Const PS_DASH = 1
Private Const PS_DOT = 2
Private Const PS_DASHDOT = 3
Private Const PS_DASHDOTDOT = 4
Private Const PS_NULL = 5
Private Const PS_INSIDEFRAME = 6
Private Const PS_USERSTYLE = 7
Private Const PS_ALTERNATE = 8
Private Const PS_STYLE_MASK = &HF
Private Declare Function SelectObject Lib "gdi32" (ByVal hdc As Long, _
    ByVal hObject As Long) As Long
Private Declare Function Ellipse Lib "gdi32" (ByVal hdc As Long, _
    ByVal X1 As Long, ByVal Y1 As Long, ByVal X2 As Long, ByVal Y2 As _
    Long) As Long
```

Next, we create the new pen when the user clicks the command button **Command1**, saving the pen's handle as **hPen**. Note that we specify the pen should be dotted by passing the **PS_DOT** constant, and we can use the Visual Basic **RGB** function to set colors:

```
Private Sub Command1_Click()
    Dim hPen As Long

    hPen = CreatePen(PS_DOT, 1, RGB(0, 0, 255))
...
```

Next, we install that pen in the device context of the picture box, **Picture1**, using **SelectObject**:

```
Private Sub Command1_Click()
    Dim hPen As Long
```

```
    hPen = CreatePen(PS_DOT, 1, RGB(0, 0, 255))
    retval = SelectObject(Picture1.hdc, hPen)
...
```

Finally, we draw the dotted blue ellipse:

```
Private Sub Command1_Click()
    Dim hPen As Long

    hPen = CreatePen(PS_DOT, 1, RGB(0, 0, 255))
    retval = SelectObject(Picture1.hdc, hPen)
    retval = Ellipse(Picture1.hdc, 10, 10, 160, 70)
End Sub
```

The result of this code appears in Figure 23.5. Now we can set the color and style in Window API drawing operations.

TIP: *Besides pens, you can also use brushes to fill figures in when you use a device context. To create a brush, you use the **CreateBrush** function.*

The code for this example is located in the dottedblue folder on this book's accompanying CD-ROM.

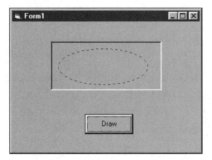

Figure 23.5   Drawing a dotted blue ellipse with Windows API functions.

Setting Drawing Modes (ROP2)

Besides setting what color and style to draw with, you can specify how a pen draws in a device context by setting the device context's *binary raster operation*, ROP2, mode. For example, if you want to draw using the inverse of the screen color at each point, you can set the ROP2 mode to **R2_NOT**. The available ROP2 modes appear in Table 23.3—take a look at that table to see what kinds of drawing effects you can create.

Table 23.3 ROP2 modes.

ROP2 Mode	Meaning
R2_BLACK (= 1)	Pixel is always black
R2_COPYPEN (= 13)	Pixel is the pen color
R2_MASKNOTPEN (= 12)	Pixel = (NOT pen) AND screen pixel
R2_MASKPEN (=9)	Pixel = pen AND screen pixel
R2_MASKPENNOT (=5)	Pixel = (NOT screen pixel) AND pen
R2_MERGENOTPEN (=12)	Pixel = (NOT pen) OR screen pixel
R2_MERGEPEN (= 15)	Pixel = pen OR screen pixel
R2_MERGEPENNOT (= 14)	Pixel = (NOT screen pixel) OR pen
R2_NOP (= 11)	Pixel remains unchanged
R2_NOT (= 6)	Pixel is the inverse of the screen color
R2_NOTCOPYPEN (= 4)	Pixel is the inverse of the pen color
R2_NOTMASKPEN (= 8)	Pixel = NOT(pen AND screen pixel)
R2_NOTMERGEPEN (= 2)	Pixel = NOT(pen OR screen pixel)
R2_NOTXORPEN (= 10)	Pixel = NOT(pen XOR screen pixel)
R2_WHITE (= 16)	Pixel is always white
R2_XORPEN (= 7)	Pixel = pen XOR screen pixel)

We'll see more about ROP2 modes in "Capturing Images From The Screen" later in this chapter.

You set the ROP2 mode with the **SetROP2** function:

```
Declare Function SetROP2 Lib "gdi32" Alias "SetROP2" (ByVal hdc As _
    Long, ByVal nDrawMode As Long) As Long
```

Here's what the arguments to that function mean:

- *hdc*—The device context to set the ROP2 mode in
- *nDrawMode*—New drawing mode

Handling The Mouse Outside Your Program's Window

Sometimes you want to work with the mouse no matter where it is on the screen. To do that, you can use the **SetCapture** and **ReleaseCapture** functions:

```
Private Declare Function SetCapture Lib "user32" (ByVal hwnd As Long) _
    As Long

Private Declare Function ReleaseCapture Lib "user32" () As Long
```

Here, *hwnd* is the handle of the window that the mouse should send mouse events to, no matter where it is in the screen. **SetCapture** captures the mouse, and **ReleaseCapture** releases it.

Let's see an example. In this case, we'll capture the mouse when the user clicks a command button, **Command1**, and let the user drag the mouse anywhere in the screen—reporting the mouse's current x and y locations in two text boxes, **Text1** and **Text2**. Set the form's **ScaleMode** to **Pixels (3)** so that we get our mouse locations in pixels.

We'll use two Boolean flags here: **blnStartCapture**, which we set to True when the user clicks the command button to capture the mouse, and **blnAmCapturing**, which we'll set to True when the user starts dragging the mouse (which means we should start reporting the mouse location in the two text boxes). Along with **SetCapture** and **ReleaseCapture**, then, we add all the declarations to the form's (General) section:

```
Dim blnStartCapture As Boolean
Dim blnAmCapturing As Boolean

Private Declare Function SetCapture Lib "user32" (ByVal hwnd As Long) _
    As Long
Private Declare Function ClientToScreen Lib "user32" (ByVal hwnd As_
    Long, lpPoint As POINTAPI) As Long
Private Declare Function ReleaseCapture Lib "user32" () As Long
```

Note also that we include the **ClientToScreen** function. You use this function to translate coordinates from window coordinates to the whole screen. We'll need to do that: the mouse coordinates passed to our mouse event handlers are in window coordinates, but we'll need screen coordinates because we're using the mouse with the whole screen.

You pass a variable of type **POINTAPI** to **ClientToScreen**, so we include that type's declaration in a new module we add to the program:

```
Type POINTAPI
    x As Long
    y As Long
End Type
```

To start the program, we set our Boolean flags to False when the program's form loads:

```
Private Sub Form_Load()

    blnStartCapture = False
    blnAmCapturing = False

End Sub
```

Now when the user clicks the command button, **Command1**, we capture the mouse with **SetCapture** and set the **blnStartCapture** flag to True:

```
Private Sub Command1_Click()
    blnStartCapture = True
    intRetVal = SetCapture(hwnd)
    Command1.Caption = "Drag the mouse"
End Sub
```

When the mouse next goes down, we'll set the **blnCapturing** flag to True and start reporting the mouse location in the two text boxes, **Text1** and **Text2**:

```
Private Sub Form_MouseDown(Button As Integer, Shift As Integer, x _
    As Single, y As Single)
    Dim ptPoint As POINTAPI

    If blnStartCapture Then
        ptPoint.x = x
        ptPoint.y = y
        retval = ClientToScreen(hwnd, ptPoint)
        Text1.Text = Str(ptPoint.x)
        Text2.Text = Str(ptPoint.y)

        blnAmCapturing = True
    End If
End Sub
```

Similarly, in the **MouseMove** event, we check to see if we're capturing the mouse, and if so, we display the mouse location in the text boxes:

```
Sub Form_MouseMove(Button As Integer, Shift As Integer, x As Single, _
    y As Single)
    Dim ptPoint As POINTAPI

    If blnAmCapturing Then
```

```
        ptPoint.x = x
        ptPoint.y = y
        retval = ClientToScreen(hwnd, ptPoint)
        Text1.Text = Str(ptPoint.x)
        Text2.Text = Str(ptPoint.y)

    End If
End Sub
```

Finally, when the user releases the mouse button, we release the mouse with **ReleaseCapture** and reset the Boolean flags:

```
Sub Form_MouseUp(Button As Integer, Shift As Integer, x As Single, _
    y As Single)

    If blnAmCapturing Then

        ReleaseCapture
        blnStartCapture = False
        blnAmCapturing = False
        Command1.Caption = "Start capture"

    End If
End Sub
```

That's it—now run the program, as shown in Figure 23.6. Click the button in the program and drag the mouse. No matter where you drag the mouse, the mouse location is displayed in the text boxes in the program. We've captured the mouse. To release the mouse, just release the mouse button.

There's one peculiarity you should know about here: starting with Windows 95, you can only capture the mouse for one mouse operation; when you finish with the mouse, it is released. That means if you start the mouse drag by pressing

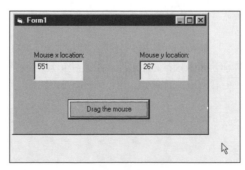

Figure 23.6   Using the mouse outside a program.

the mouse button while inside the program's window, everything is fine—the program retains control of the mouse while you drag. If, on the other hand, you press the mouse button outside the program's window and start to drag, the mouse is released.

You can remedy this problem, as we do in our screen capture program later in this chapter, by using the right mouse button for mouse operations. In that program, we have the users drag the mouse by pressing the mouse button in the program's window, dragging the mouse to the top left of the rectangle they want to capture, then use the right mouse button (while holding the left one down) to capture that rectangle.

The code for this program is located in the mousecap folder on this book's accompanying CD-ROM.

Copying Bitmaps Between Device Contexts Quickly

One of the most common reasons to use Windows API functions is to make fast bitmap transfers, which you can do with the **BitBlt** function. This function lets you copy a bitmap from one device context to another very quickly:

```
Declare Function BitBlt Lib "gdi32" Alias "BitBlt" (ByVal hDestDC As _
    Long, ByVal x As Long, ByVal y As Long, ByVal nWidth As Long, ByVal _
    nHeight As Long, ByVal hSrcDC As Long, ByVal xSrc As Long, ByVal _
    ySrc As Long, ByVal dwRop As Long) As Long
```

Here's what this function's arguments mean:

- *hDestDC*—The destination device context to copy to
- *x*—The x-coordinate of the upper-left corner of the destination rectangle
- *y*—The y-coordinate of the upper-left corner of the destination rectangle
- *nWidth*—The width of the destination rectangle and source bitmap
- *nHeight*—The height of the destination rectangle and source bitmap
- *hSrcDC*—The source device context to copy from
- *xSrc*—The logical x-coordinate of the upper-left corner of the source bitmap
- *ySrc*—The logical y-coordinate of the upper-left corner of the source bitmap
- *dwRop*—The raster operation to be performed

You can find the possible values for the **dwRop** argument in Table 23.4.

Table 23.4   *BitBlt* raster operations.

dwRop Constant	Operation
SRCCOPY = &HCC0020	destination = source
SRCPAINT = &HEE0086	destination = source OR destination
SRCAND = &H8800C6	destination = source AND destination
SRCINVERT = &H660046	destination = source XOR destination
SRCERASE = &H440328	destination = source AND (NOT destination)
NOTSRCCOPY = &H330008	destination = (NOT source)
NOTSRCERASE = &H1100A6	destination = (NOT src) AND (NOT destination)
MERGECOPY = &HC000CA	destination = (source AND pattern)
MERGEPAINT = &HBB0226	destination = (NOT source) OR destination
PATCOPY = &HF00021	destination = pattern
PATPAINT = &HFB0A09	destination = pattern OR source
PATINVERT = &H5A0049	destination = pattern XOR destination
DSTINVERT = &H550009	destination = (NOT destination)
BLACKNESS = &H42	destination = BLACK
WHITENESS = &HFF0062	destination = WHITE

We'll put **BitBlt** to work when we capture the screen in the next topic.

Capturing Images From The Screen

We'll put together the previous topics in this chapter into one substantial screen capture example: screencap. Using this program, you can capture sections of the screen and display them in a picture box.

When you run this program, press the left mouse button on the program's form, then drag the mouse to the top left of the rectangular region you want to capture. Then, using the right mouse button (while holding the left one down) draw the rectangle you want to capture. A box outlining that region will appear on the screen as you move the mouse, as shown in Figure 23.7.

When you release the mouse buttons, the region you've outline appears in the picture box in the program, as shown in Figure 23.8. You've captured an image from the screen.

Why do we have to drag the mouse before making the screen capture? There's a peculiarity in mouse capture starting in Windows 95: when you capture the

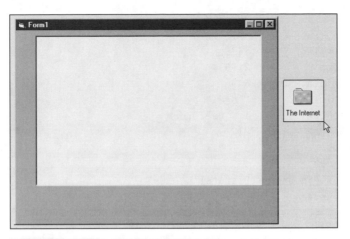

Figure 23.7   Outlining a region on the screen.

Figure 23.8   Capturing a region of the screen.

mouse, you can only hold it until you finish with a mouse operation; when you do, the mouse is released. To hold the mouse, we start the dragging process in the program's form itself and only release all mouse buttons when we're done capturing the image we want.

This program is a fairly complex one, involving lots of Visual Basic code, and it appears in Listing 23.1 for reference. This program, screencap, puts together almost all of the Windows API operations we've seen so far in this chapter, so it's worth taking a look at as an example of a substantial program that uses the Windows API.

Listing 23.1   screencap.frm

```
VERSION 6.00
Begin VB.Form Form1
```

```
        Caption         =    "Form1"
        ClientHeight    =    4755
        ClientLeft      =    1425
        ClientTop       =    2175
        ClientWidth     =    6495
        LinkTopic       =    "Form1"
        PaletteMode     =    1  'UseZOrder
        ScaleHeight     =    317
        ScaleMode       =    3  'Pixel
        ScaleWidth      =    433
        Begin VB.PictureBox Picture1
            AutoRedraw      =    -1  'True
            BackColor       =    &H00FFFFFF&
            Height          =    3735
            Left            =    480
            ScaleHeight     =    3675
            ScaleWidth      =    5595
            TabIndex        =    0
            Top             =    120
            Width           =    5655
        End
    End
End
Attribute VB_Name = "Form1"
Attribute VB_GlobalNameSpace = False
Attribute VB_Creatable = False
Attribute VB_PredeclaredId = True
Attribute VB_Exposed = False
Dim blnStartCapture As Boolean
Dim blnAmCapturing As Boolean
Dim intHandleDisplay As Integer
Dim intStartX As Integer
Dim intStartY As Integer
Dim intMouseX As Integer
Dim intMouseY As Integer
Dim intOldMouseX As Integer
Dim intOldMouseY As Integer

Private Declare Function SetCapture Lib "user32" (ByVal hwnd As Long) _
    As Long
Private Declare Function CreateDC Lib "gdi32" Alias "CreateDCA" (ByVal _
    lpDriverName As String, ByVal lpDeviceName As String, ByVal _
    lpOutput As String, lpInitData As DEVMODE) As Long
Private Declare Function SetROP2 Lib "gdi32" (ByVal hdc As Long, ByVal_
    nDrawMode As Long) As Long
Private Declare Function MoveToEx Lib "gdi32" (ByVal hdc As Long, _
    ByVal x As Long, ByVal y As Long, lpPoint As POINTAPI) As Long
```

```
Private Declare Function LineTo Lib "gdi32" (ByVal hdc As Long, ByVal x _
    As Long, ByVal y As Long) As Long
Private Declare Function DeleteDC Lib "gdi32" (ByVal hdc As Long) As Long
Private Declare Function BitBlt Lib "gdi32" (ByVal hDestDC As Long, _
    ByVal x As Long, ByVal y As Long, ByVal nWidth As Long, ByVal _
    nHeight  As Long, ByVal hSrcDC As Long, ByVal xSrc As Long, ByVal _
    ySrc As Long, ByVal dwRop As Long) As Long
Private Declare Function ReleaseCapture Lib "user32" () As Long
Private Declare Function ClientToScreen Lib "user32" (ByVal hwnd As _
    Long, lpPoint As POINTAPI) As Long

Const SRCCOPY = &HCC0020
Const R2_NOT = 6

Private Sub Form_Load()
    Dim devDevMode As DEVMODE

    blnStartCapture = False
    blnAmCapturing = False

    intHandleDisplay = CreateDC("DISPLAY", 0&, 0&, devDevMode)
End Sub

Private Sub Form_MouseDown(Button As Integer, Shift As Integer, x As _
    Single, y As Single)
    Dim ptPoint As POINTAPI

    If Button = 1 Then
        blnStartCapture = True
        intRetVal = SetCapture(hwnd)
    End If

    If blnStartCapture And Button = 2 Then

        ptPoint.x = x
        ptPoint.y = y
        retval = ClientToScreen(hwnd, ptPoint)
        intStartX = ptPoint.x
        intStartY = ptPoint.y

        intOldMouseX = intStartX
        intOldMouseY = intStartY

        blnAmCapturing = True
    End If
End Sub
```

```
Sub Form_MouseMove(Button As Integer, Shift As Integer, x As Single, y _
    As Single)

    If blnAmCapturing Then

        EraseOld x, y

        intOldMouseX = intMouseX
        intOldMouseY = intMouseY

        DrawNew x, y

    End If
End Sub

Sub Form_MouseUp(Button As Integer, Shift As Integer, x As Single, y As_
    Single)
    Dim intLeftX As Integer
    Dim intLeftY As Integer

    If blnAmCapturing Then
        ReleaseCapture
        blnStartCapture = False
        blnAmCapturing = False

        EraseOld x, y

        intLeftX = intMouseX
        If intStartX < intMouseX Then
            intLeftX = intStartX
        End If

        intLeftY = intMouseY
        If intStartY < intMouseY Then
            intLeftY = intStartY
        End If

        Picture1.Cls
        intRetVal = BitBlt(Picture1.hdc, 0, 0, Abs(intStartX - _
            intMouseX), Abs(intStartY - intMouseY), intHandleDisplay, _
            intLeftX, intLeftY, SRCCOPY)

    End If
End Sub
```

```
Private Sub EraseOld(ByVal x As Integer, ByVal y As Integer)
    Dim ptPoint As POINTAPI

    intRetVal = SetROP2(intHandleDisplay, R2_NOT)

    ptPoint.x = x
    ptPoint.y = y
    retval = ClientToScreen(hwnd, ptPoint)
    intMouseX = ptPoint.x
    intMouseY = ptPoint.y

    lngRetVal = MoveToEx(intHandleDisplay, intOldMouseX, intOldMouseY, _
        ptPoint)
    intRetVal = LineTo(intHandleDisplay, intStartX, intOldMouseY)
    intRetVal = LineTo(intHandleDisplay, intStartX, intStartY)
    intRetVal = LineTo(intHandleDisplay, intOldMouseX, intStartY)
    intRetVal = LineTo(intHandleDisplay, intOldMouseX, intOldMouseY)

End Sub

Private Sub DrawNew(ByVal x As Integer, ByVal y As Integer)
    Dim ptPoint As POINTAPI

    intRetVal = SetROP2(intHandleDisplay, R2_NOT)

    ptPoint.x = x
    ptPoint.y = y
    retval = ClientToScreen(hwnd, ptPoint)
    intMouseX = ptPoint.x
    intMouseY = ptPoint.y

    lngRetVal = MoveToEx(intHandleDisplay, intMouseX, intMouseY, _
        ptPoint)
    intRetVal = LineTo(intHandleDisplay, intStartX, intMouseY)
    intRetVal = LineTo(intHandleDisplay, intStartX, intStartY)
    intRetVal = LineTo(intHandleDisplay, intMouseX, intStartY)
    intRetVal = LineTo(intHandleDisplay, intMouseX, intMouseY)

End Sub

Private Sub Form_Unload(Cancel As Integer)
    intRetVal = DeleteDC(intHandleDisplay)
End Sub
```

Getting A Window Handle For Any Window On The Screen

To work with windows in the Windows API, you need a window handle. One way of getting a handle for any window on the screen is to use the **WindowFromPoint** function. You just pass that function the x- and y-coordinates (in screen coordinates) of a point inside the window for which you want the handle:

```
Private Declare Function WindowFromPoint Lib "user32" (ByVal xPoint As _
    Long, ByVal yPoint As Long) As Long
```

Let's see an example. Here, we'll let the users click a command button, **Command1**, with the caption Choose Window. When they do, they can move the mouse to any window on the screen, click the window, and get a handle for that window.

When the users click the Choose Window button, we'll set up a form-wide Boolean variable, **blnChoose**, to True, so we know the next time the users click the mouse, they're indicating the window for which they want a handle:

```
Dim blnChoose As Boolean
```

We set **blnChoose** to False when the form first loads:

```
Private Sub Form_Load()
    blnChoose = False
End Sub
```

To capture the mouse, we'll need **SetCapture** and **ReleaseCapture.** To convert from window to screen coordinates, we'll need **ClientToScreen**, so we declare those functions as well:

```
Private Declare Function SetCapture Lib "user32" (ByVal hwnd As Long) As _
    Long
Private Declare Function ReleaseCapture Lib "user32" () As Long
Private Declare Function WindowFromPoint Lib "user32" (ByVal xPoint As _
    Long, ByVal yPoint As Long) As Long
Private Declare Function ClientToScreen Lib "user32" (ByVal hwnd As Long,_
    lpPoint As POINTAPI) As Long
```

We also need to declare the **POINTAPI** type because **ClientToScreen** uses that type, so we add that declaration to a module we add to the program:

```
Type POINTAPI
        x As Long
        y As Long
End Type
```

Now when the user clicks the command button, we capture the mouse and set the **blnChoose** flag to True:

```
Private Sub Command1_Click()
    blnChoose = True
    intRetVal = SetCapture(hwnd)
End Sub
```

When the user clicks a window, our program's **MouseDown** event handler will be called. To determine the screen location at which the mouse went down, we use **ClientToScreen**:

```
Private Sub Form_MouseDown(Button As Integer, Shift As Integer, x As _
    Single, y As Single)
    Dim ptPoint As POINTAPI

    If blnChoose Then

        ptPoint.x = x
        ptPoint.y = y
        retval = ClientToScreen(hwnd, ptPoint)
    ...
    End If
End Sub
```

Now we can get a window handle for the window the user clicked with **WindowFromPoint**:

```
Private Sub Form_MouseDown(Button As Integer, Shift As Integer, x As
Single, y_
    As Single)
    Dim window As Long
    Dim ptPoint As POINTAPI

    If blnChoose Then

        ptPoint.x = x
        ptPoint.y = y
        retval = ClientToScreen(hwnd, ptPoint)
```

```
        window = WindowFromPoint(ptPoint.x, ptPoint.y)
    ...
      End If
End Sub
```

And that's it—now we've gotten a window handle for any window on the screen the user wants to click. Using that handle you can perform all kinds of operations on the window—resizing it, closing it, changing its style, and more, using API functions. As an example, we'll see how to get a window's title bar text in the next topic.

Getting A Window's Text

In the previous topic, we saw how to get a handle for any window on the screen when the user clicks that window. Here, we'll use the **GetWindowText** function to get the title bar text of a window:

```
Function GetWindowText Lib "user32" Alias "GetWindowTextA" (ByVal hwnd _
    As Long, ByVal lpszString As String, ByVal cch As Long) As Long
```

Here's what the arguments to this function mean:

- *hwnd*—The handle of the window you want to get the text from.

- *lpszString*—The buffer that is to receive the copied string of the window's title.

- *cch*—The maximum number of characters to be copied to the buffer. If the string is longer than the number of characters specified in *cch*, it is truncated.

This function returns the length of the text it retrieved. Let's see an example. Here, we use the window handle we got in the previous topic with **GetWindowText** to get the title bar text of any window the user clicks and display that text in a text box, **Text1**:

```
Private Sub Form_MouseDown(Button As Integer, Shift As Integer, x As _
    Single, y As Single)
    Dim window As Long
    Dim buffer As String * 1024
    Dim ptPoint As POINTAPI

    If blnChoose Then
```

```
        ptPoint.x = x
        ptPoint.y = y
        retval = ClientToScreen(hwnd, ptPoint)

        window = WindowFromPoint(ptPoint.x, ptPoint.y)
        lngRetVal = GetWindowText(window, buffer, 1024)
        Text1.Text = buffer
    End If
End Sub
```

Run the program now, as shown in Figure 23.9. When you click the Choose Window button and then click another window, the program reads the text in the clicked program's title bar and displays it in a text box, as shown in Figure 23.9. Our program is a success—now we can work with any window on the screen.

The code for this example is located in the windowinfo folder on this book's accompanying CD-ROM.

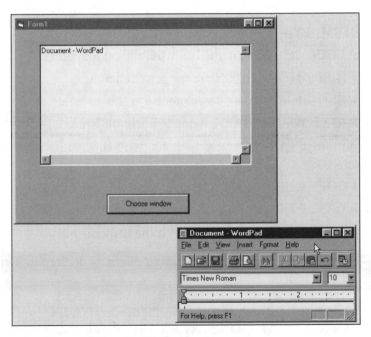

Figure 23.9   Getting a window's title bar text.

Playing Sounds With API Functions

You can use the Windows API **PlaySound** function to play sounds:

```
Function PlaySound Lib "winmm.dll" Alias "PlaySoundA" (ByVal lpszName As _
    String, ByVal hModule As Long, ByVal dwFlags As Long) As Long
```

Here's what the arguments to **PlaySound** mean:

- *lpszName*—The path and name of the file to play
- *hModule*—The module handle of the program, which you usually set to 0
- *dwFlags*—Flag settings; see the following explanation for the settings

Here are the flags you can use in the **dwFlags** parameter of the **PlaySound** function:

- **SND_SYNC**—&H0; play the sound synchronously (the default)
- **SND_ASYNC**—&H1; play the sound asynchronously
- **SND_NODEFAULT**—&H2; silence is not the default, if sound is not found
- **SND_MEMORY**—&H4; *lpszName* points to a memory file
- **SND_ALIAS**—&H10000; name is a win.ini [sounds] entry
- **SND_FILENAME**—&H20000; name is a file name
- **SND_RESOURCE**—&H40004; name is a resource name or atom
- **SND_ALIAS_ID**—&H110000; name is a win.ini [sounds] entry identifier
- **SND_ALIAS_START**—0; must be > 4096 to keep strings in same section of resource file
- **SND_LOOP**—&H8; loop the sound until next **PlaySound**
- **SND_NOSTOP**—&H10; don't stop any currently playing sound
- **SND_NOWAIT**—&H2000; don't wait if the driver is busy

Declaring this function as a **Private** function lets us declare this in the (General) section of a form:

```
Private Declare Function PlaySound Lib "winmm.dll" Alias _
    "PlaySoundA" (ByVal lpszName As String, ByVal hModule As Long, _
    ByVal dwFlags As Long) As Long
```

Now we can call **PlaySound** directly when the user clicks a command button, **Command1**; here, we pass it a value of &H20000 to indicate that we're reading the sound from a file and ignore the function's return value this way:

```
Private Sub Command1_Click()
    retVal = PlaySound("c:\windows\media\Tada.wav", 0&, &H20000)
End Sub
```

And that's it—now we're playing sounds with a Windows API function.

Allocating Memory And Storing Data

One reason programmers use Windows API calls is to work with a lot of memory, and you can use the **GlobalAlloc** (allocate memory), **GlobalLock** (lock the memory and get a pointer to it), **GlobalUnlock** (unlock the memory), and **GlobalFree** (deallocate the memory) functions for that. We'll take a look at the first two of these functions in this topic, and the last two in the following topic. We'll also see how to copy data into and out of our newly allocated memory with the **MoveMemory** function.

Here's how you use **GlobalAlloc** to allocate memory; this function returns a non-zero handle to the memory if successful:

```
Function GlobalAlloc Lib "kernel32" (ByVal wFlags As Long, ByVal _
    dwBytes As Long) As Long
```

You set the flags you want to use in **wFlags**, and the number of memory bytes you want in **dwBytes**. Here are the possible flags to use with **GlobalAlloc**:

- **GMEM_FIXED**—&H0
- **GMEM_MOVEABLE**—&H2
- **GMEM_NOCOMPACT**—&H10
- **GMEM_NODISCARD**—&H20
- **GMEM_ZEROINIT**—&H40
- **GMEM_MODIFY**—&H80
- **GMEM_DISCARDABLE**—&H100
- **GMEM_NOT_BANKED**—&H1000
- **GMEM_SHARE**—&H2000
- **GMEM_DDESHARE**—&H2000
- **GMEM_NOTIFY**—&H4000
- **GMEM_LOWER**—GMEM_NOT_BANKED
- **GMEM_VALID_FLAGS**—&H7F72
- **GMEM_INVALID_HANDLE**—&H8000

To get a pointer to the memory and so put it to use, you use **GlobalLock**, passing it the memory handle you got from **GlobalAlloc**. **GlobalLock** returns a non-zero pointer to the memory if successful:

```
Function GlobalLock Lib "kernel32" (ByVal hMem As Long) As Long
```

Besides **GlobalAlloc** and **GlobalLock**, you can move data into the memory you've allocated with **MoveMemory**:

```
Sub MoveMemory Lib "kernel32" Alias "RtlMoveMemory" (ByVal dest As _
    Any, ByVal src As Any, ByVal length As Long)
```

Here are what the arguments to **MoveMemory** mean:

- *dest*—Pointer to the destination buffer
- *src*—Pointer to the source buffer
- *length*—Number of bytes to move

Let's see an example. Here, we'll store a string of text that the user types into a text box in memory; in the next topic in this chapter, we'll read that string back. This example will give us a good general overview of working with memory and memory buffers.

We start by setting up a 40-character-long buffer for the string to store in the form's (General) declarations section:

```
Const DataLength = 40

Dim outbuffer As String * DataLength
...
```

We also declare the memory handle and pointer we'll use:

```
Const DataLength = 40

Dim outbuffer As String * DataLength

Dim hMemory As Long
Dim hMemoryPointer As Long
...
```

Finally, we declare the functions we'll use, **GlobalAlloc**, **GlobalLock**, and **MoveMemory**, as well as the memory flag we'll use, **GMEM_MOVEABLE**, which means that Windows can move the memory we are using if it needs to as part of its memory-handling operations:

```
Const DataLength = 40

Dim outbuffer As String * DataLength

Dim hMemory As Long
Dim hMemoryPointer As Long

Private Declare Function GlobalAlloc Lib "kernel32" (ByVal wFlags As_
    Long, ByVal dwBytes As Long) As Long
Private Declare Function GlobalLock Lib "kernel32" (ByVal hMem As Long) _
    As Long
Private Declare Sub MoveMemory Lib "kernel32" Alias "RtlMoveMemory" _
    (ByVal dest As Any, ByVal src As Any, ByVal length As Long)
Const GMEM_MOVEABLE = &H2
```

When the user clicks a command button, **Command1**, we will allocate and lock the memory, and store the text string now in **Text1** in it. We start by storing the text from the text box in the buffer we've named **outbuffer**:

```
Private Sub Command1_Click()

    outbuffer = Text1.Text
...
```

Next, we use **GlobalAlloc** to allocate the memory we'll use:

```
Private Sub Command1_Click()

    outbuffer = Text1.Text

    hMemory = GlobalAlloc(GMEM_MOVEABLE, DataLength)
...
```

Next, we pass the memory handle from **GlobalAlloc** to **GlobalLock** to get a pointer to the memory we've allocated:

```
Private Sub Command1_Click()

    outbuffer = Text1.Text

    hMemory = GlobalAlloc(GMEM_MOVEABLE, DataLength)
    hMemoryPointer = GlobalLock(hMemory)
...
```

Finally, we copy the data from our buffer to our newly allocated memory with **MoveMemory** (note that because **MoveMemory** is a subroutine, we use the **Call** keyword instead of assigning a return value to a variable):

```
Private Sub Command1_Click()

    outbuffer = Text1.Text

    hMemory = GlobalAlloc(GMEM_MOVEABLE, DataLength)
    hMemoryPointer = GlobalLock(hMemory)

    Call MoveMemory(hMemoryPointer, outbuffer, DataLength)

End Sub
```

And that's it—when the user clicks Command1, we copy the text string to our allocated memory.

We've stored data in allocated memory now—how do we read it back? We'll take a look at that in the next topic.

Reading Data From Memory And Deallocating Memory

In the previous topic, we stored a text string from a text box, **Text1**, in memory when the user clicked a button, **Command1**. In this topic, we'll read the string back when the user clicks another button, **Command2**, and display that string in a new text box, **Text2**. We'll also free and deallocate the memory we've used.

We'll use **MoveMemory** to read the data from memory:

```
Sub MoveMemory Lib "kernel32" Alias "RtlMoveMemory" (ByVal dest As _
    Any, ByVal src As Any, ByVal length As Long)
```

Here are what the arguments to **MoveMemory** mean:

• *dest*—Pointer to the destination buffer

• *src*—Pointer to the source buffer

• *length*—Number of bytes to move

To allocate memory, we used **GlobalAlloc** to get a handle to a memory area; to use that memory, we used **GlobalLock** to get a pointer to the memory area. To unlock memory, you pass a pointer to that memory to **GlobalUnlock**:

```
Function GlobalUnlock Lib "kernel32" (ByVal hMem As Long) As Long
```

To free memory, you pass a memory handle to **GlobalFree**:

```
Function GlobalFree Lib "kernel32" (ByVal hMem As Long) As Long
```

Let's see this at work. Here, we add the declarations of the functions we'll use to the program we developed in the previous topic, as well as a buffer, **inbuffer**, to store the data we read:

```
Const DataLength = 40
Const GMEM_MOVEABLE = &H2

Dim outbuffer As String * DataLength
Dim inbuffer As String * DataLength

Dim memHandle As Long
Dim memPointer As Long

Private Declare Function GlobalAlloc Lib "kernel32" (ByVal wFlags As Long,_
    ByVal dwBytes As Long) As Long
Private Declare Function GlobalLock Lib "kernel32" (ByVal hMem As Long) _
    As Long
Private Declare Sub MoveMemory Lib "kernel32" Alias "RtlMoveMemory" _
    (ByVal dest As Any, ByVal src As Any, ByVal length As Long)
Private Declare Function GlobalFree Lib "kernel32" (ByVal hMem As Long) _
    As Long
Private Declare Function GlobalUnlock Lib "kernel32" (ByVal hMem As Long) _
    As Long
```

Then, when the user clicks **Command2**, we can use the memory pointer we created in the program in the previous topic, **hMemoryPointer**, with **MoveMemory**, to copy the string to the buffer:

```
Private Sub Command2_Click()

    Call MoveMemory(inbuffer, hMemoryPointer, DataLength)
...
```

Now we can move the string to **Text2** from **inbuffer**:

```
Private Sub Command2_Click()

    Call MoveMemory(inbuffer, hMemoryPointer, DataLength)

    Text2.Text = inbuffer
...
```

Finally, we unlock and free the memory we've used:

```
Private Sub Command2_Click()

    Call MoveMemory(inbuffer, hMemoryPointer, DataLength)

    Text2.Text = inbuffer

    GlobalUnlock (hMemoryPointer)
    GlobalFree (hMemory)

End Sub
```

That's it—when you run the program, as shown in Figure 23.10, and click the Store Text In Memory button, the text in the top text box, **Text1**, is stored in memory. When you click the Read Text From Memory button, the string is read back and displayed in the bottom text box, **Text2**, as you see in Figure 23.10. Now we're using memory with the Windows API.

The code for this example is located in the winmemory folder on this book's accompanying CD-ROM.

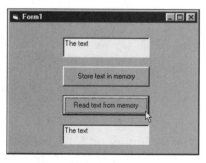

Figure 23.10   Storing and reading memory data.

Making A Window Topmost

You can use **SetWindowPos** to make a window "topmost," which means it'll always stay on top of other windows:

```
Function SetWindowPos Lib "user32" (ByVal hwnd As Long, ByVal _
    hWndInsertAfter As Long, ByVal x As Long, ByVal y As Long, ByVal _
    cx As Long, ByVal cy As Long, ByVal wFlags As Long) As Long
```

Here's what the arguments to this function mean:

- *hwnd*—Handle of the window to work with.

- *hWndInsertAfter*—Handle to the window that will precede this window in the Z-order. This parameter can be a window handle set to one of the following values: **HWND_BOTTOM** (= 1; places the window at the bottom of the Z-order), **HWND_TOP** (= 0; places the window at the top of the Z-order), **HWND_TOPMOST** (= –1; places the window above all non-topmost windows), or **HWND_NOTOPMOST** (= –2; repositions the window to the top of all non-topmost windows).

- *x*—Specifies the new position of the left side of the window.

- *y*—Specifies the new position of the top of the window.

- *cx*—Specifies the new width of the window.

- *cy*—Specifies the new height of the window.

- *wFlags*—Specifies sizing and positioning options, as shown in Table 23.5.

Table 23.5   SetWindowPos flags.

Constant	Meaning
SWP_DRAWFRAME (= &H20)	Draws a frame (defined when the window was created) around the window.
SWP_FRAMECHANGED (= &H20)	Sends a **WM_NCCALCSIZE** message to the window, even if the window's size is not being changed. If this flag is not specified, **WM_NCCALCSIZE** is sent only when the window's size is being changed.
SWP_HIDEWINDOW (=&H80)	Hides the window.
SWP_NOACTIVATE (= &H10)	Does not activate the window. If this flag is not set, the window is activated and moved to the top of either the topmost or the non-topmost group (depending on the setting of the **hWndInsertAfter** parameter).
SWP_NOCOPYBITS (= &H100)	Discards the entire contents of the client area. If this flag is not specified, the valid contents of the client area are saved and copied back into the client area after the window is sized or repositioned.
SWP_NOMOVE (= 2)	Retains current position (ignores the x and y parameters).
SWP_NOOWNERZORDER (= &H200)	Does not change the owner window's position in the Z-order.
SWP_NOREDRAW (= 8)	Does not redraw changes. If this flag is set, no repainting of any kind occurs.
SWP_NOREPOSITION (= &H200)	Same as **SWP_NOOWNERZORDER**.

(continued)

Table 23.5   SetWindowPos flags (continued).

Constant	Meaning
SWP_NOSIZE (= 1)	Retains current size (ignores the **cx** and **cy** parameters).
SWP_NOZORDER (= 4)	Retains current ordering (ignores **hWndInsertAfter**).
SWP_SHOWWINDOW (=&H40)	Displays the window.

Let's see an example. Here, we'll size a window to 100 x 100 pixels and make it a topmost window. We start by declaring **SetWindowPos** in our program, as well as the constants we'll use, **SWP_SHOWWINDOW, SWP_DRAWFRAME**, and **HWND_TOPMOST**:

```
Private Declare Function SetWindowPos Lib "user32" (ByVal hwnd As Long, _
    ByVal hWndInsertAfter As Long, ByVal x As Long, ByVal y As Long, _
    ByVal cx As Long, ByVal cy As Long, ByVal wFlags As Long) As Long

Const HWND_TOPMOST = -1
Const SWP_SHOWWINDOW = &H40
Const SWP_DRAWFRAME = &H20
```

Now when the window loads, we can make the window topmost this way:

```
Private Sub Form_Load()

    retVal = SetWindowPos(Me.hwnd, HWND_TOPMOST, 100, 100, _
        100, 100, SWP_DRAWFRAME Or SWP_SHOWWINDOW)

End Sub
```

That's all it takes. Now the window will stay on top of other windows, as you see in Figure 23.11. Our topmost program is a success.

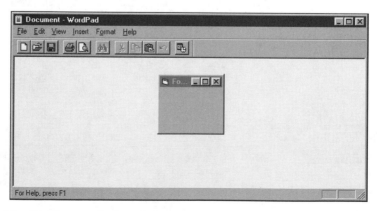

Figure 23.11   Making a window topmost.

Determining Free And Total Disk Space

The Testing Department is calling again. Your program, *SuperDuperDataCrunch*, is overflowing users' disks. Can't you check how much disk space is available before writing out your 800MB database? Hmm, you think, how would that work?

You can use the **GetDiskFreeSpace** function to check how much space there is on a disk:

```
Private Declare Function GetDiskFreeSpace Lib "kernel32" Alias _
    GetDiskFreeSpaceA" (ByVal lpRootPathName As String, _
    lpSectorsPerCluster As Long, lpBytesPerSector As Long, _
    lpNumberOfFreeClusters As Long, lpTotalNumberOfClusters As Long) _
    As Long
```

Here's what this function's arguments mean:

- *lpRootPathName*—The disk you want to check (for example, "c:\")
- *lpSectorsPerCluster*—The number of sectors per cluster on the disk
- *lpBytesPerSector*—The number of bytes per sector
- *lpNumberOfFreeClusters*—The number of free clusters
- *lpTotalNumberOfClusters*—The total number of clusters

To find the total free space, you multiply *SectorsPerCluster * BytesPerSector * NumberOfFreeClusters*. To find the total space on the drive, you multiply *SectorsPerCluster * BytesPerSector * TotalNumberOfClusters*

Let's see an example. Here, we'll determine the free space on the c: drive. We start by declaring **GetDiskFreeSpace**:

```
Private Declare Function GetDiskFreeSpace Lib "kernel32" Alias _
    "GetDiskFreeSpaceA" (ByVal lpRootPathName As String,_
    lngSectorsPerCluster As Long, lngBytesPerSector As Long, _
    lngNumberOfFreeClusters As Long, lngTotalNumberOfClusters As Long)_
    As Long
```

Next, when the form loads, we fill the variables *lngSectorsPerCluster*, *lngBytesPerSector*, *lngNumberOfFreeClusters*, and *lngTotalNumberOfClusters* with **GetDiskFeeSpace** for drive C:

```
Private Sub Form_Load()
    Dim lngSectorsPerCluster As Long
    Dim lngBytesPerSector As Long
    Dim lngNumberOfFreeClusters As Long
    Dim lngTotalNumberOfClusters As Long
```

```
    retVal = GetDiskFreeSpace("c:\", lngSectorsPerCluster, _
    lngBytesPerSector, lngNumberOfFreeClusters, lngTotalNumberOfClusters)
...
```

Finally, we can display the total number of free bytes in a label, **Label1**, this way:

```
Private Sub Form_Load()
    Dim lngSectorsPerCluster As Long
    Dim lngBytesPerSector As Long
    Dim lngNumberOfFreeClusters As Long
    Dim lngTotalNumberOfClusters As Long

    retVal = GetDiskFreeSpace("c:\", lngSectorsPerCluster, _
        lngBytesPerSector, lngNumberOfFreeClusters, _
        lngTotalNumberOfClusters)

    Label1.Caption = "Free space on drive c: " & _
        Str(lngSectorsPerCluster * lngBytesPerSector * _
        lngNumberOfFreeClusters) & " bytes"

End Sub
```

When you run the program, you'll see the number of free bytes on the computer's C: drive, something like the display in Figure 23.12.

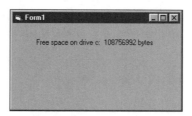

Figure 23.12   Determining free disk space.

Determining The Windows Directory

Sometimes you want to determine where Windows is installed on a system to be able to install files such as initialization files or DLLs. You can use the **GetWindowsDirectory** function to find the Windows directory:

```
Private Declare Function GetWindowsDirectory Lib "kernel32" Alias _
    "GetWindowsDirectoryA" (ByVal lpBuffer As String, ByVal nSize As _
    Long) As Long
```

Here are the arguments for the **GetWindowsDirectory** function:

- *lpBuffer*—Pointer to a buffer to store the Windows directory
- *nSize*—Size of the buffer in bytes.

Let's see an example. Here, we'll add some code to the example we started in the previous topic that displays free disk space. We add the declaration we'll need for **GetWindowsDirectory**:

```
Private Declare Function GetDiskFreeSpace Lib "kernel32" Alias _
    "GetDiskFreeSpaceA" (ByVal lpRootPathName As String, _
    lpSectorsPerCluster As Long, lpBytesPerSector As Long, _
    lpNumberOfFreeClusters As Long, lpTotalNumberOfClusters As Long) _
    As Long

Private Declare Function GetWindowsDirectory Lib "kernel32" Alias _
    "GetWindowsDirectoryA" (ByVal lpBuffer As String, ByVal nSize As _
    Long) As Long
```

Next, we set up a text buffer, get the Windows directory with **GetWindows-Directory**, and display the Windows directory in a new label, **Label2**:

```
Private Sub Form_Load()
    Dim lngSectorsPerCluster As Long
    Dim lngBytesPerSector As Long
    Dim lngNumberOfFreeClusters As Long
    Dim lngTotalNumberOfClusters As Long
    Dim strBuffer As String * 1024

    retVal = GetDiskFreeSpace("c:\", lngSectorsPerCluster, _
    lngBytesPerSector, lngNumberOfFreeClusters, lngTotalNumberOfClusters)

    Label1.Caption = "Free space on drive c: " & Str(lngSectorsPerCluster_
        * lngBytesPerSector * lngNumberOfFreeClusters) & " bytes"

    retVal = GetWindowsDirectory(strBuffer, 1024)
    Label2.Caption = "Windows directory: " & strBuffer

End Sub
```

That's it—the result appears in Figure 23.13. As you can see, we're now able to find the directory in which Windows itself is installed.

The code for this example is located in the windisk folder on this book's accompanying CD-ROM.

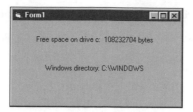

Figure 23.13   Determining the Windows directory.

TIP: If you just want to find the current, default directory, use the Visual Basic command **CurDir**. To set the current drive, use **ChDrive**, and to change directories, use **ChDir**.

Connecting To Visual C++

The Testing Department is calling again. Another company programmer has written a great routine for alphabetizing spreadsheets that would be great in your program, *SuperDuperDataCrunch*. Terrific, you say. They say, the only problem is that those routines are written in Visual C++, and you'll have to interface them to Visual Basic. Visual C++. You say, what's that?

To connect procedures written in Visual C++ (and other languages), you have to place those procedures in dynamic link libraries and use them as we've been using the Windows API procedures in this chapter. Let's see an example. There are many ways to write dynamic link libraries in Visual C++, and we'll use the simplest here to keep the code short (this Visual C++ project appears on the CD-ROM in the dynam folder). In this case, we'll create a new Visual C++ function, **addem**, which will add two integers and return the sum. We'll place **addem** in a dynamic link library, dynam.dll, put that DLL in the windows\system directory (which is where Visual Basic will search for it), and then call **addem** from Visual Basic.

We start by constructing the dynam.dll dynamic link library. We'll need a header file declaring our function, **addem.** That file, dynam.h, looks like this:

```
extern "C" {

int PASCAL EXPORT addem(int value1, int value2);

}
```

Now we can write the code for the dynamic link library itself in dynam.cpp. We start that file with the function we want to support in the dynamic link library, **addem**, which takes two integers, **value1** and **value2**, and returns their sum:

```
#include <afxwin.h>
#include "dynam.h"

extern "C"
int PASCAL EXPORT addem(int value1, int value2)
{
    return value1 + value2;
}
```

The we add the DLL support we need, including the actual Visual C++ MFC CDynamDLL object, which we'll name **DynamDLL**:

```
#include <afxwin.h>
#include "dynam.h"

extern "C"
int PASCAL EXPORT addem(int value1, int value2)
{
    return value1 + value2;
}

class CDynamDLL : public CWinApp
{
public:
    virtual BOOL InitInstance();
    virtual int ExitInstance();

    CDynamDLL(LPCTSTR pszAppName) : CWinApp(pszAppName){}
};

BOOL CDynamDLL::InitInstance()
{
    SetDialogBkColor();
    return TRUE;
}

int CDynamDLL::ExitInstance()
{
    return CWinApp::ExitInstance();
}

CDynamDLL dyamDLL("dynam.dll");
```

Finally, we create a DEF file, dynam.def, indicating that we are exporting the **addem** function from this DLL:

```
LIBRARY        DYNAM

EXPORTS
    addem
```

That's all we need. We create the dynam.dll file using Visual C++ now and copy it to the windows\system directory. Now the **addem** function is available to us in Visual Basic.

To connect the dynam.dll file to a Visual Basic project, we declare it this way:

```
Private Declare Function addem Lib "dynam" (ByVal value1 As Integer, ByVal_
    value2 As Integer) As Integer
```

Now we're free to put **addem** to work. For example, we can add two and three when the user clicks a command button, **Command1**, and display the result in a text box, **Text1**:

```
Private Sub Command1_Click()
    Text1.Text = "2 + 3 = " & Str(addem(2, 3))
End Sub
```

Running this program produces the result you see in Figure 23.14. Now we're connecting Visual Basic to Visual C++.

The code for this example, dynam.h and dynam.cpp, appear in Listing 23.2 and Listing 23.3. The Visual Basic code for this project is located in the viscpp folder on this book's accompanying CD-ROM.

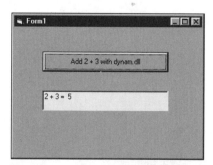

Figure 23.14   Calling a Visual C++ procedure from Visual Basic.

Listing 23.2   dynam.h

```
extern "C" {

int PASCAL EXPORT addem(int value1, int value2);

}
```

Listing 23.3   dynam.cpp

```
#include <afxwin.h>
#include "dynam.h"

extern "C"
int PASCAL EXPORT addem(int value1, int value2)
{
    return value1 + value2;
}

class CDynamDLL : public CWinApp
{
public:
    virtual BOOL InitInstance();
    virtual int ExitInstance();

    CDynamDLL(LPCTSTR pszAppName) : CWinApp(pszAppName){}
};

BOOL CDynamDLL::InitInstance()
{
    SetDialogBkColor();
    return TRUE;
}

int CDynamDLL::ExitInstance()
{
    return CWinApp::ExitInstance();
}

CDynamDLL dyamDLL("dynam.dll");
```

Chapter 24

Databases: Using DAO, RDO, And ADO

If you need an immediate solution to:	See page:
Creating And Managing Databases With The Visual Data Manager	830
Creating A Table With The Visual Data Manager	831
Creating A Field With The Visual Data Manager	831
Entering Data In A Database With The Visual Data Manager	833
Adding A Data Control To A Program	834
Opening A Database With The Data Control	835
Connecting A Data Control To A Bound Control	835
Registering An ODBC Source	836
Opening A Database With A Remote Data Control	838
Connecting A Remote Data Control To A Bound Control	838
Opening A Database With An ADO Data Control	839
Connecting An ADO Data Control To A Bound Control	840
The Data Form Wizard: Creating A Data Form	841
Using Database Control Methods: Adding, Deleting, And Modifying Records	843
Adding Records To Databases	844
Delcting Records In Databases	844
Refreshing A Data Control	845
Updating A Database With Changes	845
Moving To The Next Record	845
Moving To The Previous Record	846
Moving To The First Record	846
Moving To The Last Record	846
The Data-Bound Controls: From Text Boxes To Flex Grids	847
The ADO Data-Bound Controls	848

In Depth

This is our first chapter on databases. In this chapter, we're going to see what databases are, exploring the difference between the Microsoft database programming object sets: Data Access Objects (DAO), Remote Data Objects (RDO), and ActiveX Data Objects (ADO).

You may wonder why there are three different sets of database objects in Visual Basic. As it turns out, the reason is historical. At first, Visual Basic only supported DAO, which connected to the Microsoft Jet database engine (the database engine in Microsoft Access). Then, recognizing that there are other database types available, Microsoft created the open database connectivity (ODBC) standard and supported ODBC with Remote Data Objects in Visual Basic. Finally, Microsoft saw that the Web was available too and created Active Data Objects, which make up a flexible standard that allows connections on the same computer, over networks, and through the Web, and is intended to supercede ODBC. ADO is also called OLE DB, and in fact, it's based on COM programming techniques (which we'll see a lot more of in Chapter 26). We'll see how to work with all three of these object sets in this and the next chapter.

There are two ways to work with the DAO, RDO, and ADO object sets in Visual Basic. The first way is working with the special controls that support them: the data control (supports DAO), the remote data control (supports ODBC), and the ADO data control (supports ADO). You use those controls to connect to and move through databases, but they don't actually display data—you *bind* them to other Visual Basic controls, and those bound controls handle the display. The second way is working with the three database object sets directly in code, without controls like the data control or the ADO data control, and that's what we'll do in the next chapter.

In this chapter, then, we'll see what databases are all about and how to create and edit them with the Visual Basic Visual Data Manager tool. Next, we'll examine the data control, the remote data control, and the ADO data control to see how to connect to databases, and we'll use the bound controls to handle those databases in depth. In the next chapter, we'll see how to access the data object libraries directly and put them to work in code for additional power.

What Are Databases?

We'll begin our discussion of databases by asking just what they are. Like many other programming concepts, databases have become more complex over the years, but the fundamental concept is still a simple one. Say you were in charge of teaching a class and were supposed to hand a grade in for each student. You might make up a table much like the one in Figure 24.1 to record the grade for each student.

In fact, you've already created a database—or more specifically, a database *table*. The transition from a table on paper to one in a computer is natural: with a computer, you can sort, index, update, and organize large tables of data in an easy way (and without a great waste of paper). You can even connect tables together, creating *relational* databases.

Each individual data entry in a table, such as a student's name, goes into a *field* in the table. A collection of fields together, such as the Name and Grade

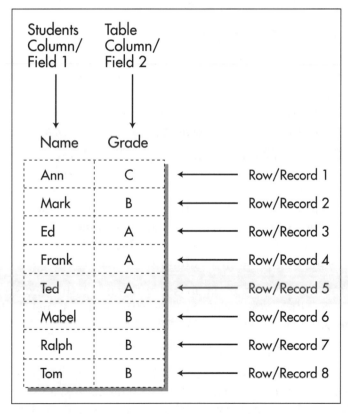

Figure 24.1   A table of data.

fields in our table, make up a *record*. Each record gets its own row in a table, and each column in that row represents a different field.

A collection of records—that is, rows of records where each column is a field— becomes a table. What, then, is a *database*? A database is just a collection of one or more tables. In fact, you can go farther than that in Visual Basic—you can have collections of databases. In DAO, those collections are called the *workspace*, and in RDO and ADO, they are referred to as the *data environment*. You can also have *indices* in databases, and those are pointers to specific fields, either in the current database or another one.

Now that you've set up a database, how do you work with the data in that database? One popular way is to use Structured Query Language (SQL), which we'll see more about in the next chapter. You use SQL to set up a *query*, which when applied to a database gives you a *record set*. This record set is made up of the records from the database that matched your query—for example, you may have asked for all students that got a grade of B or better. We'll see more about working with databases in code like this in the next chapter.

Flat And Relational Databases

So far, we've defined a certain type of database: a *flat* or *flat-file* database. There is a second type of database as well: *relational* databases. Relational databases are called *relational* because they are set up to relate the data in multiple tables together. To make a table relational, you choose certain fields to be *primary keys* and *foreign keys*.

The primary key in a table is usually the most important one—the one you might use to sort on, for instance. The foreign key usually represents the primary key in another table, giving you access to that table in an organized way. For example, we might add a field for student IDs to our student grade table. That same field, student ID, may be the primary key in the school registrar's database table, which lists all students. In our table, then, the student ID field is a foreign key, allowing us to specify individual records in the registrar's table.

We've gotten an overview of databases at this point; the next step is to look into the three different ways of working with them in Visual Basic, and we'll do that now.

DAO

When Visual Basic first started working with databases, it used the Microsoft Jet database engine, which is what Microsoft Access uses. Using the Jet engine represented a considerable advance for Visual Basic, because now you could work with all kinds of data formats in the fields of a database: text, numbers, integers, longs, singles, doubles, dates, binary values, OLE objects, currency values, Boolean values, and even memo objects (up to 1.2GB of text). The Jet engine also supports SQL, which database programmers found attractive.

To support the Jet database engine, Microsoft added the data control to Visual Basic, and you can use that control to open Jet database (.mdb) files. Microsoft also added a set of Data Access Objects (DAO) to Visual Basic:

- *DBEngine*—The Jet database engine
- *Workspace*—An area can hold one or more databases
- *Database*—A collection of tables
- *TableDef*—The definition of a table
- *QueryDef*—The definition of a query
- *Recordset*—The set of records that make up the result of a query
- *Field*—A column in a table
- *Index*—An ordered list of records
- *Relation*—Stored information about the specific relationship between tables

We'll work with these Data Access Objects in the next chapter; in this chapter, we'll work with the data control.

The Data Control

The data control enables you to move around in a database from record to record and to display and manipulate data from the records in bound controls. This control displays a set of arrow buttons the user can manipulate to move through a database, and the records from that database are displayed in bound controls. You can see a data control operating with bound controls in Figure 24.2, where we've placed our students table into a database and opened it with a data control.

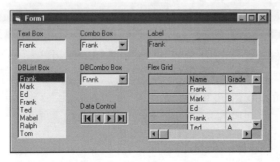

Figure 24.2   Using a data control.

In fact, you can perform most data access operations using the data control—without writing any code. Data-bound controls automatically display data from one or more fields for the current record, and the data control performs all operations on the current record. If the data control is made to move to a different record, all bound controls automatically pass any changes to the data control to be saved in the database. The data control then moves to the requested record and passes back data from the current record to the bound controls where it's displayed.

When an application begins, Visual Basic uses data control properties to open a selected database, create a DAO Database object, and create a Recordset object. The data control's **Database** and **Recordset** properties refer to those Database and Recordset objects, and you can manipulate the data using those properties. For example, if you have an SQL statement to execute, you place that statement in the data control's **RecordSource** property, and the result appears in the **Recordset** property.

RDO

Remote Data Objects (RDO) connect to databases using ODBC. You set up ODBC connections to databases using the ODBC item in the Windows Control Panel, and then use one of those connections with the RDO objects. The Remote Data Objects are designed in parallel with the Data Access Objects; for example, the database engine is rdoEngine instead of DBEngine, Recordsets have become rdoResultsets, TableDefs became rdoTables, Workspaces became rdoEnvironments, Field objects became rdoColumn objects, and so on. Although the names have changed, the command set is very similar to DAO.

Although Microsoft intends ADO to supercede RDO, many programmers will use RDO for some time to come. In this chapter, we'll take a look at RDO with the remote data control.

The Remote Data Control

Like the data control, the remote data control gives you access to a database and displays data in bound controls. Unlike the data control, however, you use the remote data control to access ODBC data sources (which can include databases built with all the popular commercial database programs).

As with the data control, if the remote data control is instructed to move to a different row, all bound controls automatically pass any changes to the remote data control to be saved to the ODBC data source. The remote data control then moves to the requested row and passes back data from the current row to the bound controls where it's displayed.

In fact, the remote data control behaves like the data control in most respects, with some differences; for example, you can treat the remote data control's **SQL** property like the data control's **RecordSource** property, but it cannot accept the name of a table by itself unless you populate the **rdoTables** collection first.

ADO

Microsoft's latest set of data access objects are the ActiveX Data Objects (ADO). These objects let you access data in a database server through any OLE DB provider. ADO is intended to give you a consistent interface for working with a wide variety of data sources, from text files to ODBC relational databases to complex groups of databases.

The way Microsoft implements connections to all those data sources is with the OLE DB set of COM interfaces, but that standard is a very complex one. Our interface to that interface, so to speak, is ADO, a set of objects with properties, events, and methods. Here are the ADOs:

- *Connection*—Access from your application to a data source is through a connection, the environment necessary for exchanging data. The Connection object is used to specify a particular data provider and any parameters.

- *Command*—A command issued across an established connection manipulates the data source in some way. The Command object lets ADO make it easy to issue commands.

- *Parameter*—Commands can require *parameters* that can be set before you issue the command. For example, if you require a debit from a charge account, you would specify the amount of money to be debited as a parameter in a Parameter object.

- *Recordset*—If your command is a query that returns data as rows of information in a table, then those rows are placed in local storage in a Recordset object.

- *Field*—A row of a Recordset consists of one or more fields, which are stored in Field objects.

- *Error*—Errors can occur when your program is not able to establish a connection, execute a command, or perform an operation, and ADO supports an Error object to hold the resulting error.

- *Collection*—ADO provides *collections*, an object that contains other objects of a particular type. ADO provides four types of collections: the Connection object has the **Errors** collection, the Command object has the **Parameters** collection, the Recordset object has the **Fields** collection, and the Connection, Command, Recordset, and Field objects all have a

Properties collection, which contains all the Property objects that apply to them.

- *Events*—ADO uses the concept of events, just like other interface objects in Visual Basic. You use event handling procedures with events. There are two types of events: **ConnectionEvents** (issued when transactions occur, when commands are executed, and when connections start or end) and **RecordsetEvents** (events used to report the progress of data changes).

ADO also includes the Remote Data Service (RDS), with which you can move data from a server to a client application or Web page, manipulate the data on the client, and return updates to the server in one round-trip.

In this chapter, we're going to use the ADO data control to handle our ADO work.

The ADO Data Control

The ADO data control is similar to the data control and the remote data control. The ADO data control is designed to create a connection to a database using Microsoft ActiveX Data Objects (ADO). At design time, you create a connection by setting the **ConnectionString** property to a valid connection string, then set the **RecordSource** property to a statement appropriate to the database manager.

You can also set the **ConnectionString** property to the name of a file that defines a connection (the file is generated by a Data Link dialog box, which appears when you click ConnectionString on the Properties window and then click either Build or Select). You then connect the ADO data control to a data-bound control such as the data grid, data combo, or data list control by setting its **DataSource** properties to the ADO data control.

At runtime, you can set the **Provider**, **ConnectionString**, and **RecordSource** properties to change the database.

We'll see how to work with the ADO control in this chapter. We'll use controls like the data control, the remote data control, and the ADO data control with bound controls.

The Data-Bound Controls

You can bind certain controls to the data control, the remote data control, and the ADO data control, and those controls are called *bound controls*. To bind a control to a database control, you use properties like **DataSource** to specify the database control, and then use properties like **DataField** or **BoundColumn** to specify what field to display in the bound control, as we'll see. Here are the controls that can function as bound controls:

- Picture boxes
- Labels
- Text boxes
- Checkboxes
- Image controls
- OLE controls
- List boxes
- Masked edit controls
- Rich text boxes
- Combo boxes

In addition, there are special controls that are designed to be used as bound controls:

- DBList
- DBCombo
- FlexGrid
- MSFlexGrid

Finally, a number of bound controls are specially built to be used with the ADO control only:

- DataList
- DataCombo
- DataGrid

We'll see these controls at work in this chapter.

That's it, then, for the overview of databases. We've seen how the process works in overview; now it's time to turn to the Immediate Solutions.

Immediate Solutions

Creating And Managing Databases With The Visual Data Manager

You can create and manage databases with the Visual Data Manager. Open this tool from the Visual Basic Add-Ins menu, as shown in Figure 24.3.

You can use this tool to create and modify databases. You create a new database with the File menu's New item and open an existing database with the Open item. Let's see an example. Here, we'll create a new database with the Visual Data Manager. Click the Table Type Recordset button, which is the button at the extreme left in the toolbar, and the Use Data Control On New Form button, which is the fourth button from the left.

Next, select the New item in the File menu. The Visual Data Manager lets you design databases in several different formats; for this example, choose Microsoft Access Version 7 MDB or later. The Visual Data Manager asks you for a name and path for this new database; we'll call it "db.mdb", so enter that name now and click on OK.

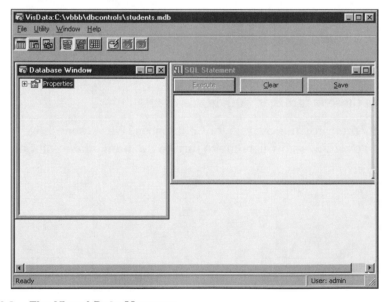

Figure 24.3   The Visual Data Manager.

That's it—now we've created a new database, db.mdb. We'll add a table to it in the next topic.

Creating A Table With The Visual Data Manager

To add a table named "students" to the db.mdb database we created in the previous topic, right-click the Properties item in the Visual Data Manager's Database window and select the New Table item, opening the Table Structure window you see in Figure 24.4.

Give this new table the name "students" by typing that into the Table Name field, as shown in Figure 24.4. That's it—it was as quick as that to create a new table.

Now that we've created a new table, we'll add the new fields in this table (Name and Grade) in the next topic.

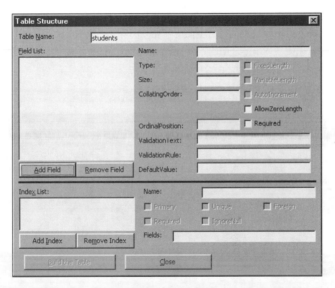

Figure 24.4   The Visual Data Manager's Table Structure window.

Creating A Field With The Visual Data Manager

To add fields to the database table named "students" we created in the previous topic, click the Add Field button in the Visual Data Manager's Table Structure window, opening the Add Field dialog box you see in Figure 24.5.

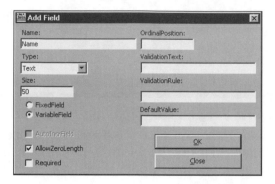

Figure 24.5 The Visual Data Manager's Add Field dialog box.

Give this new field the name "Name" by typing that into the box labeled Name and clicking on the OK button. The Add Field dialog box stays open, and the new field is added to the students table. Add another field named "Grade" in the same way. Click on OK to add the field, then click Close to close the Add Field dialog box.

Now in the Table Structure window, click the Build The Table item to build the new table with our two new fields. This creates the students table with two fields: Name and Grade, and opens that table in the Visual Data Manager's Database window, as you can see in Figure 24.6.

In the next topic, we'll enter data into our new table.

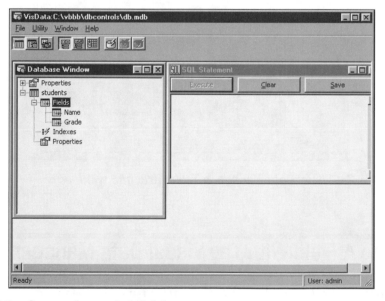

Figure 24.6 Our newly created database.

Entering Data In A Database With The Visual Data Manager

To enter data into a table in the Visual Data Manager, right-click the table's entry in the Visual Data manager's Database window and select the Open item in the menu that opens. In our case, doing so opens the Table: students dialog box you see in Figure 24.7. We'll use this dialog box to enter the data in our database's records. We'll use the data you saw in Figure 24.1, but you can also use it to edit that data.

Using the data in Figure 24.1, enter the name "Ann" and the grade "C" for the first student in the labeled boxes in the Table: students dialog box, as shown in Figure 24.7. Then click Update to add that new record to the database; when the Visual Data manager displays a message box asking if you want to add the new record to the database, click Yes.

To add a new record, click the Add button and add the name "Mark" and the grade "B", and click Update. Click Yes when the Visual Data Manager asks you if you want to add the new record to the database.

When you're done entering your records, click the Close button in the Table: students dialog box and close the database with the Close item in the Visual Data manager's File menu.

Congratulations—you've created a new database.

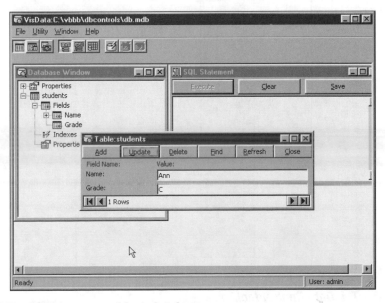

Figure 24.7   Editing a record in a database.

Adding A Data Control To A Program

The Testing Department is calling again. Now that you've created a new database file, how about using it in a program? Okay, you say, I'll look into it.

The database we've created in the previous few topics is in Microsoft Access (Jet) format, which is a format you can use with all three data access object sets: DAO, RDO, and ADO. We'll see how to use the simplest method first: connecting that database to a data control in a Visual Basic program and using that data control with data-bound controls.

The data control is the only intrinsic database control—it's already in the toolbox. This control's tool appears as the tenth tool down on the right in the toolbox in Figure 24.8. Double-click that tool now to add a data control to your form.

Stretch the data control as you want it. When you stretch the control beyond its original size, you'll see a space for text in the center of the control; set the control's **Caption** property to the name of the database table we'll be working with—students.

That's all it takes to add a data control to your program. In the next topic, we'll see how to connect the data control to a database.

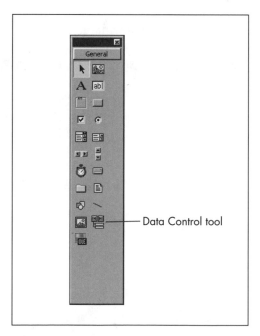

Figure 24.8   The Data Control tool.

Opening A Database With The Data Control

To connect a data control to a database, you just set the data control's **DatabaseName** property to the path and name of the Access/Jet database file you want to open. Here, we'll use the db.mdb file we've created at the beginning of this chapter. In addition, you select the table you want to work with in that file with the data control's **RecordSource** property. After connecting the control to the db.mdb database, select the students table in the drop-down list box for the **RecordSource** property in the Properties window.

You've connected the data control to a table in a database. But how do you actually see or modify the data in the database? You do that with bound controls, and we'll get an introduction to that in the next topic.

Connecting A Data Control To A Bound Control

In the previous few topics, we connected a database to a data control. To see that data, we'll use a data-bound control—a text box. We'll investigate all the data-bound controls later in this chapter—after we've gone through the ways of connecting to databases—so this is just to get us started.

To connect a text box to a data control, set the text box's **DataSource** property to the name of the data control (or remote data control or ADO control). To display a particular field in the text box, place that field's name in the text box's **DataField** property.

Let's see an example. Here, we'll use the database, db.mdb, and the data control we've developed over the previous few topics. Add a text box, **Text1**, to the program now and set its **DataSource** property to **Data1**. When you move through the database with the data control, the data control will hold the *current record*; to display a field in the current record, place that field's name in the text box's **DataField** property; here, we'll place the Name field in that property.

TIP: Set the text box's **DataSource** and **DataField** properties after adding and connecting the data control. When you do, you'll find the text box's **DataSource** and **DataField** properties can be set with drop-down list boxes in the Properties window, making that process easier.

When we run the program, we get the result in Figure 24.9. Using the data control, you can move to the beginning or end of the database, and step through record by record as well. Congratulations—now you're working with databases. The code for this example is located in the dao folder on this book's accompanying CD-ROM.

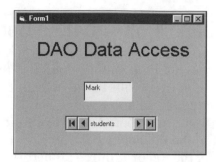

Figure 24.9   Using a data control to move through a database.

Registering An ODBC Source

The Testing Department is calling again. Your program with the data control, *SuperDuperDataBase*, is terrific, but what if you want to work with an ODBC database? Hmm, you think, is that possible?

It is, with the remote data control. You can use an ODBC data source with a remote data control, but first you have to configure a new connection for the ODBC source. You configure an ODBC connection with the 32-bit ODBC item in your computer's control panel. Open that item now, click the System DSN tab (DSN stands for *data source name*), and click the Add button to open the Create New Data Source dialog box you see in Figure 24.10.

You can see the ODBC drivers installed on your system in this dialog box. Select the one you want to use and click Finish; to install the db.mdb file we've developed in the previous few topics, we'll select the Microsoft Access Driver entry here.

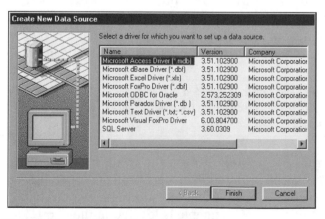

Figure 24.10   The Create New Data Source dialog box.

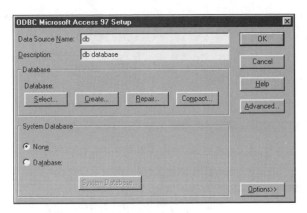

Figure 24.11   The ODBC Microsoft Access dialog box.

This opens the ODBC Microsoft Access dialog box you see in Figure 24.11. Use the Select button to select the database file, db.mdb in our example, and click on the OK button in the ODBC Microsoft Access dialog box. We give the name **db** to this source.

This creates a new ODBC connection for our file, and that connection appears in the ODBC Data Source Administrator, as shown in Figure 24.12.

Click on the OK button to close the ODBC Data Source Administrator. Now you've added a new ODBC source to your computer's data environment. We'll use this data source, **db**, in the next topic.

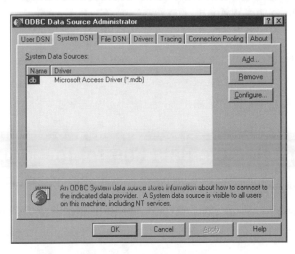

Figure 24.12   The ODBC Data Source Administrator.

Opening A Database With A Remote Data Control

To add a new remote data control to a form, follow these steps:

1. Select the Project|Components menu item.

2. Click the Controls tab in the Components dialog box that opens.

3. Select the Microsoft Remote Data Control entry in the Controls list box.

4. Click on OK to close the Components dialog box.

5. This adds the Remote Data Control tool to the toolbox; draw that control as you want it on your form.

6. Connect the remote data control to an ODBC data source with the **DataSource** property.

7. Create a result set (unlike data controls and ADO data controls, which use record sets, remote data controls use result sets) that you can work with by supplying an SQL statement in the **SQL** property.

Let's see an example. Add a remote data control, **MSRDC1**, to a form now. We'll connect it to the **db** ODBC data source we've created in the previous few topics, and you do that by setting the remote data control's **DataSourceName** property to "db".

Unlike the data control or the ADO data control, you need to create a result set to work with in the remote data control, and we create a result set by selecting the entire students table with the SQL statement **SELECT * FROM students**. Place that string in the control's **SQL** property.

Now we've connected our database to the remote data control—but how do we connect the remote data control to bound controls? We'll look at that in the next topic.

Connecting A Remote Data Control To A Bound Control

In the previous topic, we connected a database to a remote data control. To see that data, we'll use a data-bound control—a text box. We'll investigate all the data-bound controls later in this chapter—after we've gone through the ways of connecting to databases—so this is just to get us started.

To connect a text box to a remote data control, set the text box's **DataSource** property to the name of the remote data control. To display a particular field in the text box, place that field's name in the text box's **DataField** property.

Let's see an example. Here, we'll use the database, db.mdb, and the remote data control we've in the previous topic. Add a text box, **Text1**, to the program now, and set its **DataSource** property to the remote data control, **MSRDC1**.

When you move through the database with the remote data control, the remote data control will hold the *current record*; to display a field in the current record, place that field's name in the text box's **DataField** property; here, we'll place the Name field in that property.

TIP: *Set the text box's **DataSource** and **DataField** properties after adding and connecting the remote data control. When you do, you'll find the text box's **DataSource** and **DataField** properties can be set with drop-down list boxes in the Properties window, making that process easier.*

When we run the program, we get the result in Figure 24.13. Using the remote data control, you can move to the beginning or end of an ODBC database and step through record by record as well. Congratulations—now you're working with ODBC databases. The code for this example is located in the rdo folder on this book's accompanying CD-ROM.

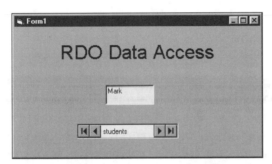

Figure 24.13 Opening a database with the remote data control.

Opening A Database With An ADO Data Control

To add a new ADO data control to a form, follow these steps:

1. Select the Project|Components menu item.
2. Click the Controls tab in the Components dialog box that opens.
3. Select the Microsoft ADO Data Control entry in the Controls list box.
4. Click on OK to close the Components dialog box.
5. This adds the ADO data control tool to the toolbox; draw that control as you want it on your form.

6. Connect the ADO data control's Connection object to a data source with the **ConnectionString** property, separating items in that string with semicolons. At the least, you should specify the **Provider** (the type of OLE DB) and **Data Source** (database name) values in the **ConnectionString**. See the following material for more information.

Let's see an example. Here, we'll connect an ADO data control to the database we've constructed in the early parts of this chapter, db.mdb. To do that, add an ADO data control, **Adodc1**, to a form, and set its **ConnectionString** property to specify the data provider type and the data source for that database like this:

```
"PROVIDER=Microsoft.Jet.OLEDB.3.51;Data Source=c:\vbbb\ado\db.mdb;"
```

TIP: One way of connecting an ADO control to a database easily is with the Data Form Wizard, which generates the connection string for you automatically. We'll see more of this wizard later in this chapter.

Next, set the ADO data control's **RecordSource** property to the table to work with, which is students in our example database, db.mdb.

Now you've connected a database to the ADO data control. To connect the ADO data control to bound controls, see the next topic.

**Connecting An
ADO Data
Control To A
Bound Control**

Connecting An ADO Data Control To A Bound Control

In the previous topic, we connected a database to an ADO data control. To see that data, we'll use a data-bound control—a text box. We'll investigate all the data-bound controls later in this chapter—after we've gone through the ways of connecting to databases—so this is just to get us started.

To connect a text box to an ADO data control, set the text box's **DataSource** property to the name of the remote data control. To display a particular field in the text box, place that field's name in the text box's **DataField** property.

Let's see an example. Here, we'll use the database, db.mdb, and the ADO data control we developed over the previous few topics. Add a text box, **Text1**, to the program now, and set its **DataSource** property to the ADO data control, **Adodc1**. When you move through the database with the ADO data control, the ADO data control will hold the *current record*; to display a field in the current record, place that field's name in the text box's **DataField** property; here, we'll place the Name field in that property.

TIP: *Set the text box's **DataSource** and **DataField** properties after adding and connecting the remote data control. When you do, you'll find the text box's **DataSource** and **DataField** properties can be set with drop-down list boxes in the Properties window, making that process easier.*

When we run the program, we get the result in Figure 24.14. Using the ADO data control, you can move to the beginning or end of databases, and step through record by record as well. Congratulations—now you're working with ADO databases. The code for this example is located in the ado folder on this book's accompanying CD-ROM.

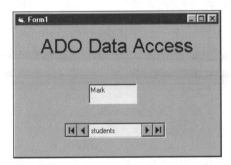

Figure 24.14   Opening a database with the ADO data control.

The Data Form Wizard: Creating A Data Form

You can use the Visual Basic Data Form Wizard to create a form using an ADO control or ADO code that lets you open and edit a database. To use the Data Form Wizard, select it in the Visual Basic Add-Ins menu (if it's not there, add it with the Add-Ins Manager in the Add-Ins menu) and follow the steps in the Data Form Wizard, one step for each successive window that appears in the Wizard:

1. Introduction window. This window asks if you want to load a profile to create the data form; click Next.

2. Database Type. This window lets you select the database format, like Microsoft Access or ODBC. For the example database we've developed in this chapter, db.mdb, select the Access type. Click Next.

3. Database. This window lets you select the database to work with. Use the Name box and the Browse button to select your database or data source. The Data Form Wizard will create the correct connection string for the ADO data control. Click Next.

4. Form. This window lets you specify the name for the form you're creating, as well as the form layout (how the data will be displayed): single record, grid, and so on, as shown in Figure 24.15. You can also

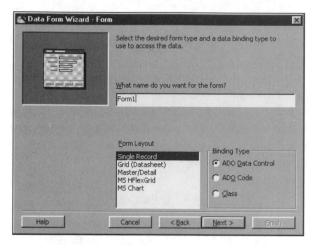

Figure 24.15   Setting up a data entry form.

specify how to bind the database to the form: with an ADO control or ADO code, or with a class (we'll see more about classes when we discuss code components in Chapter 27). For our example database, we will use an ADO control for the binding. Click Next to go to the next window.

5. Record Source. In this window, select the table name and the fields you want displayed, as shown in Figure 24.16. Click Next to go to the next window.

6. Control Selection. Specify the buttons you want in the data entry form: Add, Delete, Refresh, and so on. For the example we'll create later in this topic, leave all options selected and click Next.

7. Finished!. Click Finish in this window to create the new data form.

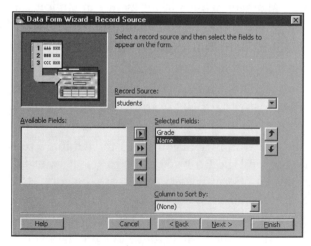

Figure 24.16   Selecting the record source.

Let's see an example to make this clearer.

Create a new project, and remove **Form1**. Next, follow the preceding steps to create a new data form named **Form1** using our db.mdb database, and set the project's startup object (using the Visual Basic Project|Properties menu item) to **Form1**.

When you run this example, the records of our database appear in the data form, as shown in Figure 24.17. You can move through the database, editing the records as you like. When you change a record, click the Update button to change the actual record in the database file itself. Now we're editing databases with our own programs in Visual Basic. The code for this example is located in the dataentry folder on this book's accompanying CD-ROM.

Figure 24.17   The ADO data entry form.

Using Database Control Methods: Adding, Deleting, And Modifying Records

The Testing Department is calling again: your *SuperDuperDataBase* program is terrific, but instead of restricting users to simply moving through a database, how about letting them edit the data in that text box, adding new records and so on? Hmm, you think, how would that work?

Like most controls, the DAO, RDO, and ADO controls have methods, events, and properties. To make these controls consistent, Microsoft has given them the same core methods, and we'll take a look at those methods in this chapter. Using these methods, users can add records to a database, change those records, delete them, and move around in the database.

In the next few topics, we'll develop the program you see in Figure 24.18, where we're editing the db.mdb database we developed in the beginning of the chapter. Because all data controls have the same core methods, we'll use a data control, **Data1**, in this example to keep this example easy. We also use two text boxes, **Text1** and **Text2**, connected to **Data1** and the Name and Grade fields in our database, respectively. Now all we have to do is to make all the buttons in the program active, and we'll do that in the following few topics.

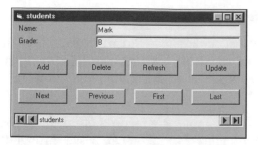

Figure 24.18   Using data control methods to add, edit, and delete records.

The code for this example is located in the dbmethods folder on this book's accompanying CD-ROM.

Adding Records To Databases

You can add a new record to a database with the **AddNew** method of the **Recordset** property of a data or ADO data control, or of the **Resultset** property of a remote data control. Let's see an example. When the user clicks the Add button in the dbmethods example we're developing in this and the previous few topics, we can add a new record like this:

```
Private Sub cmdAdd_Click()
    Data1.Recordset.AddNew
End Sub
```

This adds a new, blank record. You can enter the data you want in the record's fields, and to update the database, you click the Update button.

Deleting Records In Databases

You can delete a record in a database with the **Delete** method of the **Recordset** property of a data or an ADO data control, or of the **Resultset** property of a remote data control. Let's see an example. When the user clicks the Delete button in the dbmethods example we're developing in this and the previous few topics, we can delete a record like this:

```
Private Sub cmdDelete_Click()
    Data1.Recordset.Delete
    ...
End Sub
```

To avoid displaying a blank record, we also move to the next record this way:

```
Private Sub cmdDelete_Click()
  Data1.Recordset.Delete
  Data1.Recordset.MoveNext
End Sub
```

Refreshing A Data Control

When working with multiple databases, you can refresh the data in the current database control with the **Refresh** method of the data, ADO data control, or the remote data control. Let's see an example. When the user clicks the Refresh button in the dbmethods example we're developing in this and the previous few topics, we can refresh the control like this:

```
Private Sub cmdRefresh_Click()
  Data1.Refresh
End Sub
```

Updating A Database With Changes

After changing the fields in a record, you can update a database with the **UpdateRecord** method of the data, ADO data control, or remote data control. Let's see an example. When the user clicks the Update button in the dbmethods example we're developing in this and the previous few topics, we can update the database with the new record like this:

```
Private Sub cmdUpdate_Click()
  Data1.UpdateRecord
End Sub
```

Moving To The Next Record

You can move to the next record of a database with the **MoveNext** method of the **Recordset** property of a data or ADO data control, or of the **Resultset** property of a remote data control. Let's see an example. When the user clicks the Next button in the dbmethods example we're developing in this and the previous few topics, we can move to the next record like this:

```
Private Sub cmdNext_Click()
    Data1.Recordset.MoveNext
End Sub
```

TIP: You can use the **RecordCount** property of a Recordset or Resultset to determine how many records you have to work with, and so make sure you don't go past the end of the database.

Moving To The Previous Record

You can move to the previous record of a database with the **MovePrevious** method of the **Recordset** property of a data or ADO data control, or of the **Resultset** property of a remote data control. Let's see an example. When the user clicks the Previous button in the dbmethods example we're developing in this and the previous few topics, we can move to the previous record like this:

```
Private Sub cmdPrevious_Click()
    Data1.Recordset.MovePrevious
End Sub
```

TIP: When you use **MovePrevious**, make sure you don't try to move back before the first record of the database.

Moving To The First Record

You can move to the first record of a database with the **MoveFirst** method of the **Recordset** property of a data or ADO data control, or of the **Resultset** property of a remote data control. Let's see an example. When the user clicks the First button in the dbmethods example we're developing in this and the previous few topics, we can move to the first record like this:

```
Private Sub cmdFirst_Click()
    Data1.Recordset.MoveFirst
End Sub
```

Moving To The Last Record

You can move to the last record of a database with the **MoveLast** method of the **Recordset** property of a data or ADO data control, or of the **Resultset** property of a remote data control. Let's see an example. When the user clicks the Last button in the dbmethods example we're developing in this and the previous few topics, we can move to the last record like this:

```
Private Sub cmdLast_Click()
  Data1.Recordset.MoveLast
End Sub
```

The Data-Bound Controls: From Text Boxes To Flex Grids

After installing a data, remote data, or ADO data control, you can connect that control to other controls through a process called *data binding*. You bind controls to a data control using the data properties of the bound control. The standard bound controls and their data properties appear in Table 24.1. Using the information in that table, you can connect the listed Visual Basic controls to data controls, remote data controls, and ADO data controls.

Table 24.1   The bound controls.

Control	Properties To Set
Checkbox	**DataField** = Desired Boolean field; **DataSource** = Data control's name
Combo box	**DataField** = Desired field; **DataSource** = Data control's name
DBCombo box	**BoundColumn** = Desired field; **DataField** = Desired field; **DataSource** = Data control's name; **ListField** = Desired field to display in the combo's list; **RowSource** = Data control's name
DBList box	**DataField** = Desired field; **DataSource** = Data control's name; **RowSource** = Data control's name
FlexGrid	**DataSource** = Data control's name
Image control	**DataField** = Desired field; **DataSource** = Data control's name
Label	**DataField** = Desired field; **DataSource** = Data control's name
List box	**DataField** = Desired field; **DataSource** = Data control's name
MaskedEdit	**DataField** = Desired field; **DataSource** = Data control's name
MSFlexFrid	**DataSource** = Data control's name
Picture box	**DataField** = Desired field; **DataSource** = Data control's name
Text box	**DataField** = Desired field; **DataSource** = Data control's name
Rich text box	**DataField** = Desired field; **DataSource** = Data control's name

Note that Visual Basic also supports some additional data-bound controls to work with the ADO data control specifically, and those controls are covered in the following topic.

Let's see an example. In the program in Figure 24.19, we've added a number of controls that we bind to a data control, **Data1**. The data control, in turn, is connected to the db.mdb database we created in the beginning of the chapter. When you move through the database with the data control, the data in each bound control is updated. The code for this example is located in the dbcontrols folder on this book's accompanying CD-ROM.

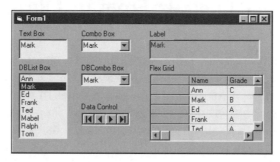

Figure 24.19   An example program showing the use of bound controls.

The ADO Data-Bound Controls

There are three data-bound controls that are specially optimized for use with the ADO data control: DataGrid controls, DataCombo controls, and DataList controls (don't confuse these controls with the non-ADO optimized data-bound controls like the DBCombo and DBList controls). These controls are specifically designed to work with ADO data controls and won't work with standard controls like the data control.

To add these controls to a program, follow these steps:

1. Select the Project|Components menu item.

2. Click the Controls tab in the Components dialog box that opens.

3. Select both the Microsoft DataGrid Control entry and the Microsoft DataList Controls entry in the Controls list box.

4. Click on OK to close the Components dialog box.

5. This adds the DataGrid, DataCombo, and DataList control tools to the toolbox; draw those controls as you want them on your form.

Here are the principal data properties you use with these three controls:

- *DataGrid*—**DataSource** = ADO data control's name. You can also set the **AllowAddNew**, **AllowDelete**, **AllowUpdate** properties to True or False to enable or disable those operations.

- *DataCombo*—**DataSource** = ADO data control's name; **DataField** = Name of the field to display in the combo's text box; **ListField** = Name of field to display in the list; **RowSource** = ADO data control's name; and **BoundColumn** = Name of the source field with which you can provide data to another control.

- *DataList*—**DataSource** = ADO data control's name; **DataField** = Name of the field to display in the current selection, **ListField** = Name of field to display in the list, **RowSource** = ADO data control's name, **BoundColumn** = Name of the source field with which you can provide data to another control.

Let's see an example. In this case, we've added an ADO data control and the three ADO data-bound controls to a program, as shown in Figure 24.20, and connected them to the ADO data control using their various properties. That's all it takes, and we're in business. The code for this example is located in the dbcontrols2 folder on this book's accompanying CD-ROM.

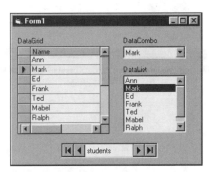

Figure 24.20   Using the ADO bound controls.

Chapter 25

Working With Database Objects In Code

If you need an immediate solution to:	See page:
A Full-Scale DAO Example	856
Using The Daocode Example To Create And Edit A Database	856
DAO: Creating A Database	857
DAO: Creating A Table With A TableDef Object	859
DAO: Adding Fields To A TableDef Object	860
DAO: Adding An Index To A TableDef Object	861
DAO: Creating A Record Set	863
DAO: Opening A Database	865
DAO: Adding A Record To A Record Set	867
DAO: Editing A Record In A Record Set	868
DAO: Updating A Record In A Record Set	868
DAO: Moving To The First Record In A Record Set	869
DAO: Moving To The Last Record In A Record Set	870
DAO: Moving To The Next Record In A Record Set	870
DAO: Moving To The Previous Record In A Record Set	871
DAO: Deleting A Record In A Record Set	872
DAO: Sorting A Record Set	872
DAO: Searching A Record Set	873
DAO: Executing SQL	874
A Full-Scale RDO Example	875
RDO: Opening A Connection	876
RDO: Creating A Result Set	877
RDO: Moving To The First Record In A Result Set	879
RDO: Moving To The Last Record In A Result Set	880

(continued)

If you need an immediate solution to:	See page:
RDO: Moving To The Next Record In A Result Set	881
RDO: Moving To The Previous Record In A Result Set	882
RDO: Executing SQL	883
A Full-Scale ADO Example	883
ADO: Opening A Connection	884
ADO: Creating A Record Set From A Connection	885
ADO: Binding Controls To Record Sets	887
ADO: Adding A Record To A Record Set	888
ADO: Refreshing The Record Set	888
ADO: Updating A Record In A Record Set	889
ADO: Moving To The First Record In A Record Set	890
ADO: Moving To The Last Record In A Record Set	890
ADO: Moving To The Next Record In A Record Set	891
ADO: Moving To The Previous Record In A Record Set	891
ADO: Deleting A Record In A Record Set	892
ADO: Executing SQL In A Record Set	893

In Depth

Programming database objects is an enormously complex topic that in itself can take up a dozen volumes. There is a career's worth of work here, so we'll have our hands full in this chapter.

Here, we're going to perform many of the tasks we first saw in the previous chapter, but while we used the data, remote data, and ADO data controls in that chapter, we'll execute those tasks in code directly in this chapter, using the Visual Basic data object libraries. Working with the data object libraries provides more flexibility, more power—and a great deal more complexity.

DAO

We'll use Data Access Object (DAO) methods to do what we did in the beginning of the last chapter: build a database and allow users to move through that database, editing it as they like. To construct a database, we'll create it, create a table with fields and add it to that database, and also construct an *index* for the database that will let us sort it.

Working with DAO, you can use the Database and Recordset Data Access Objects in your procedures. The Database and Recordset objects each have properties and methods of their own, and you can write procedures that use these properties and methods to manipulate your data.

TIP: Note that in the Learning Edition of Visual Basic, you can't declare (with the **Dim** keyword) variables as Data Access Objects in code. This means that only the data control can create Database and Recordset objects, not your code.

To open a database in DAO, you just open a Database object or create a new one. This object can represent a Microsoft Jet database (.mdb) file, an ISAM database (for example, Paradox), or an ODBC database connected through the Microsoft Jet database engine. When the Database object is available, you create a Recordset object and use that object's methods, like **MoveFirst** and **MoveNext**, to work with the database.

DAO also supports a client/server connection mode called *ODBCDirect*. ODBCDirect establishes a connection directly to an ODBC data source, without loading the Microsoft Jet database engine into memory, and is a good solution when you need ODBC features in your program.

In the ODBCDirect object model, the Connection object contains information about a connection to an ODBC data source, such as the server name, the data source name, and so on. It is similar to a Database object; in fact, a Connection object and a Database object represent different references to the same object. (In this chapter, we'll stick with the Database/Recordset model.)

RDO

With the Remote Data Objects (RDO) library of data objects, you establish an rdoConnection to an ODBC data source, then create an rdoResultset (please note, it is not an rdoRecordset). The Remote Data Objects behave like the DAO objects in many ways, because there is a core set of methods that work with both record sets and result sets.

The big difference between DAO and RDO objects is that the RDO objects are largely SQL-driven. For example, although you can move through a database using methods like **MoveNext** and **MoveLast**, just as you would with the DAO objects, programmers often update and modify RDO data sources using SQL statements directly with the rdoConnection object's **Execute** method. (In this book, we'll stick to what you can do with Visual Basic.)

ADO

As we saw in the last chapter, ActiveX Data Objects (ADO) access data from OLE DB *providers*. The Connection object is used to specify a particular provider and any parameters. To connect to a data source, you use a Connection object. Using that connection, you can create a new record set, and using the Recordset object's methods and properties, you can work with your data.

An ADO *transaction* marks the beginning and end of a series of data operations that are executed across a connection. ADO makes sure that changes to a data source resulting from operations in a transaction either all occur successfully, or not at all. If you cancel the transaction or one of its operations fails, then the result will be as if none of the operations in the transaction had occurred.

In this chapter, we'll see how to create connections using the ADO Connection object and how to open data providers, creating an ADO Recordset object. We'll read data from the data provider and see how to display and modify it. In fact, we'll see how to support data-bound controls directly in code.

Although the ADO model is a complex one, and OLE DB is even more complex, we'll see that many of the core ADO Resultset methods are the same as the DAO Resultset methods.

TIP: Note that in DAO and ADO you work with record sets, and in RDO with result sets; it's very easy to confuse the terminology here.

That's it, then, for the overview of databases. We've seen how the process works in overview; now it's time to turn to the Immediate Solutions.

Immediate Solutions

A Full-Scale DAO Example

To illustrate DAO data handling in code, we'll build a fully functional DAO project—the daocode project. This program has a File menu with the following items:

- *New Database*—Creates a new database.
- *Open Database*—Opens a database.
- *Close Database*—Closes the current database.
- *New Table*—Creates a new table.
- *Search*—Searches the database.
- *Sort*—Sorts the database.
- *Exit*—Exits the application.

Using The Daocode Example To Create And Edit A Database

To create a database file, select the New Database menu item. Next, add a table to that database with the New Table menu item, then add records to that table. When you're ready to store the database on disk, use the Close Database item.

Warning!   If you don't create a table in a database before trying to add data to a table in that database with the Add or Edit buttons, the daocode program generates an error.

In addition, the program has buttons that let users add, edit, update, and delete records, as well as letting them move through a database, as shown in Figure 25.1. Each time you want to add a record (including when you enter the first record of a new database), click the Add New Record button, type in the data for the record's fields, and click the Update Database button to update the database.

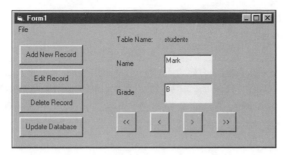

Figure 25.1   Our DAO database-building application, the daocode project.

To edit a record, open the record, click the Edit button, edit the data in the record's fields, and click the Update Database button to update the database. For simplicity, this program only creates tables with two fields, although you can place as many records as you like in each table.

We'll develop the code for this example program in the next several topics of this chapter. For reference, the main form of this example program is located in the daocode folder on this book's accompanying CD-ROM; the form the user uses to specify the names of the fields in a new table is located in the TableForm folder on CD-ROM; and the code for the form in which the user can enter a text string to search for is located in the SearchForm folder on the CD-ROM.

DAO: Creating A Database

The Testing Department is calling again. How about creating a DAO database—in code? Hmm, you think, is that possible?

It is, with the objects in the Microsoft DAO Object Library. To add a reference to that library, select the Project|References menu item, select the Microsoft DAO Object Library, and click on OK to close the References dialog box. Now we can make use of the data objects in that library to create a new database using **CreateDatabase**. **CreateDatabase** is a method of the DAO Workspace object (there are a collection of Workspace objects in the DAO DBEngine object's **Workspaces** collection). Here's how you use **CreateDatabase**:

```
Set database = workspace.CreateDatabase (name, locale [, options])
```

Here are the arguments to **CreateDatabase**:

- *name*—A string up to 255 characters long that is the name of the database file that you're creating. It can be the full path and file name, such as C:vbbb\db.mdb. If you don't supply a file name extension, .mdb is added.

* *locale*—A string that specifies a collating order for creating the database, like **dbLangGeneral** (which includes English), **dbLangGreek**, and so on.

TIP: *You can create a password for a new Database object by concatenating the password (starting with ";pwd=") with a constant in the **locale** argument, like this: **dbLangGreek & ";pwd=NewPassword"**. If you want to use the default **locale**, but specify a password, simply enter a password string for the **locale** argument: ";pwd=NewPassword".*

Here are the possible settings for the *options* argument:

* **dbEncrypt**—Creates an encrypted database.

* **dbVersion10**—Creates a database that uses the Jet engine version 1 file format.

* **dbVersion11**—Creates a database that uses the Jet database engine version 1.1 file format.

* **dbVersion20**—Creates a database that uses the Jet database engine version 2 file format.

* **dbVersion30**—The default. Creates a database that uses the Jet database engine version 3 file format (compatible with version 3.5).

Let's see an example to make this clearer. When the user selects the New database item in our example DAO program, daocode (see the first topic in this chapter), we will create a new database. First, we declare that database, **db**, as a form-wide variable:

```
Dim db As Database
```

Next, we add a Common Dialog control, **CommonDialog1**, to the program and show it to get the name of the database file the user wants to create:

```
Private Sub NewDatabase_Click()
    CommonDialog1.ShowSave
    If CommonDialog1.FileName <> "" Then
...
```

Finally, we create the new database, passing the **CreateDatabase** method the name of the database file and indicating that we want to use the default collating order by passing the constant **dbLangGeneral**:

```
Private Sub NewDatabase_Click()
    CommonDialog1.ShowSave
    If CommonDialog1.FileName <> "" Then
        Set db = DBEngine.Workspaces(0).CreateDatabase_
            (CommonDialog1.FileName, dbLangGeneral)
```

```
    End If
End Sub
```

And that's it—we've created a new, empty database. The next step is to add a table to that database, and we'll take a look at that in the next topic.

DAO: Creating A Table With A TableDef Object

How do you create a table in a DAO database? You define it with a TableDef object. After you do so, you can append fields to the table, and then you can append the new table definition to a database's **TableDefs** collection.

Let's see an example. After the users create a new database with our DAO code example, the daocode project (see the first topic in this chapter), they can create a new table using the New Table item in the File menu. That item opens the New Table dialog box you see in Figure 25.2.

Users can enter the name of the new table to create in the text boxes in the New Table dialog box, and we can use that information to create a new TableDef object, **td**, which we declare as a form-wide variable:

```
Dim td As TableDef
```

We create a new **TableDef** for the Database object we created in the previous topic, **db**, using the name for the table the user has placed in **Text1** in the New Table dialog box:

```
Sub CreateTable()
    Set td = db.CreateTableDef(TableForm.Text1.Text)
    ...
```

This code creates a new, empty TableDef object named **td**. An empty table isn't much use, though—we'll see about adding fields to this object in the next topic.

Figure 25.2   The New Table dialog box.

859

DAO: Adding Fields To A TableDef Object

How do you add fields to a DAO TableDef object? You can use that object's **CreateField** method to do that, passing that method the name of the new field and a constant indicating that field's type:

```
TableDef.CreateField(FieldName, FieldType)
```

Here are the constants specifying the possible field types:

- **dbBigInt**
- **dbBinary**
- **dbBoolean**
- **dbByte**
- **dbChar**
- **dbCurrency**
- **dbDate**
- **dbDecimal**
- **dbDouble**
- **dbFloat**
- **dbGUID**
- **dbInteger**
- **dbLong**
- **dbLongBinary** (OLE object)
- **dbMemo**
- **dbNumeric**
- **dbSingle**
- **dbText**
- **dbTime**
- **dbTimeStamp**
- **dbVarBinary**

Let's see an example to make this clearer. In the previous topic, we created a TableDef object named **td** for the daocode example project (see the first topic in this chapter), and now we can add two fields to that object, which we declare in an array named **fields** of type **Field** (which is defined in the DAO library):

```
Dim fields(2) As Field
```

The users have specified what names they want to give to those two new fields in the New Table dialog box's text boxes, so we create the new fields this way:

```
Sub CreateTable()
    Set td = db.CreateTableDef(TableForm.Text1.Text)

    Set fields(0) = td.CreateField(TableForm.Text2.Text, dbText)
    Set fields(1) = td.CreateField(TableForm.Text3.Text, dbText)
    ...
```

Now that the new fields are created, we can append them to the actual TableDef object **td**:

```
Sub CreateTable()
    Set td = db.CreateTableDef(TableForm.Text1.Text)

    Set fields(0) = td.CreateField(TableForm.Text2.Text, dbText)
    Set fields(1) = td.CreateField(TableForm.Text3.Text, dbText)
    td.fields.Append fields(0)
    td.fields.Append fields(1)
    ...
End Sub
```

That's it—we've defined two new fields, named them, and appended them to a TableDef object. Next, we'll add an index to our table to allow the user to sort the data in that object.

DAO: Adding An Index To A TableDef Object

You use an index to sort a table, and you create an index with the DAO **CreateIndex** method. The **CreateIndex** method creates an Index object, and you can make one of the fields in a table that table's index with that Index object's **CreateField** method.

Let's see an example to make this clearer. We'll create an index for our DAO example, the daocode project (see the first topic in this chapter) named **dbindex**, which we declare as a form-wide variable:

```
Dim dbindex As Index
```

We name the index when we create it; here, we'll just use the first field that the user has placed in this table as the table's index so all sort operations will sort using that field. In this example, we name our index by adding the word "index" to the name of that field this way:

```
Sub CreateTable()
    Set td = db.CreateTableDef(TableForm.Text1.Text)

    Set fields(0) = td.CreateField(TableForm.Text2.Text, dbText)
    Set fields(1) = td.CreateField(TableForm.Text3.Text, dbText)
    td.fields.Append fields(0)
    td.fields.Append fields(1)

    Set dbindex = td.CreateIndex(TableForm.Text2.Text & "index")
...
```

Next, we create a new field, **indexfield**, in the index, using the name of the first field in the table:

```
Sub CreateTable()
    Set td = db.CreateTableDef(TableForm.Text1.Text)

    Set fields(0) = td.CreateField(TableForm.Text2.Text, dbText)
    Set fields(1) = td.CreateField(TableForm.Text3.Text, dbText)
    td.fields.Append fields(0)
    td.fields.Append fields(1)

    Set dbindex = td.CreateIndex(TableForm.Text2.Text & "index")
    Set indexfield = dbindex.CreateField(TableForm.Text2.Text)
...
```

Finally, we append **indexfield** to our Index object, **dbindex**, and append that object to the TableDef object's **Indexes** collection:

```
Sub CreateTable()
    Set td = db.CreateTableDef(TableForm.Text1.Text)

    Set fields(0) = td.CreateField(TableForm.Text2.Text, dbText)
    Set fields(1) = td.CreateField(TableForm.Text3.Text, dbText)
    td.fields.Append fields(0)
    td.fields.Append fields(1)

    Set dbindex = td.CreateIndex(TableForm.Text2.Text & "index")
    Set indexfield = dbindex.CreateField(TableForm.Text2.Text)
    dbindex.fields.Append indexfield
    td.Indexes.Append dbindex
...
End Sub
```

And that's it—we've created a new index for our table. In fact, we've set up the whole TableDef object **td** now, so we can create a record set to start working with data, and we'll do that in the next topic.

DAO: Creating A Record Set

After you've finished defining a database table with a DAO TableDef object, you can append that object to a Database object, which adds that table to that database. After you've installed the new table, you can use the **OpenRecordset** method to open a record set and start working with data:

```
Set recordset = Database.OpenRecordset (source, type, options, lockedits)
```

Here are the arguments for **OpenRecordset**:

- *source*—A string specifying the source of the records for the new Recordset object. The source can be a table name, a query name, or an SQL statement that returns records. (For table-type Recordset objects in Jet-type databases, the source can only be a table name.)
- *type*—Indicates the type of Recordset to open.
- *options*—Combination of constants that specify characteristics of the new Recordset.
- *lockedits*—Constant that determines the locking for Recordset.

Here are the possible settings for *type*:

- **dbOpenTable**—Opens a table-type Recordset object.
- **dbOpenDynamic**—Opens a dynamic-type Recordset object, which is like an ODBC dynamic cursor.
- **dbOpenDynaset**—Opens a dynaset-type Recordset object, which is like an ODBC keyset cursor.
- **dbOpenSnapshot**—Opens a snapshot-type Recordset object, which is like an ODBC static cursor.
- **dbOpenForwardOnly**—Opens a forward-only-type Recordset object (where you can only use **MoveNext** to move through the database).

Here are the possible settings for *options*:

- **dbAppendOnly**—Allows users to append new records to the Recordset but prevents them from editing or deleting existing records (Microsoft Jet dynaset-type Recordset only).

- **dbSQLPassThrough**—Passes an SQL statement to a Microsoft Jet-connected ODBC data source for processing (Jet snapshot-type Recordset only).

- **dbSeeChanges**—Generates a runtime error if one user is changing data that another user is editing (Jet dynaset-type Recordset only).

- **dbDenyWrite**—Prevents other users from modifying or adding records (Jet Recordset objects only).

- **dbDenyRead**—Prevents other users from reading data in a table (Jet table-type Recordset only).

- **dbForwardOnly**—Creates a forward-only Recordset (Jet snapshot-type Recordset only). It is provided only for backward compatibility, and you should use the **dbOpenForwardOnly** constant in the *type* argument instead of using this option.

- **dbReadOnly**—Prevents users from making changes to the Recordset (Microsoft Jet only). The **dbReadOnly** constant in the *lockedits* argument replaces this option, which is provided only for backward compatibility.

- **dbRunAsync**—Runs an asynchronous query (ODBCDirect workspaces only).

- **dbExecDirect**—Runs a query by skipping **SQLPrepare** and directly calling **SQLExecDirect** (ODBCDirect workspaces only).

- **dbInconsistent**—Allows inconsistent updates (Microsoft Jet dynaset-type and snapshot-type Recordset objects only).

- **dbConsistent**—Allows only consistent updates (Microsoft Jet dynaset-type and snapshot-type Recordset objects only).

Here are the possible settings for the *lockedits* argument:

- **dbReadOnly**—Prevents users from making changes to the Recordset (default for ODBCDirect workspaces).

- **dbPessimistic**—Uses pessimistic locking to determine how changes are made to the Recordset in a multiuser environment.

- **dbOptimistic**—Uses optimistic locking to determine how changes are made to the Recordset in a multiuser environment.

- **dbOptimisticValue**—Uses optimistic concurrency based on row values (ODBCDirect workspaces only).

- **dbOptimisticBatch**—Enables batch optimistic updating (ODBCDirect workspaces only).

Let's see an example to make this clearer. In the previous few topics, we've developed a TableDef object, **td**, in our DAO code example, the daocode project. To append that object to the Database object we created, **db**, we use the **Append** method of the database object's **TableDefs** collection. After installing the table, we open it for use with the Database object's **OpenRecordset** method this way, creating a new DAO Recordset, which we name **dbrecordset**:

```
Sub CreateTable()
    Set td = db.CreateTableDef(TableForm.Text1.Text)

    Set fields(0) = td.CreateField(TableForm.Text2.Text, dbText)
    Set fields(1) = td.CreateField(TableForm.Text3.Text, dbText)
    td.fields.Append fields(0)
    td.fields.Append fields(1)

    Set dbindex = td.CreateIndex(TableForm.Text2.Text + "index")
    Set IxFlds = dbindex.CreateField(TableForm.Text2.Text)
    dbindex.fields.Append IxFlds
    td.Indexes.Append dbindex
    db.TableDefs.Append td

    Set dbrecordset = db.OpenRecordset(TableForm.Text1.Text, dbOpenTable)
End Sub
```

In this case, we're opening the new record set as a standard DAO table by passing the constant **dbOpenTable.** We also declare **dbrecordset** as a form-wide variable:

```
Dim dbrecordset As Recordset
```

At this point in the daocode project, then, we've created a new database with a table in it that has two fields, using the names that the user supplied for the fields and the table itself. And we've opened that table as a record set, so we're ready to work with it and add data to it, which we'll do in later topics in this chapter.

Besides creating a new database as we've done, however, the user may want to open an *existing* database, and we'll see how to do that in the next topic.

DAO: Opening A Database

To open an existing DAO database, you use the DAO **OpenDatabase** method, passing it the name of the database to open, and these arguments:

```
Set database = workspace.OpenDatabase (dbname, [options [, read-only _
    [, connect]]])
```

Here are the arguments for **OpenDatabase**:

- *dbname*—The name of an existing database file, or the data source name (DSN) of an ODBC data source.

- *options*—Setting options to True opens the DAO database in exclusive mode; setting it to False (the default) opens the database in shared mode.

- *read-only*—True if you want to open the database with read-only access, or False (the default) if you want to open the database with read/write access.

- *connect*—Optional. A Variant (String subtype) that specifies various connection information, including passwords.

Let's see an example to make this clearer. In our DAO code example, the daocode project (see the first topic in this chapter), the user can click the Open Database menu item to open a database. In the program, we get the name of the database the user wants to open with a Common Dialog control, and open the database like this:

```
Private Sub OpenDatabase_Click()

    CommonDialog1.ShowOpen
    If CommonDialog1.FileName <> "" Then
        Set db = _
            DBEngine.Workspaces(0).OpenDatabase(CommonDialog1.FileName)
    ...
```

Next, if you know the name of the table you want to open in the database, you can open that table by name immediately with the **OpenRecordset** method. However, because we let the user set the name of tables in the databases we create in the daocode project, we don't know the names of the tables in the database we've opened. Instead, we'll open the first user-defined table in this database.

When you open a DAO database, there are a number of system tables already in it, so to open the first user-defined table, we find the index of that table in the **TableDefs** collection by first skipping the system tables (which have the **dbSystemObject** flag set in their **Attributes** properties):

```
Private Sub OpenDatabase_Click()
    Dim table1index As Integer
    CommonDialog1.ShowOpen
    If CommonDialog1.FileName <> "" Then
        Set db = _
            DBEngine.Workspaces(0).OpenDatabase(CommonDialog1.FileName)
```

```
        tableindex = 0
        While (db.TableDefs(tableindex).Attributes And dbSystemObject)
            tableindex = tableindex + 1
        Wend
...
```

We'll open the first table after the system tables. We open a new record set for that table with the **OpenRecordset** method and fill the text boxes **Text1** and **Text2** in the program's main window with the fields of the first record in that table (note that in this example program, we are assuming the table we're opening has at least one record):

```
Private Sub OpenDatabase_Click()
    Dim tableindex As Integer
    CommonDialog1.ShowOpen
    If CommonDialog1.FileName <> "" Then
        Set db = _
            DBEngine.Workspaces(0).OpenDatabase(CommonDialog1.FileName)

        tableindex = 0
        While (db.TableDefs(tableindex).Attributes And dbSystemObject)
            tableindex = tableindex + 1
        Wend

        Set dbrecordset = db.OpenRecordset_
            (db.TableDefs(tableindex).Name, dbOpenTable)
        Set td = db.TableDefs(tableindex)

        Text1.Text = dbrecordset.fields(0)
        Text2.Text = dbrecordset.fields(1)
    End If
End Sub
```

And that's it—now we've opened a database file.

DAO: Adding A Record To A Record Set

To add a new record to a DAO record set, you use the **AddNew** method (this method takes no parameters). After you've updated the fields of the current record, you save that record to the database with the **Update** method.

Here's an example using **AddNew**. When the user clicks the Add button in our DAO code example, the daocode project (see the first topic in this chapter), we execute the **AddNew** method on the program's record set and clear the two data field text boxes:

```
Private Sub Command1_Click()
    dbrecordset.AddNew
    Text1.Text = ""
    Text2.Text = ""
End Sub
```

Now users can enter data for the new record's fields and click the program's Update button. When they click the Update Database button, the new data is written to the database.

DAO: Editing A
Record In A
Record Set

DAO: Editing A Record In A Record Set

Besides adding new records to the record set, users might want to edit the existing records. To do that, you use the **Edit** method like this in our DAO code example, the daocode project (see the first topic in this chapter):

```
Private Sub Command2_Click()
    dbrecordset.Edit
End Sub
```

After users edit the data in the record's fields (by entering new data in the text fields in the daocode project's main window), they must update the database with the new data, and they do that in the daocode project by clicking the Update Database button. That button executes the **Update** method, as we'll see in the next topic.

DAO: Updating
A Record In A
Record Set

DAO: Updating A Record In A Record Set

When the user changes the data in a record or adds a new record, we must update the database to record that change, and you use the record set **Update** method to do that:

```
recordset.Update ([type [, force]])
```

Here are the arguments in this function:

- *type*—Constant indicating the type of update, as specified in Settings (ODBCDirect workspaces only).

- *force*—Boolean value indicating whether or not to force the changes into the database, regardless of whether the data has been changed by another user (ODBCDirect workspaces only).

Let's see an example. When the user clicks the Update button in our DAO code example, the daocode project (see the first topic in this chapter), we will update the database with the new data for the current record. We get the new data for the current record from the text boxes **Text1** and **Text2**, where the user has entered that data, and load the data into the record set's fields using the **fields** collection:

```
Private Sub Command3_Click()
    dbrecordset.fields(0) = Text1.Text
    dbrecordset.fields(1) = Text2.Text
...
End Sub
```

After loading the data into the current record's fields, we save that record to the database using the **Update** method:

```
Private Sub Command3_Click()
    dbrecordset.fields(0) = Text1.Text
    dbrecordset.fields(1) = Text2.Text
    dbrecordset.Update
End Sub
```

DAO: Moving To The First Record In A Record Set

To make the first record in a record set the current record, you use the **MoveFirst** method. For example, here's how we move to the first record when the user clicks the appropriate button in our DAO code example, the daocode project (see the first topic in this chapter):

```
Private Sub Command4_Click()
    dbrecordset.MoveFirst
...
End Sub
```

After moving to the first record, we display that record's fields in the two text boxes in the program, **Text1** and **Text2**:

```
Private Sub Command4_Click()
    dbrecordset.MoveFirst
```

DAO: Moving To The First Record In A Record Set

```
        Text1.Text = dbrecordset.fields(0)
        Text2.Text = dbrecordset.fields(1)
End Sub
```

DAO: Moving To The Last Record In A Record Set

To make the last record in a record set the current record, you use the **MoveLast** method. For example, here's how we move to the last record when the user clicks the appropriate button in our DAO code example, the daocode project (see the first topic in this chapter):

```
Private Sub Command7_Click()
    dbrecordset.MoveLast
...
End Sub
```

After moving to the last record, we display that record's fields in the two text boxes in the program, **Text1** and **Text2**:

```
Private Sub Command7_Click()
    dbrecordset.MoveLast
    Text1.Text = dbrecordset.fields(0)
    Text2.Text = dbrecordset.fields(1)
End Sub
```

DAO: Moving To The Next Record In A Record Set

To move to the next record in a record set, making that record the current record, you use the **MoveNext** method. For example, in our DAO code example, the daocode project (see the first topic in this chapter), we move to the next record when the user clicks the appropriate button:

```
Private Sub Command6_Click()
    dbrecordset.MoveNext
...
```

We can check if we've gone past the end of the record set with the **EOF** property; if this property is True, we should move back one record:

```
Private Sub Command6_Click()
    dbrecordset.MoveNext
```

```
        If dbrecordset.EOF Then
            dbrecordset.MovePrevious
    ...
```

On the other hand, if the record we've moved to is a valid record, we display its fields in the program's two text boxes, **Text1** and **Text2**:

```
Private Sub Command6_Click()
    dbrecordset.MoveNext
    If dbrecordset.EOF Then
        dbrecordset.MovePrevious
    Else
        Text1.Text = dbrecordset.fields(0)
        Text2.Text = dbrecordset.fields(1)
    End If
End Sub
```

DAO: Moving To The Previous Record In A Record Set

To move to the previous record in a record set, making that record the current record, you use the **MovePrevious** method. For example, in our DAO code example, the daocode project (see the first topic in this chapter), we move to the previous record when the user clicks the appropriate button:

```
Private Sub Command5_Click()
    dbrecordset.MovePrevious
    ...
```

We can check if we've gone past the beginning of the record set with the **BOF** property; if this property is True, we should move forward one record:

```
Private Sub Command5_Click()
    dbrecordset.MovePrevious
    If dbrecordset.BOF Then
        dbrecordset.MoveNext
    ...
```

On the other hand, if the record we've moved to is a valid record, we display its fields in the program's two text boxes, **Text1** and **Text2**:

```
Private Sub Command5_Click()
    dbrecordset.MovePrevious
    If dbrecordset.BOF Then
        dbrecordset.MoveNext
```

```
      Else
          Text1.Text = dbrecordset.fields(0)
          Text2.Text = dbrecordset.fields(1)
      End If
End Sub
```

DAO: Deleting A Record In A Record Set

To delete a record in a DAO record set, you use the **Delete** method, and then you update the record set. For example, when the user clicks the Delete button in our DAO code example, the daocode project (see the first topic in this chapter), we clear the two text boxes, **Text1** and **Text2**, that display the data for the current record and delete that record:

```
Private Sub Command8_Click()
    Text1.Text = ""
    Text2.Text = ""
    dbrecordset.Delete
End Sub
```

DAO: Sorting A Record Set

To sort a record set, you can install the index you want to sort with in the record set's **Index** property. For example, we can sort the record set in our DAO code example, the daocode project, with the index we've created this way:

```
Sub Sort_Click()
    Set dbindex = td.Indexes(0)
    dbrecordset.Index = dbindex.Name
...
```

After the record set is sorted, we display the first record in the two main text boxes, **Text1** and **Text2**:

```
Sub Sort_Click()
    Set dbindex = td.Indexes(0)
    dbrecordset.Index = dbindex.Name
    Text1.Text = dbrecordset.fields(0)
    Text2.Text = dbrecordset.fields(1)
End Sub
```

DAO: Searching A Record Set

You can search a record set with an index; we just set its **Index** property to
the index we want to search and then set its **Seek** property to the string we
want to search for. Let's see an example. When the user selects the Search
menu item in our DAO code example, the daocode project (see the first topic
in this chapter), we install the index based on the first field in the record set
and show the dialog box named Search..., which appears in Figure 25.3:

```
Private Sub Search_Click()
    Set dbindex = td.Indexes(0)
    dbrecordset.Index = dbindex.Name
    SearchForm.Show
End Sub
```

After the user dismisses the Search... dialog box, we retrieve the text to search
for from that dialog box's text box and place that text in the record set's **Seek**
property, along with the command "=", which indicates we want to find exact
matches to the search text:

```
Sub SearchTable()
    dbrecordset.Seek "=", SearchForm.Text1.Text
...
```

Besides =, you can also search using <, <=, >=, and >. When the search is
complete, we display the found record in the daocode project's main text boxes,
Text1 and **Text2**:

```
Sub SearchTable()
    dbrecordset.Seek "=", SearchForm.Text1.Text
    Text1.Text = dbrecordset.fields(0)
    Text2.Text = dbrecordset.fields(1)
End Sub
```

Figure 25.3   The DAO code example's Search... dialog box.

DAO: Executing SQL

You can execute an SQL statement when you create a DAO record set using the **OpenRecordset** method by placing that SQL statement in the *source* argument:

```
Set recordset = Database.OpenRecordset (source, type, options, lockedits)
```

Here are the arguments for **OpenRecordset**:

- *source*—A string specifying the source of the records for the new Recordset. The source can be a table name, a query name, or an SQL statement that returns records. (For table-type Recordset objects in Jet-type databases, the source can only be a table name.)
- *type*—Indicates the type of Recordset to open.
- *options*—Combination of constants that specify characteristics of the new Recordset.
- *lockedits*—Constant that determines the locking for Recordset.

Here are the possible settings for *type*:

- **dbOpenTable**—Opens a table-type Recordset object.
- **dbOpenDynamic**—Opens a dynamic-type Recordset object, which is like an ODBC dynamic cursor.
- **dbOpenDynaset**—Opens a dynaset-type Recordset object, which is like an ODBC keyset cursor.
- **dbOpenSnapshot**—Opens a snapshot-type Recordset object, which is like an ODBC static cursor.
- **dbOpenForwardOnly**—Opens a forward-only-type Recordset object.

Here are the possible settings for *options*:

- **dbAppendOnly**—Allows users to append new records to the Recordset but prevents them from editing or deleting existing records (Microsoft Jet dynaset-type Recordset only).
- **dbSQLPassThrough**—Passes an SQL statement to a Microsoft Jet-connected ODBC data source for processing (Microsoft Jet snapshot-type Recordset only).
- **dbSeeChanges**—Generates a runtime error if one user is changing data that another user is editing (Microsoft Jet dynaset-type Recordset only).
- **dbDenyWrite**—Prevents other users from modifying or adding records (Microsoft Jet Recordset objects only).

- **dbDenyRead**—Prevents other users from reading data in a table (Microsoft Jet table-type Recordset only).

- **dbForwardOnly**—Creates a forward-only Recordset (Microsoft Jet snapshot-type Recordset only). It is provided only for backward compatibility, and you should use the **dbOpenForwardOnly** constant in the *type* argument instead of using this option.

- **dbReadOnly**—Prevents users from making changes to the Recordset (Microsoft Jet only). The **dbReadOnly** constant in the *lockedits* argument replaces this option, which is provided only for backward compatibility.

- **dbRunAsync**—Runs an asynchronous query (ODBCDirect workspaces only).

- **dbExecDirect**—Runs a query by skipping **SQLPrepare** and directly calling **SQLExecDirect** (ODBCDirect workspaces only).

- **dbInconsistent**—Allows inconsistent updates (Microsoft Jet dynaset-type and snapshot-type Recordset objects only).

- **dbConsistent**—Allows only consistent updates (Microsoft Jet dynaset-type and snapshot-type Recordset objects only).

Here are the possible settings for the *lockedits* argument:

- **dbReadOnly**—Prevents users from making changes to the Recordset (default for ODBCDirect workspaces).

- **dbPessimistic**—Uses pessimistic locking to determine how changes are made to the Recordset in a multiuser environment.

- **dbOptimistic**—Uses optimistic locking to determine how changes are made to the Recordset in a multiuser environment.

- **dbOptimisticValue**—Uses optimistic concurrency based on row values (ODBCDirect workspaces only).

- **dbOptimisticBatch**—Enables batch optimistic updating (ODBCDirect workspaces only).

A Full-Scale RDO Example

To illustrate RDO data handling in code, we'll build a fully functional RDO project—the rdocode project—over the next few examples. You can see that project at work in Figure 25.4. This program is designed to open the ODBC data source we set up in the previous chapter (where we created a database, db.mdb, and registered it as an ODBC data source) and let the user move around in it record by record.

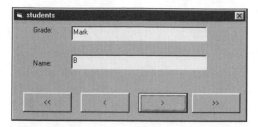

Figure 25.4   The rdocode project opening an ODBC database.

Using the buttons in the rdocode project, you can move through the database, and we'll see how to write the code for the rdocode project in the following few topics. For reference, the code for this example is located in the rdocode folder on this book's accompanying CD-ROM.

RDO: Opening A Connection

To open an RDO connection to a database, you can use the RDO **OpenConnection** method. **OpenConnection** is a method of the rdoEnvironment object, and you'll find a collection of those objects in the rdoEngine object's **rdoEnvironments** collection. To add the RDO objects to a program, select the Project|References menu item in Visual Basic, select the Microsoft Remote Data Object entry in the References dialog box, and click on OK. Now we're free to use rdoEnvironment methods like **OpenConnection**:

```
workspace.OpenConnection(datasource, [prompt, [read-only, [connect, _
    [options]]]])
```

Here are the arguments to **OpenConnection**:

- *datasource*—The name of the data source.

- *prompt*—ODBC prompting characteristic: **rdDriverPrompt** asks the user for a driver/database, **rdDriverNoPrompt** uses specified driver/database, **rdDriverComplete** specifies the connection string itself, and **rdDriverCompleteRequired** is the same as **rdDriverComplete**, with the additional requirement that the driver should disable the controls for information not needed for the connection.

- *read-only*—True if you want to open the data source as read-only.

- *connect*—The connect string.

- *options*—Set to **rdAsyncEnable** if you want to execute commands asynchronously (that is, without waiting for the command to be completed).

Let's see an example. In our RDO code example, the rdocode project (see "A Full-Scale RDO Example" earlier in this chapter), we create an rdoEnvironment object named **re** this way when the form loads:

```
Dim re As Object

Private Sub Form_Load()

    Set re = rdoEngine.rdoEnvironments(0)
...
End Sub
```

Now we open a connection named **db** to the ODBC source (we set up this ODBC source in the previous chapter) this way:

```
Dim re As Object
Dim db As rdoConnection

Private Sub Form_Load()

    Set re = rdoEngine.rdoEnvironments(0)
    Set db = re.OpenConnection("db")

End Sub
```

That's it—now we have a connection to our ODBC data source in the rdoConnection object named **db**. How do we access the records in that source? We'll look into that next.

RDO: Creating A Result Set

After opening an ODBC data source and creating an rdoConnection object, we can create an RDO result set to start working with the records in that data source. To create a result set, we can use the rdoConnection method **OpenResultset**:

```
Set resultset = rdoConnection.OpenResultset (name, [type, [locktype,_
    [options]]])
```

Here are the arguments for **OpenResultset**:

• *name*—Source for the result set; can be an rdoTable object, an rdoQuery object, or an SQL statement.

- *type*—Specifies the result set type (see the following list).

- *locktype*—Can be one of these values: **rdConcurReadOnly** (read-only), **rdConcurLock** (pessimistic concurrency), **rdConcurRowVer** (optimistic row-based concurrency), **rdConcurValues** (optimistic value-based concurrency), or **rdConcurBatch** (optimistic concurrency using batch updates).

- *options*—Set to **rdAsyncEnable** if you want to execute commands asynchronously (that is, without waiting for the command to be completed).

Here are the possible values for the *type* argument:

- **rdOpenKeyset**—Opens a dynaset-type rdoResultset object, which is like an ODBC keyset cursor.

- **rdOpenDynamic**—Opens a dynamic-type rdoResultset object, which lets the application see changes made by other users.

- **rdOpenStatic**—Opens a static-type rdoResultset object.

- **rdOpenForwardOnly**—Opens a forward-only-type rdoResultset object, where you can only use **MoveNext** to move.

Let's see an example. Here, we'll create an SQL-based result set in our RDO code example, the rdocode project (see "A Full-Scale RDO Example" earlier in this chapter), when the form loads, using the rdoConnection object we've created—**db**. In this case, we'll set up an SQL statement, **SQLSel**, to place all the fields from the data source's table named students in the result set:

```
Dim re As Object
Dim db As rdoConnection
Dim SQLSel As String

Private Sub Form_Load()

    SQLSel = "Select * from students"
    Set re = rdoEngine.rdoEnvironments(0)
    Set db = re.OpenConnection("db")
...
```

Now we use **OpenResultset** to create an rdoResultset object, **resultset**:

```
Dim re As Object
Dim db As rdoConnection
Dim resultset As rdoResultset
Dim SQLSel As String

Private Sub Form_Load()
```

```
        SQLSel = "Select * from students"
        Set re = rdoEngine.rdoEnvironments(0)
        Set db = re.OpenConnection("db")

        Set resultset = db.OpenResultset(SQLSel, rdOpenKeyset)
    ...
```

Now that we've opened a result set, we can use rdoResultset methods like **MoveFirst** to move to the first record and display the data in that record's Name and Grade fields with the rdocode project's text boxes, **Text1** and **Text2**:

```
Dim re As Object
Dim db As rdoConnection
Dim resultset As rdoResultset
Dim SQLSel As String

Private Sub Form_Load()

    SQLSel = "Select * from students"
    Set re = rdoEngine.rdoEnvironments(0)
    Set db = re.OpenConnection("db")

    Set resultset = db.OpenResultset(SQLSel, rdOpenKeyset)
    resultset.MoveFirst

    Text1.Text = resultset("Name")
    Text2.Text = resultset("Grade")

End Sub
```

And that's it—we've opened an RDO result set and displayed some of the data in that result set.

RDO: Moving To The First Record In A Result Set

To move to the first record in an RDO result set, you can use the rdoResultset method **MoveFirst**. Let's see an example. In this case, we'll move to the first record in the result set named **resultset** that we've opened in our RDO code example, the rdocode project (see "A Full-Scale RDO Example" earlier in this chapter), when the user clicks the appropriate button:

```
Private Sub cmdFirst_Click()
    On Error GoTo ErrLabel
```

```
    resultset.MoveFirst
...
    Exit Sub

ErrLabel:
    MsgBox Err.Description
End Sub
```

After moving to the new record, we display the data in that record's fields in the program's text boxes, **Text1** and **Text2**:

```
Private Sub cmdFirst_Click()
    On Error GoTo ErrLabel

    resultset.MoveFirst
    Text1.Text = resultset("Name")
    Text2.Text = resultset("Grade")

    Exit Sub

ErrLabel:
    MsgBox Err.Description
End Sub
```

RDO: Moving To The Last Record In A Result Set

To move to the last record in an RDO result set, you can use the rdoResultset method **MoveLast**. Let's see an example. In this case, we'll move to the last record in the result set named **resultset** that we've opened in our RDO code example, the rdocode project (see "A Full-Scale RDO Example" earlier in this chapter), when the user clicks the appropriate button:

```
Private Sub cmdLast_Click()
    On Error GoTo ErrLabel

    resultset.MoveLast
...
    Exit Sub

ErrLabel:
    MsgBox Err.Description
End Sub
```

After moving to the new record, we display the data in that record's fields in the program's text boxes, **Text1** and **Text2**:

```
Private Sub cmdLast_Click()
    On Error GoTo ErrLabel

    resultset.MoveLast

    Text1.Text = resultset("Name")
    Text2.Text = resultset("Grade")

    Exit Sub

ErrLabel:
    MsgBox Err.Description
End Sub
```

RDO: Moving To The Next Record In A Result Set

To move to the next record in an RDO result set, you can use the rdoResultset method **MoveNext**. Let's see an example. In this case, we'll move to the next record in the result set named **resultset** that we've opened in our RDO code example, the rdocode project (see "A Full-Scale RDO Example" earlier in this chapter), when the user clicks the appropriate button. We check to make sure we're not trying to move past the end of the record set with the **EOF** property, and if so, we make sure to move to the last record instead:

```
Private Sub cmdNext_Click()
    On Error GoTo ErrLabel

    If Not resultset.EOF Then resultset.MoveNext
    If resultset.EOF And resultset.RowCount > 0 Then
        resultset.MoveLast
    End If
...
    Exit Sub

ErrLabel:
    MsgBox Err.Description
End Sub
```

After moving to the new record, we display the data in that record's fields in the program's text boxes, **Text1** and **Text2**:

```
Private Sub cmdNext_Click()
    On Error GoTo ErrLabel

    If Not resultset.EOF Then resultset.MoveNext
    If resultset.EOF And resultset.RowCount > 0 Then
        resultset.MoveLast
    End If

    Text1.Text = resultset("Name")
    Text2.Text = resultset("Grade")

    Exit Sub

ErrLabel:
    MsgBox Err.Description
End Sub
```

RDO: Moving To The Previous Record In A Result Set

To move to the previous record in an RDO result set, you can use the rdoResultset method **MovePrevious**. Let's see an example. In this case, we'll move to the previous record in the result set named **resultset** that we've opened in our RDO code example, the rdocode project (see "A Full-Scale RDO Example" earlier in this chapter), when the user clicks the appropriate button. We check to make sure we're not trying to move past the beginning of the record set with the **BOF** property, and if so, we make sure to move to the first record instead:

```
Private Sub cmdPrevious_Click()
    On Error GoTo ErrLabel

    If Not resultset.BOF Then resultset.MovePrevious
    If resultset.BOF And resultset.RowCount > 0 Then
        resultset.MoveFirst
    End If

    Text1.Text = resultset("Name")
    Text2.Text = resultset("Grade")

    Exit Sub

ErrLabel:
    MsgBox Err.Description
End Sub
```

After moving to the new record, we display the data in that record's fields in the program's text boxes, **Text1** and **Text2**:

```
Private Sub cmdPrevious_Click()
    On Error GoTo ErrLabel

    If Not resultset.BOF Then resultset.MovePrevious
    If resultset.BOF And resultset.RowCount > 0 Then
        resultset.MoveFirst
    End If

    Text1.Text = resultset("Name")
    Text2.Text = resultset("Grade")

    Exit Sub

ErrLabel:
    MsgBox Err.Description
End Sub
```

RDO: Executing SQL

You can execute SQL statements with RDO objects when you open a result set, as we saw in "RDO: Creating A Result Set" in this chapter. You can also execute an SQL statement with the rdoConnection object's **Execute** statements like this:

```
SQLSel = "Select * from students"
rdoConnection.Execute SQLSel
```

A Full-Scale ADO Example

To illustrate ADO data handling in code, we'll build an ADO project—the adocode project. This application lets you open the db.mdb file we built in the previous chapter using ADO objects to edit records, add records, and even delete records. You can also move through the database using the arrow buttons you see in Figure 25.5.

To edit a record, just type the new value(s) into the text box(es) and click the Update button. To add a record, use the Add button, type the new value(s) into the text box(es), and click the Update button. That's all there is to it—your

Figure 25.5   The adocode project at work.

changes will be reflected in the original database. For reference, the code for this example is located in the adocode folder on this book's accompanying CD-ROM.

ADO: Opening A Connection

The Testing Department is calling again. The company is switching to using ActiveX Data Objects—how about setting up an ADO database-editing program? Already on it, you say.

The first step in editing an ADO database is to open that database, which is called a *data source* in ADO terminology, by setting up a Connection object. To use that and other ADO objects in code, you use the Project|References item, select the Microsoft ActiveX Data Objects Library item, and click on OK, adding the ADO Object Library to your program.

Now we're free to create a new ADO Connection object with the Connection object's **Open** method:

```
connection.Open ConnectionString [,UserID [, Password [, OpenOptions]]]
```

Here are the arguments for this method:

- *ConnectionString*—String containing connection information.
- *UserID*—String containing a username to use when establishing the connection.
- *Password*—String containing a password to use when establishing the connection.
- *OpenOptions*—If set to **adConnectAsync**, the connection will be opened asynchronously.

Let's see an example. When we start our ADO code example, the adocode example (see "A Full-Scale ADO Example" in this chapter), we'll establish a connection, **db**, to the database we built in the previous chapter, db.mdb:

```
Private Sub Form_Load()
    Dim db As Connection
    Set db = New Connection

    db.Open "PROVIDER=Microsoft.Jet.OLEDB.3.51;Data _
        Source=C:\vbbb\adocode\db.mdb;"
...
End Sub
```

And that's it—now we have a connection to the data source. To actually work with the data in that data source, we'll create an ADO record set in the next topic.

ADO: Creating A Record Set From A Connection

Now that you've created an ADO connection, you can open a record set from that connection using the Recordset object's **Open** method:

```
recordset.Open [Source, [ActiveConnection, [Type, [LockType, [Options]]]]]
```

Here are the arguments for this method:

- *Source*—A valid Command object variable name, an SQL statement, a table name, a stored procedure call, or the file name of a Recordset.

- *ActiveConnection*—A valid Connection object variable name or a string containing **ConnectionString** parameters.

- *Type*—Sets the Recordset type (see the following list).

- *LockType*—A value that determines what type of locking (concurrency) the provider should use when opening the Recordset (see the following list).

- *Options*—A Long value that indicates how the provider should evaluate the *Source* argument if it represents something other than a Command object, or that the Recordset should be restored from a file where it was previously saved (see the following list).

Here are the possible values for the *Type* argument:

- **dbOpenKeyset**—Opens a dynaset-type Recordset object, which is like an ODBC keyset cursor.

- **dbOpenDynamic**—Opens a dynamic-type Recordset object, which lets the application see changes made by other users.

- **dbOpenStatic**—Opens a static-type Recordset object.

- **dbOpenForwardOnly**—Opens a forward-only-type Recordset object, where you can only use **MoveNext** to move.

Here are the possible values for the *LockType* argument:

- **adLockReadOnly**—The default; read-only.
- **adLockPessimistic**—Pessimistic locking, record by record.
- **adLockOptimistic**—Optimistic locking, record by record.
- **adLockBatchOptimistic**—Optimistic batch updates.

Here are the possible values for the *Options* argument:

- **adCmdText**—Provider should evaluate *Source* as a definition of a command.
- **adCmdTable**—ADO should generate an SQL query to return all rows from the table named in *Source*.
- **adCmdTableDirect**—Provider should return all rows from the table named in *Source*.
- **adCmdStoredProc**—Provider should evaluate *Source* as a stored procedure.
- **adCmdUnknown**—Type of command in the *Source* argument is not known.
- **adCommandFile**—Record set should be restored from the file named in *Source*.
- **adExecuteAsync**—*Source* should be executed asynchronously.
- **adFetchAsync**—After the initial quantity specified in the **CacheSize** property is fetched, any remaining rows should be fetched asynchronously.

Let's see an example. In our ADO code example, the adocode example (see "A Full-Scale ADO Example" in this chapter), we create a record set, **adoRecordset**, by first declaring it as a form-wide variable:

```
Dim adoRecordset As Recordset
```

Next, we select all the records in the students table this way when the form loads, using the **Open** method:

```
Private Sub Form_Load()
    Dim db As Connection
    Set db = New Connection

    db.Open "PROVIDER=Microsoft.Jet.OLEDB.3.51;Data _
        Source=C:\vbbb\adocode\db.mdb;"
```

```
    Set adoRecordset = New Recordset
    adoRecordset.Open "select Grade, Name from students", _
        db, adOpenStatic, adLockOptimistic
...
End Sub
```

Now that we've opened our result set, we can bind that result set to various controls, like text boxes, as we'll do in the next topic.

ADO: Binding Controls To Record Sets

To bind a control to an ADO Recordset object, you just set that control's **DataSource** property to that object, and then set whatever other data properties that control needs to have set (see, for example, Table 24.1 in the previous chapter, which lists the data properties of various controls).

Let's see an example. In our ADO code example, the adocode example (see "A Full-Scale ADO Example" in this chapter), we create a record set, **adoRecordset**, and open the db.mdb database we created in the last chapter in it. We can bind the fields in that database to the text boxes **Text1** and **Text2** this way when the adocode main form loads:

```
Private Sub Form_Load()
    Dim db As Connection
    Set db = New Connection

    db.Open "PROVIDER=Microsoft.Jet.OLEDB.3.51;Data _
        Source=C:\vbbb\adocode\db.mdb;"

    Set adoRecordset = New Recordset
    adoRecordset.Open "select Grade, Name from students", _
        db, adOpenStatic, adLockOptimistic

    Set Text1.DataSource = adoRecordset
    Text1.DataField = "Name"
    Set Text2.DataSource = adoRecordset
    Text2.DataField = "Grade"

End Sub
```

That's all it takes—now we've bound two text boxes to an ADO record set.

ADO: Adding A Record To A Record Set

To add a new record to an ADO record set, you use the **AddNew** method. After you've updated the fields of the current record, you save that record to the database with the **Update** method. Here's how you use **AddNew**:

```
recordset.AddNew [Fields [, Values]]
```

Here are the arguments for this method:

- *Fields*—A single name or an array of names or ordinal positions of the fields in the new record.

- *Values*—A single value or an array of values for the fields in the new record. If *Fields* is an array, *Values* must also be an array with the same number of members. The order of field names must match the order of field values in each array.

Let's see an example. Here, we'll add a new record to the record set **adoRecordset** in our ADO code example, the adocode example (see "A Full-Scale ADO Example" in this chapter), when the user clicks the appropriate button:

```
Private Sub cmdAdd_Click()
    On Error GoTo ErrLabel
    adoRecordset.AddNew

    Text1.Text = ""
    Text2.Text = ""

    Exit Sub

ErrLabel:
    MsgBox Err.Description
End Sub
```

Note that we also clear the two text boxes that display the field data, **Text1** and **Text2**, so users can enter the data they want in the new record. When done, they press the Update button to update the data source.

ADO: Refreshing The Record Set

Sometimes you want to refresh the data in a record set—you might be dealing with multiply-connected databases, for instance, where other users are making changes as well—and you can use the ADO **Refresh** method for that. Let's see an example. Here, we'll refresh the record set **adoRecordset** in our ADO code example, the adocode example (see "A Full-Scale ADO Example" in this chapter), when the user clicks the appropriate button:

```
Private Sub cmdRefresh_Click()
    On Error GoTo ErrLabel

    adoRecordset.Requery

    Exit Sub

ErrLabel:
    MsgBox Err.Description
End Sub
```

And that's all it takes to refresh the record set.

ADO: Updating A Record In A Record Set

After changing the data in a record's fields or adding a new record, you update the data source to record the change, using the **Update** method:

```
recordset.Update Fields, Values
```

Here are the arguments for this method:

- *Fields*—A single name or an array of names or ordinal positions of the fields in the new record.

- *Values*—A single value or an array of values for the fields in the new record. If *Fields* is an array, *Values* must also be an array with the same number of members. The order of field names must match the order of field values in each array.

Let's see an example. When users want to update records in our ADO code example, the adocode example (see "A Full-Scale ADO Example" in this chapter), they click the appropriate button, and we'll update the data source this way:

```
Private Sub cmdUpdate_Click()
    On Error GoTo ErrLabel

    adoRecordset.Update
```

```
    Exit Sub

ErrLabel:
    MsgBox Err.Description
End Sub
```

That's all we need—now we're ready to update records in an ADO record set.

ADO: Moving To The First Record In A Record Set

To move to the first record in an ADO record set, you use the Recordset object's **MoveFirst** method (this method takes no parameters). Let's see an example. When the user clicks the appropriate button in our ADO code example, the adocode example (see "A Full-Scale ADO Example" in this chapter), we'll move to the first record in our record set, **adoRecordset**:

```
Private Sub cmdFirst_Click()
    On Error GoTo ErrLabel

    adoRecordset.MoveFirst

    Exit Sub

ErrLabel:
    MsgBox Err.Description
End Sub
```

And that's all the code we need to move to the first record.

ADO: Moving To The Last Record In A Record Set

To move to the last record in an ADO record set, you use the Recordset object's **MoveLast** method (this method takes no parameters). Let's see an example. When the user clicks the appropriate button in our ADO code example, the adocode example (see "A Full-Scale ADO Example" in this chapter), we'll move to the last record in our record set, **adoRecordset**:

```
Private Sub cmdLast_Click()
    On Error GoTo ErrLabel

    adoRecordset.MoveLast
```

```
      Exit Sub

ErrLabel:
    MsgBox Err.Description
End Sub
```

And that's all the code we need to move to the last record.

ADO: Moving To The Next Record In A Record Set

To move to the next record in an ADO record set, you use the Recordset object's **MoveNext** method (this method takes no parameters). Let's see an example. When the user clicks the appropriate button in our ADO code example, the adocode example (see "A Full-Scale ADO Example" in this chapter), we'll move to the next record in our record set, **adoRecordset.** Note that we make sure we don't move past the end of the record set by checking the record set's **EOF** property:

```
Private Sub cmdNext_Click()
    On Error GoTo ErrLabel

    If Not adoRecordset.EOF Then
        adoRecordset.MoveNext
    End If

    If adoRecordset.EOF And adoRecordset.RecordCount > 0 Then
        adoRecordset.MoveLast
    End If

    Exit Sub

ErrLabel:
    MsgBox Err.Description
End Sub
```

ADO: Moving To The Previous Record In A Record Set

To move to the next record in an ADO record set, you use the Recordset object's **MovePrevious** method (this method takes no parameters). Let's see an example. When the user clicks the appropriate button in our ADO code example, the adocode example (see "A Full-Scale ADO Example" in this chapter), we'll move to the previous record in our record set, **adoRecordset.** Note that we make sure we don't move past the end of the record set by checking the record set's **BOF** property:

```
Private Sub cmdPrevious_Click()
    On Error GoTo ErrLabel

    If Not adoRecordset.BOF Then adoRecordset.MovePrevious
    If adoRecordset.BOF And adoRecordset.RecordCount > 0 Then
        adoRecordset.MoveFirst
    End If

    Exit Sub

ErrLabel:
    MsgBox Err.Description
End Sub
```

ADO: Deleting A Record In A Record Set

To delete a record in an ADO record set, you use the **Delete** method:

```
recordset.Delete AffectRecords
```

Here, *AffectRecords* is a value that determines how many records the **Delete** method will affect. It can be one of the following constants:

- **adAffectCurrent**—The default; deletes only the current record.
- **adAffectGroup**—Deletes the records that satisfy the current **Filter** property setting.

Let's see an example. Here, we delete a record in our ADO code example, the adocode example (see "A Full-Scale ADO Example" in this chapter), when the user presses the appropriate button:

```
Private Sub cmdDelete_Click()
    On Error GoTo ErrLabel

    adoRecordset.Delete
...
```

In addition, we move to the next record this way:

```
Private Sub cmdDelete_Click()
    On Error GoTo ErrLabel

    adoRecordset.Delete

    adoRecordset.MoveNext
    If adoRecordset.EOF Then
        adoRecordset.MoveLast
    End If

    Exit Sub

ErrLabel:
    MsgBox Err.Description
End Sub
```

And that's it—now we've deleted a record.

ADO: Executing SQL In A Record Set

You can execute an SQL statement when you open a record set using the **Open** method by passing that statement as the *Source* argument:

```
recordset.Open [Source, [ActiveConnection, [Type, [LockType, [Options]]]]
```

Here are the arguments for this method:

- *Source*—A valid Command object variable name, an SQL statement, a table name, a stored procedure call, or the file name of a Recordset.

- *ActiveConnection*—A valid Connection object variable name or a string containing **ConnectionString** parameters.

- *Type*—Sets the Recordset type (see the following list).

- *LockType*—A value that determines what type of locking (concurrency) the provider should use when opening the Recordset object (see the following list).

- *Options*—A Long value that indicates how the provider should evaluate the *Source* argument if it represents something other than a Command object, or that the Recordset object should be restored from a file where it was previously saved (see the following list).

Here are the possible values for the *Type* argument:

- **dbOpenKeyset**—Opens a dynaset-type Recordset object, which is like an ODBC keyset cursor.

- **dbOpenDynamic**—Opens a dynamic-type Recordset object, which lets the application see changes made by other users.

- **dbOpenStatic**—Opens a static-type Recordset object.

- **dbOpenForwardOnly**—Opens a forward-only-type Recordset object, where you can only use **MoveNext** to move.

Here are the possible values for the *LockType* argument:

- **adLockReadOnly**—The default; read-only.

- **adLockPessimistic**—Pessimistic locking, record by record.

- **adLockOptimistic**—Optimistic locking, record by record.

- **adLockBatchOptimistic**—Optimistic batch updates.

Here are the possible values for the *Options* argument:

- **adCmdText**—Provider should evaluate *Source* as a definition of a command.

- **adCmdTable**—ADO should generate an SQL query to return all rows from the table named in *Source*.

- **adCmdTableDirect**—Provider should return all rows from the table named in *Source*.

- **adCmdStoredProc**—Provider should evaluate *Source* as a stored procedure.

- **adCmdUnknown**—Type of command in the *Source* argument is not known.

- **adCommandFile**—Record set should be restored from the file named in *Source*.

- **adExecuteAsync**—*Source* should be executed asynchronously.

- **adFetchAsync**—After the initial quantity specified in the **CacheSize** property is fetched, any remaining rows should be fetched asynchronously.

Here's an example where we open a record set with the SQL statement **"select * from students"**:

```
adoRecordset.Open "select * from students", db, adOpenStatic, adLockOptimistic
```

Chapter 26

OLE

If you need an immediate solution to:	See page:
Adding An OLE Control To A Form	900
Creating And Embedding An OLE Object At Design Time	900
Linking Or Embedding An Existing Document At Design Time	902
Autosizing An OLE Control	903
Determining How An Object Is Displayed In An OLE Container Control	903
Using The OLE Control's Pop-Up Menus At Design Time	904
Inserting An OLE Object Into An OLE Control At Runtime	905
Deactivating OLE Objects	907
Using Paste Special To Insert A Selected Part Of A Document Into An OLE Control	908
How To Activate The OLE Objects In Your Program	912
Activating OLE Objects With A Pop-Up Menu That Lists All OLE Verbs	912
Activating OLE Objects From Code	913
Is An Object Linked Or Embedded?	914
Handling Multiple OLE Objects	914
Using OLE Control Arrays To Handle Multiple OLE Objects	916
Loading New OLE Controls At Runtime	920
Dragging OLE Objects In A Form	924
Deleting OLE Objects	926
Copying And Pasting OLE Objects With The Clipboard	927
Zooming OLE Objects	928
Saving And Retrieving Embedded Object's Data	929
Handling OLE Object Updated Events	930
Disabling In-Place Editing	931

In Depth

For obvious reasons, Object Linking and Embedding (OLE) is a very popular programming topic. Using OLE you can give the users of your program direct access to OLE server programs like Microsoft Word or Excel. In fact, you can integrate all kinds of programs together using OLE, giving your program the power of database, spreadsheet, word processor, and even graphics programs all wrapped into one.

Visual Basic lets you do this with the OLE control. This control can display OLE objects, and those objects appear as mini-versions of the programs connected to them. For example, if you display an Excel spreadsheet in an OLE control, the control displays what looks like a small version of Excel right there in your program. The program that creates the object displayed in the OLE control is an OLE *server*, and your program, which displays the OLE object, is called an OLE *container*. In fact, the proper name for the OLE control is the OLE container control.

You can use the OLE object in the OLE control just as you would in the program that created it; for example, you can work with an Excel spreadsheet in an OLE control just as if it was open in Excel itself. How does that work? There are two primary ways of working with the OLE objects in an OLE control: opening them and editing them in place.

When you open them, the OLE server application is launched in its own window and the OLE object appears in that application. When you want to save your changes to the OLE object in the OLE control, you use the server's Update item in the File menu.

When you edit an OLE object in place, the server application is not launched in its own window; instead, the object becomes active in the OLE control itself and may be edited directly. The OLE container program's menu system is taken over by the OLE server—and you may be startled to see Microsoft Word's or Excel's menu system in your program's menu bar. To close an OLE object that is open for in-place editing, you click the form outside the object.

As an example, the Microsoft Excel spreadsheet in Figure 26.1 is open for in-place editing.

When the OLE object in an OLE control is closed, it appears in its inactive state, as shown in Figure 26.2.

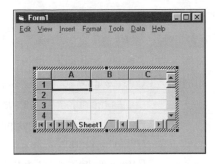

Figure 26.1   Opening an Excel spreadsheet in an OLE control for in-place editing.

OLE actions are called *verbs*; for example, opening an OLE object is accomplished with the **VbOLEOpen** verb, and editing it in place is accomplished with the **VbOLEInPlaceActivate** verb. We'll see how to handle OLE verbs in this chapter when we use the OLE control's **DoVerb** method.

What other methods does the OLE control support? Those methods and what they do appear in Table 26.1. You can also use the OLE control's **Action** method to invoke the methods in Table 26.1, and the values for this property also appear in Table 26.1. When you use the **Action** property, the control often uses other properties of the control, such as the **SourceDoc** property, to find the data it needs to perform the requested operation. Note, however, that the **Action** property is considered obsolete, and we'll use the OLE methods instead.

The term *Object Linking and Embedding* implies two ways of inserting objects into an OLE control—through linking and embedding such objects. How do those operations differ?

Linking Vs. Embedding

What's the difference between linking and embedding OLE objects in the OLE control? The main difference has to do with where the object's data (such as

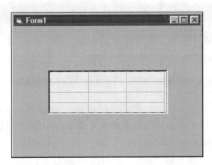

Figure 26.2   An inactive OLE object.

Table 26.1   OLE methods.

Method	Action Value	Meaning
CreateEmbed	0	Creates embedded object
CreateLink	1	Creates linked object from the contents of a file
Copy	4	Copies the object to the system Clipboard
Paste	5	Copies data from the system Clipboard to an OLE container control
Update	6	Retrieves the current data from the application that supplied the object and displays that data as a picture in the OLE container control
DoVerb	7	Opens an object for an operation, such as editing
Close	9	Closes an object and terminates the connection to the application that provided the object
Delete	10	Deletes the specified object and frees the memory associated with it
SaveToFile	11	Saves an object to a data file
ReadFromFile	12	Loads an object that was saved to a data file
InsertObjDlg	14	Displays the Insert Object dialog box
PasteSpecialDlg	15	Displays the Paste Special dialog box
FetchVerbs	17	Updates the list of verbs an object supports
SaveToOle1File	18	Saves an object to the OLE version 1 file format

the data in a spreadsheet) is stored. Data associated with a linked object is manipulated by the OLE server application that created it and is stored outside an OLE container control. Data associated with an embedded object is contained in an OLE container control, and that data can be saved with your Visual Basic application.

When you embed an object into an OLE control, that control stores the name of the application that supplied the object, along with its data. The **OLEType** property of the control is set to **Embedded** (1). When you link an object to an OLE control, that control stores the name of the application that supplied the object and a *reference* to the data. The **OLEType** property of the control is set to **Linked (0)**.

Note that because an embedded object's data is stored in your program, you're responsible for storing and reading that data if it changes. To do that, we'll use the **SaveToFile** and **ReadFromFile** methods in this chapter.

You can also specify the types of objects that an OLE control can take by setting its **OLETypeAllowed** property to **Linked (0)**, **Embedded (1)**, or **Either (2)**.

To embed objects into an OLE control at runtime, you usually use the Insert Object object of the container program's Object menu. To link objects to an OLE control, you usually copy the object in the server application and use the **Paste special** menu object in the OLE container.

TIP: *To place an object in an OLE container control, the component that provides the object must be registered in your system Registry as an OLE server.*

That's it, then, for the overview of OLE. We've seen how the process works in overview; now it's time to turn to this chapter's Immediate Solutions.

Immediate Solutions

Adding An OLE Control To A Form

The Testing Department is on the phone again. How about providing all the functionality that Microsoft Excel has in your new program? Um...you say. It would be really great, they say, if we could let users work with spreadsheets using all the Excel commands they're used to. Can you have it done by next week?

Using the OLE control, you can embed or link objects from OLE server programs like Excel into your own program. In this way, you can present your program's users with a spreadsheet that's not just like Excel—it *is* Excel.

The OLE control is an intrinsic Visual Basic control, and it appears in the toolbox when Visual Basic first starts. The OLE Control tool is the eleventh tool down on the left in the toolbox in Figure 26.3—you can't miss it; it's the one with the letters "OLE" in it.

Add an OLE control to a form now by double-clicking the OLE Control tool. When you do, the OLE control appears in the form, and a moment later, the Insert Object dialog box appears, as shown in Figure 26.4.

Now that you've created an OLE control, you can use the Insert Object dialog box to embed or link an OLE object into that control, and we'll see how that works in the next two topics in this chapter.

Creating And Embedding An OLE Object At Design Time

When you add an OLE control to a Visual Basic program, the Insert Object dialog box appears, as shown in Figure 26.4, and you can use this dialog box to create and embed a new OLE object in your OLE control. Make sure the Create New option is selected, find the name of the OLE server application you want to use, and click on OK.

For example, we've embedded a new Microsoft Excel spreadsheet in the OLE control we've added to a form at design time in Figure 26.5. This spreadsheet

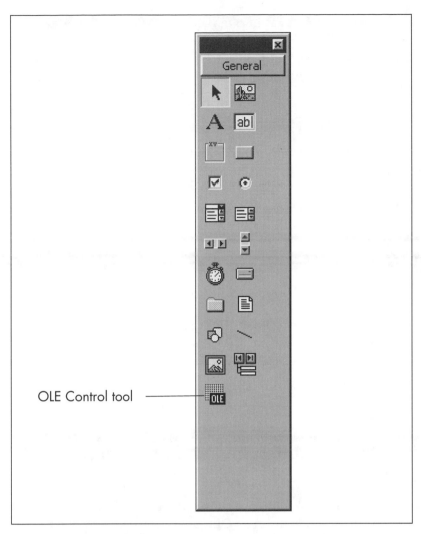

OLE Control tool ———

Figure 26.3   The OLE Control tool.

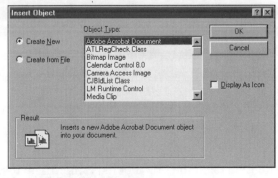

Figure 26.4   The Insert Object dialog box.

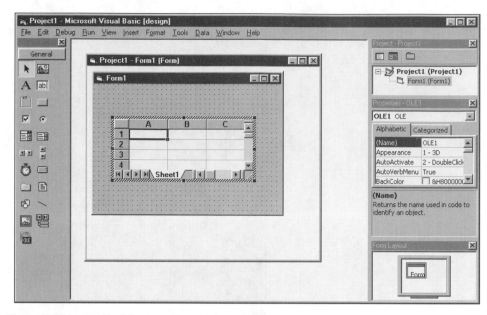

Figure 26.5   Embedding an Excel spreadsheet at design time.

is activated for in-place editing by default; to close the object, click the form itself outside the OLE control.

Linking Or Embedding An Existing Document At Design Time

When you add an OLE control to a form, the Insert Object dialog box appears in order to allow you to insert an OLE object into the new control. As we saw in the previous topic, you can create a new OLE object with the Insert Object dialog box. However, you can also embed or link to an existing file. To do so, click the Create From File option button in the Insert Object dialog box.

When you select a file by typing its path and name into the File text box or by using the Browse button, and then click on OK, that file is embedded as an OLE object in the OLE control. Embedding an existing file this way is handy if you've already got a file you want to display and work with in your program, and it saves you the time of creating the file over again from scratch in a new OLE object.

You can also link an OLE object to an OLE control using the Insert Object dialog box. To do that, click the box labeled Link In The Insert Object Dialog, then select the file as we did before to embed an object.

Autosizing An OLE Control

After you've added an OLE control to a form, you can specify how you want that control to handle OLE object insertions: for example, should the control resize itself when an OLE object is inserted in it or not? You can specify how the control should handle object insertions with the **SizeMode** property.

Here are the possible values for the **SizeMode** property:

- **vbOLESizeClip**—0 (the default); Clip. The object is displayed in actual size. If the object is larger than the OLE control, its image is clipped by the control's borders.

- **vbOLESizeStretch**—1; Stretch. The object's image is sized to fill the OLE control. (Note that the image may not maintain the original proportions of the object.)

- **vbOLESizeAutoSize**—2; Autosize. The OLE control is resized to display the entire object.

- **vbOLESizeZoom**—3; Zoom. The object is resized to fill the OLE container control as much as possible while still maintaining the original proportions of the object.

TIP: *While we're on the subject of customizing the appearance of OLE controls, we might add that you can remove the border of an OLE control by setting its **Border** property to **None** (0).*

---

*Determining
How An Object
Is Displayed In
An OLE
Container
Control*

Determining How An Object Is Displayed In An OLE Container Control

There are two ways of displaying an OLE object in an OLE control: displaying that object's content and displaying it as an icon. Throughout this chapter, we'll use the content display, which is the default, but you can also display it in icon form using the OLE control's **DisplayType** property. Here are the possible settings for **DisplayType**:

- **vbOLEDisplayContent**—0 (the default); Content. When the OLE container control contains an object, the object's data is displayed in the control.

- **vbOLEDisplayIcon**—1; Icon. When the OLE container control contains an object, the object's icon is displayed in the control.

For example, we've set the **DisplayType** property of the OLE control in Figure 26.6 to **vbOLEDisplayIcon** so it displays the icon of its OLE object, which

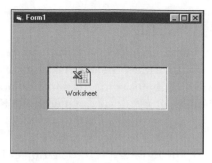

Figure 26.6   Displaying an OLE object in iconic form.

in this case is an Excel object. Note that you cannot open an iconic OLE object for in-place editing, but you can open it for editing in the OLE server program (in other words, when you double-click the object, the OLE server application opens in its own window).

TIP: Note that you must set the **DisplayType** property before you insert an OLE object into the OLE control because you cannot set the **DisplayType** property while the OLE control contains an object.

Using The OLE Control's Pop-Up Menus At Design Time

When you add an OLE control to a form, the Insert Object dialog box appears, and you can insert an object into the control at that time. However, if you don't want to insert an object right away, you can use the control's pop-up menu later. To open the OLE control's pop-up menu, just right-click the control at design time. Here are the primary items in the menu that appears:

- *Insert Object*—Open the Insert Object dialog box.

- *Paste Special*—Link to Clipboard object.

- *Delete*—Delete embedded object.

- *Create Link*—Create a link to the document in the **SourceDoc** property.

- *Create Embedded Object*—Creates an embedded object using the **Class** or **SourceDoc** property.

Note that you can link to or embed a document in the OLE control if you've set the control's **SourceDoc** property. You can also create a new embedded object if you've set the control's **Class** property; classes specify what code components (formerly called OLE automation servers) are available. (We'll see how classes work in the next chapter.)

TIP: *You can get a list of the class names available to your application by selecting the **Class** property in the Properties window and clicking the arrow button in that property's entry.*

Inserting An OLE Object Into An OLE Control At Runtime

The Testing Department is on the phone again. It's fine that you've been able to embed an OLE object in an OLE control at design time, but don't you think it would be great if you could let users embed their own OLE objects? Maybe, you say.

To let users insert their own OLE objects into an OLE control, you can display the same Insert Object dialog box that appears at design time when you created the OLE control, and you use the control's **InsertObjDlg** method to do that (this method takes no parameters).

Let's see an example. Add an OLE control, **OLE1**, to a form now, and click Cancel when the Insert Object dialog box appears. Set the OLE control's **SizeMode** property to **VbOLESizeAutoSize** (note that when you set an OLE control's **SizeMode** property to **VbOLESizeAutoSize**, the OLE server sets the size of the OLE object, so the size of the OLE control, **OLE1**, will probably change when the object is inserted). Finally, add an Insert menu to the form with one item in it: Insert Object.

When users click the Insert Object menu item, they want to insert an OLE object in **OLE1**, and we can let them create and embed a new object, embed an existing file, or embed a link to an existing file with the **InsertObjDlg** method. We do so like this:

```
Private Sub InsertObject_Click()
    OLE1.InsertObjDlg
    ...
End Sub
```

When we execute this method, **InsertObjDlg**, the program displays the Insert Object dialog box, which appears in Figure 26.4. Using this dialog box, the user can embed new objects, existing files, or link to existing files. In fact, that's all the code we need—when the **InsertObjDlg** method finishes, it inserts the new OLE object in the OLE control.

We can do one more thing here—we can check to make sure the OLE insertion operation was completed successfully. To do that, we'll use the OLE control's **OLEType** property to check if there's an OLE object in **OLE1**. This property can take the values **vbOLELinked**, **vbOLEEmbedded**, or **vbOLENone**. Here, we check that property, and if it's set to **vbOLENone**, we indicate to the user that there was an error:

```
Private Sub InsertObject_Click()
    OLE1.InsertObjDlg
    If OLE1.OLEType = vbOLENone Then
        MsgBox "OLE operation failed."
    End If
End Sub
```

Using this code allows us to insert OLE objects like the Excel spreadsheet you see in our OLE control in Figure 26.7. Here, when the object is first inserted, it's opened for in-place editing by default.

TIP: The Insert Object dialog box only lets the user perform the actions you've allowed with the **OLETypeAllowed** property; this property can be set to **Linked** (0), **Embedded** (1), or **Either** (2).

There's a problem here, however. Now that we've inserted a new OLE object and activated it, how do we deactivate it? There are no Exit items in the Excel menu system that's taken over our program's menu system. Usually you deactivate an OLE object by clicking the form around the OLE control, and we'll see how that works in the next topic.

The code for this example so far, insertole.frm version 1, appears in Listing 26.1 (version 2 will also support a Paste Special menu item). (The final version of this code, version 3, is located in the insertole folder on this book's accompanying CD-ROM.)

Listing 26.1   insertole.frm version 1

```
VERSION 6.00
Begin VB.Form Form1
    Caption         =   "Form1"
    ClientHeight    =   2115
    ClientLeft      =   165
    ClientTop       =   735
    ClientWidth     =   4680
    LinkTopic       =   "Form1"
    ScaleHeight     =   2115
    ScaleWidth      =   4680
    StartUpPosition =   3   'Windows Default
    Begin VB.OLE OLE1
        Height      =   1095
        Left        =   840
```

```
        SizeMode        =    2    'AutoSize
        TabIndex        =    0
        Top             =    360
        Width           =    3015
    End
    Begin VB.Menu File
        Caption         =    "File"
    End
    Begin VB.Menu Insert
        Caption         =    "Insert"
        Begin VB.Menu InsertObject
            Caption      =    "Insert object"
        End
    End
End
Attribute VB_Name = "Form1"
Attribute VB_GlobalNameSpace = False
Attribute VB_Creatable = False
Attribute VB_PredeclaredId = True
Attribute VB_Exposed = False

Private Sub InsertObject_Click()
    OLE1.InsertObjDlg
    If OLE1.OLEType = vbOLENone Then
        MsgBox "OLE operation failed."
    End If
End Sub
```

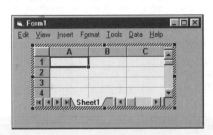

Figure 26.7   Inserting an OLE object into a program.

Deactivating OLE Objects

You've inserted and activated a new OLE object in an OLE control. However, there doesn't seem to be any way to deactivate the object now—the OLE server's menus have taken over your program's menu system, and there's no Exit item. How do you close the OLE object?

Usually you click the form around an OLE object to deactivate that object. Deactivating an OLE object is easy: you just set its **AppIsRunning** property to False. You can also use the OLE control's **Close** method to do the same thing.

As an example, we add this code to the oleinsert program we developed in the previous topic, allowing the user to deactivate OLE objects by clicking the form around the OLE control:

```
Private Sub Form_Click()
    OLE1.AppIsRunning = False
End Sub
```

Now the user can close an open OLE object just by clicking the form around the object.

Using Paste Special To Insert A Selected Part Of A Document Into An OLE Control

Using Paste Special To Insert A Selected Part Of A Document Into An OLE Control

Besides using the **InsertObjDlg** method we saw two topics ago, you can also insert OLE objects using the Paste Special menu item in most OLE container programs. Besides embedding or linking to an entire document, Paste Special allows you to link or embed just the part of that document you want.

Users select the part of the document they want to embed or link to in the OLE server application, select the Copy item in that application's Edit menu, and then select Paste Special in your container program to paste the part of the document they've selected into an OLE control. You support Paste Special with the OLE control's **PasteSpecialDlg** method (this method takes no parameters).

Let's see an example. Here, we add a Paste Special menu item to the Insert menu in the oleinsert example we developed two topics ago (see Listing 26.1). When users click that menu item, they've made a selection in an OLE server program, and we should paste that selection into our OLE control, **OLE1**. For this example, we select (using the mouse) a range of cells in an Excel spread-sheet, as shown in Figure 26.8, and copy them using Excel's Copy menu item. (You must also have saved the Excel document you're working with to disk so there is an actual document to which to link.)

In the Paste Special event handler in our oleinsert example, then, we first check to make sure there's something to paste with the OLE control's **PasteOK** property; if True, we can paste an OLE object:

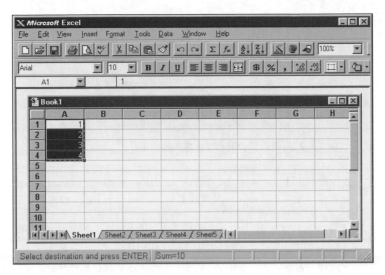

Figure 26.8   Selecting and copying a range of cells in Microsoft Excel.

```
Private Sub PasteSpecial_Click()
    If OLE1.PasteOK Then
...
```

To get the object to paste, we use **PasteSpecialDlg**:

```
Private Sub PasteSpecial_Click()
    If OLE1.PasteOK Then
        OLE1.PasteSpecialDlg
    End If
...
```

The Paste Special dialog box appears at this point, indicating that we can paste an Excel object (see Figure 26.9). We can paste this object as an embedded object if we click the Paste option button, or as a link if we click the Paste

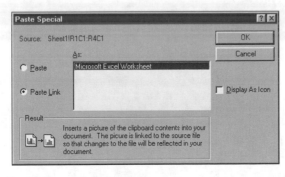

Figure 26.9   The Paste Special dialog box.

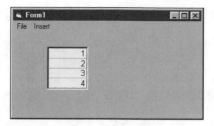

Figure 26.10   Inserting a link to part of a document.

Link option button. Here, we click Paste Link and click on OK. This pastes the new OLE link in our OLE control, **OLE1**, as shown in Figure 26.10.

We can do one more thing here—we can check to make sure the OLE paste operation was completed successfully. To do that, we'll use the OLE control's **OLEType** property to check if there's an OLE object in **OLE1**. This property can take the values **vbOLELinked**, **vbOLEEmbedded**, or **vbOLENone**. Here, we check that property, and if it's set to **vbOLENone**, we indicate to the user that there was an error:

```
Private Sub PasteSpecial_Click()
    If OLE1.PasteOK Then
        OLE1.PasteSpecialDlg
    End If
    If OLE1.OLEType = vbOLENone Then
        MsgBox "OLE operation failed."
    End If

End Sub
```

That's it—the new version of this program, oleinsert.frm version 2, appears in Listing 26.2. (The final version, Version 3—which is located in the insertole folder on this book's accompanying CD-ROM—will let the user activate OLE objects from a menu.)

Listing 26.2   insertole.frm version 2

```
VERSION 6.00
Begin VB.Form Form1
    Caption         =       "Form1"
    ClientHeight    =       2115
    ClientLeft      =       165
    ClientTop       =       735
    ClientWidth     =       4680
    LinkTopic       =       "Form1"
    ScaleHeight     =       2115
    ScaleWidth      =       4680
```

```
        StartUpPosition =   3  'Windows Default
        Begin VB.OLE OLE1
           Height        =   1095
           Left          =   840
           SizeMode      =   2  'AutoSize
           TabIndex      =   0
           Top           =   360
           Width         =   3015
        End
        Begin VB.Menu File
           Caption       =   "File"
        End
        Begin VB.Menu Insert
           Caption       =   "Insert"
           Begin VB.Menu InsertObject
              Caption        =   "Insert object"
           End
           Begin VB.Menu PasteSpecial
              Caption        =   "Paste special"
           End
        End
     End
  End
  Attribute VB_Name = "Form1"
  Attribute VB_GlobalNameSpace = False
  Attribute VB_Creatable = False
  Attribute VB_PredeclaredId = True
  Attribute VB_Exposed = False
  Private Sub Form_Click()
      OLE1.AppIsRunning = False
  End Sub

  Private Sub InsertObject_Click()
      OLE1.InsertObjDlg
      If OLE1.OLEType = vbOLENone Then
          MsgBox "OLE operation failed."
      End If
  End Sub

  Private Sub PasteSpecial_Click()
      If OLE1.PasteOK Then
          OLE1.PasteSpecialDlg
      End If
      If OLE1.OLEType = vbOLENone Then
          MsgBox "OLE operation failed."
      End If

  End Sub
```

How To Activate The OLE Objects In Your Program

You can set the conditions under which an OLE object is activated using the **AutoActivate** property. Here are the possible values for that property (we'll stick with **vbOLEActivateDoubleclick**, the default, in this chapter):

- **vbOLEActivateManual**—0; Manual. The object isn't automatically activated. You can activate an object in code using the **DoVerb** method.

- **vbOLEActivateGetFocus**—1; Focus. If the OLE container control contains an object that supports single-click activation, the application that provides the object is activated when the OLE container control receives the focus.

- **vbOLEActivateDoubleclick**—2 (the default); Double-click. If the OLE container control contains an object, the application that provides the object is activated when the user double-clicks the OLE container control or presses Enter when the control has the focus.

- **vbOLEActivateAuto**—3; Automatic. If the OLE container control contains an object, the application that provides the object is activated based on the object's normal method of activation either when the control receives the focus or when the user double-clicks the control.

For example, if you leave the OLE control's **AutoActivate** property set to **vbOLEActivateDoubleclick**, the object is activated when the user double-clicks it. In fact, what really happens is that the OLE object primary *verb* is executed, and that verb is almost always a command to open the object for in-place editing. (For a list of the OLE verbs, see "Activating OLE Objects From Code" later in this chapter.) What that means in practice is that when you double-click an OLE object in a Visual Basic OLE control, the usual response is that the OLE object is opened for in-place editing.

What if you don't want to edit the control in place? What if you prefer to launch the OLE server application in a separate window and work with the object there? In that case, you want to execute the object's **Open** verb, not its **Edit** verb. To let the user use all the OLE verbs the object supports, you enable its OLE verb pop-up menu, and we'll see how to do that in the next topic.

Activating OLE Objects With A Pop-Up Menu That Lists All OLE Verbs

To let the user select from among all the OLE verbs an object is capable of supporting, you set the **AutoVerbMenu** to True. When this property is True

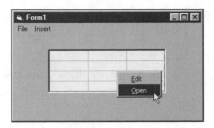

Figure 26.11   Pop-up menu listing the OLE verbs an Excel OLE object supports.

(the default), and the user right-clicks an inactive OLE object, a pop-up menu appears listing the OLE verbs the object supports.

For example, when you right-click an inactive Excel object in the OLE container example we've developed in the last few topics, a pop-up menu appears, displaying the possible OLE verbs you can us (see Figure 26.11). Selecting a verb in the pop-up menu executes that verb; here, the **Edit** verb opens the OLE object for in-place editing, and the **Open** verb launches Excel and opens the OLE object in Excel.

Warning!   When the AutoVerbMenu property is True, Click events and MouseDown events don't occur when the OLE container control is clicked with the right mouse button.

Activating OLE Objects From Code

In the previous few topics, we've seen how to add an OLE object to an OLE control and how to deactivate it. In fact, we've even seen how the object is activated when the user double-clicks it. But how can we activate an OLE object in code? To do that, you use the OLE control's **DoVerb** method:

```
OLEControl.DoVerb ([verb])
```

Here are the possible values for the *verb* argument—an OLE object's primary verb is considered its default verb, and it usually opens the object for in-place editing:

- **vbOLEPrimary**—0; the default action for the object.

- **vbOLEShow**—1; activates the object for editing. If the application that created the object supports in-place activation, the object is activated within the OLE container control.

- **vbOLEOpen**—2; opens the object in a separate application window. If the application that created the object supports in-place activation, the object is activated in its own window.

- **vbOLEHide**—3; for embedded objects, hides the application that created the object.

- **vbOLEUIActivate**—4; if the object supports in-place activation, activates the object for in-place activation and shows any user interface tools. If the object doesn't support in-place activation, the object doesn't activate and an error occurs.

- **vbOLEInPlaceActivate**—5; if the user moves the focus to the OLE container control, creates a window for the object and prepares the object to be edited. An error occurs if the object doesn't support activation on a single mouse click.

- **vbOLEDiscardUndoState**—6; used when the object is activated for editing to discard all record of changes that the object's application can undo.

Let's see an example. Here, we add a new item, Activate Object, to the File menu in the oleinsert example we've developed over the previous few topics. If the user clicks this item, we want to activate the OLE object in the **OLE1** control, and we'll do that by executing its primary verb:

```
Private Sub ActivateObject_Click()
    OLE1.DoVerb 0
End Sub
```

For example, if there's an inactive Excel spreadsheet in the OLE control, selecting the Activate Object menu item will open it for in-place editing. The final code for this example is located in the oleinsert folder on this book's accompanying CD-ROM.

*Is An Object
Linked Or
Embedded?*

Is An Object Linked Or Embedded?

You can use an OLE control's **OLEType** property to determine how if an OLE object is linked or embedded. If the object is linked, **OLEType** will be set to **Linked (0)**. If the object is embedded, **OLEType** will be set to **Embedded (1)**.

*Handling
Multiple OLE
Objects*

Handling Multiple OLE Objects

So far, we've only dealt with a single OLE object in our example program, oleinsert. However, when you start working with multiple OLE controls in a program, there are some issues that you might not think of at first. For example, if you have two OLE controls in a form, and the user selects your program's Insert Object menu item, which control do you insert the new OLE object into?

You usually handle this problem by checking to see which control is the active control—that is, the control with the focus—in the program. In this way, the user clicks a control to give it the focus and uses the Insert Object menu item. Then you can use the Visual Basic form **ActiveControl** property to see which control to use.

Let's see an example. Here, we'll create a new program, olemultiple, with two OLE controls, **OLE1** and **OLE2**. We'll develop this program over the next few topics to handle multiple OLE objects and even load new OLE controls in if the user wants to work with more than two objects at once.

For now, add two OLE controls, **OLE1** and **OLE2** (setting their **SizeMode** properties to **VbOLESizeAutoSize**), to a new program, olemultiple. When the Insert Object dialog box comes up for each control, just click Cancel to make sure we don't insert any OLE objects before runtime. Add two menus as well: a File menu with the item Activate Object and an Insert menu with two items, Insert Object and Paste Special.

When users select the Activate Object menu item, they want to activate the OLE object with the focus, and we can do that with the OLE control's **DoVerb** method. To determine which control to activate, we use the form's **ActiveControl** property. In fact, we can even make sure that the active control is really an OLE control by checking its type using the **TypeOf** keyword:

```
Private Sub ActivateObject_Click()
    If TypeOf ActiveControl Is OLE Then
...
End Sub
```

If the control with the focus is an OLE control, we activate the object in that control, executing its primary verb:

```
Private Sub ActivateObject_Click()
    If TypeOf ActiveControl Is OLE Then
        ActiveControl.DoVerb 0
    End If
End Sub
```

In the same way, we can insert a new OLE object into the OLE control with the focus using the **InsertObjDlg** method when the user clicks the Insert Object menu item:

```
Private Sub InsertObject_Click()
    If TypeOf ActiveControl Is OLE Then
        ActiveControl.InsertObjDlg
        If ActiveControl.OLEType = None Then
            MsgBox "OLE operation failed."
        End If
    End If
End Sub
```

And we can perform Paste Special operations on the OLE control with the
focus when the user selects the Paste Special menu item:

```
Private Sub PasteSpecial_Click()
    If TypeOf ActiveControl Is OLE Then
        If ActiveControl.PasteOK Then
            ActiveControl.PasteSpecialDlg
        End If
        If ActiveControl.OLEType = None Then
            MsgBox "OLE operation failed."
        End If
    End If
End Sub
```

In fact, we can even deactivate our OLE objects when the user clicks the form
outside any OLE control with the **AppIsRunning** property:

```
Private Sub Form_Click()
    OLE1.AppIsRunning = False
    OLE2.AppIsRunning = False
End Sub
```

Note that this last subroutine contains some awkward code: we need to address each OLE control by name (what if we had 50 OLE controls?), and ad-
dressing each control by name precludes the possibility of loading in new OLE
controls at runtime (you need a control array for that). We'll look at these two
issues in the next topic.

Using OLE Control Arrays To Handle Multiple OLE Objects

When you've got a number of OLE objects to work with in a program, it helps
to store them in an OLE control array because you can address those objects
using an array index instead of by name, and that allows you to loop over

them. Let's see an example. Here, we will modify the olemultiple example we started in the previous topic to use an array of OLE controls instead of individual OLE controls. As the program stands, we have to address each OLE control by name like this, where we deactivate any active objects when the user clicks the form:

```
Private Sub Form_Click()
    OLE1.AppIsRunning = False
    OLE2.AppIsRunning = False
End Sub
```

To install the OLE control array in the olemultiple example, delete the two OLE controls already there, **OLE1** and **OLE2**. Add two OLE controls named **OLEControls** now, answering Yes when Visual Basic asks if you want to create a control array. Set these new controls' **SizeMode** properties to **AutoSize**. Because we'll load new OLE controls into this program under user control in the next topic, we keep track of the total number of OLE controls in an integer named **intTotalOLEControls**:

```
Dim intTotalOLEControls As Integer
```

And we set **intTotalOLEControls** to 2 when we start the program:

```
Private Sub Form_Load()
    intTotalOLEControls = 2
End Sub
```

Now when the user clicks the form to deactivate any running OLE objects, we can simply loop over the OLE controls in the **OLEControls** array:

```
Private Sub Form_Click()
    Dim intLoopIndex As Integer

    For intLoopIndex = 0 To intTotalOLEControls - 1
        OLEControls(intLoopIndex).AppIsRunning = False
    Next intLoopIndex
End Sub
```

Now we're able to insert two OLE objects into the olemultiple program, as shown in Figure 26.12. However, standard OLE container programs should be able to load new OLE controls on demand to handle additional objects as the user requires, and we'll see how to do that in the next topic.

The code for this example, olemultiple.frm version 1, appears in Listing 26.3 (version 2 will let the user load additional OLE controls as required). (Version 3,

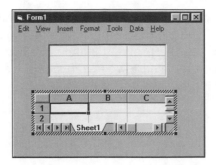

Figure 26.12   Inserting multiple OLE objects into a program.

the final version of this example, is located in the olemultiple folder on this book's accompanying CD-ROM.)

Listing 26.3   olemultiple.frm version 1

```
VERSION 6.00
Begin VB.Form Form1
    Caption         =   "Form1"
    ClientHeight    =   3015
    ClientLeft      =   165
    ClientTop       =   735
    ClientWidth     =   4680
    LinkTopic       =   "Form1"
    ScaleHeight     =   3015
    ScaleWidth      =   4680
    StartUpPosition =   3  'Windows Default
    Begin VB.OLE OLEControls
        Height          =   1215
        Index           =   1
        Left            =   840
        SizeMode        =   2   'AutoSize
        TabIndex        =   1
        Top             =   1680
        Width           =   3015
    End
    Begin VB.OLE OLEControls
        Height          =   1215
        Index           =   0
        Left            =   840
        SizeMode        =   2   'AutoSize
        TabIndex        =   0
        Top             =   240
        Width           =   3015
    End
```

```
    Begin VB.Menu File
        Caption          =    "File"
        Begin VB.Menu ActivateObject
            Caption          =    "Activate object"
        End
        Begin VB.Menu CreateNewOLEControl
            Caption          =    "Create new OLE control"
        End
    End
    Begin VB.Menu Insert
        Caption          =    "Insert"
        Begin VB.Menu InsertObject
            Caption          =    "Insert object"
        End
        Begin VB.Menu PasteSpecial
            Caption          =    "Paste special"
        End
    End
End
Attribute VB_Name = "Form1"
Attribute VB_GlobalNameSpace = False
Attribute VB_Creatable = False
Attribute VB_PredeclaredId = True
Attribute VB_Exposed = False
Dim intTotalOLEControls As Integer
Dim intXOffset, intYOffset As Integer

Private Sub ActivateObject_Click()
    If TypeOf ActiveControl Is OLE Then
        ActiveControl.DoVerb 0
    End If
End Sub

Private Sub Form_Load()
    intTotalOLEControls = 2
End Sub

Private Sub InsertObject_Click()
    If TypeOf ActiveControl Is OLE Then
        ActiveControl.InsertObjDlg
        If ActiveControl.OLEType = None Then
            MsgBox "OLE operation failed."
        End If
    End If
End Sub
```

```
Private Sub PasteSpecial_Click()
    If TypeOf ActiveControl Is OLE Then
        If ActiveControl.PasteOK Then
            ActiveControl.PasteSpecialDlg
        End If
        If ActiveControl.OLEType = None Then
            MsgBox "OLE operation failed."
        End If
    End If
End Sub

Private Sub Form_Click()
    Dim intLoopIndex As Integer

    For intLoopIndex = 0 To intTotalOLEControls - 1
        OLEControls(intLoopIndex).AppIsRunning = False
        OLEControls(intLoopIndex).Visible = True
    Next intLoopIndex
End Sub
```

Loading New OLE Controls At Runtime

The olemultiple example we've developed in the previous two topics is designed to handle multiple OLE objects, but so far we only can handle two such objects because there are only two OLE controls in the program. OLE container programs, however, may be expected to handle more than two OLE objects, so we'll take a look at how to load additional OLE controls as required at runtime.

Let's see an example. We'll modify the olemultiple example now to let the user load in multiple OLE controls as required. To do that, add a new menu item, Create New OLE Control, to that program's File menu. When the user selects this item, we start by incrementing the total number of OLE controls, which we've stored in the variable **intTotalOLEControls**:

```
Private Sub CreateNewOLEControl_Click()
        intTotalOLEControls = intTotalOLEControls + 1
    ...
```

Next, we load a new OLE control, adding it to our array of OLE controls, **OLEControls**:

```
Private Sub CreateNewOLEControl_Click()
        intTotalOLEControls = intTotalOLEControls + 1
```

```
        Load OLEControls(intTotalOLEControls - 1)
...
```

Now we position the new OLE control at upper left in the program, make it visible, and let the user insert an OLE object into it with the **InsertObjDlg** method:

```
Private Sub CreateNewOLEControl_Click()
        intTotalOLEControls = intTotalOLEControls + 1

        Load OLEControls(intTotalOLEControls - 1)
        OLEControls(intTotalOLEControls - 1).Move 0, 0
        OLEControls(intTotalOLEControls - 1).Visible = True
        OLEControls(intTotalOLEControls - 1).InsertObjDlg
...
```

Finally, we can check if the object insertion operation was completed successfully and inform the user if not:

```
Private Sub CreateNewOLEControl_Click()
        intTotalOLEControls = intTotalOLEControls + 1

        Load OLEControls(intTotalOLEControls - 1)
        OLEControls(intTotalOLEControls - 1).Move 0, 0
        OLEControls(intTotalOLEControls - 1).Visible = True
        OLEControls(intTotalOLEControls - 1).InsertObjDlg

        If OLEControls(intTotalOLEControls - 1).OLEType = None Then
            MsgBox "OLE operation failed."
        End If
End Sub
```

And that's it—now we let the user add OLE controls as needed, using the Create New OLE Control menu item, as you can see in Figure 26.13. As you can also see in Figure 26.13, however, the placement of our new OLE object is less than optimal. Ideally, of course, the user can specify where in a container program the new OLE object should go, and we'll take a look at that in the next topic, where we let the user drag OLE controls in a form.

The code for this example, olemultiple.frm version 2, appears in Listing 26.4. (The final version, version 3—which is located in the olemultiple folder on this book's accompanying CD-ROM—will let the user drag and position OLE controls.)

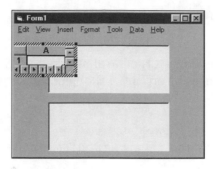

Figure 26.13   Loading a new OLE control at runtime.

Listing 26.4   olemultiple.frm version 2

```
VERSION 6.00
Begin VB.Form Form1
   Caption         =    "Form1"
   ClientHeight    =    3015
   ClientLeft      =    165
   ClientTop       =    735
   ClientWidth     =    4680
   LinkTopic       =    "Form1"
   ScaleHeight     =    3015
   ScaleWidth      =    4680
   StartUpPosition =    3 'Windows Default
   Begin VB.OLE OLEControls
      Height       =    1215
      Index        =    1
      Left         =    840
      SizeMode     =    2  'AutoSize
      TabIndex     =    1
      Top          =    1680
      Width        =    3015
   End
   Begin VB.OLE OLEControls
      Height       =    1215
      Index        =    0
      Left         =    840
      SizeMode     =    2  'AutoSize
      TabIndex     =    0
      Top          =    240
      Width        =    3015
   End
   Begin VB.Menu File
      Caption      =    "File"
      Begin VB.Menu ActivateObject
         Caption   =    "Activate object"
```

```
            End
        Begin VB.Menu CreateNewOLEControl
            Caption          =   "Create new OLE control"
        End
    End
    Begin VB.Menu Insert
        Caption          =   "Insert"
        Begin VB.Menu InsertObject
            Caption          =   "Insert object"
        End
        Begin VB.Menu PasteSpecial
            Caption          =   "Paste special"
        End
    End
End
Attribute VB_Name = "Form1"
Attribute VB_GlobalNameSpace = False
Attribute VB_Creatable = False
Attribute VB_PredeclaredId = True
Attribute VB_Exposed = False
Dim intTotalOLEControls As Integer
Dim intXOffset, intYOffset As Integer

Private Sub ActivateObject_Click()
    If TypeOf ActiveControl Is OLE Then
        ActiveControl.DoVerb 0
    End If
End Sub

Private Sub CreateNewOLEControl_Click()
        intTotalOLEControls = intTotalOLEControls + 1

        Load OLEControls(intTotalOLEControls - 1)
        OLEControls(intTotalOLEControls - 1).Move 0, 0
        OLEControls(intTotalOLEControls - 1).Visible = True
        OLEControls(intTotalOLEControls - 1).InsertObjDlg

        If OLEControls(intTotalOLEControls - 1).OLEType = None Then
            MsgBox "OLE operation failed."
        End If
End Sub

Private Sub Form_Load()
    intTotalOLEControls = 2
End Sub
```

```
Private Sub InsertObject_Click()
    If TypeOf ActiveControl Is OLE Then
        ActiveControl.InsertObjDlg
        If ActiveControl.OLEType = None Then
            MsgBox "OLE operation failed."
        End If
    End If
End Sub


Private Sub PasteSpecial_Click()
    If TypeOf ActiveControl Is OLE Then
        If ActiveControl.PasteOK Then
            ActiveControl.PasteSpecialDlg
        End If
        If ActiveControl.OLEType = None Then
            MsgBox "OLE operation failed."
        End If
    End If
End Sub

Private Sub Form_Click()
    Dim intLoopIndex As Integer

    For intLoopIndex = 0 To intTotalOLEControls - 1
        OLEControls(intLoopIndex).AppIsRunning = False
    Next intLoopIndex
End Sub
```

Dragging OLE Objects In A Form

In most OLE container programs, such as Microsoft Word, users can position OLE objects as they like in order to create a composite document. To let users position OLE objects in a form as they would like, we can support dragging those controls using their **Drag** method:

```
OLEControl.Drag action
```

Here are the possible values for the *action* argument:

- **vbCancel**—Cancels the drag operation.
- **vbBeginDrag**—Starts the drag operation
- **vbEndDrag**—Ends the drag operation.

Let's see an example. We'll modify the olemultiple example program that we've developed in the previous few topics to let the user drag OLE controls. When the user presses the mouse in an OLE control, we will start the drag operation, and we do that by recording the location of the mouse in two new form-wide variables, **intXOffset** and **intYOffset**:

```
Dim intXOffset, intYOffset As Integer
```

Here's how we set those variables and begin the drag operation when the user presses the mouse button:

```
Private Sub OLEControls_MouseDown(Index As Integer, Button As Integer, _
    Shift As Integer, X As Single, Y As Single)
    intXOffset = X
    intYOffset = Y
    OLEControls(Index).Drag vbBeginDrag
End Sub
```

Now when the user drags the control to a new location in the form, we will move the control to that new location using the form's **DragDrop** event handler:

```
Private Sub Form_DragDrop(Source As Control, X As Single, Y As Single)
    Source.Move X - intXOffset, Y - intYOffset
End Sub
```

If the user doesn't move the control far enough, however, the control itself gets a **DragDrop** event when the user drops it, because Visual Basic is assuming the user is dropping the control on top of itself. To handle that case, we set up a **DragDrop** event handler for the OLE control itself, convert the coordinates we are passed in that event handler from coordinates local to the OLE control to coordinates based on the form's client area, and move the control to its new location:

```
Private Sub OLEControls_DragDrop(Index As Integer, Source As Control, _
    X As Single, Y As Single)
    Source.Move X + OLEControls(Index).Left - intXOffset, Y + _
        OLEControls(Index).Top - intYOffset
End Sub
```

And that's it—now the user can drag and drop the OLE controls in our olemultiple example, as shown in Figure 26.14. The final code for this example is located in the olemultiple folder on this book's accompanying CD-ROM.

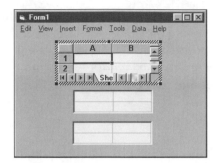

Figure 26.14   Letting the user drag OLE controls to position them.

Deleting OLE Objects

Besides adding OLE objects, OLE container programs should also allow the user to delete those objects. You can delete an OLE object in an OLE control with the control's **Delete** method (this method takes no parameters). Let's see an example. Here, we add code to a menu item, Delete Object, to delete an OLE object in the currently active OLE control. First, we check to see if the type of control that's currently active (that is, has the focus) is an OLE control:

```
Private Sub DeleteObject_Click()
    If TypeOf ActiveControl Is OLE Then
...
    End If
End Sub
```

If the active control is an OLE control, we delete the OLE object in that control with the control's **Delete** method:

```
Private Sub DeleteObject_Click()
    If TypeOf ActiveControl Is OLE Then
        ActiveControl.Delete
    End If
End Sub
```

This method deletes the OLE object in the control and does not, as the name of this method might make you think, delete the control itself.

Copying And Pasting OLE Objects With The Clipboard

You can copy an OLE object to the Clipboard with an OLE control's **Copy** method, and you can paste an OLE object in the Clipboard to an OLE control with that control's **Paste** method. Neither of these methods takes any parameters. Let's see an example. Here, we can copy the OLE object in the OLE control **OLE1** when the user clicks a command button, **Command1**, and paste that object into another OLE control, **OLE2**, when the user clicks a second command button, **Command2**.

When the user clicks **Command1**, then, we just copy the OLE object in **OLE1** to the Clipboard (note that an OLE object should be running when you copy it to the Clipboard):

```
Private Sub Command1_Click()
    OLE1.Copy
End Sub
```

When the user clicks **Command2**, we should paste the OLE object from the Clipboard to **OLE2**. First, we check to make sure there is an object in the Clipboard that the **OLE2** control will accept, using that control's **PasteOK** method:

```
Private Sub Command2_Click()

        If OLE2.PasteOK Then
...
        End If
```

If it's okay to paste into **OLE2**, we use that control's **Paste** method to paste the OLE object in the Clipboard into **OLE2**:

```
Private Sub Command2_Click()

        If OLE2.PasteOK Then
            OLE2.Paste
        End If
...
```

Finally, we check to make sure the paste operation was completed successfully:

```
End SubPrivate Sub Command2_Click()

        If OLE2.PasteOK Then
            OLE2.Paste
```

```
        End If
        If OLE2.OLEType = None Then
            MsgBox "OLE operation failed."
        End If

End Sub
```

Zooming OLE Objects

The Testing Department is on the phone again. The OLE control you're using to show a picture of the company's glorious founder is great, but can't it be larger?

You can zoom (that is, enlarge or shrink) OLE objects using the **SizeMode** property of OLE controls. Here are the possible values for the **SizeMode** property:

- **vbOLESizeClip**—0 (the default); Clip. The object is displayed in actual size. If the object is larger than the OLE control, its image is clipped by the control's borders.

- **vbOLESizeStretch**—1; Stretch. The object's image is sized to fill the OLE control. (Note that the image may not maintain the original proportions of the object.)

- **vbOLESizeAutoSize**—2; Autosize. The OLE control is resized to display the entire object.

- **vbOLESizeZoom**—3; Zoom. The object is resized to fill the OLE container control as much as possible while still maintaining the original proportions of the object.

Let's see an example. Add a new OLE control to a form, setting its **SizeMode** property to **VbOLESizeZoom**. Next, we add a button, **Command1**, with the caption Zoom and add this code to enlarge **OLE1** when the user clicks that button:

```
Private Sub Command1_Click()
    OLE1.Width = 3 * OLE1.Width
    OLE1.Height = 3 * OLE1.Height
End Sub
```

That's all it takes. As an example, we're zooming the Excel spreadsheet you see in Figure 26.15.

Figure 26.15   Zooming an OLE object.

Saving And Retrieving Embedded Object's Data

Because an embedded OLE object's data is stored in your program, you are responsible for storing and retrieving that data if it's changed. Otherwise, when a form containing an OLE container control is closed, any changes to the data associated with that control are lost.

To save updated data from an object to a file, you use the OLE container control's **SaveToFile** method. Once the data has been saved to a file, you can open the file and restore the object with the **ReadFromFile** method. Let's see an example. When the user clicks a button, **Command1**, we can open a new file, data.ole, for binary output:

```
Private Sub Command1_Click ()
    Dim intFileNumber as Integer

    intFileNumber = FreeFile
    Open "data.ole" For Binary As #intFileNumber
...
```

Now we can save the OLE object in an OLE control, **OLE1**, to that file this way using **SaveToFile**:

```
Private Sub Command1_Click ()
    Dim intFileNumber as Integer

    intFileNumber = FreeFile
    Open "data.ole" For Binary As #intFileNumber
    OLE1.SaveToFile intFileNumber

    Close #intFileNumber
End Sub
```

Warning!   If you save multiple OLE objects to a file, you should read them from the file in the same order you wrote them.

Later, we can read the stored OLE object back to **OLE1** with the **ReadFromFile** method when the user clicks another button, **Command2**. First, we open the data.ole file:

```
Private Sub Command2_Click ()
    Dim intFileNumber as Integer

    intFileNumber = FreeFile
    Open "data.ole" For Binary As #intFileNumber
...
```

Then we read the OLE object back into **OLE1** with the **ReadFromFile** method:

```
Private Sub Command2_Click ()
    Dim intFileNumber as Integer

    intFileNumber = FreeFile
    Open "data.ole" For Binary As #intFileNumber
    OLE1.ReadFromFile intFileNumber

    Close #intFileNumber
End Sub
```

And that's it—now we've stored and retrieved an OLE file to and from disk (which is called *persisting* the object).

Handling OLE Object Updated Events

You can determine when an OLE object has been updated with the OLE control's **Updated** event. Your program is passed a variable named *code* in the **Updated** event handler to indicate what operation updated the OLE object's data:

```
Sub OLEobject_Updated (code As Integer)
```

Here are the possible settings for *code*:

- **vbOLEChanged**—0; the object's data was changed.
- **vbOLESaved**—1; the object's data was saved by the application that created the object.

- **vbOLEClosed**—2; the file containing the linked object's data was closed by the server application that created the object.

- **vbOLERenamed**—3; the file containing the linked object's data was renamed by the server application that created the object.

Disabling In-Place Editing

If you don't want an OLE control to allow its OLE object to open for in-place editing, you can set the control's **MiscFlags** property. Here are the possible values for that property:

- **vbOLEMiscFlagMemStorage**—1; causes the control to use memory to store the object while it's loaded.

- **vbOLEMiscFlagDisableInPlace**—2; overrides the control's default behavior of allowing in-place activation for objects that support it.

Using **vbOLEMiscFlagMemStorage** makes data storage operations faster than the default operations (which store data on disk as a temporary file). This setting can, however, use a lot of memory. If an object supports in-place activation, you can use the **vbOLEMiscFlagDisableInPlace** setting to make the object launch its server in a separate window.

Chapter 27

Creating Code Components (OLE Automation)

If you need an immediate solution to:	See page:
Using A Code Component From A Client Application	938
Creating An Object From A Class	940
Using A Code Component's Properties And Methods	942
Creating A Code Component	942
Setting A Code Component's Project Type: In-Process Or Out-Of-Process	945
Adding A Property To A Code Component	946
Adding A **Get/Let** Property To A Code Component	947
Adding A Method To A Code Component	950
Passing Arguments To A Code Component Method	951
Passing Optional Arguments To A Code Component Method	953
Testing A Code Component With A Second Instance Of Visual Basic	954
Creating And Registering An In-Process Code Component	957
Creating And Registering An Out-Of-Process Code Component	958
Using The Class **Initialize** Event	958
Using The Class **Terminate** Event	958
Global Objects: Using Code Components Without Creating An Object	959
Destroying A Code Component Object	960
Using Forms From Code Components	961
Creating Dialog Box Libraries In Code Components	962
Designing Multithreaded In-Process Components	963
Designing Multithreaded Out-Of-Process Components	963

In Depth

You can think of a code component—formerly called *OLE automation servers*—as a library of objects, ready to be used by other applications (called client applications). For example, you might have a terrific routine to sort records that you want to use in a dozen different programs. You can put that routine in a code component, register it with Windows, and then you're free to use the routine in that code component in other programs—just as with an ActiveX control, the other programs can call the code components methods and properties.

A code component is like an ActiveX control or document that doesn't create a visual display in a host application. Code components provide access to methods and properties through code, not a direct graphical user interface (although code components themselves can support a user interface—for example, you might have a library of dialog boxes that form a code component).

In fact, code components are the third part of the standard ActiveX object set (collectively called ActiveX components) that Visual Basic supports: ActiveX controls, ActiveX documents, and code components. You build code components as ActiveX EXEs or ActiveX DLLs, much as you do with ActiveX controls or documents (the difference is that the DLLs are in-process code components, and the EXEs are out-of-process code components).

Code Components: Classes And Objects

When you create a code component, you add code in *class module(s)*, and when you register the code component with Windows, you make the class(es) available to client applications. Those applications, in turn, can add a *reference* to your code component and create an object of the class they want to use with the **New**, **CreateObject**, or other Visual Basic instruction (we'll see in detail how to create objects later in this chapter). When the client application has an object corresponding to one of your classes, it can use that class's properties and methods.

That's how it works—it's all about reusing your code. You get an object corresponding to a class in a code component like this, where we're creating an object, **objCalendar**, of the class **CalendarClass** from the hypothetical code component named **PlannerCodeComponent**:

```
Dim objCalendar As Object
Set objCalendar = CreateObject("PlannerCodeComponent.CalendarClass")
...
```

Then you can use that object's properties and methods to give you access to the code in the class, something like this:

```
Dim objCalendar As Object
Set objCalendar = CreateObject("PlannerCodeComponent.CalendarClass")

objCalendar.Days = 365                        'Use a property
intWorkDays = objCalendar.CalculateWorkDays   'Use a method
...
```

TIP: *In fact, code component objects can themselves contain other objects (called dependent objects), and you create object variables of those types using the code component object's methods.*

If you've created your code component as an ActiveX EXE, that code component is an out-of-process server and runs separately from the client application; if you've created your code component as an ActiveX DLL, that code component is an in-process server, which means it'll run as part of the client application's process.

There's even a way to use code components *without* creating an object. To make it easy to create code components that can be used with desktop tools like the Microsoft Office Suite, Visual Basic allows you to label objects in a code component as *global*, which means they're part of a global object. In practice, this means that you don't have to create an object to use the methods and properties of this code component—you just add a reference to the code component in the client application, and you can use the component's properties and methods as though they were part of the client application.

A client application and an in-process component share the same memory space, so calls to the methods of an in-process code component can use the client's stack to pass arguments. That's not possible for an out-of-process component; there, method arguments must be moved across the memory boundary between the two processes, which is called *marshaling*.

Code Components And Threads

When you start working with another application, as code components do, you share threads of execution with that application in a joint process. As a default, the Microsoft Component Object Model (COM) deals with this situation by *serializing* thread operations. That is, the operations are queued and processed, one at a time, until they all have been completed.

That process is safe, and you don't have to think about it except for performance issues. In a multithreading operating environment, serialization protects single-threaded objects from overlapping client operations. However, serializing single-threaded components also means that operations can be blocked, and can stay blocked for some time, which can be frustrating (especially when short operations are blocked by long ones).

Visual Basic has two ways to avoiding blocked calls: multithreading and **SingleUse** objects.

Multithreading Code Components

You make in-process and out-of-process code components multithreaded by changing their *threading model*. Visual Basic uses its *apartment-model* threading to ensure thread safety when you're working with multiple threads. In apartment-model threading, each thread is like an apartment—all objects created on the thread work in an apartment, and they are not "aware" of the objects in other apartments. This threading model also eliminates conflicts when accessing global data from multiple threads by giving each apartment its own copy of that global data. You can use apartment-model threading without having to eliminate visual elements such as forms and controls, because all such Visual Basic objects are thread-safe.

You can specify the apartment threading model (instead of the single-threaded model) for in-process code components to make them multithreaded. To make out-of-process code components multithreaded, you have two options (both use the apartment thread model): thread pooling and the thread-per-object model. With thread pooling, you can specify how many threads you want available for your code components, and those threads are used in a round-robin way (that is, the first object is created on the first thread in the pool and thread allocation keeps going thread by thread, starting over with the first thread when the others in the pool are used). If you specify the thread-per-object model, each new object is created with its own thread.

SingleUse Code Components

You can also handle serialization conflicts by creating **SingleUse** code components, in which every new object of your code component class creates a new instance of the component. You do this by setting the class's **Instancing** property. The **Instancing** property indicates how you want your class to interact with client applications, if at all. Here are the possible values of that property:

- **Private**—Other applications aren't allowed access to type library information about the class and cannot create instances of it. Private objects are only for use within your component.

- **PublicNotCreatable**—Other applications can use objects of this class only if your component creates the objects first. Other applications cannot use the **CreateObject** function or the **New** operator to create objects from the class.

- **MultiUse**—Other applications are allowed to create objects from the class. One instance of your component can provide any number of objects created in this fashion. An out-of-process component can supply multiple objects to multiple clients; an in-process component can supply multiple objects to the client and to any other components in its process.

- **GlobalMultiUse**—Similar to **MultiUse**, with one addition: properties and methods of the class can be invoked as if they were simply global functions. It's not necessary to explicitly create an instance of the class first, because one will automatically be created.

- **SingleUse**—Other applications are allowed to create objects from the class, but every object of this class that a client creates starts a new instance of your component. Not allowed in ActiveX DLL projects.

- **GlobalSingleUse**—Similar to **SingleUse**, except that properties and methods of the class can be invoked as if they were simply global functions. Not allowed in ActiveX DLL projects.

Overall, then, the reason you use code components is to make it easy to reuse your code in other applications, and we'll see how that works now in the Immediate Solutions section.

Immediate Solutions

Using A Code Component From A Client Application

The Testing Department is on the phone again. Wouldn't it be great to use Microsoft Excel as part of your new program? Maybe, you say. It's easy, they say, just treat Excel as a code component.

You can treat OLE automation servers like Excel as code components, adding them to your program and using them as you like. To do that, you add a reference to the code component to your program, create an object from that code component, then use the properties and methods of that object.

Let's see an example. Here, we'll use Microsoft Excel 7 in a Visual Basic program to add 2 and 2 and display the result in a text box. Start by adding a reference to Excel with the Project|References menu item, selecting the item labeled Microsoft Excel Object Library, and clicking on OK.

After you've added a reference to a code component, you can use the Object browser to take a look at the properties and methods in that component, as in Figure 27.1, where we are examining the Excel code library.

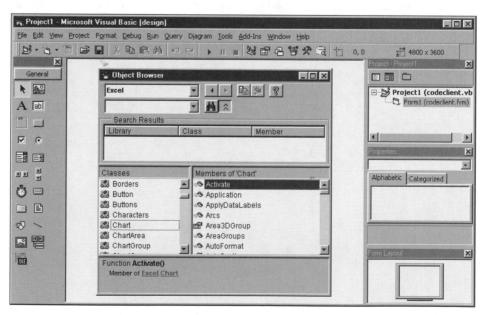

Figure 27.1   Using the Object browser to examine the Microsoft Excel code library.

Add a button, **Command1**, with the caption "Add 2 + 2 using Microsoft Excel" to the program now, as well as a text box, **Text1**, where we can display the results of the addition. When the user clicks the button, we start by creating an object, **objExcel**, from the Excel library (Excel will stay hidden throughout the program) using the Visual Basic **CreateObject** function (for other ways to create an object, see the next topic):

```
Private Sub Command1_Click()
    Dim objExcel As Object
    Set objExcel = CreateObject("Excel.Sheet")
...
```

Now that we have our new object, we can use its properties like this, where we place 2 in both cells (1,1) and (2,1):

```
Private Sub Command1_Click()
    Dim objExcel As Object
    Set objExcel = CreateObject("Excel.Sheet")

    objExcel.Cells(1, 1).Value = "2"
    objExcel.Cells(2, 1).Value = "2"
...
```

To add these values together, we place an Excel formula in the cell beneath these two, cell (3,1) to add those values:

```
Private Sub Command1_Click()
    Dim objExcel As Object
    Set objExcel = CreateObject("Excel.Sheet")

    objExcel.Cells(1, 1).Value = "2"
    objExcel.Cells(2, 1).Value = "2"

    objExcel.Cells(3, 1).Formula = "=R1C1 + R2C1"
...
```

Finally, we display the resulting sum in the text box in our program, **Text1**, and quit Excel like this:

```
Private Sub Command1_Click()
    Dim objExcel As Object
    Set objExcel = CreateObject("Excel.Sheet")

    objExcel.Cells(1, 1).Value = "2"
    objExcel.Cells(2, 1).Value = "2"
```

```
      objExcel.Cells(3, 1).Formula = "=R1C1 + R2C1"
      Text1.Text = "Microsoft Excel says: 2 + 2 = " & objExcel.Cells(3, 1)

      objExcel.Application.Quit
End Sub
```

The result appears in Figure 27.2, where we learn that 2 plus 2 equals 4. Congratulations, you've created your first code component client application. The code for this example is located in the codeclient folder on this book's accompanying CD-ROM.

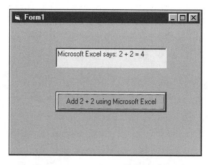

Figure 27.2   Using Microsoft Excel as a code component.

Creating An Object From A Class

When you want to create an object from a code component, you first add a reference to that code component using the Visual Basic Project|References menu item (note that the code component must be registered with Windows, which most applications will do automatically when installed). Next, you create that object in code, and there are three ways to create objects from code components in Visual Basic (we'll use the **CreateObject** technique in this chapter):

- Declaring the variable using the **New** keyword (in statements like **Dim**, **Public**, or **Private**), which means Visual Basic automatically assigns a new object reference the first time you use the variable (for example, when you refer to one of its methods or properties). This technique only works with code components that supply *type libraries* (as the code components created with Visual Basic do). These type libraries specify what's in the code component.

- Assigning a reference to a new object in a **Set** statement by using the **New** keyword or **CreateObject** function.

- Assigning a reference to a new or existing object in a **Set** statement by using the **GetObject** function.

Let's see some examples. Here, we'll assume we've already added a reference to the code component containing the classes we'll work with. If the code component you're using supplies a type library, as the ones built with Visual basic do, you can use the **New** keyword when you declare the object to create it. As an example, here we're creating an object named **objSorter** of the **Sorter** class:

```
Dim objSorter As New Sorter
objSorter.Sort
```

The object is actually only created when you refer to it for the first time.

Whether or not a code component supplies a type library, you can use the **CreateObject** function in a **Set** statement to create a new object and assign an object reference to an object variable. To use **CreateObject**, you pass it the name of the class you want to create an object of. For example, here's how we created a new object named **objExcel** from the Microsoft Excel code component library in the previous topic, using **CreateObject**:

```
Dim objExcel As Object
Set objExcel = CreateObject("Excel.Sheet")
```

Note the way we specify the class name to create the object from—as **Excel.Sheet** (that is, as *CodeComponent.Class*). Because the code components you create with **CreateObject** don't need a type library, you must refer to the class you want to use as *CodeComponent.Class* instead of just by class, as you can with **New**.

You can also use the **GetObject** function to assign a reference to a new class, although it's usually used to assign a reference to an existing object. Here's how you use **GetObject**:

```
Set objectvariable = GetObject([pathname] [, class])
```

Here's what the arguments of this function mean:

- *pathname*—The path to an existing file or an empty string. This argument can be omitted.
- *class*—The name of the class you want to create an object of. If *pathname* is omitted, then *class* is required.

Passing an empty string for the first argument makes **GetObject** work like **CreateObject**, creating a new object of the class whose name is in *class*. For example, here's how we create an object of the class **ExampleClass** in the code component **NewClass** using **GetObject** (once again, we refer to the class we're using as *CodeComponent.Class*):

```
Set objNewClass = GetObject("", "NewClass.ExampleClass")
```

Using A Code Component's Properties And Methods

Now that you've created an object from a code component, how do you use its properties and methods? You access them in the same way you would the properties and methods of intrinsic Visual Basic objects. For example, we created a client application at the beginning of this chapter that created an object, **objExcel**, from the Microsoft Excel library, and then we used that object's properties as you would any Visual Basic property—with the dot operator:

```
Private Sub Command1_Click()
    Dim objExcel As Object
    Set objExcel = CreateObject("Excel.Sheet")

    objExcel.Cells(1, 1).Value = "2"
    objExcel.Cells(2, 1).Value = "2"

    objExcel.Cells(3, 1).Formula = "=R1C1 + R2C1"
    MsgBox "Microsoft Excel says: 2 + 2 = " & objExcel.Cells(3, 1)

    objExcel.Application.Quit
End Sub
```

Creating A Code Component

The Testing Department is on the phone again. The sorting routine you've written is great, but how about making it available to the rest of the company's programmers? Sure, you say, I'll print it out now. Not that way, they say, create a code component.

How do you create a code component? There are two types of code components: in-process components and out-of-process components:

• When you create a code component as an ActiveX DLL, it will run as an in-process component, in the same process as the client application.

- When you create a code component as an ActiveX EXE, it will run as an out-of-process component, in a different process as the client application.

And, as it turns out, there are two ways to create each type of code component in Visual Basic. From the New Project window, you can create an ActiveX DLL or ActiveX EXE by selecting the appropriate icon and clicking on OK, which creates the files you'll need. Or you can set the project type using the Project|Properties menu item in a standard project to convert it to an ActiveX DLL or ActiveX EXE project.

We'll take a look at the second way here, because that will give us some insight into how code components are constructed (to use the shorter method, all you have to do is to click the ActiveX DLL or ActiveX EXE icon in the New Project window). Create a new standard Visual Basic project now, and select the Project|Properties menu item, opening the Project Properties dialog box you see in Figure 27.3.

In this case, we'll name the new project NewClass, so just enter that name in the Project Name field now. In addition, you can't use a form as a startup object in a code component, so select (None) in the Startup Object box, as shown in Figure 27.3. We'll make this example an ActiveX EXE project, so select that type in the Project Type box, as shown in the figure. Now click on OK to close the Project Properties window.

TIP: *You can use **Sub Main** as the startup object in a code component, adding code to that procedure if you wish. For example, you may want to display a form when your code component first loads, in which case you could do that from **Sub Main** (although doing so is not recommended for ActiveX DLLs).*

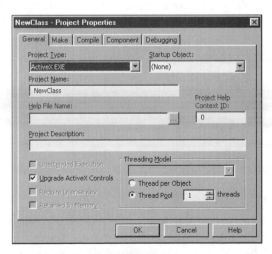

Figure 27.3   The Project Properties dialog box.

Even though we don't have a startup object now, we still have a form, Form1, in our project (which you won't have if you create an ActiveX DLL or EXE project directly from the New Project window), and you can remove that form in your code component projects as you like. We'll leave it in the NewClass project to show how to use forms in code components later in this chapter.

At this point, then, we've created a new code component. However, this new code component doesn't have any classes in it, so we'll add one now. To add a class to our code component, we add a class module. To do that, select the Project|Add Class Module menu item, select the Class Module icon in the Add Class Module dialog box that appears, and click Open.

This creates a new class module and brings us up to exactly where we'd be if we had used the ActiveX EXE icon in the New Project window instead of creating this project ourselves. When you save the new class module in a file, the file will have the extension .cls, for class.

Now set the class module's **Name** property to the name you want to use for your new class—we'll use **ExampleClass** here. That's it—we've created a new class. However, there's not much going on in this class, so we'll add a property, **NewValue**, to the class **ExampleClass** here. To do that, just add this code to the class module:

```
Option Explicit

Public NewValue As Single
...
```

Declaring a variable as **Public** in a class module makes it available as a property to client applications, as we'll see when we discuss properties later in this chapter. To set the value of our new property to, say, 1, we add code to the class's **Initialize** event, which occurs when the code component is first loaded:

```
Option Explicit

Public NewValue As Single

Private Sub Class_Initialize()
    NewValue = 1
End Sub
```

And that's it—we've created a new code component and a new class that supports a property. To make this component available to client applications, just create its EXE file using the Make NewClass.exe item in the File menu, and run that EXE file to register the code component with Windows. We'll see how to put this new code component to work in the following topics in this chapter.

The code for this example, ExampleClass.cls version 1, appears in Listing 27.1. (The final version, version 4, is located in the ExampleClass folder on this book's accompanying CD-ROM.)

Listing 27.1 ExampleClass.cls version 1

```
VERSION 1.0 CLASS
BEGIN
  MultiUse = -1  'True
  Persistable = 0  'NotPersistable
  DataBindingBehavior = 0  'vbNone
  DataSourceBehavior = 0  'vbNone
  MTSTransactionMode = 0  'NotAnMTSObject
END
Attribute VB_Name = "ExampleClass"
Attribute VB_GlobalNameSpace = False
Attribute VB_Creatable = True
Attribute VB_PredeclaredId = False
Attribute VB_Exposed = True
Option Explicit

Public NewValue As Single

Private Sub Class_Initialize()
    NewValue = 1
End Sub
```

Setting A Code Component's Project Type: In-Process Or Out-Of-Process

Setting A Code Component's Project Type: In-Process Or Out-Of-Process

There are two types of code components: in-process components and out-of-process components:

- When you create a code component as an ActiveX DLL, it will run as an in-process component, in the same process as the client application.

- When you create a code component as an ActiveX EXE, it will run as an out-of-process component, in a different process as the client application.

There are advantages to both types. For example, an in-process component can run faster, but an out-of-process component can be self-registering (just run the EXE file to register the component with Windows).

Adding A Property To A Code Component

The Testing Department is on the phone again. Your new code component's class is great, by why doesn't it do anything? How about adding a property to it? Hmm, you think, how does that work?

You can add properties to a class in a code component in two ways: by declaring them as **Public** variables or by using **Let** and **Get** functions. We'll take a look at the first technique here and the second technique in the next topic in this chapter.

The first way of creating properties in a class module is very easy: you just declare the property you want as a **Public** variable in the class module's (General) declarations area. Making a variable public in a class module makes it a property of that module. Besides declaring variables **Public** in a class module, you can also declare them as **Private**, which means they are not available outside the module, and as **Friend**. When you declare variables as **Friend** variables, they are available to the other objects in your code component, but not to client applications (in other words, **Friend** works as a sort of local **Public** declaration).

Let's see an example. In "Creating An Object From A Class" earlier in this chapter, we created a class named **ExampleClass** and added a property to that class—**NewValue**—by simply declaring that property as a public variable:

```
Option Explicit

Public NewValue As Single
...
```

In addition, we initialized the value of that property when the class was first loaded with the **Initialize** event:

```
Option Explicit

Public NewValue As Single

Private Sub Class_Initialize()
    NewValue = 1
End Sub
```

That's one way of adding a property to a class, but note that client applications have full access to this property—they can read it and set it anytime and any way they wish. If you want to restrict access to the values a property can be set to (for example, making sure a **Date** property only holds legal dates), use the property **Get** and **Let** methods covered in the next topic.

TIP: *Setting properties for an out-of-process component can be slow. If your client application sets many properties and then calls a method, it's probably better to pass those values to the method directly rather than setting them as properties.*

Adding A **Get/Let** Property To A Code Component

The Testing Department is on the phone again. Why isn't your new code component safe? Programmers are setting your **DayOfTheMonth** property and then having all kinds of trouble. Well, you say, they shouldn't set it to values greater than 31. It's your job to watch for that, they say.

If you want to have control when client applications set or get the properties in your class's properties, you use **Get** and **Let** methods to let the client application get or set the property. To set up a property with **Get/Let** methods in a class module, open the class module's code window and select the Add Procedure item in the Tools menu, opening the Add Procedure dialog box you see in Figure 27.4. Select the Property option button in the Type box and the Public option button in the Scope box, and click on OK to close the Add Procedure dialog box. This adds the **Get/Let** procedures for this property, and it's up to you to customize them.

Let's see an example. In this case, we'll add a new property, **SafeValue**, to the class named **ExampleClass** that we've developed in the previous few topics in this chapter. This new property will be a **Single** that can only be set to values greater than 0. To add this new property to **ExampleClass**, open that class module's code window and select the Add Procedure item in the Tools menu. Set this property's name to **SafeValue**, as you see in Figure 27.4, select the Property and Public option buttons, as also shown in that figure, and click on OK. When you click on OK, Visual Basic adds two new procedures to the class module for this property:

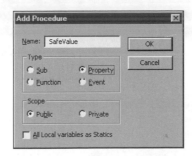

Figure 27.4   The Visual Basic Add Procedure dialog box.

```
Public Property Get SafeValue() As Variant

End Property

Public Property Let SafeValue(ByVal vNewValue As Variant)

End Property
```

When client applications want to get the value in the **SafeValue** property, the **SafeValue Get** procedure is called; when they want to set the value in the **SafeValue** property, the **SafeValue Let** procedure is called.

TIP: *In addition to **Get/Let** procedures, you can even have **Set** procedures, which you use if your property is itself an object. This is a relatively advanced topic, worth looking into only if you want to set up properties that are themselves objects with data members and methods.*

Visual Basic has given this new property the default type of **Variant**, which you can change to the appropriate type for your property. In this case, we'll make **SafeValue** a **Single** value this way:

```
Public Property Get SafeValue() As Single

End Property

Public Property Let SafeValue(ByVal vNewValue As Single)

End Property
```

At this point, we're ready to add code to support the **SafeValue** property. For example, we can store the actual value in this property in an internal variable named, say, **sngInternalSafeValue**:

```
Option Explicit

Public NewValue As Single
Private sngInternalSafeValue As Single
...
```

Now when client applications ask for the value in the **SafeValue** property, we pass back the value in **sngInternalSafeValue:**

```
Public Property Get SafeValue() As Single
    SafeValue = sngInternalSafeValue
End Property
```

On the other hand, if client applications try to set the value in **SafeValue**, we'll check first to make sure that value is greater than 0 before storing it in **sngInternalSafeValue**:

```
Public Property Let SafeValue(ByVal vNewValue As Single)
    If vNewValue > 0 Then
        sngInternalSafeValue = vNewValue
    End If
End Property
```

In this way, we can control what values are stored in the properties in code components. The code for this example, ExampleClass.cls version 2, appears in Listing 27.2. (The final version, version 4, of this code is located in the ExampleClass folder on this book's accompanying CD-ROM.)

TIP: *Setting properties for an out-of-process component can be slow. If your client application sets many properties and then calls a method, it's probably better to pass those values to the method directly rather than setting them as properties.*

Listing 27.2   ExampleClass.cls version 2

```
VERSION 1.0 CLASS
BEGIN
  MultiUse = -1  'True
  Persistable = 0  'NotPersistable
  DataBindingBehavior = 0  'vbNone
  DataSourceBehavior  = 0  'vbNone
  MTSTransactionMode  = 0   'NotAnMTSObject
END
Attribute VB_Name = "ExampleClass"
Attribute VB_GlobalNameSpace = False
Attribute VB_Creatable = True
Attribute VB_PredeclaredId = False
Attribute VB_Exposed = True
Option Explicit

Public NewValue As Single
Private sngInternalSafeValue As Single

Private Sub Class_Initialize()
    NewValue = 1
End Sub

Public Property Get SafeValue() As Single
    SafeValue = sngInternalSafeValue
End Property
```

```
Public Property Let SafeValue(ByVal vNewValue As Single)
    If vNewValue > 0 Then
        sngInternalSafeValue = vNewValue
    End If
End Property
```

Adding A Method To A Code Component

You can add a method to a class in a code component as easily as you add a property. Methods can be either public subroutines or functions, and you can add them to a class module with the Tools menu's Add Procedure item.

Besides declaring procedures **Public** in a class module, you can also declare them as **Private**, which means they are not available outside the module, and as **Friend**. When you declare procedures as **Friend** procedures, they are available to the other objects in your code component, but not to client applications (that is, **Friend** works as a sort of local **Public** declaration).

Let's see an example. Here, we'll add a method to the class named **ExampleClass** that we've been developing in the previous few topics. This new method, **ReturnSaveValue**, will return the value currently in the class's **SafeValue** property. To add this method, open the **ExampleClass**'s code window and select the Tools menu's Add Procedure dialog box. Using that dialog box, add a new public function named **ReturnSafeValue**. When you close the dialog box by clicking on OK, Visual Basic adds this code to the class module:

```
Public Function ReturnSafeValue()

End Function
```

As it stands, this function returns a Variant, so we change that to make it return a value of the same type as the **SafeValue** property, which is **Single**:

```
Public Function ReturnSafeValue() As Single

End Function
```

Now we're ready to write the code for this method, which just returns the value in the **SafeValue** property, and that value is stored in the **sngInternalSafeValue** variable:

```
Public Function ReturnSafeValue() As Single
    ReturnSafeValue = sngInternalSafeValue
End Function
```

And that's all it takes—now we've added a new method to the class named **ExampleClass**.

Passing Arguments To A Code Component Method

You can pass arguments to class methods just as you can to other procedures—just specify an argument list in the method's declaration.

Because of marshaling, certain method arguments should be declared **ByVal** for out-of-process components and **ByRef** for in-process components. When you're declaring methods for objects provided by an out-of-process component, use **ByVal** to declare arguments that will contain object references. In addition, if you expect client applications to pass large strings or **Variant** arrays to a method, and the method does not modify the data, declare the parameter **ByVal** for an out-of-process component, but **ByRef** for an in-process component.

Let's see an example. In this case, we'll add a method named **Addem** to the class named **ExampleClass** that we've developed over the previous few topics. This function will take two integer arguments, add them, and return their sum.

To add this new function, open **ExampleClass**'s code window, and select Add Procedure in the Tools menu, adding a public function named **Addem**:

```
Public Function Addem()

End Function
```

Here, we modify the declaration of the function to indicate that it takes two integers and returns another integer:

```
Public Function Addem(Operand1 As Integer, Operand2 As Integer) As _
    Integer

End Function
```

Finally, we add the two arguments passed to us in **Addem** and return the sum:

```
Public Function Addem(Operand1 As Integer, Operand2 As Integer) As _
    Integer
    Addem = Operand1 + Operand2
End Function
```

And that's all it takes—now we've added a new method to **ExampleClass**, which takes two arguments, adds them, and returns the result. Our arguments example is a success.

The code for this example, ExampleClass.cls version 3, appears in Listing 27.3. (The final version, version 4, is located in the ExampleClass folder on this book's accompanying CD-ROM.)

Listing 27.3   ExampleClass.cls version 3

```
VERSION 1.0 CLASS
BEGIN
  MultiUse = -1  'True
  Persistable = 0  'NotPersistable
  DataBindingBehavior = 0  'vbNone
  DataSourceBehavior  = 0  'vbNone
  MTSTransactionMode  = 0  'NotAnMTSObject
END
Attribute VB_Name = "ExampleClass"
Attribute VB_GlobalNameSpace = False
Attribute VB_Creatable = True
Attribute VB_PredeclaredId = False
Attribute VB_Exposed = True
Option Explicit

Public NewValue As Single
Private sngInternalSafeValue As Single

Private Sub Class_Initialize()
    NewValue = 1
End Sub

Public Property Get SafeValue() As Single
    SafeValue = sngInternalSafeValue
End Property

Public Property Let SafeValue(ByVal vNewValue As Single)
    If vNewValue > 0 Then
        sngInternalSafeValue = vNewValue
    End If
End Property

Public Function ReturnSafeValue() As Single
    ReturnSafeValue = sngInternalSafeValue
End Function
```

```
Public Function Addem(Operand1 As Integer, Operand2 As Integer) As Integer
    Addem = Operand1 + Operand2
End Function
```

Passing Optional Arguments To A Code Component Method

You can set up code component methods to accept *optional* arguments, just as the Windows calls in Chapter 23 did. To make an argument in an argument list optional, you use the Visual Basic **Optional** keyword when declaring a subroutine or function (note that if you declare an argument in an argument list **Optional**, all following arguments must be **Optional** as well).

Let's see an example. Here, we create a hypothetical code component method, a subroutine named **DrawRect**, to draw a rectangle. We pass the width and height to that subroutine, as well as an optional argument to set the rectangle's color. If the programmer using **DrawRect** does not specify a color for the rectangle, we'll make it black.

To start, we declare the subroutine, making the color argument optional:

```
Public Sub DrawRect(intWidth As Integer, intHeight as Integer, Optional_
    lngColor As Long)
...
```

Now we declare a rectangle from some hypothetical type named **RectangleType** and set its width and height from the arguments passed to us:

```
Public Sub DrawRect(intWidth As Integer, intHeight as Integer, Optional_
    lngColor As Long)
    Dim rectangle as New RectangleType

    rectangle.width = intWidth
    rectangle.height = intHeight
...
```

We can also make use of the optional color argument—*if* it was passed to us. You can test if an argument was passed with the **IsMissing** function, allowing us to set the rectangle's color this way if we were passed a color:

```
Public Sub DrawRect(intWidth As Integer, intHeight as Integer, Optional_
    lngColor As Long)
    Dim rectangle as New RectangleType
```

```
        rectangle.width = intWidth
        rectangle.height = intHeight

        If Not IsMissing(lngColor) Then
            rectangle.color = lngColor
    ...
```

On the other hand, if we were not passed a color value for the rectangle, we use black like this for the default color:

```
Public Sub DrawRect(intWidth As Integer, intHeight as Integer, Optional_
    lngColor As Long)
    Dim rectangle as New RectangleType

    rectangle.width = intWidth
    rectangle.height = intHeight

    If Not IsMissing(lngColor) Then
        rectangle.color = lngColor
    Else
        rectangle.color = vbBlack
    End If

End Sub
```

In fact, there's an easier way to specify a default value—you just append "= *DefaultValue*" to the argument in the argument list as in this case, where we make **vbBlack** the default for the **lngColor** argument:

```
Public Sub DrawRect(intWidth As Integer, intHeight As Integer, Optional_
    lngColor As Single = vbBlack)
    Dim rectangle As New RectangleType
...
End Sub
```

That's it—now we've made use of optional arguments in our class methods.

Testing A Code
Component
With A Second
Instance Of
Visual Basic

Testing A Code Component With A Second Instance Of Visual Basic

The Testing Department is on the phone again. Didn't you test your code component before releasing it? You say, *test* it?

You can test a code component while developing it by registering it with Windows temporarily and letting Visual Basic handle all the details. All you have to do is to open the Project|Properties menu item, click the Debugging tab, make sure the option button labeled Wait For components To Be Created is selected, click on OK to close the Properties dialog box, and run the program. This registers your code component with Windows temporarily and makes it available to client applications until you stop the code component execution.

How do you make use of the code component you're testing in a client application? One easy way is to start a second copy of Visual Basic and run the client program there after adding a reference to the code component you're testing. Let's see an example. Here, we'll test the **NewClass** code component that we've developed in the previous few topics in a client application. That project supports a class, **ExampleClass**, which has properties and methods, and we'll put them to use in the client application. Load that code component into Visual Basic, as well as the client application, after setting the debugging options as indicated in the previous paragraph.

Now start a second instance of Visual Basic and begin the new client application (a standard EXE project), which we'll call **ExampleClassApp**, by adding a reference to our code component, **NewClass**, using the Project|References menu item.

Next, we'll create an object of the **ExampleClass** class named, say, **objExample** (make this object a form-wide variable by declaring it in the (General) area):

```
Dim objExample As ExampleClass
```

When the form loads, we create that object using **CreateObject** this way; note the way we specify the class name to create the object from—as **NewClass.ExampleClass** (that is, as *CodeComponent.Class*)—when we use **CreateObject**:

```
Private Sub Form_Load()
    Set objExample = CreateObject("NewClass.ExampleClass")
...
End Sub
```

You can also take care of any needed initialization in the **Form Load** event handler, as in this case, where we set the new object's **SafeValue** property to 3:

```
Private Sub Form_Load()
    Set objExample = CreateObject("NewClass.ExampleClass")
    objExample.SafeValue = 3
End Sub
```

There are two properties and two methods in **ExampleClass**, so we add four command buttons to the client application, as well as a text box, **Text1**, to show the results of testing these properties and methods. When the user clicks **Command1**, we can read and display the value in the **objExample**'s **NewValue** property:

```
Private Sub Command1_Click()
    Text1.Text = "The NewValue property = " objExample.NewValue
End Sub
```

When the user clicks **Command2**, we set the **objExample**'s **SafeValue** (which is supported with **Get** and **Let** methods) to 5 and then display the new value:

```
Private Sub Command2_Click()
    objExample.SafeValue = 5
    Text1.Text = "The SafeValue property was set to 5 and returns: " &_
        objExample.SafeValue
End Sub
```

We'll test the **ReturnSafeValue** method when the user clicks **Command3**. That method takes no parameters and returns the value in the **SafeValue** property:

```
Private Sub Command3_Click()
    Text1.Text = "The ReturnSafeValue method returns: " & _
        objExample.ReturnSafeValue
End Sub
```

Finally, when the user clicks **Command4**, we test the **Addem** method, which adds two numbers, by adding 2 and 2:

```
Private Sub Command4_Click()
    Text1.Text = "Adding 2 + 2 with Addem yields: " & _
        objExample.Addem(2, 2)
End Sub
```

That's all it takes. Now run the client application we've just developed, as shown in Figure 27.5. You can see the client application running in that figure and testing the **ExampleClass**'s properties and methods; behind it is the copy of Visual Basic in which we've developed the client application, and behind that is the copy of Visual Basic in which the code component, **NewClass** (which contains the **ExampleClass** class), is running. Our test is a success. The code for the client application is located in the exampleclassapp folder on this book's accompanying CD-ROM.

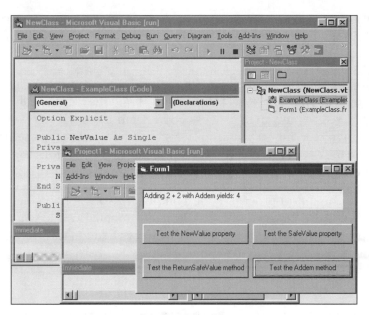

Figure 27.5   Testing a code component by running a second copy of Visual Basic.

Creating And Registering An In-Process Code Component

In the previous topic, we showed how to test code components using two copies of Visual Basic—but how do you create and register the real code component for use in actual client applications? There are two ways to create the actual code component: one if you're creating an in-process code component (an ActiveX DLL), and one if you're creating an out-of-process code component (an ActiveX EXE). We'll take a look at in-process code components here and out-of-process code components in the next topic.

To create the in-process server's DLL file, select the Make *ProjectName*.dll item in the Visual Basic File menu. To register that DLL file with Windows, you use a Windows utility like regsvr32.exe like this:

```
c:\>c:\windows\system\regsvr32 ProjectName.dll
```

You can also let the Package and Deployment Wizard (see Chapter 30) register the DLL file when it's installed.

Creating And Registering An Out-Of-Process Code Component

How do you create and register the real code component for use in actual client applications? There are two ways to create the actual code component: one if you're creating an in-process code component (an ActiveX DLL), and one if you're creating an out-of-process code component (an ActiveX EXE). We took a look at in-process code components in the previous topic, and we'll look at out-of-process code components here.

To create the out-of-process code component's EXE file, select the Make *ProjectName*.exe item in the Visual Basic File menu. How do you register that out-of-process code component with Windows? You just run the EXE file—that's all it takes. You code component is now ready to use.

Using The Class **Initialize** Event

The **Initialize** event occurs when a client application creates an instance of a class, and you can use this event to initialize the object that's being created. No arguments are passed to this event's handler. Here's an example. When we created the class **ExampleClass** in the **NewClass** code component earlier in this chapter, we set up a property named **NewValue** and initialized it to 1 in the **Initialize** event handler like this:

```
Option Explicit

Public NewValue As Single

Private Sub Class_Initialize()
    NewValue = 1
End Sub
```

Using The Class **Terminate** Event

An object's **Terminate** event occurs when the object goes out of scope, or when you set it to the **Nothing** keyword (see "Destroying A Code Component Object" later in this chapter). You can use this event to clean up after the object, such as releasing allocated memory or resources.

Here's an example that you can add to the class **ExampleClass** in the **NewClass** code component developed earlier in this chapter. In this case, we'll use the **Terminate** event to display a message box to the users indicating that the **ExampleClass** object they've created is being terminated:

```
Private Sub Class_Terminate()
    MsgBox "Terminating now!"
End Sub
```

Warning! *If you use the Visual Basic **End** statement in a program, the program is stopped immediately and you won't get a **Terminate** event for any of the program's objects.*

Global Objects: Using Code Components Without Creating An Object

Sometimes it's difficult to create objects from code components in client applications, because the client application doesn't support coding to let you do so. To handle such cases, Visual Basic supports **GlobalMultiUse** code components. After adding one of these code components to a client application, you don't need to create an object before using its properties and methods.

Properties and methods of a **GlobalMultiUse** object (or *global* object) are added to the *global name space* of any project that uses the object. In the client application, then, you can add a reference to the component, and the names of the global object's properties and methods will be recognized globally. You make a code component a **GlobalMultiUse** object with the **Instancing** property.

The **Instancing** property indicates how you want your class to interact with client applications, if at all; here are the possible values of that property:

- **Private**—Other applications aren't allowed access to type library information about the class and cannot create instances of it. Private objects are only for use within your component.

- **PublicNotCreatable**—Other applications can use objects of this class only if your component creates the objects first. Other applications cannot use the **CreateObject** function or the **New** operator to create objects from the class.

- **MultiUse**—Other applications are allowed to create objects from the class. One instance of your component can provide any number of objects created in this fashion. An out-of-process component can supply multiple objects to multiple clients; an in-process component can supply multiple objects to the client and to any other components in its process.

- **GlobalMultiUse**—Similar to **MultiUse**, with one addition: properties and methods of the class can be invoked as if they were simply global functions. It's not necessary to explicitly create an instance of the class first, because one will automatically be created.

- **SingleUse**—Other applications are allowed to create objects from the class, but every object of this class that a client creates starts a new instance of your component. Not allowed in ActiveX DLL projects.

- **GlobalSingleUse**—Similar to **SingleUse**, except that properties and methods of the class can be invoked as if they were simply global functions. Not allowed in ActiveX DLL projects.

Warning!   The properties and methods of a global object only become part of the global name space when the component is used in other projects. Inside the project where you've created the GlobalMultiUse class, objects created from the class are not automatically added to the global space.

Here's an example using a hypothetical nonglobal component named **Calendar**. When you add a reference to that class, you usually have to create an object from it and then can use the object's properties and methods this way:

```
Dim objCalendar As New Calendar

Private Sub cmdCalculateResult_Click()
    Text1.Text = objCalendar.GetDate
End Sub
```

On the other hand, if **Calendar** is a **GlobalMultiUse** component, you just need to add a reference to it and then you can use its properties and methods without creating an object:

```
Private Sub cmdCalculateResult_Click()
    Text1.Text = GetDate
End Sub
```

Destroying A Code Component Object

The Testing Department is on the phone again. The objects created with your new code component are great, but they seem to use up a lot of memory. How can you free that memory?

There are two ways to destroy an object. It's destroyed automatically when it goes out of scope. If you don't want to wait for that to happen, you can just set its variable using the Visual Basic **Nothing** keyword, which destroys the object and releases its memory:

```
Set objBigObject = Nothing
```

Using Forms From Code Components

You can show forms from code component classes just as you would in a standard Visual Basic project—you use the **Show** method:

```
FormName.Show [style [, ownerform]]
```

Here are the arguments for **Show**:

- *style*—Integer that determines if the form is modal (**vbModal** = 1) or modeless (**vbModeless** = 0). (For more on using modeless forms in in-process code components, see the next topic.)

- *ownerform*—String that specifies the component that owns the form you want to show (for instance, you can use the keyword **Me** here).

Forms that you show from code components can support controls in the normal Visual Basic way. Let's see an example. When we created the **NewClass** code component in the beginning of this chapter, we left the default form, Form1, in the project. To show that form, we just add a new method, **ShowForm**, to the **ExampleClass** class in **NewClass**, and we show **Form1** in that method:

```
Public Sub ShowForm()
    Form1.Show
End Sub
```

In addition, we'll add a label with the caption "Code Component Form" in Form1. Now in the client application, we can make use of this new method to show Form1 this way:

```
Private Sub Command5_Click()
    objExample.ShowForm
End Sub
```

The result appears in Figure 27.6. Now we're displaying forms from classes in code components. The final code for this example is located in the ExampleClass folder on this book's accompanying CD-ROM.

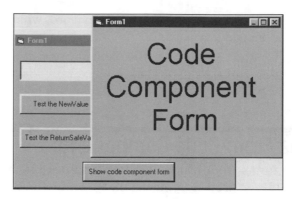

Figure 27.6   Displaying a form from a code component.

Creating Dialog Box Libraries In Code Components

You can use code components to provide libraries of modal and modeless dialog boxes (for more on creating dialog boxes, see Chapter 4). There is one consideration, however, that we should address. It turns out that modeless dialog boxes (that is, dialog boxes that can be open at the same time the user is working in another form) displayed by in-process code components (ActiveX DLLs) cannot work unless they can communicate with the client application's internal message loop. This means that in-process components can only display modeless dialog boxes in client processes that support such communication. You can test if the client application supports this communication by checking the Visual Basic App object's **NonModalAllowed** property.

Let's see an example. Here's some code that might appear in an in-process code component that displays a dialog box. If the application supports access to its message loop, we can show the dialog box, Form1, as modeless by passing the constant **vbModeless** to the **Show** method:

```
Public Sub ShowForm()
    If App.NonModalAllowed Then
        Form1.Show vbModeless
...
```

Otherwise, you should display the dialog box as modal:

```
Public Sub ShowForm()
    If App.NonModalAllowed Then
        Form1.Show vbModeless
    Else
```

```
        Form1.Show vbModal
    End If
End Sub
```

Designing Multithreaded In-Process Components

At the beginning of this chapter, we discussed some thread serialization concerns for code components; in particular, we saw that to avoid blocked threads, you can use multithreaded code components. We'll see how that works for in-process components in this topic and take a look at out-of-process components in the next topic.

To make an in-process code component multithreaded, select the Project| Properties menu item and click the General tab. For ActiveX DLLs, you can select two options in the Threading Model box: Single Threaded or Apartment Threaded. Selecting Apartment Threaded makes the in-process code component multithreaded.

TIP: Set the threading model before you add controls to your project. When you change the threading model for an existing project, errors will occur if the project uses single-threaded ActiveX controls. Visual Basic doesn't allow the use of single-threaded controls in apartment-threaded projects.

Designing Multithreaded Out-Of-Process Components

At the beginning of this chapter, we discussed some thread serialization concerns for code components; in particular, we saw that to avoid blocked threads, you can use multithreaded code components. We saw how that worked for in-process components in the previous topic. In this topic, we'll take a look at out-of-process components.

To make an out-of-process code component multithreaded, select the Project|Properties menu item and click the General tab. For ActiveX EXEs, you can select two options in the Threading Model box: Thread Per Object or Thread Pool.

To make the project multithreaded, you can specify that each new object is created on a new thread with the Thread Per Object option, or you can limit your component to a fixed pool of threads by setting up a thread pool. A thread pool size of 1 makes the out-of-process code component single-threaded, whereas a larger thread pool makes the project apartment-threaded.

TIP: *Set the threading model before you add controls to your project. When you change the threading model for an existing project, errors will occur if the project uses single-threaded ActiveX controls. Visual Basic doesn't allow the use of single-threaded controls in apartment-threaded projects.*

Chapter 28

Advanced Form, Control, And Windows Registry Handling

If you need an immediate solution to:	See page:
Passing Controls To Procedures	970
Passing Control Arrays To Procedures	970
Determining The Active Control	971
Determining Control Type At Runtime	972
Creating/Loading New Controls At Runtime	973
Changing Control Tab Order	975
Changing Control Stacking Position With Z-Order	976
Drag/Drop: Dragging Controls	976
Drag/Drop: Dropping Controls	978
Handling "Self-Drops" When Dragging And Dropping	981
Drag/Drop: Handling **DragOver** Events	982
OLE Drag/Drop: Dragging Data	983
OLE Drag/Drop: Dropping Data	986
OLE Drag/Drop: Reporting The Drag/Drop Outcome	989
Using The Lightweight Controls	990
Passing Forms To Procedures	992
Determining The Active Form	992
Using The Form Object's **Controls** Collection	993
Using the **Forms** Collection	994
Setting A Form's Startup Position	995
Keeping A Form's Icon Out Of The Windows 95 Taskbar	995
Handling Keystrokes In A Form Before Controls Read Them	995
Making A Form Immovable	996

(continued)

If you need an immediate solution to:	See page:
Showing Modal Forms	996
Saving Values In The Windows Registry	997
Getting Values From The Windows Registry	997
Getting All Registry Settings	999
Deleting A Registry Setting	999

In Depth

This is our chapter on advanced form and control techniques—and working with the Windows Registry. We'll see many new techniques here, including dragging and dropping controls (and even how to drag and drop the data in controls, using OLE drag and drop). Programmers are often surprised when an advanced technique doesn't work in the same way that a basic technique does in Visual Basic. For example, a programmer might want to pass a control array to a procedure—and immediately run into problems because that process doesn't work the same way as passing a normal array to a procedure. Here's how you pass a normal array to a procedure; first, you set up the array this way where we set up an integer array named **intArray**:

```
Private Sub Form_Load()
    Dim intArray(4) As Integer
    intArray(0) = 0
    intArray(1) = 1
    intArray(2) = 2
    intArray(3) = 3
    intArray(4) = 4
...
```

Then you pass the array to a procedure named, say, **ShowValues**, by specifying the name of the array with empty parentheses:

```
Private Sub Form_Load()
    Dim intArray(4) As Integer
    intArray(0) = 0
    intArray(1) = 1
    intArray(2) = 2
    intArray(3) = 3
    intArray(4) = 4
    ShowValues intArray()
End Sub
```

In the procedure, you can work with the passed array as a normal array like this:

```
Private Sub ShowValues(TargetArray() As Integer)
    For Each intValue In TargetArray
```

```
        MsgBox intValue
    Next
End Sub
```

Extrapolating the preceding technique to control arrays, you might think that you'd pass a control array to a procedure in the same way. For example, if you had an array of command buttons named **CommandArray**, you might think you can pass it to a procedure, **SetCaption**, like this:

```
Private Sub Form_Load()
    SetCaption CommandArray()
End Sub
```

In the **SetCaption** procedure, you'd want to work with the control array as with a normal array, as in this case where we change the caption of each button to "Button":

```
Private Sub SetCaption(TargetControl() As Control)
    For Each ButtonObject In TargetControl
        ButtonObject.Caption = "Button"
    Next
End Sub
```

However, it doesn't work like that—in many ways, control arrays are really treated in Visual Basic like objects, not normal arrays. What that means here is that you have to pass the control array as an object (without the parentheses), like this:

```
Private Sub Form_Load()
    SetCaption CommandArray
End Sub
```

Then in the procedure, you declare the control array as an **Object**, not as an array of type **Control**. However, you can treat it as an array like this:

```
Private Sub SetCaption(TargetControl As Object)
    For Each ButtonObject In TargetControl
        ButtonObject.Caption = "Button"
    Next
End Sub
```

This is the kind of technique we'll take a look at in this chapter—programming topics that might cause trouble unless you know the ins and outs of the situation. In addition, we'll take a look at two other broad programming areas: dragging and dropping controls, and working with the Windows Registry.

Drag And Drop And OLE Drag And Drop

One of the techniques we'll take a look at is *dragging and dropping* controls. We've seen this technique in a few places in the book already, but we'll make our examination of this topic systematic in this chapter. We'll see how to let the user drag and drop controls using the mouse. Users have only to press the mouse button over a control to start the process, and they can drag and drop controls in our applications as they like. This ability allows them to customize those applications.

Besides dragging and dropping controls in an application, it's recently become popular to be able to drag data *between* applications. We'll see how to do that here with *OLE drag* operations, which will let us drag data between the controls in our application, or to another application entirely; for example, we'll see how to let the user drag text directly from a text box in our program to another text box—or to a word processor like Microsoft Word.

The Windows Registry

Another popular aspect of Windows programming these days is the Windows Registry, a built-in part of Windows that provides long-term storage for program settings. For example, you can save the file names the user has most recently opened in a Most Recently Used (MRU) list at the bottom of the File menu. You can also store other settings for the program, such as window size and location, and use them when the program starts again.

That's it for the overview of what's in this chapter—now it's time to turn to the Immediate Solutions section for advanced form, control, and Windows Registry handling.

Immediate Solutions

Passing Controls To Procedures

One easy way to handle a large number of controls is to set up a procedure that handles the controls in a generic way and pass the controls to that procedure. How do you pass a control to a procedure? You just declare it as type **Control** in the argument list of the procedure you're passing it to.

Let's see an example. Here, we'll pass a command button, **Command1**, to a procedure, **SetCaption**, to set that button's caption to "Button" when the form containing the button first loads:

```
Private Sub Form_Load()
    SetCaption Command1
End Sub
```

In the **SetCaption** procedure, you declare the passed button as type **Control**:

```
Private Sub SetCaption(TargetControl As Control)
    TargetControl.Caption = "Button"
End Sub
```

And that's it—now we're passing controls to procedures.

Passing Control Arrays To Procedures

It's reasonable to think that control arrays are really arrays, but in fact, you sometimes have to treat them as objects, not arrays (which is why you can create event handlers for control arrays—something you certainly couldn't do if they were just Visual Basic arrays). For example, when you want to pass a control array to a procedure, you pass it as an **Object**, not an array of type **Control**.

Let's see an example. Here, we pass a control array of buttons, **CommandArray**, to a procedure, **SetCaption** (note that you omit the empty parentheses after **CommandArray**, which you would include if that array were a normal array and not a control array):

```
Private Sub Form_Load()
    SetCaption CommandArray
End Sub
```

Now in **SetCaption**, we declare the passed array as type **Object**:

```
Private Sub SetCaption(TargetControl As Object)

End Sub
```

Then we can use the passed control array as we would any control array; here we set the caption of each command button in the array to "Button":

```
Private Sub SetCaption(TargetControl As Object)
    For Each ButtonObject In TargetControl
        ButtonObject.Caption = "Button"
    Next
End Sub
```

That's it—now we can pass control arrays to procedures.

Determining The Active Control

The Testing Department is on the phone again. How about letting the user customize your program by clicking a control and then selecting a menu item to, say, set the control's background color? Well, you say, how do I know which control the user has clicked before using the menu item? Use the **ActiveControl** property, they say.

The **ActiveControl** property of forms indicates which control on the form is currently active. Using this property, you can determine which control currently has the focus.

TIP: *Besides forms, the Screen object also has an **ActiveControl** property, so if you have a number of forms, you can determine the active control with the Screen object's **ActiveControl** property.*

Let's see an example. In this case, when the user clicks the form, we'll set the active control's **Caption** property to "Active Control":

```
Private Sub Form_Click()
    ActiveControl.Caption = "Active Control"
End Sub
```

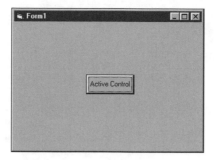

Figure 28.1   Indicating the active control in a form.

The result of this code appears in Figure 28.1, where we indicate the active control when the user clicks the form.

There's a problem with this code, however—the form might contain all kinds of controls, some of which (like text boxes) don't even have a **Caption** property. If the user clicks the form when one of those controls is the active control, an error will result. To fix this potential problem, we can check the type of the active control before working with it, and we'll see how to do that in the next topic.

*Determining
Control Type
At Runtime*

Determining Control Type At Runtime

In the previous topic, we set the caption of the currently active control (that is, the control with the focus) to "Active Control" when the user clicked the form, but realized there was a problem if the active control was one that didn't have a **Caption** property.

To determine what type of control you're working with at runtime, you can use **TypeOf** keyword, which you can use to determine the type of any object. At first, it seems odd that you might not know what kind of control you're working with, but cases like the current one—where we're using the control now stored in the form's **ActiveControl** property—are very common in Visual Basic programming.

In the previous topic, we set the caption of the active control when the user clicked the form like this:

```
Private Sub Form_Click()
    ActiveControl.Caption = "Active Control"
End Sub
```

Now we can add code to check the active control's type (possible types for Visual Basic controls include **CommandButton**, **CheckBox**, **ListBox**, **OptionButton**, **HScrollBar**, **VScrollBar**, **ComboBox**, **Frame**, **PictureBox**, **Label**, **TextBox**, and so on) this way, making sure the active control is a command button before changing its caption:

```
Private Sub Form_Click()
    If TypeOf ActiveControl Is CommandButton Then
        ActiveControl.Caption = "Active Control"
    End If
End Sub
```

Creating/Loading New Controls At Runtime

The Testing Department is on the phone again. Your program, *SuperDuperData-Crunch*, just doesn't have enough buttons to please some users. You ask, how's that again? Let's add some way to let the user create new buttons at runtime, they say.

To load new controls at runtime, you must have a control array. This makes a lot of sense, actually, because you can set up event handlers for the controls in a control array, and a new control just represents a new index in such an event handler. If you didn't have a control array, you'd need to set up an event handler for the new control that named the new control by name—before it existed—which the Visual Basic compiler couldn't do.

When you have a control array, you just use the **Load** statement:

```
Load object
```

In this case, *object* is the new control in the control array. Let's see an example. Here, we'll place four buttons in a form and add a fifth when the user clicks the form. When the user does click the form, we should add a new button, and we start that process by calculating the index for the new control in the control array. That new control's index, which we'll call **intNextIndex**, is the index after the current end of the control array, and we determine that with the **Ubound** property:

```
Private Sub Form_Click()
    Dim intNextIndex As Integer

    intNextIndex = CommandArray.UBound + 1
    ...
```

Then we use the **Load** statement to create this new control:

```
Private Sub Form_Click()
    Dim intNextIndex As Integer

    intNextIndex = CommandArray.UBound + 1
    Load CommandArray(intNextIndex)
...
```

Controls are originally loaded as invisible (in case you want to work with it off screen first), so we make our new button visible by setting its **Visible** property to True:

```
Private Sub Form_Click()
    Dim intNextIndex As Integer

    intNextIndex = CommandArray.UBound + 1
    Load CommandArray(intNextIndex)
    CommandArray(intNextIndex).Visible = True
...
```

Now we can treat this new button as any other button; here, we set its caption to "New button" and place it in the center of the form this way:

```
Private Sub Form_Click()
    Dim intNextIndex As Integer

    intNextIndex = CommandArray.UBound + 1
    Load CommandArray(intNextIndex)
    CommandArray(intNextIndex).Visible = True
    CommandArray(intNextIndex).Caption = "New button"
    CommandArray(intNextIndex).Move ScaleWidth / 2 - _
        CommandArray(intNextIndex).Width / 2, ScaleHeight / 2 - _
        CommandArray(intNextIndex).Height / 2
End Sub
```

In addition, we can handle events from the new button in the event handler for the whole button array, because the index of the control that caused the event is passed to us in that event handler:

```
Private Sub CommandArray_Click(Index As Integer)
    MsgBox "You clicked button " & Index
End Sub
```

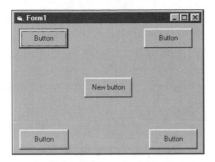

Figure 28.2   Adding a new control to a form at runtime.

The result of this code appears in Figure 28.2, where we've added a new button by just clicking the form. The code for this example is located in the loadcontrols folder on this book's accompanying CD-ROM.

Changing Control Tab Order

The Testing Department is calling again. About the keyboard interface you've set up for your program, *SuperDuperDataCrunch*—can't you let the user customize the tab order for the controls? Sure, you say, what's tab order? They explain, that's the order in which the focus moves from control to control when the user presses the Tab button.

Each control that can accept the focus has a **TabIndex** property, and when the user presses the Tab key, the focus moves from control to control, following the tab order as set by the control's **TabIndex** properties. (The first control in the tab order has **TabIndex** = 0.) You can change the tab order at runtime by changing the value in your controls' **TabIndex** properties.

Let's see an example. Here, we add three buttons to a form, **Command1**, **Command2**, and **Command3**, which, by default, have the **TabIndex** properties 0, 1, and 2, respectively. To change that tab order when the user clicks the form, we can use buttons' **TabIndex** properties like this, where we reverse the tab order:

```
Private Sub Form_Click()
    Command1.TabIndex = 2
    Command2.TabIndex = 1
    Command3.TabIndex = 0
End Sub
```

Changing Control Stacking Position With Z-Order

The Aesthetic Design Department is on the phone. It takes an awfully long time to load and change pictures of the company's founders in that large picture box you have in your program: isn't there a better way?

There is. Instead of loading the images into a picture box when needed, you can place a number of picture boxes on top of each other and display them one at a time by setting the picture boxes' *Z-order*. Z-order is the stacking order for controls, and you can set controls' Z-orders with the **ZOrder** method:

```
Control.ZOrder position
```

The *position* argument is an integer that indicates the position of the control relative to other controls of the same type. If *position* is 0 or omitted, *Control* is placed at the front of the Z-order, on top of the other controls. If *position* is 1, *Control* is placed at the back of the Z-order.

Let's see an example. Here, we place two picture boxes, **Picture1** and **Picture2**, in a form, with **Picture2** on top of **Picture1**. When the user clicks the form, we can move **Picture1** to the top with the **ZOrder** method:

```
Private Sub Form_Click()
    Picture1.ZOrder 0
End Sub
```

Drag/Drop: Dragging Controls

The Aesthetic Design Department is on the phone again. There are still some customization issues with your program, *SuperDuperDataCrunch*. Can't you let the users drag all the controls and place them where they want? Hmm, you say, how does that work?

To enable a control for drag operations, make sure its **DragMode** property is set to **Manual** (= 0, the default), not **Automatic** (= 1); when **DragMode** is manual, we can handle drag operations from code. When the user presses the mouse in a control, you can start a drag operation with the **Drag** method:

```
Control.Drag action
```

Here, the *action* argument can take these values:

• **vbCancel**—0; cancels the drag operation.

- **vbBeginDrag**—1; begins dragging the control.
- **vbEndDrag**–2; ends the drag operation.

The user can then drag the control to a new position on the form and release it, causing a **DragDrop** event in the form, and you can move the control in that event. Here, the control that's been dropped is passed in the **Source** argument, and the position of the mouse is passed as (**X, Y**):

```
Private Sub Form_DragDrop(Source As Control, X As Single, Y As Single)

End Sub
```

Let's see an example. In this case, we'll add six text boxes to a form in a control array named **Textboxes**, and when the form first loads, we display the text "Drag me" in each text box:

```
Private Sub Form_Load()
    For Each objText In Textboxes
        objText.Text = "Drag me"
    Next
End Sub
```

We also add a **MouseDown** event handler to the text box control array so we can start the dragging operation when the user presses the mouse button in the control:

```
Private Sub Textboxes_MouseDown(Index As Integer, Button As Integer, Shift _
    As Integer, X As Single, Y As Single)

End Sub
```

When the user drops the control, we'll be given the location of the mouse in the form, but to position the control correctly, we also need the original position of the mouse in the control. That is, if the user pressed the mouse button in the middle of the control, we need to move the middle of the control (not the control's origin, the upper-left corner) to the new mouse location. Therefore, we need to save the mouse's original location in the control when the user presses the mouse button. We'll save the mouse's original location in two integers, **intXOffset** and **intYOffset**, making these form-wide variables:

```
Dim intXOffset, intYOffset As Integer
```

Here's how we save those integers and start the drag operation with the **Drag** method:

```
Private Sub Textboxes_MouseDown(Index As Integer, Button As Integer, Shift _
    As Integer, X As Single, Y As Single)
    intXOffset = X
    intYOffset = Y
    Textboxes(Index).Drag vbBeginDrag
End Sub
```

Now the user is dragging the control—and we'll see how to let the user drop it in the next topic.

Drag/Drop: Dropping Controls

When the user drops a control on a form, you get a **DragDrop** event:

```
Private Sub Form_DragDrop(Source As Control, X As Single, Y As Single)

End Sub
```

Here, the control that's been dropped is passed in the **Source** argument, and the position of the mouse is passed as (**X, Y**). You can use the control's **Move** method to move the control to the new position.

Let's see an example. In the previous topic, we let users drag a text box in a form. When they drop it, we'll get a **DragDrop** event in the form and can move the text box to the new location—after taking into account the original mouse position in the control with the x and y offsets, **intXOffset** and **intYOffset**:

```
Dim intXOffset, intYOffset As Integer

Private Sub Form_Load()
    For Each objText In Textboxes
        objText.Text = "Drag me"
    Next
End Sub

Private Sub Textboxes_MouseDown(Index As Integer, Button As Integer, Shift _
    As Integer, X As Single, Y As Single)
    intXOffset = X
    intYOffset = Y
    Textboxes(Index).Drag vbBeginDrag
End Sub

Private Sub Form_DragDrop(Source As Control, X As Single, Y As Single)
    Source.Move X - intXOffset, Y - intYOffset
End Sub
```

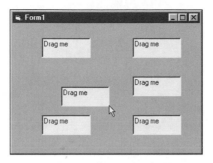

Figure 28.3   Dragging and dropping controls in a form.

And that's all it takes—now you can drag and drop controls in a form, as shown in Figure 28.3.

However, there's a problem here. When you move a text box to an entirely new location in the form, the drag/drop operation goes smoothly. However, if you drag the text box just a short distance, that text box jumps back to its original position when you release it—what's going on?

Here's what's happening: if you drag the text box just a short distance and drop it, Visual Basic thinks you're dropping it on itself, and instead of triggering a form **DragDrop** event, it triggers a **DragDrop** event for the text box itself. To complete our drag/drop example, we'll take care of this "self-drop" problem in the next topic.

The code for this example, dragcontrols.frm version 1, appears in Listing 28.1. (Version 2, which is located in the dragcontrols folder on this book's accompanying CD-ROM, will take care of the "self-drop" problem.)

Listing 28.1   dragcontrols.frm version 1

```
VERSION 6.00
Begin VB.Form Form1
   Caption         =    "Form1"
   ClientHeight    =    3195
   ClientLeft      =    60
   ClientTop       =    345
   ClientWidth     =    4680
   LinkTopic       =    "Form1"
   ScaleHeight     =    3195
   ScaleWidth      =    4680
   StartUpPosition =    3   'Windows Default
   Begin VB.TextBox Textboxes
      Height       =    495
      Index        =    5
      Left         =    1920
      TabIndex     =    5
```

```
         Top             =    1920
         Width           =    1215
      End
      Begin VB.TextBox Textboxes
         Height          =    495
         Index           =    4
         Left            =    1920
         TabIndex        =    4
         Top             =    1200
         Width           =    1215
      End
      Begin VB.TextBox Textboxes
         Height          =    495
         Index           =    3
         Left            =    1920
         TabIndex        =    3
         Top             =    240
         Width           =    1215
      End
      Begin VB.TextBox Textboxes
         Height          =    495
         Index           =    2
         Left            =    360
         TabIndex        =    2
         Top             =    1920
         Width           =    1215
      End
      Begin VB.TextBox Textboxes
         Height          =    495
         Index           =    1
         Left            =    360
         TabIndex        =    1
         Top             =    1080
         Width           =    1215
      End
      Begin VB.TextBox Textboxes
         Height          =    495
         Index           =    0
         Left            =    360
         TabIndex        =    0
         Top             =    240
         Width           =    1215
      End
   End
End
Attribute VB_Name = "Form1"
Attribute VB_GlobalNameSpace = False
Attribute VB_Creatable = False
```

```
Attribute VB_PredeclaredId = True
Attribute VB_Exposed = False
Dim intXOffset, intYOffset As Integer

Private Sub Form_Load()
    For Each objText In Textboxes
        objText.Text = "Drag me"
    Next
End Sub

Private Sub Textboxes_MouseDown(Index As Integer, Button As Integer,_
    Shift As Integer, X As Single, Y As Single)
    intXOffset = X
    intYOffset = Y
    Textboxes(Index).Drag vbBeginDrag
End Sub

Private Sub Form_DragDrop(Source As Control, X As Single, Y As Single)
    Source.Move X - intXOffset, Y - intYOffset
End Sub
```

Handling "Self-Drops" When Dragging And Dropping

In the previous two topics, we handled drag/drop operations for controls in a form, but there was a problem. If the user doesn't move a control very far, we get a **DragDrop** event for the control itself, because Visual Basic acts as though the user is dropping the control on itself, not on the form. We can handle this case by adding a **DragDrop** event handler to the control itself.

Let's see how this works in an example. We'll add a **DragDrop** event handler for the text boxes in the previous example, the dragcontrols project:

```
Dim intXOffset, intYOffset As Integer
...
Private Sub Form_DragDrop(Source As Control, X As Single, Y As Single)
    Source.Move X - intXOffset, Y - intYOffset
End Sub

Private Sub TextBoxes_DragDrop(Index As Integer, Source As Control, X As_
    Single, Y As Single)
...
End Sub
```

Now when the user drags a control a little way and drops it on top of itself, we can move the control to its new position. Note that we are passed mouse coordinates local to the control in the **DragDrop** event and have to translate them to form-based coordinates to use the **Move** method:

```
Dim intXOffset, intYOffset As Integer
...
Private Sub Form_DragDrop(Source As Control, X As Single, Y As Single)
    Source.Move X - intXOffset, Y - intYOffset
End Sub

Private Sub TextBoxes_DragDrop(Index As Integer, Source As Control, X As_
    Single, Y As Single)
    Source.Move X + Textboxes(Index).Left - intXOffset, Y + _
        Textboxes(Index).Top - intYOffset
End Sub
```

That's all it takes—now users can move the text boxes in the dragcontrols example around as they like. The code for this example is located in the dragcontrols folder on this book's accompanying CD-ROM.

Drag/Drop: Handling **DragOver** Events

When the user drags a control over a form or control, a **DragOver** event is triggered like this:

```
Sub Form_DragOver(source As Control, x As Single, y As Single, state As_
    Integer)
```

Here are the arguments this event handler is passed:

- *source*—The control being dragged.

- *x, y*—Position of the mouse in the target form or control. These coordinates are set in terms of the target's coordinate system (as set by the **ScaleHeight**, **ScaleWidth**, **ScaleLeft**, and **ScaleTop** properties).

- *state*—The transition state of the control being dragged in relation to a target form or control: **Enter** = 0, source control is being dragged into the target; **Leave** = 1, source control is being dragged out of the target; **Over** = 2, source control has moved in the target.

Let's see an example. Here, we'll turn the text boxes in the dragcontrols example that we've developed in the previous few topics blue as the user drags a control over them. To do that, we add a **DragOver** event to the text boxes in the **Textboxes** control array:

```
Private Sub Textboxes_DragOver(Index As Integer, Source As Control, X As _
    Single, Y As Single, State As Integer)

End Sub
```

Here, we simply add code to turn the text box blue when we drag another control over it:

```
Private Sub Textboxes_DragOver(Index As Integer, Source As Control, X As _
    Single, Y As Single, State As Integer)
    Textboxes(Index).BackColor = RGB(0, 0, 255)
End Sub
```

And that's it—now we're handling **DragOver** events, as shown in Figure 28.4.

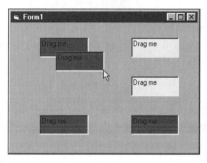

Figure 28.4   Handling DragOver events.

OLE Drag/Drop: Dragging Data

The Testing Department is on the phone again. A lot of new word processors are allowing users to drag data from application to application—how about your new *SuperDuperTextPro* program? It's not possible, you say. Yes it is, they say, use OLE drag/drop.

In OLE drag/drop operations, you can let the user drag data between controls, and even between programs. Here's how it works: when the user presses the mouse button, you start the OLE drag operation with the **OLEDrag** method (this method has no parameters). This causes an **OLEStartDrag** event, and you are passed an object of type DataObject in that event's handler. You use that object's **SetData** method to set the data you want the user to drag:

```
DataObject.SetData [data], [format]
```

Here, *data* is a variant that holds the data you want the user to drag, and *format* indicates the data format, which can be one of these values:

- **vbCFText**—1; text (TXT) files
- **vbCFBitmap**—2; bitmap (BMP) files
- **vbCFMetafile**—3; Windows metafile (WMF) files
- **vbCFEMetafile**—14; enhanced metafile (EMF) files
- **vbCFDIB**—8; device-independent bitmap (DIB)
- **vbCFPalette**—9; color palette
- **vbCFFiles**—15; list of files
- **vbCFRTF**—16639; Rich Text Format (RTF) files

You're also passed a parameter named **AllowedEffects** in the **OLEStartDrag** event's handler, and you need to set that parameter to one of the following values:

- **vbDropEffectNone**—0; drop target cannot accept the data.
- **vbDropEffectCopy**—1; drop results in a copy of data from the source to the target. (Note that the original data is unaltered by the drag operation.)
- **vbDropEffectMove**—2; drop results in data being moved from drag source to drop source. (Note that the drag source should remove the data from itself after the move.)

When the user drops the data onto an appropriate target, which is a form or control with its **OLEDropMode** property set to **Manual** (= 1), an **OLEDragDrop** event occurs, and you are passed a DataObject in that event's handler. To get the dragged data, you use the DataObject's **GetData** method:

```
DataObject.GetData (format)
```

The *format* parameter here may be set to the same values as the *format* parameter for **SetData**. Let's see an example. In this case, we'll add two text boxes, **Text1** and **Text2**, to a form, and let the user drag the text from **Text1** to **Text2**. We start at design time by placing the text "OLE Drag!" into **Text1** so the user will have something to drag when the program runs.

TIP: *The user will also be able to drag the text from* **Text1** *to any OLE-drag-enabled word processor, like Microsoft Word.*

When the user presses the mouse button in **Text1**, then, we start the OLE drag/drop operation with the **OLEDrag** method:

```
Private Sub Text1_MouseDown(Button As Integer, Shift As Integer, X As _
    Single, Y As Single)

    Text1.OLEDrag

End Sub
```

This triggers an **OLEStartDrag** event for **Text1**:

```
Private Sub Text1_OLEStartDrag(Data As DataObject, AllowedEffects As Long)

End Sub
```

Here, we'll let the user drag the text from the text box **Text1**, and we do that by placing that text into the data object passed to us in the **OLEStartDrag** event handler:

```
Private Sub Text1_OLEStartDrag(Data As DataObject, AllowedEffects As Long)

    Data.SetData Text1.Text, vbCFText
...
End Sub
```

We also must set the **AllowedEffects** parameter to the OLE drag/drop operations we'll allow:

```
Private Sub Text1_OLEStartDrag(Data As DataObject, AllowedEffects As Long)

    Data.SetData Text1.Text, vbCFText
    AllowedEffects = vbDropEffectMove

End Sub
```

And that's it—now users can drag the text from the text box. To let them drop that text in the other text box, **Text2**, we'll enable that text box for OLE drops in the next topic.

OLE Drag/Drop: Dropping Data

The testing department is on the phone again. It's fine that you've allowed users to drag data from controls in your program, but how about letting them *drop* that data as well? Coming right up, you say.

To let users drop OLE data, you use the **OLEDragDrop** event (this event occurs only if the object's **OLEDropMode** property is set to **Manual** = 1):

```
Sub object_OLEDragDrop(data As DataObject, effect As Long, _
    button As Integer, shift As Integer, x As Single, y As Single)
```

Here are the parameters passed to this event handler:

- *data*—A DataObject object containing data in formats that the source will provide.

- *effect*—A Long integer set by the target component identifying the action that has been performed, if any. This allows the source to take appropriate action if the component was moved. See the next list for the possible settings.

- *button*—An integer that gives the mouse button state. If the left mouse button is down, *button* will be 1; if the right button is down, *button* will be 2; and if the middle button is down, *button* will be 4. These values add if more than one button is down.

- *shift*—An integer that gives the state of the Shift, Ctrl, and Alt keys when they are depressed. If the Shift key is pressed, *shift* will be 1; for the Ctrl key, *shift* will be 2; and for the Alt key, *shift* will be 4. These values add if more than one key is down.

- *x, y*—The current location of the mouse pointer. The x and y values are in terms of the coordinate system set by the object (in other words, using the **ScaleHeight**, **ScaleWidth**, **ScaleLeft**, and **ScaleTop** properties).

Here are the possible values for the *effect* parameter:

- **vbDropEffectNone**—0; drop target cannot accept the data.

- **vbDropEffectCopy**—1; drop results in a copy of data from the source to the target. (Note that the original data is unaltered by the drag operation.)

- **vbDropEffectMove**—2; drop results in data being moved from drag source to drop source. (Note that the drag source should remove the data from itself after the move.)

To get the dragged data in the **OLEDragDrop** event, you use the DataObject's **GetData** method, which returns the data stored in the format you've selected, if there is any:

```
DataObject.GetData (format)
```

The *format* parameter here indicates the data format and may be set to one of these values:

- **vbCFText**—1; text (TXT) files
- **vbCFBitmap**—2; bitmap (BMP) files
- **vbCFMetafile**—3; Windows metafile (WMF) files
- **vbCFEMetafile**—14; enhanced metafile (EMF) files
- **vbCFDIB**—8; device independent bitmap (DIB)
- **vbCFPalette**—9; color palette
- **vbCFFiles**—15; list of files
- **vbCFRTF**—16639; Rich Text Format (RTF) files

Let's see an example. In the previous topic, we've allowed the user to drag the text from a text box, **Text1**, to another text box, **Text2**, whose **OLEDropMode** property is set to **Manual** = 1. To place the dropped data into **Text2**, we just add a call to **GetData** to that text box's **OLEDragDrop** event handler:

```
Private Sub Text1_MouseDown(Button As Integer, Shift As Integer, X As _
    Single, Y As Single)

    Text1.OLEDrag

End Sub


Private Sub Text1_OLECompleteDrag(Effect As Long)
    MsgBox "Returned OLE effect: " & Effect
End Sub

Private Sub Text1_OLEStartDrag(Data As DataObject, AllowedEffects As Long)

    Data.SetData Text1.Text, vbCFText
    AllowedEffects = vbDropEffectMove

End Sub
```

```
Private Sub Text2_OLEDragDrop(Data As DataObject, Effect As Long, _
    Button As Integer, Shift As Integer, X As Single, Y As Single)
    Text2.Text = Data.GetData(vbCFText)
End Sub
```

And that's it—now run the program, as shown in Figure 28.5. When you do, you can drag the text from the text box on the left, **Text1**, to the text box on the right, **Text2**, as shown in that figure. Our OLE drag/drop example is a success.

The code for this example, oledrag.frm version 1, appears in Listing 28.2 (version 2, which is located on in the oledrag folder on this book's accompanying CD-ROM, will report back to **Text1** what happened when **Text2** accepted the data).

Listing 28.2   oledrag.frm version 1

```
VERSION 6.00
Begin VB.Form Form1
    Caption         =   "Form1"
    ClientHeight    =   3195
    ClientLeft      =   60
    ClientTop       =   345
    ClientWidth     =   4680
    LinkTopic       =   "Form1"
    ScaleHeight     =   3195
    ScaleWidth      =   4680
    StartUpPosition =   3  'Windows Default
    Begin VB.TextBox Text2
        Height          =   495
        Left            =   2760
        OLEDropMode     =   1  'Manual
        TabIndex        =   1
        Top             =   1200
        Width           =   1215
    End
    Begin VB.TextBox Text1
        Height          =   495
        Left            =   480
        OLEDropMode     =   1  'Manual
        TabIndex        =   0
        Text            =   "OLE Drag!"
        Top             =   1200
        Width           =   1215
    End
End
Attribute VB_Name = "Form1"
```

```
Attribute VB_GlobalNameSpace = False
Attribute VB_Creatable = False
Attribute VB_PredeclaredId = True
Attribute VB_Exposed = False


Private Sub Text1_MouseDown(Button As Integer, Shift As Integer, X As _
    Single, Y As Single)
    Text1.OLEDrag

End Sub


Private Sub Text1_OLEStartDrag(Data As DataObject, AllowedEffects As Long)

    Data.SetData Text1.Text, vbCFText
    AllowedEffects = vbDropEffectMove

End Sub

Private Sub Text2_OLEDragDrop(Data As DataObject, Effect As Long, _
    Button As Integer, Shift As Integer, X As Single, Y As Single)
    Text2.Text = Data.GetData(vbCFText)
End Sub
```

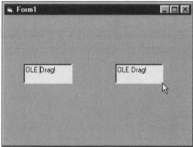

Figure 28.5 ***Dragging text data from one text box to another using OLE drag/drop.***

OLE Drag/Drop: Reporting The Drag/Drop Outcome

OLE Drag/Drop: Reporting The Drag/Drop Outcome

When the user drops data into a target component during an OLE drag/drop operation, you can make sure the source component is informed of that fact with the **OLECompleteDrag** event:

```
Sub object_CompleteDrag([effect As Long])
```

Here, the *effect* parameter can take these values:

- **vbDropEffectNone**—0; drop target cannot accept the data.

- **vbDropEffectCopy**—1; drop results in a copy of data from the source to the target. (Note that the original data is unaltered by the drag operation.)

- **vbDropEffectMove**—2; drop results in data being moved from drag source to drop source. (Note that the drag source should remove the data from itself after the move.)

Let's see an example. Here, we'll add code to our oledrag example that we've developed in the previous few examples to report what happened when users drop the data they've dragged from **Text1** into **Text2** using **Text1**'s **OLECompleteDrag** event:

```
Private Sub Text1_OLECompleteDrag(Effect As Long)
    MsgBox "Returned OLE effect: " & Effect
End Sub
```

Now the program displays the OLE effect value when the user drops the OLE data, as shown in Figure 28.6. The code for this example is located in the oledrag folder on this book's accompanying CD-ROM.

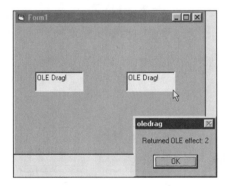

Figure 28.6   Reporting the results of an OLE drag/drop operation.

Using The Lightweight Controls

The Testing Department is on the phone again. Your program, *SuperDuperData-Crunch*, sure is using up a lot of memory. Can't you do something about it? You ask, any suggestions? They say, how about using lightweight controls to replace the 200 command buttons in the program?

To save memory, you can use the Microsoft *lightweight* controls, also called the *windowless* controls because they don't include all the internal machinery needed to support a window and window procedure. The lightweight controls come in the ActiveX control group named MSWLess.ocx.

You add them to a project with the Project|Components menu item, clicking the Controls tab and selecting the Microsoft Windowless Controls entry in the Component's dialog box.

TIP: *If that entry does not appear in the Components dialog box, you must register MSWLess.ocx with Windows using the utility regsvr32.exe that comes with Windows and Visual Basic.*

You can add the lightweight controls to a program, as shown in Figure 28.7, where you see the complete set of lightweight controls.

From the Visual Basic programmer's point of view, there are really only two differences between the standard Visual Basic controls and the lightweight controls: the lightweight controls do not have a **hWnd** property, and they do not support Dynamic Data Exchange (DDE). Besides those two differences, using a lightweight control is just like using a standard control; for example, you can add items to the **WLlist1** list box this way when the form loads:

```
Private Sub Form_Load()
    WLList1.AddItem "WLlist1"
End Sub
```

Or you can have the computer beep using the Visual Basic **Beep** statement when the user clicks the command button **WLCommand1**:

```
Private Sub WLCommand1_Click()
    Beep
End Sub
```

Figure 28.7   The windowless lightweight controls.

Passing Forms To Procedures

Can you pass forms to procedures in Visual Basic? You certainly can—just declare them with the keywords **As Form** in the argument list.

Let's see an example. Here, we set up a subroutine named **SetColor** that will set the background color of forms you pass to that subroutine, and we pass the current form to **SetColor** when that form loads:

```
Private Sub Form_Load()
    SetColor Me
End Sub
```

In the **SetColor** subroutine, we declare the passed form this way, giving it the name **TargetForm**:

```
Public Sub SetColor(TargetForm As Form)

End Sub
```

Now we're free to use the passed form as we would any form:

```
Public Sub SetColor(TargetForm As Form)
    TargetForm.BackColor = RGB(0, 0, 255)
End Sub
```

Determining The Active Form

You've got a multiform program and need to work with the controls on the currently active form (that is, the form with the focus)—but how do you determine which form is the active form?

You can use the Visual Basic Screen object's **ActiveForm** property to determine which form is active. For example, say we had a clock program with two forms, Form1 and Form2, each with a label control, **Label1**, in which we can display the current time using a timer, **Timer1**. However, we'll only update the time in the active form, which the user can switch simply by clicking the forms with the mouse.

To display the time, we add the timer, **Timer1**, to Form1, and set its **Interval** property to 1000 (as measured in milliseconds). Now we can use the **Label1** control in the currently active form in the timer's **Timer** event this way:

```
Private Sub Timer1_Timer()
    Screen.ActiveForm.Label1.Caption = Format(Now, "hh:mm:ss")
End Sub
```

We also make sure the second form, Form2, is shown when the program loads with Form1's **Load** event:

```
Private Sub Form_Load()
    Form2.Show
End Sub
```

You can see the result of this code in Figure 28.8. When you click one of the two forms, that form displays and updates the time, until you click the other form, which makes that other form take over.

The code for this example is located in the twoclocks folder on this book's accompanying CD-ROM. (This is the form with the name **Form1** in our example; **Form2** in this program is just a standard form with a label control, **Label1**, in it.)

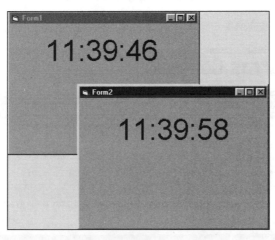

Figure 28.8   Determining the active form.

Using The Form Object's **Controls** Collection

Using The Form Object's Controls Collection

If you want to work with all the controls in a form indexed in an array, use the form's **Controls** collection. You can loop over all controls in a form using this collection. Let's see an example. Here, we fill a form with command buttons and then set the caption of each control to "Button" when the user clicks the form:

```
Private Sub Form_Click()
    For Each ButtonControl In Form1.Controls
        ButtonControl.Caption = "Button"
    Next
End Sub
```

That's all the code we need. Now the user can click the form to set the captions of all the buttons at once, as shown in Figure 28.9.

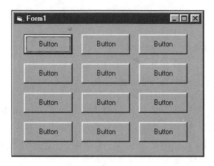

Figure 28.9   Using the Controls collection to set captions

Using the **Forms** Collection

In the previous topic, we saw that you can loop over all the controls in a form using the form's **Controls** collection. You can also loop over all the forms in an application using the Visual Basic Global object's **Forms** collection.

Let's see an example. Here, we'll display three forms, **Form1**, **Form2**, and **Form3**, displaying Form2 and Form3 when Form1 loads:

```
Private Sub Form_Load()
    Form2.Show
    Form3.Show
End Sub
```

Now when the user clicks a button in Form1 named, say, **CloseAll**, we can hide all open forms this way using the **Forms** collection:

```
Private Sub CloseAll_Click()
    For Each Form In Forms
        Form.Hide
    Next Form
End Sub
```

Setting A Form's Startup Position

You can set the position of a form when it is first displayed by positioning it in the Visual Basic IDE's forms window, or by setting the **StartUpPosition** property at design time (this property is not available at runtime):

- **vbStartUpManual**—0; no initial setting specified
- **vbStartUpOwner**—1; center on the item to which the form belongs
- **vbStartUpScreen**—2; center form in the whole screen
- **vbStartUpWindowsDefault**—3 (the default); position in the upper-left corner of the screen

Note, of course, that you can also position a form in the form's **Load** event handler by setting its **Left** and **Top** properties.

Keeping A Form's Icon Out Of The Windows 95 Taskbar

The Aesthetic Design Department is on the phone again. The dialog boxes in your program, *SuperDuperTextPro*, are fine, but there's one little problem: when you display a dialog box, its icon appears in the Windows 95 taskbar, and according to company specs, dialog boxes should not add an icon to the taskbar, even when they're displayed. Oh, you say.

It's easy to keep a dialog box's icon—or other form's icon—out of the Windows 95 taskbar; just set that form's **ShowInTaskbar** property to False at design time (this property is read-only at runtime). In fact, that's the most common use for this property—to keep dialog box icons out of the taskbar.

Handling Keystrokes In A Form Before Controls Read Them

There's a subtle war for possession of the focus between forms and controls in Visual Basic. If you click a form, giving the focus to that form, what really happens is that a control in that form (if there are any) gets the focus. But what if you really wanted to give the focus to the form as a whole to use the form's keystroke events?

It turns out that you can indeed make sure the form gets keystrokes even before the control with the focus gets them by setting the form's **KeyPreview** property to True (the default is False). You can set this property at runtime or design time.

Let's see an example. Here, we add a text box, **Text1**, to a form. When the users click the form, we'll start intercepting keystrokes before they go to the text box. Following the Christmas example developed earlier in this book, we'll remove all occurrences of the letter "L" when the user types that letter (making the text box a No-"L" text box).

Here's how we start intercepting keystrokes when the user clicks the form:

```
Private Sub Form_Click()
    KeyPreview = True
End Sub
```

Now we'll get the keystrokes first, as the user presses them, no matter what control has the focus. We can remove the letter "L" before it's passed on to the text box in our example this way:

```
Private Sub Form_KeyPress(KeyAscii As Integer)
    If KeyAscii = Asc("L") Then
        KeyAscii = 0
    End If
End Sub
```

*Making A Form
Immovable*

Making A Form Immovable

The Aesthetic Design Department is calling. They like the screen position they've set for the windows in your program—is there any way to make sure the user can't move them?

There is. You can set the form's **Moveable** property to False. Note, however, that you can only set this property at design time.

*Showing Modal
Forms*

Showing Modal Forms

The Testing Department is on the phone again. When you show that form full of options, you shouldn't let users go back to the main form until they've chosen the options they want. Hmm, you think, how does that work?

You can make a form *modal*, which means that the user has to dismiss it from the screen before working with the other forms in your application. You usually make only dialog boxes modal, but you can make any form modal if you wish. To make a form modal, pass the constant **vbModal** to the **Show** method:

```
Private Sub Command1_Click()
    Form2.Show vbModal
End Sub
```

Saving Values In The Windows Registry

Placing data in the Windows Registry saves that data for the next time your program runs, and the kind of data you save there usually represents settings for your program, such as window size and location. You can use the Windows Registry directly from Visual Basic. To save a setting in the Windows Registry, you use the **SaveSetting** statement:

```
SaveSetting appname, section, key, setting
```

Here are the arguments for **SaveSetting**:

- *appname*—String containing the name of the application to which the setting applies.
- *section*—String containing the name of the section where the key setting should be saved.
- *key*—String containing the name of the key setting being saved.
- *setting*—Expression containing the value to set the key to.

Here's how it works: to save a setting in the Windows Registry, you pass your application's name, a section name, a key name, and the setting for that key. Using section names allows you to break up an application's set of keys into different groups, which can be handy in terms of organization. Those keys are the actual variables that you save settings to. We'll see an example showing how to get and save settings with the Windows Registry in the next topic.

Getting Values From The Windows Registry

You can get settings that you've placed in the Windows Registry with the **GetSetting** function, which returns the value of that setting, or the default value as specified in the list that follows:

```
GetSetting(appname, section, key[, default])
```

Here are the arguments passed to this function:

- *appname*—String containing the name of the application or project whose key setting is requested.

- *section*—String containing the name of the section where the key setting is found.

- *key*—String containing the name of the key setting to return.

- *default*—Expression containing the value to return if no value is set in the key setting. (If omitted, default is assumed to be a null string, "".)

Let's see an example. In Chapter 5, we developed the MRU application, which supports a Most Recently Used (MRU) menu item in the File menu. This item displayed the most recently opened file's name using data stored in the Registry.

We stored the MRU file name in a Registry section named "Settings" and gave that file name the key "Doc1". When the program's form first loads, then, we got the file name last stored there, if there was one, with **GetSetting** this way:

```
Private Sub Form_Load()
    Dim FileName As String
    FileName = GetSetting(App.Title, "Settings", "Doc1")

    If FileName <> "" Then
        Load mnuMRU(1)
        mnuMRU(1).Caption = FileName
        mnuMRU(1).Visible = True
    End If
End Sub
```

On the other hand, when the user opens a file, we store that file's name in the Windows Registry this way so we can add it to the MRU menu item later:

```
Private Sub mnuOpen_Click()
    With dlgCommonDialog
        .DialogTitle = "Open"
        .CancelError = False
        .Filter = "All Files (*.*)|*.*"
        .ShowOpen
        If Len(.FileName) = 0 Then
            Exit Sub
        End If

        If GetSetting(App.Title, "Settings", "Doc1") = "" Then
            Load mnuMRU(1)
        End If
```

```
            mnuMRU(1).Caption = .FileName
            mnuMRU(1).Visible = True
            SaveSetting App.Title, "Settings", "Doc1", .FileName
        End With
End Sub
```

And that's all there is to it—using **SaveSetting** and **GetSetting**, you can access the Windows Registry directly in a simple way.

Getting All Registry Settings

You can use the **GetAllSettings** to get a list of key settings and their values from a section in the Windows Registry. Here's how you use **GetAllSettings**:

```
GetAllSettings(appname, section)
```

Here are the arguments for **GetAllSettings**:

- *appname*—String containing the name of the application whose key settings you want.

- *section*—String containing the name of the section whose key settings you want.

The **GetAllSettings** function returns a variant whose content is a two-dimensional array of strings, and these strings contain all the key settings in the indicated section and their values.

Deleting A Registry Setting

You can delete Registry settings with the **DeleteSetting** statement:

```
DeleteSetting appname, section[, key]
```

Here are the arguments for **DeleteSetting**:

- *appname*—String expression containing the name of the application you want to work with.

- *section*—String expression containing the name of the section where the key you are deleting is stored. (If only *appname* and *section* are provided, the specified section is deleted along with all related key settings.)

- *key*—String expression containing the name of the key setting being deleted.

Chapter 29

Error Handling And Debugging

If you need an immediate solution to:	See page:
Writing Error Handlers	1009
Using **On Error GoTo** *Label*	1012
Using **On Error GoTo** *line#*	1014
Using **On Error Resume Next**	1015
Using **On Error GoTo 0**	1015
Using **Resume** In Error Handlers	1016
Using **Resume** *Label* In Error Handlers	1017
Using **Resume** *line#* In Error Handlers	1018
Using **Resume Next** In Error Handlers	1019
Getting An Error's Error Code	1020
Getting An Error's Description	1021
Determining An Error's Source Object	1022
Handling Errors In DLLs: The **LastDLLError** Property	1023
Creating An Intentional (User-Defined) Error	1023
Nested Error Handling	1024
Creating An Error Object Directly In Visual Basic	1026
Trappable Cancel Errors In Common Dialogs	1028
Debugging In Visual Basic	1029
Setting Debugging Breakpoints	1031
Single-Stepping While Debugging	1032
Examining Variables And Expressions	1033
Adding Debug Watch Windows	1034
Using The Immediate Window While Debugging	1035

(continued)

If you need an immediate solution to:	See page:
Clearing All Debugging Breakpoints	1036
Executing Code Up To The Cursor While Debugging	1036
Skipping Over Statements While Debugging	1036

In Depth

This is our chapter on runtime errors and bugs. With a process called *trapping*, Visual Basic lets you catch many runtime errors, and we'll see how to do that here. And when we catch a runtime error, we'll see how to recover from that error without crashing the program. Just about every Visual Basic programmer is familiar with bugs—they're those annoying logic errors that occur when what the computer does doesn't appear to be the same as what you asked it to do. We'll ferret out bugs in this chapter with the Visual Basic debugger.

We'll also see how to get and interpret error codes—including translating them to English, how to write error handlers, how to use the **Resume** statement to continue program execution, and quite a few other powerful topics. Handling runtime errors is usually a part of any commercially released Visual Basic program because Visual Basic handles runtime errors by displaying information only useful to the programmer. Visual Basic lets you handle runtime errors by trapping them with special code, and these errors are referred to as *trappable* errors. You'll find a list of the Visual Basic trappable errors in Table 29.1.

TIP: *Getting "out of memory" errors has driven more than one programmer to distraction, How can I be out of memory? I have 512MB of RAM! In fact, Microsoft sometimes treats this error as a generic error, and programs can issue this error when the actual error cause is unknown.*

Table 29.1   The Visual Basic trappable error codes and messages.

Code	Message
3	Return without GoSub
5	Invalid procedure call
6	Overflow
7	Out of memory
9	Subscript out of range
10	This array is fixed or temporarily locked
11	Division by zero
13	Type mismatch
14	Out of string space

(continued)

Table 29.1   The Visual Basic trappable error codes and messages (continued).

Code	Message
16	Expression too complex
17	Can't perform requested operation
18	User interrupt occurred
20	Resume without error
28	Out of stack space
35	Sub, Function, or Property not defined
47	Too many code resource or DLL application clients
48	Error in loading code resource or DLL
49	Bad code resource or DLL calling convention
51	Internal error
52	Bad file name or number
53	File not found
54	Bad file mode
55	File already open
57	Device I/O error
58	File already exists
59	Bad record length
61	Disk full
62	Input past end of file
63	Bad record number
67	Too many files
68	Device unavailable
70	Permission denied
71	Disk not ready
74	Can't rename with different drive
75	Path/File access error
76	Path not found
91	Object variable or With block variable not set
92	For loop not initialized
93	Invalid pattern string
94	Invalid use of Null
97	Can't call Friend procedure on an object that is not an instance of the defining class

(continued)

Table 29.1 The Visual Basic trappable error codes and messages (continued).

Code	Message
98	A property or method call cannot include a reference to a private object, either as an argument or as a return value
298	System resource or DLL could not be loaded
320	Can't use character device names in specified file names
321	Invalid file format
322	Can't create necessary temporary file
325	Invalid format in resource file
327	Data value named not found
328	Illegal parameter; can't write arrays
335	Could not access system registry
336	ActiveX Component not correctly registered
337	ActiveX Component not found
338	ActiveX Component did not run correctly
360	Object already loaded
361	Can't load or unload this object
363	ActiveX Control specified not found
364	Object was unloaded
365	Unable to unload within this context
368	The specified file is out of date. This program requires a later version
371	The specified object can't be used as an owner form for Show
380	Invalid property value
381	Invalid property-array index
382	Property Set can't be executed at runtime
383	Property Set can't be used with a read-only property
385	Need property-array index
387	Property Set not permitted
393	Property Get can't be executed at runtime
394	Property Get can't be executed on write-only property
400	Form already displayed; can't show modally
402	Code must close topmost modal form first
419	Permission to use object denied
422	Property not found

(continued)

Table 29.1   The Visual Basic trappable error codes and messages (continued).

Code	Message
423	Property or method not found
424	Object required
425	Invalid object use
429	ActiveX Component can't create object or return reference to this object
430	Class doesn't support Automation
432	File name or class name not found during Automation operation
438	Object doesn't support this property or method
440	Automation error
442	Connection to type library or object library for remote process has been lost
443	Automation object doesn't have a default value
445	Object doesn't support this action
446	Object doesn't support named arguments
447	Object doesn't support current locale setting
448	Named argument not found
449	Argument not optional or invalid property assignment
450	Wrong number of arguments or invalid property assignment
451	Object not a collection
452	Invalid ordinal
453	Specified DLL function code resource not found
454	Code resource not found
455	Code resource lock error
457	This key is already associated with an element of this collection
458	Variable uses a type not supported in Visual Basic
459	This component doesn't support the set of events
460	Invalid Clipboard format
461	Specified format doesn't match format of data
480	Can't create AutoRedraw image
481	Invalid picture
482	Printer error
483	Printer driver does not support specified property
484	Problem getting printer information from the system. Make sure the printer is set up correctly

(continued)

Table 29.1   The Visual Basic trappable error codes and messages (continued).

Code	Message
485	Invalid picture type
486	Can't print form image to this type of printer
520	Can't empty Clipboard
521	Can't open Clipboard
735	Can't save file to TEMP directory
744	Search text not found
746	Replacements too long
31001	Out of memory
31004	No object
31018	Class is not set
31027	Unable to activate object
31032	Unable to create embedded object
31036	Error saving to file
31037	Error loading from file

With regard to debugging, Visual Basic provides programmers with a set of tools that is hard to beat. You can debug your programs interactively, working through your code line by line as the program runs. This powerful technique lets you work behind the scenes in a way that is invaluable to finding out what's going wrong. You can also specify where to begin debugging a program with *breakpoints*, which are lines of code that you tag to make the program halt and debugging start.

In this chapter, we'll see how to set and use breakpoints, execute code line by line, execute code up to a specified line, watch variables as they're changing, and more. Taking care of your program's bugs before you release it is important—the user might be able to handle runtime errors with the aid of our error handlers, but not errors in program logic.

Testing Your Programs

Before you release your programs for others to use, you'll probably want to test them first. This can involve a large investment of time—one that programmers are reluctant to make. It helps if you're smart in the way you go about testing your programs. For example, if your program operates on numeric data, you should test the bounds of variable ranges—it's easy to forget that the limits of Visual Basic integers, which are only 2-byte variables, are –32,768 to

32,767. Entering values like those, or values outside that range, can help test possible danger points. There is a bounds check you can perform for every crucial variable in your program. (Of course, you should check mid-range values as well, because a certain combination of values might give you unexpected errors.)

In addition, file operations are notorious for generating errors. What if the disk is full and you try to write to it? What if the file the user wants to read in doesn't exist? What if the output file turns out to be read-only? You should address and check all these considerations.

Besides the inherent programming checks, determining the logic danger-points of a program is also very important. For example, if your program has an array of data and you let the user average sections of that data by entering the number of cells to average over, what would happen if the user entered a value of 0? Or –100? Besides testing the software yourself, releasing beta versions of the software to be tested by other programmers or potential users is often a good idea.

If you do a lot of programming, you'll start to feel, sooner or later, that inevitably some user is going to come up with exactly the bad data set or operation that will crash your program. You might even start dreading the letters forwarded on to you from the Customer Relations Department. It's far better to catch all that before the program goes out the door, which is what beta testing your software is all about. The longer you test your program under usual—and unusual—operating circumstances, the more confidence you'll have that things are going as they should.

That's it for the overview of what's in this chapter—now it's time to turn to the Immediate Solutions section.

Immediate Solutions

Writing Error Handlers

Visual Basic has specific built-in ways to handle runtime errors, called *trappable errors*. When such an error occurs, you can direct the execution of your program to an *error handler*, which is a section of code written specifically to deal with errors.

Let's see an example to make this clearer. One area of programming very susceptible to runtime errors is file handling; we'll write our example here to open a file and display its contents in a text box—as well as to handle file errors. When the user clicks a button, **Command1**, we can show an Open dialog box using a Common Dialog control, **CommonDialog1**:

```
Private Sub Command1_Click()
    With CommonDialog1

        .ShowOpen
...
    End With
End Sub
```

The user enters the name of the file to open in that dialog box. We open the file, read the text in the file, and display it a multiline text box with scroll bars, **Text1** (with its **Multiline** property set to True and its **Scrollbars** property set to Both); then we close the file:

```
Private Sub Command1_Click()
    With CommonDialog1

        .ShowOpen
        Open .FileName For Input As #1
        Text1.Text = Input$(LOF(1), #1)

        Close #1

    End With
End Sub
```

Errors can occur here for a number of reasons—for example, the user may have typed in the name of a nonexistent file. To handle errors like that, we add an **On Error GoTo** statement like this, where we indicate that our error handler code will start at the label **FileError**:

```
Private Sub Command1_Click()

    On Error GoTo FileError

    With CommonDialog1

        .ShowOpen
        Open .FileName For Input As #1
        Text1.Text = Input$(LOF(1), #1)

        Close #1

    End With
```

Next, we add that label, **FileError**, and indicate with a message box that a file error occurred:

```
Private Sub Command1_Click()

    On Error GoTo FileError

    With CommonDialog1

        .ShowOpen
        Open .FileName For Input As #1
        Text1.Text = Input$(LOF(1), #1)

        Close #1

    End With

FileError:
    MsgBox "File Error"
End Sub
```

We also have to prevent execution of the normal code continuing into the error handler, so we add an **Exit Sub** statement to the code before that error handler:

```
Private Sub Command1_Click()
```

```
On Error GoTo FileError

With CommonDialog1

    .ShowOpen
    Open .FileName For Input As #1
    Text1.Text = Input$(LOF(1), #1)

    Close #1

End With

Exit Sub

FileError:
    MsgBox "File Error"
End Sub
```

So far, we've used very rudimentary code in our error handler, but error handlers get much more complex. As we'll see in this chapter, you can get the actual error code of the trappable error (as listed in Table 29.1) using the Visual Basic Err object's **Number** property. You can make that number the basis of a **Select Case** statement to take the appropriate action depending on which error occurred.

For example, here we handle two types of errors specifically—the case where the user clicked the Cancel button in the Common Dialog (you must set the Common Dialog control's **CancelError** property to True for the Common Dialog control to generate an error when the user clicks the Cancel button) and the File Not Found error:

```
Private Sub Command1_Click()

    On Error GoTo FileError

    With CommonDialog1

        .ShowOpen
        Open .FileName For Input As #1
        Text1.Text = Input$(LOF(1), #1)

        Close #1

    End With

    Exit Sub
```

```
FileError:
    Select Case Err.Number
        Case cdlCancel
            MsgBox "Please select a file."
            Resume
        Case 53
            MsgBox "File not found"
        Case Default
            MsgBox "File Error"
    End Select

End Sub
```

We'll see how to write error handlers like this one—and see what statements like **Resume** do—in this chapter. The code for this example is located in the errors folder on this book's accompanying CD-ROM.

Using **On Error GoTo** *Label*

The Visual Basic **On Error GoTo** statement is the foundation of handling trappable errors. When you execute an **On Error GoTo** *Label* statement in your code, execution is transferred to the code starting at *Label* if a trappable error has occurred. The code following that label is your error handler.

Let's see an example to make this clear. In the previous topic, we executed a statement indicating that our error handler code starts at the label **FileError** this way:

```
Private Sub Command1_Click()

    On Error GoTo FileError
    ...
```

Now if an error occurs, we'll transfer program execution to the code that follows the label **FileError**. That means that for all this code, error trapping is enabled:

```
Private Sub Command1_Click()

    On Error GoTo FileError

    With CommonDialog1
```

```
        .ShowOpen
        Open .FileName For Input As #1
        Text1.Text = Input$(LOF(1), #1)

        Close #1

    End With

    Exit Sub
...
```

The actual error-handling code itself follows the label **FileError** like this:

```
Private Sub Command1_Click()

    On Error GoTo FileError

    With CommonDialog1

        .ShowOpen
        Open .FileName For Input As #1
        Text1.Text = Input$(LOF(1), #1)

        Close #1

    End With

    Exit Sub

FileError:
    Select Case Err.Number
        Case cdlCancel
            MsgBox "Please select a file."
            Resume
        Case 53
            MsgBox "File not found"
        Case Default
            MsgBox "File Error"
    End Select

End Sub
```

TIP: Note that if you want to turn off error trapping at some point in your code, you can execute the statement **On Error GoTo 0** (see "Using **On Error GoTo 0**" coming up later in this chapter). You can also redirect error trapping to a new error handler by executing a new **On Error GoTo Label** statement.

Using **On Error GoTo** *line#*

Besides using a label to start an error handler (see the previous topic), you can refer to an error handler by line number in Visual Basic, using the **On Error GoTo** *line#* statement. Numbering code lines is part of Visual Basic history all the way back to the original days of the Basic language, and, in fact, many programmers don't know that you can number the lines of code in Visual Basic. For example, here's how we set up an error handler that starts at line 16 in our code (you can enter the line numbers directly in the code as shown in the following code), using the **On Error GoTo** *line#* statement:

```
Private Sub Command1_Click()
1
2    On Error GoTo 16
3
4    With CommonDialog1
5
6        .ShowOpen
7        Open .FileName For Input As #1
8        Text1.Text = Input$(LOF(1), #1)
9
10        Close #1
11
12   End With
13
14   Exit Sub
15
16
17   Select Case Err.Number
        Case cdlCancel
            MsgBox "Please select a file."
            Resume
        Case 53
            MsgBox "File not found"
        Case Default
            MsgBox "File Error"
    End Select

End Sub
```

Now when there's a trappable error, program execution jumps to line 16 to execute our error handler. Note that numbering lines has long been obsolete in Visual Basic; for most purposes, it's better to stick with **On Error GoTo** *Label*.

Using **On Error Resume Next**

The **On Error Resume Next** statement provides an easy way to disregard errors, if you want to do so. Once you execute this statement, execution continues with the next line of code if the current line generates an error, and the error is disregarded.

Let's see an example. Here we set the **Text**, **Caption**, **Min**, and **Max** properties of the currently active control on a form when the user clicks that form. Because no one control has all those properties, this code would generate an error in a message box to the user:

```
Private Sub Form_Click()
    ActiveControl.Text = "Active control"
    ActiveControl.Caption = "Active Control"
    ActiveControl.Min = 0
    ActiveControl.Max = 100
End Sub
```

However, we can place an **On Error Resume Next** statement in the code to suppress all the trappable errors:

```
Private Sub Form_Click()
    On Error Resume Next
    ActiveControl.Text = "Active control"
    ActiveControl.Caption = "Active Control"
    ActiveControl.Min = 0
    ActiveControl.Max = 100
End Sub
```

The result here is that whichever of these four properties the active control does have is set, without any errors.

Warning!   Note, however, that code like this is not good programming form, of course; it's better to check what the type of the active control is before setting its properties instead of simply disregarding errors.

Using **On Error GoTo 0**

To turn off error trapping, you can use the **On Error GoTo 0** statement. For example, here we turn on error trapping to catch the case where the user clicks the Cancel button in a Common Dialog control's Font dialog box, but we then turn error trapping off if the user did not press Cancel (to make the Cancel button generate a trappable error, set the Common Dialog control's **CancelError** property to True; this is the standard way of catching the Cancel button when working with Common Dialogs):

```
Private Sub Command1_Click()
    On Error GoTo Cancel
    CommonDialog1.Flags = cdlCFBoth Or cdlCFEffects
    CommonDialog1.ShowFont
    On Error GoTo 0

    Text1.FontName = CommonDialog1.FontName
    Text1.FontBold = CommonDialog1.FontBold
    Text1.FontItalic = CommonDialog1.FontItalic
    Text1.FontUnderline = CommonDialog1.FontUnderline
    Text1.FontSize = CommonDialog1.FontSize
    Text1.FontName = CommonDialog1.FontName
Cancel:
End Sub
```

*Using Resume
In Error
Handlers*

Using **Resume** In Error Handlers

When you're writing code for an error handler, you can return control to the main body of the procedure using the **Resume** statement. Program execution starts again with the line that caused the error, and this can be very valuable if you're able to fix the error in the error handler.

Let's see an example. In this example, we open a file that the user has selected with an Open Common Dialog. If the user clicked the Cancel button instead, we can insist that the user select a file by displaying a message box with the text "Please select a file" and use the **Resume** statement to display the Open dialog box once again. We do that by trapping the error generated when the user clicks the Cancel button in the Open dialog box (set the Common Dialog control's **CancelError** property to True to make sure a trappable error is generated when the user clicks the Cancel button):

```
Private Sub Command1_Click()

    On Error GoTo FileError

    With CommonDialog1

        .ShowOpen
        Open .FileName For Input As #1
```

```
            Text1.Text = Input$(LOF(1), #1)

            Close #1

        End With

        Exit Sub

FileError:

    Select Case Err.Number
        Case cdlCancel
            MsgBox "Please select a file."
            Resume
        Case 53
            MsgBox "File not found"
        Case Default
            MsgBox "File Error"
    End Select

End Sub
```

Using **Resume** *Label* In Error Handlers

When you're writing code for an error handler, you can return control to a particular line in the main body of the procedure using the **Resume** *Label* statement. To label a line, you just place the label's text directly into the code, followed by a colon.

Let's see an example. Here, we use the **Resume** *Label* statement to retry a File Open operation if the user clicked the Cancel button in the Open dialog box. We do this by using the label **TryAgain** (to make the Open Common Dialog return a trappable error if the user clicks the Cancel button, set the Common Dialog control's **CancelError** property to True):

```
Private Sub Command1_Click()

    On Error GoTo FileError

    With CommonDialog1
TryAgain:
        .ShowOpen
        Open .FileName For Input As #1
        Text1.Text = Input$(LOF(1), #1)
        Close #1
```

```
        End With

        Exit Sub

FileError:

    Select Case Err.Number
        Case cdlCancel
            MsgBox "Please select a file."
            Resume TryAgain
        Case 53
            MsgBox "File not found"
        Case Default
            MsgBox "File Error"
    End Select

End Sub
```

Using **Resume *Label*** is useful if you're able to fix a trappable error in an error handler and want to resume execution at some specific line in the code (not necessarily the next line in the code).

Using **Resume *line#*** In Error Handlers

You can use the **Resume** statement (see the previous two topics) with an actual line number in Visual Basic. For example, here's how we'd write the example from the previous topic using line numbers instead of a **Resume *Label*** statement:

```
Private Sub Command1_Click()
1
2    On Error GoTo 16
3
4    With CommonDialog1
5
6        .ShowOpen
7        Open .FileName For Input As #1
8        Text1.Text = Input$(LOF(1), #1)
9
10       Close #1
11
12   End With
13
14   Exit Sub
```

```
15
16
17
18   Select Case Err.Number
        Case cdlCancel
            MsgBox "Please select a file."
            Resume 6
        Case 53
            MsgBox "File not found"
        Case Default
            MsgBox "File Error"
     End Select

End Sub
```

In this case, we're specifying that execution should continue starting at line 6 after we've indicated to the users that they should select a file to open instead of just clicking the Cancel button.

Using **Resume Next** In Error Handlers

Besides **Resume**, **Resume** *Label*, and **Resume** *line#*, you can also use the **Resume Next** statement in an error handler. This statement resumes program execution in the line after the one that caused the error.

Let's see an example. Here we set the **Text**, **Caption**, **Min**, and **Max** properties of the currently active control on a form when the user clicks that form. Because no one control has all those properties, this code would generate an error in a message box to the user:

```
Private Sub Form_Click()

    ActiveControl.Text = "Active control"
    ActiveControl.Caption = "Active Control"
    ActiveControl.Min = 0
    ActiveControl.Max = 100

End Sub
```

We can handle and suppress these errors with an error handler, which we start at the label **SetError**:

```
Private Sub Form_Click()
    On Error GoTo SetError
```

```
        ActiveControl.Text = "Active control"
        ActiveControl.Caption = "Active Control"
        ActiveControl.Min = 0
        ActiveControl.Max = 100

        Exit Sub

SetError:
    ...
```

In this case, we handle the error by moving on to the next line of code like this with **Resume Next**:

```
Private Sub Form_Click()
    On Error GoTo SetError
    ActiveControl.Text = "Active control"
    ActiveControl.Caption = "Active Control"
    ActiveControl.Min = 0
    ActiveControl.Max = 100

    Exit Sub

SetError:
    Resume Next
End Sub
```

The result here is that whichever of these four properties the active control does have is set, without any errors.

Warning!   Note, however, that code like this is not good programming form, of course; it's better to check what the type of the active control is before setting its properties instead of simply disregarding errors.

Getting An Error's Error Code

To determine what trappable error has occurred, you can use the Visual Basic Err object's **Number** property, which holds the error code; see Table 29.1 at the beginning of this chapter for a list of trappable errors and their numeric codes.

Let's see an example. Here, we use the Err object's **Number** property to set up a **Select Case** statement, handling trappable errors in different ways. If the error occurred because the users clicked the Cancel button in the Open dialog box, we indicate to the users that they should select a file and retry the operation. If the error occurred because the users entered the name of a file that was subsequently not found (trappable error 53), we indicate that to them. Otherwise, we just display the generic message "File error" in a message box:

```
Private Sub Command1_Click()

    On Error GoTo FileError

    With CommonDialog1

        .ShowOpen
        Open .FileName For Input As #1
        Text1.Text = Input$(LOF(1), #1)

        Close #1

    End With

    Exit Sub

FileError:
    Select Case Err.Number
        Case cdlCancel
            MsgBox "Please select a file."
            Resume
        Case 53
            MsgBox "File not found"
        Case Default
            MsgBox "File Error"
    End Select

End Sub
```

TIP: *These days, it's considered bad programming practice to simply display an error number to the user—the user might not know, for example, that error 31001 means "out of memory." To translate an error code into an error description, you can pass that code to the Visual Basic **Error** function, which returns the text error message for that error, and you can display that. You can also use the Err object's **Description** property, as we'll see in the next topic.*

Getting An Error's Description

To let the user know what kind of trappable error has occurred, you can use the Visual Basic Err object's **Description** property. Let's see an example. In this code, we'll trap errors and handle two of them expressly: the case where the user has clicked the Cancel button in the Open Common Dialog, and the case where a "File Not Found" error occurs. Otherwise, we'll just display the Visual Basic error message in the **Default** case of a **Select Case** statement:

```
Private Sub Command1_Click()

    On Error GoTo FileError

    With CommonDialog1

        .ShowOpen
        Open .FileName For Input As #1
        Text1.Text = Input$(LOF(1), #1)
        Close #1

    End With

    Exit Sub

FileError:

    Select Case Err.Number
        Case cdlCancel
            MsgBox "Please select a file."
            Resume
        Case 53
            MsgBox "File not found"
        Case Default
            MsgBox Err.Description
    End Select

End Sub
```

Using **Err.Description**, you can inform the user that an error occurred—and indicate what error occurred with readable text.

Determining An Error's Source Object

You can determine the object that caused the error using the Visual Basic Err object's **Source** property. This property holds the name of the object or application that caused the error. For example, if you connect to Microsoft Excel and it generates an error, Excel sets **Err.Number** to its error code for that error, and it sets **Err.Source** to **Excel.Application**.

Handling Errors In DLLs: The **LastDLLError** Property

Errors during calls to Windows dynamic link libraries (DLLs) do not create trappable errors and so cannot be trapped with Visual Basic error trapping. In practice, this means that when you call a DLL procedure, you should check each return value for success or failure. In the event of a failure, check the value in the Err object's **LastDLLError** property.

Creating An Intentional (User-Defined) Error

There are cases in programs where you might want to create an error; although no Visual Basic trappable error has occurred, some situation may have occurred that's incompatible with your program's logic. You can create an error intentionally, called *raising* an error, with the Visual Basic Err object's **Raise** method:

```
Err.Raise number, [source [, description [, helpfile [, helpcontext]]]]
```

Here are the arguments for the **Raise** method:

- *number*—Long integer that identifies the nature of the error (see the paragraphs that follows for more details).
- *source*—String expression naming the object or application that generated the error; use the form project.class. (If the source is not specified, the name of the current Visual Basic project is used.)
- *description*—String expression describing the error.
- *helpfile*—The path to the Help file in which help on this error can be found.
- *helpcontext*—The context ID identifying a topic within helpfile that provides help for the error.

When setting the error number for the error, bear in mind that Visual Basic errors are in the range 0 to 65535. The range 0 to 512 is reserved for system errors, but the range 513 to 65535 is available for user-defined errors.

Let's see an example. Here, we'll generate an error, error number 2000, when the user clicks a command button, **Command1**, and then indicate the error has occurred with a message box. First, we raise error 2000:

```
Private Sub Command1_Click()
    On Error GoTo CaptionError

    Err.Raise 2000
    ...
```

Then we display the error in a message box in an error handler:

```
Private Sub Command1_Click()
    On Error GoTo CaptionError

    Err.Raise 2000

    Exit Sub

CaptionError:

    MsgBox "Error number " & Err.Number

End Sub
```

The result appears in Figure 29.1. Now we're raising errors intentionally in Visual Basic.

TIP: You can also use the Visual Basic **Error** statement to raise an error like this: **Error errnumber**. However, the **Error** function is considered obsolete now, replaced by the **Raise** method of the Err object.

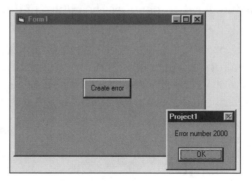

Figure 29.1   Generating an error on purpose.

Nested Error Handling

If a trappable error occurs in a procedure, you can handle that error in an error handler. But what if you call another procedure, and an error occurs before control returns from that procedure? If the called procedure has an error handler, the code in that error handler will be executed. However, if the called procedure does not have an error handler, control will return to the error handler in the calling procedure. In this way, control moves back up the calling chain to the closest error handler.

Let's see an example. Here, we set up an error handler in a subroutine and then call another subroutine, **LoadText**, to load text from a file the user specifies into a text box, **Text1**:

```
Private Sub Command1_Click()

    On Error GoTo FileError

    LoadText

    Exit Sub

FileError:

    Select Case Err.Number
        Case cdlCancel
            MsgBox "Please select a file."
            Resume
        Case 53
            MsgBox "File not found"
        Case Default
            MsgBox Err.Description
    End Select

End Sub
```

Here's the **LoadText** subroutine, which uses an Open Common Dialog to get the name of the file to open, opens the file, and loads the file's text into **Text1**:

```
Public Sub LoadText()
    With CommonDialog1

        .ShowOpen
        Open .FileName For Input As #1
        Text1.Text = Input$(LOF(1), #1)
        Close #1

    End With
End Sub
```

If an error occurs in **LoadText**, which has no error handler itself, control returns back to the calling subroutine, and the code in the error handler there is executed. In this way, you don't have to worry about calling procedures without error handlers when you're trying to trap errors.

Creating An Error Object Directly In Visual Basic

You can create an error object directly and use it as a return value from your procedures. To create that object, you use the Visual Basic **CVErr** function, passing it the error code for the error you want to create.

Let's see an example. Here, we'll set up a function, **MakePositiveNumber**, which takes a string representing an integer (for example, 25) and returns the integer represented by that string (for example, 25). If you pass **MakePositive-Number** a string representing a negative integer (for example, –25), the function will return an error object (actually a **Variant** of subtype **Error**).

We start by declaring **MakePositiveNumber**, indicating that it will accept a string and return a variant (that variant can be either a number or an error object):

```
Public Function MakePositiveNumber(strData As String) As Variant
...
```

Next, we use the Visual Basic **Val** function to create an integer from the string passed to us (to keep this example short, we're assuming the string passed to **MakePositiveNumber** does indeed represent a valid positive or negative integer):

```
Public Function MakePositiveNumber(strData As String) As Variant
    Dim intValue As Integer

    intValue = Val(strData)
...
```

If the integer is less than 0, we return an error with the error code 5 (which in Visual Basic means "Invalid procedure call") using **CVErr** this way:

```
Public Function MakePositiveNumber(strData As String) As Variant
    Dim intValue As Integer

    intValue = Val(strData)

    If intValue < 0 Then
        MakePositiveNumber = CVErr(5)
...
```

Otherwise, we return the positive integer this way:

```
Public Function MakePositiveNumber(strData As String) As Variant
    Dim intValue As Integer

    intValue = Val(strData)
```

```
    If intValue < 0 Then
        MakePositiveNumber = CVErr(5)
    Else
        MakePositiveNumber = intValue
    End If
End Function
```

Now we'll put **MakePositiveNumber** to work. When the user clicks a command button, **Command1**, we can take the string in a text box, **Text1**, use **MakePositiveNumber** to convert it to a number, and display the result in another text box, **Text2**:

```
Private Sub Command1_Click()
    Dim varNumber As Variant

    varNumber = MakePositiveNumber(Text1.Text)

    Text2.Text = Str(varNumber)
End Sub
```

We can check for error return values with the Visual Basic **IsError** function, which returns True if you pass it an error object. If **MakePositiveNumber** did return an error, we convert that error into a number with the Visual Basic **CInt** function, and if that error is 5, indicating that the passed string represented a negative number, we display a message box informing the user that the number to convert must be positive:

```
Private Sub Command1_Click()
    Dim varNumber As Variant

    varNumber = MakePositiveNumber(Text1.Text)

    If IsError(varNumber) Then
        If CInt(varNumber) = 5 Then
            MsgBox "Number must be positive"
        End If
    Else
        Text2.Text = Str(varNumber)
    End If
End Sub
```

And that's it—we've created and used our own error objects. When you run the program and try to convert a negative value, as shown in Figure 29.2, the program displays an error. The code for this example is located in the errobject folder on this book's accompanying CD-ROM.

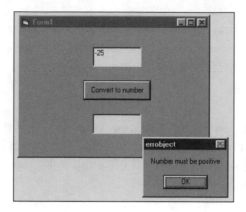

Figure 29.2   Using a user-defined error object in Visual Basic.

Trappable Cancel Errors In Common Dialogs

The usual way to work with the Cancel button in Common Dialogs is to use trappable errors. You set the Common Dialog control's **CancelError** property to True, and the Common Dialog control will generate an error when the user clicks the Cancel button.

Let's see an example. Here, we'll use a Common Dialog to open a text file the user has selected and display it in a text box, **Text1**. If the user has clicked the Cancel button, the trappable error **cdlCancel** is generated, and we display a message box asking the user to select a file and try the operation again by showing the Open dialog box again:

```
Private Sub Command1_Click()

    On Error GoTo FileError

    With CommonDialog1

        .ShowOpen
        Open .FileName For Input As #1
        Text1.Text = Input$(LOF(1), #1)

        Close #1

    End With

    Exit Sub
```

```
FileError:
    Select Case Err.Number
        Case cdlCancel
            MsgBox "Please select a file."
            Resume
        Case Default
            MsgBox "File Error"
    End Select

End Sub
```

Debugging In Visual Basic

Visual Basic offers a powerful suite of debugging options—notably the ability to single-step through your code as it's executing. The standard way to debug is to place a breakpoint at a particular line in your code, and when execution reaches that line, it will halt and Visual Basic will enter the Debug state, giving you access to your code and variables. You can examine the contents of those variables and work through your code line by line, watching program execution behind the scenes.

For example, we might write the following code, which is meant to increment the value in a text box, **Text1**, each time you click a button:

```
Private Sub Command1_Click()
    Dim intCounter As Integer

    intCounter = intCounter + 1
    Text1.Text = intCounter

End Sub
```

What actually happens is that the value 1 appears in the text box each time you click the button—it's time to debug. To start that process, we place a breakpoint at this line in our code:

```
Private Sub Command1_Click()
    Dim intCounter As Integer

    intCounter = intCounter + 1
    Text1.Text = intCounter

End Sub
```

You place a breakpoint in code by moving the text insertion caret to that line and either selecting Toggle Breakpoint in the Debug menu or pressing F9. (Breakpoints toggle, so to remove the breakpoint, select Toggle Breakpoint in the Debug menu or press F9 again.)

Now when you run the program and press the button, execution halts at the breakpoint, and the code window appears. You can examine the contents of variables by selecting them on the screen with the mouse and clicking the Quick Watch item in the Debug menu (besides individual variables, you can select an entire expression). This opens a window displaying the current value of the variable or expression you've selected.

To move through your program step-by-step, you can select these stepping options in the Debug menu:

- *Step Into*—Single-step through the code, entering called procedures if encountered.

- *Step Over*—Single-step through the code, stepping over procedure calls.

- *Step Out*—Step out of the current procedure.

Examining the contents of the **intCounter** variable shows that it's being reset to 0 each time the code runs, and we realize that we should declare that variable as static this way:

```
Private Sub Command1_Click()
    Static intCounter As Integer

    intCounter = intCounter + 1
    Text1.Text = intCounter

End Sub
```

That's the process in overview—we've debugged the code. For more details on the debugging process, and to examine other debugging processes like selected code execution, see the following topics in this chapter.

TIP: *Want to save a little time debugging? Often the crucial aspect of debugging is watching the values in your variables change as your program executes, and sometimes doing that without the debugger is easy enough: just add some temporary text boxes or message boxes to your program and use them to display the values you want to watch. This is an expedient shortcut for simple bugs—but if it doesn't fit the bill for you, turn to the debugger.*

Setting Debugging Breakpoints

Breakpoints are the foundation of Visual Basic debugging. When you set breakpoints in a program and run that program, program execution continues until one of the breakpoints is encountered and program execution stops, making Visual Basic enter the Debug state. You place a breakpoint in code by moving the text insertion caret to that line and either selecting Toggle Breakpoint in the Debug menu or pressing F9. (Breakpoints toggle, so to remove the breakpoint, select Toggle Breakpoint in the Debug menu or press F9 again.) When you place a breakpoint in code, it appears at design time in red, as shown in Figure 29.3.

When you run the program and reach the breakpoint, execution stops and Visual Basic appears in the Debug state, as shown in Figure 29.4. You can see the breakpoint highlighted in Visual Basic in that figure, and the arrow in the left margin of the code window points to the current line of execution.

You can execute the lines following a breakpoint by single stepping, and we'll take a look at that process in the next topic.

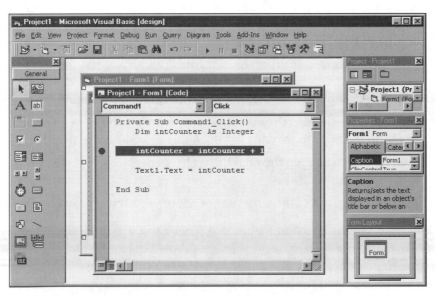

Figure 29.3   Setting a breakpoint in code at design time.

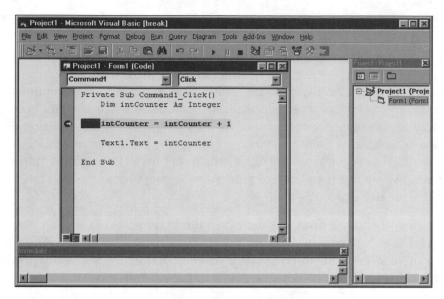

Figure 29.4   A breakpoint in Visual Basic's Debug state.

Single-Stepping While Debugging

When you've stopped a program at a breakpoint, you get an inside look at what's going on. When the code is stopped at a breakpoint, you can move through the code with the single-stepping options in the Debug menu:

- *Step Into*—Single-step through the code, entering the code in called procedures if procedure calls are encountered (shortcut: press F8).

- *Step Over*—Single-step through the code, stepping over procedure calls (shortcut: press Shift+F8).

- *Step Out*—Step out of the current procedure (shortcut: press Ctrl+Shift+F8).

For example, take a look at Figure 29.4. There, we are stopped at a breakpoint, but we can single-step to the next line, as shown in Figure 29.5. As you can see in that figure, the arrow at left in the code window has moved to the next line, and we've executed the previous line of code. Single stepping in this way, you can move through your code to debug it.

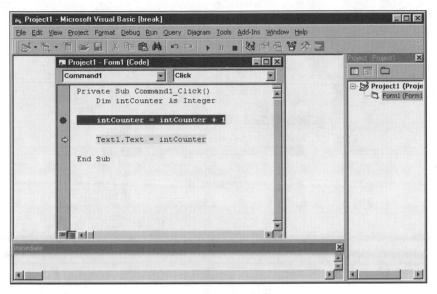

Figure 29.5   Single-stepping in Debug mode.

Examining Variables And Expressions

Just single-stepping through a program when debugging it wouldn't be of that much use—we should be able to examine the value in the various program variables as well. You can do that with a "quick watch" window.

To examine the value in a variable or expression in the code window when stopped at a breakpoint, select the variable or expression you want to examine with the mouse and select the Quick Watch item in the Debug menu, or press Shift+F9. This opens the Quick Watch window you see in Figure 29.6. You can see the value in the variable named **intCounter** in that window.

Besides quick watches, you can open a whole watch window, as we'll see in the next topic.

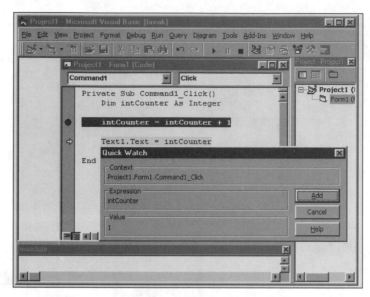

Figure 29.6   Examining a variable with a Quick Watch window.

Adding Debug Watch Windows

You can add a watch window to your debugging session and display the values of selected variables or expressions in that window continuously as you execute your program line by line.

To add a watch window, select the variable or expression you want to watch with the mouse and click the Add Watch item in the Debug menu. This opens the Add Watch dialog box; make sure the variable or expression you want to watch is entered in the Expression box and click on OK. When you do, Visual Basic adds a watch window to the debug session, as you can see at bottom in Figure 29.7, where we're watching the value in the variable **intCounter**.

Being able to continuously watch the values in your program's variables as the program executes can be a great asset in debugging, because you can see unexpected values as they appear.

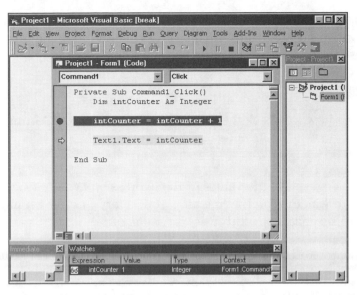

Figure 29.7   A debug watch window.

Using The Immediate Window While Debugging

When debugging, you can use the Immediate window to examine expressions or variables immediately, just by typing them in. The Immediate window appears at lower left when Visual Basic is in its Debug state, as shown in Figure 29.8.

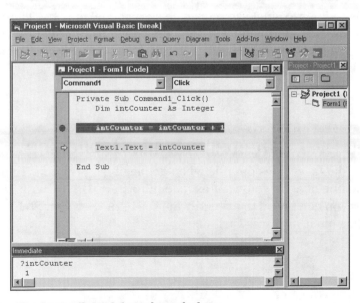

Figure 29.8   The Immediate debugging window.

Using The Immediate Window While Debugging

You can enter an expression to evaluate in the Immediate window if you precede it with a question mark and then press the Enter key. For example, here's how we check the value in a variable named **intCounter**:

```
?intCounter
```

And here's how we check the value of the expression **intCounter + 1**:

```
?intCounter + 1
```

Visual Basic displays the values of the expressions you're examining in the Immediate window (on the line after your query), as shown in Figure 29.8, where we see that **intCounter** holds a value of 1.

Clearing All Debugging Breakpoints

Clearing All Debugging Breakpoints

If you have a large number of breakpoints in a program, you might be relieved to learn that you can clear them all at once with the Clear All Breakpoints menu item in the Debug menu. The shortcut for this menu item is Ctrl+Shift+F9.

Executing Code Up To The Cursor While Debugging

Executing Code Up To The Cursor While Debugging

It can be tedious to single-step through a great deal of code. There is another option, however—you can click a line of code to place the blinking text insertion caret at that line and select the Run To Cursor item in the Debug menu, or press Ctrl+F8. When you do, execution continues to the line you've selected.

Skipping Over Statements While Debugging

Skipping Over Statements While Debugging

You can skip over lines of code when debugging a program. To do that, just click the line of code you want execution to start with (after having skipped the lines you don't want to execute) and select the Set Next Statement item in the Debug menu, or press Ctrl+F9.

Chapter 30

Deploying Your Program: Creating Setup Programs, Help Files, And Online Registration

If you need an immediate solution to:	See page:
Creating Your Application's EXE File	1043
Using The Package And Deployment Wizard	1043
Step 1: Package Type	1044
Step 2: Build Folder	1044
Step 3: Files	1045
Step 4: Distribution Type	1045
Step 5: Installation Title	1046
Step 6: Icons	1046
Step 7: Install Locations	1047
Step 8: Shared Files	1048
Step 9: Finished!	1048
Creating Help Files With The Microsoft Help Workshop	1049
Creating A Help Project's RTF File	1051
Entering Text In A Help File	1052
Creating A Help Hotspot	1053
Creating A Help Hotspot Target	1055
Titling A Help Page	1057
Adding Help Topics To The Help Index	1058
Creating Help Pop-Up Links	1058
Creating Help "Tool Tips" Targets	1059
Compiling Help Files With The Help Workshop	1060
Displaying A Help File From Visual Basic	1061

(continued)

If you need an immediate solution to:	See page:
Building Online Help Into Your Application	1063
Creating Online User Registration	1065
Uploading Online Registration Information To An FTP Server	1066
Concluding The FTP Transfer Of The Online Registration Information	1068

In Depth

You've created your application, and it's a doozy. It runs fine—on your computer. But what's next? How do you get your application out the door and onto other people's computers?

That's what this chapter is all about. Here, we're going to reap the benefits of all our work by deploying applications to users. We'll see how to create setup programs, Help files, and even online registration.

Application deployment is a topic many books skip, but it's of vital interest to many programmers. After all, the EXE files you create might run fine on your computer, which has a full installation of Visual Basic on it, but what about other computers? You can't just copy the EXE files to another computer and expect them to run: Visual Basic applications require a great deal of support in terms of dynamic link libraries and possibly other components like ActiveX controls you may have used. How do you install all that? We'll see how that works in this chapter.

Setup Programs

You use setup programs to install your application on other computers, and Visual Basic has a good tool that will help us here: the Package And Deployment Wizard. Using this wizard, you can create setup files that you can distribute on CDs, multiple disks, or even across the Internet.

TIP: *It's important to make sure that you don't distribute licensed material or components without permission, of course. Check with the manufacturer of the DLL or OCX files you want to distribute first, making sure its policy allows distribution.*

In this chapter, we'll see how easy it is to create setup programs with the Package And Deployment Wizard. Once you've created your application's EXE file, you're all set—the Package And Deployment Wizard will analyze what files your application needs and include them in the data file for your setup program. The data itself is stored in a cabinet file, with the extension .cab, and the setup.exe program will unpack and deploy the contents of that file as needed.

Help Files

Help files are an asset to any application, and just about all serious applications come with a Help system of some sort. In this chapter, we'll see how to create Windows Help files of the kind you can display on the user's computer with standard Windows calls.

To create a Windows Help file, you use the Windows Help Workshop, which creates a Help *project*. You place the actual Help text in a rich text (RTF) file, and add that file to the Help project. Why rich text? The Help Workshop uses RTF files so that you can embed jumps, called *hotspots*, that work like hyperlinks, and commands directly into your Help file, encoding those items with rich text footnotes, hidden text, and so forth. We'll see how this works in this chapter. When you're done with your RTF file, you use the Help Workshop to compile it into an HLP file.

Now that you have an HLP file, how do you open it from Visual Basic? Here, we'll use the Windows API **WinHelp** function, which allows you a great deal of flexibility when opening Help files. You can even make the Package And Deployment Wizard include your Help files and data files in the setup program, as we'll see in this chapter.

Online Registration

Keeping in touch with an application's users is important for many programmers, which is why online registration has become so popular. Using online registration, the user has only to select a menu item to register the application with you.

In this chapter, we'll use the FTP protocol to let users connect and register their applications in a few easy steps. Using FTP is probably the most common method for handling online registration and provides us with a better and more robust alternative to using another alternative, email, because the Visual Basic email support relies on the Microsoft MAPI system, which the user may not have enabled.

When users decide to register online, the program will display an information dialog box, asking them to enter their name and email address. When they click a button labeled Register, the program will establish an FTP connection to your server (connecting to the Internet, if necessary, first) and upload the information the users provided, along with the date and time. In this way, you can keep track of your application's users.

The "Designed For Microsoft Windows" Logo

If you're serious about your application and want to release it commercially, you might want to fulfill the requirements for the Microsoft "Designed for Microsoft Windows" logo. To add this logo to your application, that application must pass a fairly rigorous set of tests (you submit the application on a CD for testing).

Even if you are not trying to get the logo, it's worth taking a look at some of the requirements an application must fill to get that logo, because they provide some insight into what Microsoft considers good programming practice. For example, your application must:

- Be a 32-bit multitasking program, stable and functional on all current versions of Windows and Windows NT.

- Digitally sign ActiveX controls that it provides and support Authenticode signing of all its downloadable code.

- Provide an OLE container or object server, and allow users to drag objects to any container. Object servers and OLE containers must pass tests of basic functionality, and an Object command must be placed on a container's Insert menu.

- Use new Microsoft installer technology, which makes it easy to meet the other install/uninstall requirements.

- Provide a graphical 32-bit setup program that detects software versions, creates shortcuts, supports CD-ROM AutoPlay, supports Add/Remove Programs, and checks operations in advance.

- Support the Universal Naming Convention, long file names, and hard drives larger than 2GB.

- Support users who upgrade their computers from one version of Windows to another by providing a migration DLL (when necessary).

- Provide keyboard access to all features and provide some kind of notification of the keyboard focus location.

- Provide and register a fully automated uninstaller that appears in Add/Remove Programs and that when run, removes all application files, references in the Start menu, and Registry entries.

- Not install executables or DLLs in the root directory, but must use the \Program Files directory instead.

- Separate user data from application code and query the Registry for the names of suitable directories in which to save user data.

- Not overwrite core components when installing, or decrement or remove core components when uninstalling. It must register all shared components during installation.

- Register native data types and support informational keys in the Registry. It must not add any entries to the Win.ini or System.ini files.

That's just a partial list—you can get more information directly from Microsoft.

That's it for the overview of what's in this chapter. Now it's time to turn to the Immediate Solutions section.

Immediate Solutions

Creating Your Application's EXE File

The first step in deploying your application is to create its EXE (or DLL or OCX) file. You probably already know how to create your project's EXE file, but for the record, you just select the Make *projectname*.exe (or .dll or .ocx) item in the File menu.

TIP: The Package And Deployment Wizard will actually create your application's executable file for you if that file doesn't exist (it first asks whether you want it to).

After your application's executable file is created, you're ready to create a setup program to deploy it with.

Using The Package And Deployment Wizard

The Visual Basic Package And Deployment Wizard is an add-in that lets you deploy your application. If you don't see it in the Visual Basic Add-Ins menu, use the Add-In Manager (which appears in the Add-Ins menu) to insert it in that menu.

TIP: It's important to make sure that you don't distribute licensed material or components without permission, of course. Check with the manufacturer of the DLL or OCX files you want to distribute first, making sure their policy allows distribution.

Open the application you want to distribute in Visual Basic now, and open the Package And Deployment Wizard, as shown in Figure 30.1. As you can see in that figure, there are several options here: you can create a new setup program, deploy a setup package to a distribution site, or manage the scripts you can use with this wizard.

We'll create a setup program for our alarm clock application, the alarm project, which we developed in Chapter 13, in the next few topics in this chapter, progressing step-by-step through the Package And Deployment Wizard. Select the top button in the Package And Deployment Wizard now to create a setup program for the Alarm application.

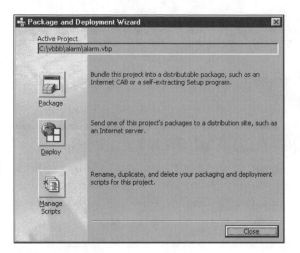

Figure 30.1   The Package And Deployment Wizard.

Step 1: Package
Type

Step 1: Package Type

In the first step of the Package And Deployment Wizard, you select the package type you want to create. In this case, make sure the Standard Setup Package item is selected in the Package Type box.

Selecting this item means that we will create a deployment package that can be installed using a setup.exe file. After you've selected the Standard Setup Package item, click the Next button to move on to Step 2 in the Package And Deployment Wizard.

Step 2: Build
Folder

Step 2: Build Folder

In Step 2 of the Package And Deployment Wizard, you select the folder in which your deployment package will be created. By default, this folder is named Package and Package And Deployment is added to your Visual Basic project's folder. For example, in the alarm project, which is in the C:\vbbb\alarm folder, the deployment package will be created in the folder C:\vbbb\alarm\Package. If you want to build the deployment package in another folder, select that folder now.

When you're ready, click the Next button to move on to the next step in the Package And Deployment Wizard.

Step 3: Files

In Step 3 of the Package And Deployment Wizard, you can select what files will be included for distribution. This includes your application's executable file and all the needed support files—the Package And Deployment Wizard determines what support files your application needs and adds them automatically.

The Package And Deployment Wizard presents a list of files it will include in your deployment package in this step, and you can deselect ones you don't want to include. You can also include additional files in your deployment package, such as Help or application-specific data files, by clicking the Add button and specifying those files.

TIP: *If you're going to install your application on a computer that already has Visual Basic installed, you can deselect the standard DLL and OCX files that come with Visual Basic because you won't have to deploy them. Doing so will avoid annoying questions about replacing those files when you install your application.*

When you're ready, click the Next button to move on to the next step in the Package And Deployment Wizard.

Step 4: Distribution Type

In Step 4 of the Package And Deployment Wizard, you specify how you want to distribute your application—as one single cabinet (.cab) file, or over multiple disks—as shown in Figure 30.2. If you select deployment with multiple disks, you can specify the capacity of each disk, from 360K to 2.88MB, and the

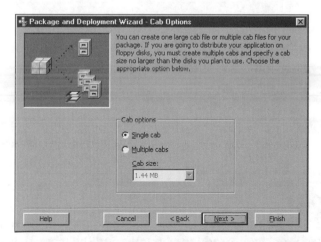

Figure 30.2   Selecting the distribution type in the Package And Deployment Wizard.

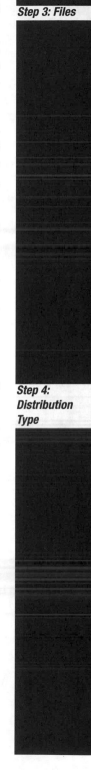

Package And Deployment Wizard will create a CAB file for each disk and let you know how many disks you need. Here, we'll select the single cab option for the alarm clock application we're working with.

When you're ready, click the Next button to move on to the next step in the Package And Deployment Wizard.

Step 5: Installation Title

In Step 5 of the Package And Deployment Wizard, you enter the installation title for your application, as shown in Figure 30.3. This title will appear on the setup program's "wash" screen (which covers the whole screen) when the user installs the application.

Here, we'll use the title "Alarm", as shown in Figure 30.3, while creating the deployment package for our alarm clock application, but you may also want to include your company's name in the title, if applicable.

When you're ready, click the Next button to move on to the next step in the Package And Deployment Wizard.

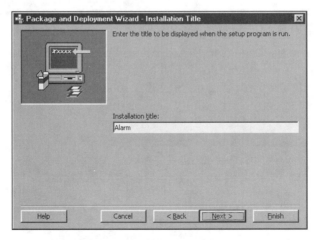

Figure 30.3   Selecting a deployment package's installation title.

Step 6: Icons

In Step 6 of the Package And Deployment Wizard, you indicate what new program group(s) you want to add to Windows and the icons to use. In this case, where we're building a deployment package for our alarm application, we're

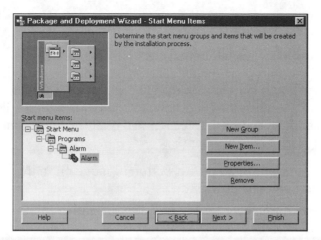

Figure 30.4   Selecting program groups and icons to install in the Package And Deployment Wizard.

only going to add one program group, Alarm, and use the icon from the alarm.exe file, as shown in Figure 30.4 (these are the defaults the Package And Deployment Wizard has selected for us).

When you're ready, click the Next button to move on to the next step in the Package And Deployment Wizard.

Step 7: Install Locations

In Step 7 of the Package And Deployment Wizard, you indicate where you want the parts of your application installed on the target computer. By default, your application is placed into the directory the user specifies, which is represented in the Package And Deployment Wizard with the macro $(AppPath), and the other files, like DLL files, are installed where your application expects to find them (such as the windows\system directory).

You can change the default installation location of your applications files in this step; for example, if you want your Help files to go into the installation folder's Help subfolder, specify that they should be installed in the $(AppPath)\Help folder.

When you're ready, click the Next button to move on to the next step in the Package And Deployment Wizard.

Step 8: Shared Files

In Step 8 of the Package And Deployment Wizard, you can indicate which files you want to register as shared files. These files may be used by several applications in the target computer and will be uninstalled only if all applications that use them are uninstalled. If in doubt, it's better to register files as shared—especially common DLLs and OCXs. (And if really in doubt, don't forget to test your application's setup program.)

When you're ready, click the Next button to move on to the next step in the Package And Deployment Wizard.

Step 9: Finished!

Step 9 in the Package And Deployment Wizard is the last step in creating your application's deployment package. Just click the Finish button to create the CAB file(s), the setup.exe program itself, and the setup.lst file, which holds a list of the files to install and where they go (setup.exe reads setup.lst to know what to install where).

When you click Finish, the Package And Deployment Wizard also displays a packaging report indicating that the alarm.cab file has been created (click Close to close the packaging report dialog box and click Close again to close the Package And Deployment Wizard).

And that's all it takes—now the user can run the setup.exe program to install your application, as shown in Figure 30.5. When the setup program runs, it

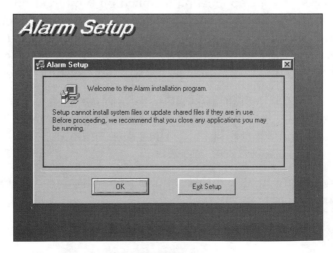

Figure 30.5   Installing the alarm application.

handles all the details of checking for adequate disk space, asking the user where to install the application, and installs the necessary files for you, using the CAB file and the setup.lst file. It's that simple.

You've completed the process: using the Package And Deployment Wizard, you can now create setup programs to distribute your application.

Creating Help Files With The Microsoft Help Workshop

The Testing Department is calling again. Your new program, *SuperDuper-Graphics4U*, is really fine, but no one seems to be able to use it. But, you say, it's so intuitive and simple: just use Alt+F8 to draw a line, Ctlr+Shift+Esc to draw a circle, and.... Add a Help file, they say.

You can create Help files with the Microsoft Help Workshop, hcw.exe, which comes with Visual Basic, and appears in Figure 30.6. To see how the Help Workshop works, we'll create a basic Help file for an application named "Helper" over the next few topics in this chapter.

TIP: *You can create more advanced Help files than the one we'll create in this chapter, complete with tabs and clickable tree views of Help topics, by creating a Help contents file (extension .cnt) with the Help Workshop, setting up a hierarchy of Help topics and headers as you want.*

To create the Help file, helper.hlp, for the helper application, we will create a Help project, helper.hpj, in the Help Workshop. This project keeps track of the

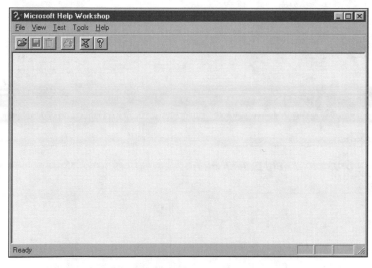

Figure 30.6   The Microsoft Help Workshop.

files in our Help system, and in this example, we'll just have one such file: helper.rtf, which will hold the data for our Help file. In that RTF file, we'll set up the Help topics to display to the user, along with the hotspots in the Help file that will connect those topics.

After adding helper.rtf in the helper.prj file, you can compile that RTF file to create helper.hlp. And to open the helper.hlp Help file, you can use the Windows API function **WinHelp** as follows:

```
Private Declare Function WinHelp Lib "user32" Alias "WinHelpA" (ByVal hwnd _
    As Long, ByVal lpHelpFile As String, ByVal wCommand As Long, ByVal _
    dwData As Long) As Long
```

To create a new Help project, select the New item in the Help Workshop's File menu now, select the Help Project item in the New dialog box that opens, and click on OK. Using the Save As menu item in the Help Workshop, save the new Help project as helper.hpj. The new Help project appears in the Help Workshop in Figure 30.7.

Now that we've created a new Help project, we'll add the actual Help text to that project, and we do that by creating an RTF file, as we'll see in the next topic.

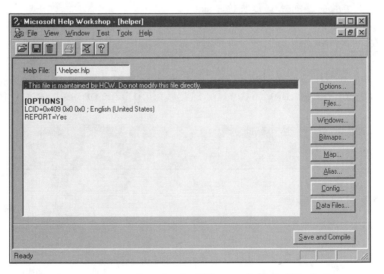

Figure 30.7   Creating a Help project in the Microsoft Help Workshop.

Creating A Help Project's RTF File

The real work of creating a Help file takes place in the Help file's RTF file. This rich text file holds not only the text for your Help files but also holds the commands used in your Help file.

For example, you use Help file RTF commands to create Help *hotspots*, which work like hyperlinks, and pop-up links, which work like tool tips. As we'll see in the following topics, you use rich text format codes to support these and other Help features. For example, here are some rich text format codes and what they do as far as the Help workshop is concerned:

- **\footnote**—Footnote; handles special topic commands
- **\page**—Page break; ends the current topic
- **\strike**—Strikethrough; indicates a hotspot
- **\ul**—Underline; indicates a link to a pop-up topic
- **\uldb**—Double underline; indicates a hotspot
- **\v**—Hidden test; indicates the topic ID to jump to

We'll see how these format codes are used in the following topics. In fact, we'll build our Help file's RTF file, helper.rtf, with Microsoft Word, and we won't have to deal with these codes directly.

Using Microsoft Word, we create the file helper.rtf now (save the file in RTF format). Next, we add it to our Help project in the Help Workshop by clicking the Files button in the Help Workshop, clicking the Add button in the Topic Files dialog box that appears, selecting helper.rtf, and clicking on OK. This adds helper.rtf to our Help project, as you see in the Help Workshop in Figure 30.8.

In the following topics in this chapter, we'll see how to create the text in the helper.rtf file to build our Help file. The actual RTF file we create is located in the helper folder on this book's accompanying CD-ROM (note that the RTF codes in that listing will not be visible in Microsoft Word, which interprets and formats the text with those codes).

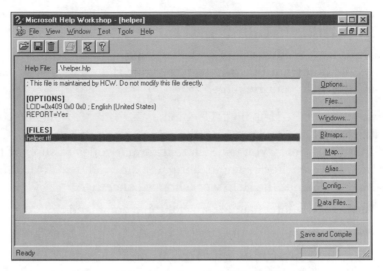

Figure 30.8   Adding helper.rtf to the helper.hpj Help project.

Entering Text In A Help File

The text in a Help file is divided into pages, and only one page is displayed at a time. To divide your text into pages in Microsoft Word, you enter a page break with the Insert|Break menu item or by pressing Ctrl+Enter. The first page in the RTF file is the first page displayed when your Help file is opened.

Let's see an example. Here, we will make the first page of the helper.hlp file we're creating a welcome page by entering this text directly into helper.rtf and following it with a page break:

```
Contents
```

```
Welcome to helper example application. This help file gives you help on the
menu items in helper.
```

Now this text will greet the user when the helper.hlp file is first opened, as shown in Figure 30.9.

Actually, this text is not really enough by itself—we should allow users some way to jump to the Help pages they want to look at, and we'll do that in the next topic.

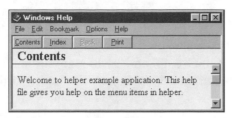

Figure 30.9   The opening text in our Help file.

Creating A Help Hotspot

To let the user move around in a Help file, you use *Help hotspots*, which act much like hyperlinks. Help hotspots appear underlined in Help files, and when the user clicks a hotspot, the Help system jumps to the target of that hotspot and opens the associated Help page.

To see how hotspots work, we'll add two hotspots to the opening Help page we developed in the last topic. Here, we'll let the user jump to two new pages, as shown in Figure 30.10—a Help page giving help about the application's File menu items, and another page giving help about the application's Help menu.

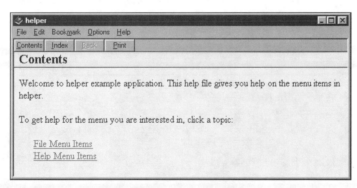

Figure 30.10   Adding two Help hotspots to a Help file.

To add those hotspots to the helper.rtf file, we add this text:

```
Contents

Welcome to helper example application. This help file gives you help on
the menu items in helper.

To get help for the menu you are interested in, click a topic:
```

```
File Menu Items
Help Menu Items
```

To make the "File Menu Items" and "Help Menu Items" into Help hotspots, we give them a double underline, using the Microsoft Word Format menu:

```
Contents

Welcome to helper example application. This help file gives you help on
the menu items in helper.

To get help for the menu you are interested in, click a topic:

File Menu Items
===============

Help Menu Items
===============
```

Now that we've created two Help hotspots, we will connect a label, called a *jump tag*, to the hotspots to indicate where we want to jump to when the user clicks the hotspots. In this case, we add the jump tags **FILE_MENU_ITEMS** and **HELP_MENU_ITEMS** to our hotspots this way, marking them as *hidden text* with the Word Format menu (hidden text appears in a Word document with a dotted underline):

```
Contents

Welcome to helper example application. This help file gives you help on
the menu items in helper.

To get help for the menu you are interested in, click a topic:

File Menu ItemsFILE_MENU_ITEMS
===============...............

Help Menu ItemsHELP_MENU_ITEMS
===============...............
```

The text for our helper.rtf file so far appears in Microsoft Word in Figure 30.11.

Because we've made the new jump tags hidden text, they will not appear visually in the Help file; however, when the user clicks a Help hotspot, the Help system will look for the page that has the same tag as the hotspot that the user clicked. How do you give a Help page a tag? We'll look at that topic next.

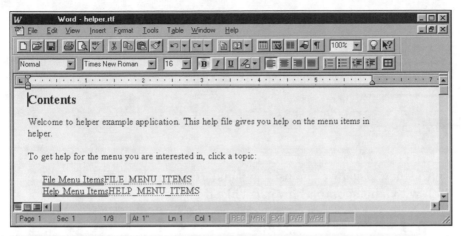

Figure 30.11   Creating help jumps and their targets in Microsoft Word.

Creating A Help Hotspot Target

To connect a Help hotspot with a page in a Help file, you place the blinking insertion caret in Word at the very beginning of the target page in the Help file's RTF file, and select Word's Insert|Footnote menu item to insert a new footnote.

In the Footnote And Endnote dialog box that appears, click Custom Mark in the Numbering box, enter the special footnote character "#" (that is, type that character # into the Custom Mark box), and click on OK. This inserts a new footnote in the document and opens a window showing the document's footnotes at the bottom of the window. To connect a Help hotspot to the current page, you simply enter the hotspot's tag as the footnote text.

Let's see an example. In the previous topic, we created two Help hotspots, and in this topic, we'll create the target the Help system will jump to when the user clicks the File Menu Items hotspot; the tag for this hotspot is **FILE_MENU_ITEMS**.

To create the page to jump to when the user clicks the File Menu Items hotspot, we insert a page break to start a new page and add the title "File Menu Items" to that page:

```
Contents

Welcome to helper example application. This help file gives you help on the
menu items in helper.
```

```
To get help for the menu you are interested in, click a topic:

File Menu ItemsFILE_MENU_ITEMS
═══════════════..............
Help Menu ItemsHELP_MENU_ITEMS
═══════════════..............
--------------------------------Page Break----------------------------
File Menu Items
...
```

On this new page, we can list the menu items in the application's File menu, each with a hotspot to a new page, like this:

```
Contents

Welcome to helper example application. This help file gives you help on the
menu items in helper.

To get help for the menu you are interested in, click a topic:

File Menu ItemsFILE_MENU_ITEMS
═══════════════..............
Help Menu ItemsHELP_MENU_ITEMS
═══════════════..............
--------------------------------Page Break----------------------------
File Menu Items

Select the menu item you want to get help on:

     NewNEW
     ═══...
     OpenOPEN
     ════....
     CloseCLOSE
     ═════.....
```

To connect the **FILE_MENU_ITEMS** jump tag with the new page, then, place the insertion caret at the beginning of that page, select the Insert|Footnote menu item, and give the footnote the custom mark # and the text **FILE_MENU_ITEMS**, as shown in Figure 30.12.

Now we've connected the File Menu Items hotspot to the next Help page we've just created; when the user clicks the File Menu Items hotspot, shown in Figure 30.10, we'll jump to this new page, shown in Figure 30.13.

Using footnotes, you can do more than just create Help hotspots; you can title a Help page, and we'll see how to do that in the next topic.

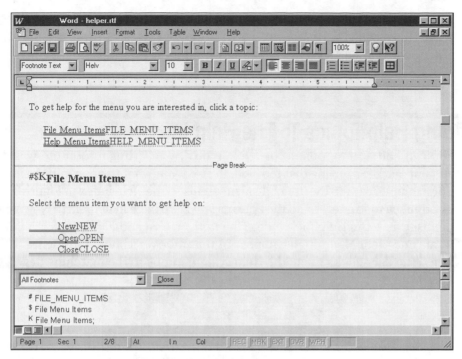

Figure 30.12   Setting up a Help hotspot target.

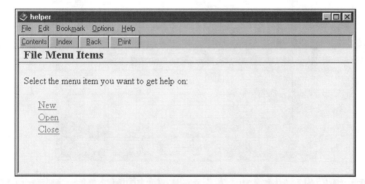

Figure 30.13   Jumping to a Help target page.

Titling A Help Page

You can add a title to a Help page. To do that, you add a footnote to a Help page, giving it the custom mark "$", and give the footnote the text you want to use as the page's title.

Let's see an example. In this case, we will add the title "File Menu Items" to the appropriate page in the helper.rtf file that we've been developing for the previous few topics. To do that, position the insertion caret at the beginning of the File Menu Items page, add a footnote with the custom mark "$", and give that footnote the text "File Menu Items", as shown in Figure 30.12.

Adding Help
Topics To The
Help Index

Adding Help Topics To The Help Index

You can add a Help topic to the Help index by inserting a footnote with the custom mark "K", giving that footnote the text you want to appear in the index. For example, we add the item File Menu Items to the Help index in Figure 30.12, by adding a footnote, "K", to the appropriate Help page in helper.rtf. Now when the user uses the Help file's index, the items we've added, such as File Menu Items and Help Menu Items, appear in that index, as shown in Figure 30.14. When the user clicks them, the Help system jumps to the matching page.

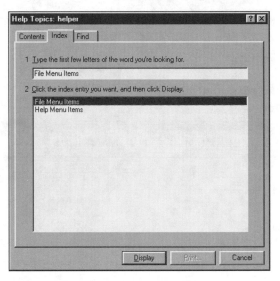

Figure 30.14   Adding items to the Help system's index.

Creating Help
Pop-Up Links

Creating Help Pop-Up Links

You can create Help pop-ups, which work much like tool tips in a Visual Basic program. As an example, we've added the pop-up you see in Figure 30.15, which explains the term "file" with a pop-up. Pop-ups appear in Help files with a dotted underline; when the user clicks that pop-up, the associated text is displayed in a tool-tip-like window.

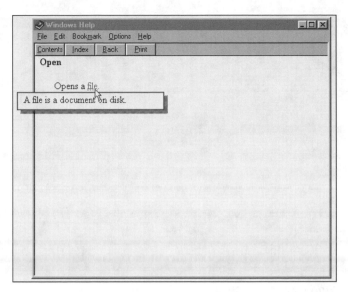

Figure 30.15   Adding a Help pop-up.

Adding a pop-up is just like adding a Help hotspot, but instead of double-underlining the hotspot, you just use a single underline. Let's see an example. Here, we'll create the pop-up you see at work in Figure 30.15. To do that, just underline the term you want to create a pop-up for, using the Visual Basic Format menu, and add the hidden text jump tag. We'll use **FILE_POPUP** for the jump tag here, like this:

```
Open
```

```
    Opens a fileFILE_POPUP.
              ----..........
```

Because we've used a single underline instead of a double one, the Help system will display the text that has the tag **FILE_POPUP** instead of actually jumping to that page. We'll see how to create that page in the next topic.

Creating Help "Tool Tips" Targets

To create a target page for a Help pop-up, you use footnotes with the custom mark "#", just as you would for any Help hotspot. To complete the example we started in the previous topic, we add a new page to our helper example's RTF file with the footnote "#" and the footnote text **FILE_POPUP**, as shown in Figure 30.16.

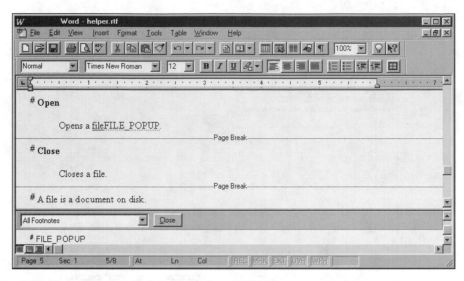

Figure 30.16   Adding a Help pop-up to an RTF file.

Finally, we place the text we want to display when the pop-up appears into the new page, as also shown in Figure 30.16. Now when the user clicks the underlined item in the Help system, the pop-up will appear, as shown in Figure 30.15.

*Compiling Help
Files With The
Help Workshop*

Compiling Help Files With The Help Workshop

Now that you've created your RTF file with the Help text and hotspots you want to use, along with your Help project in the Help Workshop, how do you create the actual HLP file? You use the Help Workshop's Compile item in the File menu. That menu item brings up the Compile A Help File dialog box you see in Figure 30.17; click Compile to create the Help file, which in the case of the example we've developed over the previous few topics is helper.hlp.

Figure 30.17   The Compile A Help File dialog box in the Help Workshop.

Congratulations—you've created a new Help file. But how do you launch it from Visual Basic? We'll look at that next.

Displaying A Help File From Visual Basic

The Testing Department is calling. Your new Help file is very helpful, but now you've got to display it from your Visual Basic application. Makes sense, you think, but how do you do that?

To display a Help file from a Visual Basic program, you can use the Windows API function **WinHelp**:

```
Declare Function WinHelp Lib "user32" Alias "WinHelpA" (ByVal_
    hwnd As Long, ByVal lpHelpFile As String, ByVal wCommand As Long,_
    ByVal dwData As Long) As Long
```

Here's what the arguments to this function mean:

- *hwnd*—Handle of the window opening the Help file

- *lpHelpFile*—Name of the Help file to open

- *wCommand*—Open command; see the list that follows

- *dwData*—Additional data as required for the Help file opening operation

Here are the possible values you can use for the *wCommand* argument:

- **HELP_CONTEXT** = &H1
- **HELP_QUIT** = &H2
- **HELP_INDEX** = &H3
- **HELP_CONTENTS** = &H3&
- **HELP_HELPONHELP** = &H4
- **HELP_SETINDEX** = &H5
- **HELP_SETCONTENTS** = &H5&
- **HELP_CONTEXTPOPUP** = &H8&
- **HELP_FORCEFILE** = &H9&
- **HELP_KEY** = &H101
- **HELP_COMMAND** = &H102&
- **HELP_PARTIALKEY** = &H105&

- **HELP_MULTIKEY** = &H201&
- **HELP_SETWINPOS** = &H203&

Let's see an example. Here, we'll open the helper.hlp Help file in an application named "helper" when the user selects the Help item in the application's Help menu. To start, we declare **WinHelp** and the constants it can use:

```
Const HELP_CONTEXT = &H1
Const HELP_QUIT = &H2
Const HELP_INDEX = &H3
Const HELP_CONTENTS = &H3&
Const HELP_HELPONHELP = &H4
Const HELP_SETINDEX = &H5
Const HELP_SETCONTENTS = &H5&
Const HELP_CONTEXTPOPUP = &H8&
Const HELP_FORCEFILE = &H9&
Const HELP_KEY = &H101
Const HELP_COMMAND = &H102&
Const HELP_PARTIALKEY = &H105&
Const HELP_MULTIKEY = &H201&
Const HELP_SETWINPOS = &H203&


Private Declare Function WinHelp Lib "user32" Alias "WinHelpA" (ByVal_
    hwnd As Long, ByVal lpHelpFile As String, ByVal wCommand As Long,_
    ByVal dwData As Long) As Long
```

Then, when the user selects the appropriate menu item, we display the helper.hlp file with **WinHelp** this way:

```
Private Sub mnuHelp_Click()
    retVal = WinHelp(Form1.hwnd, "c:\vbbb\helper\helper.hlp",_
        HELP_INDEX, CLng(0))
End Sub
```

And that's it—now the user can open the helper.hlp file from the Visual Basic helper application, as shown in Figure 30.18.

Now we're supporting Help files in our Visual Basic applications. The code for this example is located in the helper folder on this book's accompanying CD-ROM.

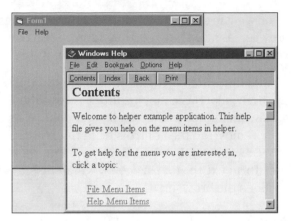

Figure 30.18   *Opening a customized Windows Help file from a Visual Basic program.*

Building Online Help Into Your Application

The Testing Department is calling again. The company's software is changing too fast to keep up with creating new Help files and sending them out to users all the time—what can we do? You suggest, how about some *online* Help files?

You can build support for online Help files into Visual Basic applications easily by using the Web browser control. Using that control, you can connect the users directly to the company Web site and let them view Help files in HTML format.

Let's see an example. Using the Visual Basic Application Wizard, create a new project named "onlinehelp". When the Application Wizard asks about Internet connectivity, as shown in Figure 30.19, click the Yes option button and enter the

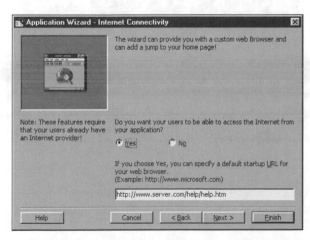

Figure 30.19   *Adding an online Help page to a Visual Basic application.*

Help Web page you want to display to the user as the startup page for the program's built-in Web browser, as also shown in that figure. Then complete building the application with the Application Wizard by clicking the Finish button.

To make the application's Web browser look less like a browser and more like online Help, use the Visual Basic menu editor to move the Web Browser menu item from the View menu to the Help menu and change its caption to Online Help. In addition, remove all the controls from the **frmBrowser** form except for the Web browser control, **brwWebBrowser**. Finally, take all code out of the **frmBrowser** form except for this code, which displays the starting page when the user opens the browser:

```
Public StartingAddress As String

Private Sub Form_Load()
    Me.Show

    If Len(StartingAddress) > 0 Then
        brwWebBrowser.Navigate StartingAddress
    End If

End Sub
```

And that's it—now when the user selects the Online Help item in the Help menu, the Web browser appears and connects to the Help page you've selected online, as shown in Figure 30.20. Congratulations—now you're supporting online Help

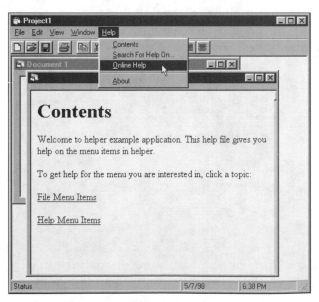

Figure 30.20   Supporting online Help in a Visual Basic application.

in your application. The code for this example is located in the FrmBrowser folder on this book's accompanying CD-ROM.

Creating Online User Registration

The Testing Department has sent an email. Isn't there some way to keep track of your application's users? How about adding online registration to your application? Hmm, you think, how does that work?

To let your application's users register their new purchase easily, you can add online registration to your program. When users click the Online Registration menu item in the Help menu, a dialog box appears asking them to enter their name and email address. When they do and click a button marked Register, the application connects to the Internet and sends the recorded information to you.

We'll see how this works in the next few topics in this chapter, where we use the FTP protocol to upload user registrations directly to an FTP site. This example, the onlinereg application, lets the user select a menu item, Register Online, in the Help menu, and displays an online registration form, Form2, as shown in Figure 30.21. When users enter their name and email address in the registration form and click the button labeled Register, the program sends the data in that form to an FTP server.

We'll write the code for the registration form, Form2, now. When users enter their name and email address and click the Register button, we start by writing that information out to a temporary file, along with the name of the application the users are registering, as well as the time and date:

Figure 30.21   The onlinereg application's online registration form.

```
Private Sub Command1_Click()
    Open "c:\temp.dat" For Output As #1
    Print #1, "Registering SuperDuperDataCrunch" & vbCrLf
    Print #1, "Name: " & Text1.Text & vbCrLf
    Print #1, "email: " & Text2.Text & vbCrLf
    Print #1, "Time: " & Format(Now)
    Close #1
...
End Sub
```

This code stores the user information to the temp.dat file, like this:

```
Registering SuperDuperDataCrunch

Name: steve

email: steve@steveco.com

Time: 5/5/99 10:02:23 AM
```

This is the data that we will upload to the FTP server in the next topic.

TIP: Note that the file name here, temp.dat, may well conflict with an existing file. To make sure that does not happen, you can use the Visual Basic **GetTempName** method to get a name for the temporary file in which to store the user's registration data.

Uploading Online Registration Information To An FTP Server

In the previous topic, we've stored the registration information we want to upload to the FTP server in a file, temp.dat. To upload the user registration data, we add an Internet transfer control, **Inet1**, to the onlinereg application's registration form, Form2 (see Chapter 21 for more details on the Internet transfer control).

After writing the registration form to disk, we connect to the FTP server to upload the data to by using the Internet transfer control like this, where we set the control's **URL** property to the address of the FTP server and set the **UserName** and **Password** properties as required:

```
Private Sub Command1_Click()
    Open "c:\temp.dat" For Output As #1
    Print #1, "Registering SuperDuperDataCrunch" & vbCrLf
```

```
Print #1, "Name: " & Text1.Text & vbCrLf
Print #1, "email: " & Text2.Text & vbCrLf
Print #1, "Time: " & Format(Now)
Close #1

Inet1.URL = "ftp://ftp.server.com"
Inet1.UserName = "steve"
Inet1.Password = "secret"
...
```

Here we are using the connection protocol used by many FTP servers, which sets the current FTP directory based on the username you log in with. If you need to set the current directory yourself, use the FTP CD command, using the Internet transfer control's **Execute** method.

TIP: *You may want to encode any password that you embed in your code for security purposes.*

To actually upload the file temp.dat, we use the Internet transfer control's **Execute** method to execute the FTP Put command like this, where we name the file reg.dat when uploaded to the server:

```
Private Sub Command1_Click()
    Open "c:\temp.dat" For Output As #1
    Print #1, "Registering SuperDuperDataCrunch" & vbCrLf
    Print #1, "Name: " & Text1.Text & vbCrLf
    Print #1, "email: " & Text2.Text & vbCrLf
    Print #1, "Time: " & Format(Now)
    Close #1

    Inet1.URL = "ftp://ftp.server.com"
    Inet1.UserName = "steve"
    Inet1.Password = "secret"
    Inet1.Execute , "PUT c:\temp.dat reg.dat"

End Sub
```

This uploads the file with the user registration information to the FTP site you've selected:

```
Registering SuperDuperDataCrunch

Name: steve

email: steve@steveco.com

Time: 5/5/99 10:02:23 AM
```

TIP: *Note that we've uploaded the file and named it reg.dat on the FTP server; using that name for all uploads will cause a conflict. You should use a unique file name for each separate file; for example, you can incorporate the date and time of day in the file name.*

Now that we've uploaded the registration data, we need to terminate the FTP connection and delete the temporary file, and we'll do that in the next topic.

Concluding The FTP Transfer Of The Online Registration Information

In the previous few topics, we've sent user registration data to an FTP site in the onlinereg application. Now that the upload operation is complete, we will close the FTP connection in the Internet transfer control's **StateChanged** event handler:

```
Private Sub Inet1_StateChanged(ByVal State As Integer)

    If State = icResponseCompleted Then
        Inet1.Execute , "Close"
...
```

In addition, we delete the temporary file we've created and hide the registration form this way:

```
Private Sub Inet1_StateChanged(ByVal State As Integer)

    If State = icResponseCompleted Then
        Inet1.Execute , "Close"

        Dim FileSystemObject As Object
        Set FileSystemObject = CreateObject("Scripting.FileSystemObject")
        FileSystemObject.DeleteFile "c:\temp.dat"

        Form2.Hide
    End If
End Sub
```

And that's it—we've uploaded the user registration data to the specified FTP site. Congratulations, now you're supporting online registration. The code for this example is located in the onlinereg folder, and the code that displays that form is located in the Form1 folder, both on this book's accompanying CD-ROM.

Index

Special Characters

& (ampersand)
  & operator, use of, 37
  access characters, 168–171, 235
* (asterisk), 101
$(AppPath) macro, 1047
32-bit MAPI DLLs, installing, 718
+ operator, 37
| (pipe symbol), 356
2D, 3D area charts, 385–387
2D, 3D bar charts, 387
2D, 3D combination charts, 390–392
2D, 3D line charts, 384–385
2D, 3D step charts, 388–390
_ (underscore), 38

A

Abs function, 113
Access characters, 155, 168–171, 235, 447
Action property, 346, 720, 897
Activating OLE objects, 912–914
Active control, determining, 971–972
Active form, determining, 992–993
ActiveControl property, 608, 915, 971–972
ActiveForm property, 608, 992–993
ActiveX components, 650, 652. See also ActiveX controls; ActiveX documents; Code components.
ActiveX Control Interface Wizard, 669, 675, 680
ActiveX controls, 650–651, 652
  adding to DHTML pages, 713–715
  adding to projects, 66–67
  adding to toolbox, 664
  constituent controls, 651, 659–661
  creating, 653–658
  embedding in Web pages, 657
  event handlers, 659

events
  adding, 678–680
  Initialize event, 672
  Paint event, 657
  ReadProperties event, 671–672
  Terminate event, 672
  WriteProperties event, 671–672
files created for, 651
graphics, 655, 657
methods
  adding, 674–678
  Initialize method, 655
  RaiseEvent method, 679
properties
  adding at design time, 666–670
  Ambient property, 666
  AutoRedraw property, 657
  displaying, 47
  Extender property, 666
  Let and **Get** procedures, 667–668, 669
  making properties persistent, 671–674
property pages, 680–681
PropertyBag objects, 671, 693–694
referenced in VBP files, 25
registering with Windows, 67, 656, 664
testing, 655–656, 661–664
ActiveX Data Objects. *See* ADO (ActiveX Data Objects).
ActiveX Designers, 77
ActiveX DLLs, 935, 945
  methods, passing arguments to, 951–953
  registering, 957
  threading models, 936, 963
ActiveX Document Migration Wizard, 683
ActiveX documents, 651, 652. *See also* DHTML pages; Web pages.
  constituent controls, 684–689, 689
  converting Visual Basic projects to, 683

  creating, 682–683
  DLLs vs. EXE files, 652, 684
  DOB files, 686, 690–691
  events
    ReadProperties event, 693–694
    WriteProperties event, 693–694
  files created for, 651
  integrating Web browsers into, 691–692
  opening from Internet, 691–692
  properties, 693–694
  testing, 683, 690–691
  VBD files, 686, 690–691
ActiveX EXEs, 935, 945
  creating, 943–945
  methods, passing arguments to, 951–953
  properties, setting, 947
  registering, 958
  threading models, 936, 963
ActiveX MAPI controls, 697
Add Field dialog box, Visual Data Manager, 832
Add Form dialog box, 58–59, 178
Add-In Manager, 66
Add-Ins menu, IDE, 43, 66
Add method
  Buttons collection, 482–484
  collections, 110
  ListImages collection, 507
  ListItems collection, 520–521
  ListSubItems collection, 527–528
  Nodes collection, 512, 513
  Panels collection, 485
  Tabs collection, 533
Add Procedure dialog box, 667, 674–680, 947–949, 950
AddItem method, 254–255, 265
AddNew method, 844, 867–868
AddressCaption property, 720
AddressEditFieldCount property, 720
AddressLabel property, 720
AddressModifiable property, 720

ADO (ActiveX Data Objects), 827–828, 854. *See also* ADO data control; DAO (Data Access Objects); RDO (Remote Data Objects).
  adding records, 844, 888
  adocode example project, 883–894
  collections, 827
  creating record sets, 885–887
  data-bound controls, 840–841, 847–848, 887
  data environment, 824
  deleting records, 844–845, 892–893
  navigating data, 845–847, 890–892
  opening connections to databases, 884–885
  opening databases, 839–840
  refreshing data, 845, 888–889
  Remote Data Service (RDS), 828
  SQL commands, executing, 893–894
  transactions, 854
  updating data, 845, 889–890
ADO data-bound controls, 848–849
ADO data control, 828. *See also* ADO (ActiveX Data Objects).
  methods
    AddNew method, 844
    Delete method, 844–845
    MoveFirst method, 846
    MoveLast method, 846–847
    MoveNext method, 845–846
    MovePrevious method, 846
    Refresh method, 845
    UpdateRecord method, 845
  properties
    ConnectionString property, 828, 840
    DataSource property, 840
    Provider property, 828, 840
    Recordset property, 844, 845, 846
    RecordSource property, 828, 840
Adocode example project, 883–894
Advanced Optimizations dialog box, 64, 65. *See also* Compiler options; Optimization.
Advapi32.dll, 774
Alarm clock example program, 417–419
Alias clause, DLL procedure declarations, 776
Align item, Format menu, 52
Align property, 470, 494
Aligning controls, 51–52, 53–54, 442, 453
Aligning coolbars, 494
Aligning picture boxes, 317
Aligning status bars, 485
Aligning text, 200–201, 216–217, 446

Alignment property, 488
Allocating memory, 805–806, 807
AllowAddNew property, 849
AllowCustomize property, 482
AllowDelete property, 849
AllowUpdate property, 849
Ambient properties, 666
Ambient property, 666
Animation
  Animation control, 742–743
  arrays of Picture objects, 623, 634–635
  Move method, 132
  multimedia MCI control, 769
  picture boxes, 320–321
  in status bar panels, 489
  timer control, 419–421
Animation control, 742–743
ANSI character set, limiting fonts to, 360
Apartment-model threading, 936
API Viewer add-in tool, Visual Basic, 779
App object, 962
AppActivate function, 112
Appearance property, 439
AppIsRunning property, 908
Application deployment, 1044–1048
Application Wizard
  adding status bars to forms, 484
  adding toolbars to forms, 123–125
  designing menus, 157
  integrating Web browsers into projects, 691–692
  online help system, 1063–1064
  profiles, 23
  projects, creating, 22–28
Applications (Windows applications). *See* Windows applications.
Arcs, drawing, 460, 597–599
Area charts, 385–387
Arguments, passing, 679, 776, 951–953, 953–954
Arrange method, 141
Arranging MDI child windows, 140–141
Array function, 95, 96
Arrays. *See also* Control arrays.animation sequences, 623, 634–635
  array bounds checking, 63–65
  Array function, 95
  dynamic arrays, 94–95
  looping over elements, 108
  lower bound, 94
  Option Base statement, 94
  passing to procedures, 967–968
  standard arrays, 93–94
Arrows property, 295–296

As Form keywords, 992
As keyword, variable type, specifying, 11
Asc function, 90, 101
Atn function, 113
Attachment... properties, MAPIMessages control, 720
Auto List Members feature, IDE, 70, 72
AutoActivate property, 912
AutoPlay property, 743
AutoRedraw bitmap, 648
AutoRedraw property
  ActiveX controls, 657
  controls, 584
  drawing graphics from **Load** event, 588
  forms, 129, 584
  layering graphics, 611–612
  picture boxes, 328
  printing graphics, 610
AutoSize property, 317, 445, 488, 619
AutoVerbMenu property, 912–913
Available disk space, determining, 813–814
AVI files, playing, 742–743, 759–761
Axis titles in charts, 382

B

B argument, **Line** method, 593
Back button, Web browsers, 704
Back command, multimedia MCI control, 748, 769
BackColor property, 230, 585, 617
Background color. *See* **BackColor** property.
Bands, coolbar, 467, 494–495
"Bang" menus, 175–176
Bar charts, 2D and 3D, 387
BAS files (module files), 22
Best coding practices, 36–38
Bevel property, 488
Binary data, 425, 732–733
Binary files, 543, 554, 561–563
Binary raster operation mode (ROP2), 788–789
BitBlt Windows API function, 190, 793–794
Bitmaps, 190–192, 793–794
Blackness pen setting, 604
Blurring images, 646–647
BOF property, 871–872
Bold property, 590
Bolding text in RTF boxes, 209–211
Bookmarks, 78–79
Boolean variable type, 89

Border property, 903
BorderColor property, 585
Borders. *See* **BorderStyle** property;
  BorderWidth property.
BorderStyle property
  flex grid control, 400
  forms, 123
  image controls, 618
  line control, 456
  picture boxes, 619
  shape control, 452
BorderWidth property, 452, 456
Bound controls. *See* Data-bound
  controls.
BoundColumn property, 849
Bounds (array bounds)
  bounds checking, 63–65
  lower bound, 94
Boxes, drawing, 593–594
Break state, entering, 116
Breakpoints, 1031, 1036
Browser forms, customizing, 692. *See*
  also Web browsers.
BuddyControl property, 307
Bulleted text, RTF boxes, 214–215
Button groups, toolbars, 478
ButtonClick event, toolbars, 471–472
Buttons. *See* Checkboxes; Command
  buttons; Option buttons; Toolbars.
Buttons collection, toolbars, 482–484
ByRef keyword, 97, 98, 776, 951–953
Byte variable type, 89
ByVal keyword, 97, 98, 776, 951–953

C

C/C++ code
  C/C++ data types, 776–778
  linking programs to, 816–818
CAB files, 1045–1046
Calculator (ActiveX control example),
  660–661
Call keyword, 775
Cancel button, Common Dialog
  controls, 347–348, 1028–1029
Cancel property, 244–245
CancelError property, 347–348, 1028–
  1029
CanStep property, 769
Caption property
  buttons, 229, 235
  data control (DAO), 834
  forms, 121
  frame control, 439
  label control, 443

menus, 166
  tab strip tabs, 533
Capturing images from screen, 794–799
Case statement. *See* **Select Case**
  statement.
Casting. *See* Converting data between
  variable types.
CBool function, 90
CByte function, 90
CCur function, 90
CD (FTP command), 730
CDate function, 90
CDbl function, 90
CDec function, 90
CDs (music), playing, 753–755
CDUP (FTP command), 730
CellFont... properties, flex grid
  control, 401
Cells. *See* Flex grid control
Change event
combo boxes, 253, 267
  DateTimePicker control, 430
  directory list box control, 568
  drive list box control, 567–568
  list boxes, 253
  scroll bars, 289–290
  slider controls, 301
  text boxes, 145, 207
  updown controls, 308–309
Characters
  restricting input characters, 206–207
  Windows or ANSI character sets,
    limiting fonts to, 360
Chart control, 372–373, 375
  adding data to, 376–379
  adding to forms, 375
  area charts, 385–387
  bar charts, 387
  colors, setting, 382
  combination charts, 390–392
  data series, 379–381
  line charts, 381, 384–385
  pie charts, 382–383
  properties
    ChartData property, 376–377
    ChartType property, 375
    Column property, 377–378
    ColumnCount property, 377–378
    Data property, 377–378
    DataGrid property, 379
    Row property, 377–378
    RowCount property, 377–378
    RowLabel property, 378
  SetData methods, 379
  step charts, 381, 388–390
  titles, 382

ChartData property, 376–377
ChDir command, 816
ChDir statement, 572
ChDrive command, 816
Check buttons in toolbars, 477
Checkboxes, 227
  adding and removing at runtime, 242
  background color, 229–230
  binding to data controls, 847
  button releases, 244
  caption, 229
  combining with option buttons,
    249–250
  in control arrays, 233–234, 242
  disabling, 236–237
  displaying images in, 237, 239–240,
    241, 616
  events
    Click event, 232–233
    GotFocus event, 235
    Key... events, 244
    LostFocus event, 235
    Mouse... events, 244
  focus, 234, 236
  graphical checkboxes, 248
  keyboard access, 235
  methods
    Move method, 239
    SetFocus method, 234
  moving, 239
  passing to procedures, 243
  properties
    BackColor property, 230
    Caption property, 229, 235
    Default property, 234, 236
    DisabledPicture property, 237
    DownPicture property, 241, 248
    Enabled property, 237
    Font property, 231–232
    ForeColor property, 231
    Height property, 239
    Index property, 233–234
    Left property, 239
    Name property, 233–234
    Picture property, 239–240, 248
    Style property, 230, 237, 239–
      240, 241, 616
    TabIndex property, 236
    TabStop property, 236
    ToolTipText property, 238
    Top property, 239
    Value property, 245–246
    Visible property, 237–238
    Width property, 239
  resizing, 239
  responding to button clicks, 232–233

showing and hiding, 237–238
state of checkbox, 245–246
tab order, 236
text attributes, 230–232
tool tips, 238
Checked property, 179
Checkmarks, 178–179, 264
Child property, 495–496
Choose function, 106
Chr function, 90, 101
CInt function, 90
Circle method
  drawing arcs, 460, 597–599
  drawing ellipses, 460, 596–597
  forms and picture boxes, 324, 459,
    594–595
  printing graphics, 610–611
Circles, drawing, 324–325, 450, 459,
  594–595
Class modules, 128, 934, 946. *See also*
  Classes, code components; Modules.
Class property, 904
Classes, code components, 934–935
  adding to components, 944
  creating objects, 940–942
  Initialize event, 958
  Instancing property, 936–937,
    959–960
  Terminate event, 958–959
Clear method, 264, 272
Clearing combo box items, 272
Clearing drawing area, 585
Clearing images, 621
Clearing list box items, 264–265
Clearing slider control selections, 306
ClearSel method, 306
Click event
  buttons, 232–233
  combo boxes, 253, 267–268
  coolbar controls, 496–497
  label control, 446
  list boxes, 253, 256–257
  multiselect list boxes, 261
  picture boxes, 318
  tab strips, 536
  Web browser navigation, 701
Client area, 119
ClientToScreen Windows API
  function, 790, 800–802
Clip property, 626
Clipboard, 204–205, 332–333, 609, 610,
  927
Clipboard object
  methods
    GetData method, 332

GetText method, 205
    SetData method, 332
    SetText method, 205
  password controls, security of, 206
ClipControls property, 611–612
ClipHeight, **ClipWidth** properties, 626
ClipX, **ClipY** properties, 626
CLng function, 90
Clock example program, 415–416
Close command, multimedia MCI
  control, 748, 753
Close method, 578–579, 898, 908
Close statement, 564
Cls method, 330, 585, 621, 648
Code components, 651, 652, 934
  classes, 934–935, 944, 958–959
  creating, 942–945
  dialog box libraries, 962
  forms, showing, 961
  global objects, 935, 959–960
  in-process servers (ActiveX DLLs),
    935, 936, 945, 951–953, 957, 963
  methods, 942, 950, 951–953
  objects, 934–935, 940–942, 960–961
  out-of-process servers (ActiveX
    EXEs), 935, 936, 943–945, 947,
    951–953, 958, 963
  properties, 942, 946, 947–949
  references to, adding, 938
  SingleUse code components, 936–937
  testing, 954–956
  threading models, 936, 963
  type libraries, 940, 941
  using in projects, 938–940
Code windows, 6, 49
Col property, 393
Collapse event, 517
Collection ADO object, 827
Collections, 110. *See also names of*
  specific collections.
  looping over elements in, 108
  methods
    Add method, 110
    Item method, 110
    Remove method, 110
Color constants, Visual Basic, 586–587
Color dialog box, 348–350
Color property, 358
Colors
  Color dialog box, 348–350
  color-related properties, 585
  converting images to grayscale,
    637–640
  custom colors, allowing definition
    of, 350

drawing pen, 604–606
fill color, 453, 585, 601–602
four-byte integer color
  specifications, 588
IDE, customizing, 50–51
of points, retrieving, 604
propagating color values among
  pixels, 645
QBColor function, 586
RGB function, 586
system color constants, 587–588
Visual Basic color constants, 586–587
ColPosition property, 402
Cols property, 393
Column property, 377–378
ColumnClick event, 529
ColumnCount property, 377–378
Columns
  flex grid control, 402–403
  list views, 525–528
Columns property, 263, 629
Combination charts, 2D and 3D, 390–392
Combo boxes, 252–253
  adding items, 266
  adding to toolbars, 479–481
  binding to data controls, 847
  clearing items, 272
  events
    Change event, 253, 267
    Click event, 253, 267–268
    DblClick event, 253
    DblClick events, 268
  image combo boxes, 277–279
  index of new items, 276–277
  ItemData array, 275–276
  locking, 272–273
  methods
    AddItem method, 265
    Clear method, 272
    RemoveItem method, 269
  number of items, 273–274
  numeric data, connecting to list
    items, 275–276
  properties
    Enabled property, 273
    List property, 265
    ListCount property, 273–274
    ListIndex property, 267–268, 270
    Locked property, 272
    NewIndex property, 276–277
    Sorted property, 271
    Style property, 265, 273
    Text property, 265, 267, 270–271
    TopIndex property, 274–275
    Visible property, 273

removing items, 269
restricting user input, 271, 272–273
selected items, 267–268, 270–271, 275
sorting, 271–272
topmost item, 274–275
types of, 265
Web browser navigation, 700–701
Comdlg32.dll, 774
ComEvent... errors, 426–427
Command ADO object, 827
Command buttons, 227
  adding and removing at runtime, 242
  background color, 229–230
  button releases, 244
  in control arrays, 233–234, 242
  disabling, 236–237
  displaying images, 237, 239–240, 241, 616
  events
    Click event, 232–233
    GotFocus event, 235
    Key... events, 244
    LostFocus event, 235
    Mouse... events, 244
  focus, 234, 236
  keyboard access, 235
  methods
    Move method, 239
    SetFocus method, 234
  moving, 239
  passing to procedures, 243
  properties
    BackColor property, 230
    Cancel property, 244–245
    Caption property, 229, 235
    Default property, 234, 236
    DisabledPicture property, 237
    DownPicture property, 241
    Enabled property, 237
    Font property, 231–232
    ForeColor property, 231
    Height property, 239
    Index property, 233, 234
    Left property, 239
    Name property, 233, 234
    Picture property, 239–240
    Style property, 230, 237, 239–240, 241, 616
    TabIndex property, 236
    TabStop property, 236
    ToolTipText property, 238
    Top property, 239
    Visible property, 237–238
    Width property, 239
  resizing, 239

responding to button clicks, 232–233
setting caption, 229
showing and hiding, 237–238
tab order, 236
text attributes, 230–232
tool tips, 238
using as Cancel buttons, 244–245
Command property, 741
Command strings, sending to modem, 423–424
Commands. *See also* Menu items.
  FTP commands, 730, 735
  multimedia MCI control commands, 748–749
  OLE primary verbs, executing, 914
  SQL commands, executing, 874–875, 883, 893–894
  in text boxes and RTF boxes, 198–199
Commenting conventions, 33–34
CommEvent property, 409, 422, 424, 426–427
Common Controls, Windows. *See* Windows Common Controls.
Common Dialog controls, 342–343
  adding to forms, 345
  Cancel button, trapping button clicks, 347–348, 1028–1029
  Color dialog box, 348–350
  displaying dialog boxes, 345–346
  displaying Windows Help, 368–370
  File Open dialog box, 350–357, 544–545
  File Save As dialog box, 350–357
  Font dialog box, 358–362
  methods
    ShowColor method, 348–350
    ShowFont method, 358
    ShowHelp method, 368
    ShowOpen method, 350–351
    ShowSave method, 350–351
  Print dialog box, 363–368
  properties
    Action property, 346
    CancelError property, 347–348
    Copies property, 364
    DefaultExt property, 355
    FileName property, 350–351, 354
    FileTitle property, 351, 354
    Filter property, 356–357
    Flags property, 350, 352–353, 358, 360–361, 365–366
    FromPage property, 364
    hDC property, 364
    HelpCommand property, 368
    HelpFile property, 368

InitDir property, 355–356
MaxFileSize property, 354
Min, **Max** properties, 361–362, 366
Orientation property, 367–368
PrinterDefault property, 363
ToPage property, 364
title bar text, 346–347
CommPort property, 408, 423
Communications control, 407–408
  adding to forms, 421
  buffers, 422
  handshaking, 425
  modem command strings, sending, 423–424
  OnComm event, 409, 422, 424, 426–427
  properties
    CommEvent property, 409, 422, 424, 426–427
    CommPort property, 408, 423
    EOFEnable property, 409, 422
    Handshaking property, 425
    InBufferCount property, 409, 424
    InBufferSize property, 408, 422
    Input property, 409, 422, 423, 424
    InputLen property, 409, 422, 424
    OutBufferCount property, 409, 425
    OutBufferSize property, 408, 422
    Output property, 409, 423–424, 425
    PortOpen property, 408, 423, 427
    RThreshold property, 408, 422
    Settings property, 408, 423
    SThreshold property, 408, 422
  reading data, 409, 424
  sending data, 409, 425
  serial port, 408, 423, 427
Comparison operators, precedence of, 103
Compiler options
  array bounds checking, 64
  fast code, optimizing for, 75
  listed in VBP files, 15
  Pentium FDIV error check, 65
  Pentium Pro processor, optimizing for, 76
  small code, optimizing for, 75
Compiling Help files, 1060
Components, 58, 176–178. *See also* ActiveX controls; Code components.
Components dialog box, 67, 77, 664
Compose buffer, MAPIMessages control, 719
Compose method, 719, 721

Conditional statements. *See also*
  Choose function; **Switch** function.
  If...Else statement, 104
  nesting, 37
  Select Case statement, 105
Connection object, ADO, 827, 884–885
Connection object, RDO, 854, 877–879, 883
ConnectionEvents, ADO, 828
Connections, serial. *See* Communications control.
ConnectionString property, 828, 840
Const statement, 85
Constants, 33, 36–37, 85–86, 778–779
Constituent controls, 651, 659–661, 684–689
Container controls, 322, 439–443
Containers, 611–612
Control arrays
  buttons, 233–234, 242
  controls, loading at runtime, 973–975
  multiple OLE objects, 916–924
  passing to procedures, 968, 970–971
  Ubound property, 973
Control boxes, 122
Control buttons, 146
Control type, 970
Control variable type, 970
ControlBox property, 122
Controls. *See also* Data-bound controls;
  Keyboard interface.
  active control, determining, 971–972
  adding code to, 49
  adding using toolbox, 48
  aligning, 51–52, 53–54, 453
  basing ActiveX controls on, 657–658
  binding to ADO record sets, 887
  clearing drawing area, 585
  creating and loading at runtime, 973–975
  determining type of, 972–973
  device contexts, 780
  drag and drop operations, 976–983
  events
    DragDrop event, 981–982
    DragOver event, 982–983
    Paint event, 584
  grouping, 322, 442–443
  lightweight (windowless) controls, 990–991
  methods
    Cls method, 585
    Move method, 131–132
    ZOrder method, 976

  moving, 131
  naming conventions (prefixes), 29–32
  passing to procedures, 970
  properties
    ActiveControl property, 971–972
    AutoRedraw property, 584, 610
    BackColor property, 585
    BorderColor property, 585
    DataSource property, 887
    DragMode property, 976
    FillColor property, 585
    ForeColor property, 585
    hDC property, 780
    managing using Properties window, 46–47
    OLEDropMode property, 984
    Parent property, 136
    TabIndex property, 130, 975
    TabStop property, 19, 130
    Visible property, 132
  redrawing graphics, 584
  showing and hiding, 132
  sizing, 51–52, 131
  tab order, 129–130, 236, 975
  Z-order position, 976
Controls collection, 993–994
Conventions. *See* Programming conventions, Microsoft.
Converting data between variable types, 90, 102
Coolbars, 466–467, 493–497
Coordinate systems, 133, 583, 606–607, 790
Copies property, 364
Copy method, 573, 719, 898
Copy Pen pen setting, 605
Copying images, 609, 635–636
Copying OLE objects, 927
Copyright information, adding to projects, 59
Core Windows DLLs, 774
Cos function, 113
Cosecant function, 114
Cotangent function, 114
CPP files, in DLLs, 816
Create New Data Source dialog box, 836
CreateBrush Windows API function, 788
CreateCompatibleBitmap Windows API function, 190
CreateCompatibleDC Windows API function, 190
CreateDatabase method, 857–858
CreateDC function, 780–781
CreateEmbed method, 898

CreateField method, 861–863
CreateIndex method, 861–863
CreateLink method, 898
CreateObject function, 940–941
CreatePen Windows API function, 786
CSng function, 90
CStr function, 90
CTL files (ActiveX control class files), 651
Ctrl key, 112, 172–173
CurDir command, 816
Currency variable type, 89, 116
Current directory, 353
Current form, referencing, 128
Current time, displaying, 415
CurrentX, **CurrentY** properties, 588
Custom colors, 350
Customize dialog box, IDE, 68
Customize Toolbar dialog box, Application Wizard, 469
CVar function, 90
CVErr function, 90, 1026–1027

D

DAO (Data Access Objects), 824–825, 853–854. *See also* ADO (ActiveX Data Objects); Data control, DAO; RDO (Remote Data Objects).
  adding records, 844, 867–868
  creating databases, 857–859
  creating record sets, 863–865
  DAO Object Library, 857
  daocode example project, 856–875
  data-bound controls, 835, 847–848
  deleting records, 844–845, 872
  editing records, 868
  indexes on tables, creating, 861–863
  navigating data, 845–847, 869–872
  OpenDatabase method, 865–867
  opening databases, 865–867
  refreshing data, 845
  searching record sets, 873
  sorting records, 872
  SQL statements, executing, 874–875
  tables, 859, 860–861
  updating data, 845, 868–869
  workspace, 824
DAO Object Library, 857
Daocode example project, 856–875
Darkening images, 641
Dashed lines, drawing using line control, 456
Data. *See also* Databases.
  adding to charts, 376–379

dragging and dropping between applications, 983–990
entering in databases, 833
reading from memory, 808, 809
receiving and sending, 424, 425
sensitive data, protecting, 37
storing in memory, 806, 808
Data Access Objects. *See* DAO (Data Access Objects).
Data-bound controls, 828–829
  with ADO data control, 840–841, 848–849
  with data control (DAO), 826, 835
  list of, 847–848
  with remote data control, 826, 838–839
  Data control, DAO, 825–826. *See also* ADO data control; Remote data control.
  adding to programs, 834
  connecting to bound controls, 835
  methods
    AddNew method, 844
    Delete method, 844–845
    MoveFirst method, 846
    MoveLast method, 846–847
    MoveNext method, 845–846
    MovePrevious method, 846
    Refresh method, 845
    UpdateRecord method, 845
  properties
    Caption property, 834
    Database property, 826
    DatabaseName property, 835
    Recordset property, 826, 844, 845, 846
    RecordSource property, 826, 835
Data conversion, 90, 102
Data forms, 841–843
Data property, 377–378
Data series, 379–381
Data Tips, 70, 72
Data types. *See* Variable types.
Database access, 830, 836–837. *See also* ADO (ActiveX Data Objects); DAO (Data Access Objects); Data-bound controls; RDO (Remote Data Objects).
Database object, DAO, 825, 853, 857–859, 863–865, 874–875
Database property, 826
DatabaseName property, 835
Databases. *See also* ADO (ActiveX Data Objects); DAO (Data Access Objects); RDO (Remote Data Objects).
  adding records, 844, 867–868, 888

adocode example project, 883–894
components of, 823
connecting to flex grid controls, 403–404
creating, 830–833, 857–859
daocode example project, 856–875
deleting records, 844–845, 872, 892–893
moving between records, 845–847
navigating, 845–847, 869–872, 879–883, 890–892
opening, 835, 838, 839–840, 865–867
opening connections to, 876–877, 883–885
rdocode example project, 875–884
refreshing data, 845
relational databases, 776
updating, 845, 868–869, 889–890
DataCombo control, properties
  BoundColumn property, 849
  data properties, 849
  DataField property, 849
  DataSource property, 849
  ListField property, 849
  RowSource property, 849
DataField property, 835, 838–839, 840–841, 849
DataGrid control, 849
DataGrid property, 379
DataList control, 849
DataObject object, 984, 987
DataSource property
  ADO data control, 840
  controls, 887
  DataCombo control, 849
  DataGrid control, 849
  DataList control, 849
  flex grid control, 393, 404
  remote data control, 838
  text boxes, 835, 838–839, 840–841
DataSourceName property, 838
Date... methods, 574
Date function, 115
Date$ function, 413
Date values, 114–115, 413–415
Date variable type, 89
DateAdd function, 115
DateClick event, MonthView control, 428–429
DateDiff function, 115
DatePart function, 115
DateSerial function, 90, 115
DateTimePicker control, 410, 429–430
DateValue function, 90, 115
Day function, 90

DBCombo boxes, binding to data controls, 847
DBEngine DAO object, 825
DblClick event
  combo boxes, 253, 268
  label control, 446
  list boxes, 253, 256–257
  multiselect list boxes, 261
  option buttons, 233
DBList boxes, binding to data controls, 847
DDB function, 116
Deactivating OLE objects, 916
Deallocating memory, 809, 810
Debug menu, IDE, 43
Debug toolbar, IDE, 61, 62
Debugging, 1007, 1029–1030
  breakpoints, 1031, 1036
  examining expressions and variables, 1033–1036
  executing code to cursor, 1036
  Immediate window, 1035–1036
  Quick Watch window, 1033
  single-stepping, 1032
  skipping statements, 1036
  using message boxes, 1030
  Watch window, 1034
Decimal variable type, 89
Declaring arrays, 93–95
Declaring constants, 85–86
Declaring DLL procedures, 775–776
Declaring DLLs, 818
Declaring functions, 97–98
Declaring methods in code components, 950
Declaring properties in class modules, 946
Declaring subroutines, 96–97
Declaring variables, 11, 86–87
  implicit declaration, 87
  Option Explicit statement, 38, 88
  Option Private Module statement, 91
  variable scope, 90–91
  variable types, 88–89
Declaring Windows API functions, 775–776
DEF files, in DLLs, 818
Default property, 234, 236
Default values, optional arguments, 954
DefaultExt property, 355
Defensive programming, 37
DELETE (FTP command), 730
Delete method
  data controls, 844–845

FileObject, 574
MAPIMessages control, 719, 720
OLE control, 926
OLE objects, 898
Recordset objects, 872, 892–893
DeleteDC function, 782
DeleteFile method, 574
DeleteSetting Windows API function, 999
Deleting OLE objects, 926
Deployment package, 1044–1048
Description property, 1021–1022
Design standards, 155–156, 163–165, 172–173
Design time grid, 53–54, 453
Design time properties, 46
"Designed for Microsoft Windows" logo, 1041–1042
Device contexts
    controls, 780
    copying bitmaps between, 793–794
    deleting, 782
    drawing in, 782–788
    for entire screen, 781–782
    printers, 365
    ROP2 (binary raster operation) mode, 788–789
    windows, 780
Devices. *See* Media Control Interface (MCI) devices.
DeviceType property, 744–745
DHTML controls, 710
DHTML (Dynamic HTML), 696, 710, 715. *See also* DHTML Page Designer; DHTML pages.
DHTML Page Designer
    opening, 706
    Table Operation drop-down box, 715–716
    text, entering, 709–710
    toolbar, inserting HTML tags, 710
    toolbox, 710–711, 712–713, 716–717
DHTML pages
    ActiveX controls, 713–715
    HTML controls, 712–713
    HTML tags, 710
    hyperlinks, 716–717
    images, 710–711
    tables, 715–716
    testing, 717
    text, 709–710
Dialog boxes
    Cancel buttons, 244–245
    creating, 146–147
    designing, 122

displaying icons in taskbar, 995
libraries of, 962
modal display of, 147, 962, 996–997
Dim statement, 11, 86, 93–94, 138
DIR (FTP command), 730
Directories
    changing, 572, 816
    creating and deleting, 572
    current directory, 353, 816
    default directory, 816
    downloading from Web pages, 731, 732
    Windows installation directory, 814–815
Directory list box control, 568, 569–571
DisabledPicture property, 237
Disabling buttons, 236–237
Disabling forms at runtime, 151
Disabling menu items, 180–181
Disk space available, determining, 813–814
Display screen. *See* Screen; Screen object.
DisplayType property, 903–904
Distances, changing measurement scale, 17
<DIV> DHTML tag, 710
DLL files, 1043
DLL procedures, 775–776
DLLs (Dynamic Link Libraries)
    ActiveX components, 652
    ActiveX documents, 684
    C++ DLLs, linking to, 816–818
    code components (ActiveX DLLs), 935, 936, 945, 951–953, 957, 963
    components of, 816–818
    core Windows DLLs, 774
    declaring, 818
    DHTML pages, 706
    error handling, 1023
    vs. EXE files, 652, 684
Do loop, 107
DOB files (ActiveX document files), 651, 686
Dockable toolbars, 44
Document views, 144
DocumentProperties Windows API function, 780
Documents, 141, 144–145. *See also* ActiveX documents; MDI child forms; MDI forms.
Done event, 741, 763–764, 768
Dotted lines, drawing, 456
Double-clicking. *See* **DblClick** event.
Double variable type, 89
DoVerb method, 898, 913–914
Down picture, adding to buttons, 241

DownClick event, 308–309
DownloadComplete event, 701
Downloading files, 728–736
DownLoadMail property, 721, 725
DownPicture property, 241, 248
Drag and drop operations
    columns in flex grid controls, 402–403
    controls, 976–983
    frames, 440–442
    OLE objects, 983–990
Drag method, 440–441, 924–925
DragDrop event, 925, 977, 978–982
DragMode property, 976
DragOver event, 982–983
Drawing area, clearing, 585
Drawing boxes, 593–594
Drawing circles, 324–325, 450, 459, 594–595
Drawing freehand lines, 599–600
Drawing images, 622–623
Drawing lines, 325–326, 455–458, 591, 782–783
Drawing mode, setting, 604–606, 788–789
Drawing ovals, 450
Drawing pen, setting, 604–606, 786–788
Drawing points, 326, 604
Drawing position, setting, 782–783
Drawing rectangles, 449
Drawing rounded rectangles, 451
Drawing rounded squares, 451
Drawing scales, setting, 606–607
Drawing squares, 449
Drawing style, setting, 602–603
Drawing width, setting, 602–603
DrawMode property, 604–606
DrawStyle property, 602–603
DrawWidth property, 602–603
Drive list box control, 567–568, 569–571
Drive property, 567–568
Drop-down combo boxes, 265
Drop-down list combo boxes, 265
Dynamic arrays, 94–95
Dynamic HTML. *See* DHTML (Dynamic HTML).
Dynamic HTML Application item, New Project dialog box, 706
Dynamic Link Libraries. *See* DLLs (Dynamic Link Libraries).

E

Edit menu, 43, 78–79, 164–165
Edit method, 868
Edit toolbar, 61, 62

Editing images, 623
Editing OLE objects, 896, 912
Eject command, multimedia MCI
control, 748, 755
Ejecting CDs, 755
Elapsed time, displaying, 417, 752
Ellipse Windows API function, 784
Ellipses, drawing, 460, 596–597, 784
Ellipsis (...) in names of menu items, 155
ElseIf statement, 104
Email functionality. *See also*
MAPIMessages control; MAPISession
control.
composing messages, 721–722
MAPI controls, adding to projects, 718
MAPI session, initiating, 721
reading messages, 725–726
sending messages, 722–723
Visual Basic support for, 007
Embedded OLE objects, 897–899, 902,
905–907, 908–911, 929–930
Embedding ActiveX controls in Web
pages, 657
Embossing images, 642–644
Enabled property
buttons, 237
combo boxes, 273
forms, 151
menu items, 181
scroll bars, 292
text boxes, 202
timer control, 412
Encapsulation, 37
End Function keywords, 99
End statement, 116
End Sub keywords, 97
EndDoc method, 611
Ending programs, 116, 136
Engraving images, 644–645
Enlarging OLE objects, 928
Enterprise Edition, Visual Basic, 2
EOF function, 556
EOF property, 870–871
EOFEnable property, 409, 422
Erase statement, 96
Erasing images, 621
Err object
Description property, 1021–1022
LastDLLError property, 1023
Number property, 1020–1021
Raise method, 1023–1024
Source property, 1022
Error ADO object, 827
Error function, 1021

Error handlers
disabling error trapping, 1015–1016
disregarding errors, 1015
nested error handling, 1024–1025
resuming execution, 1016–1020
using labels, 1012–1013
using line numbers, 1014
writing, 1009–1012
Error objects, creating, 1026–1027
Error property, 764–768
Error strings, multimedia MCI control,
765–767
ErrorMessages property, 764–768
Errors
comEvent... errors, 426–427
determining which error occurred,
1020–1021
in DLLs, 1023
error description, 1021–1022
list of trappable errors, 1003–1007
Pentium FDIV error, 65
source of error, 1022
trapping Cancel button in Common
Dialogs, 347–348, 1028–1029
user-defined errors, 1023–1024
Errors collection, ADO, 827
Event handlers, 6, 659, 713
Events, 678–680. *See also names of*
specific events.
Events ADO objects, 827
Exclamation point (!) in menu item
names, 156, 176
Exclusive OR pen. *See* Xor Pen
pen setting.
EXE files
ActiveX components, 652
ActiveX documents, 684
code components (ActiveX EXEs),
935, 945
creating, 943–945
methods, passing arguments to,
951–953
properties, setting, 947
registering, 958
threading models, 936, 963
creating, 44, 1043
vs. DLLs, 652, 684
icon, specifying, 61
name, setting, 61
Execute method, 697, 698, 727, 729–730,
735
Exit Function keywords, 98
Exit item, File menu, 164
Exit Sub keywords, 97
Exp function, 113

Expand event, tree views, 517
Expanded property, 518
Expressions
date and time format expressions, 115
examining values of (debugging),
1033–1036
operator precedence, 102–104
values of constants, 85
Extender objects, 666
Extender property, 666

F

F argument, **Line** method, 602
Fast code, optimizing for, 75
FDIV error, Pentium, 65
Fetch method, 719, 725
FetchMsgType property, 719
FetchSorted property, 719, 720
FetchUnreadOnly property, 719
FetchVerbs method, OLE objects, 898
Field ADO object, 827
Field DAO object, 825
Fields, database, 823, 831–832, 860–861
Fields collection, ADO, 827
Figures. *See* Graphics.
File list box control, 569
File menu, 43, 44, 164
File name extensions, 352, 355
File names
maximum length, setting, 354
retrieving in File Open, File Save As
dialog boxes, 350–351, 354, 544–545
temporary, 1066
File Open dialog box, 350–357, 544–545
File Save As dialog box, 350–357
File statistics, 574–575
File Transfer Protocol. *See* FTP (File
Transfer Protocol).
File types, specifying, 356–357
FileLen function, 548
FileName property
Common Dialog controls, 350–351,
354
file list box control, 569
multimedia MCI control, 745
FileObject, 573–574
Files
closing, 564
copying, 572. *See also* Clipboard
object.
creating, 352, 546–548
deleting, 574
file numbers, 548

file statistics, 574–575
FileObject, 572–575
FileSystemObject, 543, 572–577
length of, 548–549
moving, 573–574
opening, 549–550, 565, 566, 745. *See also* File Open dialog box.
saving, 564–565, 566. *See also* File Save As dialog box.
temporary file names, 1066
TextStream objects, 575–579
transferring. *See* FTP (File Transfer Protocol).
FileSystemObject, 543, 572–577
FileTitle property, 351, 354
Fill color, 601–602
Fill pattern, 602
FillColor property
controls, 585
forms, 585, 601–602
picture boxes, 601–602
shape control, 453
FillStyle property
forms and picture boxes, 602
shape control, 452
Filters, 356–357
Financial functions, 116
Fix function, 90, 113
Fixed-length strings, 101
FixedCols, **FixedRows** properties, 393, 400
Flags property, 350, 352–353, 358, 360–361, 365–366
Flat scroll bars, 283–284, 294–296. *See also* Scroll bars.
Flex grid control, 373–374
adding to forms, 392–393
borders, 400
columns, dragging, 402–403
connecting to databases, 393, 403–404, 847
data entry, 394, 395, 397–399
events
KeyPress event, 395
LeaveCell event, 399
MouseDown event, 402
formatting cells, 401
grid lines, 400
labeling rows and columns, 400
properties
BorderStyle property, 400
CellFont... properties, 401
Col, **Cols** properties, 393
ColPosition property, 402
DataSource property, 393, 404

FixedCols, **FixedRows** properties, 393, 400
GridLines property, 400
GridLineWidth property, 400
MouseCol property, 402
Row, **Rows** property, 393
Sort property, 401
Text property, 393, 394
TextArray property, 400
resetting focus on specific cells, 396
sorting data, 401
using as spreadsheet, 393–399
Flipping images, 333–334, 630–631
Focus
cells in flex grid control, 396
giving to Windows applications, 112
label controls, 447
resetting after button click, 218, 234
setting when form loads, 234
tab order of controls, 129–130, 975
Font... properties
buttons, 232
Color dialog box, 358–359
label control, 445
picture boxes, 329
Font dialog box, 358–361
Font object, 590
Font property, 231–232
FontCount property, 591, 608
Fonts
customizing in IDE, 50–51
determining fonts available, 590–591
setting attributes for buttons, 231–232
setting attributes in RTF boxes, 212–214
Fonts property, 590–591, 608
Footnotes, in Help files, 1065
For Each loop, 108
For loop, 108
ForeColor property
buttons, 231
forms and controls, 585
Foreign keys, 776
Form designers, 48
Form Editor toolbar, IDE, 61, 62–63
Form Layout window, IDE, 47–48
Form-level variables, 7, 8, 91
Form Load event, 8, 588. *See also* **Initialize** event.
Format function, 90, 101, 102
Format$ function, 115, 414–415
Format menu, 43, 52–53
Formatting date and time values, 114–115, 413–415, 429
Formatting flex grid control cells, 401

Formatting string expressions, 102
Formatting text, 329–330, 445–446, 589, 710. *See also* RTF boxes.
Forms, 10. *See also* MDI forms.
active form, determining, 992–993
adding code to, 49
adding controls, 48
adding menus to, 165–168
arrays of forms, 142–143
background color, 617
browser forms, 692
clearing drawing area, 585
components of, 118–119
Controls collection, 993–994
coordinate systems, 133, 606–607
creating at runtime, 138
current form, referencing in code, 128
displaying in Web pages, 682–683. *See also* ActiveX documents.
drag and drop operations, 924–925, 982–990
drawing in forms, 459, 591–600, 602–607
enabling and disabling at runtime, 151
events
DragDrop event, 925, 977, 978–981
DragOver event, 982–983
MouseDown event, 186
Paint event, 584
Resize event, 608–609
form-level variables, 91
icons in Windows 95 taskbar, 995
keystrokes, intercepting, 995–996
layers, 611–612
loading, 136
LoadPicture function, 617
making immovable, 996
managing using Project Explorer, 45
maximizing and minimizing at runtime, 122, 151
methods
Arrange method, 141
Circle method, 459
Cls method, 585, 621
Hide method, 137
Line method, 458
Move method, 978
Point method, 604
PSet method, 604
Show method, 136, 147, 961, 962
moving controls, 131
multiple forms, 134–136
passing to procedures, 150–151, 992
positioning off screen, 69

predefined forms, 57, 58–59
printing graphics, 610–611
properties
　AutoRedraw property, 129, 584,
　　610, 611–612
　BackColor property, 585, 617
　BorderColor property, 585
　BorderStyle property, 123
　Caption property, 121
　ControlBox property, 122
　CurrentX, **CurrentY** properties,
　　588
　DrawMode property, 604–606
　DrawStyle property, 602–603
　DrawWidth property, 602–603
　Enabled property, 151
　FillColor property, 585, 601–602
　FillStyle property, 602
　Font... properties, 580
　ForeColor property, 585
　Height property, 133
　Image property, 648
　KeyPreview property, 995–996
　Left property, 133
　MDIChild property, 139
　Moveable property, 996
　Picture property, 617, 648
　ScaleHeight property, 133
　ScaleLeft property, 133
　ScaleMode property, 17, 133,
　　606–607, 636
　ScaleTop property, 133
　ScaleWidth property, 133
　ShowInTaskbar property, 995
　StartUpPosition property, 995
　Top property, 133
　Width property, 133
　WindowState property, 151
redrawing, 129, 584
resizing graphics, 608–609
showing and hiding controls, 132
showing and hiding forms, 136, 137
showing from code components, 961
startup forms, 55, 61, 69, 137
startup position, 995
title bar text, 121, 802–803
Z-order position, 810–812
Forward button, Web browsers, 704
Forward method, 719
Frame control, 435
　adding to forms, 439
　aligning controls, 442
　dragging and dropping, 440–442
　grouping controls, 246, 442–443
　location and size, 440

methods
　Drag method, 440–441
　Move method, 440
properties
　Appearance property, 439
　Caption property, 439
　Height property, 440
　Left property, 440
　ToolTipText property, 439
　Top property, 440
　Width property, 440
Frames, 717, 769. *See also* Frame control.
Frames property, 769
Free disk space, determining, 813–814
FreeFile function, 548
Freehand line drawing, 599–600
Freeing memory, 647–648, 809
Friend keyword, 13, 96, 946, 950
FRM files (form files), 16, 22, 26
From property, 770
FromPage property, 364
Front layer of forms, 611
FTP (File Transfer Protocol), 697,
　727–734, 1066–1068. *See also* Internet
　transfer control.
Functions
　calling, 98
　declaring, 97–98
　DLL functions, 775–776
　variable values, preserving, 99–100
FV function, 116

G

Gdi32.dll, 774
GET (FTP command), 730
GET (HTTP command), 735
Get/Let properties, code components,
　947–949
Get procedure, 667–668, 669, 947–949
Get statement, 558–564
GetAllSettings Windows API
　function, 999
GetCapture Windows API function,
　790–793, 800–802
GetChunk method, 729
GetData method, 332, 610, 984, 987
GetDC method, 780
GetDiskFreeSpace Windows API
　function, 813–814
GetFile method, 573
GetNumTicks method, 299
GetObject function, 941–942
GetSetting Windows API function,
　192–193, 997–998

GetTempName method, 1066
GetText method, 205
GetWindowsDirectory Windows API
　function, 814–815
GetWindowText Windows API
　function, 802–803
Global items, 10
Global object, Visual Basic, 994
Global objects, 935, 959–960
Global variables, 10, 37, 91
GlobalAlloc Windows API function,
　805, 807
GlobalFree Windows API function,
　809, 810
GlobalLock Windows API function,
　805, 806, 807
GlobalMultiUse value, 937, 960
GlobalSingleUse value, 937, 960
GlobaUnlock Windows API function,
　808–809
GoBack method, 704
GoForward method, 704
GoHome method, 701, 705
GoSearch method, 705
GotFocus event, 235
Graphical buttons, 248
GraphicCell array, 629
Graphics
　adding to ActiveX controls, 655, 657
　bitmaps, 190–192, 793–794
　copying to Clipboard, 609
　drawing
　　boxes, 593–594
　　circles, 324–325, 450, 459, 594–595
　　clearing drawing area, 585
　　freehand lines, 599–600
　　images, 622–623
　　lines, 591–592, 782–783
　　in picture boxes, 323–326
　　points, 604
　　setting drawing mode, 604–606,
　　　788–789
　　setting drawing pen, 604–606,
　　　786–788
　　setting drawing position, 782–783
　　setting drawing scales, 606–607
　　setting drawing style, 602–603
　　setting drawing width, 602–603
　　text, 588–589
　fill color and patterns, 601–602
　freeing memory used by, 647–648
　layering, 611–612
　manipulating at pixel level, 635–647
　pasting from Clipboard, 610
　printing, 610–611

redrawing, 584
resizing, 608–609
Graphics controls, vs. graphics
methods, 582–583
Graying out menu items, 180–181
Grayscale images, 637–640
Grid controls, 373–374. *See also* Flex
grid control.
Grid lines, 53, 453
GridLines property, 400
GridLineWidth property, 400
Grippers, 467
Grouping buttons in toolbars, 478
Grouping controls in frame controls,
442–443
Grouping controls in picture boxes, 322
Grouping option buttons, 246

H

Handle property, 336
Handles
device context handles, 780
memory handles, 805, 806
picture box handles, 336
window handles, 800–802, 811
Handshaking property, 425
Hayes-type modem commands, 423–424
HDC property, 336, 364, 780
HEAD (HTTP command), 735
Header files, included in DLLs, 816–818
Height property
buttons, 239
forms, 133
frame control, 440
label control, 443
picture boxes, 338, 607
Screen object, 608
shape control, 454
Help button, displaying in Common
Dialog controls, 353
Help files, 1040
compiling, 1060
displaying, 368–370, 1061–1062
Help projects, 1049–1050
index, 1058
online help, 1063
RTF files, creating, 1051–1060
Help menu, 44, 165
Help Workshop, 369, 1049–1050, 1060
HelpCommand property, 368
HelpFile property, 368
Hex function, 90
HideSelection property, 204

Hiding and showing controls, 132
Hiding and showing menus and menu
items, 184
Hiding and showing scroll bars, 292
Hiding and showing shapes, 455
Hiding and showing windows in IDE, 73
Highlighting, turning on and off, 204
Histograms, 387
Home button, Web browsers, 705
Horizontal scroll bars, 286. *See also*
Scroll bars.
Horizontal Spacing item, Format menu,
52–53
Hotspot targets, Help files, 1055–1057
Hotspots, Help files, 1053–1055
Hour function, 90
HPJ files, 1049–1050
HTM files, 707
HTML controls, 712–713
HTML tags, 710
HTTP (Hypertext Transport Protocol),
697–698, 735–737
Hungarian prefix notation, 776–777
HWnd property, 336, 759, 761, 991
HWndDisplay property, 759, 761
Hyperbolic trigonometric functions, 114
Hyperlinks, in DHTML pages, 716–717

I

Icon mode, list views, 519
Icon property, 522–523
Icons
adding to list view items, 522–524
for applications, specifying, 1046
custom mouse icon, setting, 608
of forms, in Windows 95 taskbar, 995
of OLE objects, displaying, 903–904
IDE (Integrated Development
Environment)
ActiveX Designers, 77
Add-Ins, 65–66
Auto List Members feature, 70, 72
bookmarks, 78–79
code windows, 49
components of, 42–43
customizing, 50–51, 67–69
Data Tips, 70, 72
design time grid, 53–54, 453
form designers, 48
Form Layout window, 47–48
hiding and displaying windows, 73
menu bar, 43–44
Object Browser, 79, 938

procedure definitions, viewing, 74
Project Explorer, 45
Project menu, 76–77
Properties window, 46–47
Quick Info feature, 70, 72
Syntax Checking, 71, 72
text, searching files for, 74
toolbars, 44, 61, 67–69
toolbox, 48
variable definitions, viewing, 74
VBW files (project files), 16
If...Else statement, 104
Illusion of motion in images, 645–646
Image combo boxes, 277–279
Image controls, 312, 617–618
adding to forms, 338–339
binding to data controls, 847
events supported by, 618
freeing memory used by graphics, 648
loading images at runtime, 619–620
vs. picture boxes, 614–615
properties
BorderStyle property, 618
Picture property, 339–340, 618,
648
Stretch property, 339–340, 618,
633
stretching images to fit control,
339–340, 633
Image element, DHTML, 710
Image list control, 501
adding images to list, 507
adding to forms, 507
animation using timer control,
419–421
image properties
Index property, 507
Key property, 507, 509–510
ListImages collection, 327, 507
size of images, 508
using with image combo boxes,
277–278
using with other controls, 508–509
using with picture boxes, 326–327
using with tab strips, 534
using with toolbar buttons, 475
using with tree views, 515–517
Image maps, 318–319
Image property, 316, 336, 515, 648
ImageList property, 476, 508, 534
Images
adding to ActiveX controls, 655
adding to controls, 616
adding to DHTML pages, 710–711
adding to forms, 617

adding to image list control, 507
adding to toolbar buttons, 475–476
adding to tree views, 515–517
capturing from screen, 794–799
Clipboard, copying and pasting, 609
dimensions of in picture boxes, 607
displaying in controls, 616
displaying in status bars, 489
displaying in Windows Common
    Controls, 616
editing using picture clip controls, 623
erasing, 621
filling, 601–602
flipping, 630–631
freeing memory used by graphics,
    647–648
loading at runtime, 619–620
manipulating at pixel level, 635–647
printing, 610–611
saving to disk, 620
selecting in picture clip controls,
    625–630
setting drawing mode, 604–606
setting drawing scales, 606–607
setting drawing style, 602–603
storing in memory, 621–622
stretching, 632–633
stretching and flipping in picture
    boxes, 333–334
<IMG> HTML tag, 710
Immediate menus, 175–176. *See also*
    Toolbars.
Immediate window, 1035–1036
In-place editing, OLE objects, 896, 912,
    931
In-process servers (ActiveX DLLs),
    935, 945
    methods, passing arguments to, 951–953
    registering, 957
    threading models, 936, 963
Inbox, Microsoft Exchange, 725
InBufferCount property, 409, 424
InBufferSize property, 108, 409
Indenting menu items, 168–169
Indenting program code, 38
Indenting text in RTF boxes, 211–212,
    214–215
Index object, DAO, 825, 861–863
Index property, 233–234, 471, 475, 507,
    872, 873
Indexes, Help files, 1058
Indices
    combo box items, 269, 272, 276–277
    database indices, 824, 861–863
    list box items, 255–256, 258, 259,
        276–277

loop indices, referencing, 108
Information hiding, 37
Initial directory, File Open and File
    Save As dialog boxes, 355–356
Initialize event, 655, 672, 958. *See also*
    Form Load event.
Initializing form-wide variables, 8
Initializing variables, 87
Input, **InputLen** properties, 409, 422,
    423–424
Input # statement, 555
Input boxes, 149–150
Input$ statement, 557
InputBox function, 149–150
Insert Object dialog box, 900, 902,
    905–907, 920–924
Insertable objects, 66–67
Insertion point, moving in RTF boxes,
    217–219
InsertObjDlg method, OLE control,
    898, 905
Installation directory (Windows),
    814–815
Installation location for applications,
    1047
Instancing property, 935–937, 959–960
InStr function, 101
Int function, 90, 113
Integer variable type, 89
Integrated Development Environment.
    See IDE (Integrated Development
    Environment).
Internet Explorer. *See* Microsoft
    Internet Explorer.
Internet transfer control, 727–728
    adding to programs, 728
    FTP operations, 697, 727–734,
        1066–1068
    HTTP operations, 697–698, 734–736
    methods
        Execute method, 697, 698, 727,
            729–730, 735, 1067
        GetChunk method, 730
        OpenURL method, 697, 728–729,
            730, 732–733, 734–736
    properties
        Password property, 727
        StillExecuting property, 727
        URL property, 1066
        UserName property, 727
    StateChanged event, 727, 729, 1068
Interval property, 412
Inverse trigonometric functions,
    calculating, 114
Invert pen setting, 604
IPmt function, 116

IRR function, 116
IsArray function, 93, 96
IsDate function, 93
IsEmpty function, 93
IsError function, 93, 1027
IsMissing function, 91, 93, 953–954
IsNull function, 93
IsNumeric function, 93
IsObject function, 93
Italic property, 590
Item method, 110
ItemClick event, 529
ItemData array, 275–276

J

Jet database engine, 824–825
Jump tags, Help files, 1054

K

Kernel32.dll, 774
Key property
    image list images, 507, 509–510
    status bar panels, 490
    toolbar buttons, 125, 471
    tree view nodes, 512
Keyboard interface, 155
    access characters, 168–171, 235, 447
    shortcut keys, 171–173
    tab order of controls, 129–130, 975
KeyDown event, 204, 207
KeyPress event, 206, 395, 701
KeyPreview property, 995–996
Keystrokes
    intercepting at form level, 995–996
    sending to Windows applications,
        110–112
KeyUp event, 207

L

Label control, 425–436
    access keys, controls without
        captions, 447
    adding to forms, 443–444
    aligning text, 446
    binding to data controls, 847
    events
        Click event, 446
        DblClick event, 446
    formatting text, 445–446

properties
AutoSize property, 445
Caption property, 443
Font... properties, 445
Height property, 443
Top property, 443
UseMnemonic property, 447
Width property, 443
WordWrap property, 445
text, displaying, 203
vs. text boxes, 444–445
Labels in error handlers, 1012
LargeChange property, 287, 298–299
LastDLLError property, 1023
Layers, 611–612, 810–812
LBound function, 96
LCase function, 90, 101
Learning Edition, Visual Basic, 2
LeaveCell event, 399
Left function, 101
Left property
buttons, 239
forms, 133
frame control, 440
label control, 443
shape control, 454
Len function, 101, 204
Let procedure, 667–668, 669, 947–949
Libraries, 940, 941, 962. *See also* DLLs
(Dynamic Link Libraries).
Lightening images, 640–642
Lightweight controls, 990–991
Line charts, 384–385
Line control, 437–438, 455–457, 459
Line Input statement, 556–557
Line method
B argument, 593
drawing boxes, 593–594
drawing freehand lines, 599–600
drawing lines, 591–592
F argument, 602
forms, 458
picture boxes, 325–326
Line numbers, in error handling, 1014
Lines. *See also* Graphics.
automatic alignment, turning off,
456–457
drawing freehand lines, 599–600
drawing in device contexts, 782–783
drawing in forms and picture boxes,
591
drawing in picture boxes, 325–326
drawing using line control, 437–438,
455–458
drawing using **Line** method, 458,
591–594, 599–600

grid lines, 53
LineTo Windows API function, 782–783
Linking OLE objects, 897–899, 902,
905–907, 908–911
List boxes, 252–253
binding to data controls, 847
checkmarks, 264
clearing list, 264–265
events
Change event, 253
Click event, 253, 256–257, 261
DblClick event, 253, 256–257, 261
indices of items, 255–256, 258, 259,
276–277
ItemData array, 275–276
methods
AddItem method, 254–255
Clear method, 264
RemoveItem method, 257–258
multiselect list boxes, 257, 261–262
number of items, 254, 259
numeric data, connecting to items,
275–276
properties
Columns property, 263
List property, 254–256, 257
ListCount property, 254–255, 259
ListIndex property, 255–256
MultiSelect property, 261–262
NewIndex property, 276–277
Selected property, 257
Sorted property, 258
Style property, 264
TopIndex property, 274–275
removing items, 257–258
scrolling horizontally, 263
Selected array, 260
selected items, 255, 256–257, 259–260,
262, 275
sorting items, 258
topmost item, 274–275
List mode, list views, 519
List property, 254–256, 257, 265
List views, 504
adding to forms, 518
columns, 525–526, 527–528, 530
events
ColumnClick event, 529
ItemClick event, 529
items, 520–521, 522–523, 529
ListItem properties
Icon property, 522–523
Text property, 527–528
ListItems collection, 520–521
ListSubItems collection, 527–528
view modes, 504, 519, 524–525

View property, 524, 525
ListCount property, 254–255, 259,
273–274
ListField property, 849
ListImages array, 327
ListImages collection, 507
ListIndex property, 255–256, 267–268,
270
ListSubItems collection, 527–528
Literal suffix symbols, numeric values, 88
Load event, 588
Load statement, 136, 188, 242, 973–975
LoadFile method, 223, 565
LoadPicture function
adding down pictures to buttons, 241
controls, 616, 620
forms, 617
image controls, 620
picture boxes, 316, 566, 619, 620
Picture objects, 620, 621
setting **Picture** property at runtime,
240, 248
LoadResPicture function, 316
Localization, 316
LocationName property, 701, 705
Locked property, 202, 272
Locking memory, 805, 806, 807
LOF function, 549, 557
Log function, 113
Logarithm (to base N) function,
calculating, 114
Logical operators, precedence of, 103
Long variable type, 89
Loop index, referencing, 108
Loop statements
Do loop, 107
For Each loop, 108
For loop, 108
nesting, 37
With statement, 109
While loop, 109
LostFocus event, 235
LS (FTP command), 730
LSet function, 101
LTrim function, 101
Lz32.dll, 774

M

Magic numbers, 36–37. *See also* Constants.
Main( ) procedure, 54, 55, 943
Make *ProjectName*.exe item, File
menu, 44
Make Same Size item, Format menu, 52

MAPI controls, 697, 718. *See also* MAPIMessages control; MAPISession control.

MAPIMessages control, 697, 719. *See also* Email functionality.
 compose buffer, 719
 methods
  Compose method, 721
  Copy method, 719
  Fetch method, 719, 725
  methods supported, 719
  Send method, 722–723
  SignOff method, 722–723
 properties
  FetchMsgType property, 719
  FetchSorted property, 719
  FetchUnreadOnly property, 719
  MsgCount property, 725
  MsgIndex property, 719, 721, 726
  MsgNoteText property, 719, 726
  properties supported, 720
  SessionID property, 721, 725
 read buffer, 719

MAPISession control, 697, 719. *See also* Email functionality.
  DownLoadMail property, 721, 725
  SessionID property, 721, 725
  SignOn method, 721, 725

Marshaling, 935, 951
Mask Not Pen pen setting, 604
Mask Pen Not pen setting, 604
Mask Pen pen setting, 605
MaskedEdit control, 847
Math functions, built-in, 113
Max property
 Common Dialog controls, 361–362, 366
 scroll bars, 286–287
 slider controls, 298
 updown controls, 308
MaxFileSize property, 354
Maximize buttons, on forms, 122
Maximizing forms at runtime, 151
MaxLength property, 201
MCI_ commands, 710–710
MdDir statement, 572
MDI child forms, 120. *See also* MDI forms.
 creating, 139
 loading, 137
 referenced in FRM files, 26
MDI forms, 119–120. *See also* MDI child forms.
 adding picture boxes, 322–323
 arranging child windows, 140–141

arrays of child windows, 142–143
 coordinating data between child windows, 144–145
 displaying child windows, 139
 menus, 181, 182–183
 multiple documents, opening, 141–142
MDI (Multiple Document Interface). *See* MDI child forms; MDI forms.
MDIChild property, 139
Me keyword, 128
Measurement units, 17, 53, 133, 606–607
Media Control Interface (MCI) devices, 740–741, 744. *See also* Multimedia MCI control.
Memory
 allocating, 805–806, 807
 deallocating, 809, 810
 locking, 805, 806, 807
 reading data from, 808, 809
 retrieving pointers to, 806, 807
 storing data in, 806, 808
 unlocking, 808–809
 used by code components, freeing, 960–961
 used by graphics, freeing, 647–648
Menu bar, 43–44, 68, 119. *See also* Menu items; Menus.
Menu control prefixes, 33
Menu Editor. *See also* Menu items; Menus.
 access characters, 168–171
 checkmarks, 179
 creating menus, 165–168
 deleting menu items, 168
 disabling (graying out) menu items, 180
 inserting menu items, 168
 menu separators, 168
 rearranging menu items, 168–169
 submenus, 173–175
Menu items. *See also* Menu Editor; Menus.
 access characters, 155, 168–171
 adding and deleting at runtime, 107–109
 adding code to, 167–168
 checkmarks, 178–179
 connecting toolbar buttons to, 473
 creating, 166–168
 deleting, 168
 design standards, 163–165
 disabling (graying out), 180–181
 ellipses in item names, 155
 exclamation points in item names, 156, 176

hiding and showing, 184
 indenting and outdenting, 168–169
 inserting, 168
 keyboard shortcuts, 155
 moving to menu bar, 68
 naming conventions, 155–156
 properties
  Checked property, 179
  Enabled property, 181
  Visible property, 184, 188
 rearranging, 168–169
 shortcut keys, 171–173
Menu separators, adding, 168
Menus
 access characters, 155, 168–171
 adding bitmaps to, 190–192
 "bang" menus, 175–176
 components of, 154–155
 creating, 166
 designing, 155–156, 157, 163–168
 hiding and showing, 184
 IDE menus, 67–69
 immediate menus, 175–176
 listing open windows, 182–183
 in MDI forms, 181
 menu control prefixes, 33
 menu separators, 168
 ModifyMenu Windows API function, 190
 naming conventions, 155–156
 pop-up menus, 184–185, 186–187
 predefined menus, 56–57, 59, 176–178
 properties
  Caption property, 166
  Name property, 166
  Visible property, 184
  WindowList property, 183
 submenus, 173–175
Merge Not Pen pen setting, 605
Merge Pen Not pen setting, 605
Merge Pen pen setting, 605
Message boxes, 148–149, 1030
Messages. *See* Email functionality.
Metafiles, drawing to, 623
Methods. *See also* names of specific methods; Procedures.
 adding to ActiveX controls, 674–678
 in code components, 942, 950, 951–954
 viewing in Object Browser, 79
Microsoft DAO Object Library, 857
Microsoft Exchange utility, 697, 718, 721, 723, 725
Microsoft Help Workshop, 369, 1049–1050, 1060

Microsoft Internet Explorer. *See also*
Web browser control.
  testing ActiveX controls, 655–656,
    661–662
  testing ActiveX documents, 690
  testing DHTML pages, 717
  Web browsers, creating, 696
Microsoft Win32 Software
  Development Kit, 779
Microsoft XML parser, 698
MID files, playing, 757–759
Mid function, 101
Min/max buttons, 122
Min property
  Common Dialog controls, 361–362,
    366
  scroll bars, 286–287
  slider controls, 298
  updown controls, 308
Minimize buttons, 122
Minimizing forms, 151
Minute function, 90
MIRR function, 116
MiscFlags property, 931
MKDIR (FTP command), 730
Modal display, 147, 996–997
Mode property, 741, 750
Modem command strings, 423–424
ModifyMenu Windows API function, 190
Modular program design, 37
Module-level variables, 91
Modules, 10. *See also* Class modules.
  BAS files (module files), 22
  DLL procedures, declaring, 775
  managing using Project Explorer, 45
  module-level variables, 91
Month function, 90
MonthView control, 410, 428–429
Motion, illusion of, adding to images,
  645–646
Mouse events
  button controls, 244
  capturing outside program's
    window, 789–793
  drawing freehand lines, 599–600
  OLE controls, 913
  right mouse button events, 186
Mouse location, reporting in pixels, 607
Mouse pointer, 220–221, 608
MouseCol property, 402
MouseDown event
  buttons, 244
  capturing outside program's
    window, 792
  drag and drop operations, 977

flex grid control, 402
forms, 186
picture boxes, 318
MouseIcon property, 608
MouseMove event
  capturing outside program's
    window, 791–792
  freehand lines, drawing, 599–600
MousePointer property, 608
MouseUp event
  buttons, 244
  capturing outside program's
    window, 793
Move method
  buttons, 239
  controls, 131–132
  FileObject, 573
  forms, 978
  frame control, 440
  shape control, 454–455
Moveable property, 996
MoveFile method, 573
MoveFirst method
  data controls, 846
  rdoResultset object, 879–880
  Recordset object, ADO, 890
  Recordset object, DAO, 869–870
MoveLast method
  data controls, 846–847
  rdoResultset object, 880–881
  Recordset object, ADO, 890–891
  Recordset object, DAO, 870
MoveMemory Windows API function,
  805, 806, 808, 809
MoveNext method
  data controls, 845–846
  rdoResultset object, 881–882
  Recordset object, ADO, 891
  Recordset object, DAO, 870–871
MovePrevious method
  data controls, 846
  rdoResultset object, 882–883
  Recordset object, ADO, 891–892
  Recordset object, DAO, 871–872
MoveToEx Windows API function,
  782–783
MPG files, playing, 761–763
Mpr.dll, 774
MSFlexGrid control, 847
MsgBox function, 148–149, 150
MsgConversationID property, 720
MsgCount property, 720, 725
MsgDateReceived property, 720
MsgID property, 720
MsgIndex property, 719, 720, 721, 726

MsgNoteText property, 719, 720, 726
MsgOrigAddress property, 720
MsgRead property, 720
MsgReceiptRequested property, 720
MsgSent property, 720
MsgSubject property, 720
MsgType property, 720
MSWLess.ocx ActiveX control group, 991
Multiline property, 200, 201
Multimedia, 740, 771–772. *See also*
  Multimedia MCI control.
Multimedia MCI control, 740–741
  adding to forms, 743–744
  animation, 769
  AVI files, 759–761
  CDs, playing from CD-ROM drive,
    753–755
  closing, 753
  commands, 747–749
    Back command, 769
    Close command, 753
    Eject command, 755
    Open command, 741, 744–745
    Pause command, 749–750
    Step command, 769
    Stop command, 749–750, 753
  controlling at runtime, 741, 747–749
  current operation, 750–752
  device, opening, 744–745
  elapsed time, 752
  ending point in file, 770
  error handling, 764–768
  events
    Done event, 741, 763–764, 768
    StatusUpdate event, 741, 750
  files, opening, 745
  MID files, 757–759
  MPG files, 761–763
  notification of command execution,
    763–764
  overhead, 771
  vs. **PlaySound** Windows API
    function, 771
  properties
    CanStep property, 769
    Command property, 741, 744–745,
      747–749
    DeviceType property, 744–745
    Error property, 764–768
    ErrorMessages property, 764–768
    FileName property, 745
    Frames property, 769
    hWndDisplay property, 759, 761
    Mode property, 741, 750
    Notify property, 741, 763–764

Orientation property, 743
Position property, 752
properties using current time
    format, 746
From property, 770
To property, 770
TimeFormat property, 746, 770
UpdateInterval property, 750
Visible property, 749
Wait property, 771
recorded data, saving to disk, 753
resuming playback, 749–750
showing and hiding, 749
starting point in file, 770
stopping playback, 749
time formats, 746–747
trappable errors, 767–768
waiting until current operation is
    complete, 771
WAV files, 755–757
Multiple Document Interface. *See* MDI
child forms; MDI forms.
Multiple documents, opening, 141
Multiple forms, 134–136
Multiple OLE objects, 914–924
Multiselect list boxes, 257, 261–262, 264
MultiSelect property, 261–262, 429
MultiUse value, 937, 959

N

Name property, 166, 233–234, 590
Names of variables, misspelling, 38. *See
also* Naming conventions.
Naming conventions. *See also*
    Programming c
    onventions, Microsoft.
    constant prefixes, 33
    control prefixes, 29–32
    Data Access Object prefixes, 32
    menu control prefixes, 33
    menus and menu items, 155–156
    variable prefixes, 28–29
    variable scope prefixes, 28
Navigate method, 700
Nested conditionals and loops, 37
Nested error handling, 1024–1025
Netapi32.dll, 774
New keyword, 87, 94, 138, 940–941
NewIndex property, 276–277
NewPage method, 611
Next command (multimedia MCI
    control), 748
NodeClick event, 518

Nodes, tree view, 511–518. *See also*
    Tree views.
Nodes collection, tree views, 511–512
NonModalAllowed property, 962
Nop pen setting, 605
Not Copy Pen pen setting, 604
Not Mask Pen pen setting, 604
Not Merge Pen pen setting, 604
Not Xor Pen pen setting, 605
Nothing keyword, 958–959, 961
Notification of multimedia control
    command execution, 763–764
Notify property, 741, 763–764
Now function, 115, 414
NPer function, 116
NPV function, 116
Number property, 1020–1021
Numeric values
    connecting data to list box items,
        275–276
    converting between string and
        numeric values, 102
    date and time values, 114–115
    financial functions, 116
    math functions, built-in, 113
    trigonometric functions, calculated,
        114

O

Object Browser, 79, 938
<OBJECT> HTML tag, 657
Object references, 951–953
Object type, 970–971
Object variable type, 89, 970–971
Objects
    adding code to, 49
    code components, 934–935, 940–942,
        960–961
    insertable objects, 66–67
    predefined objects, Visual Basic,
        56–59, 176–178
Oct function, 90
OCX files (ActiveX control files), 931,
    1043
ODBC data sources, 836–837
ODBCDirect, 853–854
OLE automation servers. *See* Code
    components.
OLE container control. *See* OLE
    control.
OLE containers, 896
OLE control, 896–897
    adding to forms, 900

border, removing, 903
Class property, 904
display options, 903–904
events
    OLECompleteDrag event, 989–990
    OLEDragDrop event, 984, 986–989
    OLEStartDrag event, 983
    Updated event, 930–931
loading at runtime, 920–924
methods
    Close method, 908
    Delete method, 926
    Drag method, 924–925
    InsertObjDlg method, 905
    OLEDrag method, 983–985
    Paste method, 927
    PasteOK method, 927
    PasteSpecialDlg method, 908–911
    ReadFromFile method, 898,
        929–930
    SaveToFile method, 898, 929–930
pop-up menu, 904
primary verbs, executing, 914
properties
    Action property, 897
    ActiveControl property, 915
    AppIsRunning property, 908, 916
    AutoActivate property, 912
    AutoVerbMenu property, 912–913
    Border property, 903
    DisplayType property, 903–904
    MiscFlags property, 931
    OLEDropMode property, 986
    OLEType property, 898, 906, 914
    OLETypeAllowed property, 899,
        906
    PasteOK property, 908–909
    SizeMode property, 903, 905, 928
    SourceDoc property, 897, 904
    resizing options, 903, 905
OLE DB. *See* ADO (ActiveX Data
    Objects).
OLE (Object Linking and Embedding),
    896–897, 897–899. *See also* OLE
    control; OLE objects.
OLE objects
    activating, 912–914
    clipboard, copying and pasting, 927
    deactivating, 907–908, 916
    deleting, 926
    determining if object has been
        updated, 930–931
    determining whether linked or
        embedded, 914
    displaying content or icons, 903–904

DoVerb method, 913–914
drag and drop operations, 924–925, 983–990
editing in place, 896, 912, 931
embedded objects, 897–899, 929–930
enlarging, 928
existing files, linking or embedding, 902, 904, 905–907, 908–911
linking, 897–899
methods supported, 898
multiple objects, 914–924
new objects, creating and embedding, 900, 905–907
opening, 896, 912
shrinking, 928
verifying insertion in OLE control, 905–906
OLE servers, 896
OLE verbs, 897, 912–914
OLECompleteDrag event, 989–990
OLEDrag method, 983–985
OLEDragDrop event, 984, 986–989
OLEDropMode property, 984, 986
OLEStartDrag event, 983
OLEType property, 898, 906, 914
OLETypeAllowed property, 899, 906
On Error GoTo 0 statement, 1015–1016
On Error GoTo *Label* statement, 1012–1013
On Error GoTo *line#* statement, 1013
On Error Resume Next statement, 1015
OnComm event, 409, 422, 424, 426–427
Online help system, 1063–1064. *See also* Help files.
Online user registration, 1040, 1065–1068
Open command, 741, 748
Open method, 742, 884–887, 893–894
Open statement, 546, 549–550
OpenConnection method, 876–877
OpenDatabase method, 865–867
Opening OLE objects, 896, 912
OpenRecordset method, 863–865, 866–867
OpenResultset method, 877–879
OpenTextFile method, 576–577
OpenURL method, 697, 728–729, 730, 732–733, 734–736
Operator precedence, 102–104
Optimization, 64–65, 75–76
Option Base statement, 94, 96
Option buttons, 227
adding and removing at runtime, 242
background color, 229–230
button releases, 244

combining with checkboxes, 249–250
in control arrays, 233–234, 242
disabling, 236–237
displaying images in, 237, 239–240, 241, 616
events
Click event, 232–233
DblClick event, 233
GotFocus event, 235
Key... events, 244
LostFocus event, 235
Mouse... events, 244
focus, 234, 236
graphical option buttons, 248
grouping, 246
keyboard access, 235
methods
Move method, 239
SetFocus method, 234
moving, 239
passing to procedures, 243
properties
BackColor property, 230
Caption property, 229, 235
Default property, 234, 236
DisabledPicture property, 237
DownPicture property, 241, 248
Enabled property, 237
Font property, 231–232
ForeColor property, 231
Height property, 239
Index property, 233–234
Left property, 239
Name property, 233–234
Picture property, 239–240, 248
Style property, 230, 237, 239–240, 241, 616
TabIndex property, 236
TabStop property, 236
ToolTipText property, 238
Top property, 239
Value property, 247–248
Visible property, 237–238
Width property, 239
resizing, 239
responding to button clicks, 232–233
setting caption, 229
showing and hiding, 237–238
state of buttons, 247–248
tab order, 236
text color, 230–231
tool tips, 238
Option Compare statement, 101
Option Explicit statement, 38, 88
Option Private Module statement, 91

Optional arguments, 97, 98, 953–954
Optional keyword, 97, 98, 953–954
Orientation property, 295, 297, 367–368, 743
Origin of coordinate systems, 583
Out-of-process servers (ActiveX EXEs), 935, 945
creating, 943–945
methods, passing arguments to, 951–953
properties, setting, 947
registering, 958
threading models, 936, 963
Outbox, Microsoft Exchange, 723
OutBufferCount, **OutBufferSize** properties, 409, 425
Outdenting menu items, 169
Output property, 409, 423–424, 425
Ovals, drawing, 450
Overhead
image storage, 508
lightweight controls, 990–991
memory used by graphics, freeing, 647–648
multimedia MCI control, 771
optimizing, 75–76
picture boxes vs. image controls, 615
Variant variable type, 38, 89

P

Package And Deployment Wizard, 1039, 1043–1048
Page Designer, DHTML. *See* DHTML Page Designer.
Page orientation, setting, 367–368
Paint event, 584, 611–612, 657
PaintPicture method. *See also* **Render** method.
flipping images, 630–631
picture boxes, 333–334, 335, 619
printing graphics using Printer object, 610–611
stretching images, 632–633
Pairs of scroll bars, coordinating, 293
PanelClick, **PanelDblClick** events, 490
Panels, status bars, 127, 485–490
Paragraphs, indenting, 211–212
ParamArray keyword, 97, 98, 968
Parameter ADO object, 827
Parent property, 136
Parentheses, 104
Parsers, 698
Password control, 205–206

Password property, 727
PasswordChar property, 205–206
Passwords, 858
Paste method, OLE control, 898, 927
Paste Special menu item, OLE objects,
908–911
PasteOK property, 908–909, 927
PasteSpecialDlg method, OLE
control, 898, 908–911
Pasting OLE objects from Clipboard, 927
Pasting pictures from Clipboard, 610
Path property, 568, 569
Patterns (fill patterns), 602
Pause command, multimedia MCI
control, 748, 749
PDL (program design language), 35–36
Pens, 604–606, 786–788
Pentium FDIV error, disabling checks
for, 65
Pentium Pro processor, optimizing for,
76
Performance
DLLs vs. EXE files, 684
optimizing, 64–65, 75–76
properties for out-of-process
servers, setting, 947
Variant variable type, 89
Persistent properties, 671–674, 693–694
Picture boxes, 313–314, 618–619. *See
also* Picture objects.
accessing images, 316
adjusting size to fit image, 317
aligning, 317
animation, 320–321
AVI files, displaying, 759–761
binding to data controls, 847
clearing images, 330
Clipboard, copying and pasting,
332, 609, 610
dimensions of images, 607
drawing in, 324–326, 450, 459,
588–589, 591–600
events
Click event, 318
mouse events, 318–319
Resize event, 608–609
filling images, 601–602
flipping images, 333, 630–631
freeing memory used by graphics,
647–648
grouping controls, 322
vs. image controls, 614–615
image lists, 326–327
image maps, 318–319
loading images at runtime, 619–620

methods
Circle method, 324
Cls method, 330, 621
Line method, 325–326
LoadPicture function, 619, 620
PaintPicture method, 333–334,
335, 619
Point method, 331, 604
Print method, 327, 588–589
PSet method, 326, 604
SavePicture method, 620
MPG files, displaying, 761–763
opening files, 566
pixel-level image manipulation, 331,
635–647
printing images, 335–336
properties
Align property, 317
AutoRedraw property, 620
AutoSize property, 317, 619
BorderStyle property, 619
CurrentX, **CurrentY**
properties, 327–328, 588
DrawMode property, 604–606
DrawStyle property, 602–603
DrawWidth property, 602–603
FillColor property, 601–602
FillStyle property, 602
Font... properties, 329, 589
Handle property, 336
hDC property, 336
Height property, 338, 607
hWnd property, 336, 759, 761
Image property, 316, 336, 648
Picture property, 316, 320, 619, 648
ScaleHeight, **ScaleWidth**
properties, 338, 607
ScaleMode property, 337–338,
606–607, 636
Width property, 338, 607
resizing graphics, 608–609
resizing to fit image, 619
saving files, 338, 566, 620
setting drawing mode, 604–606
setting drawing scales, 606–607
setting drawing style, 602–603
stretching images, 333, 632–633
text, 327, 329–330
units of measurement, 337–338
Windows handles, 336
Picture clip controls
adding to forms, 623–624
GraphicCell array, 629
properties
Clip property, 626

ClipHeight property, 626
ClipWidth property, 626
ClipX, **ClipY** properties, 626
Columns property, 629
Rows property, 629
selecting images in, 625–628, 629–630
Picture control, 190
Picture objects. *See also* Picture boxes.
arrays of, for animation sequences,
623, 634–635
drawing images using, 622–623
images
loading into, 620, 621
storing in memory, 621–622
LoadPicture function, 620, 621
Render method, 622–623
Picture property
buttons, 239–240, 248
forms, 617
freeing memory used by graphics, 648
image controls, 339–340, 618
picture boxes, 316, 320, 619
status bar panels, 489
Pictures, adding to buttons, 239–240, 241
Pie charts, 382–383
Pixels
accessing in picture boxes, 331
binary raster operation mode
(ROP2), 788–789
drawing, 604
mouse location, reporting, 607
pixel-level image manipulation,
635–647
retrieving color of, 604
Play command (multimedia MCI
control), 748
Play method, 742
PlaySound Windows API function,
770–805, 771, 776
Pmt function, 116
Point method, 331, 604
Pointers to memory, retrieving, 806, 807
Points, 326, 604
Pop-up links, Help files, 1058–1060
Pop-up menus, 184–185, 186–187, 904,
912–913
PortOpen property, 408, 423, 427–428
Position attribute, 710, 715
Position property, 752
Positioning startup forms, 69
Positioning windows in Z-order, 810–812
POST (HTTP command), 735
PPmt function, 116
Precedence (operator precedence),
102–104

Predefined dialog boxes, 146–147
Predefined elements, Visual Basic, 58, 176–178. *See also* Visual Component Manager.
Predefined forms, 57
Predefined menus, 59, 176–178
Prefixes
    constant prefixes, 33
    control prefixes, 29–32
    Data Access Object prefixes, 32
    Hungarian prefix notation, 776–777
    menu control prefixes, 33, 156
    variable prefixes, 28–29
    variable scope prefixes, 28
Preserve keyword, 95
Prev command (multimedia MCI control), 748
Primary keys, 776
Primary verbs, executing for OLE objects, 914
Print # statement, 550–551
Print dialog box, 363–368
Print method, 588–589, 610–611
Print Setup dialog box, 365
Printer object
    flipping images, 630–631
    fonts available, 590–591
    printing from Print dialog box, 363
    printing graphics, 610–611
    stretching images, 632–633
PrinterDefault property, 363
Printers, 365
Printers collection, 611
PrintForm method, 364, 610
Printing images, 335–336
Printing text, 223–224
Private keyword
    declaring constants, 85
    declaring DLL procedures, 775
    declaring methods in code components, 950
    declaring properties in class modules, 946
    declaring subroutines, 96
    declaring variables, 86
    defined, 11
    scope of procedures, restricting, 13
Private value, 937, 959
Private variables, 91
Procedure-level variables, 91
Procedure scope, 13
Procedures. *See also* Methods.
    arguments, passing by value or reference, 776, 951–953
    arrays, passing as arguments, 967–968

buttons, passing as arguments, 243
commenting conventions, 33–34
control arrays, passing as arguments, 968, 970–971
declared as **Static**, 13
design of, 37
DLL procedures, 775–776
forms, passing as arguments, 150–151, 992
functions, 97–98
global variables, passing as arguments, 37
procedure-level variables, 91
procedure scope, 13
subroutines, 96–97
variable values, preserving, 99–100
viewing definition in IDE, 74
in Windows API, 778–779
Product information, adding to projects, 59
Professional Edition, Visual Basic, 2
Profiles, Application Wizard, 23
Program design language (PDL), 35–36
Programming conventions, Microsoft
    best coding practices, 36–38
    commenting conventions, 33–34
    constant prefixes, 33
    control prefixes, 29–32
    Data Access Object prefixes, 32
    indentation of code, 38
    menu control prefixes, 33
    program design language (PDL), 35–36
    software design process, 34–35
    variable prefixes, 28–29
    variable scope prefixes, 28
Programming defensively, 37
Programs, Visual Basic
    entering break state, 116
    linking to Visual C++ code, 816–818
    online user registration, 1065–1068
    terminating, 116, 136
    using custom ActiveX controls, 664
    windows, hiding, 136
Progress bars, 466–467, 491–493
Project Explorer window, 45, 77
Project groups, Visual Basic, 662–664
Project menu, IDE, 43, 76–77
Project Properties dialog box, 54, 55, 61, 137, 655–656, 683
Project types supported by Visual Basic, 2–3
Projects, Visual Basic. *See also* IDE (Integrated Development Environment).
    adding ActiveX controls, 66–67
    adding ActiveX Designers, 77
    adding OLE controls, 900

adding Web browsers, 696
BAS files (module files), 22
components of, 9–10
converting to ActiveX documents, 683
creating using Application Wizard, 22 28
custom ActiveX controls, 664
FRM files (form files), 16–22
GlobalMultiUse objects, 959–960
insertable objects, adding to projects, 66–67
integrating Web browsers into, 691–692
optimizing, 75–76
saving to disk, 13–14
scope, 11–13
software design process, 35–36
splash screens, 24
startup forms, 55, 61, 69, 137
startup procedure, 54
VBP files (project files), 15
VBW files (project files), 16
version information, 59
Prompts in message boxes, 148
Properties. *See also names of specific properties.*
    ActiveX controls, 666–674
    ActiveX documents, 693–694
    code components, 942, 946, 947–949
    design-time vs. runtime, 46
    managing using Properties window, 46–47
    out-of-process servers, 947
    viewing in Object Browser, 79
Properties collection, ADO, 828
Properties window, IDE, 46–47
Property Page Wizard, 680–681
Property pages, 680–681
PropertyBag objects, ActiveX controls, 671, 693–694
PropertyChanged method, 671–672, 693–694
Provider property, 828, 840
PSet method, 326, 604, 610–611
Public keyword
    declaring arrays, 93
    declaring constants, 85
    declaring global items, 10
    declaring methods in code components, 950
    declaring properties in class modules, 946
    declaring subroutines, 96
    declaring variables, 86
    defined, 11

PublicNotCreatable value, 937, 959
PUT (FTP command), 730
PUT (HTTP command), 735
Put statement, 552–553, 554, 564
PV function, 116
PWD (FTP command), 730

Q

QBColor function, 586
QueryDef DAO object, 825
Quick Info feature, 70, 72
Quick Watch window, 1033
QUIT (FTP command), 730

R

Radio buttons. *See* Option buttons.
Raise method, 1023–1024
RaiseEvent method, 679
Random access files, 542, 552–553, 558–561, 563–564
Randomize statement, 454
Raster operations, 788–789, 794
Rate function, 116
RDO (Remote Data Objects), 826, 854. *See also* Remote data control.
    adding records, 844
    creating result sets, 877–879
    data-bound controls, 838–839, 847–848
    data environment, 824
    deleting records, 844–845
    navigating databases, 845–847
    navigating result set, 879–883
    opening database connections, 876–877
    opening databases, 838
    rdocode example project, 875–884
    refreshing data, 845
    SQL statements, executing, 883
    updating databases, 845
Rdocode example project, 875–884
RdoConnection object, 854, 877–879, 883
RdoEnvironment object, 876–877
RdoResultset object, 879–883
RdoTables collection, 827
Read buffer, MAPIMessages control, 719
Read method, 578
Read-only text boxes, 202
ReadFromFile method, OLE control, 898, 929–930
Reading from binary files, 561–563
Reading from random access files, 558–561

Reading from sequential files, 555–557
Reading RTF files into RTF boxes, 223
ReadLine method, 578
ReadProperties event, 671–672, 693–694
Record command, multimedia MCI control, 748
Record sets, ADO
    adding records to, 888
    binding controls to, 887
    creating, 885–887
    deleting records, 892–893
    navigating, 890–892
    refreshing, 888–889
    updating records, 889–890
Record sets, DAO
    adding records, 867–868
    creating, 863–865
    deleting records, 872
    editing records, 868
    navigating, 869–872
    searching, 873
    sorting records, 872
    updating records, 868–869
Records
    database records, 823–824
        adding, 844, 867–868, 888
        deleting, 844–845, 872, 892–893
        editing, 868
        entering data using Visual Data Manager, 833
        navigating, 845–847, 869–872, 879–883, 890–892
        refreshing and updating data, 845
        searching, 873
        sorting, 872
        updating, 868–869, 889–890
    random access files, 563–564
Recordset object, ADO, 827
    methods
        AddNew method, 888
        Delete method, 892–893
        MoveFirst method, 890
        MoveLast method, 890–891
        MoveNext method, 891
        MovePrevious method, 891–892
        Open method, 885–887, 893–894
        Refresh method, 888–889
        Update method, 889–890
Recordset object, DAO
    creating record set, 863–865
    methods
        AddNew method, 867–868
        Delete method, 872
        Edit method, 868
        MoveFirst method, 869–870
        MoveLast method, 870

MoveNext method, 870–871
MovePrevious method, 871–872
OpenRecordset method, 866–867
Update method, 868–869
    properties
        BOF property, 871–872
        EOF property, 870–871
        Index property, 872, 873
        Seek property, 873
Recordset property, 826, 844, 845, 846
RecordsetEvents, ADO, 828
RecordSource property, 826, 828, 835
Rectangle Windows API function, 785–786
Rectangles, drawing, 449, 785–786
RECV (FTP command), 730
ReDim statement, 11, 86, 94, 96
Redrawing form contents, 129
Redrawing graphics, 584
Reference, passing arguments by, 776
References to code components, adding, 938
Refresh button, Web browsers, 705
Refresh method, 705, 845
Refreshing record sets, 888–889
Refreshing screen. *See* Redrawing graphics.
Registering ActiveX controls with Windows, 656, 664
Registering in-process servers, 957
Registering ODBC data sources, 836–837
Registering out-of-process servers, 958
Registering programs online, 1040, 1065–1068
Registry, Windows. *See* Windows Registry.
Regsvr32.exe utility, 664
Relation DAO object, 825
Remote data control, 826–827. *See also* ADO data control; Data control; RDO (Remote Data Objects).
    data-bound controls, 838–839
    methods
        AddNew method, 844
        Delete method, 844–845
        MoveFirst method, 846
        MoveLast method, 846–847
        MoveNext method, 845–846
        MovePrevious method, 846
        Refresh method, 845
        UpdateRecord method, 845
    properties
        DataSource property, 838
        DataSourceName property, 838
        Resultset property, 844, 845, 846
        SQL property, 827, 838
    rdoTables collection, 827

Remote Data Objects. *See* RDO (Remote Data Objects).
Remote Data Service (RDS), 828
Remove method, 110
RemoveItem method, 257–258, 269
RENAME (FTP command), 730
Render method, 622–623. *See also* **PaintPicture** method.
Replacing text in RTF boxes, 221
ReplayAll method, 719
Reply method, 719
Report mode, list views, 519
Resize event, 608–609
Resizing buttons, 239
Resizing graphics, 608–609
ResolveName method, 720
Resource files, 316
RestoreToolbar method, 482
Result set (RDO), 877–883
Resultset property, 844, 845, 846
Resume *Label* statement, 1017–1018
Resume *line*# statement, 1018–1019
Resume Next statement, 1019–1020
Resume statement, 1016–1017
Return values, 98, 150, 775
RGB function, 216–217, 586
Rich text. *See* RTF boxes.
Right function, 101
Right mouse events, 186, 793
RightMargin property, 212
RMDIR (FTP command), 730
RmDir statement, 572
Rnd function, 113
ROP2 (binary raster operation) mode, 788–789
Rounded rectangles and squares, 451
Row property, 377–378, 393
RowCount property, 377–378
RowLabel property, 378
Rows property, 393, 629
RowSource property, 849
RSet function, 101
RTF boxes
  binding to data controls, 847
  creating, 198
  inappropriate use of, 198–199
  methods
    Find method, 221
    LoadFile method, 223, 565
    SaveFile method, 222, 564–565
    SelPrint method, 223–224
    Span method, 208
  moving insertion point, 217–219
  opening files, 223, 565
  printing text, 223–224

properties
  BulletIndent property, 214–215
  RightMargin property, 212
  SelAlignment property, 216–217
  SelBold property, 209–211
  SelBullet property, 214–215
  SelCharOffset property, 219–220
  SelColor property, 216–217
  SelFontName property, 213
  SelFontSize property, 213
  SelHangingIndent property, 211–212
  SelIndent property, 211–212
  SelItalic property, 209–211
  SelRightIndent property, 211–212
  SelRTF property, 208
  SelStrikethru property, 209–211
  SelUnderline property, 209–211
  Text property, 208–209
  TextRTF property, 208–209
replacing text, 221
saving files, 222, 564–565
searching for text, 221
selecting text, 208–209
setting text attributes, 209–215, 216–217, 219–220
RTF files, 222, 223, 1051–1052
RTF text, 198
RThreshold property, 408, 422
RTrim function, 101
Run menu, IDE, 43

S

Save command (multimedia MCI control), 748
Save method, 719
SaveFile method, 222, 564–565
SavePicture function, 566, 620
SavePicture statement, 338
SaveSetting Windows API function, 193–195, 997
SaveToFile method, 898, 929–930
SaveToolbar method, 482
SaveToOle1File method, 898
Saving pictures to disk, 338
Saving RTF files, 222
ScaleHeight property, 133, 338, 607
ScaleLeft property, 133
ScaleMode property
  forms, 17, 133, 606–607
  picture boxes, 337–338, 606–607
  pixel-level manipulation of images, 636

ScaleTop property, 133
ScaleWidth property, 133, 338, 607
Scope, 11, 13, 28, 37, 90–91
Screen
  capturing images, 794–799
  capturing mouse events outside program window, 789–793
  coordinates, translating to window coordinates, 790
  device context for entire screen, 781–782
  refreshing, 584
Screen object, 590–591, 608, 971–972, 992–993
Scroll bars, 283–284. *See also* Flat scroll bars.
  adding to forms, 286
  adding to text boxes, 201–202, 293–294
  current value, 289
  events
    Change event, 289–290
    Scroll event, 291–292
  large changes, 287
  pairs, coordinating, 293
  properties
    Enabled property, 292
    LargeChange property, 287
    Min, **Max** properties, 286–287
    SmallChange property, 288
    Value property, 289
    Visible property, 292
  range of values, 286
  showing and hiding, 292
  small changes, 288
Scroll event, 291–292, 302–303
ScrollBars property, 201, 293–294
Scrolling list boxes horizontally, 263
Search and replace, in RTF boxes, 221
Search button, Web browsers, 705
Secant function, calculating, 114
Second function, 90
Security: password controls, 206
Seek command (multimedia MCI control), 748
Seek property, 873
SelAlignment property, 216–217
SelBold property, 209–211
SelBullet property, 214–215
SelCharOffset property, 219–220
SelColor property, 216–217
Select Case Is keyword, 105
Select Case statement, 105
Selected array, 260
Selected property, 257
SelectObject Windows API function, 190, 786–787

SelectRange property, 303
Self drops, handling, 981–982
SelFontName property, 213
SelFontSize property, 213
SelHangingIndent property, 211–212
SelIndent property, 211–212
SelLength property, 204, 303
SelPrint method, 223–224
SelRightIndent property, 211–212
SelRTF property, 208
SelStart property, 204, 303
SelStrikethru property, 209–211
SelText property, 204
SelUnderline property, 209–211
SEND (FTP command), 730
Send method, 719, 722–723
SendKeys function, 111–112
Sensitive data, protecting, 37
Sequential files, 541–542, 550–552, 554–558
Serial port access, 408, 423, 427
Serialized thread operations, 936
SessionID property, 721, 725
Set procedures, 948
Set statement, 940–942
SetCapture Windows API function, 790–793, 800–802
SetData method, 332, 379, 609, 984
SetFocus method, 234
SetROP2 Windows API function, 789
SetText method, 205
Settings, Windows Registry. *See* Windows Registry.
Settings property, 408, 423
SetWindowPos Windows API function, 810–812
Sgn function, 113
Shape control, 436–437
  adding to forms, 448–449
  automatic alignment, turning off, 453
  borders, 452
  drawing shapes, 449–451
  filling shapes, 452–453
  hiding and showing shapes, 455
  Move method, 454–455
  moving shapes at runtime, 454
  properties
    BorderStyle property, 452
    BorderWidth property, 452
    FillColor property, 453
    FillStyle property, 452
    Height property, 454
    Left property, 454
    Shape property, 449, 450, 451
    Top property, 454
    Width property, 454

Shape property, 449, 450, 451
Shared files, specifying, 1048
Shell32.dll, 774
Shift key, 112, 303–306, 304
Shortcut keys, 155, 171, 172–173
Show method
  dialog box display, 962
  forms, 136, 961
  MAPIMessages control, 720
  modal dialog box display, 147, 996–997
ShowHelp method, 368
Showing and hiding buttons, 237–238
Showing and hiding controls, 132
Showing and hiding IDE windows, 73
Showing and hiding menus and menu items, 184
Showing and hiding multimedia MCI control, 749
Showing and hiding scroll bars, 292
Showing and hiding shapes, 455
ShowInTaskbar property, 995
ShowOpen, ShowSave methods, 350–351
Shrinking OLE objects, 928
SignOff method, 722–723
SignOn method, 721, 725
Simple combo boxes, 265
SimpleText property, 491
Sin function, 113
Single-stepping, 1032
Single-threaded objects, 936
Single variable type, 89
SingleUse value, Instancing property, 937, 960
SIZE (FTP command), 730
Size property, 590
SizeMode property, 903, 905, 928
Sizing controls, 51–52, 131
Sizing handles on controls, 51
Slider control, 284
  adding to forms, 296–297
  clearing selection, 306
  current value, 301–303
  events
    Change events, 301
    handling, 301–303
    KeyDown event, 204
    Scroll event, 302–303
  groove clicks, 298–299
  methods
    ClearSel method, 306
    GetNumTicks method, 299
    Move method, 297
  orientation, 297

properties
  LargeChange property, 298–299
  Min, Max properties, 298
  Orientation property, 297
  SelectRange property, 303
  SelLength property, 303
  SelStart property, 303
  SmallChange property, 299
  TickFrequency property, 299–300
  TickStyle property, 300
  Value property, 301, 302
range of values, 298, 303–306
tick marks, 299–300
tick style, 300
SLN function, 116
Small changes, 288
Small code, optimizing for, 75
Small icons, adding to list views, 522–524
SmallChange property, 288, 299
SmallIcon mode, list views, 519
SMPTE (Society of Motion Picture and Television Engineers) time formats, 746
Software design process, 35–38
Sort property, 401
Sorted property, 258
Sorting combo boxes, 271–272
Sorting flex grid control, 401
Sorting list boxes, 258
Sound command, multimedia MCI control, 748
Source property, 1022
SourceDoc property, 897, 904
Space function, 101
Spacing controls, 51–53
<SPAN> DHTML tag, 710
Span method, 208
Splash screens, 24
Spreadsheet, creating, 393–399
SQL property, 827, 838
SQL statements, executing, 874–875, 883, 893–894
Sqr function, 113
Squares, drawing, 449–450
Src attribute, 710
Src property, 710
Standard arrays, 93–94
Startup forms, 55, 61, 69
Startup objects, 943
Startup position of forms, specifying, 995
Startup procedure, 54
StateChanged event, 727–728, 729
Static keyword
  declaring arrays, 93
  declaring procedures, 13
  declaring subroutines, 96

declaring variables, 86
defined, 11
preserving variable values, 99–100
Status bars, 465–466
  adding panels, 485, 490
  adding to forms, 126–127, 184
  aligning, 485
  appearance, customizing, 488
  click events, 490
  creating using picture boxes, 322
  displaying images, 489
  displaying status information, 487
  displaying text, 486
  panel properties
    Alignment property, 488
    AutoSize property, 488
    Bevel property, 488
    Key property, 490
    Picture property, 489
    SimpleText property, 491
    Style property, 487
    Text property, 486
  PanelClick, **PanelDblClick**
    events, 490
  Panels collection, 485
  properties
    Align property, 485
    Style property, 491
  without panels, 491
StatusUpdate event, 741, 750
Step charts, 2D and 3D, 388–390
Step command, multimedia MCI
  control, 748, 769
Step keyword, 591, 594, 604
SThreshold property, 408, 422
StillExecuting property, 727
Stop button, Web browsers, 705
Stop command, multimedia MCI
  control, 748, 749, 753
Stop method, 705
Stop statement, 116
Stopwatch example program, 416–417
Str function, 90, 102
StrComp function, 101
StrConv function, 101
Stretch property, 339–340, 618, 633
Stretching images, 333–334, 632–633
StrikeThrough property, 590
Strikethru text in RTF boxes, 209–211
String function, 101
String variable type, 89, 101
Strings
  converting between string and
    numeric values, 102
  formatting date and time values, 115

passing as arguments to code
  components, 951–953
string-handling functions, 101–102
variable-length vs. fixed-length, 101
Style property
  buttons, 230, 237, 239–240, 241
  combo boxes, 265, 273
  images, displaying in controls, 616
  list boxes, 264
  status bar panels, 487
  status bars, 491
  toolbar buttons, 474–475, 477, 479
  tree views, 511
Sub Main procedure, 54, 943
Sub procedures, 674–678
Submenus, 173–175
Submit button, 712–713
Subnodes, adding to tree views, 513–515
Subroutines, 96–97, 99–100, 775–776
Subscript characters, RTF boxes, 219–220
Suffix symbols, numeric values, 88
Superscript characters, RTF boxes,
  219–220
Switch function, 106
SYD function, 116
SyncBuddy property, 307
Syntax Checking, IDE, 71, 72

T

Tab order in text-entry forms, 236
Tab order of controls, 129–130, 236, 975
Tab strips, 504–505
  adding tabs, 532–533
  adding to forms, 531–532
  Click events, 536
  connecting images to tabs, 534
  displaying correct tab, 536
  displaying other controls, 535–536
  properties
    Caption property, 533
    ImageList property, 534
  tab captions, 533
  Tabs collection, 533
TabIndex property, 130, 236, 975
Table Operation drop-down box,
  DHTML Page Designer, 715–716
Table Structure window, Visual Data
  Manager, 831–832
TableDef object, DAO, 859, 860–863
Tables, DHTML pages, 715–716
Tables (database tables). *See also*
  Fields.
  adding fields to, 860–861

creating, 859
creating using Visual Data Manager,
  830
defined, 823
indexes, 861–863
opening, 866–867
TabStop property, 19, 130, 236
Tan function, 113
Target URL, setting, 716–717
Taskbar, Windows 95, 995
Templates folder, Visual Component
  Manager, 56–57, 176–178
Temporary file names, 1066
Terminate event, 672, 958–959
Terminating programs, 116
Testing ActiveX controls, 655–656,
  661–662, 662–664
Testing ActiveX documents, 683, 690–691
Testing code components, 954–956
Testing DHTML pages, 717
Testing programs, 1007–1008
Text
  adding to DHTML pages, 709–710
  aligning, 200–201, 216–217, 446
  customizing IDE, 50–51
  determining fonts available, 590–591
  displaying in status bars, 486
  drawing using **Print** method, 588–589
  entering in flex grid control, 394
  Font object, 590
  font properties, 589
  formatting, 329–330, 445–446, 589, 710
  highlighting, turning off, 204
  printing, from RTF boxes, 223–224
  replacing in text boxes, 204
  in RTF boxes, 208–209
  searching for in IDE, 74
  selecting, 204, 208–209
  setting attributes, 209–211
  setting color, 216–217
  superscripts and subscripts, in RTF
    boxes, 219–220
  in text boxes, 203
  title bar text, 121, 802–803
Text boxes. *See also* Combo boxes.
  adding scroll bars, 201–202, 293–294
  adding to forms, 198
  aligning text, 200–201
  binding to data controls, 835, 838–
    839, 840–841, 847
  clipboard, copying and pasting,
    204–205
  data entry in flex grid control, 397–399
  events
    Change event, 145, 207

KeyDown event, 207
KeyPress event, 206
KeyUpevent, 207
highlighting, turning on and off, 204
inappropriate use of, 198–199
vs. label controls, 444–445
limiting number of characters, 201
multiline text boxes, 200
password control, 205–206
properties
  Alignment property, 200–201
  DataField, **DataSource**
    properties, 835, 838–839, 840–841
  Enabled property, 202
  HideSelection property, 204
  Locked property, 202
  MaxLength property, 201
  Multiline property, 200, 201
  PasswordChar property, 205–206
  ScrollBars property, 201, 293–294
  SelLength property, 204
  SelStart property, 204
  SelText property, 204
  Text property, 203
read-only text boxes, 202
replacing text, 204
restricting input characters, 206–207
selecting text, 204
setting text, 203
word wrap, 200
Text data, sending, 425
Text property
combo boxes, 265, 267, 270–271
flex grid control, 393, 394
RTF boxes, 208–209
status bar panels, 486
text boxes, 203
TextArray property, 400
TextHeight method, 589
TextRTF property, 208–209
TextStream objects, 542, 575–579
TextWidth method, 589
Thread-per-object model, 936
Thread pooling, 936
Threading models, 936, 963
Thumb of scroll bars, 283
Tic-tac-toe game (ActiveX document
  example), 684–689
Tick marks, slider controls, 299–300, 300
TickFrequency property, 299–300
TickStyle property, 300
Time formats, 114–115, 413–415, 746–747
Time function, 115
Time$ function, 413
TimeFormat property, 746, 770

Timer control, 406–407
accuracy of, 413
adding to forms, 412
animation using image list control,
  419–421
current time, displaying, 415
elapsed time, displaying, 417
example programs, 415–419
formatting date and time values,
  413–415
initializing, 412
properties
  Enabled property, 412
  Interval property, 412
Timer event, 412, 413
using with progress bar, 492–493
Timer event, 412, 413
TimeSerial function, 90, 115
TimeValue function, 90, 115
Title bar text, 121, 346–347, 802–803
Title bars, 118
Titles for Help pages, 1057–1058
To property, 770
Toggle buttons in toolbars, 477
Tool tips, 45, 238, 1058–1060
Toolbars, 465
adding buttons, 471, 482–484
adding combo boxes, 479–481
adding images to buttons, 475–476
adding to forms, 469
aligning, 470
button groups, 478
button properties
  Index property, 471, 475
  Key property, 125, 471
  Style property, 474–475, 477, 479
  ToolTipText property, 481
ButtonClick event, 471–472
Buttons collection, 482–484
check buttons, 477
connecting buttons to menu items,
  473
creating using picture boxes, 322
in forms, 119, 123–125–126
handling button clicks, 472
in IDE, 44, 61, 67–69
methods
  RestoreToolbar method, 482
  SaveToolbar method, 482
properties
  Align property, 470
  AllowCustomize property, 482
  ImageList property, 476
separators, 474–475
tool tips, 481
user customization, 482

Toolbox, DHTML Page Designer,
  710–711, 712–713, 716–717
Toolbox, Visual Basic, 48, 664
Tools menu, IDE, 43
ToolTipText property, 238, 439, 481
Top property
buttons, 239
forms, 133
frame control, 440
label control, 443
shape control, 454
ToPage property, 364
TopIndex property, 274–275
Total disk space, determining, 813–814
Trademark information, adding to
  projects, 59
Transactions, ADO, 854
Transferring files. *See* FTP (File
  Transfer Protocol).
Trappable errors
Cancel button, Common Dialogs,
  1028–1029
creating error objects, 1026–1027
determining source of error, 1022
determining which error occurred,
  1020–1021
disabling error trapping, 1015–1016
disregarding errors, 1015
in DLLs, 1023
list of, 1003–1007
multimedia MCI control, 767–768
nested error handling, 1024–1025
resuming execution, 1016–1020
retrieving error description, 1021–1022
user-defined errors, 1023–1024
using labels, 1012–1013
using line numbers, 1014
writing error handlers, 1009–1012
Tree views, 502
adding images, 515–517
adding to forms, 510–511
events
  Collapse event, 517
  Expand event, 517
  NodeClick event, 518
expanding and collapsing nodes,
  517–518
node properties
  Expanded property, 518
  Image property, 515
  Key property, 512
nodes, 511–512
properties, **Style** property, 511
style, selecting, 511
subnodes, 513–515
Trigonometric functions, 114

Trim function, 101
TwipsPerPixelX property, 608
TwipsPerPixelY property, 608
Type casting. *See* Converting data between variable types.
Type keyword, 11, 86, 93
Type libraries, code components, 940, 941
Type of control, determining at runtime, 972–973
TypeOf keyword, 972–973
Types. *See* Variable types.

U

UBound function, 96
Ubound property, 973
UCase function, 90, 101
Underline property, 590
Underlining text in RTF boxes, 209–211
Units of measurement, 17, 53, 133, 328, 337–338, 606–607
Unload statement, 137, 189, 242
Unlocking memory, 808–809
UpClick event, 308–309
Update method, 868–869
Update method, OLE objects, 898
Updated event, 930–931
UpdateInterval property, 750
UpdateRecord method, 845
Updown controls, 284, 307–309
UpDown property, 410, 430
URL property, 1066
URLs, 700–703, 716–717
UseMnemonic property, 447
User controls. *See* ActiveX controls.
User-defined coordinate systems, 133, 607
User-defined data types, 89
User-defined errors, 1023–1024
User registration, online, 1065–1068
User32.dll, 774
UserName property, 727

V

Val function, 90, 102
Value, passing arguments by, 776
Value property
   checkboxes, 245–246
   DateTimePicker control, 430
   MonthView control, 429
   option buttons, 247–248
   progress bars, 492

scroll bars, 289
slider controls, 301, 302
Variable-length arrays, 968
Variable-length strings, 101
Variable scope, 11, 37
Variable scope prefixes, 28
Variable type prefixes, 28–29
Variable types, 88–89
   C/C++ data type correspondences, 776–778
   converting between types, 90, 102
   default type, 88
   field types, DAO TableDef object, 860
   Hungarian prefix notation, 776–777
   list of, 7–8
   specifying using **As** keyword, 11
   used in Windows API, 778–779
   variable prefixes, 28–29
   verifying type, 91, 93
   Windows-defined data types, 777–778
Variables
   commenting conventions, 33–34
   declaring, 11, 86–87
      implicit declaration, 87
      Option Explicit statement, 38, 88
      Option Private Module statement, 91
      variable scope, 90–91
      variable types, 88–89
   default initialization, 87
   examining values of (debugging), 1033–1036
   form-level variables, 91
   form-wide variables, 7, 8
   global variables, 10, 91
   literal suffix symbols, 88
   module-level variables, 91
   names, misspelling, 38
   preserving values, 99–100
   procedure-level variables, 91
   variable scope, 11, 37, 90–91
   variable scope prefixes, 28
   variable type, verifying, 91, 93
   variable type prefixes, 28–29
   variable types, 7–8
   viewing definition in IDE, 74
Variant arrays, 951–953
Variant variable type, 38, 88–89, 89
VBD files (ActiveX document specification files), 651, 686, 690–691
VbOLEInPlaceActivate verb, 897
VbOLEOpen verb, 897
VBP files (project files), 15, 25
VBW files (project files), 16
Version control, 39

Version information, 59
Version.dll, 774
Vertical scroll bars, 286. *See also* Scroll bars.
Vertical Spacing item, Format menu, 52–53
View menu, 43, 73, 165
View modes, list views, 504, 519, 524–525
View property, 524, 525
Visible property
   buttons, 237–238
   combo boxes, 273
   controls, 132
   menu items, 184, 188
   menus, 184
   multimedia MCI control, 749
   pop-up menus, 184
   scroll bars, 292
Visual Basic
   best coding practices, 36–38
   commenting conventions, 33–34
   editions of, 2
   naming conventions, 28–33
   project types supported by, 2–3
Visual Basic API Viewer, 779
Visual Basic Application Wizard
   adding status bars to forms, 484
   adding toolbars to forms, 123–125, 469
   designing menus, 157
   integrating Web browsers into projects, 691–692
   online help system, 1063–1064
   profiles, 23
   projects, creating, 22–28
Visual Basic color constants, 586–587
Visual Basic Global object, 994
Visual Basic Integrated Development Environment. *See* IDE (Integrated Development Environment).
Visual Basic Menu Editor. *See* Menu Editor.
Visual Basic project groups, 662–664
Visual C++ code, 816–818
Visual Component Manager, 56–57, 58, 65–66, 176–178
Visual Data Manager, 830–833

W

Wait property, 771
Watch window, 1034
WAV files, playing, 755–757
Web browser control, 696. *See also* Web browsers.

events, **DownloadComplete** event,
701
methods
  GoBack method, 704
  GoForward method, 704
  GoHome method, 701, 705
  GoSearch method, 705
  Navigate method, 700
  Refresh method, 705
  Stop method, 705
online help system, 1063–1064
properties, **LocationName**
  property, 701, 705
Web browsers. *See also* Web browser
  control.
  allowing navigation to URLs, 700–703
  creating, 696, 699–700
  integrating into Visual Basic
    programs, 691–692
  specifying home page, 701
  standard buttons, 705
  URLs, specifying, 700–703
Web pages. *See also* ActiveX documents.
  DHTML pages, testing, 707, 717
  directories, downloading, 731, 732
  embedding ActiveX controls in, 657
  including Visual Basic code in, 706
Weekday function, 90
Weight property, 590
While loop, 109
Whiteness pen setting, 605
Width property
  buttons, 239
  forms, 133
  frame control, 440
  label control, 443
  picture boxes, 338, 607
  Screen object, 608
  shape control, 454
Win32 Software Development Kit
  (Microsoft), 779
Win32api.txt, 778–779
Window coordinates, translating to
  screen coordinates, 790
Window handles, 800–802, 811
Window list, adding to menus, 182–183
Window menu, 44, 165, 182–183
WindowFromPoint Windows API
  function, 800–802
Windowless controls, 990–991
WindowList property, 183

Windows
  capturing mouse events outside of,
    789–793
  device contexts, retrieving, 780
  forcing to topmost position, 810–812
  hiding, 136
  specifying Z-order position, 810–812
  title bar text, 121, 802–803
  window handles, retrieving, 800–802
Windows, IDE, 73
Windows 95 taskbar, 995
Windows API
  core Windows DLLs, 774
  sounds, playing, 804–805
  Visual Basic API Viewer add-in tool,
    779
  window handles, retrieving, 800–802
Windows API functions. *See also*
  names of specific functions
  calling, 775
  correspondences between data
    types and Visual Basic variable
    types, 776–778
  declarations, adding to Visual Basic
    programs, 779
  declaring, 775–776
Windows applications. *See also*
  headings beginning with OLE.
  "Designed for Microsoft Windows"
    logo, 1041–1042
  dragging data between applications,
    983–990
  giving focus to, 112
  sending keystrokes to, 110–112
Windows character set, limiting
  fonts to, 360
Windows Common Controls
  coolbars, 466–467, 493–497
  displaying images, 616
  ImageList property, 508
  progress bars, 466–467, 491–493
  status bars, 126–127, 465–466, 484–491
  toolbars, 126, 222, 465, 466–484
Windows Help, displaying from
  Common Dialog controls, 868–870.
  See also Help files.
Windows installation directory, 814–815
Windows Registry
  deleting settings, 999
  Most Recently Used (MRU) files
    list, 192–195

registering ActiveX controls, 664
retrieving settings, 192–193,
  997–998, 999
storing settings, 193–195, 997
WindowState property, 151
WinHelp Windows API function,
  1061–1062
Winmm.dll, 774
With statement, 109
WithEvents keyword, 86, 94
Wizards. *See also* Visual Basic
  Application Wizard.
  ActiveX Control Interface Wizard,
    669, 675, 680
  ActiveX Document Migration
    Wizard, 683
  Data Form Wizard, 840, 841–843
  Package and Deployment Wizard,
    1020, 1043–1048
  Property Page Wizard, 680–681
Word wrap in text boxes, 200
WordWrap property, 445
Workspace object, DAO, 825, 857–858
Write # statement, 550–551
Write method, 577
WriteLine method, 577
WriteProperties event, 671–672, 693–694
Writing to binary files, 554
Writing to random access files, 552–553
Writing to sequential files, 550–551

X1, **X2** properties, 455, 457
XML (Extended Markup Language),
  697, 698
Xor Pen pen setting, 604, 605

Y1, **Y2** properties, 455, 457
Year function, 90

Z

Z-order position, 810–812, 976
Zooming OLE objects, 928
ZOrder method, 976

What's On The CD-ROM

The companion CD-ROM contains the source code and project files used in the *Visual Basic 6 Black Book*.

Also included are demo copies of the following programs:

- CoffeeCup HTML Editor++ 98—An HTML editor with built in Java and animated GIFs.
- CoffeeCup ImageMapper++—A fully functional image mapper.
- Site Sweeper—Program that provides an automatic, comprehensive analysis of your Web site.
- QuickSite
- SQL-Station
- Setup Factory
- AutoPlay Menu Studio
- VBAdvantage
- Olectra Resizer
- Q-Diagnostic Software

Requirements

To run all the projects discussed in the book, you will need to have Visual Basic 6 installed.

Platform

486 or higher processor

Operating System

Windows 95, 95, or NT

RAM

16MB